Using FoxPro® 2

LISA C. SLATER
STEVEN E. ARNOTT

with NANCY JACOBSEN
and JOSEPH A. GOTTHELF

Foreword by Dr. David L. Fulton,
President of Fox Software

Using FoxPro 2

Copyright © 1992 by Que® Corporation.

All rights reserved. Printed in the United States of America. No part of this book may be used or reproduced in any form or by any means, or stored in a database or retrieval system, without prior written permission of the publisher except in the case of brief quotations embodied in critical articles and reviews. Making copies of any part of this book for any purpose other than your own personal use is a violation of United States copyright laws. For information, address Que Corporation, 11711 N. College Ave., Carmel, IN 46032.

Library of Congress Catalog No.: 90-64401

ISBN: 0-88022-703-6

This book is sold *as is*, without warranty of any kind, either express or implied, respecting the contents of this book, including but not limited to implied warranties for the book's quality, performance, merchantability, or fitness for any particular purpose. Neither Que Corporation nor its dealers or distributors shall be liable to the purchaser or any other person or entity with respect to any liability, loss, or damage caused or alleged to be caused directly or indirectly by this book.

95 94 93 92 4 3 2

Interpretation of the printing code: the rightmost double-digit number is the year of the book's printing; the rightmost single-digit number, the number of the book's printing. For example, a printing code of 92-1 shows that the first printing of the book occurred in 1992.

Screen reproductions in this book were created by means of the program Collage Plus from Inner Media, Inc., Hollis, NH.

This book is based on Fox Software's FoxPro Version 2.0.

Publisher: Lloyd J. Short

Acquisitions Editor: Rick Ranucci

Managing Editor: Paul Boger

Product Development Manager: Thomas H. Bennett

Book Designers: Scott Cook and Michele Laseau

Production Team: Claudia Bell, Brad Chinn, Mark Enochs, Denny Hager, Audra Hershman, Phil Kitchel, Bob LaRoche, Laurie Lee, Anne Owen, Cindy L. Phipps, Caroline Roop, Kevin Spear, Bruce Steed, Johnna VanHoose, Phil Worthington, Christine Young

CREDITS

Product Director
Walter R. Bruce III

Production Editor
Kelly D. Dobbs

Editors
Jo Anna Arnott
Donald R. Eamon
Mike La Bonne
Susan M. Shaw

Technical Editor
Sherrie Bruhn

Composed in Cheltenham and MCP Digital by Que Corporation.

ABOUT THE AUTHORS

LISA C. SLATER

Lisa C. Slater is an independent consultant as SoftSpoken, specializing in optimizing database management strategy and code for programmers working in FoxPro. She is the archivist for CompuServe's FoxForum, where she regularly encounters and solves the problems of a varied group of FoxPro users and developers. Slater regularly writes for *DataBased Advisor* and *FoxTalk* magazines and has been a speaker at the Fox Software Developers Conference.

Slater earned an A.B. in history and literature from Harvard University. She can be reached on CompuServe at 72077,2417.

STEVEN E. ARNOTT

Steven E. Arnott is a software developer with Korenthal Associates, Inc., New York City, authors of PhDbase—a fuzzy search tool for FoxPro, Clipper, and dBASE—and 4Print, the popular LaserJet printing utility. He has worked primarily in the xBase language for the past five years and has developed several major applications in the areas of finance, manufacturing, and physicians' credentialing.

Arnott received a B.B.A. in accounting from Pace University. He can be reached on CompuServe at 70247,2614.

ABOUT THE AUTHORS

NANCY JACOBSEN

Nancy Jacobsen, who contributed materials to Chapters 3 and 4, is a software developer, consultant, desktop publisher, and writer. She specializes in FoxPro and Ventura Publisher applications. Jacobsen has been a speaker for the Fox Software Developers Conference for the past two years and has written several articles for *FoxTalk* and *DataBased Advisor* magazines.

Jacobsen currently resides in San Rafael, California and holds an A.B. in anthropology from the University of California, Berkeley. She can be reached on CompuServe at 72230,2664.

JOSEPH A. GOTTHELF

Joseph A. Gotthelf, who contributed materials to Chapters 5, 6, and 7, is a software developer who has more than nine years of experience in personal computer hardware and software consulting. He has written several articles for *DataBased Advisor.*

Gotthelf studied physics at Rutgers University and completed electrical engineering coursework at Drexel University. He can be reached on CompuServe at 74017,3670.

TRADEMARK ACKNOWLEDGMENTS

Que Corporation has made every effort to supply trademark information about company names, products, and services mentioned in this book. Trademarks indicated below were derived from various sources. Que Corporation cannot attest to the accuracy of this information.

CompuServe is a registered trademark of H&R Block.

dBASE is a registered trademark and dBASE IV is a trademark of Ashton-Tate Corporation.

FoxBASE, FoxBASE +, and FoxBASE+/Mac are registered trademarks and FoxPro and Rushmore are trademarks of Fox Holdings, Inc.

Hewlett-Packard is a registered trademark and LaserJet is a trademark of Hewlett-Packard Company.

IBM, PC, XT, AT, PS/2, and PC DOS are registered trademarks of International Business Machines Corporation.

Lotus, 1-2-3, and Symphony are registered trademarks of Lotus Development Corporation.

Macintosh and Mac are registered trademarks of Apple Computer, Inc.

Microsoft, Microsoft Excel, MS-DOS, and Multiplan are registered trademarks of Microsoft Corporation.

Paradox is a registered trademark of Ansa-Borland.

Ventura Publisher is a registered trademark of Ventura Software, Inc.

WordPerfect is a registered trademark of WordPerfect Corporation.

Trademarks of other products mentioned in this book are held by the companies producing them.

ACKNOWLEDGMENTS

More people than we can name helped us create this book, but we would like to offer some special thanks:

to Jonathan, Joshua, and Derek Slater; Kevin Jamieson; Marcia Cooper; Larry Lynette; and Stan and Jeanne Cooper (Lisa's family) for love and patience that passes all understanding

to Gladys Arnott; Nancy Arnott; and Sheila, Robert, Megan, and Matthew LaLima (Steve's family) for their constant love and support

to Walt Bruce and Kelly Dobbs, our editors at Que, for going beyond the call of duty to encourage us to write the best possible *Using FoxPro 2*

to Sherri Bruhn, our technical editor, for her many valuable recommendations and her keen eye

to Jim Korenthal, Tracey Siesser, and Lew Horowitz for their patience, guidance, inspiration, and moral support

to the BobRed Company, for the Market Research and Product Line Development used in Omnipresent Widgets Limited

to George Goley, whose examples showed us that anything and everything can be done in FoxPro

to Jordan Powell for spurring our work on interface design principles; Peter Colclough for organizing our thoughts on the API; and Jim McKinney for helping us imagine the person who needed to read *Using FoxPro 2*

to Jeff Winchell for providing research on performance issues

to Glenn Hart and Pat Adams for general support whenever we asked for it and specific recommendations whenever we needed them to the FoxForumFolk for asking the questions we wrote this book to answer and all the Fox Software forum sysops—Toni Taylor, Kristine Ulrich, Roger Bischoff, Jackie Jaynes, Cathy Selhorst, and others—for steering the Forum calmly on its endless-but-endlessly-interesting journey

... and, last but very far from least,

to Dr. Dave Fulton, Walt Kennamer, Janet Walker, and all of Fox Software for giving us a wonderful product and all the Betazoids for helping Fox **make it so** <g>.

FOREWORD

I was delighted when I heard that Lisa and Steve planned to write *Using FoxPro 2*. Both of them were among the most productive FoxPro 2.0 beta testers and understand FoxPro 2.0 in great depth. Both are also active on our CompuServe forum and have become adept at teaching other people about FoxPro 2.0, a skill that is well displayed here.

Lisa observed to me earlier this year that FoxPro 2.0 does away with the long-standing division between programmers and end users. I believe that comment is exactly on point. The new power tools (the Project Manager, Screen Builder, Menu Builder, and the Report and Label Writers) blur this traditional programmer-end user distinction. Programmers will likely find themselves doing more work by *pointing and clicking,* and end users will probably find themselves sliding effortlessly into writing a few lines of code.

Lisa and Steve approach FoxPro through the new power tools, which is clearly the right approach. These new features are not always the center of attention in product reviews, but I believe they are among the most significant of the innovations in FoxPro 2.0. *Using FoxPro 2* does an excellent job of "pulling them all together" and illustrating how to use FoxPro efficiently and easily.

I recommend *Using FoxPro 2* highly, especially to knowledgeable end users who previously may have been intimidated by powerful database products. This is the book for you.

David L. Fulton

Perrysburg, Ohio

CONVENTIONS

The conventions used in this book have been established to help you learn to use the program quickly and easily.

- Material the user types is in **boldface** or on a line by itself.
- Menu bar selections have initial capital letters: File, Edit, Database, Record, Program, and Window.
- FoxPro commands and field names are in all capital letters.
- Screen messages and samples of program code appear in a `special typeface`.
- *Italic* type is used to emphasize the authors' points or to introduce new terms.
- Version 2 icons in the margins indicate features new with Version 2.0 of FoxPro.
- Mouse icons indicate functions that can be performed by using the mouse.

Because xBase is a very English-like language, the commands and functions that make up the FoxPro dialect are usually common English words. For this reason, direct instructions you give FoxPro are capitalized in the text so that you can distinguish them from their normal English usage.

For example, "Every GET involved in one READ may be DISABLEd by using the Enter command or global SHOW GETS DISABLE command." In this sentence, the words you use to give FoxPro instructions are capitalized; in one case, (DISABLEd) only the part of the word properly used in the FoxPro instructions, not the entire construct used to form the English sentence, is capitalized.

However, sections of FoxPro instructions are set off from the rest of the text by the following typeface:

```
ACTIVATE WINDOW rwindow
@ 1,1 GET m.var WHEN my_udf()
READ
RELEASE WINDOW rwindow
```

One line or an entire program may be included. When you see this typeface, you notice that different standards for capitalization are used in different sections of the book. Here, FoxPro commands and keywords are capitalized, but a few words—names of memory variables and other items created by the programmer—are not. This convention is common, but some people do the opposite, and some people capitalize no letters at all.

In this book, each author has followed his or her personal style of capitalization, giving you a fairly representative look at the conventions commonly used by xBase programmers.

You should become comfortable with these different styles so that you can understand other people's programs wherever you see them. Sharing your work is the best way to learn! It is not important which style you pick for yourself. It is important that you adopt one convention and use it consistently so that your programs are readable and easy to maintain.

If you find one style difficult to use consistently or hard to read, try another one. FoxPro includes a tool (FoxDoc) that can standardize the capitalization in your programs for you after you write them—using any style you prefer. You learn about FoxDoc in Chapter 18.

Many features of FoxPro 2 were in flux while this book was being written, in the early stages of the product's release. If you have trouble duplicating the results you see in the examples, your problem may be because of your *build date* (the exact date that your copy of FoxPro 2 was created), rather than because of anything you are doing wrong or differently.

You can find out your build date by looking at the date of your FOXPRO.EXE or FOXPROL.EXE file in your main FoxPro 2 directory. From within FoxPro, you can type the following in the Command window and press Enter:

```
WAIT WINDOW VERSION(1)
```

If your copy of FoxPro is dated from within the original release (July 12 or 19), some techniques in this book will not work for you until you obtain an updated version. You can call Fox Software, and they will ship the update to you at no charge. You also can download files to update your copy from the FoxForum on CompuServe. Read Appendix H for information about contacting Fox Software and joining the FoxForum and about other available sources of help.

CONTENTS AT A GLANCE

CONTENTS

III Building FoxPro 2 Applications

IV FoxProgramming: Enhanced Use of the Design Tools and Beyond

V Getting To Know FoxPro 2 Commands and Functions

Introduction

Welcome to *Using FoxPro 2*. This book gives you the tools to understand your own information management needs and to fulfill them with FoxPro 2's powerful capabilities.

Like any database management system, or *DBMS*, FoxPro is a program that enables you to create *tables*, which are collections of similar pieces of information. Your phone book, a listing of employees in your department, and your grocery list are all tables. In a DBMS, the process of collecting and storing this information, or data, in tables is called *data input*, or *data entry*. You can sort and organize tables, even large ones, in many different ways. You can retrieve and locate individual data elements quickly and accurately.

In a relational DBMS, such as FoxPro, many tables can work together in a *database* to produce complex results or forms of *output*. Output usually is an answer to a question you pose about your data. This question, often referred to as a *query*, requires the DBMS to summarize and classify the information in your tables and to generate a representation (or report) of the answer so that you can use the information productively. In FoxPro 2, queries and output can take almost any form.

FoxPro is one of several DBMS software products often referred to as *xBase* because these products evolved from the dBase language. Almost all dBase III and IV syntax and programs work the same way in FoxPro as they work in dBase. FoxPro, however, also includes many commands and features not found in any other xBase dialect.

This book is your guide to database management in FoxPro 2's unique style.

What Is FoxPro 2?

When FoxPro was introduced in 1989, the program altered the face of MS-DOS database management. Fox Software took the interface design and flexibility of its Macintosh DBMS, FoxBASE+/Mac, and transferred these features to the PC world, without losing the speed advantage that is the hallmark of all its products. The company had already made it possible for people working on both platforms to share the same data, using FoxBASE+/Mac and FoxBASE+ for the PC. In FoxPro, Fox Software began to blur the distinctions between the ways programs looked and the ways in which people used them on the two platforms.

With FoxPro 2, the face is the same—but the heart has undergone some fundamental changes. FoxPro 1 brought some of the aspects of working on a Macintosh to the PC database world, proving that you can have many of the benefits of a graphical interface without the graphics. Now FoxPro 2 makes users reassess some other assumptions and constraints in a new light:

- The traditional boundary between an *end-user* and a *programmer* becomes difficult to maintain, because beginners can generate useful applications without writing any lines of program code, and experts can become more productive by using the same techniques to develop extensive systems.
- The classic distinction between *interactive* use of the DBMS and a controlled, *programmatic* use is dispelled, because programs can be written to exactly mimic the interactive environment or even to coexist peacefully within that environment.
- The standard difference between the system's internal mechanisms and external capabilities is hard to see because the same features you use to create your programs can be provided within the programs.
- The assumed limitations of data management on personal computers are overcome, because innovative file-handling and searching techniques enable you to process vast amounts of information as fast or faster than on large mainframes.

In fact, no matter how accustomed you are to database management programming, FoxPro 2 challenges some of your established theories and practices. No matter how new you are to the DBMS world, or even to computers, this program gives you access to sophisticated manipulation of your own data.

FoxPro 2 can give you a new and exciting way of looking at the information you possess—and what you can accomplish with it.

What Is New in FoxPro 2?

By now, you should realize that FoxPro 2 is more than just a "second release." This program is really a new product. Besides about 150 new or significantly enhanced commands and system memory variables, FoxPro 2 offers the following advances:

- A Screen Builder enables object-oriented design of data-entry screens and other displays. A Menu Builder allows completely configurable access to the System menu for your applications or for your own interactive use. You can *attach* code to a screen object or menu option and let FoxPro generate the lines of program code to support it.

- A Project Manager tracks all the elements of one application and creates one compiled file for you, only recompiling those elements that have changed since your last *build*. With the optional Distribution Kit, successor to the old Runtime, you also can create executable versions.

- The Report Writer supports integrated report variables that eliminate the need for most UDFs (user-defined functions) in reports. Report and label forms are defined in a new (table) format that makes them easier to change. Along with most other output commands in FoxPro, they can use a new Printer Driver system.

- The RQBE (Relational Query By Example) provides an interactive environment for retrieving information. Underlying the RQBE, the new SQL-SELECT command has been integrated with the FoxPro programming language, allowing access to SQL without any special mode or switches.

- The addition of Rushmore technology enables pinpointed searches using complex criteria to retrieve data sets from very large tables with incredible speed.

- Indexes now can contain multiple *tags*, or orders, within each file. They can be opened and updated along with their associated tables. They also can be processed much faster than before, because the same information (or much more) is stored in a more compact format.

- One-to-many relationships can be created easily (even interactively) and used in new and powerful ways in reports and BROWSEs.

- The External Routine Application Program Interface (API) enables C and assembly language routines to supplement FoxPro with any capabilities not found in its native command set.

- A second version of FoxPro (the Extended version) is included along with the Standard version. Although the Standard version can use LIM 4.0-compatible expanded memory to great advantage, the Extended version uses *all* available *extended* memory, effectively removing many limits on system capacity that can be imposed by memory constraints.
- The Standard version of FoxPro runs in less memory than before and uses a new *segment-loader* technology to avoid *disk-trashing* calls to the overlay file. The Extended version requires no overlay files.

Along with these obvious changes, nearly every feature of the interface has been enhanced with improvements in almost every menu option and dialog.

How Should You Read This Book?

In keeping with the assertion that no separate classes of users exist when working with FoxPro, and because so much in FoxPro 2 will be new to everyone, no sections of this book are specifically aimed at beginners or experts. Instead, the discussions address each subject at an entry level—no previous knowledge is assumed. The discussion of each FoxPro tool or feature starts out with simple examples and progresses to complex ones. For some tools, this progression takes two consecutive chapters; others are handled in one chapter or section.

If you are new to database management, start at the beginning and work through the book at a slow pace. (Start by following the instructions in Appendix A if you have not yet installed FoxPro 2 on your computer.) Part I gives you a good basis for mastering all the material in this book if you investigate the contents thoroughly. In Parts II, III, and IV, you may want to read about each tool until you feel out of your depth. You can return to finish these final sections at a later time. Part V introduces you to the families of commands and functions in the FoxPro language that provide the basis for the more complex examples.

If you are familiar with FoxPro and/or database management, you should still skim Part I for interface and database design hints specific to FoxPro 2 before moving on. In Parts II, III, and IV, you progress quickly through the initial explanation of the new querying and application-building tools, spending most of your time with the tips and tricks offered as part of the discussion of each one. Turn to Part V for a more comprehensive grasp of the enhancements to the language that you can use to design similar techniques of your own.

If you are a FoxPro programmer, you may want to start with Part III, which concentrates on developing applications in FoxPro 2 using the new tools. You can turn to the other chapters as the need to understand each new feature arises.

What Is Covered in This Book?

Because FoxPro 2 has such extensive capabilities, this book maintains a fairly rapid pace through the different features available. The book is divided into five major parts and several appendixes.

Introducing FoxPro 2

In Part I of this book, you get an initial tour of FoxPro and database fundamentals.

Chapter 1, "Understanding FoxPro Fundamentals," tells you how to start FoxPro and takes you through the development of a simple application, from the creation of its table through a sample query and report. No programming is needed. This chapter also introduces you to some of the features of the interface, using a number of the sample applications supplied with FoxPro 2 for practice.

Chapter 2, "Understanding the FoxPro 2 Interface," is your complete guide to manipulating the objects and elements you see in FoxPro's rich interactive environment. You learn about editing text, managing windows, executing instructions directly as FoxPro commands as well as through the menu-driven system, and accessing FoxPro's extensive on-line help system.

Chapter 3, "Exploring Databases and Tables," covers table structure and use. You learn how to enter new data into a table interactively and how to distinguish between different types of data. You also learn how to get output in different forms and how to set criteria for the data included in the output.

Chapter 4, "Database Management Fundamentals," takes a more comprehensive look at what a database is and does. You learn about the index files used to order data and how tables are used together in relationships. You also learn about important design considerations you should keep in mind while designing a database—including ways to make the database accessible to, and comfortable for, the people who have to use it.

Getting Productive with FoxPro 2 Databases

After you know something about putting data into a database, Part II shows you how to pull complex and organized answers out.

Chapters 5, "Using the RQBE as the Gateway to Queries," and 6, "Investigating Your Data with Advanced Queries," are devoted to FoxPro 2's new *RQBE* (Relational Query By Example), which can be used to create queries from multiple tables without programming.

Chapter 7, "Querying with SQL and Searching with Rushmore," builds on what you learn about the RQBE by exploring the new *SQL SELECT* command that underlies the RQBE. You learn the complete syntax of the SELECT command and how to use it to issue increasingly complex queries on your own. This chapter also covers other searching and querying techniques, including FoxPro 2's *Rushmore technology*, which enables you to retrieve subsets of data at startling speeds.

Chapter 8, "Organizing the Answers with BROWSE," gives you an in-depth look at another one of FoxPro's powerful commands: *BROWSE*. You learn to use BROWSE to view your data, including query results, on-screen, in almost endless configurations.

Chapters 9, "Putting the Answers To Work in Reports and Labels," and 10, "Using the Report Writer and Label Designer," teach you to put your data and query results to other productive uses, creating tangible output in any format you require.

Building FoxPro 2 Applications

In Part III, you learn to build programs to control the process of filling, maintaining, and querying databases by creating *applications* so that many people can use the same information in a consistent way.

Chapter 11, "Coordinating a FoxPro 2 Application," is devoted to the principles of interface design. This chapter presents some model criteria for choosing among the bewildering array of options you have available in FoxPro 2 and tells you how to decide which ones meet the needs of a particular project. This chapter also gives you a quick introduction to the power tools presented in Part III, so you can see how each one helps you achieve your goals.

Chapters 12 and 13 cover the *Screen Builder*, in which you create visual formats for data entry and other communication. In Chapter 12, "Creating Application Elements," you learn to control this complex tool, and in Chapter 13, "Using Complex Screen Sets To Control Data Entry," you find out how to coordinate your results with the other elements of applications.

Chapter 14, "Organizing and Packaging Your Applications," continues this process. Using the *Menu Builder*, you learn to provide users with choices of all the tasks your application can accomplish. Using the *Project Manager* and the *Distribution Kit*, you learn to manage your application's files for yourself and when you make them available to others. You also learn how to structure a program from its subsidiary elements, as collected in a Project.

Chapter 15, "Discovering More FoxPro 2 Productivity Features," covers a whole host of supporting tools available in the FoxPro interface and in the applications that you design (Resource files, the Filer, the color system, macro keystrokes, the desk accessories on the System menu, printer drivers, and the API).

FoxProgramming: Enhanced Use of the Design Tools and Beyond

In Part IV, you find out how to get the most out of FoxPro's application development process.

Chapter 16, "Understanding Program Structure," is your introduction to programming principles. You learn to plan a program, what its basic elements are, and how to accomplish the basic programming tasks required for your work in FoxPro 2.

Chapter 17, "Using Advanced FoxProgramming Techniques," continues this process. You learn to organize large-scale programs that incorporate many other programs—creating programs that are easily maintained and that can "flex" to accommodate the environments in which they are run. You learn how easily you can create *template* programs, which can generate other programs for you.

Chapter 18, "Enhancing the Applications You Program," covers tools of special interest to developers, including the creation of custom help systems, error handling during development and from within an application, and *FoxDoc*, a device to help you document and maintain your programs.

Getting To Know FoxPro 2 Commands and Functions

In Part V, you get an introduction to the rich command language that is the basis for the power and capability of FoxPro. No attempt is made to cover every command available. You explore some techniques and related *families* of commands in depth so that you can proceed to investigate others in a similar manner when you are ready.

Chapter 19, "Using Commands and Functions To Manipulate Data," teaches you how single data elements are handled in FoxPro and how you move through the items in a table or database to locate and edit the ones you want.

Chapter 20, "Using Arrays and the Low-Level File Functions," concentrates on the commands and functions used to handle a table as an entity or to coordinate tables in a database. This chapter also covers arrays, which are structures similar to tables that are maintained only in memory (rather than permanently on your disk) and can be used in similar ways.

Using the Appendixes

The various Appendixes provide handy references to topics of special interest on using FoxPro in your environment.

Appendix A, "Installing FoxPro 2," tells you how to take FoxPro out of the box and get the program working on your system, including using the optional Distribution Kit.

Appendix B, "Using FoxPro 2 in a Network Environment," introduces some topics pertinent to the multi-user version of FoxPro only.

Appendix C, "Optimizing FoxPro 2's Performance," tells you how to get the most out of FoxPro with reference to your hardware configuration and gives you some techniques to help you gauge and fine-tune performance.

Appendix D, "Customizing the CONFIG.FP File," teaches you how to use the special configuration file that FoxPro reads on start-up so that you can set your FoxPro environment up in your own style.

Appendix E, "Using Command Line Options and the FoxPro 2 Loaders," explains the different ways in which you can load FoxPro and what difference this makes to your use of the program.

Appendix F, "Key Codes, Key Labels, and Special Key Usage in FoxPro 2," contains a comprehensive reference chart of the different ways keystrokes are interpreted and acted on by FoxPro 2 and information on keyboard handling in the program.

Appendix G, "Installation Disk Files and File Extensions," tells you about the files you find when you have installed FoxPro 2 on your disk and how to interpret the various file extensions that FoxPro 2 uses for them and for the files you create yourself.

Appendix H, "Finding Available Help," tells you how to contact Fox Software and other people who work with FoxPro when you want to solve a problem or just share what you have been doing.

Appendix I, "Example Database Structures and Procedures," provides some short programs that support the sample tables and applications created in this book.

What Hardware Does FoxPro 2 Need?

FoxPro 2 requires at least 480k free RAM and at least 7 megabytes (6 for its minimum installed files, 1 for temporary files used during processing) of free space on your hard disk. The program runs much more smoothly if you give it more memory—using LIM 4.0-compatible expanded or extended memory. You need much more free RAM to use FoxPro 2's capability to handle many simultaneous activities in multiple windows to its fullest extent.

If you are using FoxPro 2 on a network, each workstation should have this memory free after the network shell is loaded. Workstations do not need local hard disks, but they greatly enhance performance. Most currently available networks are supported.

To take full advantage of FoxPro's output capabilities, you also should have a printer. FoxPro 2 includes improved support for network printers.

Where Can You Go from Here?

No one book can cover all the aspects of FoxPro 2. As you get more serious about programming, you should have as many different perspectives as possible. Que's *FoxPro Programmer's Reference*, by John Hawkins, is an excellent companion volume to this book. Hawkins takes an encyclopedia approach to FoxPro, presenting full command syntax and extensive examples grouped by programming task.

Appendix H, "Finding Available Help," gives you more ideas about sharing your interests and discoveries and broadening your resources as you learn about FoxPro.

Let this book take you on your initial tour of the powerful tools and features of FoxPro 2. With this database management system, your ultimate destination is as any place you want to go.

Introducing FoxPro 2

1

CHAPTER

Understanding FoxPro Fundamentals

In this chapter, you learn how to navigate among FoxPro 2 features by using the sample application programs provided on the installation disks.

An *application* is a collection of instructions and information designed to perform a specific task, such as accounting or telecommunication. (The main FoxPro executable file 2 is a large application.) The sample applications you examine include some organizers for personal information and facts. Although the applications are in themselves convenient devices, more importantly, these applications present an impressive display of the powerful tools available in FoxPro 2.

After you explore some sample applications, you learn how to create an application. This application includes a *table*—the basic database management tool for collecting information—that you use in all practice sessions.

You don't have to be a programmer to create an application. You *generate* an application by using *FoxApp*, one of FoxPro 2's special tools.

Although you do not actually write the program (FoxApp writes the program for you), you may find this exercise both easy and fun.

If you are a programmer, this section helps to introduce you to some new methods that you use in FoxPro 2 and the polished and complex results that you produce with the relatively few lines of programming code you need to enter.

Getting Ready To Work

If you didn't install a copy of FoxPro 2, refer to the installation instructions in Appendix A to help you install the program. FoxPro 2 uses a mouse extensively. If you have a mouse, make sure that you install the driver software and that the mouse is working, *before* starting up FoxPro.

Throughout this book, you create and store data files on-disk, including scratch files that you may want to delete immediately and working files that comprise the model application you refer to frequently.

Separate data files from the main program as delivered on the installation disks. Keep separate, backup copies of the data files, and you can make backups much easier if you also aren't making copies of the program files at the same time. DOS, the disk operating system that sends information back and forth between the different components of the hardware system, also runs slowly if many files are searched each time you look for only one file.

Separate data files from the main program by creating separate subdirectories on the disk. If you explore the hard disk after installation, you may notice that FoxPro 2 creates many subdirectories to hold the subsidiary files.

To hold the data files, make a subdirectory that you refer to as the MODEL directory by using the following procedures:

After the computer is turned on and has gone through the startup sequence, make the drive holding FoxPro 2 the default drive. To do so, at the DOS prompt type the drive letter, a colon, and then press Enter. This procedure looks like the following line:

C:\>**C:**

Now type the letters **MD** (for make directory), a backslash (\), the name of the **FOXPRO 2** main directory, another backslash (\), and the word **MODEL**. You should not use any spaces. If you used the default directory during installation, type the following line and press Enter:

MD\FOXPRO2\MODEL

During practice sessions, assume that you started FoxPro 2 from this data directory to make saving information in this directory easier.

To start FoxPro 2 from a data directory (or any directory other than the main program directory), DOS must be able to find the FoxPro 2 program files on the PATH. Type **PATH** at the DOS prompt to see whether you already have a path installed. DOS returns a line that begins with *PATH=*, followed by a list of directories similar to the following line:

```
PATH=C:\;C:\DOS;C:\UTILS
```

Add the FoxPro 2 main directory to the path by typing a line similar to the following:

```
PATH=C:\;C:\DOS;C:\UTILS;C:\FOXPRO2
```

If DOS didn't return a path, you can create a path by typing the following line:

```
PATH=C:\FOXPRO2
```

Substitute the appropriate drive and directory in the new path to fit your needs.

Now, when you are ready, start FoxPro 2 from the MODEL data directory by typing the following lines at the DOS prompt and using the appropriate drive and directory, as in the following (*CD* stands for change directory):

```
CD\FOXPRO2\MODEL
FOX
```

The name *FOX* is one of several *loader* programs available to start FoxPro 2. The loaders and the switches enable you to specify important configuration options at startup. Refer to Appendix E for this information.

You can put the preceding lines in a *batch file* (starting with the PATH line), so that you can start FoxPro from DOS with one line or one letter. You can have several batch files to start FoxPro from different data directories. You also can specify FoxPro2 as part of the DOS path after you start up the computer, by editing the *AUTOEXEC.BAT*, a special batch file that executes when the computer boots up.

In Chapter 2, you learn about the FoxPro Editor, which enables you to create and edit batch files directly in the Editor.

Exploring the Program

The FoxPro 2 sign-on screen presents seven choices in a row across the top as shown in figure 1.1. In the next chapter, you discuss these choices and how you access them. Practice choosing a few options and see what happens.

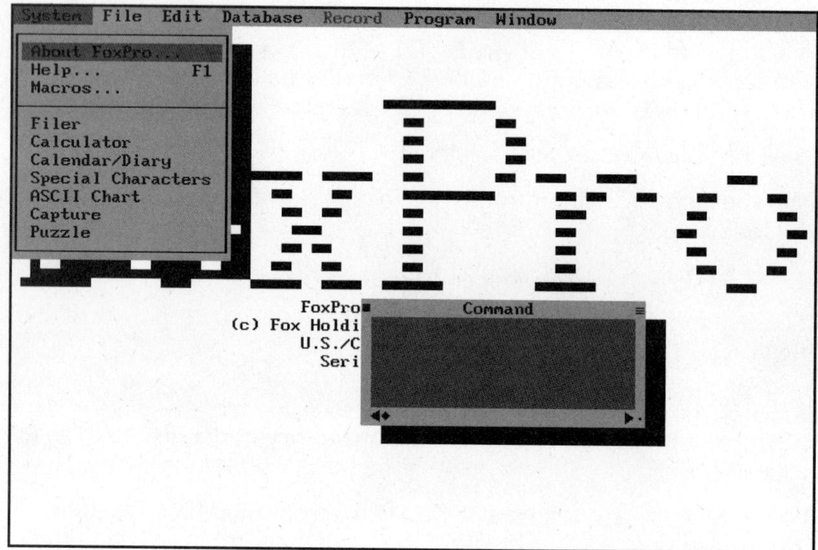

FIG. 1.1

The FoxPro 2 sign-on screen when the System option is accessed.

For now, you need to know only that you can use the keyboard to choose an option by pressing the Alt key simultaneously with a highlighted letter in the choice you want (the letter is shown on your screen in a different intensity or color). To access the first option (System), press Alt-S (or Alt-s) and a box of subsidiary choices appears. You then can press the single highlighted letter (without pressing Alt) of any subsidiary choices. Try this procedure and look at the list of choices (see fig. 1.1).

Mouse users also can *click* the words on-screen to activate the choices. *Click* means to press and quickly release the left mouse button (or right, when indicated). *Double-click* means to make two presses, in rapid succession, of the left mouse button. *Click-drag* means to move the mouse pointer while holding down the left mouse button.

Press Alt-W or click Window to access the Window choices. You see another list. Press V (or click View) to select the last item and then M (for Miscellaneous), and the screens in figures 1.2 and 1.3 appear in succession.

You can make many choices here. One item (the box labeled Date) is *highlighted*, which means that you can edit the item in the box. Press the Tab key or the Shift-Tab keys, and you can cycle the highlight through the list to edit the choices one at a time. (You also can click the choice you want.) Press the Tab key until the `[ ] Clock` check box is highlighted. After you press Enter or the space bar or click the item, the *check box* (the square brackets) now contains an `X`, and the clock appears in the upper right corner of the screen.

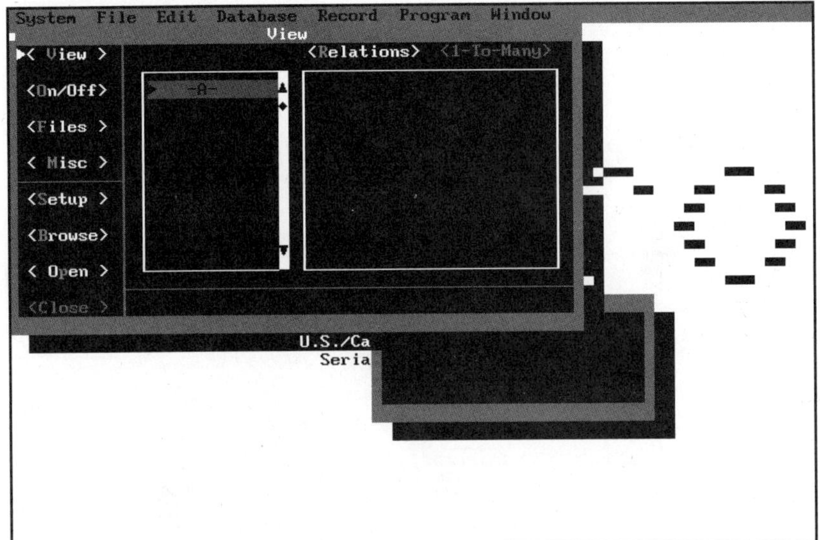

FIG. 1.2

View was accessed from the Window options by pressing Alt-W and then V.

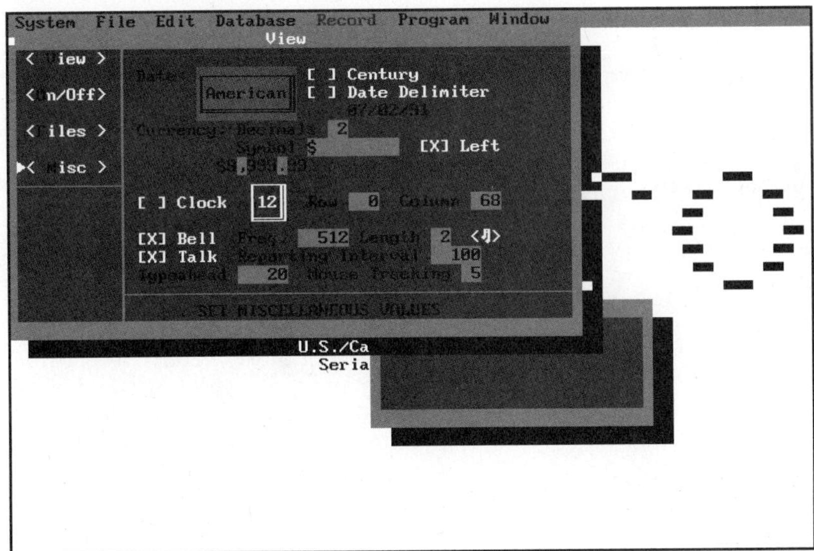

FIG. 1.3

View's Miscellaneous panel is selected.

If you don't like the clock's on-screen position, you can change the position by typing different numbers in the Row and Column items. (You learn how to change the colors in a following chapter.) Figure 1.4 shows the clock turned on and moved slightly from the default position. The Enter key was pressed on the box initially labeled 12 to change the time format to military time. Using the arrow keys, move the highlight to the 24 as shown and then press Enter or the space bar to select the box, or you can click on 24 with the mouse.

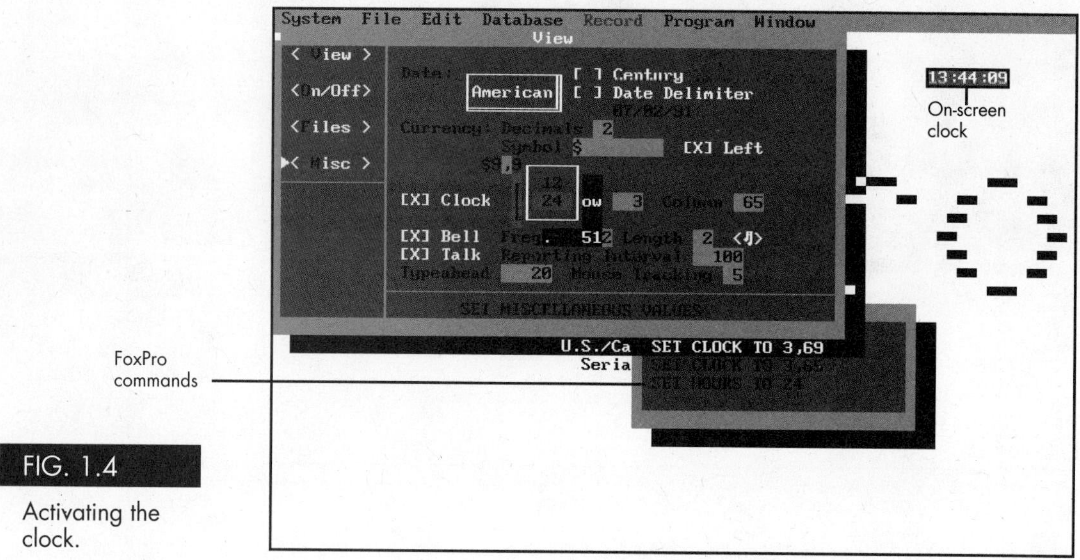

FIG. 1.4

Activating the clock.

In figure 1.4, words appear in a box to the lower right as you make these selections. These words are FoxPro 2 *commands*; all the selections that you made issued these commands. FoxPro echoes commands so that you can read each command as each is executed. Noting these commands as you make the selections is a good way to learn how to issue commands directly.

If you use a mouse, you may want to try changing the Mouse Tracking *setting*, or value, before leaving the Misc panel. This value ranges from 1 to 10 (1 is the least responsive setting) and initially is set in the mid-range. Type different values and move the mouse around on the pad or desk; if you type **1**, you must move the mouse much farther before the mouse cursor moves on-screen than if you type **10**. Choose a value comfortable to you.

What happens if you make a mistake? Figure 1.5 shows a value outside the allowable range entered into the Mouse Tracking box and the error message that results. Just click or press any key to enter a new value.

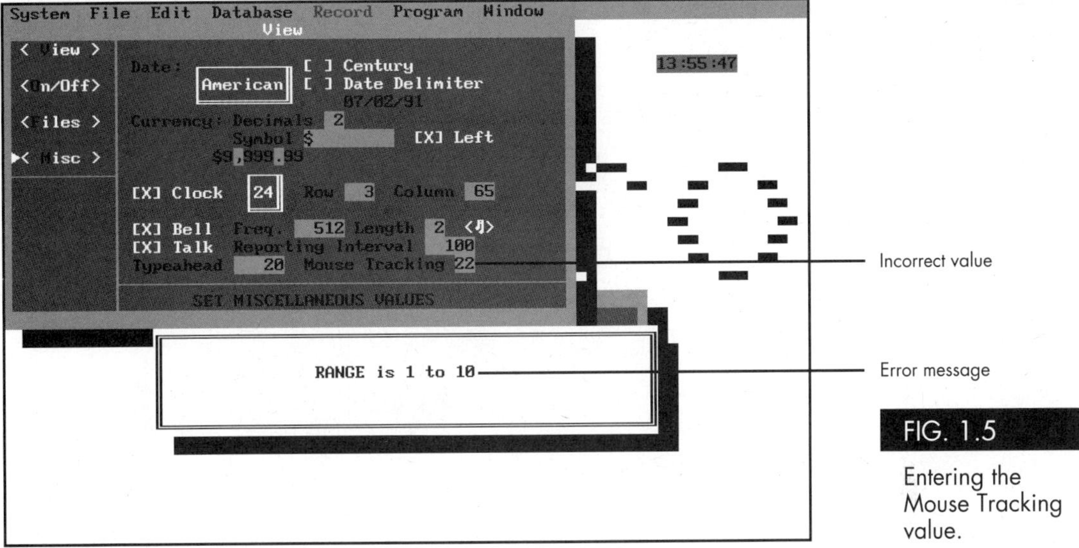

FIG. 1.5

Entering the Mouse Tracking value.

Press Esc and the View/Misc panel disappears. To load the sample application, press Alt-P (Program) and then D (Do).

Starting To Organize

After you press D, you see a screen much like figure 1.6. If you started FoxPro from the MODEL data directory, as previously instructed, the box on the upper right shows the current drive letter, and, in the next box down (the middle right), the word `MODEL` (the current directory) appears. Press Enter with the `[..]` entry highlighted, or double-click the brackets, to move up one level in the drive's directory structure. You are now in the main FoxPro 2 program directory. Use the mouse or the cursor keys to move the highlight to the SAMPLE directory, as shown, and then double-click or press Enter to access this directory.

After you locate and enter the SAMPLE directory's list of files, press the letter O. The highlight moves to the first file that begins with the letter O, as shown in figure 1.7. ORGANIZE.APP is the file you want, so after the file is highlighted, press Enter to run the ORGANIZE application.

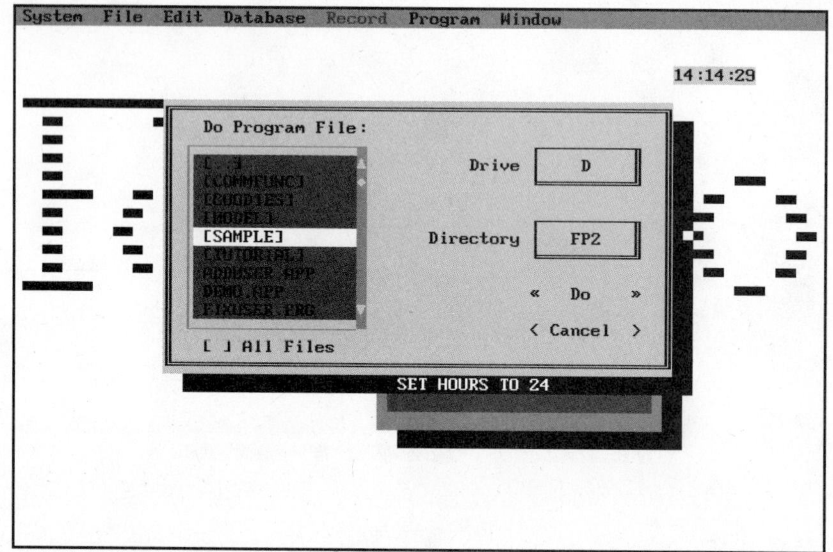

FIG. 1.6

Getting a list of Program Files available.

T I P

If you didn't start FoxPro 2 from the MODEL directory or didn't create the MODEL directory under the main FOXPRO 2 program directory, as suggested, you may need to search for the SAMPLE files. Use the Drive and Directory items (press Enter after the items are highlighted and select, just as you did to change the time format for the clock).

If you cannot find the SAMPLE directory and files under the main FOXPRO 2 directory, you may not have created these when you installed FoxPro. If necessary, refer to the installation instructions in Appendix A.

Using another FoxPro application, you also can install—at any time—a choice of optional products from *within* FoxPro. Use the preceding instructions to access the Program menu, choose the Do option, and then choose the main FoxPro 2 drive and directory. Press Tab or click the list of files you see on the left side. Press I or use the cursor keys or mouse until the file INSTALL.APP is highlighted. Press Enter to start installation of optional files.

You also can install options if, after you practice, you want fresh copies of sample data. The INSTALL process warns you if your computer lacks the space to install all the optional files. Ignore this warning, however, if you install these files over existing copies of the same files.

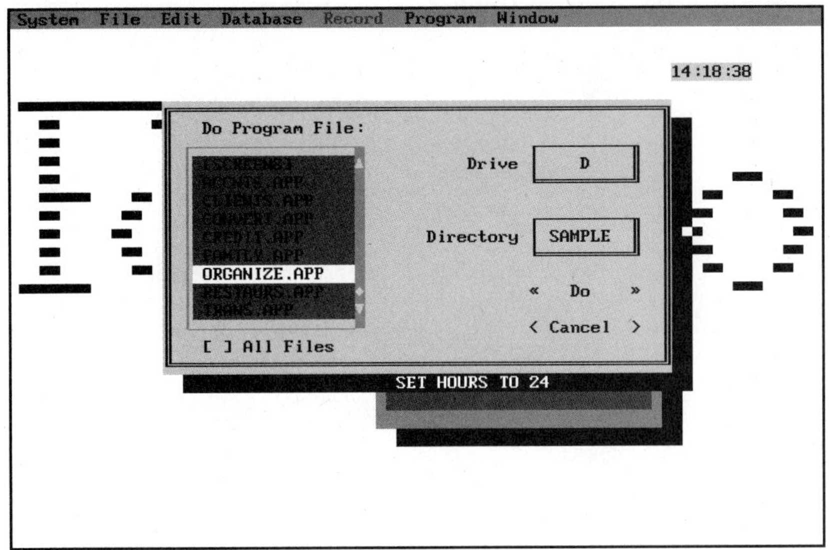

FIG. 1.7

The ORGANIZE.APP program highlighted.

The file list disappears, and you see a brief flash of the list of choices on the top line. Depending on the date of the version of FoxPro 2 you are using, the message `Organizer is installed under System menu popup` appears, but the screen doesn't seem to change. Press Alt-S and look at the System options again. The two new options are now installed on the menu popup, beneath Puzzle. These options, Conversions and Organize, are two of the sample applications that come with FoxPro 2.

The *Conversions* menu option is a delightful program that functions as a desk accessory, much like the Calendar and Calculator programs native to FoxPro 2 System options. This option converts different kinds of measurements from one unit to another.

Organize is a group of programs that help you manage personal information. When you press O, you see a list of Organize subsidiary programs: Restaurants, Client Manager, Money Manager (which also contains subsidiary programs), and Family & Friends. Press M to see the list (see fig. 1.8). Although these programs all work in similar ways, for now, just look at the Client Manager.

After you press M to see the Money Manager applications, press the right- or left-arrow key to go back one level to the main Organize list. Press L to enter the Client Manager, and a screen similar to figure 1.9 appears.

The Client Manager enables you to collect information about clients and to view and balance financial transactions you entered for clients, using the Money Manager Transactions application.

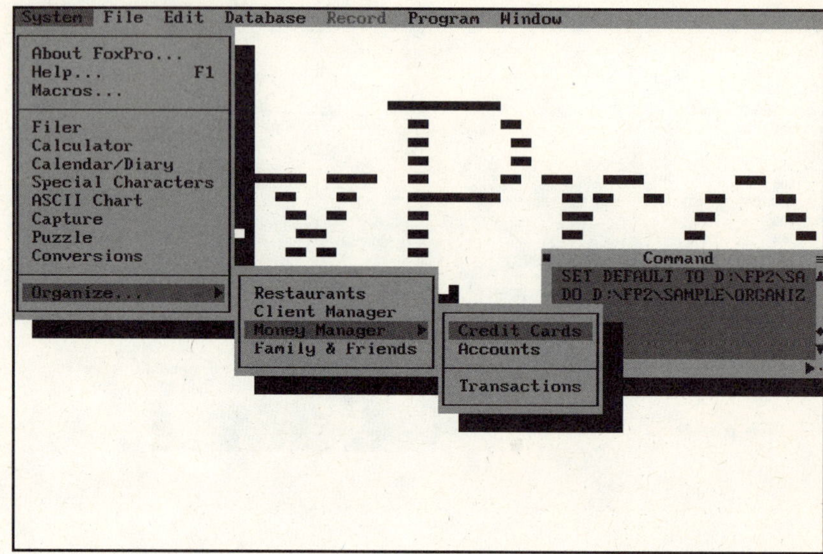

FIG. 1.8

The Organizer applications.

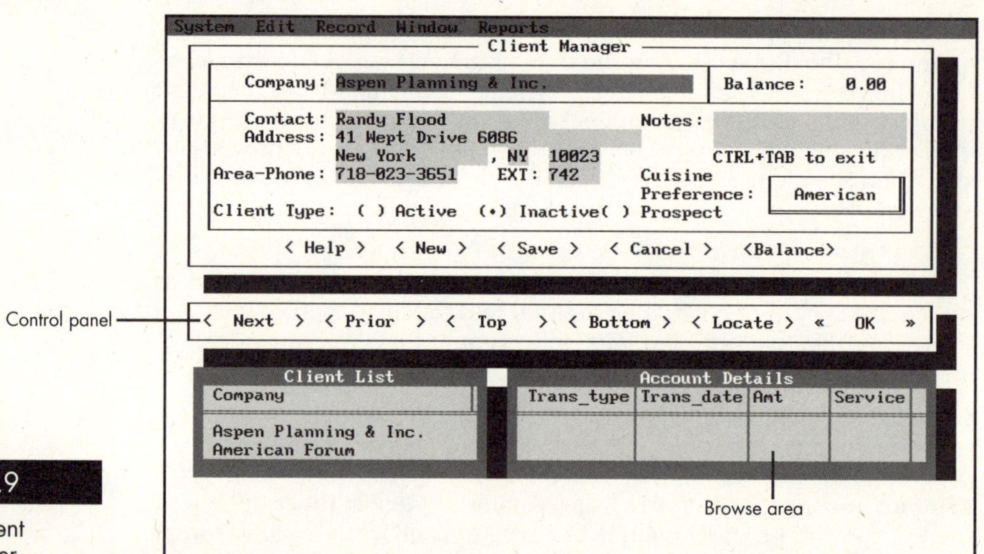

FIG. 1.9

The Client Manager.

On the top section of the screen, you edit information for this client. The middle section contains a control panel of options that enables you to move through the Client table. The bottom section contains *BROWSE*, one of FoxPro's most versatile features for displaying lists of items. On the lower left, you see the current Client Browse. On the lower right, you see the Account Browse (empty in this figure) that enables you to make a detailed perspective on the client's financial transactions.

> **CAUTION:** Some Organizer programs and features may not run on some systems, depending on the amount of memory the system has. If you see an `Insufficient memory` message from FoxPro while trying to follow some of the instructions, then follow along by using the accompanying screen displays shown in the text.
>
> You can use the System About option to learn about the system configuration and the way FoxPro sees the system. To fine-tune the system for use with FoxPro, check Appendixes C and D ("Optimizing FoxPro 2's Performance" and "Customizing the CONFIG.FP File").

Initially, the cursor is placed in the first item to edit (Company), as shown by the highlight. You can press Tab or click items that you want to edit.

When you select the Cuisine Preference box for editing, a list of choices pops up, similar to the time format options box for the Clock you previously edited. A similar list appears if you select the two-character State item.

The Notes box enables you to enter free-form information about a client.

You cannot edit the Balance figure as you press Tab to move through the items in the Client Manager. You can calculate the Client balance by selecting the `<Balance>` push button, specifying a month, and choosing whether to calculate a balance for one client or for all records. To understand the Balance feature, select Balance and, while the Balance features are displayed, use the System Help option. A help index appears (see fig. 1.10), or (depending on the version of the Organize application), you may see a Help topic on the Balance option. If you see the index, select the `▌ Balance` topic by highlighting the topic and pressing Enter. Read the information on this and on all other topics that interest you. Press Esc to return to the Client Manager.

To see the screen exactly as shown in figure 1.10, use the Window Move option from the top bar.

By pressing Ctrl-F1 or clicking different places, you can *cycle* through the different areas of the screen (you find the Cycle option under Window in the top bar). Use the cursor keys or the mouse to move through the different items in each area, and use the control panel to move through the different clients. As you do so, notice the changes in the Client and Account Browses.

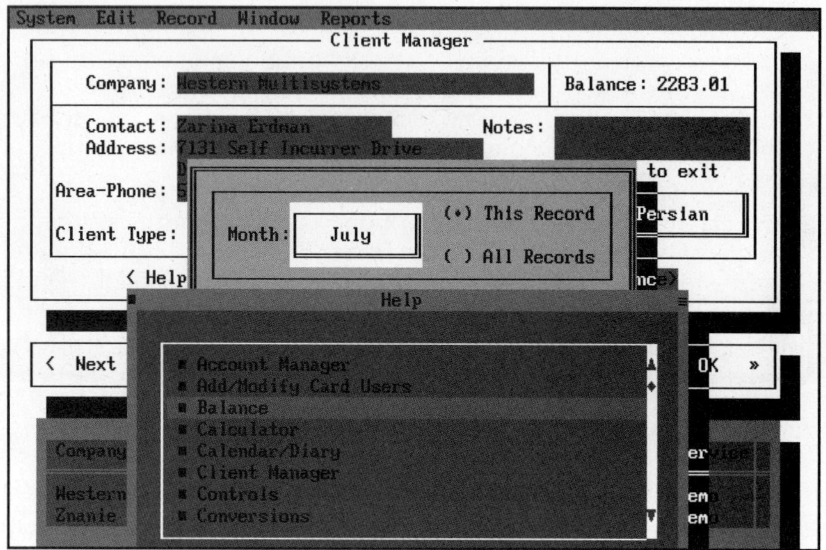

FIG. 1.10

The Balance feature and the Organizer Help index.

Find a client for whom some transactions are listed, cycle to the Account Browse, and move the cursor to the Memo item under the Service heading. Press Ctrl-PgDn or double-click the mouse on the down arrow to see another level of detail (see fig. 1.11). You access a box that contains the Service information which, like the Notes box in the Client table, can contain any free-form text you type.

Press Esc, and the Service text disappears. From the top bar, choose the Reports option (Alt-P) and select Reports, Labels, and Mail Merge. For each subsidiary option, press Ctrl-Enter at the next screen to accept all the default choices. This exercise shows the versatility with which FoxPro displays and outputs information from data.

In Chapter 3, “Exploring Databases and Tables,” you learn more about maintaining tables. You can completely clear the Organizers of sample data and fill them with information for personal use.

You aren’t limited to keeping or sending information by using the structures provided by the Organizer tables. You also can create similar applications from scratch with a table that holds records in a format that you design.

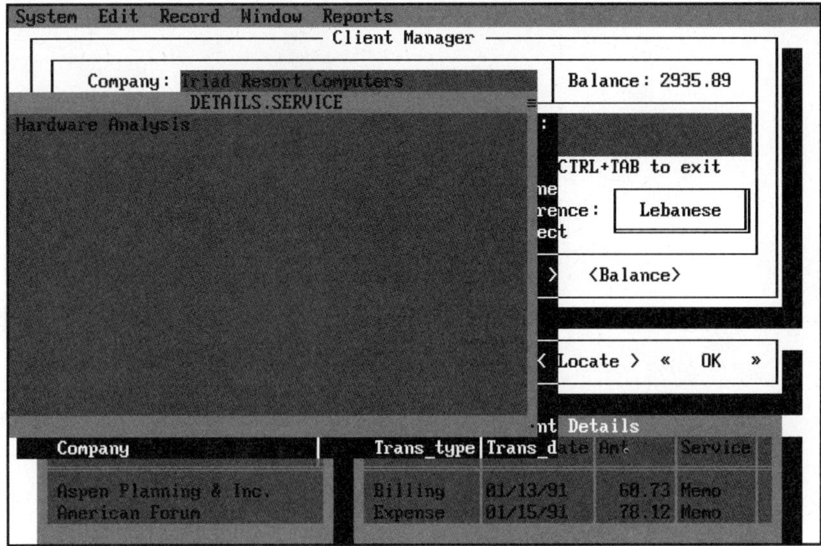

FIG. 1.11

The Service memo accessed through the Account Browse.

If you still are in one of the Organizer Reports output options and you want to leave the Client Manager, press Esc and then press Esc again (or use the System OK option).

Starting Applications

Press Alt-P and then D to access the list of programs. Because you are in the SAMPLE directory, you can press Enter with the top entry ([..]) in the list highlighted to move to the main FOXPRO program directory. In the main FOXPRO directory, find the file FOXAPP.APP in the file list. Press Enter with the highlight positioned on—or double-click—this file name to start FoxApp.

The screen in figure 1.12 appears, with the cursor positioned in an empty box waiting for a Database name to be entered. Type the drive and directory of *your* MODEL directory (the directory you use for all data), followed by a backslash (\) and the word **PRODUCT**, as shown in figure 1.12.

When you run FoxApp from the Program Do option, the directory returns to the FoxApp default setting. To make sure that FoxApp sends the files to the appropriate place, you must type the full drive and directory of the files you want to create.

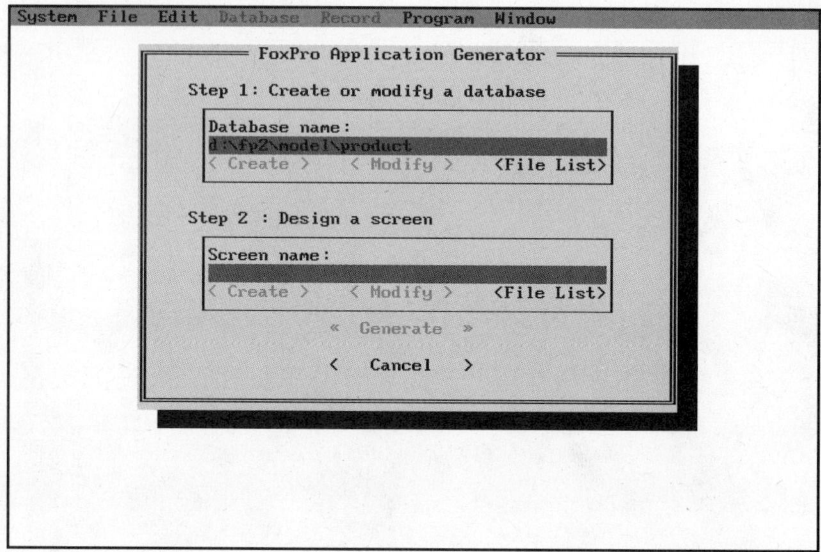

FIG. 1.12

Beginning work in FOXAPP.

After you finish typing, press Enter and, by replacing the file name with a line similar to `C:\FP2\MODEL\PRODUCT.DBF`, FoxApp confirms the name of the table you are creating. The default extension for tables, DBF, is added. FoxApp also fills out the Screen Name box with the same file name and SCX, the default extension for screens.

The Create item under the table name now is highlighted. Press Enter and a screen similar to figure 1.13 appears.

In this step, you actually describe the table structure to FoxPro. As you discover in Chapter 3, "Exploring Databases and Tables," a table is a kind of list, and each item on the list is a *record*. In the Product table, each record is an item in the product line of the imaginary Omnipresent Widget Company.

Each record can incorporate many different pieces, or *fields*, of information about the item it represents. In the Product table, you store a name and a company code for each product. You also create a place to store a digitized photo of each product in a special kind of FoxPro field, *memo field*. (Memo fields can store anything you want. The Notes field and Service field that you saw briefly in the Client Manager are both memo fields.)

The next time you create a table, you learn how to name fields, the kinds of fields available, and what these fields do. For this brisk run-through, however, just type the Name, choose the Type from the list that appears, and add the Width for the three necessary fields, as shown in the following instructions and figure 1.13. Press Tab or click the available spaces so that you put everything in the correct place.

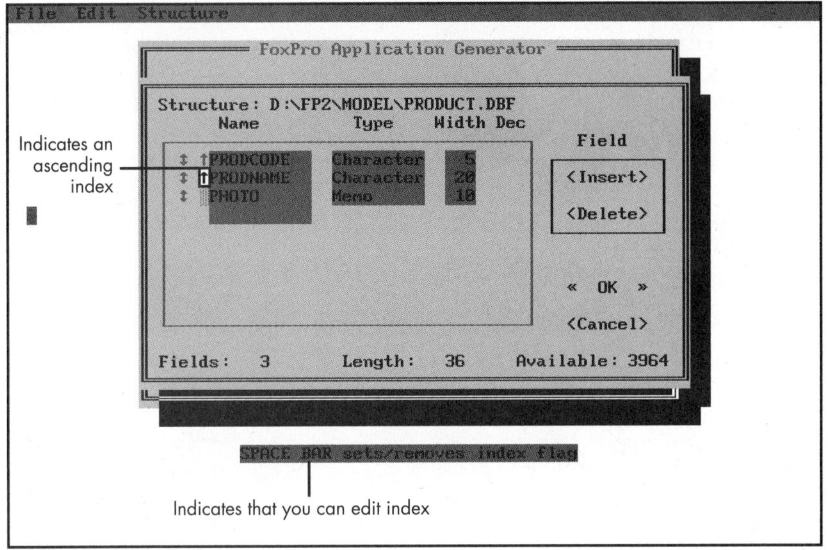

FIG. 1.13

Creating the Product table structure.

- As the first field Name, type **PRODCODE** (FoxPro uses all uppercase, no matter how you type it). After you type the name, a small shaded box appears just to the left. Use the left-arrow key, or Shift-Tab while you're in the PRODCODE space, and press the space bar (or double-click the shaded box). A small up arrow appears instead of the shaded box. As you learn in following chapters, this arrow represents an index, which enables FoxPro to show you the data in order by product code. Leave the Type at the default of Character and type **5** for the Width.
- The second field is **PRODNAME**. Again, double-click the shaded box, or highlight and press the space bar, so that the small up arrow appears. This field also is a Character type, and the Width should be **20**.
- For the third field Name, type **PHOTO**. Press Tab to move to the Type entry and press the space bar or click it to choose Memo from the list of data types that appears but don't add an index to this field. Memo fields have a fixed width of 10, so FoxPro doesn't ask you to enter the width.

Now press Ctrl-Enter, a shortcut for choosing the default (chevron enclosed) *end task* option that you can use almost everywhere in FoxPro, or press Enter with the `K` item highlighted (or click it with the mouse) to save the table definition. FoxApp asks whether you want to `Input data records now?` Press N or click `<No>` and you return to the main FoxApp screen. After using FoxApp to generate the information, you enter the data into the application screen.

Although a table now exists, you can use FoxApp to modify this table if you need to make changes. If you are satisfied that you followed the instructions and that the table is structured as shown in figure 1.13, press Tab twice to Create a screen in which you can enter the Product records. FoxApp places the cursor in the Screen Name space, in case you want to rename the file. Press Enter to accept the default name and press Enter again, if necessary, with the `<Create>` push button highlighted. You see a message from FoxApp that announces the screen is now created.

Although FoxApp already did all the work, choose the `<Modify>` push button highlighted now and make at least one change in the prepared screen. After you click `<Modify>` or press Enter, the screen in figure 1.14 appears.

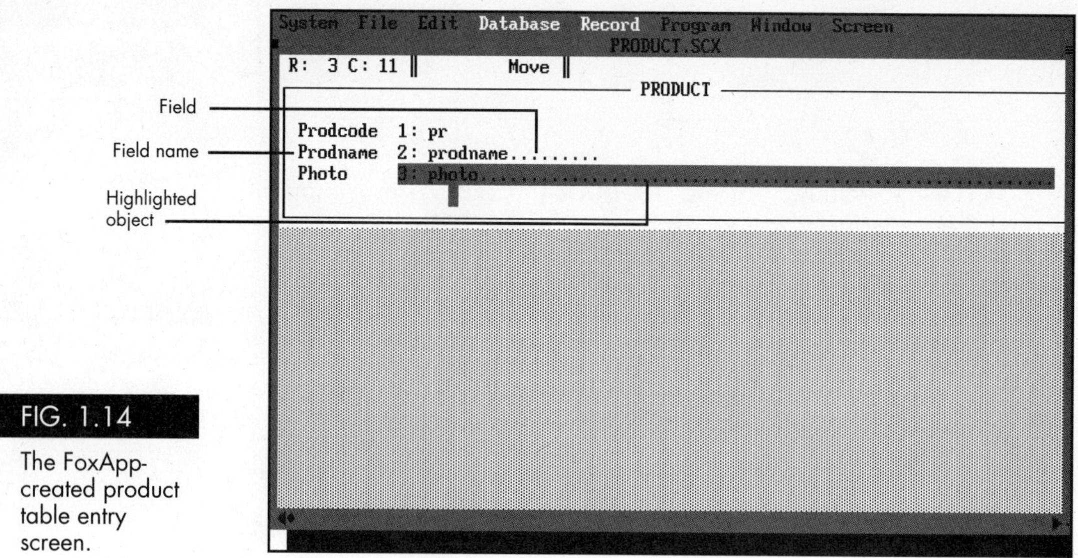

FIG. 1.14

The FoxApp-created product table entry screen.

You see the three field names you just created, each next to a space for you to enter data. One thing you surely know about the Product table: you are not going to do any direct data entry to the Photo field because you cannot type digitized images in from the keyboard. Eliminate this item from the data-entry screen.

To delete this item, move the cursor to the PHOTO field name at the bottom left, and press the space bar, or click it. After `PHOTO` is highlighted, press the Delete key, and PHOTO is deleted. Also delete the space FoxApp prepared for the data entry, to the right (highlighted in figure 1.14).

Now the screen looks unbalanced. To make the screen look better, highlight `PRODNAME` and press the down-arrow key once to move `PRODNAME` down. Press Enter to fix `PRODNAME` in the new position. Do the same for the data-entry space to the right.

You have wasted space here that you can delete. To delete this space, access the Screen option on the top bar by pressing Alt-C and press Enter on Screen Layout to see the varied display of options shown in figure 1.15. (You learn more about these options in Chapter 12.) You can solve the excess space problem if you change the Width item on the left. Type **35**, and the space disappears. After you type the number, press Enter, click «`OK`», or press Ctrl-Enter to look at a smaller screen (see fig. 1.16).

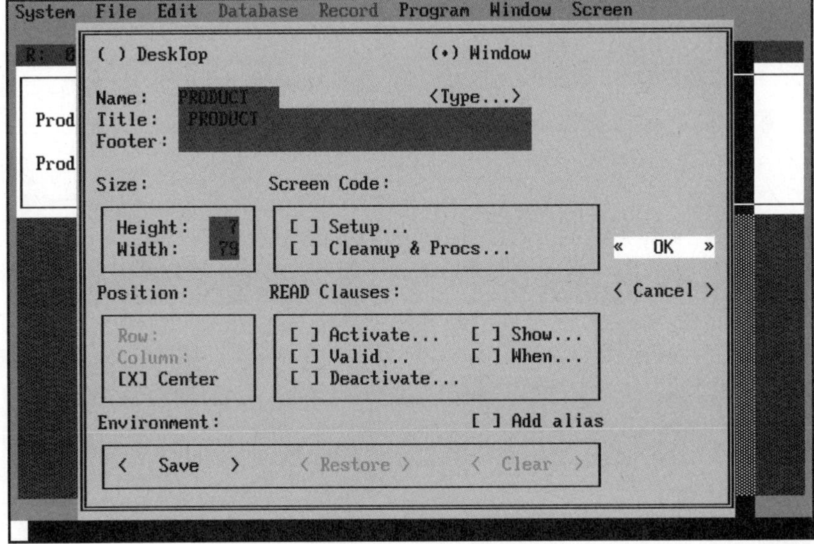

FIG. 1.15

The Screen Layout options.

Press Alt-F to access File options from the top bar and choose Close. After FoxPro asks whether you want to save the changes, select Yes.

You are now back at the main FoxApp screen, and you can click the «`Generate`» push button on the bottom of the screen (or press Ctrl-Enter). FoxApp asks for a name for the application with a file list similar to the one you used to find a program to Do. The name PRODUCT.APP is fine for this application, but make sure that you use the Drive and Directory options, if necessary, to get into the MODEL directory so that you save the file in the correct place. (If you prefer, you also can use the File list to move between directories.)

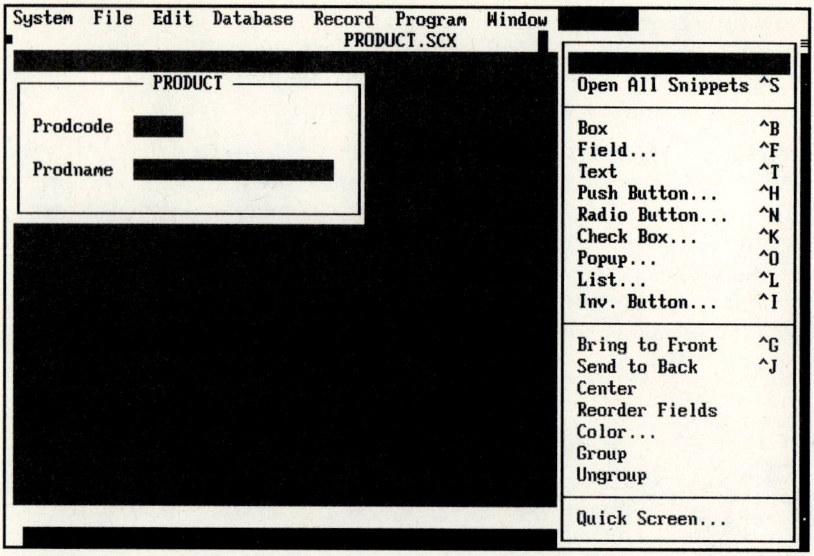

FIG. 1.16

The revised Product table data-entry screen and the Screen Builder options.

FoxApp then begins to generate the application, and you see a number of messages flash across the screen. After FoxApp is finished, a message tells you where the application is stored and that you can press any key or click the mouse to start the application for the first time. When you start an application, the screen you see looks like figure 1.17.

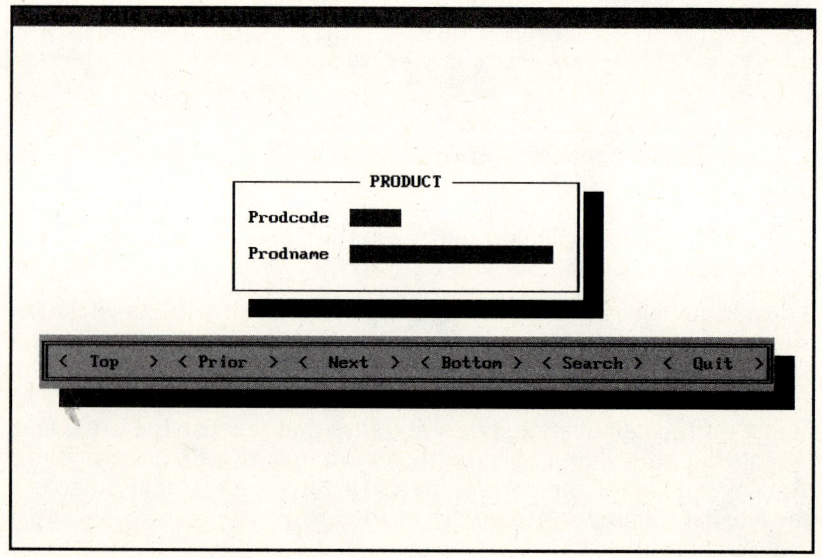

FIG. 1.17

The Product table application screen.

The Product table application screen contains a data-entry area and a panel of controls with which you use to move through the file. The screen also has a new list of options on the top bar. Table 1.1 lists the products manufactured and sold by Omnipresent Widgets. Type these items into the data-entry area now so that you can use them in examples throughout this book. As you type each record, use the option you find under Application on the top bar, as shown in figure 1.18, to Add a new record.

Table 1.1 The Omnipresent Widget Product Line

Record Number	Product Code	Product Name
1	WGT2	Mainframe Widgets
2	WGT1	Laptop Widgets
3	DSQ0	Dream Sequencers
4	BBM0	Bobometers
5	LLD0	Log Ladles (pine)
6	JLD0	Jeli-Do Nuts & Bolts
7	WZL1	Pine Weazlettes
8	WZL2	Lemon Weazlettes
9	WZL3	Floral Weazlettes
10	WZL4	Unscented Weazlettes

NOTE

You don't type the *record numbers* in the preceding chart. Each record in a table has a number that FoxPro assigns internally. The record numbers are provided here for your convenience. Record numbers are not fixed and may change if some records are permanently removed from the database. But, at any time, the highest record number is the same as the *total* number of records in the database.

Make sure that you enter the information carefully. In particular, assign each product code three *capital* letters followed by a digit, as shown in the list. Now, the generated application enables you to add any characters you type in either field. Soon, you learn ways of *validating* data, or of making sure that data fits certain criteria as you enter information. For now, however, this application is not protected by these techniques.

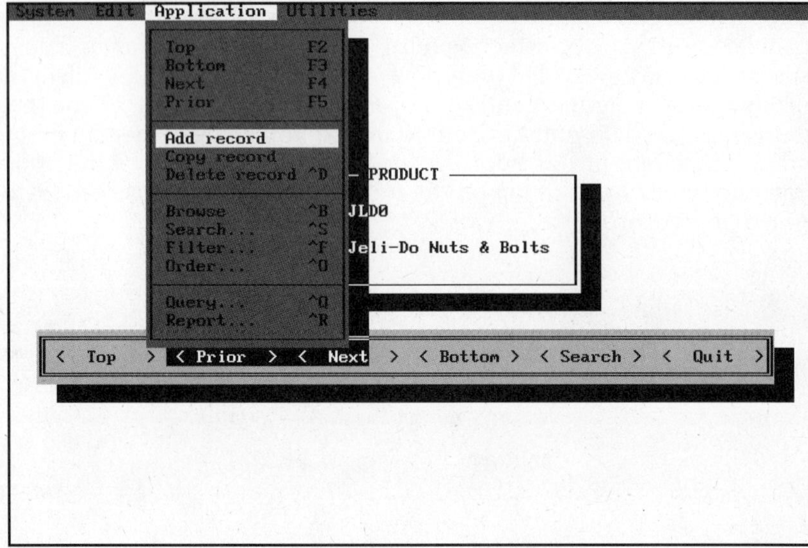

FIG. 1.18

The FoxApp application options.

Now that the table contains information, see what you can do. Use the Application Search option to explore or click the control panel to find some text within the available fields, as shown in figure 1.19. After you find a desired record, you may want to display the word in the context of the product list in various sequences by using the Browse and Order options from the Application choices. Try the Browse option first; then change the Order and Browse the product list again.

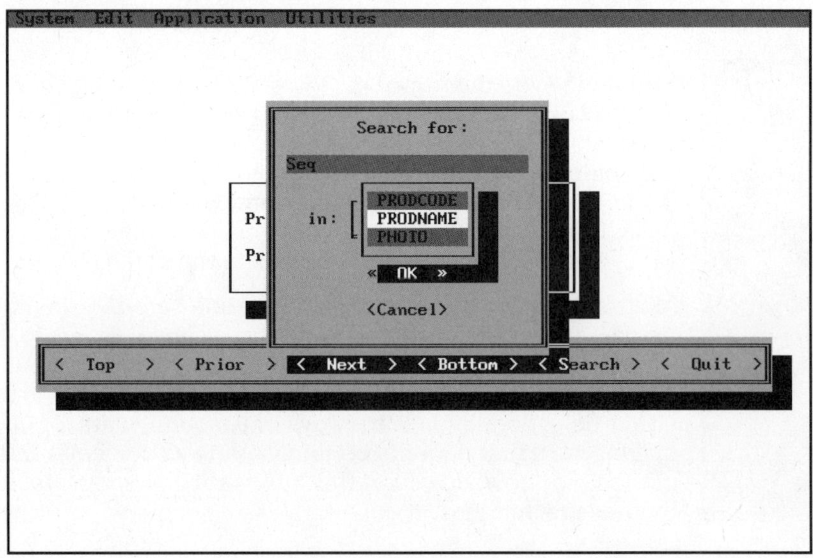

FIG. 1.19

The FoxApp Application Search screen.

Next, try Application's Query option. You are asked to specify a Query name; you can accept the default of PRODUCT.QPR. You then see the screen shown in figure 1.20.

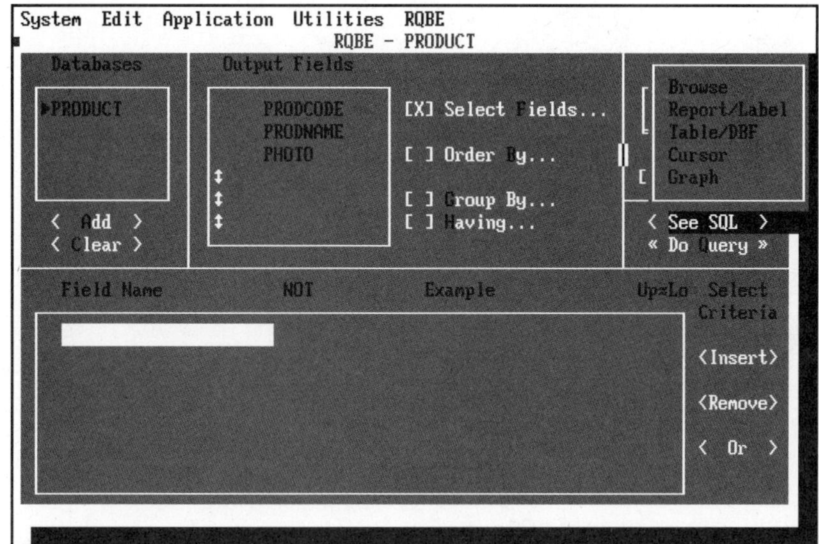

FIG. 1.20

FoxPro's RQBE, with the Report/ Label option about to be chosen.

This screen is FoxPro's *RQBE* (*Relational Query By Example*) design screen. The RQBE enables you to select records by almost unlimited criteria and then display the selected record in many ways. You learn about RQBE and *SQL* (*Structured Query Language*), the command set that underlies FoxPro 2's RQBE, in several sections of this book. RQBE is worth a look during this tour because, along with the Screen Builder with which you have briefly worked, this tool represents a powerful new feature of FoxPro 2. If you access the System Help option while the RQBE screen shows, you can read a good synopsis of RQBE's elements.

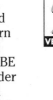

For now, however, just click or press the Tab key to move to the Output To box in the top right corner and press the space bar to choose Report/Label from the list of options that appears. Mark the `Options` check box. From the screen that appears next (see fig. 1.21), press R and then Q to prepare an RQBE Quick Report. Press Enter to accept the default layout. Press Ctrl-Enter to finish selecting Options, and you are returned to the main RQBE screen.

The sample records are entered in no particular order. Arrange the records in alphabetical order for the report. Press B (for `Order By`), and the screen in figure 1.22 appears. Use the down-arrow key to move the highlight to the `PRODUCT.PRODNAME` entry in the Selected Output list on the left side of the screen, as shown in the figure. Press Enter (or double-click the entry), and `PRODUCT.PRODNAME` moves to the Ordering Criteria box on the right side. Press Ctrl-Enter to return to the main RQBE screen. (Notice that in the `Order By` check box, an `X` now appears).

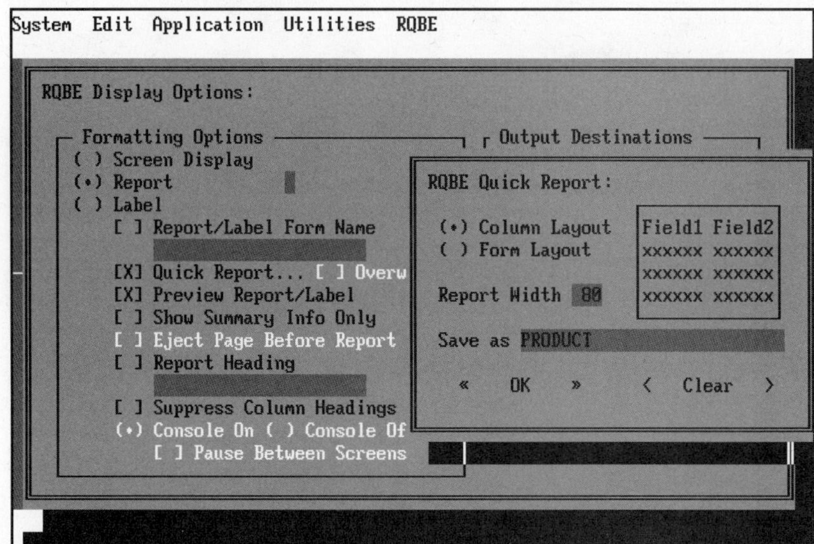

FIG. 1.21

Choosing RQBE output options.

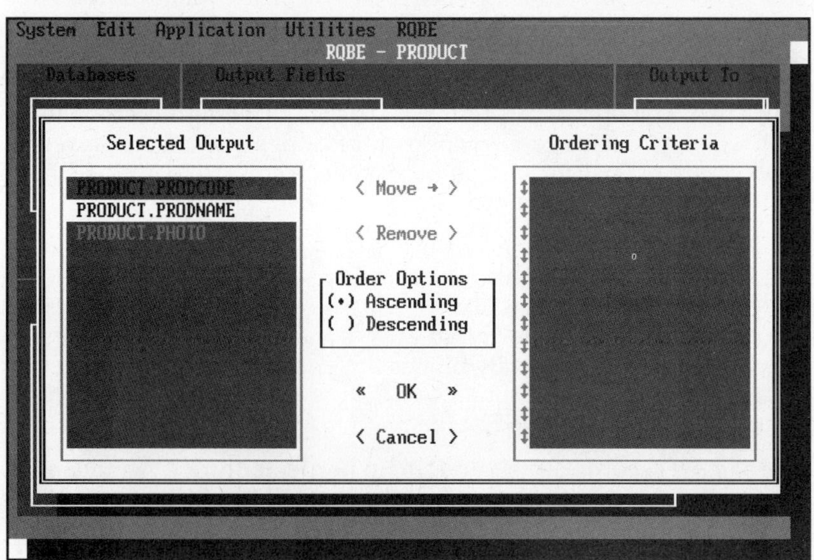

FIG. 1.22

Ordering output in the RQBE.

Now press Q, and the report is delivered to the screen, as shown in figure 1.23, with all records alphabetically ordered by product name. Enter the Options again and press P to remove the `Preview Report/Label` option. Then press T to send the report `To the Printer`.

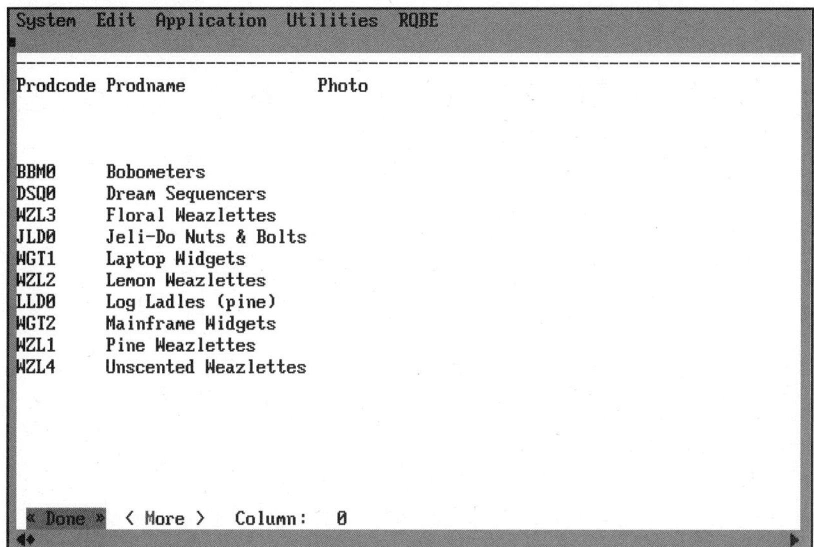

FIG. 1.23

The RQBE-generated report previewed on-screen.

You have not exhausted the capabilities of a generated application in this quick tour; this application represents only a small fraction of what FoxPro can do. Return to this application at your leisure and experiment with the different choices FoxApp provides with little work on your part.

FoxApp is just another FoxPro 2 application, similar to the Product application you just generated with FoxApp and similar to the Organizers. If you use the Program Do sequence that you were using to search for files, and if you installed the necessary optional products, then you see a FOXAPP directory under the GOODIES directory, beneath the main FOXPRO 2 directory. The FoxApp directory and the sub-levels contain the source files for FOXAPP. Later in this book, you examine them directly to see how FOXAPP does the work.

Learning More About FoxPro

FoxPro 2's installation disks contain many other sample materials that this book cannot fully cover. Besides FOXAPP, you find the following items under the GOODIES directory:

- A complete simple application in the LASER directory
- A directory, FNDATION, that holds sophisticated examples for programmers
- A HELPTREE directory that contains a program to add advanced features to the FoxPro 2 HELP system

Take a close look at the self-running DEMO.APP program you can DO from the main FOXPRO program directory (the same way you started FoxApp). You find the source files in the DEMO directory, under GOODIES. DEMO.APP gives you a quick introduction to all FoxPro 2 features and the power tools available under the FoxPro program.

Ending a FoxPro Session

You may decide that you practiced enough in FoxPro for the day or that you are ready to go to Chapter 2 to begin to learn how these intriguing sample applications are created. When you leave FoxPro, however, use the Quit option on the File menu popup. Never turn off or reboot a computer without first Quitting FoxPro.

Occasionally (because of a program or disk crash or a power failure), you must end a FoxPro session abnormally. When this kind of disaster strikes, you will see a number of temporary work files with the extension TMP on the disk. FoxPro usually deletes these files at the end of a session; the number and location of these files depends on the tasks you performed and on other aspects of the configuration. Refer to Appendix D for the kinds of temporary files and how to manage these files by using a CONFIG.FP file. When found, you can delete the files. You also can run the CHKDSK command from DOS to clean up any lost clusters that may result from an abnormal exit (see the DOS manual for details, or for more information, see *MS-DOS 5 User's Guide*, Special Edition or *Using MS-DOS 5*, both published by Que Corporation).

Cleaning up temporary files is easy but often restoring precious data files that become corrupted in a disk crash or other abnormal exits from FoxPro isn't easy. Therefore, backing up data is as vital as using the Quit option to safely end a FoxPro session. Whether you use a special backup utility program or DOS commands to make a second copy of the data doesn't matter; just find a comfortable routine and develop the habit of backing up important data files.

Chapter Summary

In this chapter, you learned how to navigate among FoxPro 2 features by using some of the sample application programs. You learned how to create an application. You practiced starting the program and entering data in the Product table that you created. In the next chapter, you step back a little to discuss the FoxPro 2 *interface*, the ways in which you interact with the program.

2

CHAPTER

Understanding the FoxPro 2 Interface

In this chapter, you learn about the elements that make up the FoxPro 2 interface. The interface of any computer program is composed of all the ways the program communicates directly with you. This interface, through which information travels between you and the program, includes the following characteristics:

- The items you can expect to see on-screen
- The language and formats or style of presentation the program commonly uses to ask you questions and inform you of tasks in progress
- The methods you can use to respond to the program's requests
- The clues (such as colors, positions on-screen, or sounds) the program uses to help you understand the task you are currently doing and the options available to you

These items, formats, methods, and clues are in use no matter what task you are performing with the program. Therefore, the more comfortable you become with the interface, the more productive you become.

Some parts of the FoxPro 2 interface may be familiar if you previously used other computer programs, and other parts may be unique to FoxPro. Because of the rich assortment of choices in the interface, you need to take the time to understand how these choices are organized and presented.

If you like to dive in without much introduction, then go right ahead. In the following chapter, "Exploring Databases and Tables," you can go right to work creating and using data. You can return to this chapter if some aspect of the interface puzzles you.

In subsequent chapters of this book, when you design FoxPro applications for other people to use, you find that you have powerful tools to create application interfaces by using the same items, formats, methods, and clues that FoxPro uses. The better you understand the interface, therefore, the better you can design easily understood applications.

Familiarizing Yourself with the FoxPro Screen

If you followed the introductory information in Chapter 1, then you installed FoxPro and know how to load the program from the DOS command line. If you haven't installed FoxPro, read Appendix A, "Installing FoxPro 2," to make sure that you are prepared to use the program.

If you have not yet done so in Chapter 1, refer to the first chapter to create a subdirectory of the main FoxPro 2 directory, MODEL, to store the data and other files for practice sessions and for the model application. Include the main FoxPro 2 directory in the DOS path, as described in Chapter 1. Now change the current drive and directory so that you are in the MODEL directory. Make sure that the mouse driver is loaded and load FoxPro.

After you load FoxPro 2, you see a sign-on screen (see fig. 2.1).

Across the top of the screen, you see a line known as the *menu bar.* Like other software—and restaurant—menus, this menu presents a list of options available to you. Each option is a *pad* of the menu bar. In the next section, you learn how to choose options or *menu pads* and navigate through the choices contained in each.

NOTE

Remember that the *driver* (the software that interprets information from the mouse) is not part of FoxPro. By using a program provided by the manufacturer of the mouse, you need to make this driver available before you load FoxPro. To encourage mouse use, Fox Software offers inexpensive mice and includes some standard drivers on the FoxPro installation disks.

You can use FoxPro 2 with or without a mouse or other pointing tool. For many people, however, mouse use in FoxPro is both fun and intuitive. Even if you have never used a mouse, make arrangements to test a mouse with this program. Throughout this book, both keyboard and mouse alternatives are provided for each action you take. With a little experimenting, you may find that a mixture of using the keyboard and the mouse best suits your work habits.

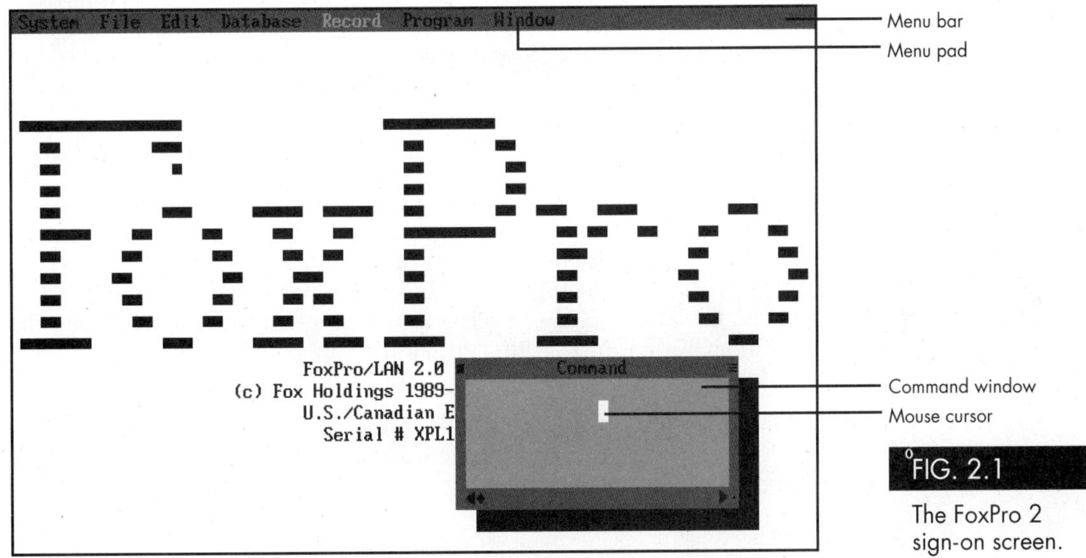

FIG. 2.1

The FoxPro 2 sign-on screen.

In the bottom right quarter of the screen shown in figure 2.1, and in approximately the same position on-screen when you load FoxPro, you see a small box with a border. This box is known as a *window*. Windows are used in FoxPro to present and separate different kinds of tasks and information. In this chapter, you learn about the different kinds of FoxPro windows, the kinds of information these windows contain, and the work you accomplish with each window.

The FoxPro window you now see is the *Command* window. As an alternative to making menu choices, you can type FoxPro command language instructions directly into this window. This chapter helps you learn the typing and editing keystrokes you use in the Command window and elsewhere within FoxPro, and techniques for typing instructions in the Command window.

In figure 2.1, you also see a small rectangle in the bottom half of the screen. This rectangle is the *mouse cursor*. If you are using a mouse, the mouse cursor shows you where the mouse is currently positioned (otherwise, the mouse cursor doesn't appear). If you think the mouse is working but you do not see the mouse cursor, move the mouse around on the mouse pad or on a hard surface until you can see the cursor.

The mouse cursor may be a different shape from the rectangle in figure 2.1. Some PCs are equipped with graphics cards that display a graphical arrow cursor as a mouse pointer.

Understanding the FoxPro Menu System

FoxPro 2 uses two kinds of menus. Some menus are simple lists of available options from which you make a choice and then continue with your business. Other menus are part of a menu system, which organizes the options according to the kind of function each menu performs. The menu bar in figure 2.1 is part of a menu system. Each pad in the menu bar represents a different kind of function that you can perform in FoxPro.

In this section, you investigate the FoxPro menu system, and you learn how to use the menus to communicate with FoxPro without knowing the FoxPro command language.

Learning How To Use the Menu System

A *menu system* has four components: a menu bar, menu pads, menu popups and menu options.

The menu *bar*, the glue that holds the menu system together, contains one or more menu pads, which divide the menu options into different categories. The menu *options* are displayed in a *popup window*, which appears as though attached to the related menu pad.

Figure 2.2 shows the FoxPro menu system with the System menu popup active. Solid lines in the menu popup, such as the line between Macros and Filer, divide the options by function. Here, the solid line separates the desktop accessories, such as the Calculator and the Capture utility, from the other System menu options, such as Help.

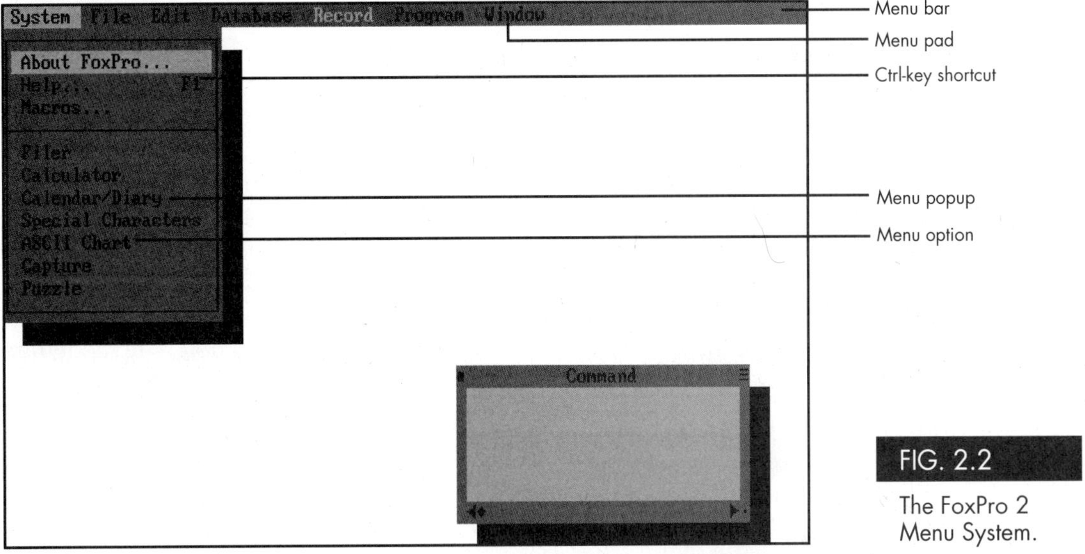

FIG. 2.2

The FoxPro 2 Menu System.

The ellipsis (...) that follows some options indicates that FoxPro requires more information about what you want to do. The method through which this additional information is collected is usually a *dialog*. Dialogs are explained in a following section of this chapter.

Notice that each menu pad name and option description contains a highlighted letter. If you are using a color monitor, the letter appears in a color different from the rest of the text. On a monochrome monitor, this letter is supposed to appear brighter than the other letters. This letter is part of a *hot key*, which enables you to quickly select the pad or option. You learn more about hot keys later in this section.

TIP

On some monochrome and EGA monitors, you may have to adjust the monitor's contrast setting to see the hot-key letter. Move the contrast control to the highest setting and then slowly reduce the contrast until you can distinguish the hot-key letter from the rest of the text.

You can select some menu options directly from the keyboard without activating the menu. If an option can be selected in this way, then a *control-key shortcut* appears on the menu popup to the right of the option description. In figure 2.2, you see that pressing the F1 function key selects the FoxPro Help facility. You learn more about control-key shortcuts in the following section.

Selecting Menu Options

Two ways are available to select a menu option in FoxPro. One way is to activate the menu and choose the option from a menu popup. This step can be performed by using either the keyboard or the mouse. The other way is to enter the option's control-key shortcut (if a shortcut is available) from the keyboard.

The simplest way to activate the FoxPro menu is to press either the Alt key or the F10 function key. These keys perform the same function as the slash (/) key in the Lotus 1-2-3 spreadsheet program. The menu bar becomes active, and the first menu pad is highlighted. From here, you can activate a particular menu pad and the related popup by either moving the highlight bar to the pad name and pressing the space bar or by typing the hot-key letter. You then can select the desired menu option in the same way, by either highlighting the option name and pressing the space bar or by typing the hot-key letter. Mouse users also can activate the menu bar by double-clicking the right-hand button.

You also can activate a particular menu popup by holding down the Alt key and pressing the pad's hot-key letter. For example, Alt-F activates the File popup. The F10 key, however, does not work in the same way and should not be used for this purpose.

You can deactivate the menu at any time by pressing the Esc key or by clicking the mouse on an area of screen other than the menu system. FoxPro reactivates the previously active window. You also can deactivate the menu by pressing the Alt key (F10) again, explicitly deactivating the menu in this way. This step is preferable in multitasking environments, such as Windows and DESQview, which may interfere with the way FoxPro uses the Alt key. When you switch to another program in DESQview or Windows and then come back to FoxPro, the System menu bar is automatically activated.

After you activate a menu popup, you can activate other menus by using the left- and right-arrow keys to move from one menu pad to the next or by using a hot key.

You can select certain menu options by using a control-key shortcut. Except for the FoxPro Help facility, which is selected by pressing F1, keystroke shortcuts are activated by holding down the Ctrl key and pressing an assigned letter or function key. This step is the fastest way to access an option; however, this procedure requires you to memorize the assigned keystrokes. You may want to memorize only the shortcuts for the options that you use frequently, especially if you do not have a mouse.

The following quick reference guide lists all of the FoxPro 2 control-key shortcuts as they appear in the related menu popups. Remember that the caret (^) means that you *hold down the Ctrl key while pressing the appropriate key.*

Table 2.1 Menu Option Shortcuts

Pad Name	Option	Key Shortcut
System	Help	F1
Edit	Undo	^U
	Redo	^R
	Cut	^X
	Copy	^C
	Paste	^V
	Select All	^A
	Find...	^F
	Find Again	^G
	Replace and Find Again	^E
Record	Continue	^K
Program	Do...	^D
	Resume	^M
Window	Move	^F7
	Size	^F8
	Zoom ↑	^F10
	Zoom ↓	^F9
	Cycle	^F1

You can easily activate a menu popup by using a mouse. Place the mouse cursor on the desired menu pad and click the left mouse button. Then move the mouse cursor to the desired option and click the left button again.

The FoxPro menu system is *context-sensitive*, which means that options are enabled only if the options serve a purpose. When you first run FoxPro, for example, you cannot activate the Record menu pad because all the options on this pad's popup act on an open table. Because a table isn't yet open, these options serve no useful purpose and presently cannot be selected.

For similar reasons, one or more options on a popup may be disabled. If you activate the Database popup when no table is open, most options cannot be selected because the options need an open table on which to operate. Those enabled options bring forward the FoxPro Open File dialog to enable you to select a table.

FoxPro displays disabled options in a color (on color monitors) or intensity (on monochrome monitors) that makes the options appear dimmer than enabled options. The default colors for disabled options are cyan letters on a low-intensity white background.

Working with FoxPro 2 Menu Options

When working in FoxPro, the menu bar usually contains seven menu pads. Each pad's menu popup contains options of a different kind.

In the following sections, you see an overview of each menu pad in the form of a table. Consider these tables as a reference guide to the menu options. How you use the menus is covered in subsequent chapters.

You also learn about various menu options that may not be apparent. Where applicable, you are referred to the chapter in which these options are discussed in greater detail.

The System Menu Pad

The System menu popup as shown in table 2.2 presents an eclectic group of options, the most important of which is the FoxPro 2 Help facility. This feature provides instructions on the proper use of FoxPro's many commands and functions. The Help facility is covered in the final section of this chapter.

The System menu also contains the desk accessories, such as the *Filer* and *Calculator*, and the keyboard macro utility, which enables you to save and replay keystroke sequences. These desk accessories are covered in Chapter 15, "Discovering More FoxPro 2 Productivity Features."

Table 2.2 The System Menu Popup

Option	Purpose
About FoxPro...	View information about the version of FoxPro 2, Resource and configuration files in use, available memory and disk space, and so on
Help...	Access the FoxPro 2 Help facility

Option	Purpose
Macros...	Create and edit keyboard macros; create, save, and restore sets of macros, including a special default set
Filer	Display file names; use DOS file functions, such as Copy, Move, Delete, and Rename; search files for text strings
Calculator	Perform basic mathematical functions on-screen and store the results for pasting into a field or file
Calendar/Diary	Display a calendar for any month of any year; attach appointment and other notes to a particular date; store the date selected for use in a field or file
Special Characters	Insert graphic characters into a field or file
ASCII Chart	Display the complete ASCII character set
Capture	Mark and copy text from the screen or window to a field or alternate window
Puzzle	A FoxPro 2 toy. Check out this game!

The File Menu Pad

The File menu popup enables you to create, open, save, and print files. File also enables you to quit FoxPro 2 and return to DOS.

Table 2.3 The File Menu Popup

Option	Purpose
New...	Create a database, program, text, index, report, label, screen, menu, query, or project file
Open...	Open an existing database, program, view text, index, report, label, screen, menu, query, or project file
Close	Close the active window
Save	Save a file with the current name
Save as...	Save a file with the current name or a different name; create a view file when the view window is open
Revert	Cancel all changes to the file in the current editing session

continues

Table 2.3 Continued

Option	Purpose
Printer Setup...	Set certain printer output options, such as the print device and page margins
Print	Print the contents of any open text window, a file, or the FoxPro 2 Clipboard
Quit	Return to DOS

One file that you can create with the New command is a query file. A *query file* contains search expressions, which you build by using the *RQBE* (Relational Query By Example) dialog. RQBE is a powerful searching tool new to version 2 of FoxPro. The RQBE and queries are covered in Chapters 5 and 6.

Notice that the Close option doesn't close a database file; Close closes the active window. If you are editing a text file in the window, then the file closes as a result of closing the window. If you made changes to the text file since you opened or last saved the file, then FoxPro asks whether you want to save these changes.

Save and Save As both save files by writing the files to the disk. Save As, however, enables you to save the file with a different name. This feature is useful when a file was created without a specified file name. (In which case, FoxPro assigns the name *UNTITLED* to the file. This option also is useful to create—rather than replace—a new file with a name similar to an existing file).

Although the File popup menu contains a Print option, you usually use this option only to print straight ASCII text files, such as FoxPro programs. Reports, labels, and other results from the FoxPro data are printed by using the Report and Label options on the Database Menu.

The Edit Menu Pad

In table 2.4, you see that most options on the Edit menu popup have control-key shortcuts, which enable you to quickly access the editor's features from the keyboard. The primary purpose of the Edit pad, therefore, is to act as a reference guide for typists and to provide mouse users with access to the editor's functions. The FoxPro editor is explored in a following section of this chapter.

Table 2.4 The Edit Menu Popup

Option	Purpose
Undo	Cancel the most recent change in a field or file
Redo	Restore changes previously undone
Cut	Remove text from a field or file and place the text on the Clipboard
Copy	Copy text from a field or file to the Clipboard
Paste	Insert the current contents of the Clipboard into a field or file
Clear	Delete text without placing the text on the Clipboard
Select All	Select all text in the current editing window or select the contents of a current field in a Browse or Edit window
Goto Line...	Move the cursor to a specific line number in a text file or memo field
Find...	Search a file or memo field for the first occurrence of a text string
Find Again	Find the next occurrence of the text string
Replace and Find Again	Same as Find Again, except that the located text is replaced by the replacement text entered in the Find dialog
Replace All	Replace all occurrences of a text string
Preferences	Set certain text formatting options, such as word wrap and tab spacing

Like other text editors, the FoxPro 2 editor uses default settings, such as the number of spaces to insert into the file when you press the Tab key. You can configure the editor to use settings that are appropriate for a task through the Preferences option. You can specify that these new settings apply only to the current file or to all files that have the same extension as the current file (for example, all files that end in TXT).

The Database Menu Pad

The Database menu popup contains some options, such as Browse and Report, that you use all the time and other options, such as Append From and Copy To, that you may never use (see table 2.5).

Table 2.5 The Database Menu Popup

Option	Purpose
Setup	Set display options for the records in the current work area or modify the structure of the table
Browse	View/Edit records in the current table
Append From...	Add records to the current table from another table or from a file of a different format
Copy To...	Copy records from the current table to a new table
Sort...	Sort the records in the current table by using a specified field as the sort key
Total...	Create records in another table containing totals of numeric fields in the current table
Average...	Calculate the average of numeric fields in the current table
Count...	Calculate the number of records in the current table that meet a specified criterion
Sum...	Calculate totals of numeric fields in the current table
Calculate...	Perform financial and statistical operations on fields in the current table
Report...	Print reports by using an existing report form
Label...	Print labels by using an existing label form
Pack	Permanently remove records marked for deletion from the current table
Reindex	Recreate all open index files related to the current table

All these options work on an open table, and most of the options are therefore disabled when a table is not open in the current work area. The options enabled, such as Browse, bring up the Open File dialog to enable you to select and open a table.

Browse is the real workhorse of FoxPro. If you are familiar with the limited functionality of the BROWSE command in dBASE IV or FoxBASE+, then you are in for a treat as you begin to learn the power of FoxPro 2's browse facility. The ways in which you can use Browse are limited only by your imagination. This remarkable FoxPro 2 feature is covered in Chapter 8, "Organizing the Answers with BROWSE."

You use the Report and Label options to print reports and labels by using existing report and label forms. To create these forms, select the New option from the File Menu. Chapters 9 and 10 cover the features of reports and labels.

The Record Menu Pad

The Record menu popup enables you to perform basic database management operations—such as Add, Edit, Replace, and Delete—on one or more records. You also can locate a record by entering a search expression in the dialog that appears after you select Locate or Seek.

Table 2.6 The Record Menu Popup

Option	Purpose
Append	Enable new records to be added to the current table from the keyboard
Change	Edit existing records in the current table
Goto...	Move the record pointer to another record in the table
Locate...	Find the first record that meets a specified criterion
Continue	Find the next record that meets the criteria specified in the Locate command
Seek...	Use an active index file to quickly find a record
Replace...	Exchange the current contents of one or more fields with a specified value
Delete...	Mark records for deletion at a later time
Recall...	Restore records marked for deletion to active status

Seek uses a FoxPro 2 index file. Indexed searches are fast (usually taking less than one second), regardless of the table's size.

Locate, however, searches the database by scanning each record without using the active index. Although the range of records to be scanned can be restricted, search times using Locate are therefore proportionate to the size of the database, and usually longer than when using Seek. FoxPro's new Rushmore technology, a data access technique that collects sets of records by using all available indexes rather than one active index, makes Locate a better choice than Seek under some conditions. Rushmore and the ways in which you use this feature are discussed in Chapter 7, "Querying with SQL and Searching with Rushmore."

Along with an investigation of the RQBE and of Rushmore's effect on search techniques, the Seek and Locate features are used and discussed throughout the programs in this book.

The Program Menu Pad

The Program menu popup options listed in table 2.7 enable you to create, compile, and run programs. New to FoxPro 2, the Generate option tells FoxPro to create a program by using a special screen or menu definition table that you create with Screen Builder or Menu Builder, which are covered in Chapters 12, 13, and 14.

Table 2.7 The Program Menu Popup

Option	Purpose
Do...	Execute a FoxPro program
Cancel	Cancel a program paused by using the Suspend command
Resume	Resume execution of a paused program
Compile...	Create an executable version of a FoxPro program
Generate...	Create a FoxPro program from a screen or menu definition table
FoxDoc	Create technical documentation for a FoxPro program
FoxGraph...	Create 2- and 3-dimensional graphs from a table or database

FoxDoc is a powerful documentation tool for FoxPro programmers. After you tell FoxDoc the name of a project file or the name of the first program in the system, this tool creates formatted source code listings, a tree diagram, a variable cross-reference, and several other useful reports. Most FoxPro programmers consider FoxDoc an invaluable aid. The final section of Chapter 18, "Enhancing the Applications You Program," is devoted to FoxDoc.

The Window Menu Pad

The Window menu pad is FoxPro's window control center (see table 2.8). Besides the options shown in the following table, the Window popup lists the names of windows you previously defined and enables you to activate a window by selecting the window name from the menu.

Zoom, an option new to FoxPro 2, minimizes a window so that text and other objects aren't obscured on-screen, yet still remain visible and easily accessible. Besides minimizing, you also can move a window out of the way by *docking* the window. Docking and other methods of manipulating windows are covered in the following section.

Table 2.8 The Window Menu Popup

Option	Purpose
Hide	Remove the active window from the screen display
Clear	Remove all displayed text in the active window
Move	Move the active window to another position on-screen
Size	Change the size and shape of the active window
Zoom ↑	Expand the active window to fill the screen
Zoom ↓	Shrink the active window to minimum size (all you can see is the title bar)
Cycle	Activate the next window in the list of defined windows
Color...	Use the FoxPro 2 Color Picker to set the screen display colors
Command	Activate the Command window
Debug	Activate the FoxPro 2 program debugging window
Trace	Activate the FoxPro 2 program trace window
View	Activate the View window

The Context-Sensitive Menu Pads

Occasionally, while working in FoxPro 2, the menu pads that appear in the menu bar may change. Some pads are added only if the options contained in the related menu popups are pertinent to the current screen. Besides providing quick access to certain options, these popups also serve as a quick-reference guide to features related to the current task.

Figure 2.3 shows the FoxPro 2 menu bar, with a browse window open. The Browse menu popup shows you many options that add power and flexibility to the browse editing mode. After you close the Browse window, the menu pad disappears from the menu bar.

In some contexts, FoxPro also eliminates some of the usual pads from the menu bar. These pads reappear when you can use them again.

Examining FoxPro 2 Windows

You may have previously noticed that the menu popups you produce by selecting menu bar options at times cover up—but do not really erase—other information on-screen. This condition occurs because menu popups are a special kind of FoxPro *window*.

Browse menu pad

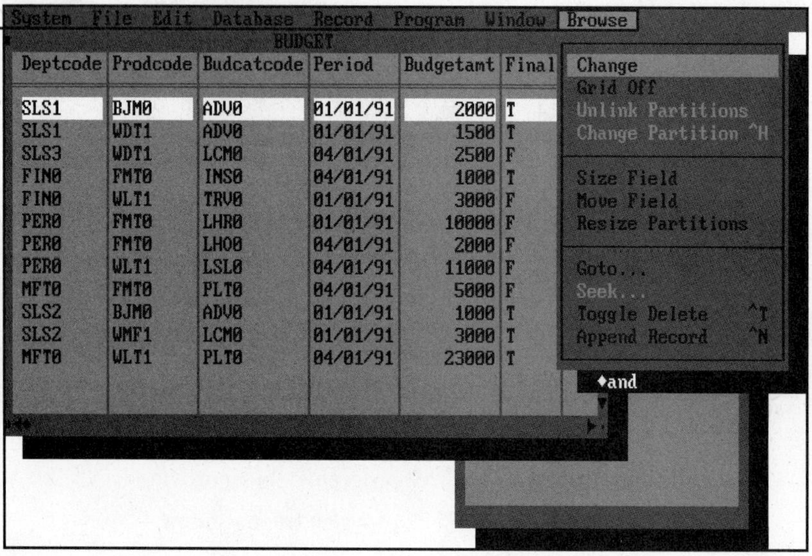

FIG. 2.3

The Browse menu popup.

Consider a window as a self-contained object. Many people find that thinking of the screen as a *desktop* is a good analogy, with the windows as pieces of paper or other items arranged on this desktop. You can move windows around and remove old or add new windows; you also can change a window's dimensions, contents, or other attributes without affecting the underlying *desk* surface. This section introduces the window elements that tell you the kind of window at which you are looking and what you can do with the window.

Understanding the Parts of a Window

Figure 2.4 shows you a typical assortment of windows in use during a FoxPro session. As you see, many FoxPro windows have *shadows* (a dark line to the bottom and the right of the window) to help you remember that these objects are separate from the screen. The windows also are surrounded by a *border* that serves as a visual boundary between this window and the screen and other windows that may be open.

Using the System pad on the menu bar, open the Filer and the Calculator as you learned in the preceding section. Now select New from the File... pad on the menu bar. As the three dots indicate, further choices appear in the form of a *dialog*. Dialogs are explained in a subsequent section of this chapter, but for now just click the File option or press F (to open a new text file window). With the mouse, click the «OK» push button in the dialog or press Enter while «OK» is highlighted, and the UNTITLED text file window appears.

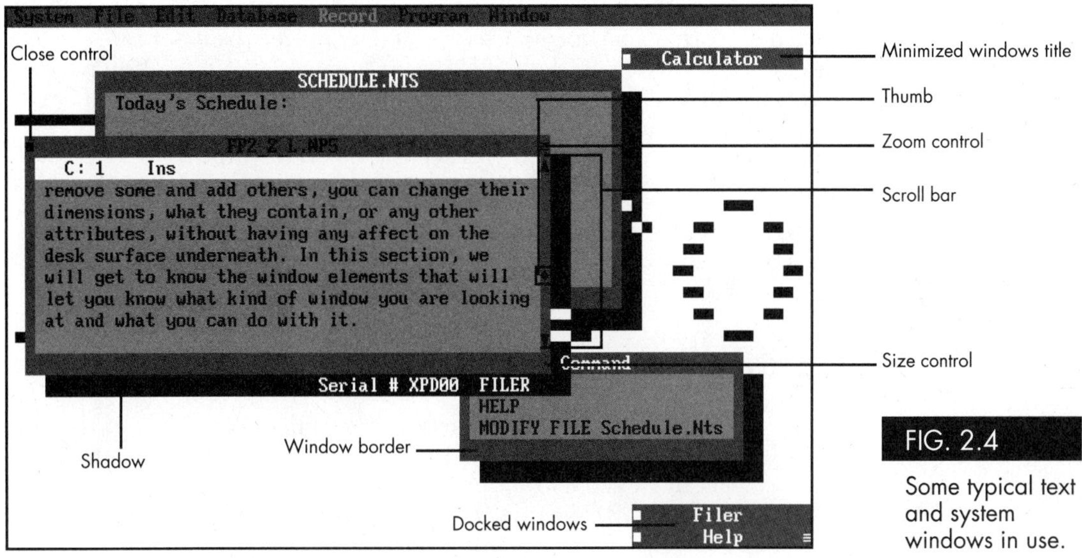

FIG. 2.4

Some typical text and system windows in use.

Besides the Command window, you probably now see three windows on-screen, and each window probably appears on top of the previous window. As you activate these windows, notice that each window has a *title*, centered in the top window border, that indicates the window's function. One window has a title differently colored or highlighted from the other windows (see fig. 2.4). This color marks the currently *active*, or in use, window. Only one window is active at a time. The last window you opened usually is the window on top of the stack and is active until you make a new choice.

After you select the Window pad, you may notice that the newly opened Filer, Calculator, and UNTITLED file are added to the list of windows available. You can *cycle* through the available windows, making different windows active by performing one of the following procedures:

- Select the desired window from the Window menu popup (by pressing the highlighted letter in or next to the name, by moving the highlight bar with the up- and down-arrow keys until the name is selected and pressing Enter, or by clicking on the name with the mouse).

- Click directly on the window you want to activate with the mouse.
- Press Ctrl-F1 to move between the windows until you activate the window you want.

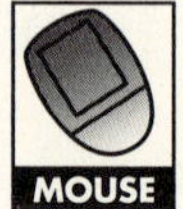

Try the different window-activation techniques by using the mouse and the keyboard in different combinations. You may find clicking the Window pad and selecting the window by highlighted letter a more natural way to perform this procedure, or you may prefer to select the Window pad by using Alt-W and then clicking on the window name. You may prefer clicking directly on the window you want to activate but in some situations, such as when the screen is crowded, you may use Ctrl-F1 to bring windows forward until you see the desired window.

You can make the Command window active by using a special keyboard shortcut. You can press Ctrl-F2 at any time to bring forward the Command window.

Controlling the Window

Using the Window menu popup, activate the Filer. You see that the Filer provides many options for file management that you may want to keep readily available, even if you don't want this menu cluttering the screen. An easy way to set up this kind of screen is to *minimize* the window so that the Filer remains on-screen but uses little space. Minimize the Filer now by taking one of the following actions:

- With the mouse, double-click the top border near the Filer title.
- From the Window menu popup, choose the Zoom ↓ option.
- Press Ctrl-F9.

You bring the Filer back to the normal size by repeating one of the preceding actions.

You may prefer to keep the Filer on the desk, either minimized or normal size, but also want the menu out of the way to make room to edit the UNTITLED text file. You can *move* a window by performing one of the following actions:

- With the mouse, *click-drag* (click and hold down the mouse button as you move the mouse) the title to near the center of the window's or box's top border.
- Choose the Move option from the Window menu popup.
- Press Ctrl-F7.

If you are moving a window by using the keyboard, the border *flashes* (blinks on and off), and you can press the up-, down-, left-, and right-arrow keys until the window is in the preferred position. Press Enter to end the move.

FoxPro 2 uses a special way, *docking*, to minimize and push a window out of the way at the same time. When you dock a window, you stow the window neatly in minimized size in the lower right corner of the screen. You dock a window by double-clicking on the window title while holding down the Shift key or by pressing Shift-Ctrl-F9.

You just learned an important and consistent FoxPro interface principle, where you perform an action by using the mouse and—where a keyboard equivalent exists—adding a Shift key to either the mouse click or to the keypress are equivalent actions.

FoxPro often uses the space bar to imitate a mouse click to select items, such as currently highlighted menu popup options. Wherever a double-click or a shift-click enables you to perform an additional action, you can duplicate a mouse double-click with a double space bar or a Shift-space bar keypress.

Figure 2.4 shows two docked system windows. If you dock more than one window, the windows stack in a vertical pile.

To make a window consistently appear in a different part of the screen, minimize and move the window to the desired position. The next time you minimize this window, the window moves to the selected position.

Activate the Command window. You see that, besides a differently colored title, an active window may have extra elements in the bor der, usually referred to as *controls*. These controls provide convenient window-manipulation for mouse users.

The bottom border contains a small triangle facing left at the left corner (◀), another triangle facing right at the right corner(▶), and a diamond (♦) on the border and between the two triangles. These three items make up a window's *scroll bar*. These characters indicate that you can move to the left and to the right to see more information in the window. A window also may have a second scroll bar along the right border, which indicates that you can scroll up and down to see more information in this window.

You use the scroll bars by clicking with the mouse on either triangle to scroll smoothly through the window. Notice that the diamond (referred to here as the scroll bar's *thumb*) moves to provide a rough indication of the current position in the window, relative to the top or bottom of the information list. You also can click any point of the scroll bar or click-drag the thumb, which changes your relative position with rapid jumps.

You cannot activate the scroll bars directly from the keyboard, but all windows that show scroll bars enable you to move rapidly through the window contents by using the PgUp and PgDn keys. You also can move to the top or bottom of a window that contains text by using the Ctrl-Home and the Ctrl-End key combinations.

The Command window border contains a few more controls that you need to recognize and learn to use.

In the upper right corner of the border is a small box composed of three horizontal lines (≡), which is the window's *zoom control.* Clicking on the zoom control enables you to make the currently active window fill all the space available on-screen. This feature is useful for editing text on a full screen. Clicking the zoom control again returns the window to the original size.

You also can zoom a window to full screen size from the Window menu popup, by using the Zoom ↑ option, or by pressing Ctrl-F10. You can return a window to the previous size by repeating the action.

To change a window to a size other than the default size FoxPro gives (not a full-screen window), you can use the control that appears as a small dot (•) in the bottom right corner of the border, to *size* the window any way you want. With the mouse, click-drag the control to stretch or shrink the window. You can size a window from the Window menu popup by using the Size option or by pressing Ctrl-F8. After you take either step, the border flashes, and you can use the arrow keys to size the window, as you did when you moved the window, until you press Enter to signify that you are finished. The cursor temporarily disappears while the arrow keys assume the sizing or moving function.

An important difference exists between zooming a window, either up to full-screen or down to minimum, and sizing a window to either of these extremes and anywhere between. By storing the information in the *Resource* file, FoxPro can remember a custom size that you give as a window's new default size. The FoxPro Resource file (discussed in Chapter 15), holds many other personal preferences besides window positions. Consider this file as the way FoxPro arranges the screen to suit your work habits. *Zooming* a window doesn't affect FoxPro's default size for this window.

Activate the Calculator window and notice the solid square control (■) in the upper left corner of the border. This symbol is the *close* control. You can click this control to close a window, or you can choose the equivalent Close option from the File menu popup. After activating each window in turn, try both methods to close the Calculator and Filer windows. You also can close these windows by pressing Esc. Notice that you also can activate or close a minimized or docked window.

You also can *hide* a window by Shift-clicking the close control. Make the Filer window active and try this procedure. Alternatively, you can hide a window with the option on the Window menu popup. You still can activate a hidden window for use even when the window is hidden. Choose the window from the current Window menu popup list, and the window reappears.

Activate the UNTITLED text file window now. Type your name in the window. Practice changing the size and hiding the window. Now bring back and try to close the window by using any of the preceding methods.

After you type your name (or anything else) in the text file window, you receive a new kind of window with a message, as shown in figure 2.5. (The buttons in the figure appear *only after the Esc key is pressed* to close a text file after you make changes.)

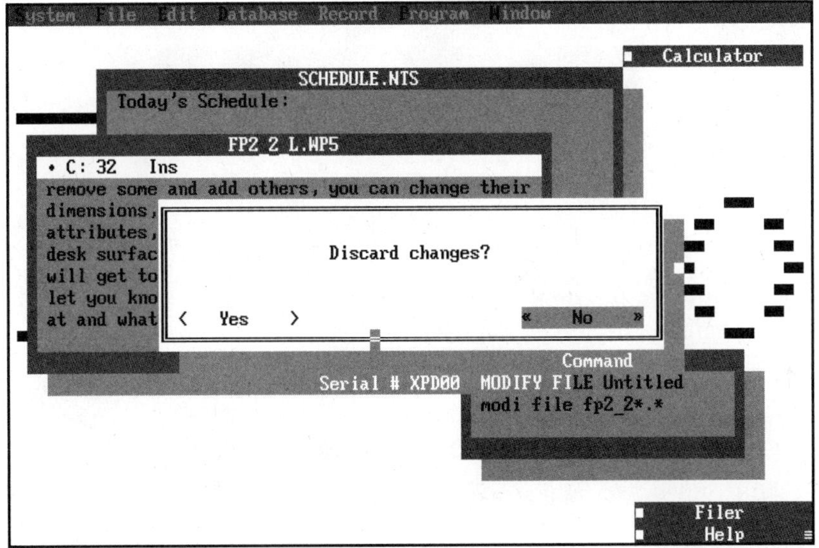

FIG. 2.5

A sample Alert window with prompt and buttons.

Working with Different Window Types

This window, although asking for information and a response, looks different from the dialog that opens a new file. This window has a different border style and colors or intensities. FoxPro uses this kind of window, referred to as an *Alert*, to tell you that something may be wrong. Here, the Alert wants to know whether you mean to *save* the information you typed to a text file before closing the window; if you do not save these changes, the information is lost. FoxPro asks a question, known as a *prompt* or *message*, and enables you to make some possible responses by clicking on a form known as *buttons*.

Depending on the method you use to try to close the text file window, the Alert you see may produce a slightly different prompt or different choices from the prompt in figure 2.5. Responding to an Alert, however, is similar in each case: like buttons on a physical machine, these buttons offer choices. You must press one button to signify your intent. You press a button by clicking with the mouse or by using the Tab key to move the highlight to the button and pressing Enter. You also have a *default button*, usually indicating the safest choice you can make, which you can choose by pressing Enter or Ctrl-Enter when you see the Alert. The default button is surrounded by *chevrons* («, »)—for example, `«No»`. By pressing Esc, you also can *cancel* the process that brought about the Alert.

TIP FoxPro offers keyboard shortcuts that, in one step, close the window and save all the work in the window. Press either Ctrl-W or Ctrl-Enter to close and save. Refer to Appendix F and table 2.1 for more information on key combinations that close a window.

Not every Alert requires you to make a choice. You see an error message from FoxPro if you type a command in the Command window that FoxPro doesn't understand. Try activating the Command window, typing your name, and pressing Enter to see this kind of Alert message. This Alert message requires that you read a message only, which you then remove by pressing any key that usually produces on-screen characters (Shift, Ctrl, CapsLock, and other keys that produce no output don't work), or by clicking the mouse anywhere on-screen.

Not all messages that FoxPro gives you are warnings. FoxPro has a special kind of dialog that contains informational messages or instructions that require minimal response. These items usually appear in a small window in the upper right corner of the screen and look entirely different from Alerts. Again, by pressing any key, you can remove this kind of window after you read the contents.

To see an informational message window, activate the Command window, type **DISPLAY MEMORY**, and press Enter. You are prompted to `Press any key to continue` in a small message window which provides a pause so that you can read each screen of information.

Alerts, dialogs, and other message windows and some windows with special contents, such as the Filer, cannot be resized but can be moved by normal methods. (You may want to move an Alert to examine a window or other object on-screen that is beneath the obscuring item before you answer the prompt.) Try moving an Alert, message window, or dialog by click-dragging the top border or by pressing Ctrl-F7. Although these borders appear different from other window borders, the borders respond normally. You cannot, however, specify new default positions by moving dialogs and Alerts (when these items next appear, they return to the original position). To momentarily check the screen beneath *all* the open windows, such as when checking the memory display you just called on-screen, press the Ctrl, Shift, and Alt keys together. As long as you hold down this key combination, all open windows—even the menu bar—remain hidden.

Learning About More Window Options

You may want to tidy the screen after displaying memory on-screen or (as in an upcoming chapter, after you learn to direct FoxPro's output) in a window. Choose the Window popup option to Clear, and the information disappears from the screen.

If you hold down the Shift key while you use either the mouse or the keyboard to select the Window pad on the menu bar, you see a subtle change in the options in the Window menu popup list. The Hide option now reads Hide All, and the Clear item changes to Show All. (You cannot select both items at the same time.) This step is another effective way to banish clutter from the screen and yet keep working objects within easy reach.

You still have another way to explore how you can affect the appearance of FoxPro 2 windows: you can change window and object *colors*. Although you more fully investigate methods for changing the colors of FoxPro interface elements in a following chapter, you can immediately change the colors of all standard interface elements if the present combination appears unpleasant or difficult to read on some hardware. Even if you use a monochrome monitor and video card, you may want to vary intensities to make certain elements more legible.

Choose the Color option of the Window menu popup, and a special dialog, the *Color Picker*, appears. In the upper right corner is a special *popup control*; pushing this kind of button makes a list of choices appear. Click on this button with the mouse or press the Tab key until the button is highlighted and then press Enter. A list of screen objects pops up, as shown in figure 2.6.

You see several kinds of interface objects that you may recognize, such as Alerts and dialogs. Select an object you know by clicking the object with the mouse or moving the highlight in the popup to the object and—while the object is highlighted—pressing Enter or the space bar. The popup list closes, and the chosen object is named on the button. The list of characteristic parts of the object includes one item marked with a bullet (•) to indicate that you are selecting colors for the object, and the grid of color pairs includes one item marked with chevrons (« and ») to indicate the current colors for the item.

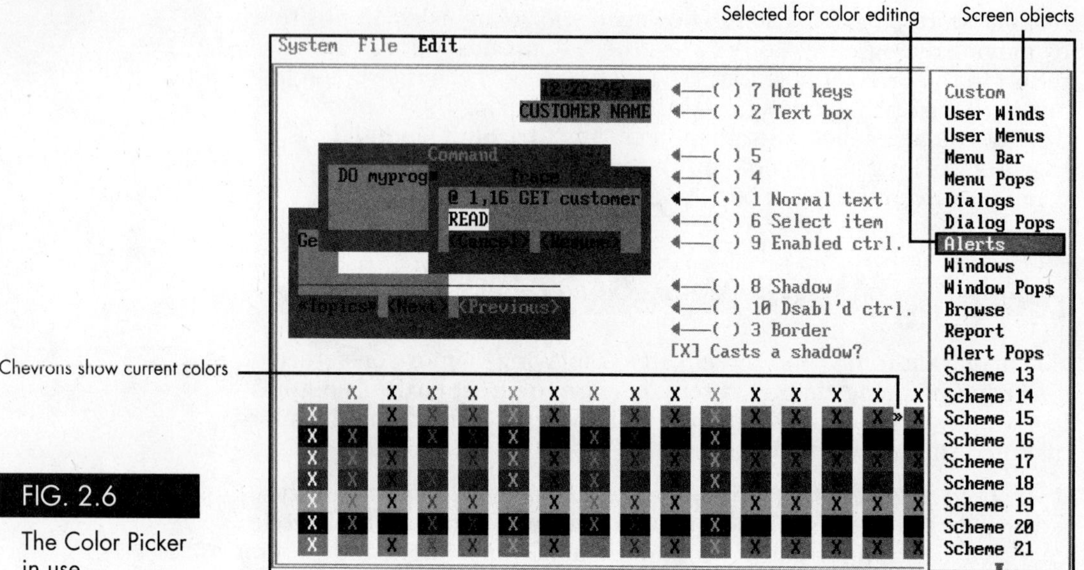

FIG. 2.6

The Color Picker in use.

With the Tab key, move the highlight to the currently selected item, `Normal text`, and press the space bar. The chevrons blink, and you can use the arrow keys to move the selection to a new color pair. As you move among the pairs, watch in the sample window as the normal text sample changes colors. Pick new colors in this object for normal text by pressing the space bar or Enter (or just click with the mouse). Register the selection (it won't be permanent) by clicking on the `«OK»` button, pressing Enter while the object is highlighted, or by pressing Ctrl-Enter. Call up a new instance of this kind of object in the interface. You see the selection reflected in the new dialog or Alert window that appears.

The new color selections remain in effect for this kind of object until you change them again or until you quit FoxPro. To save the selections more permanently, read the "FoxPro Color Control" section of Chapter 15.

Putting System Windows in Perspective

So far, the windows you have examined are windows that FoxPro creates internally and produces when needed. In following chapters, you learn to design windows that can have the same attributes as windows designed by the system, such as the capability of being moved, having a particular border style, or a window definition that includes any combination of these attributes.

The following table is a quick reference to the options available for both system-defined and user-defined windows in the FoxPro 2 interface.

Table 2.9 Window Manipulation

Window Action	Menu Item	Key Shortcut	Mouse Method
Open a window	Various System pad options, Open dialog on the File popup	None	None
Cycle between windows	Cycle option of Window pad	Ctrl-F1 (Ctrl-F2 for Command window)	Click inside window you want to activate
Minimize a window	Zoom ↓ on Window popup	Ctrl-F9	Double-click on top window border
Move a window	Move on Window popup	Ctrl-F7	Click-drag on top border
Dock a window	None	Shift-Ctrl-F9	Shift, double-click on top border
Move quickly through window contents	None	PgDn, PgUp, Ctrl-End, and Ctrl-Home in window border	Scroll bars on and bottom and right text
Zoom to full-size	Zoom ↑ on Window popup	Ctrl-F10	Zoom control on right corner of border
Size a window corner	Size on Window popup	Ctrl-F8	Size control on upper right
Close a window	Close on File popup	Ctrl-W or Ctrl-Enter to save contents; Esc or Ctrl-Q to cancel last changes	Close control on upper left corner
Close all windows	Close All on Shifted File popup	None	None
Hide a window	Hide on Window popup	None	None

continues

Table 2.9 Continued

Window Action	Menu Item	Key Shortcut	Mouse Method
Clear output from a window	Clear on Window popup	None	None
Hide all windows	Hide All on shifted Window popup	Ctrl-Shift-Alt (temp.)	None
Show all windows	Show All on shifted Window popup	None	None
Change window or window element colors	Color... on Window popup	None	None

Understanding Dialog Logic

A *dialog* is a special kind of FoxPro window that gathers information needed to complete a FoxPro command or expression. The box appears whenever you select a menu option followed by an ellipsis (...). Dialogs are visually distinguished from other kinds of windows by a double-line border and the special objects they contain. While in a dialog, you are required to finish one or more tasks before you can go to other options.

In this section, you learn to recognize the various components of a dialog and how to use a dialog to complete menu selections.

Identifying the Components of a Dialog

Dialogs consist of *control objects* that enable you to specify, confirm, and cancel actions. Each object has a different appearance, which provides a visual clue as to the function in the dialog.

The FoxPro 2 Report dialog shown in figure 2.7 contains four kinds of objects: *check boxes*, *radio buttons*, *push buttons*, and *text boxes*.

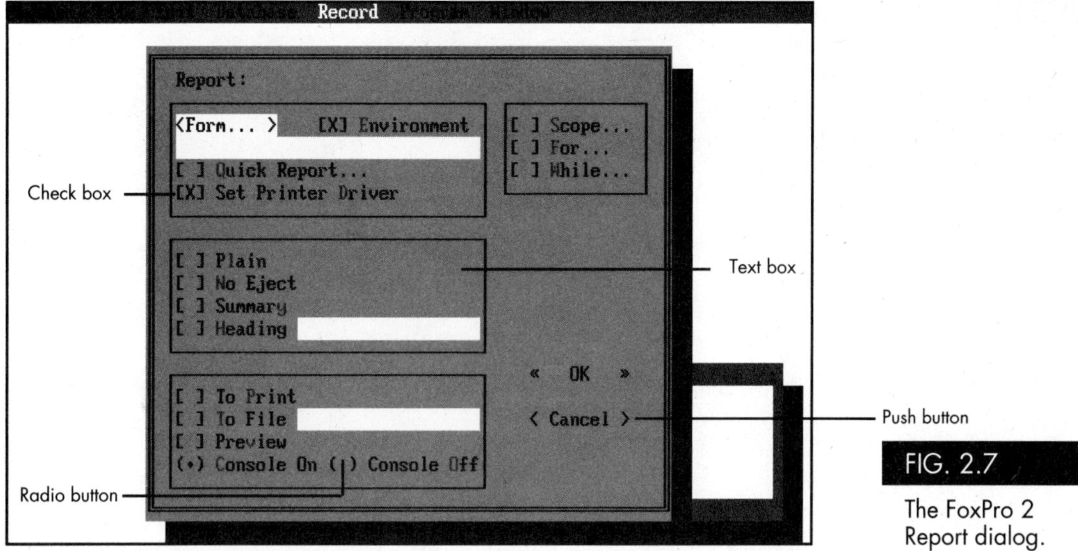

FIG. 2.7

The FoxPro 2 Report dialog.

Check Boxes

A check box appears as a pair of square brackets followed by text. The text describes what happens if you check the box. A check box that is checked, or marked, shows an X between the brackets.

Check boxes enable you to turn on or off different options. Selecting a check box is like flipping a light switch. An option that is *on* is turned *off*, and vice-versa.

Related check boxes are usually grouped together in a box drawn with a single solid line. Although related, each check box is a separate object. You can mark more than one check box in a group at the same time, and marking one box usually has no effect on the other boxes. A check box may become disabled, however, if another check box with which this option is incompatible is marked.

Radio Buttons

A radio button appears as a pair of parentheses followed by text. Radio buttons always come in groups of two or more. The selected button appears with a bullet (•) between parentheses.

Radio buttons enable you to choose among several related options. Unlike a group of check boxes, a group of radio buttons forms a single FoxPro object. Because only one radio button in the group may be marked at a time, each radio button responds to actions performed on the other buttons in the group. When you change a selection from one button in a group to another button, the selected symbol (•) moves from the old button to the new button.

Push Buttons

A push button appears as text enclosed by angle brackets (< and >). A push button always triggers an action. If the text is followed by an ellipsis (...), another dialog appears after the text button is pushed. Most dialogs contain at least two push buttons, «Okay» and <Cancel>.

As shown in the preceding paragraph, every dialog has one push button enclosed in chevrons (« and »). This button is the *default action* button. You can trigger the default action from the keyboard by holding down the Ctrl key and pressing Enter.

If the default action push button is disabled, you haven't provided FoxPro with at least one item of information, such as a file name, which is needed to complete the command or expression.

Text Boxes

Text boxes enable you to enter text from the keyboard. These items usually appear in conjunction with another dialog object, such as a check box, to provide information that either cannot be obtained through the menus or that is easier to specify directly, such as the name of an output report file.

Note that, although a text box may appear a certain width, you can type past the right edge of the box; the text scrolls to the left as you type.

Scrollable Lists

When FoxPro needs the name of a file or database field, you are presented with a list. If the list contains more entries than can be displayed on-screen, you can scroll the list to bring into view the other entries. Scrollable lists contain up and down *arrowheads* and a diamond-shaped *scroll bar* to the right of the list. If you have a mouse, you can use these controls to quickly scroll around the list. At the top of a list of file names, for example, you see one or more items enclosed in square brackets. These items are the names of directories on the disk. The double period object (..) is a DOS convention that enables you to move up one level in the directory tree. The other directory names shown, if any, are subdirectories one level below the current directory. If you select a new directory name, the list changes to display the files in this directory.

You can select an item from the list either by using the cursor keys to highlight the item name and pressing Enter or by double-clicking on the name with the mouse.

Popup Controls

Popup controls appear as boxes drawn with a single line across the top and left side, and a double line across the bottom and the right side of the box. You use popup controls to change the items shown in a list that appears when you select the control. This list is similar to menu popups, and you move through the options in the same way.

The popup controls shown in figure 2.8 enable you to change the drive and directory from which the list of file names is constructed. When FoxPro asks for the name of a database field, the popup control enables you to select a different database from which to select a field.

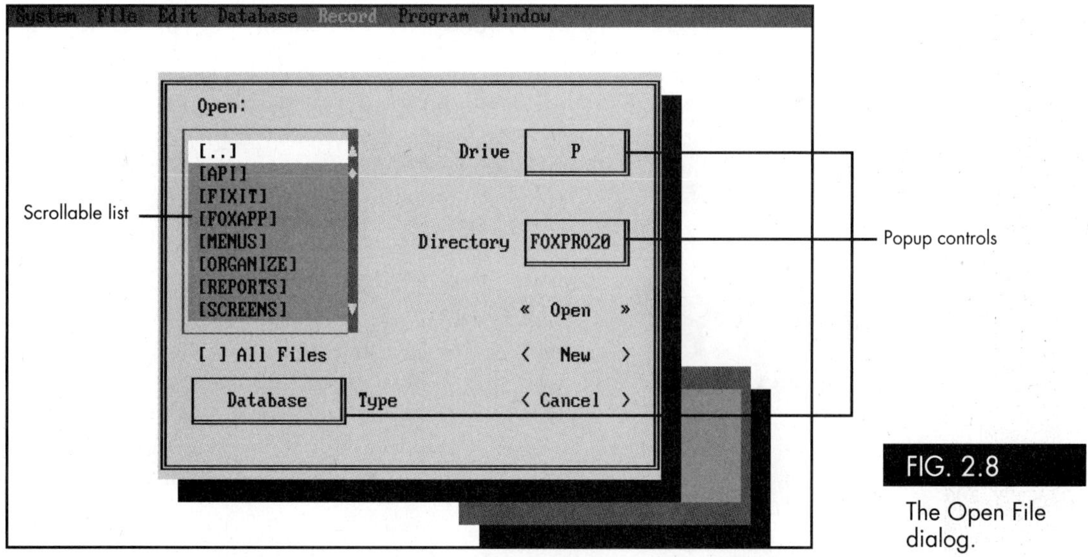

FIG. 2.8

The Open File dialog.

Using a Dialog and Confirming Choices

From the keyboard, you use the Tab key to move to the next object and Shift-Tab to move to the preceding object. When the highlight bar rests on the last object in the dialog, Tab takes you back to the first object. When the highlight bar is on the first object, Shift-Tab moves the highlight bar to the last object.

A mouse makes a big difference when you work with dialogs. Just position the mouse cursor on an object and click the left button to select the object. If you spend a great deal of time using dialogs, a mouse can save you both time and frustration. If you do not have a mouse, many dialog control objects have highlighted hot keys you can use from the keyboard, just as the menu popups do. After you activate the list, you also can move through lists by typing the initial letters of the choice.

TIP The highlighted hot keys help you move from object to object. After you select an object that requires further typing (whether a box that accepts text or a list or popup that accepts characters to move through the choices) the hot keys are disabled so that typing isn't interrupted.

After you set up the dialog options, you tell FoxPro that you're finished by selecting the default text box, which is usually «`OK`». You can select this text button from the keyboard by using the Tab or pressing Shift-Tab to highlight the button and pressing Enter or by clicking the option with the mouse. If you decide to cancel the operation, then press Esc or click on `<Cancel>`. No matter where the highlight is in a dialog, you also can press Ctrl-Enter to activate the default closing option.

Editing Keystrokes and Mouse Movement

Until now, you have done little typing in FoxPro except to select menu options and, if you are using a mouse, you may not even have used the keyboard much for this procedure.

Entering text is an important part of database management. You type commands, express calculations, enter data, phrase queries, answer dialog questions, and write programs—all by entering text. Throughout this process, you use an *editor* (or, you use certain consistent shortcuts to modify and manipulate the text *as* you enter the information).

As usual in FoxPro, the editor's features are available both to mouse and to keyboard users. Where both alternatives exist, you can use either method.

In FoxPro, editing shortcuts remain the same *no matter what kind of text you are entering*, although a few features differ slightly in different text-editing situations. In this section, you *practice* with FoxPro's editor in a text file that can contain any kind of notes, but remember that you soon can make good use of the same features in the Command window and during data entry.

Creating, Opening, and Saving a File

First you must create a text file for editing practice.

You previously used the File New menu popup option to open an UNTITLED text file in this chapter. If the file is not still open, re-open the file. With this text file as the active window, type your name.

File New always creates a window that you see on-screen with the title, `UNTITLED` as the name of the new file. In most cases, File New also shows a default file extension. If you choose to create a New Label, the Label Designer window that appears is titled `UNTITLED.LBX`. (Default file extensions for different kinds of files are available from the on-line Help system discussed in a following section of this chapter.)

Try to close this editing window now (by using the Close option on the File menu popup or by clicking the window's close control). Because you made changes to the file, an Alert tells you that you selected an option to close the file without first saving the changes. Save the changes, and a dialog appears. You can access this dialog directly (without seeing the Alert) if you try to close the window by using the Save or Save As menu items or by using any appropriate keyboard shortcuts previously described in this chapter.

Because this file was created with the New option, FoxPro asks you to name the new file. You can assign any valid DOS file name and choose another file extension (if you want), and the dialog enables you to place the file in any drive or directory in the system. Use the popup controls and the scrolling list previously described to choose the drive where the FoxPro 2 files are located (here, use the default) and the MODEL directory. Type the file name **MODEL.TXT** (capitalization does not matter).

The text file is now closed, but you need to retrieve the file again to practice a few more procedures.

Any file you previously created is available from the File Open menu popup option. A dialog asks you to specify the kind of file for which you are looking and enables you to search through the drives and directory to find the file. (If you assigned a file extension that doesn't appear by default for this kind of file, then use the `All Files` check box to make the file appear in the scrolling list.) Notice that, in figure 2.9, a file *currently open* appears in different colors or different intensity, to indicate that the file is open and cannot be selected.

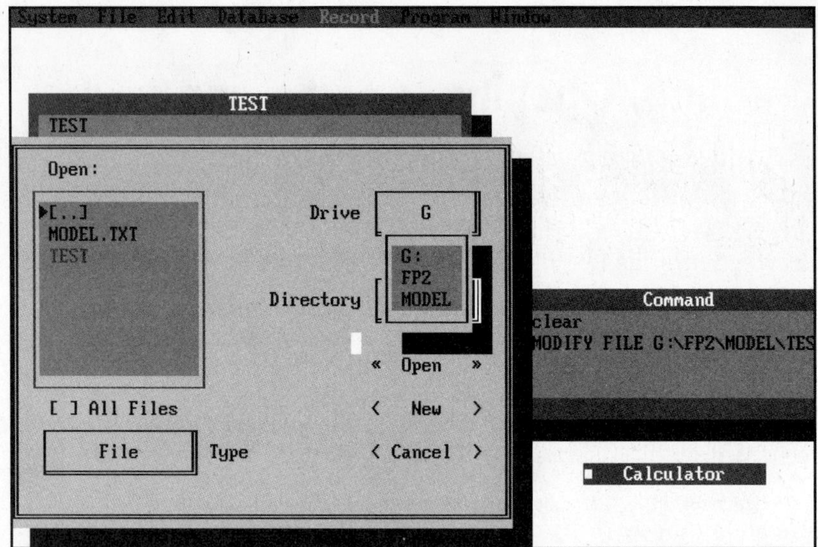

FIG. 2.9

The File Open dialog in use.

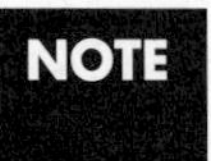

The word `TEST` should appear in a different color (or shading) than `MODEL.TXT` in the PCX file, although these words may not show differently here.

Practice opening and saving this file by using different interface techniques. You can save the same information to several different names (by using the File Save As option to bring up the file-naming dialog you previously saw) and open several windows at once.

The FoxPro 2 editor is flexible in the amount of text it can handle. The only real limits on the size of a file you can edit, or on the number of items you can edit in different windows simultaneously, are imposed by the system configuration and available memory.

Like the editing techniques you learn in this chapter, this process of opening saving files remains consistent for all kinds of FoxPro files. You select a different file type in the File New or Open dialogs. When you Save a file, the file is saved in the appropriate format.

Moving through and Editing Text

If you already know another editing or word processing program, then you may feel comfortable navigating in the FoxPro 2 editor. The following chart provides a handy reference for moving the cursor through the text.

Table 2.10 Cursor-Movement Reference Table

Move Cursor	Menu Item	Key Method	Mouse Method
One character	See note *	Right-, left-arrow keys	See note**
One word		Ctrl+right-, left-arrow keys	
One line		Up-, down-arrow keys	
One window		PgUp, PgDn	
Beginning of line		Home	
End of line		End	
Beginning of file		Ctrl-Home	
End of file		Ctrl-End	

* The Edit menu pad has several items that enable you to move to any position in the file by searching for text. The menu also contains a Goto Line option that enables you to move rapidly through the file in some situations.

** Mouse movement of the cursor to any position in the text is simple: click the mouse on the spot you want the cursor to appear, and you can use the scroll bar or bars to move rapidly through the text by using the mouse.

With the UNTITLED text window active, and by using any technique in the preceding chart, move the cursor to the end of your name and type a few sentences describing yourself, without pressing Enter. Notice that the text *wraps* (or, words too long to fit at the right margin of the first line jump down to the next line) in the window. Resize the text window and watch the word wrapping feature change line lengths when the amount of room available changes.

The FoxPro editor defaults to *inserting*, rather than *overwriting*, text and uses the cursor shape as a single line (_) in Insert mode. Use the arrow keys to move the cursor between the first and last names. Type a middle name and note that the text to the right moves to the right to make room. Now press the Insert key; a solid block cursor (■) appears. Use the arrow keys to return the cursor to the first letter of your middle name and give a new name by typing over the previous middle name you typed.

Press backspace, and you delete the characters to the *left* of the cursor (erasing your new middle name). You can press Ctrl-backspace to erase the whole word at one time. Press the Delete key to delete a character directly under the cursor, moving characters on the right to the left to fill the gap created by the deletion. Pressing the Delete key repeatedly therefore erases characters to the *right* of the cursor.

Move the cursor to the end of the name. Press Insert (if you haven't already put the editor back into Insert mode) and insert a carriage return after your name by pressing Enter. Now, resize the text window; the first two lines don't flow together regardless of the space available. The word wrap feature recognizes carriage returns that you enter so that you can press Enter to separate paragraphs and make sections of text distinct from one another.

Now that you know how to type and move around in the text, you can learn to *select*, or mark, sections of text of various lengths. You will see selected text highlighted in different colors or intensity. You then can edit selected text by using the techniques described in this section. These techniques are summarized in table 2.11.

You select text from the keyboard by using the same cursor movements mentioned previously but here, you add the Shift key. You select text with the mouse by holding Shift down as you click-drag the mouse across the desired text. In both cases, text is selected *from the original cursor position through the new cursor position*.

Some other tricks are available for text selection with the mouse. You find these techniques listed in table 2.11.

If you type while text is selected, you *replace* the selected text (delete the selected text). Pressing the Delete, Enter, or backspace key also deletes selected text. You can *unselect* text by moving the cursor.

A special kind of text removal, known as *cutting*, eliminates selected text from the current position but—instead of deleting the text—cutting stores the cut text in memory. Press Ctrl-X to cut text. You can then *paste* the text (press Ctrl-V), either to another position in the same text or to text you are editing in a different window.

You also can *copy* a selected block of text (press Ctrl-C). This step does not change the selected block, but makes the same text available for pasting in another or multiple locations.

CAUTION: After cutting or copying a text selection, FoxPro 2 puts this text in memory to a system variable known as *_CLIPTEXT*, which is FoxPro's Clipboard. Only one selection can be present in _CLIPTEXT at a time (only one Clipboard is available). If you cut or copy a new selection, then you *replace* the data _CLIPTEXT currently contains with new material. Variables are explained in Chapter 16, which covers program structure, although you use these variables in earlier chapters. *System variables* are special variables with standard meanings and values. FoxPro creates these variables without intervention on the part of the user. You saw these system variables listed when you displayed memory on-screen in a previous section of this chapter.

If you make a mistake when you delete or cut text, or regret an editing action, FoxPro 2's editor has an almost unlimited memory for past editing actions. You can *undo* and *redo* these mistakes with Ctrl-U and Ctrl-R.

Table 2.11 Editing Techniques

Editing Action	Menu Item	Key Method	Mouse Method
Select Text, any length, from current position to new cursor position	None	Shift+editing keys from Cursor Movement Table. Continuing to move cursor while holding the Shift key down continues to change the length of selection until another action is performed.	Click-drag or Shift-click anywhere to select from cursor position to place you clicked on
Select a word at a time	None	See above	Double-click (drag for additional whole words)
Select a line at a time	None	See above	Triple-click (drag for additional whole lines)

continues

Table 2.11 Continued

Editing Action	Menu Item	Key Method	Mouse Method
Unselect whole selection	None	Any key from Cursor Movement Table	Click outside selected text
Select All Text	Select All on Edit popup	Ctrl-A	None
Delete text (and to the right)	None	Delete key	None
Delete text to the left	None	Backspace key	None
Delete selected text	None	Delete, Backspace, Enter, or type any text	None
Cut selected text	Cut on Edit popup	Ctrl-X	None
Copy selected text	Copy on Edit popup	Ctrl-C	None
Paste selected text	Paste on Edit popup	Ctrl-V	None
Undo last edit action	Undo on Edit popup	Ctrl-U	None
Redo last "Undone" edit action	Redo on Edit popup	Ctrl-R	None

Searching for Text

One of the most productive techniques available in any text editor is the capability of *finding* and *replacing* specific text. Searching for text enables you to move instantly to any phrase or symbol in the text. If you specify a Replace phrase, you can change any instance, or all instances, of the search text when found.

Use Ctrl-F or the Find option in the Edit popup to activate the appropriate dialog in FoxPro 2. As you see in figure 2.10, this dialog enables you to specify search and replace text and also the following options:

- Whether a search is *case* sensitive (should *Edit* in the search phrase find *edit* in the text?)
- Whether the *whole word* must be the same for a match (should *and* in the search phrase find *understand* in the text?)
- Whether the search goes *forward* or *backward* from the current cursor position in the file
- When the beginning or the end of a file is reached

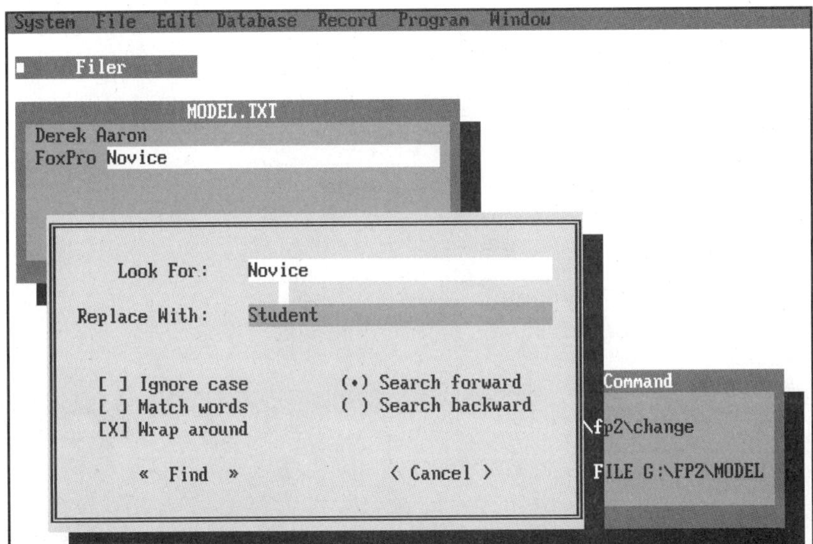

FIG. 2.10

The Find and Replace dialog with a search phrase high-lighted.

After the search phrase is found, this phrase is selected in the text. Here, you can either press Ctrl-G to find the next incidence (the Edit Find Again option), replace the selected text with Ctrl-E and move to the next incidence (the Edit Replace and Find Again option), or just continue editing from this point in the text. You even can use the Edit Replace All option to find and replace all occurrences of the search phrase in this text at one time. (If you perform a Replace or Replace All with no replace text specified, the search phrase is deleted.)

Notice that, in figure 2.10, the search phrase is highlighted. As is common in FoxPro 2 dialogs, if an item you need to type contains text when you move into the dialog, the text is selected. Dialogs obey the editing rules just as other text entry situations do; if you start typing immediately while text is selected, you overwrite the old entry. If you use the cursor-movement keys, then the text becomes unselected for editing. You can reselect the text with Ctrl-A or paste in a previously copied phrase.

Try the selecting and searching techniques with the MODEL.TXT file. Under your name, type **FoxPro Novice**. Select the word `Novice` by any of the available methods and then press Ctrl-C to copy the word. Use any cursor-movement technique so that Novice is no longer selected. Press Ctrl-F to bring up the Find dialog and press Ctrl-V to copy the word Novice to the search phrase. Choose a description of yourself and type this description as a replace phrase. Confirm the choice and you return to the MODEL.TXT window with `Novice` highlighted. Press Ctrl-E, and the replacement phrase appears to replace the word Novice. A bell rings, and a small message window informs you that the search phrase cannot be found again.

Searching for and Typing Special Characters

You may often want to use special graphics characters and search in the text for these characters or nonprinting characters. You may want to use a graphics border around some text, (see fig. 2.11) or search for the first incidence of a carriage return in the text.

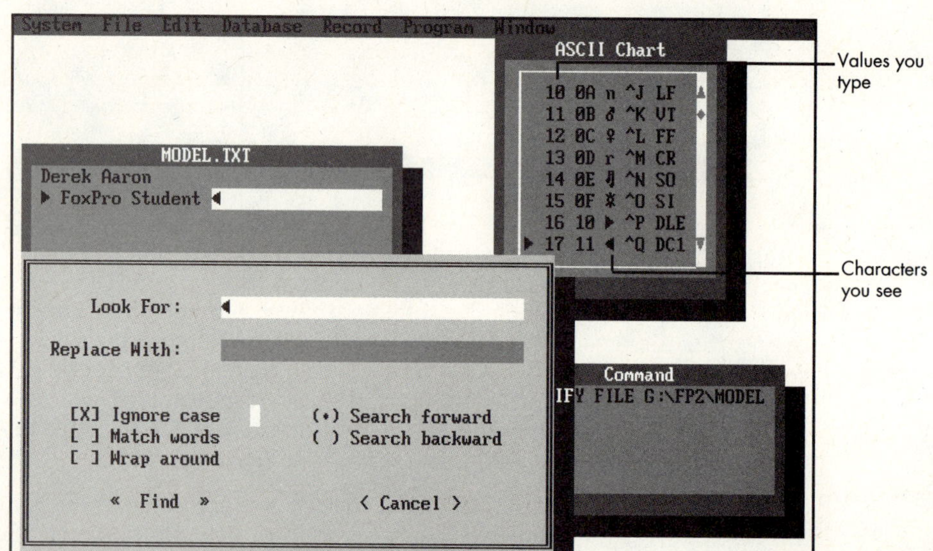

FIG. 2.11

The ASCII chart helps you type special characters.

By performing one of the following methods, FoxPro 2 makes easy the search for nonprinting characters that you commonly use in text entry:

- Type **\r** to search for a carriage return
- Type **\n** to search for a line feed
- Type **\t** to search for a tab character

  (Because the backslash is used to indicate the special nature of the character that follows, you must type \\ to search for the backslash.)

Like many other editing programs and word processors, FoxPro 2 enables you to type other special characters by combining the Alt key with the characters' *ASCII value*, by using the separate numeric keypad on the keyboard (not, however, the numbers that form part of the standard typewriter keyboard) to type the digits. ASCII is a code used by computers to represent text. You can use each character that is assigned a unique numeric value in the ASCII system. You enter the small graphics triangle used in figure 2.11, (▲), by holding down the Alt key while typing **16** on the numeric keypad. After you release the Alt key, the character appears at the cursor position. You can choose the ASCII Chart from the System menu popup to look up the ASCII value of characters.

Notice that in the ASCII chart shown in figure 2.11, the same graphics character also can be expressed as a control character, and this procedure is often easier to remember than the ASCII value. In the chart, the control character is written as `^Q`, which you usually type by pressing the key combination Ctrl-Q. Because, however, many control characters (including this example) are used with special meanings in FoxPro 2, the editor provides a method to enable you to type these characters. Type a left-single-quote (‘) followed by the character (here, **Q**). Because of the special use of the ‘ character (similar to the backslash), you must type the character twice to enter a left-single-quote.)

In "Using the FoxPro 2 Help System," a following section, you find a quick-use reference for typing some graphics characters.

Editing Options and the Edit Preferences Dialog

Until now, you were editing a text file with all the editor's default settings, but you can alter many of these features by using the Edit popup's *Preference* selections (see fig. 2.12).

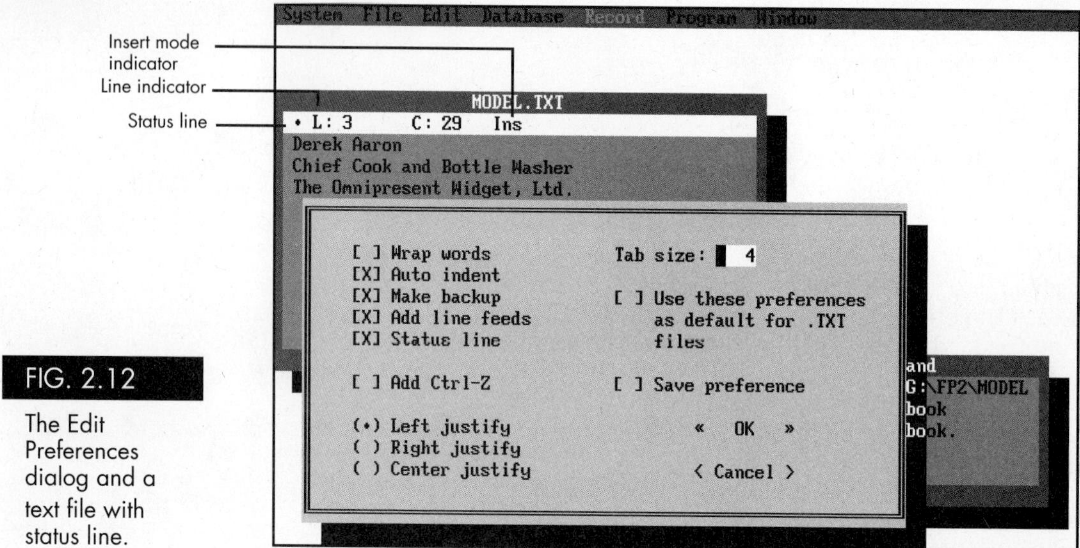

FIG. 2.12

The Edit Preferences dialog and a text file with status line.

Many settings are self-explanatory. You can tell Tabs to indent the text a number of spaces other than the default of 4, and you can turn off the word-wrap feature. You can turn off the feature that backs up files by copying the last version of the file to another file name with a BAK extension.

Note that when the `Wrap Words` and `Auto Indent` check boxes are both marked (the default for text file editing), you can indent a whole paragraph by altering the position of the first character in the first line (by adding spaces or a tab or by removing spaces or tabs with a backspace). If you begin a paragraph with a number (for example, to write an outline) or other text followed by a tab, the wrapped paragraph is aligned with the text following the tab.

Mark the `Status Line` check box and return to the text file. You see a new line added to the text editing window, as shown in figure 2.12. If you changed the file since the last Save, a bullet (•) appears in the corner of the status line to remind you these changes aren't yet saved to disk. The `C:` followed by a number tells you the current screen *column* (characters across, counted from the left) position of the cursor, and `Ins` or `Over` tells you if you are in Insert or Overwrite mode. If you turn off `Wrap Words`, as you do to write programs, an `L:` followed by a number tells you the cursor's position counted in lines from the top of the text (or *rows*, as FoxPro usually calls lines on the screen). After you turn off Wrap Words, you also can use the Goto Line option on the Edit menu to move quickly to any line number.

The Edit Preferences dialog enables you to store all combinations of these features. You can make this feature set available for this file only (by checking off `Save preference` and confirming the dialog choices in the standard way) or for all files that you create or open with the same extension (by checking off both `Save preference` and `Use these preferences as default for .TXT files` before confirming the choices).

If you are comfortable in another text editor or word processor now, then you may be accustomed to different sets of keystrokes to accomplish many editing tasks. Or you may have some tasks that you do over and over for which the FoxPro editor has no shortcuts. In either case, you can further customize the editor by using *macros*. Macros assign sequences of keystrokes, including the editing keystrokes you learned about in this section, to a key combination that you can remember and use easily. You learn about macros in Chapter 15.

Typing Command Instructions

Besides selecting options from menus, you also can execute FoxPro commands by typing in the Command window. If you haven't used a command language before, then you may feel a little intimidated at first.

Few commands you enter can harm the data, and FoxPro usually gives you a chance to cancel an action that results in the permanent loss of data, such as removing deleted records or overwriting a file. However, be aware that a way exists to tell FoxPro that you're sure you know what you're doing, and you don't want to be prompted to confirm actions. You do this by typing **SET SAFETY OFF** in the Command window or by including this command in a program and then running the program. The default value for the SAFETY setting is ON, which means that FoxPro forces you to confirm a choice before executing the command. If you have doubts, type **SET SAFETY ON** in the Command window and press Enter.

Using the Command Window

The Command window is a special kind of FoxPro window. When you run FoxPro, the Command window appears on the desktop, ready to accept instructions.

In a previous section, you activated the Filer utility. You may have noticed that the word `FILER` appeared in the Command window. FoxPro enters the FILER command for you.

When you choose an option from a menu, FoxPro uses the selections to build a command language instruction. These command expressions usually appear in the Command window and then execute. Think of the Command window as the low-level interface to the FoxPro database engine, through which all requests are processed. The menu system is the high-level interface, that constructs and then enters FoxPro commands in the Command window. If you note the expressions that FoxPro constructs for you, you can begin to learn the FoxPro command language, with FoxPro acting as a tutor.

You may wonder why you need to learn how to enter commands when FoxPro enters these commands for you. You need to learn to use the Command window to type commands for the following three reasons:

- Often, you can type a command easier and faster than you can deal with menus and dialogs, especially if you don't have a mouse.
- Not all of FoxPro's more than 700 commands and functions are available through menu selections. Not enough room exists for all these commands. At some point, you may want to use the commands that you must enter.
- The more you know about the command language, the more confident you become in mastering the intricacies of database management and FoxPro 2. If you decide to try writing FoxPro programs, you have the tools needed to start.

Entering, Repeating, and Editing Commands

Commands are entered on a single line, although you can tell FoxPro to regard a subsequent line as part of the current line. When you press Enter, FoxPro tries to execute the command on the same line as the cursor. The position of the cursor on the line is not important; FoxPro includes the entire line as part of the command.

The Command window is an editing window that you move around by using the same keystrokes you learned in the section of this chapter that covered the FoxPro editor. All the editor's functions, such as Cut and Paste, are available while you work in the Command window.

You can repeat a previously entered command by moving the cursor to the command and pressing Enter. You also can add or delete parts of a command. If you enter a command incorrectly, you don't have to retype the command. Just use the editor to correct the error and press Enter.

Some commands, such as BROWSE, have a multitude of options. The entire command may be so long that the text scrolls off-screen. FoxPro doesn't care about this situation and happily executes the command regardless of length, but you can break a long command in two or more lines and make the command easier to read.

If you end a line with a semicolon, FoxPro doesn't try to execute the command and regards everything typed on the following line as a continuation of the previous line. You can use any number of lines to type a command, but remember that the last line *must not* end in a semicolon.

FoxPro joins two command segments separated by a semicolon exactly as the segments are typed. If you start a new FoxPro *word* after the semicolon, make sure that you precede the semicolon with a space.

TIP

When you design queries with the RQBE (which you learn in Chapters 5 and 6), FoxPro writes lines of code for you that can be long and complex, nicely formatted in multiple lines. Examining a query is a good way to learn how to format long command lines.

Interpreting and Responding to Error Messages

The command language has strict syntax rules. You must correctly spell the command, and you must provide all information required to execute the command. If you use the COPY TO command to copy records from the current database to another, then you have to include the name of the other database. If you don't, then FoxPro displays a Syntax error message in an Alert window, as shown in figure 2.13. Press any key or click the mouse to clear the message from the screen and return to the Command window.

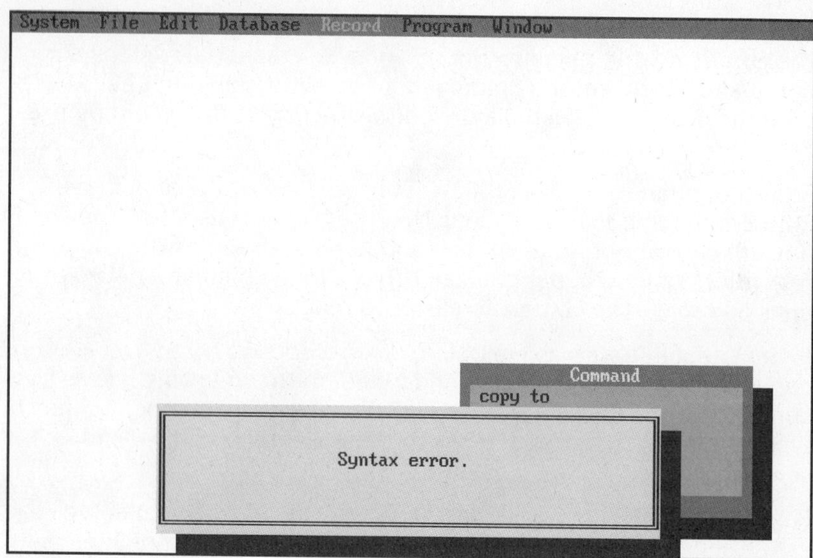

FIG. 2.13

A FoxPro error message in an Alert window.

When you make a mistake, FoxPro attempts to tell you what is wrong. Sometimes what you type appears correct, but FoxPro cannot execute the command because you use a field name that isn't part of the current database. This error usually results in a `Variable not found` message, and FoxPro 2 tries to identify the incorrect word in the line by including the word in the error message. All the error messages are brief, and some messages can be rather cryptic until you learn what to look for when you see them.

If you receive an error message from FoxPro while entering commands in the Command window, then first check what you typed for misspelled words, missing information, or missing commas in a list of field names. If you have doubts that what you typed is correct, then try to execute the command by using menu selections and compare the entry you type to the entry FoxPro enters in the Command window.

In the following section, you learn to use the Help file to aid you in tracking down problems. The Help file has one entry that contains a complete listing of all the error messages. The file has separate entries that show you the correct syntax for all the commands and functions and includes examples that help you learn how to use the commands and functions. You even can copy the examples from the Help window, paste them into the Command window, and press Enter to execute the command!

Using the FoxPro 2 Help System

By now you realize that FoxPro 2 contains many menu options and dialogs. You may at some point be asked to make a choice and have absolutely no idea what to do. Fortunately, help for the action you are currently performing is never more than a few keypresses away.

Open the Edit menu popup and press F1, the FoxPro 2 help key, and you see a Help window with an entry on Text Editing similar to the window shown in figure 2.14.

Except when the System menu is active, mouse users can press Alt while clicking the left mouse button to access the Help system. If you press Alt and click the left button while the System menu is active, you are returned to the last active window, and the menu deactivates.

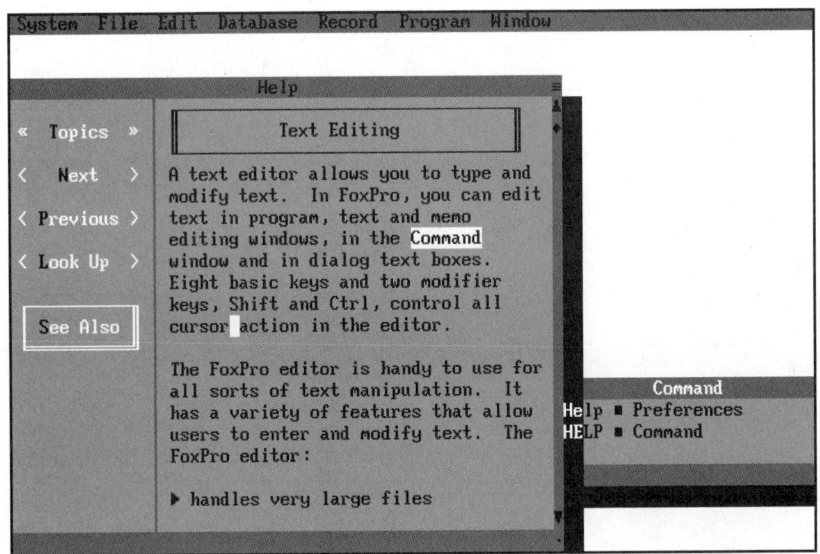

FIG. 2.14

The help window.

This Help window contains information on one FoxPro 2 topic. Down the left side are controls that enable you to access other topics in the Help Index, including a <Look Up> button that you can press whenever you have text selected within the Help window or in any other text you may be editing. (Although you cannot modify the help text on-screen, you can select text and search within help text just like any other FoxPro window.)

FoxPro 2 help is *context-sensitive*, which means that FoxPro tries to give you information relevant to the text you select or the action you perform. If FoxPro cannot find a match, the Help index appears, positioned as closely as possible to a matching entry. You can move around in the index with the usual cursor movements, or you can start typing the initial letters of the choice. The Index tries to find a match, until you select a topic to investigate. If the `<Look Up>` button can't find a match, a similar list appears from which you can choose a topic.

The Help Index is extremely complete because the Index is revised when you make changes to the product; the Help Index is the most up-to-date source of FoxPro information available. Be sure that you use the topic "Changes Since Documentation" to annotate your copy of the manuals and to learn about new features added after the manuals went to press. FoxPro has an entry for every command or function, and also topics (marked with an (▶) at the *top* of the index), which are all introductory or general in nature. Topics marked with an (■), at the *bottom* of the list, are designed to describe different aspects of the FoxPro 2 interface. In between these two groups are, arranged alphabetically, the individual commands and functions that make up the FoxPro programming language.

Figure 2.15 shows you an abbreviated version of the Help index so that you can contrast the different kinds of Help topics. Take some time to look through the topics and practice moving through the Help file, using the `<Look Up>` function and the `See Also` popup control to jump to related topics.

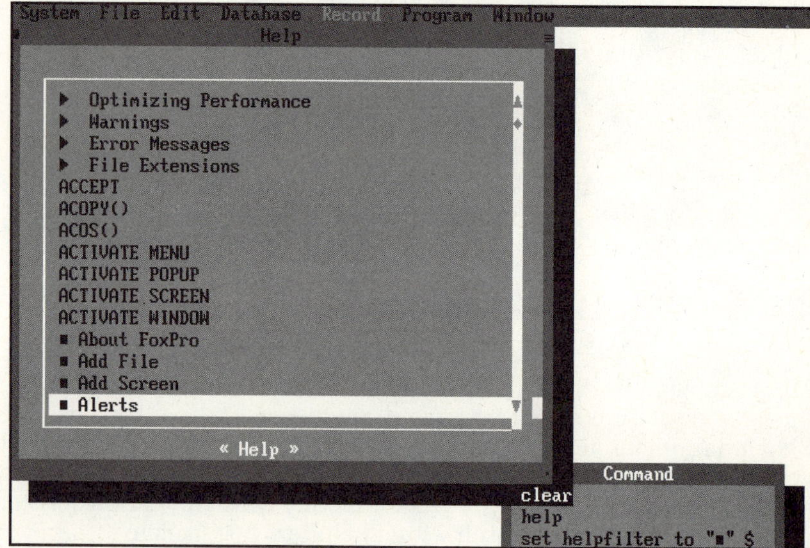

FIG. 2.15

Selections from the Help index, showing different kinds of topics.

While you are in the Help index, also practice searching for a topic by typing the first few characters of the topic's name. You can easily reach the introductory topics by using one of the methods of typing special characters, which you learned in the text editing section. Press Alt-16 (which generates the ▲ character), remembering to use the numeric keypad, and you jump to the introductory topics section of the index.

You also can ask FoxPro directly for help on any topic by typing HELP in the Command window and following the command with the topic name or the first few characters in the name. Activate the Command window and type **HELP HELP** and see what happens. Then type **HELP ■ F** (press and hold down the Alt key and type **254** to produce the small box character), and you are placed in the first matching topic (in the middle of the interface topic group). Try the `<Next>` and `<Previous>` buttons to look through other interface topics. Return to the Command window and type **HELP ► F** (use the Alt-16 key combination or type ' followed by a **p**), and you are returned to the general introductory topic list where you can refer to the File Extensions list available.

Now that you learned how to use the Command window, the text editor, and the Help file, you can begin to learn FoxPro commands. Most of the entries for FoxPro commands and functions in the Help file hold examples of the action's use, along with the explanatory text. You can copy and paste in the Command window and edit the example to suit your needs. If an Alert window appears because FoxPro didn't understand a command, just press F1 again and look for the answer.

Chapter Summary

In this chapter, you learned to interpret and respond to the various objects that make up the FoxPro 2 interface.

You now know where to find options in the FoxPro System menu, System, and how to summon the options you want. You are familiar with various kinds of windows that FoxPro uses to exchange information with you, and how the windows differ in use and appearance. You know how to change the appearance and positions of the windows to set up the FoxPro desk as a comfortable workspace.

You now are aware of the editing keystrokes available in FoxPro and can begin to use these keystrokes to issue instructions in the FoxPro command language by using the Command window and Help system. You know how to open, close, and save all kinds of files.

You can put these skills together to do some real work. In the following chapter, you start to put raw data into a FoxPro 2 database and pull out organized information.

3

CHAPTER

Exploring Databases and Tables

In Chapter 1, "Understanding FoxPro Fundamentals," you learned how to create a table (the Product table) using FoxApp, and you learned that a table is a kind of list in which each item on the list is known as a record. Each record, in turn, contains pieces of information which are contained in fields. It's useful to think of tables as lists of items that have something in common.

The word database is often used interchangeably with the word table. When used in this book, however, a *database* is a collection of tables that work together to accomplish a common purpose.

Understanding What a Database Is and Does

As a basic example, a dictionary is a database that holds information about words. Dictionaries usually contain a table of phonetic conventions, a table of abbreviations used in the word listings, a table of words and definitions, and a variety of specialty tables—such as commonly used abbreviations, historical names, fictional names, and other information the publisher thinks may fulfill the purpose of the dictionary. Although combining the extra tables with the definitions list is possible, arranging these tables separately makes more sense.

In FoxPro, a *database* consists of the tables needed for an application.

In figure 3.1, you see the components of a dictionary which are treated as separate tables in a database. In figure 3.2, you see how a database in FoxPro looks. If you wrote a dictionary in FoxPro, the FoxPro dictionary database may consist of tables similar to the tables in figure 3.2. You can arrange the dictionary (the *output*—or results—from the database) to look like any other dictionary.

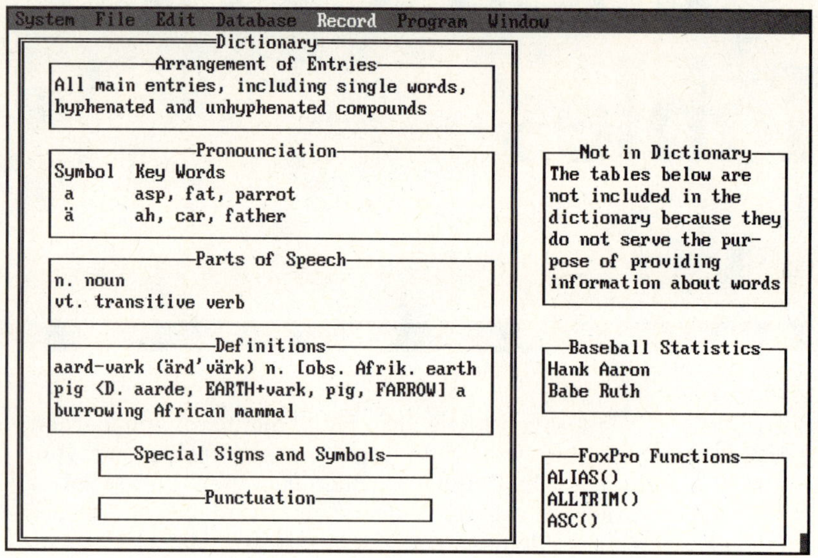

FIG. 3.1

The Dictionary as a database.

Understanding the Role of a Table in a Database

The purpose of the model application example used here is to provide the managers of the Omnipresent Widget Company with the information needed to manage the company. Although the complete application consists of many tables that represent all facets of the company, for now this book concentrates only on the sub-application that helps the managers handle the on-going budget process. To accomplish this task, the managers need information by product, by department, and by budget category. A total of four tables are needed.

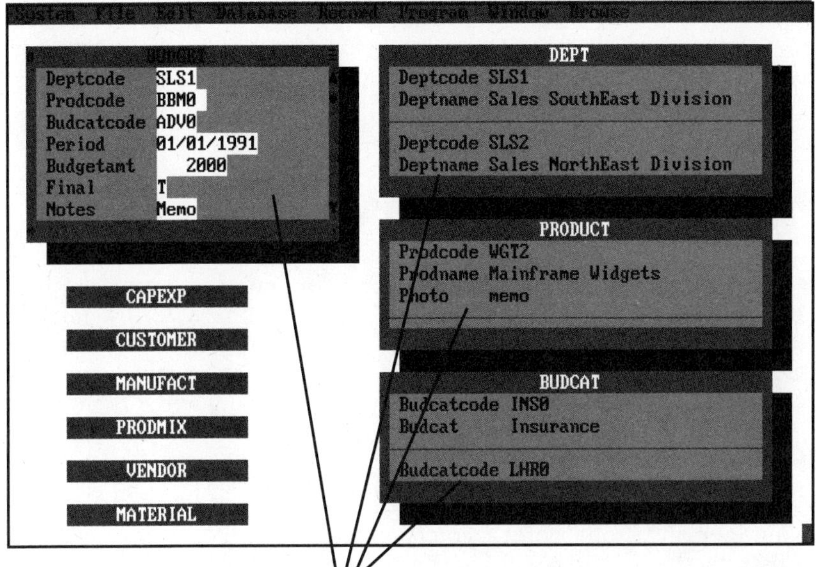

FIG. 3.2

How a database looks in FoxPro.

The next table you create is the main table, Budget. You use FoxPro's View window, rather than FoxApp, to create this table. No matter which way you create a table in FoxPro, you need to understand the basics of a table's structure and elements.

Designing a Structure and Assigning Data Types

As you previously learned, records in a table consist of pieces of information stored in fields. Designing a table structure involves creating table fields for the pieces of information you collect for each record in the table, which assumes that you already know how you plan to use the table and what information you need to collect. You learn more about determining your needs in Chapter 4.

You also need to know two items about each piece of information: the type of data and what you reasonably need to use as a value.

Different kinds of information are handled differently by FoxPro. FoxPro has several options for manipulating most kinds of data. FoxPro can convert a field that contains a word or a phrase to upper- or lowercase or a mixture of cases, tell you the length of the phrase, or tell you the first three letters of the word or phrase. If the field contains numeric data, however, you can use FoxPro to perform arithmetic operations on the data. In this book, you find examples of data manipulation, which is always determined by data type.

Understanding Data Types

Character fields are composed of letters, digits, punctuation marks and line drawing, foreign alphabet, and special symbol characters. Character fields are limited to 254 characters in a field. You can enter these characters from the keyboard, either by typing them directly (using the labeled keys), by pressing a combination of the Alt key and a number key, or by choosing the character from the Special Characters table under the System menu pad.

The Alt-number combination generates a character based on the ASCII code number of the character—you can see the ASCII code for a character by referring to the ASCII Chart option on the System menu popup.

FoxPro treats character data as strings of individual characters. If you add together the contents of two character fields, you get a combined string of the two fields—*"dog"*+*"cat"* equals *"dogcat"* (this process is known as *concatenation*).

NOTE

All computer information—program, text, image, and other files—is stored in binary format. The character symbols discussed here are a subset of *binary data*, or ASCII characters. *ASCII* is an agreed-upon convention in the computer industry that enables programs to share character data.

For special purposes, a character field also can contain non-ASCII binary data, such as a series of special codes or instructions to be sent to the printer. Usually, however, you use the memo data type to store non-ASCII binary data, which is generally not manipulated directly by FoxPro but imported from and exported to the hard disk to serve special needs.

Numeric fields contain only numbers, the minus and plus signs, and the decimal point. Numbers are limited to 20 digits (including signs, decimal point, and the number of decimals). FoxPro treats numeric data as *numbers*, which means that when you add two numbers together, you get the sum of the numbers, such as *2 + 2 = 4*.

Although you can enter 20 numbers in a field, FoxPro tracks only the first 16 significant digits, which means that if you enter 17 digits, the number is not correct (digits after 16 are replaced by 0). You can, however, accurately enter 16 digits, a sign, and a decimal point.

Don't assume that you put data in a numeric field just because the data contains digits. If you plan no computations on this data, you are better off treating the information as a string of characters. Zip codes and Social Security numbers are both composed of digits, but using these numbers (usually by sorting records into a certain order, including the - character to represent a dash rather than a minus sign) is easier if entered in a character—rather than a number—field. If you have doubts about the eventual contents of the field (suppose that you may need to include Canadian zip codes, which have both alpha and numeric characters), use a character field.

TIP

Although you can't manually enter more numbers than the digits allowed by a field, you can try to place a number into a field larger than the field size by using FoxPro commands. You also can try to place a number which has no mathematical value (the result of dividing a number by zero, for example, has no mathematical value) into a field. If a number is too large or is the result of dividing by zero, FoxPro either fills the field with asterisks, or a number appears on-screen that looks like `.990E+03`. The number form in the latter case is *scientific notation* and evaluates to the beginning number times 10 to the power indicated after the E. Here, the result is .990 times 10^3 (.990 times 1000) or 990. Asterisks and scientific notation numbers can lead to problems. The best approach is to make the numeric fields large and avoid dividing by zero.

Date fields can contain valid dates only, in numeric form, between 01/01/100 and 12/31/9999. FoxPro enables you to use many forms to represent a date. You can show the dates with the full century, as in 01/01/1991, or with the last two digits of the year, as in 01/01/91. You also can show dates in American, British, Italian, or other formats. In a following section, you can experiment with different date formats and see how the dates change to reflect these formats. No matter what date form you display on-screen or how you enter dates, FoxPro stores a date internally in the numeric form *YYYYMMDD* (year, 4 digits; month, 2 digits; day, 2 digits).

Because dates are stored internally as numbers, FoxPro can use dates to perform *date math* (such as figuring out what date is 30 days from today) and convert numeric dates into character dates for reports (such as January 1, 1991).

Logical fields contain true (the letter *T*) or false (the letter *F*) only. You also can enter Y for true and N for false, but the field always stores the value as T or F. You can think of a logical field as an *on/off switch* to specify whether some condition is satisfied. The sample Budget table will contain a logical field named FINAL, which you use to determine whether you can edit a record.

Memo fields contain text or *any* binary data, such as images or programs. FoxPro can perform a large number of simple and complex operations on memo fields. For now, however, use these fields only to add free-form additional notes to the contents of a record.

NOTE The default extension for a FoxPro table is DBF. When a table contains one or more memo fields, FoxPro creates a companion file (a memo file) with the same file name but adds the extension FPT. (No matter how many memo fields a table has, FoxPro creates only one memo file to hold all the memo fields.) An important matter to remember is that, when you move files from one location to another, you must keep these files together. To make a copy of the table, you also need a duplicate memo file. When you open a table, FoxPro opens the related memo file. If the companion memo file is missing, an error message appears.

Although floating-point numeric fields are available when you create a table structure, FoxPro handles these fields as numeric data. For this reason—and because FoxPro *may* use these fields differently in the future—use regular numeric fields.

Picture fields are included only for compatibility with Fox Software's Macintosh products and cannot be used by the current MS-DOS version of FoxPro 2. Fox Software plans for a Windows version of FoxPro also include use of the picture type.

All data types except memos are limited to a field length that you determine (up to FoxPro's maximum length for each field type). The field length you choose depends on what values each field may contain. If you have a character field for customer name, for example, you may need 25 or 30 character spaces—possibly more—available to enter the full names of all the customers. Try to learn, in advance, as much as possible about the values for each field because as you increase field length, you also increase the amount of disk space each record requires. If you now know that a character field *never* uses more than 10 characters (such as a code you created), set the field length for 10.

You can make memos as large as available disk space permits. Each memo field takes 10 bytes per record, but the associated entries in the FPT file can vary in length.

Creating a Table Using the FoxPro View Window

You can create a table using FoxApp (as you did in Chapter 1), but the View window gives you greater flexibility in which you can arrange other aspects of the work environment at the same time.

In figures 3.1 and 3.2, you see two ways to visually represent the nature of a database. In FoxPro, the View window gives you another more useful way to show a database in action (see Fig. 3.3).

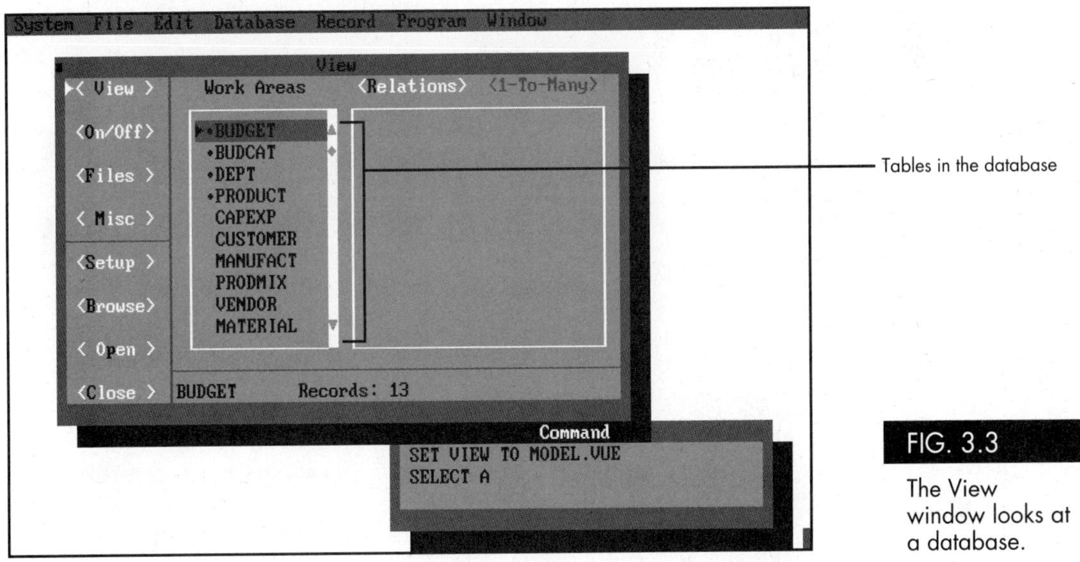

FIG. 3.3

The View window looks at a database.

Besides providing a bird's-eye view of the tables you are using, the View window enables you to enter data, view table contents, create and modify individual tables, and bring together individual tables to build a database. You also can use View to change a variety of miscellaneous FoxPro settings. In Chapter 1, you used the `<Misc>` button of the View window to activate the clock and to change other settings. In a following section of this chapter, you see how changing settings affects the way data is displayed on-screen and entered on the keyboard.

To use the View window, select View from the Window menu popup by pressing Alt-W and then V or by clicking the Window menu pad and then the View option. You see an empty View window similar to the window shown in figure 3.4. In the left column, you see the View window options, the center column is a list of work areas, and the right column is currently empty.

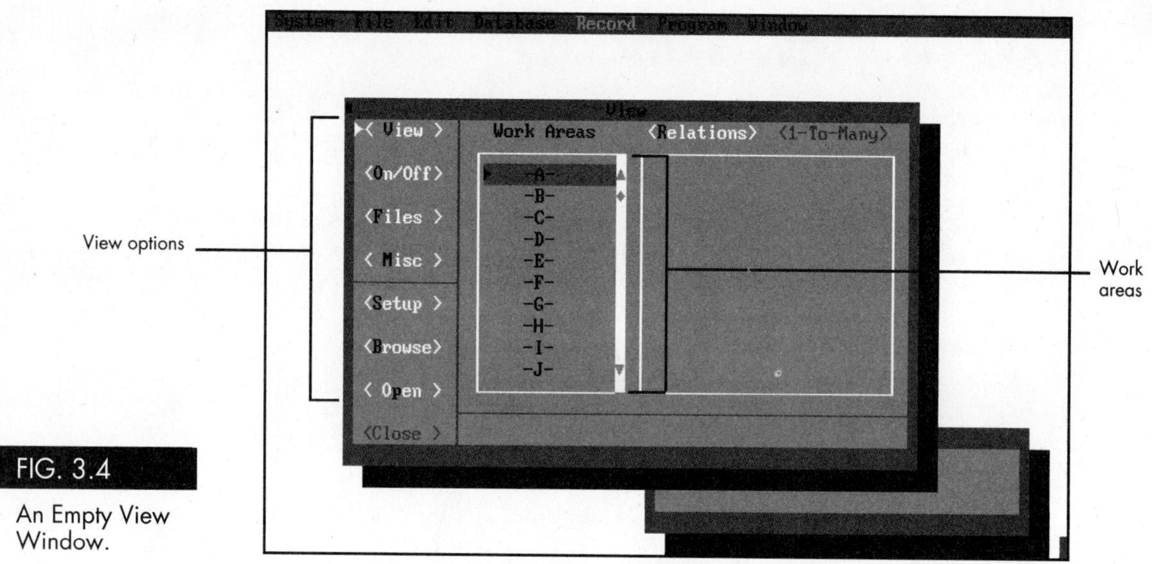

FIG. 3.4

An Empty View Window.

In FoxPro, the various tables that comprise a database are *opened* (made available for use) in 25 possible work areas. You can refer to work areas as 1 through 25 or as A through J, 11 to 25 (as the View window does). Each work area holds one table at a time.

After a table is opened in a work area, the work area and the table become virtually synonymous. You can refer to or select either term by using the table's alias. An *alias* is similar to a nickname for a table or work area. When you use the View window, FoxPro shows you the table's alias when opened in a work area.

When you open a table with the View window, FoxPro makes the name of the table the alias by default. If, however, you open the same table in different work areas or open two different tables with the same name in different work areas, FoxPro assigns an alias comprised of the table name, and a letter to distinguish between the two files. If you open the Product table in work area A, the alias becomes PRODUCT. If you change to work area B and open the PRODUCT table again or open another Product table (say from a different DOS directory), the alias in work area B becomes PRODUCT_A.

If you want, you can open a file by using FoxPro commands, either in a program or in the Command window, and specify a different alias for the default.

One work area is always the *currently selected work area*. In the View window, you can make a work area the currently selected work area by using the Tab key to move to the Work Areas column, using the arrow keys to highlight the desired work area, and pressing the space bar or clicking the work area you want with the mouse. The currently selected work area is marked with a ► immediately to the left of one table name in the Work Areas column.

After a work area is currently selected, the table open in the work area becomes the controlling table for many FoxPro operations. In Chapter 4, "Database Management Fundamentals," you learn how to establish connecting relationships between tables. These relationships are always established between the controlling table and other tables in the database.

Now, use the View window to create the Budget table of the database. Because you are opening the Budget table in work area A, make work area A the currently selected area and choose the Open option by pressing P, tabbing to the `<Open>` button in the left column and pressing Enter. You also can click on the `<Open>` button with the mouse.

The Open File dialog appears, as shown in figure 3.5.

To open an existing table, you can select the table from the list of available files. Because you are creating a table, however, use the Tab key to move to the `<New>` button and press Enter or click on the `<New>` button with the mouse. You see the Table Structure dialog shown in figure 3.6.

This dialog may look familiar because you used the same box in Chapter 1 to create the Product table. The title of the dialog reads `Structure: Untitled` because you haven't yet named this table.

Now, create the fields in the table by entering the field names, type, width and decimals (optional) as shown in figure 3.6. Remember that you can move from the name to the type to the width by pressing Tab (or Shift-Tab to move back) or clicking with the mouse. After you enter some fields, you also can move up and down within each column by using the arrow keys. Table 3.1 explains the characteristics of each field.

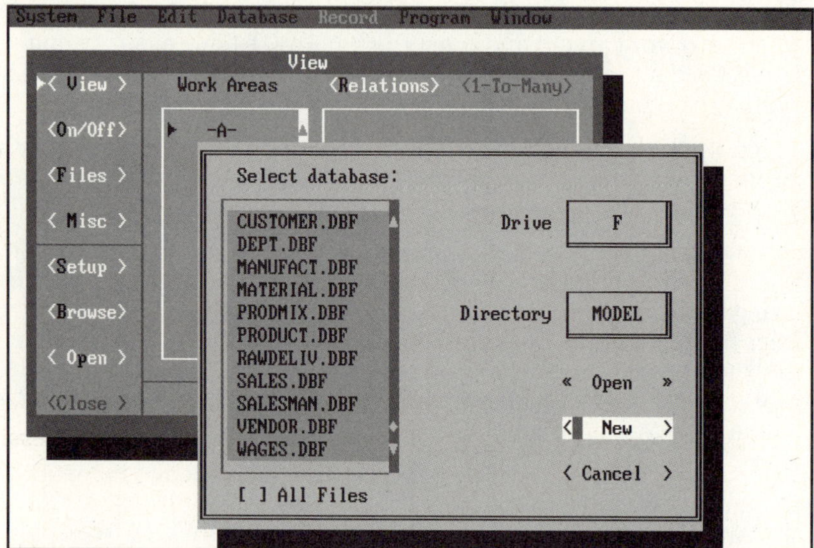

FIG. 3.5

The File Open dialog in use for table selection.

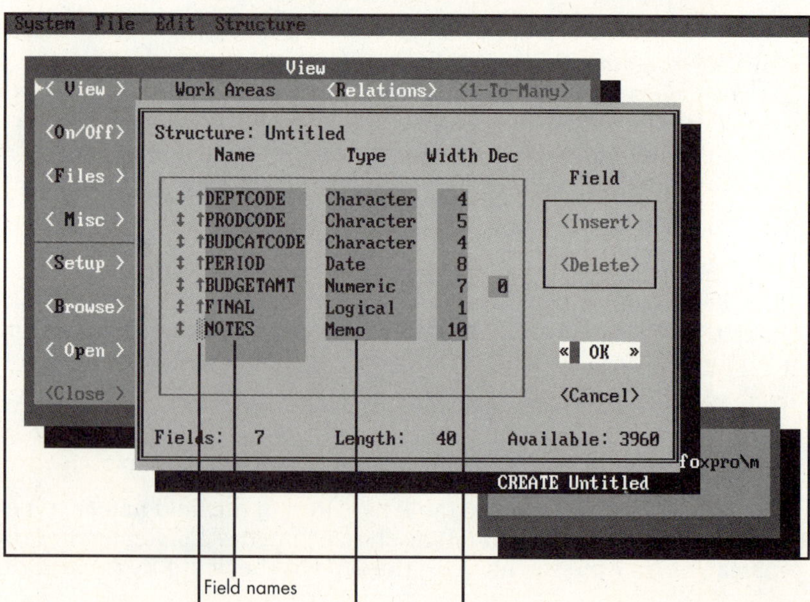

FIG. 3.6

The table Structure dialog.

Table 3.1 The Structure of the Budget Table

Field Name	Type	Width
DEPTCODE	Character	4
PRODCODE	Character	5
BUDCATCODE	Character	4
PERIOD	Date	8*
BUDGETAMT	Numeric	7
FINAL	Logical	1*
NOTES	Memo	10*

* Widths are determined by FoxPro.

Note that the shaded box to the left of the name represents an *index tag* (tags are explained in a following section). You can access this box by pressing Shift-Tab immediately after entering the name or by pressing Tab after all the fields are entered, until you reach the box you want. You also can click directly on this column with the mouse. After you land on the shaded box, you can press the space bar or Enter or click with the mouse to fill the box with either an up arrow, a down arrow, or an empty shaded box. (A keypress or mouse click cycles through these three available options.)

You explore indexes in a following section of this chapter and in Chapter 4. From working with the Product table in Chapter 1, you already know that an index enables you to view the data in a different order than the *natural order* (the order in which the records are entered). The up arrow creates an *ascending* tag (lowest to highest), the down arrow creates a *descending* tag (highest to lowest), and the empty shaded box creates no index tag on this field. When you create the Budget table, you want to create index tags for all the fields except the memo field, which doesn't accept an arrow in the shaded box.

After you enter the PERIOD, FINAL, and NOTES fields (date, logical, and memo data types), notice that you cannot adjust the width. Date type fields default to a width of 8, logical types to a width of 1, and memo types to a width of 10. With date and memo types, these limiting factors can become confusing.

As previously discussed in this chapter, you can display and enter date type fields in many forms—including a full century form, such as 01/01/1991 which has a width of 10. Yet FoxPro uses a width of 8 no matter how dates appear on-screen, FoxPro stores the date internally in the form *YYYYMMDD* (year, month, day). You can accept this default and still know that you can display or enter dates in the form you require.

NOTE

Ascending and *descending* have different meanings depending on the data type. For numeric data, the order ascends from the smallest number to the largest. For dates, the order ascends chronologically from the earliest date to the latest date. For logical data, the order ascends from false to true.

With character data, however, the ordering is not so simple and intuitive. Character data ascends from the lowest ASCII code number to the highest—this order is not strictly alphabetical. The order is case sensitive—uppercase letters precede lowercase letters—and spaces make a difference. An ascending character order can look like the following list (the numbers also are entered in character fields):

1

10

2

20

APPLE

GO THERE

GOPHER

apple

banana

Now you know why you see so much computer data where numbers are entered as *02* and codes and other information are entered only in upper- or lowercase. Remember these conventions when you are indexing, although of course, FoxPro provides features to make the process simple.

Again, memo data types also are limited in size only by the available space on the hard disk—certainly a far greater width than the default of 10. Here, the data in a memo field is stored in the companion memo file; the 10 character field in the main file is used by FoxPro to make the connection to the memo file.

As you create the field entries, you can change the order in which the entries appear, which is the same order in which they are saved in the table. Click-drag on the double-headed arrow (↕) on any field to move it up or down in the relative order. With the keyboard, press the Ctrl key with either the up- or down-arrow key while a field's information is highlighted. (The kind of characteristic—Index, Name, Type, Width, or Dec—that you highlight doesn't matter.)

After the table Structure dialog is completed so that this dialog exactly resembles figure 3.6, press Ctrl-Enter or Tab to the «OK» button and press Enter or click on the button to save the work. You now see the Table Naming dialog shown in figure 3.7. Type the name **Budget** at the cursor and press Enter or Tab. The «Save» button now becomes available. To name the table, Tab to the button and press Enter or click the button with the mouse.

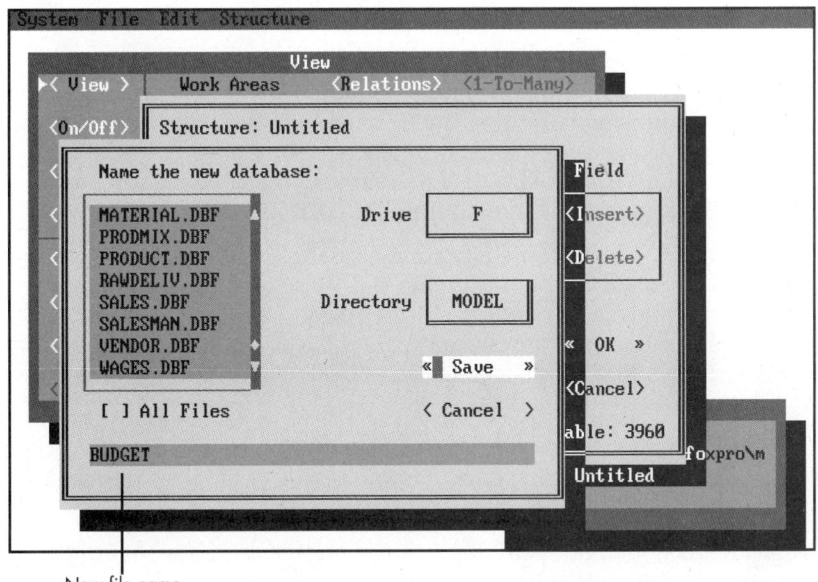

FIG. 3.7

The Table Naming dialog.

FoxPro asks you to input data now. If you click the «Yes» button, you can begin to add records to the table (which you learn to do in a following section of this chapter). For now, select <No> to exit to the View window.

The table BUDGET opens in work area A.

Saving Your Place with a View File

Because you learned how to create the Budget table and now understand the different kinds of data a file can contain, you can create the rest of the tables in the model database. You can find the structures and the *index keys* (or orders) that you need for each table in Appendix I.

Throughout this book, you are referred to many—although not all—of these tables in the examples, which you create to use in the practice sessions. You also draw on the tables that form the parts of the sample applications provided with FoxPro 2. Often you may want to have two or more tables open at the same time, and you become accustomed to seeing the contents of both tables appearing in a particular order for a particular task.

Each time you start to work, you may open all the tables you need and set the order, much as you open the drawers of a desk and arrange notebooks, pens, and other tools for easy access. Using a special type of file known as a View, FoxPro 2 also enables you to "walk away and then come back" and still have all the tools just as you left them.

If you closed the Budget table after creating the table in the preceding section, open Budget again now, using the View window. Choose a second work area and also open the Product table. Create or open as many other tables (and all appropriate index tags) in the model database as you want, using a new work area for each table.

With the View window active, choose the File Save As menu option. You see the dialog as shown in figure 3.8, although the screen may look different, depending on how many sample tables you have open and in what sequence you opened them.

Type **Model** as a filename and confirm the choice and the state of the open files as saved. If you look in the Command window for the executed command, you see that FoxPro added the default extension VUE for a View file.

Now, when you want to begin work after you load FoxPro, you can use the File Open option or the SET VIEW TO <*filename*> command in the Command window to restore these files (and other factors of what in FoxPro is known as the environment) just as you want them.

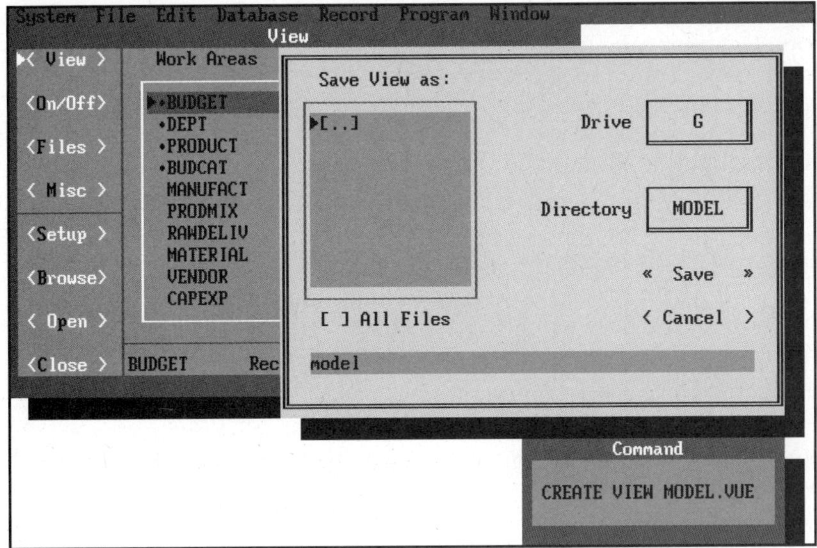

FIG. 3.8

The View window with the Save View As dialog.

View files are unusual because you cannot use File New to create a View file. You can access this capability by using File Save As while the View window is currently active or by typing the **CREATE VIEW** command in the Command window.

Bringing Data in with FoxPro Browse

Now that you can set up the open files the way you want them, you can begin to fill the files with data. In this section, you learn some quick techniques for adding records to the files by using FoxPro 2's Browse feature.

Using any method you prefer, open the Product and Budget tables. If the View window is not currently available, make the View window active now.

Highlight the Product table in the list. If you press Enter, you open a Browse of Product records.

You also can double-click with the mouse to open a Browse of the Product table. One click selects the Product table (makes Product the active work area), and the second click opens the Browse. Because the space bar is used in FoxPro to imitate mouse clicks for keyboard users, you also can press the space bar once to select the table and again to open the Browse. Watch the commands being executed in the Command window as you press the space bar.

You see that the Browse is an arrangement of the Product records, with the various fields listed across (in columns) and the various records listed down (in rows). You can use the usual editing keys to move around in the Browse window. The current record (the record you are editing) is highlighted in different colors or in a different intensity than the other records, and the current field also is presented differently. (Use the Tab key to move between fields.)

Because, for the moment, you are only going to refer to the Product table for reference, size and then place the window to one side. Then select the Budget table and open another Browse table (try using the View window's Browse button this time.) Resize the Budget browse so that you can comfortably see all the fields. The screen setup should resemble figure 3.9.

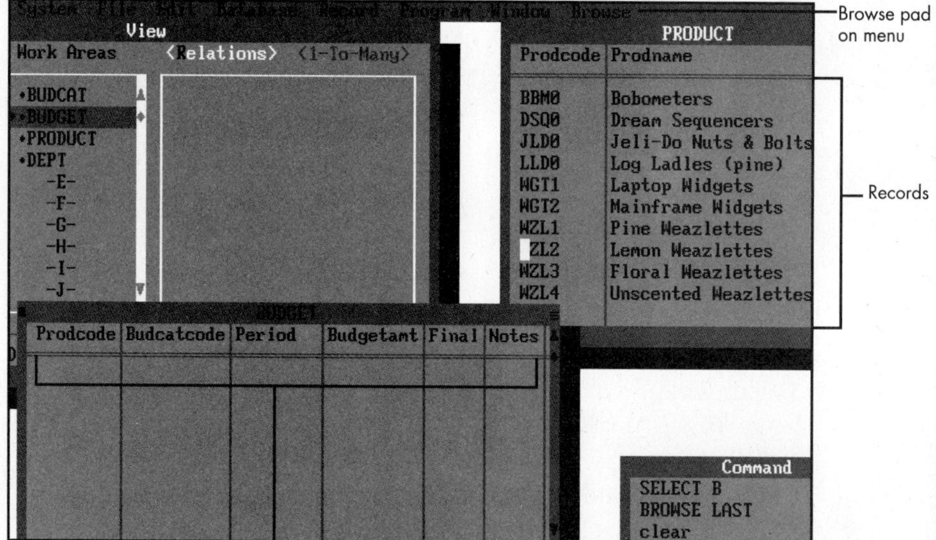

FIG. 3.9

An empty Budget Table Browse active and ready for data entry.

Note that you have a new option on the menu bar, the Browse pad. Browse is one of FoxPro 2's most powerful and versatile features, and you learn much more about how to arrange the Browse contents in subsequent chapters. For now, use the last two entries on the menu popup, Toggle Delete and Append Record, to add information to the file.

The key shortcut for appending, or adding, a new record to the table is Ctrl- N. The key shortcut for toggling delete is Ctrl-T. The deleting process marks a record in a special way so that the record becomes *invisible* by FoxPro for many tasks, although the record is not physically removed from the database. (You learn more about deleted records in the following section.)

A *toggle* is a switch used to alternate between two mutually exclusive states. Here, you can delete a record by pressing Ctrl-T and then you can *turn off* the delete marker by pressing Ctrl-T again. You can tell that a record is deleted in a Browse because the record is marked with a *bullet* (•) to the left of the first field.

No mouse equivalent exists for Ctrl-N. You can toggle the delete-state of records, however, by using a single click immediately to the left of the first field in the Browse. Clicking elsewhere on a record makes the record the current active record.

Figure 3.10 shows the Budget table with information added. Take the time to append records and type the sample information so that you can use this data for display and queries in this and in the following chapters. (You can find a complete listing for the sample records in Appendix I.) The DEPTCODE, PRODCODE, and BUDCATCODE fields come from other supporting tables in the database, including the Product table currently on-screen (you can refer to this Browse as you type to see what each product code means). In following operations, you use these codes to identify groups of records that belong together, so make sure that you type the codes accurately. Delete records to get rid of errors or just to practice.

The PERIOD field is a date field; all dates are shown as the first day of a quarter. Type a nonsense date, such as 13/13/91, or some non-numeric characters in the BUDGETAMT field to see the way FoxPro prevents you from typing an obviously invalid entry. The FINAL field is a logical field that accepts only True or False values (although logical fields also enable you to type Y or N, which are appropriately converted to True or False values).

In later chapters, you learn to do much more complex validation of information as it is entered by using criteria that you define. You do not have to type information into code fields like PRODCODE, either; you can tell FoxPro to do look-ups of such fields from the support tables they come from.

Notice that the last field, NOTES, is designed to enable executives to jot down reminders about the budget lines as these lines are entered. Because NOTES is a memo field, you cannot edit NOTES directly in the Browse window. To edit this field, position the cursor in the four-character *placeholder* in the Browse and press Ctrl-PgDn to access a text editing window where you can type notes. With the mouse, you can double-click the Memo placeholder to bring up the memo editing window. You can edit and save a memo field as you save any other text. After you enter information into a memo field, you can see that the placeholder in the Browse window now displays a capital `M` on-screen.

During text entry in the NOTES field, take a moment to look at the Edit Preferences menu option. You can see that the available options for a memo differ slightly from the options for a regular text file.

After you return to the Browse, notice that you also can press Ctrl-F or use the Edit Find option to search for information in a Browse. Because this procedure can check all character and numeric fields, Edit Find is extremely convenient for moving quickly through a large table to find information. You can only search forward in a Browse, however, although the option to *Wrap around* in a search permits you to find data in records that precede the current record.

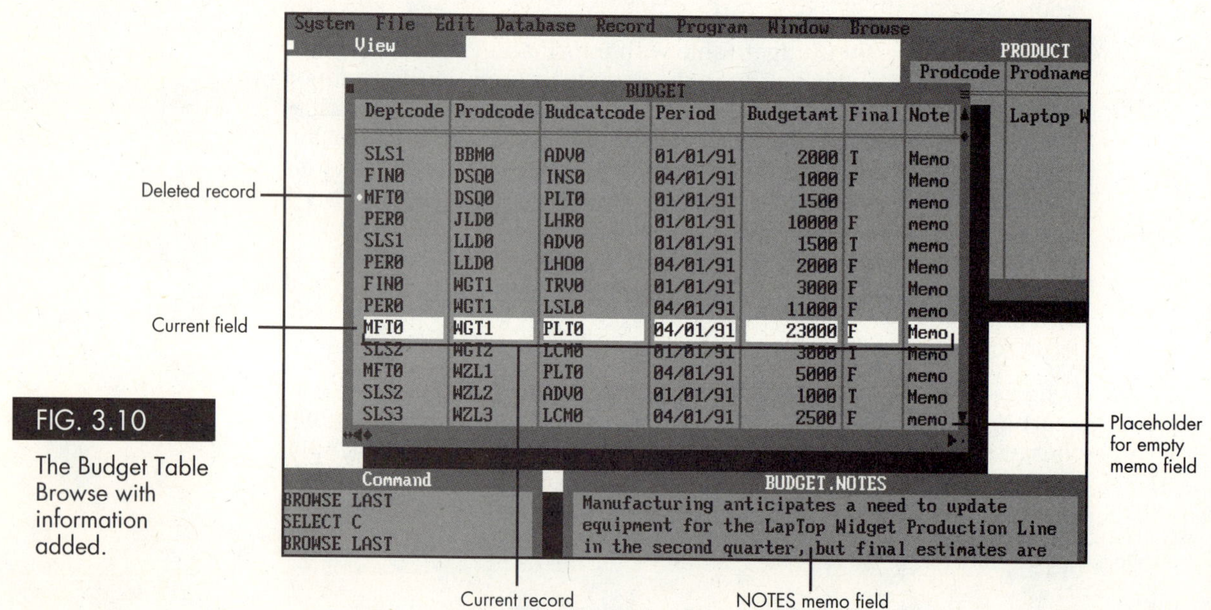

FIG. 3.10

The Budget Table Browse with information added.

The View window contains many features that you haven't yet explored. Some of these features are useful for quick editing, such as the work you are now doing in the Browse. Open the View window and then click the `<Misc>` button to see the check boxes in figure 3.11. Of particular interest to our Browse session are the `Bell`, `Date Delimiter`, and `Century` check boxes. Change the settings of these features to see what happens to Browse. If you change the bell Frequency or Length (rather than simply turning off the bell), you can choose the little musical note to the right of these items to immediately hear the change you make. If the `Bell` check box is marked (the default state), you hear this sound while you edit information in the Browse each time you completely fill a field, and the cursor moves to the next field.

Just for practice, mark the `Clock` check box and choose a custom position on the screen for the clock. As always, you can learn the syntax for these commands by watching as they are echoed to the Command window.

You may want to experiment with the Mouse Tracking option, which can be set between 1 and 10 (a setting of 10 is the highest level of sensitivity).

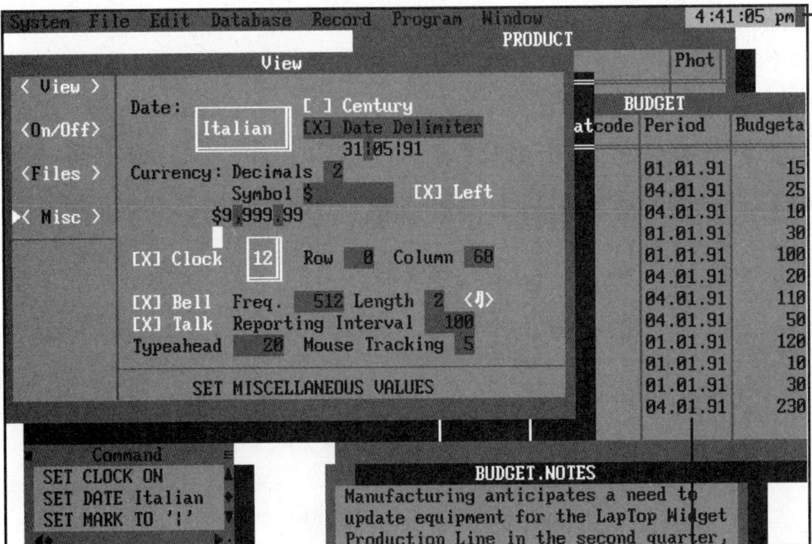

FIG. 3.11

The View Miscellaneous Settings Panel.

Now choose the `<View>` window button for On/Off settings. A number of the check boxes also have particular application to the editing session. Turn DELETED on (DELETED is on when the check box is filled with an X) and return to the Budget browse; the deleted records are no longer visible. Turn CARRY on and append a new record to this browse; you see that the information on the previous record is carried over. Set CONFIRM on and go back to entering information in the Browse; when you reach the limit of a field, you need to press Enter rather than moving by default to the next field.

The View window has a fourth panel, Files. Although you do not yet need to change these settings, look at the settings as you experiment with the View features. If you don't know what a particular item does, use the Help system. You can express most of the options in View as commands that begin with the word SET, such as SET DELETED ON/OFF. (To find out about this setting, look under SET DELETED in the Help file.)

Packing a File

You learned that you can delete records in a file, but that the records aren't really erased. In the following section, you learn that if you do not want deleted records accessed along with others when the SET DELETED ON command is used, you can make the records *invisible* for the purposes of a count or any other output that you ask FoxPro to create.

Ordinarily, therefore, you do not need to physically remove deleted records from a table. This knowledge is important because actually removing records is more work for FoxPro (and more interruption for you) for the following reasons:

- FoxPro must create a temporary file while removing records, and if the file is large, you may not have enough disk space. A good rule of thumb for the free space needed on a disk is three times the size of the file, including associated memo files.
- Removing records takes time (this time depends on the size of the file and the speed of the system).
- If you are running the network version of FoxPro, no one else can access this file until you complete the process of removing the unwanted records.

However, as part of regular maintenance procedures, you may want to remove the records entirely from the table. The physical removal is known as *packing* a file. This option is available from the Database menu pad.

You can pack the Budget table now. If you left the TALK check box in the default setting of ON in the View window, you see a message that tells you how many records remain in the file after packing.

Besides removal of records, which can allow for a significant savings of disk space, packing a file has another benefit: if the packed table contains memo fields (as the Budget table does), the table also has an associated file with the extension FPT in which memos are stored. FoxPro assigns space for each memo field in a standard size known as the file's *blocksize*. Although you can adjust the blocksize for a given file, some space is wasted as you add information to a particular memo field because each piece of information is not an exact blocksize in length or a multiple of the blocksize.

During the file-packing procedure, FoxPro 2 consolidates the entries in the memo file and eliminates this wasted space.

You may even want to perform this consolidation when you do not want to remove the deleted records, which you can do by issuing the PACK MEMO command in the Command window. If for some reason you need to remove deleted records from the file but do not want to consolidate the memo file, you can issue the command PACK DBF.

Structural index files, which are discussed in Chapter 4, also can contain wasted space that the PACK command can reclaim.

Understanding PACK is essential for proper maintenance of a database, but like other *housekeeping* chores PACK is not terribly illuminating. Now that you took the trouble of putting data into the Budget table, the database is ready to work for you by pulling information back out of the table.

Getting Quick Results to the Screen and Printer

As you learn in Chapter 1 and as you learn in more detail in Chapter 8, the Browse window with which you are working with is a powerful tool for viewing the information in tables. You also need, however, to print information and display on-screen or print information in many different forms.

Quick Results on the Screen

If the View window and the Browse window for the Budget file are not currently open on-screen, open them now.

When you created the Budget file, you set index tags on all the fields except the NOTES field (a memo field). You now can see how these tags work with a Browse. Select the View window again and choose the Setup option. You see the Setup dialog.

In the left column, you see the table Structure, defined when you created the table. In the middle column, you see the fields you indexed with up arrows to the left (as you set these fields when you created the table).

Just as you can currently select only one table or one work area—no matter how many indexes are open and in use—only *one* index at a time is ordering the records. A bullet (•) appears to the left of this index, known as the *master* or *controlling* index in the Setup panel. If no bullet appears, the records in the browse appear in the original order in which the records were entered in the table. You can see what the browse looks like if you list the records in date order. Use the Tab key to move to the Indexes column and use the arrow keys to highlight the PERIOD index (or click on the word `PERIOD` with the mouse). Now tab to the `<Set Order>` button and press Enter (or press O or click on the button with the mouse), and the bullet appears to the left of the name, as shown in figure 3.12. Click the `«OK»` button to exit the Setup dialog.

Now return to the Browse window. The records appear in *ascending date order* (earliest date to latest date), as shown in figure 3.13. Return to the Setup dialog box, select another index, choose `<Set Order>` and again return to the Browse. The records now appear in ascending order (lowest value to highest value) by whichever field you chose (such as DEPTCODE or PRODCODE).

Quick Results to the Printer

In Chapter 1, you saw a quick demonstration of printing reports by using FoxPro 2's RQBE. In following chapters, you learn how to produce both easy and complicated reports, with FoxPro's Report Writer. Other options are available that may suit your needs at a particular moment.

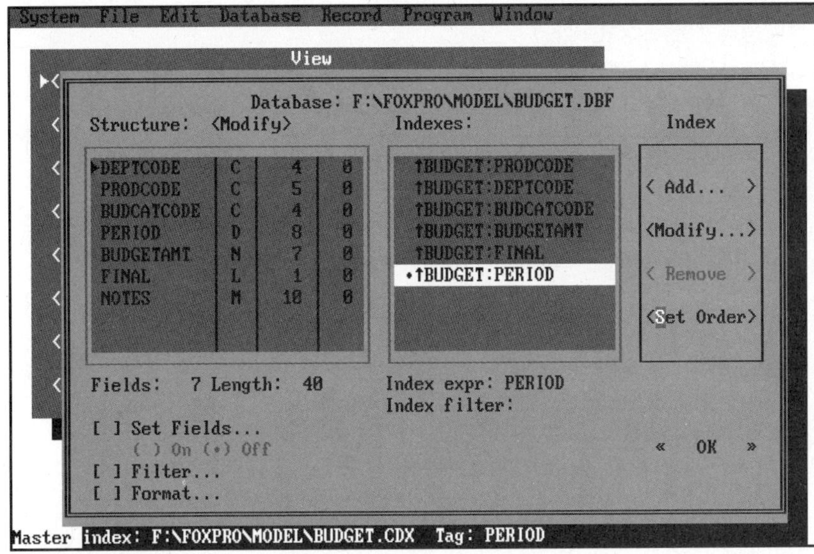

FIG. 3.12

The Setup dialog—index order by PERIOD selected.

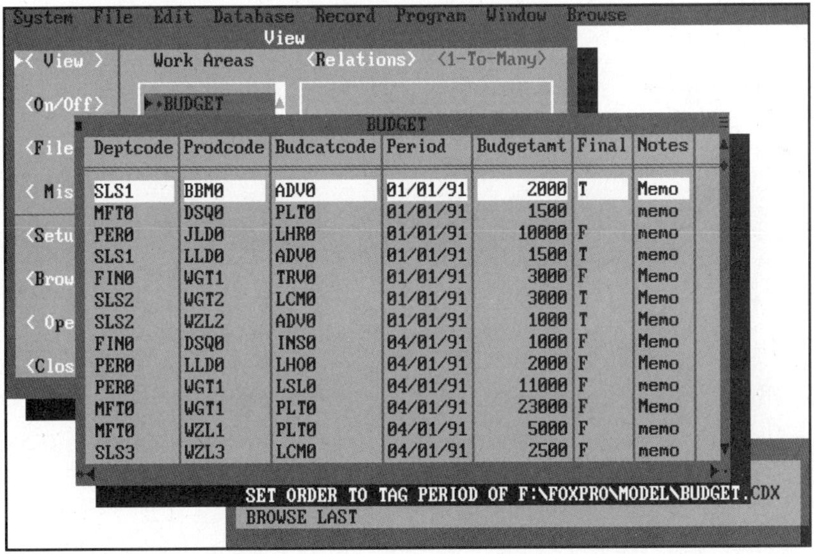

FIG. 3.13

The Browse with records in date order.

FoxPro, however, provides simple ways to print the same information you just saw in the Browse. Press Ctrl-F2 to bring forward the Command window (or select the Command window from the Window menu pad). Make sure that the printer is ready and, in the Command window, type **LIST TO PRINTER** and press Enter (see fig. 3.14). If you have a laser printer, type **EJECT** to tell the printer to eject the page. On an impact printer, EJECT advances the page to the top of the next page.

```
System  File  Edit  Database  Record  Program  Window
Record#  DEPTCODE PRODCODE BUDCATCODE PERIOD      BUDGETAMT FINAL NOTES
      1  SLS1     BBM0     ADV0       01/01/1991       2000 .T.   Memo
      2  FIN0     DSQ0     INS0       04/01/1991       1000 .F.   Memo
      3  MFT0     DSQ0     PLT0       01/01/1991       1500 .F.   memo
      4  PER0     JLD0     LHR0       01/01/1991      10000 .F.   memo
      5  SLS1     LLD0     ADV0       01/01/1991       1500 .T.   memo
      6  PER0     LLD0     LHO0       04/01/1991       2000 .F.   Memo
      7  FIN0     WGT1     TRV0       01/01/1991       3000 .F.   Memo
      8  PER0     WGT1     LSL0       04/01/1991      11000 .F.   memo
      9  MFT0     WGT1     PLT0       04/01/1991      23000 .F.   Memo
     10  SLS2     WGT2     LCM0       01/01/1991       3000 .T.   Memo
     11  MFT0     WZL1     PLT0       04/01/1991       5000 .F.   memo
     12  SLS2     WZL2     ADV0       01/01/1991       1000 .T.   Memo
     13  SLS3     WZL3     LCM0       04/01/1991       2500 .F.   memo

                              Command
LIST TO PRINTER
LIST FIELDS PRODCODE,BUDGETAMT TO PRINTER
LIST TO PRINTER FOR PRODCODE="WGT1"
LIST TO PRINTER FOR BUDGETAMT>=5000
LIST FILES TO PRINTER
```

LIST TO PRINTER is echoed on-screen

FIG. 3.14

The LIST commands in the Command window.

Now you can try some more LIST options. Suppose that you want a report that shows only the PRODCODE and the BUDGETAMT. Type **LIST FIELDS PRODCODE, BUDGETAMT TO PRINTER** (and, if needed add the **EJECT** command).

To produce a list for only records that use the PRODCODE *WGT1*, type **LIST TO PRINTER FOR PRODCODE = "WGT1"** (which means "Information in the field PRODCODE is equal or is the same as the string of characters *WGT1*").

Notice that *WGT1* is character data and must be enclosed in quotation marks. You use quotation marks to distinguish character data from FoxPro commands and from the names of fields. Notice that because the comparison is case sensitive, you also must type WGT1 in uppercase.

Now type **LIST TO PRINTER FOR BUDGETAMT >= 5000**. The >= is defined as *greater than or equal to.* Numbers need no quotation marks; FoxPro can work directly with numbers.

Type **LIST TO PRINTER FOR PERIOD = {04/01/91}**. Here, you need curly braces to distinguish dates from numbers.

As you try these options, you also can return to the Setup dialog and change the index order, as you did with the Browse. The order of records in printed change in exactly the same way. If desired, continue to experiment with the `<Misc>` button's options in the View window—changing the SET CENTURY ON/OFF setting or the date format from AMERICAN to BRITISH. Now, try changing the DELETED option in the ON/OFF option of the View window—if you have any deleted records, you see these records disappear when DELETED is set to ON and reappear when set to OFF.

Now, highlight the word `LIST` from the commands in the Command window and press F1. You see FoxPro's Help for the LIST command with all the different options (see fig. 3.15). Try LIST FILES TO PRINTER and you see a list of all the tables in the working directory. Try LIST STRUCTURE TO PRINTER and you see the structure of the Budget file.

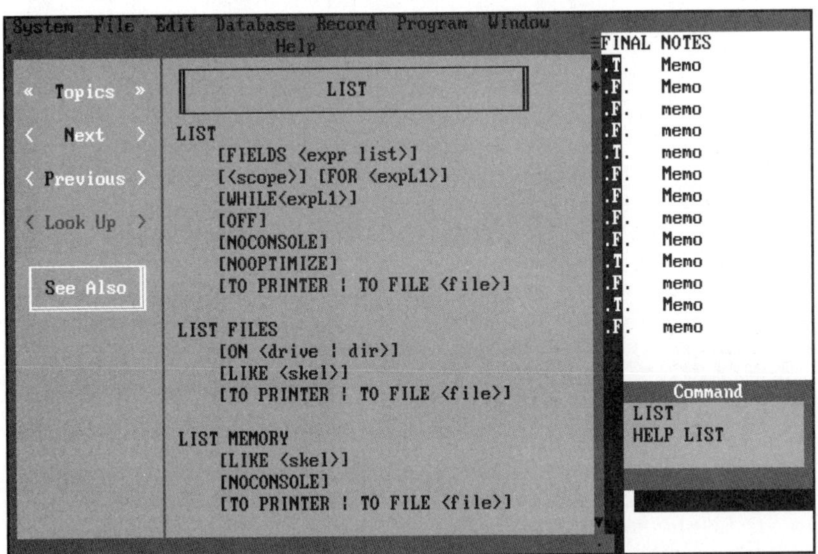

FIG. 3.15

The FoxPro Help entry on the LIST command.

The LIST command displays the same information on-screen during the printing process, or on-screen only if you omit TO PRINTER from the command. If you don't see this display, press Ctrl-Alt-Shift (hold down all three keys at one time) to temporarily remove windows which may obscure the screen. You can use the NOCONSOLE key word to print records but not show the records on-screen. The output from the LIST command usually goes to the screen but you learn in a following section how to make a window active for output. When you do this, Ctrl-Alt-Shift hides all windows except the active window.

Another convenient way to list the contents of tables to a screen is by using the DISPLAY command, which pauses after each screen or window of information. The DISPLAY command is nearly identical to list except that this command defaults to show the current record only; LIST displays on-screen or prints all records, subject to the conditions you previously set. Type **DISPLAY ALL** to see all records on-screen.

As you see, the LIST command does not show the contents of a memo field by default. You can include the name of the memo field in a FIELDS list with any other fields you LIST or DISPLAY by typing **LIST FIELDS BUDGETAMT, NOTES**. You also can print or display the contents of one memo field with other fields by typing another FoxPro command used for output—the **?** (question mark). Switch back to the browse window for the Budget file and select an entry for which the word `memo` in the notes field begins with a capital `M`, which indicates that this memo contains text or other data. Now switch to the Command window and type the following:

```
SET PRINT ON
? NOTES, PERIOD
SET PRINT OFF
```

If you just want to show the entry on-screen, leave out the SET PRINT ON and SET PRINT OFF commands. The former command sends all output to the printer until the latter command is used to turn off the SET PRINT ON command.

Like LIST, the ? command has many options—some quite sophisticated—for producing output. Check the help file for reference.

LIST and DISPLAY are both affected by the active printer driver setup, and a STYLE special clause on the ? command is available which enables you to adjust the output even further if a printer driver is loaded. Refer to the *Printer Drivers* booklet in the FoxPro documentation and to Chapter 15 for more information on printer drivers.

Quick Results to a File

You often want a more permanent record of a report for subsequent use or to print at a later date. You also can use the LIST command to send a report to a file on disk by using the TO FILE *<filename>* clause.

In the Command window, type **LIST TO FILE LISTFILE** and then type **MODIFY FILE LISTFILE.TXT** and you see the file in an editing window as it is stored on disk. If you want, you now can edit the file! Note that—because you did not specify a file extension—FoxPro creates a file with the extension TXT. You can create any file name you want by specifying the entire name, as in LISTFILE.PRN. Press Escape to exit the LISTFILE.TXT window.

To print the contents of the file, type the following command in the Command window: **TYPE LISTFILE.TXT**, followed by **EJECT** if you are printing to a laser printer. You also can print a file by choosing Print from the File menu pad, using the Windows popup button to choose File, and entering the name of the file to print in the File text region. Mark the `Page eject after` check box if you have a laser printer or to advance the paper to the top of the next page.

In FoxPro 2, the TYPE command was enhanced and is now affected by the printer driver you load. TYPE also has new keywords that enable you to activate word wrap and indentation for memo fields.

Rearranging and Extracting Data from Tables

By now, you know a bit about how indexes work. You learn more about how to create and maintain indexes in Chapter 4, but you can already see how useful indexes are for rearranging data. With the FOR option of the LIST command, you now are starting to see how you can extract data from tables so that you may deal only with the specific range of information useful to you at the moment. Many ways are available to perform this process in FoxPro, but all ways primarily rely on the same basic concepts.

When extracting data, you set certain conditions that the data must meet before the data is included in the information you want. Essentially, you are defining a *subset* of all possible data.

In Chapter 1, you used FoxPro's RQBE feature to rearrange and extract data. You get a lot more practice with this feature in following chapters and you learn that RQBE handles many of the details for you. For now, however, you are looking at rearranging and extracting data as it applies to many of the FoxPro table commands, such as the BROWSE and LIST commands you previously used.

Extracting Records by Using a SCOPE Clause

A scope clause tells a FoxPro command to limit its action to a specified range of contiguous records (contiguous as defined by the current index order). If all conditions of the SCOPE clause are met, records are included. If you previously tried the DISPLAY ALL command, the ALL clause told DISPLAY to show all the records.

Table 3.2 The Scope Clauses

Scope	Effect
ALL	Acts on all records in the table
NEXT *<n>*	Acts on the next *<n>* (*number*) of records, starting at the current record. If you are located at the first record in an ordered table, the command LIST NEXT 10 gives you a list of the first 10 records. If you are at or near the end of the table, NEXT gives you as many records as exist (up to 10 records) in this range.
RECORD *<n>*	Acts only on the one record number you specify. Therefore, LIST RECORD 5 lists only the information for record number 5. ***Warning:*** this clause acts on the *physical* record number 5, not on the fifth record in the current table order.
REST	Acts on all remaining records in a file, starting with the current record and continuing through the last record in the table

Extracting Records by Using FOR, WHILE, and SET FILTER TO

FOR and WHILE clauses, like SCOPE clauses, instruct a FoxPro command to limit the actions of a command to only records that meet certain conditions. SET FILTER TO is a FoxPro command.

The FOR clause tells a FoxPro command "Work on all the records in this table FOR which the following conditions are true."

The WHILE clause begins at the current record and tells FoxPro to "Work on records in sequence WHILE the conditions are true," or "Work on records in sequence *until* the conditions are *no longer* true."

You use SET FILTER TO a little differently—to tell FoxPro to ignore all records that don't meet certain conditions. SET FILTER TO is used *before* a command so that the command *sees* only data which already meets certain conditions. This command works much like the FOR command, except SET FILTER TO selects the records before a command or series of commands is issued. These conditions stay in effect until removed with another SET FILTER TO command (if you include no conditions, all records are *seen*).

Not only are the conditions for each FILTER, FOR, and WHILE clause comprehensive and possibly complicated, but you also can combine the three clauses—with each other and with the SCOPE clauses—to create extremely precise sets of conditions. One possibility, for example, is to create a combination of commands and clauses like the following:

SET FILTER TO <*conditions*>

LIST NEXT 5 FOR <*conditions*> WHILE <*conditions*>

Although designing these combinations can become complicated, in practice a less complex combination of conditions can handle most needs.

If you previously used other xBase dialects, you know that FILTERs and FOR clauses are seldom used because the database manager is forced to scan the entire table and evaluate conditions for each record. If a table contains several hundred records, this process can take a long time.

If you can phrase the conditions in the form of an expression that includes one or more index expressions, FoxPro 2 can quickly extract the desired subset of records by using the exclusive *Rushmore* technology. You learn how this technology works in Chapter 7. For now, however, remember that FOR and FILTER clauses are efficient and usable options in FoxPro 2.

Defining Conditions

Conditions are a simple concept. Nearly every moment, you make choices based on whether certain conditions are met. If you dine out, you must first choose a restaurant and then select a number of items from a menu. You can phrase these conditions in the following way: "I want to eat Italian food, but I have only $10 to spend. I want to eat pasta with alfredo sauce, and I want to leave the restaurant by 9 p.m. so that I am home in time to watch a *Twin Peaks* rerun."

First, you narrow the available options from all the possible meals on earth to decide on the meals available in a certain restaurant. Then you winnow the food choices from all the meals available from the restaurant's menu. In *FoxProse*, this kind of narrowing down may look like the following text:

```
SET FILTER TO FOOD = ITALIAN AND PRICES = INEXPENSIVE

EAT FOR ITEM = PASTA AND SAUCE = ALFREDO AND
PRICE <= $10 WHILE TIME <= 9 PM.
```

In the preceding listing, <= means *less than or equal to* as >= means *greater than or equal to* in the LIST exercises. Of course, = also means *equal to*. These examples are FoxPro *logical operators* (symbols that FoxPro interprets to make comparisons between data items).

In FoxPro, conditions are defined (or constructed) by comparing one or more data items in a variety of ways. You previously defined conditions in the LIST exercises by typing the commands directly into the Command window. FoxPro also provides a tool known as the Expression Builder for defining conditions.

You can quickly see how to use the Expression Builder to define the conditions for a filter. If the View window and the Browse window for the Budget file are not currently open on-screen, open View, Browse, and Budget now.

Choose the Setup option again from the View window to bring forward the Setup dialog as illustrated in figure 3.12. Look at the `Filter` check in the lower left corner. Press I or use the Tab key to move to this box or click with the mouse to activate the Expression Builder dialog, as shown in figure 3.16.

At the cursor, type **PRODCODE = "WGT1"**. (You previously used this condition in the LIST exercises with the FOR option, which tells FoxPro to create a temporary table that includes *only* the budget items which have product codes of WGT1.) Press Ctrl-Enter or click `«OK»` to save the work. When you return to the Setup dialog, you can see the condition displayed on-screen, beside the `Filter` check box. Return to the View window.

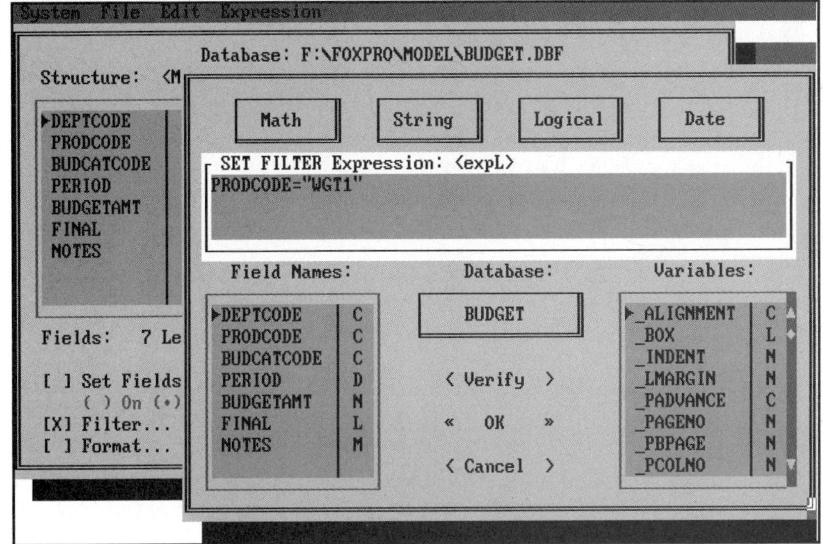

FIG. 3.16

The Expression Builder dialog.

Select the Browse window again. Only items with *WGT1* product codes are listed, and no other items are available. To LIST ALL now, only the items visible in the Browse print in the reports. To return to all the items in the table, reselect `Filter`, reenter the Expression Builder, and delete the condition you set. Try this step now. After you return to the Browse, all the items are listed again.

You learn more about defining conditions and using the Expression Builder in Chapter 10. You also learn the *syntax* FoxPro uses for making comparisons, but you already know how the Expression Builder works!

For now, select the Database menu popup from the menu bar and select any option. You see that almost all the options—from Append From through Label—have SCOPE, FOR, and WHILE options that use the Expression Builder. The Setup option on the Database menu is the same as Setup in the View window, and you can use this option to set a filter in the same way.

Chapter Summary

In this chapter, you began to take control of the data tables.

You saw how the tables fit into a wider picture of related tables, and you know how to create a table to meet specific needs. You learned how to rearrange information for a particular purpose and how to extract subsets of data that meet specific requirements.

Using the mouse or keyboard to move around, select menus, and pop-up and drop-down menus and boxes in FoxPro is fun, but the *real* point is that FoxPro gives you the power to control the information you need to do the job. In the following chapter, "Database Management Fundamentals," you concentrate on ways to organize and define information, creating properly structured tables and databases so that FoxPro can manage the data.

4

CHAPTER

Database Management Fundamentals

In this chapter, you learn to design a database by looking at a database as one part of an *information* system. The purpose of an information system is to provide the information you need to accomplish specific results.

Raw data has little value. An information system makes basic information useful by collecting, organizing, processing, and presenting data in a way that makes sense to the reader.

Critically important areas on which you must focus are the *results* you ultimately want to achieve and to realize that the purpose of the information system is to support you in managing information. An emphasis on results gives you a context in which to make decisions, and you find that this emphasis filters down to the smallest details of database design and management.

Information systems frequently fail due to an inadequate understanding and definition of the results. Results can be defined as both *comprehensive* and *detailed*. A comprehensive system design includes consideration of future growth, increasingly sophisticated information users, and potential changes in the operating environment. These changes may include both changes in the people who use—and the equipment used—to run the system. A detailed system's design includes an exacting analysis of what information is wanted or needed and a plan for the information's proper use.

In the model presented here, the Omnipresent Widget company is developing an information system that tells you how well the company is performing and provides the company with information that helps to identify both problems and opportunities. Omnipresent Widget uses this information to monitor growth and change so that the company can respond quickly and appropriately to changes in the marketplace. The company is generating information that gives both a wide view of the company's performance and a narrow view of how individual products, salespeople, and how departments are functioning.

The first three sections of this chapter show you how the Omnipresent Widget database designers—and you—can design the structure of a database and get all the elements to work together internally. In the third section, you learn about getting the database to function as a whole within an information system.

Constructing Databases

Chapter 3 defines a database as a collection of tables that work together to accomplish a common purpose and describes tables as collections or lists of records, with each record holding individual pieces of information in fields.

How do you determine which pieces of information you want in a table? How do you determine the tables you want in a database? How do the tables work together to accomplish a purpose? What do you want to know, and how do you put together a system that gives you this information?

Two approaches are available for constructing a database. In one approach, the *top down* approach, you define the results, define the specific purpose of the database in terms of supporting these results, and look at what you specifically want to know. In the other approach, the *bottom up* approach, you organize specific pieces of information into larger and larger groups. When constructing a complete database system, you must use both approaches at the same time.

Although this process may sound complicated, you already know how to do this! The process is often referred to as *getting organized*. The following mental exercise illustrates this process.

Suppose that a tornado sweeps through your home and office, picks up every scrap of paper, and deposits the whole mess on the living room floor. You now must sort through this chaos and reorganize all the information. Because the material may not have been as organized as you liked, and you also accumulated a great deal of junk, you can use this opportunity to start with a clean slate. Think about how you want to organize the material. Without the inertia of the old systems, you find a new freedom to create systems that work better.

You may start with a *home* pile and an *office* pile. These piles represent databases. You then can break down the home database into separate piles such as home finances, family matters, and community affairs. These piles are the *tables*, which you can break down into even more precise tables.

Take a minute and notice how you are thinking and making choices. You are organizing the material based on how you want your life organized—based on the results. Although you are putting together pieces of information one at a time (building *up* piles), you also are working *down* from a mental image of what you want to know and how you want to access the information. You probably aren't sorting all the blue pieces of paper into one pile and the yellow pieces into a second pile—this sorting process, although a form of organizing, is not very useful.

Concentrating on Output

The purpose of a database management system is to produce useful *output*, or information that you can review and analyze. Computer systems provide output in many different forms, usually on-screen and on paper. Although the information with which you work is the same, you can present the data differently, as you saw with BROWSE and with the printed reports when using LIST.

Before constructing a database, think of every report you imagine may be useful. A handy tip is to think in terms of printed reports. Design the system by sketching the reports on pieces of paper. Make these sample reports look exactly as you want to see the printed product. Think of the possible subsets of information and the order in which you want this information to appear. Be creative. Don't limit yourself at this stage; you always can make compromises at a later date.

Suppose that you want a list of customers. One report may consist of a list of all customers in alphabetical order. Another report may be a list of only certain customers in alphabetical order. Another report may be a list of customers sorted by salesperson. You may want mailing labels (just another form of report) sorted by ZIP code, or you may want a list of all the products that each customer purchased in the preceding year.

You begin to see information you need in the output, and you can work back from these results to determine the information you need to collect (or input) to produce this output. You must collect information that does the following:

- Tells you something you want to know
- Gives you a means of ordering information
- Gives you a means of extracting subsets of information
- Gives you a means of relating, or connecting, one set of information to other sets of information
- Is used in processing other input (say, for example, calculating sales tax on a sale)

When you complete this process, you have determined all the pieces of information you need to output and most of the pieces of information you need to input or provide within an application. In the following section, you look at the task of organizing and distributing these pieces of information into tables.

Organizing Information into Tables

Suppose that you are again back on the living room floor with the piles of paper. You need to sort this data into fields, records, tables, and databases.

The goal is to organize information economically into tables (without unnecessary duplication or wasted space) and in a way that enables each table to operate as independently as possible. You may think that putting all the information into a single table is the most efficient sorting method. You soon see, however, that much of the power and flexibility of FoxPro depends on separate tables that work together.

Remember that a table is a collection of items that share common traits. These traits may differ from the way you organize paper files. In a paper-based system, for example, you may have a customer file that contains a variety of different kinds of information. You may have a cover sheet with name, address, assigned salesperson, and miscellaneous information, correspondence to and from the customer, copies of all invoices, payments, and adjusting memos. Several problems exist with this method.

- Duplicated information takes space. On a computer system, duplication takes up disk space, which is always at a premium.

- If you ever want to look at the correspondence of all customers (for example, to analyze the number of complaints about a certain product or the number of letters received by date), you may need to keep another file that contains a copy of every piece of correspondence. Similarly, if you want to extract information about invoices, you need a separate invoice file.
- Duplicated information makes changing data difficult. In a paper-based system, if you have a customer file and an invoice file—and both contain the customer's complete name and address—you have to make changes in both files when the address changes. A better method is to make changes in one place because the change is quicker and because the fewer changes you make, the fewer mistakes occur.
- Suppose that you are entering customer data on a form and you want to assign an available salesperson to this customer. You do not want to have to thumb through all the customer files to get this information. You want a separate list of salespeople to which you can refer.

In a relational database management system, such as FoxPro, you create one table for each kind of information and *relate* the tables (similar to keeping cross-reference lists for paper files). You can easily present the information together—just as if all the information were in the same table. When needed, you also can work with each table independently.

Deciding which kinds of information belong together in one table can take thought and perhaps some experimentation. This decision also depends a great deal on specific circumstances. *Customers* are generally the same kind of *items*, although different kinds of customers exist. Although you may have different kinds of customers, all customers usually can stay in the same table with a code that identifies each kind of customer entry. If you have a business where you keep completely different kinds of information for each of two groups of customers, however, you may choose to create separate tables for the two customer groups.

In another example, you may consider sales, adjustment memos, and payments as different items that require different fields in separate tables. On the other hand, you may consider all the fields *accounting transactions* and place all the fields in one table, with codes to distinguish each kind of transaction.

To make the most efficient use of record and disk space, you occasionally may need to separate into different tables some items that seem similar. Addresses always require the same types and numbers of fields. Normally customers have one or two addresses (billing and shipping), so you may place fields in each customer record for both billing and shipping addresses. Some customers, however, may have seven addresses. You may not know in advance how many addresses a customer has. If you set up separate fields for all possible address combinations and numbers, you waste disk space for all the customers who have only one or two addresses. You also may run up against FoxPro's limit of 255 fields per table. A more sensible approach is to put addresses into a separate address table. Each record in the address table contains one address and two additional fields that identify the customer to whom each address belongs and the kind of address of each entry.

You can address other considerations by looking at the Budget, Product, and Dept tables. Use the View window to open the Budget and Product tables in separate work areas. Open Browse windows for both tables, adjusting the size for each so that you can see both tables at once. You need only to look at one record at time, so this process is easier to manage if you use the Browse menu pad and select the Change option to give you a vertical listing.

In figure 4.1, you see the two tables—and the Dept table, which you have not yet created—opened. The structure of the Dept table is similar to the structure of the Product table and the other tables that support the Budget table in the model database, as you learn when you use FoxPro's Screen Builder to create the table in Chapter 12. A good idea is to consider the Budget and Product tables in the context of the larger database. To see the Dept table's structure, along with the structure of the other supporting tables, refer to Appendix I.

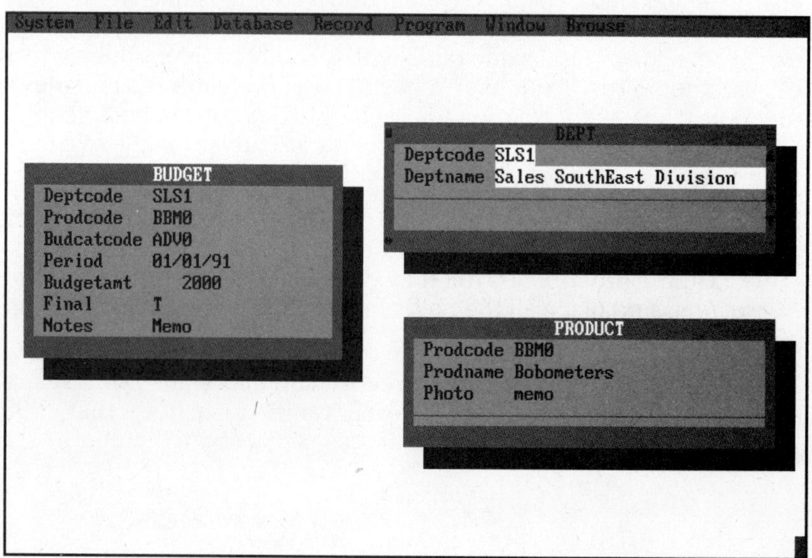

FIG. 4.1

The Budget, Product, and Dept Tables.

Why are these tables separate? Why do you need a separate Product table? Why don't you just store the product name in each record of the Budget table?

Theoretically (although with some difficulty), you can stuff all this information into one table, the Budget table, which is the center of activity for this particular database task.

You can use the following two basic rules to help you decide when to place data in separate tables:

- Create separate tables for sets of information which are essentially *independent* of each other.
- Create separate tables to provide the most *economic* use of table and disk space.

The Product table contains the Photo memo field, which holds additional product-specific data completely independent of the Budget table. If the Product table isn't separate, you need to store the photo elsewhere. Although you may store the product name in the Budget table, you may not want to include the photo in every report. Photos are a good reason for separate tables because storing this data in binary form in memo fields takes large amounts of disk space. This rule also applies to other data.

You save more disk space and data-entry time by eliminating the repetition of the long product names in the Budget table. Another argument for separate tables is that, during data entry, you may want to look up available products and choose a product from a list. A separate table makes this process simple. In a similar way, you may want to validate a previously entered product to make sure that you are using information that already exists and is defined as acceptable input. Otherwise, you may end up entering the same product name with different spellings or abbreviations, and the associated records may not be properly grouped together when you order or extract data.

Sorting information into tables is not a cut-and-dried process. In relational database terminology, this process is known as *normalization*. As you gain more experience with database management concepts, you may want to read more about normalization, but for now, if you concentrate on economy and independence of tables and apply common sense, you are off to a good start.

Understanding How Tables Connect and Interact

If you read the previous sections, you learned that often you need to separate data into independent tables and that these tables also need to work together to perform the tasks of a database. How tables work together is the subject of this section.

You provide connections between tables by creating cross-referencing links. In the model database, the Budget table is linked to the Product, Department (Dept) and Budget Category (Budcat) tables by using information present in these tables. The Budget table links to the Product table by using a field that has the same name, Prodcode, in both tables. The two fields do not necessarily need to use the same name in every case; the important part is that the contents of the field are shared by the tables. Here, the value *WGT1*—not the field name Prodcode—provides a connecting link between records in the two tables.

In FoxPro, the connecting link between tables is created through a key expression common to both tables. You use key expressions to distinguish between records in the same table, providing unique identifiers for each record. Each record in the Product table has a unique Prodcode. The Prodcode field, when used in the Budget table, provides the key to the proper information, such as a product name, in the Product table for the current Budget record.

After you establish connections between tables, the way tables interact seems almost magical. As you scan through one table, the associated information from tables connected to this table is immediately *on line* and can be viewed, reported, or processed simultaneously. The equivalent in a paper-based system is the ability to thumb through the customer files and have the selected invoices and correspondence for each customer pop up on the desk for immediate use, and finally popping back into the files after you move on to the next customer's file.

To make the connection between tables, you give FoxPro instructions that may be translated into English as "As you process records in a table, look for this reference in the connected table, and bring me the related information." In a following section of this chapter, you learn how to create these instructions, known as *relations*, and you also learn the rules that apply to these instructions.

Connections are made in only one direction between tables. The connection is established between the table in the currently selected work area and other tables and is active if you stay in this work area. You may temporarily activate another work area, but when you return to the controlling table, the connections are reestablished.

The controlling table can make connections with many tables at the same time, and the connection can look up both individual records in these tables or sets of information. If the Budget table is the controlling table and is looking up product names in the Product table, FoxPro finds only one record in the product table which applies. This example is known as a *many-to-one relationship*.

If the Product table is the controlling table and you are looking up information in the Budget table, you may need to see several Budget records in relation to the current Product record. This example is known as a *one-to-many relationship*.

You also may find that a one-to-one relationship, in which records in two tables *pair up*, is common.

Because FoxPro is indeed looking up information in tables connected to the controlling table, FoxPro needs a fast way to perform this chore. Consequently, the look-up tables must be ordered, almost always by using an index on the expression that forms the connecting link. You may order the controlling table, or you may leave the controlling table unordered, depending on the goals you are trying to accomplish.

Organizing Information into Records

When you were "Concentrating on Output" in the previous section of the same name, you discovered several kinds of information that you need to collect and enter into the system. The information that you store in record fields do the following:

- Tells you something you want to know; stores the actual data, such as name, address, contact, and so on
- Gives you a means of ordering the information in a table. If you want to alphabetize customers, you need a field that can be indexed to produce alphabetical output (such as last name or an alphabetizing code). To produce mailing labels by ZIP code, you want a separate ZIP code field (rather than making the ZIP code a part of a long address line). You also may use a combination of fields in index expressions.
- Gives you a means of extracting subsets of information in the table. If you want to produce a report for each salesperson, you need a separate field for a salesperson name or code.

- Gives you a means of relating or connecting one table with other tables—the connecting links or keys discussed previously
- Helps you process information in other fields (If you don't have a lookup table that provides the sales tax percentage for each location, you may have to enter this figure into each record.)

Create fields that enable you to fulfill all these purposes, assigning appropriate data types, optimum field lengths, index tags, and the most useful order (ascending or descending) for all fields as you go along.

When you are working in a table, often you want an easy way to locate the specific record with which to work, such as to change or delete a table's information. To find a specific record, you need a unique identifying code for each record. You only need to create this code if you (or FoxPro) needs to find one—and only one—record among many records. The Product table needs this code, known as a *primary key*, because each physical product is unique, and you want to find a specific product to change or delete. When you relate the Budget table to the Product table, you also may want FoxPro to find one and only one Product record with the right information for this Budget record.

Depending on how you want the system to work, you can mix and match the way records are located by you and by FoxPro. When you or another user of the system enters data, for example, you can use a searching method based upon conditions to find many records that provide a *near match*, rather than a unique code. The Budget table is a good example of a table in which you may want to find several possible matches as the result of one search.

When you choose to access records by using unique codes, make sure that the table order is set to the index expression that matches the primary key. This step enables you to use FoxPro's speedy indexes to find the record quickly.

Choosing the values the primary key will have is another area where you may need to think a bit and perhaps experiment. The main consideration is that you have to choose values that provide unique keys for as many records as you think you may have. If you limit the key to one uppercase letter, you have only 26 unique keys from which to choose.

Furthermore, if you want to be able to use the primary key during data entry, choose values you can easily remember (character-based codes are best for this purpose) and as short as possible. You can base these product codes on three characters that serve to identify a class of products plus a digit that identifies products within the class (you can, for example, type **WGT1** for Laptop Widgets and **WGT2** for Mainframe Widgets).

By now, you have most of the information needed to create tables. However, as you read the rest of this chapter, you learn other considerations that affect your current preliminary table and record design.

Using Indexes

In Chapter 3, you saw how you can use indexes to order the data in a useful way for viewing and reporting. The capability of ordering data also is useful to FoxPro, especially for connecting tables and increasing processing speed. FoxPro's incredible speed and much of the ease of use are a result of the capability of creating and manipulating unusually efficient indexes to access data.

Understanding Indexes

You and FoxPro use indexes to perform the following:

- Order data for processing or output
- Look up information quickly in tables

FoxPro has two different basic types of indexes. Both index types are separate files from the data tables. The first index, the *compound* index has the file extension CDX. This kind of index may contain multiple individual indexes, or *tags*. The second kind of index file, the *individual* index, has the file extension IDX and contains only one individual index.

Indexes contain only as much information as is needed to perform the kind of search you specify in an index expression (or expressions, in the case of CDX files), plus *pointers* to the corresponding records in the table. When you open index files along with the table, you can update the information in the table when records in the table are edited in any way.

The compound (CDX) index is a very fast and efficient new feature of FoxPro 2. A compound index's capability of containing multiple indexes means that you can dispense with much tedious effort of tracking the indexes you need to use. An added advantage is that these indexes require only one MS-DOS file handle, which means that CDX files can decrease the burden placed on the operating system, which opens and manages files for FoxPro (and also all the other application programs).

A special kind of compound index, known as a *structural* index, is available. This index is the kind you already created in the Structure dialog (when you created the Budget and Product tables). This file must always use the same file name as the table and is opened by FoxPro whenever you open the table.

The individual (IDX) indexes are the type of index FoxPro once used exclusively and are included in FoxPro 2 mainly to ensure compatibility with previous Fox products and with FoxBase+/Mac. However, IDX indexes can be useful if you need a quick index for a temporary purpose. When you create individual indexes, be sure that you always use the COMPACT option, which produces a smaller and faster index. However, if you create an individual index that must be used by an earlier Fox product or by FoxBase+/Mac, don't use COMPACT because these versions of FoxPro cannot read compressed indexes.

Choosing Indexes

When you created the Budget table, you indexed on all the fields except the MEMO field, which you cannot (and should never) directly index. In many tables, however, you may have fields which you won't need to keep in any particular order. You may never, or rarely, want to order the data by street address or by customer contact person.

Because keeping all open indexes updated properly may slow FoxPro a bit, limit the number of tags in the structural index (or in other indexing schemes, which are discussed in a following section this chapter) to the fields on which you regularly need to order or search.

Similarly, although you can have multiple indexes of all kinds open with the same table, you may find that limiting this practice is usually more efficient. Because FoxPro can build indexes very rapidly, you usually use the structural index for the most common indexing needs and create temporary IDX indexes *on the fly* when needed.

To open multiple indexes for a table (remember that the structural index is opened by default) you can use the Setup dialog from the View window or the Database menu pad. You also can use the Setup dialog to create additional indexes that you can either add to a new or existing compound index or assign to an individual index. Type the following FoxPro commands to open indexes:

> USE <*table*> INDEX <*index file list*>
>
> SET INDEX TO <*index file list*>

You use the first command to open the indexes at the same time the table is opened. You use the second command to open indexes after you open the table. In each case, the *index file list* consists of one or more index file names, separated by commas. Both these commands contain additional options that enable you to set the order of the indexes as you open them and to access a previously created ascending index in descending order (and a descending index in ascending order). The SET INDEX command also enables you to add new indexes to the current index file list, if you use the key word **ADDITIVE**.

In a following section of this chapter, you use the Setup dialog to create an additional index for the Budget table and to experiment with opening multiple indexes for the table.

TIP

CDX files, both structural and non-structural, have a complex format. When you add tags at different times or add large groups of records, CDX files can grow far faster than the new data being added may warrant because some space is wasted. Chapter 3 explain how you can remove this file bloat and wasted space in memo files, by using the PACK command. If you want to *slim down* the CDX files at other times, you can either use the REINDEX command or DELETE TAG ALL (which eliminates the file) and then re-create each individual tag.

The latter approach, although seemingly convoluted, is preferable because you also can use this procedure to rebuild a CDX file that is missing or damaged.

Adding and deleting tags to a CDX file, however, requires extensive use of the CDX in a network environment. (See Appendix B for items of special concern to users of Multi User or LAN FoxPro.) When the CDX is a structural index, you also need exclusive use of the associated table. Weigh these factors for each situation when you work out your file maintenance practices.

Setting Index Order

A table's current order is controlled by the master index, which is established when you choose Set Order in the Setup dialog, use the FoxPro command SET ORDER TO, or set the order with the USE and SET INDEX TO commands. Other open indexes, however, are active in the sense that these indexes are constantly updated as changes are made in the table.

> **CAUTION:** Remember that indexes not kept open when the table is edited are *not* kept current! You need to rebuild or re-create these indexes when you're ready to use them. In FoxPro 2, with compound indexes, no real reason exists to maintain indexes that you don't keep open and updated along with tables. Create temporary IDX file indexes for infrequent reports or other special purposes just before you need the index. Delete these indexes after you finish the task.

When a structural index is opened along with the table, FoxPro sets the order to *0* (natural order). FoxPro takes this approach for several reasons. Because tags are in the index in the order they were created, the first one may not be the one with which you really want to start. Moreover, FoxPro performs many operations more efficiently when no order is in effect.

In Chapter 3, you experimented with changing the index order in the Setup dialog for the Budget table. You can continue to use the Setup dialog for this purpose, and you can choose the order by using any open indexes.

The SET ORDER command and ORDER options of the USE and SET INDEX TO commands give you the option of referring to an individual index or tag within a compound index by its name, which is the most efficient way to perform this function.

To maintain compatibility with previous versions of Fox products and FoxBase+/Mac, FoxPro also provides the option of referring to indexes by number. However, the numbering system can be extremely complex if you use a large number of tags and mix together index types. Look up the CDX( ), KEY( ), TAG( ) and other associated functions (in the *Commands and Functions* volume of the FoxPro 2 documentation), which you use together to determine the order number of a given index expression out of all the indexes currently available, if you want to refer to indexes by number.

In FoxPro 2, using the DESCENDING or ASCENDING keyword on the Set Order To or Set Index To commands enables you to *flip* the order of records in an index, no matter how the index was created. To check the original index expression, either in the Command window or in a program, you can check the value of the following expression:

```
SET("ORDER")
```

If the index was created in descending order, this expression returns a value of `"DESCENDING"`.

Note that using the DESCENDING and ASCENDING keywords on SET ORDER TO and SET INDEX TO don't physically alter the index for future use (unlike the Setup/Index/Modify option of the View window), which both speeds and doubles the flexibility of the indexes.

Understanding Index Expressions

Indexing always was one of Fox's most efficient ways of managing data. In the past, you needed elaborate index schemes to accomplish tasks you now can handle by using a simple DESCENDING key word or FoxPro 2's RQBE. In FoxPro 2, indexing isn't really more complicated than the way you already learned in this book—indexing on fields within a structural index by using the Structure or Setup dialogs.

These indexing possibilities, however, are even more extensive. Although the indexes you created so far ordered the tables on the basis of a field name, indexes create orders on the basis of a key expression. The field names you used in previous indexes are just simple key expressions.

A slightly more complex FoxPro index expression is a combination of fields. This kind of compound key creates a *cascading* index order. To display on-screen—or to print—the information for the Budget table in product order and in department order for each product, you use an index expression similar to *PRODCODE + DEPTCODE*. These cascading orders can get much deeper, subject only to the overall limit on the length of an index key expression (this limit varies according to the kind of index you use). You can easily create an index that you first index by product, then by date, and finally by budget amount.

NOTE Compound index expressions must use the *same data type* components. You cannot mix a character field and a date field in these fields' native states. You can use various FoxPro functions, however, to translate one or more of the components into other data types. (You see an example of this kind of translation in the index you create in a following part of this section.)

You also learn in Chapter 3 that indexing character data can lead to unexpected results because character data is ordered by ASCII code number. To index on a character field which may contain upper- or lowercase letters, you can produce a correct order (by most alphabetizing standards) if you first use another FoxPro function UPPER( ) to translate the field into uppercase.

Index expressions can become even more complicated and can include memory variables and user-defined functions. These functions are discussed in Chapter 10—where you learn to use these features in the Report Writer—and in even greater depth in the programming sections of this book. Index expressions may even contain fields from other connected tables. You also can create a *conditional index*, which enables you to include only records that meet certain conditions that you set. To create a conditional index, use the FOR clause of the INDEX ON command (or the equivalent selection in the Setup dialog). This command works in the same way as the FOR clause on the LIST command, which you used in Chapter 3 to extract a subset of data from a larger table.

Now, you can experiment with creating additional indexes for the Budget table. If not already open, open the Budget table and the View window now.

Select the Budget table and choose Setup from the View window or the Database menu popup. Now, create a completely separate index of the IDX type to see how this kind of index works. In the far right column, you see the Index options. Click the `<Add>` button to add a new index to the existing list.

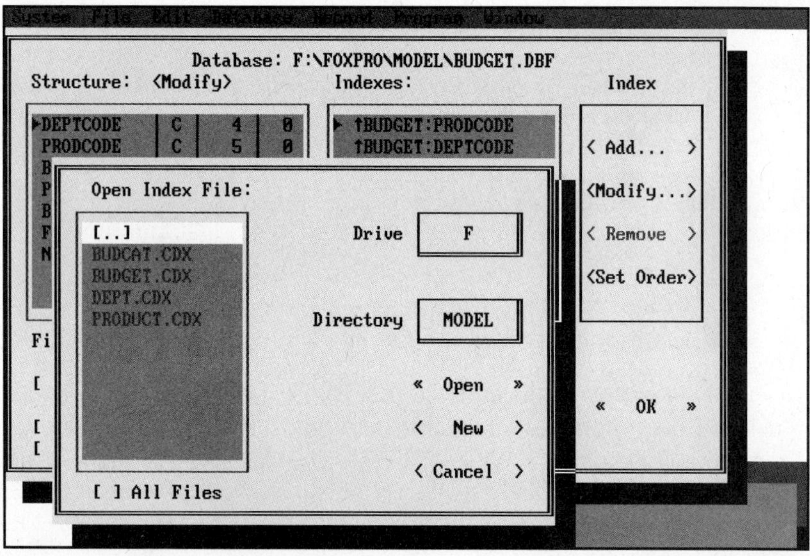

FIG. 4.2

The Open Index dialog.

In figure 4.2, you see the Open Index dialog. So far, you have not yet created additional index files for the Budget table; you relied on the structural index. Choose `<New>` to create an index and you see the Index dialog, as shown in figure 4.3.

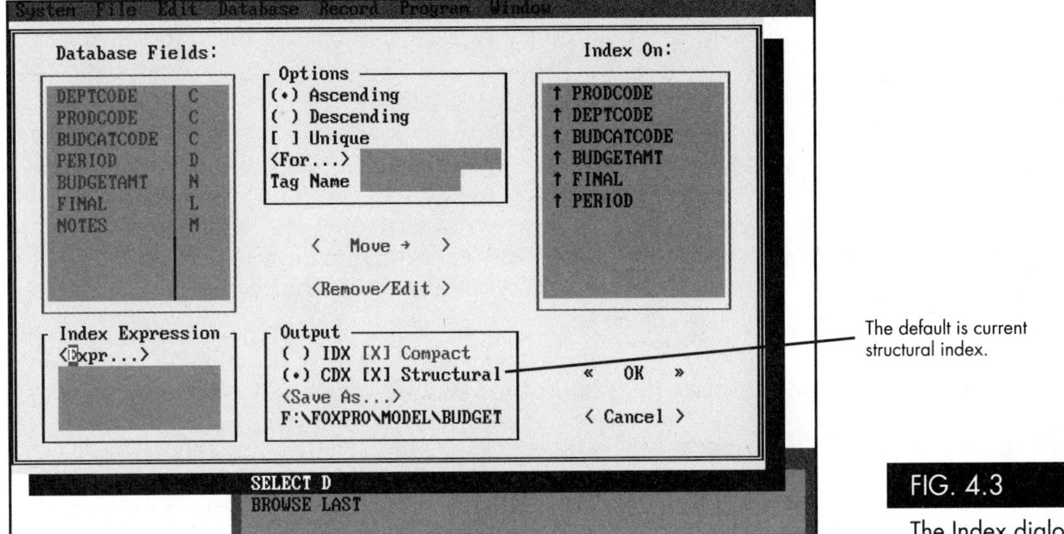

FIG. 4.3

The Index dialog.

You can use the Index dialog to add, delete, or modify index tags within the structural index, to create IDX indexes, or to create or modify additional CDX indexes. As you see, a large number of options are available in this dialog.

Notice that the Index dialog assumes that you want to add indexes to the existing structural index. In the upper left corner of the window, you see the Database Fields list. This list shows all the fields in the current database. The fields already used as index expressions are dimmed to indicate that you cannot select these fields. In the upper right corner, you see the Index On list that shows all the current index expressions. Indexes comprised of only field names correspond to the dimmed fields in the Database Fields list.

In the top and center of the Index dialog, you see the Options box. The selections in this box determine whether a specific index is Ascending or Descending, or whether the index is Unique. A *unique* index type contains only one instance of each value for the key expression. In the Budget table, you can create an index similar to the following line:

INDEX ON Prodcode UNIQUE TO Budgprods

When this index controls the use of the Budget table, only one entry is shown (the first entry typed into the table) for each product. Likewise, if multiple records have a blank Prodcode field, only the first record is displayed on-screen. If some products do not appear in the indexed table, you know *no* entries exist in the Budget table for these products.

The <For> button in the Options box enables you to create a condition for a specific index, and the *Tag* name is the name given to a specific tag within a compound index file. Usually, the tag name defaults to the field name. If you create a new or more complex tag, you are prompted to enter a new name.

Experiment with using only the sections of the Index dialog you have learned about so far. In the Index On list, select any index so that the index is highlighted. Now move to the top center and click the Descending radio button. You see the arrow for this field change to a down arrow. Now select the Ascending radio button and the arrow changes back.

Select the <For> option and you see the Expression Builder you saw briefly in Chapter 3 (Expression Builder is covered in greater detail in subsequent chapters of the book). If you enter an expression here, you build a condition. The index you create includes only records that match the condition. If you type **BUDGETAMT >= 5000**, only records whose budget amount is greater than or equal to 5,000 are included in the resulting index. Because you use these indexes in subsequent chapters, click <For> again and delete any expression you entered.

Now, select any index in the Index On box and click the <Remove> push button. Notice that the index disappears from the list on the right side of the screen and appears undimmed in the list on the left. Select the index in the left list and choose <Move →>. The list is dimmed in the left window and shows up in the right window.

Look at the options in the lower part of the dialog. On the left is an Index Expression box, with a text box used to create a compound index key. In the center is the Output text box, where you name an index file if you don't want to use the structural index. Choose the IDX radio button (to create an individual index) and notice how the dialog changes. In the Options box, only the Unique and <For> buttons are selectable. All IDX indexes are created in ascending order and don't use Tag names.

All the fields are now undimmed on the left and no fields exist in the Index On list because you haven't yet used fields in this new index file.

Move to the Index Expression box and use the <Expr> button to bring forward the Expression Builder. Now you can create the PRODCODE + BUDGETAMT index discussed previously. Type the expression **PRODCODE + BUDGETAMT** or select each field from the fields list on the lower left and type + (plus sign) between the fields. Choose <Verify> to see whether you created a valid index expression. You haven't because Prodcode is a character field and Budgetamt is a numeric field; you can't mix the two in an expression. Retype the expression to look like the following line:

PRODCODE+STR(BUDGETAMT,7,0)

You type this line in the Expression Builder text box shown in figure 4.4. Select <Verify>—it works! You just used the FoxPro STR( ) function to translate or transform a numeric field into character data. Now that all elements in the index expression are the same data type, the expression is valid.

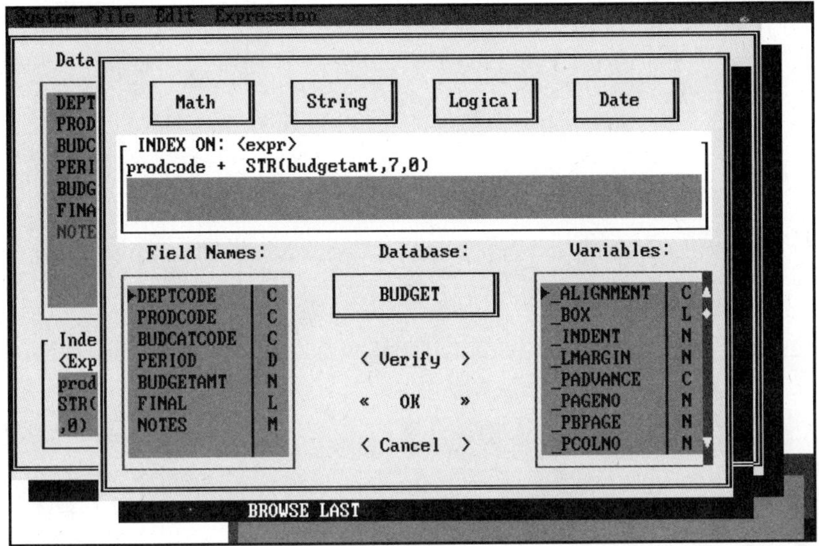

FIG. 4.4

The Index On Expression Builder dialog.

Select «OK» to complete the work here.

When you return to the Index dialog, you see this expression in the Index Expression box. Choose <Move →> to move the expression to the top right (Index On) list.

You have one more option. You can either name the new file in the Save As box or select «OK». If you don't type the name of the new file in the box, FoxPro names the file (see fig. 4.5), using the same Save File dialog you used for other types of files.

When you return to the Setup dialog (see fig. 4.6), you see that the new index was added to the Indexes list, and the table's order is set to the new index (you see the • character next to the new index file name). Return to the View window and Browse the Budget table. Note that the records are listed in product code order and that within each product code, the budget amounts are listed in ascending order.

Indexes are powerful tools and also are the cornerstones upon which many of FoxPro's other powerful tools are built. An entire chapter of this book easily could be devoted to indexing alone. By now, however, you have a firm grasp of how to make indexes work; therefore, you can go on to see some of the tasks indexes can perform for you.

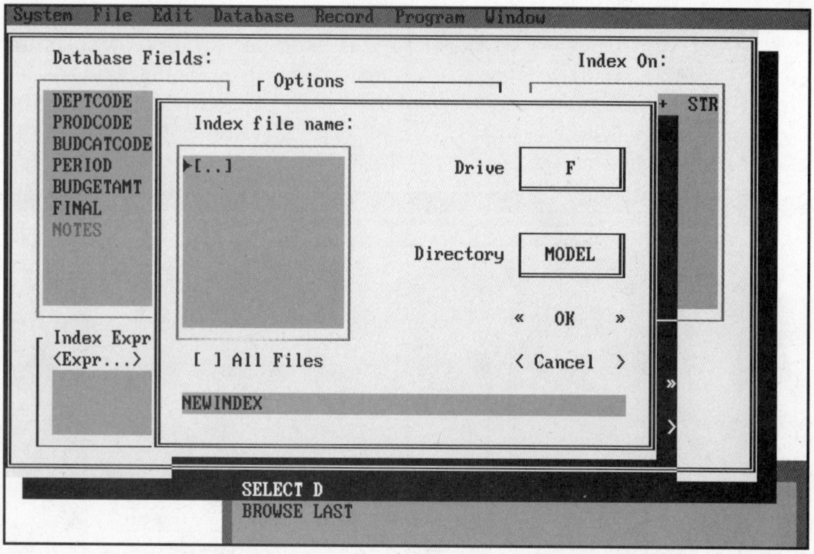

FIG. 4.5

The Index File Name dialog.

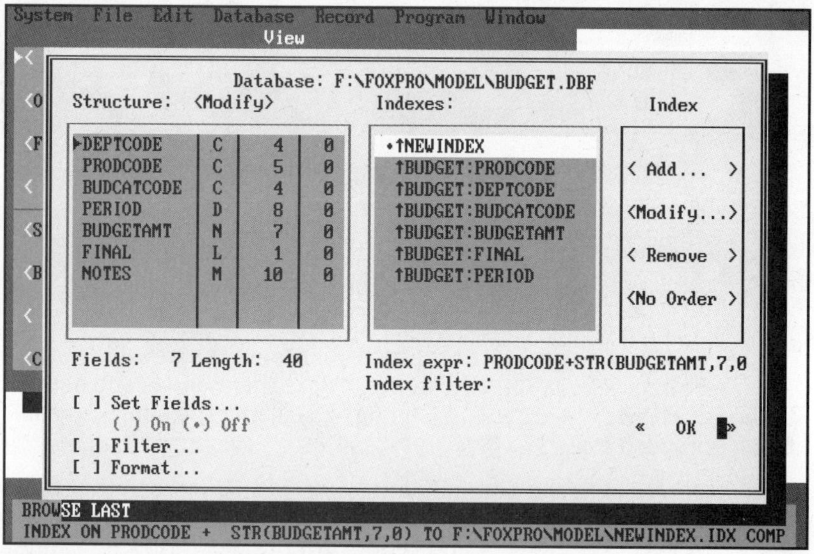

FIG. 4.6

Returning to the Setup dialog.

Linking Tables

In this section, you learn how to establish the *links*, or relations, that connect tables in a FoxPro database.

Using SET RELATION

Open the View window and close all open tables.

Select work area A and open the Product table. Choose `<Setup>` and Set Order to the PRODCODE index. Now select work area B, open the Budget table, choose `<Setup>` and Set Order to the PRODCODE index.

You are going to set a relation between the Product table as the controlling table and the Budget table. For a relation to be set, the subsidiary table (in this case Budget) must be indexed on the connecting link. You are going to link by PRODCODE, the only field that contains information shared by both tables. (If you want to, you can use the PRODNAME field to establish a link, but this action isn't very useful because no matches are found in the Budget table.)

The View window should now look like the illustration in figure 4.7.

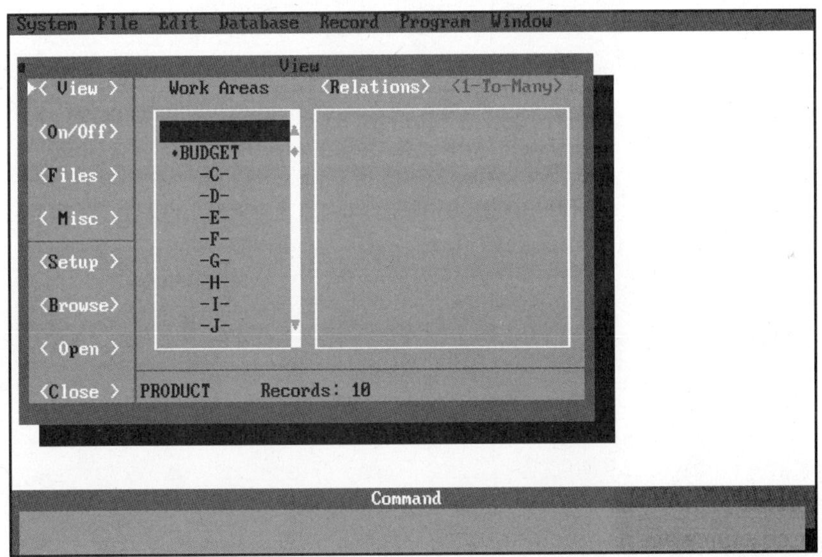

FIG. 4.7

The PRODUCT and BUDGET tables opened in the View window.

As you learned previously in this chapter, the controlling table must be the currently selected table when a relation (connection) is established. This relation is active except when the subsidiary table is the currently selected table. You can work in the subsidiary table, moving through the records—temporarily—and the link will become active again when you change work areas.

Select the Product table and choose Relations by pressing R, tabbing to the on-screen word `Relations`, or clicking on the word with a mouse.

The View window now looks like the illustration in figure 4.8.

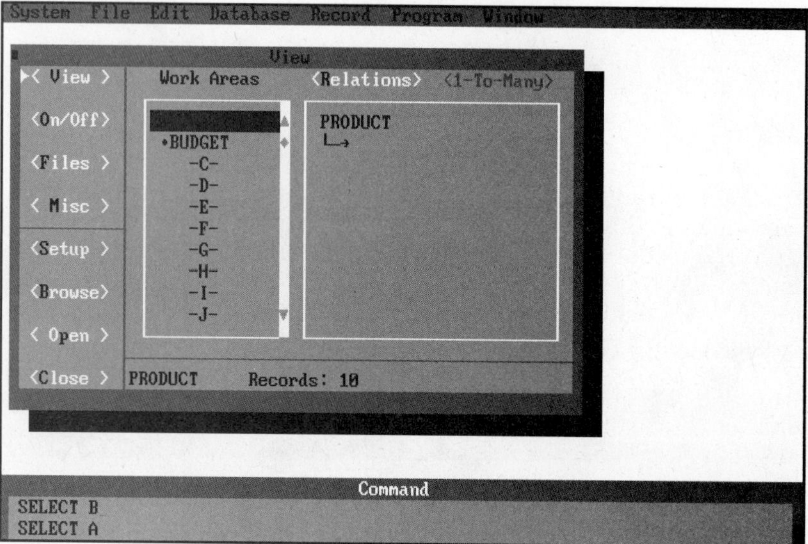

FIG. 4.8

The PRODUCT table, chosen as the controlling table.

The beginning of the relation is complete, with the Product table now established as the controlling table. Select the subsidiary table, Budget, by highlighting the name in the list and pressing Enter, or by clicking on the name with the mouse. The Expression Builder appears to enable you to create an expression on which to create the relation, as shown in figure 4.9.

You are going to link the tables on the field PRODCODE, or so it appears. By design (and this idea is a good design element), a PRODCODE field happens to be in both databases. As previously explained, however, the name of the field is not important. The link is created by using an expression (which may be a field) from the controlling table (Product) that contains values that match the contents of the currently selected index of the subsidiary table (Budget). If Budget were currently indexed on the field ANY_FIELD and ANY_FIELD contained data like *WGT1* and other product codes, you can establish a link with no trouble. When entering this Set Relation expression, you still use PRODCODE because this field is the field in the controlling table that generates data to match in the subsidiary table.

Although the preceding paragraph may seem confusing, just remember that a link asks FoxPro to look up information in another table. When you set a relation, you are asking FoxPro to look at an expression and go find a match to the expression in the index of the related table.

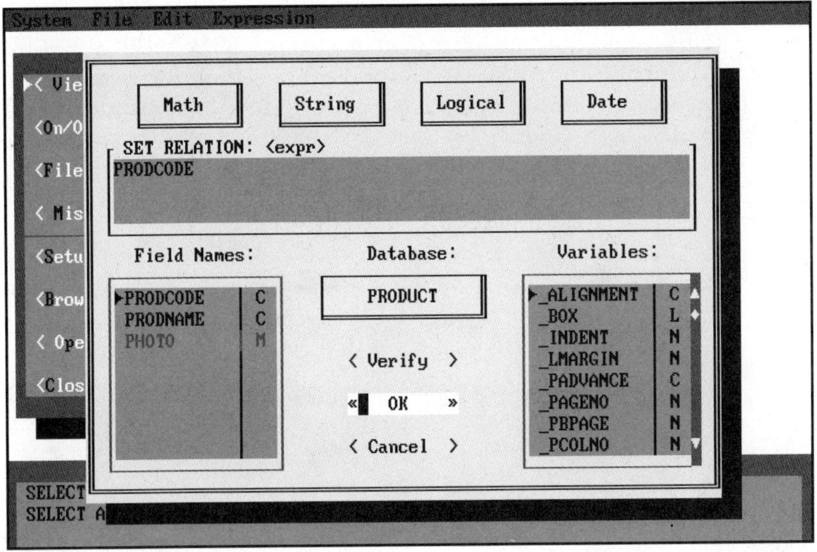

FIG. 4.9

The Expression Builder in the process of setting a relation.

Enter the expression into the Expression Builder text box, either by typing **PRODCODE** or by tabbing to the list of fields in the lower left, selecting PRODCODE and pressing Enter, or by clicking PRODCODE with the mouse. Now click the «OK» button to complete the work.

After you return to the View window, the screen resembles the illustration in figure 4.10.

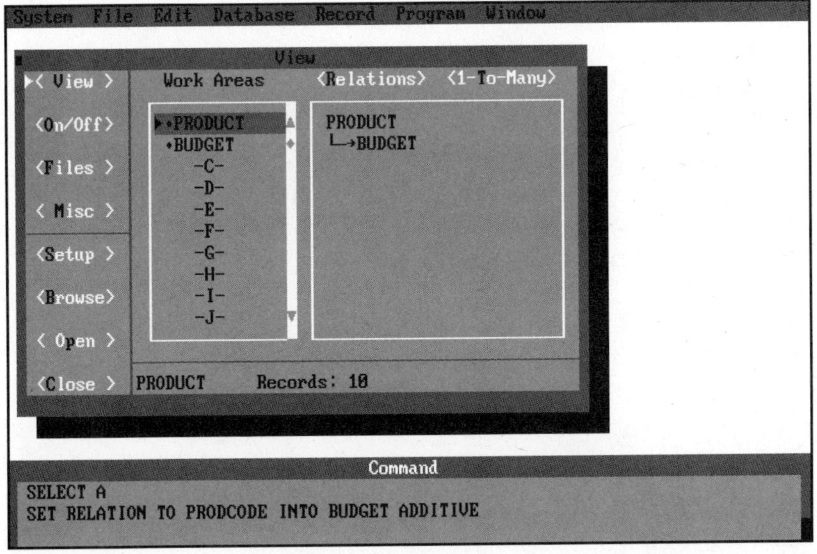

FIG. 4.10

The View window after setting a relation.

Now look at what you accomplished. Select and then Browse the Budget table. Everything looks normal. Resize and move the table out of the way, but where you can still see it. Now select and then Browse the PRODUCT table. Look at the Budget Browse window! This window has changed to show only the records that match the current product code in the Product table Browse window (see fig. 4.11). Select a new record in the Product table and watch the Budget table Browse change to show a different group of matching records.

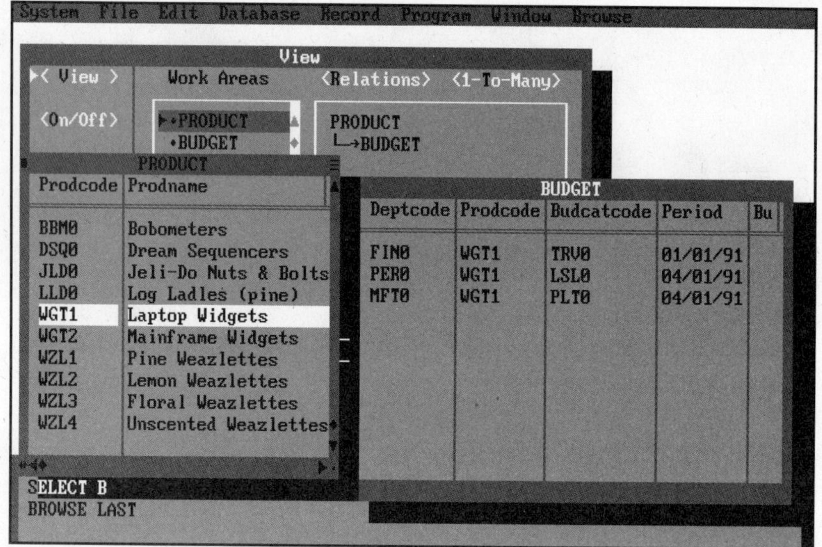

FIG. 4.11

The PRODUCT and BUDGET tables in relation.

Remember that the connection is not maintained when the subsidiary table is the currently selected table. You can quickly see how this process works by returning to the View window, selecting the Budget table, and issuing a new Browse command by double-clicking or pressing Enter with Budget highlighted or by using the `Browse` push button. Notice that you now can see all the records in the table. Select the Product table Browse again, and you see the nonmatching records in the Budget table Browse disappear. (You must issue a new Browse command, rather than selecting a Browse window, to see the change reflected on-screen.)

Keep the View window and the Product and Budget files open now, for use in the following section, or save the setup as a new VUE file so that you can return to this precise setup shortly.

Using SET SKIP To Manipulate the One-To-Many Relationship

As you learned in the preceding sections, you can use SET RELATION to link two tables, and the tables *move* together in relationship. As you move through the *controlling* (or parent) file, the first record that matches in the *subsidiary* (or child) file is accessed. If more than one matching record exists, the other records aren't available from the current work area.

The *parent and child* metaphor is useful because it implies that each parent may have many children, but each child has only one parent.

In previous versions of FoxPro, if you wanted to process all the child records that match the parent table's current record in a one-to-many relationship, you had to select—and then work in—the subsidiary table, perhaps using a WHILE clause to stay *within* the group of child records that matched the current parent entry. In FoxPro 2, however, you can establish the one-to-many relationship in a special way—by using the SET SKIP command, which permits you to access all the child records while remaining in the parent work area.

In this special version of the One to Many relationship, each record in the controlling table is joined to all the matching records in the subsidiary table to create *virtual* records, comprised of the information in the controlling record and information from all the child records that match the controlling record. When you create a Browse, a report, or other representation of a database, you see what appears as many entries for one parent record as that record has subsidiary records in the child table. (However, if no matching child records exist, one entry still exists for the parent.)

The capabilities of the one-to-many relationship also are provided by some other new features of FoxPro 2. Usually, you can provide the same result with less effort by using the RQBE and SELECT statements, which are shown elsewhere in the book. Occasionally, however, this feature may prove useful—particularly when you *process* data in a particular order as opposed to extracting data for reporting purposes.

Return to the View window, with the Product and Budget table open and a relation set between the Product table and the Budget table. Make sure the Product table is the currently selected table.

Notice that, after you select the Product table, in the top right corner of the screen the `<1 To Many>` push button is active. Select this option now by pressing T, tabbing to the button and pressing Enter, or clicking on the button with the mouse.

You now see the Establish 1-To-Many Relationship dialog as illustrated in figure 4.12. Notice that the *parent-and-child* metaphor is reflected in the terminology used in this dialog.

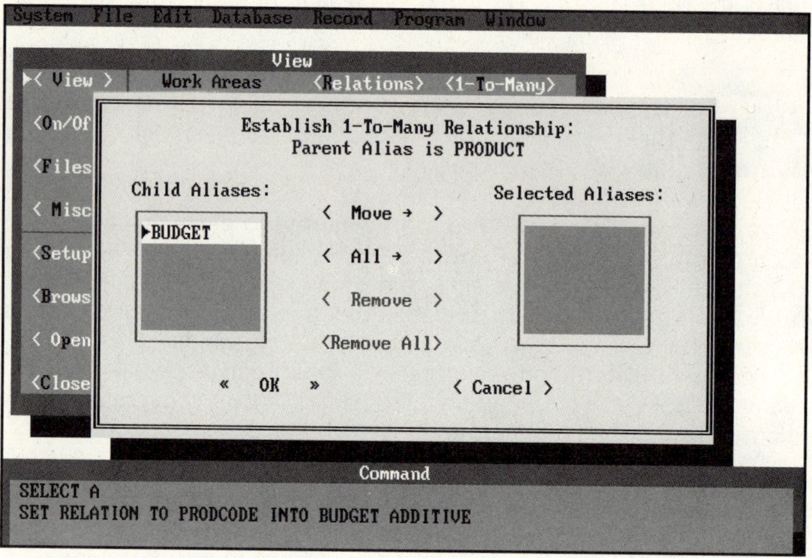

FIG. 4.12

The Establish One-to-Many Relationship dialog.

You see only one entry in the Child Aliases list because you established a relation only between the Product table and the Budget table. You also can establish relations between the Product table and additional tables. If you establish these relations with other tables, the new aliases appear in the list. For now, however, you want to establish only the one-to-many relationship between Product and Budget. Select `<All →>` to move Budget into the Selected Aliases list and then click `«OK»` to complete the work.

To observe the effects of a one-to-many relationship, you need to issue a few instructions in the Command window.

Make sure that Product is the currently selected table. Activate the Command window by pressing Ctrl-F2 or by selecting the Command option from the Window menu popup and type the following text:

BROWSE FIELDS PRODCODE, PRODNAME, BUDGET.BUDGETAMT, BUDGET.PERIOD

Press Enter to execute the command. You learn more about Browse commands in following chapters of this book. This command instructs FoxPro to create a Browse which shows the product code and product name from the Product table and the budget amount and the period from the Budget table. Here, you use a FIELDS clause—similar to the FIELDS clause used on a LIST command in Chapter 3—to explicitly include a memo field. In this case, the FIELDS list specifies the alias of the fields included from a related table. The Browse is shown in figure 4.13.

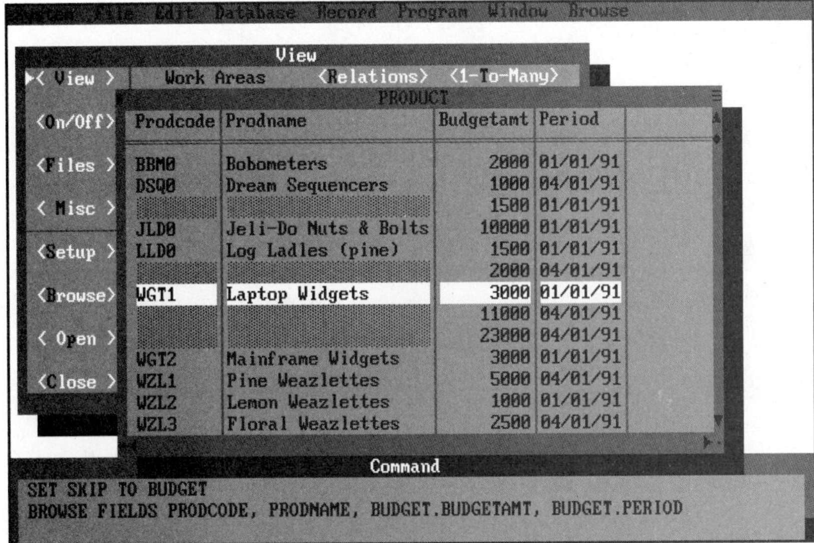

FIG. 4.13

The Browse feature of the Product table, linked with the Budget table in a one-to-many relationship.

As you see, the Browse now treats both tables as if they are one table. For each record in the controlling (parent) file, additional entries are shown until all the child records are displayed on-screen. (These additional entries use shaded blocks, instead of repeating the information in the parent table's fields, to help you distinguish between entries that belong to different parent records.)

Maintaining Relational Integrity

By now you have a good feel for how the Product and Budget tables are connected when the Product table is the controlling table. Now consider the following question:

> *What happens if you delete one of the products from the Product table or change a product code and do not make a corresponding adjustment in the Budget table?*

If you change WGT1 to ABCD, all the records in the Budget table with the product code of WGT1 are now, in a sense, *orphaned*. When FoxPro looks up information in the Budget file, these records cannot be found or included in reports or other output based on the WGT1 relationship.

The consequences of orphaned records can become serious. In some situations, such as in an accounting application, not being able to find specific records may lead to out-of-balance accounting files.

Maintaining viable links is called *relational integrity*, and the most important rule is that whenever you change or delete a field used anywhere in an application to link to another table, make sure that the related tables are updated to reflect this change.

If you change WGT1 to ABCD in the PRODUCT table, go to the BUDGET table and change all occurrences of WGT1 to ABCD. If you delete WGT1, go to the BUDGET table and replace WGT1 with another valid product code.

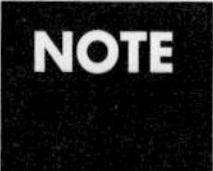

In certain situations, orphaned records in a table are acceptable. You may create orphaned records if you are absolutely clear that this kind of condition exists.

You have much more to learn about linking files and other ways to perform the linking. In special cases, you may link two files with identical sets of records by the record number—by using the RECNO( ) function—rather than by linking with a key expression. You now have, however, all the basic tools needed to set, take advantage of, and maintain relations between tables.

Setting Up a Database Management System

The focus of this book is to use FoxPro to design database applications—for you, for an organization, or for clients. Yet, as indicated at the beginning of this chapter, a database application is just one part of a complete information system, and the best database application in the world can fail if improperly used.

This section addresses the issue of designing and implementing a database application so that the application can function properly in a real-world environment.

Understanding the Scope of the Project

You're now back to the central issue of what you want in a database management system. In a community or an organization, this issue really is *what does everybody want?* For a database management system to succeed, all the people who need information must be able to get this information in a form and in a time frame that makes this data useful. All the people from whom information is collected—and all the people who enter the information into the computer—also need suitable tools and schedules so that the work can be completed. As you start the project of designing and implementing a new system, the task can be made considerably easier if you solicit the support, commitment, and participation of all who may be involved in the operation of the system. Although the support of top management is critical to ultimate success, the support of clerks and secretaries can be just as important. Often, top management can provide the *big picture* of what's needed and the person who does the job can tell you *how the work is really done*. Often, top management doesn't understand how information is collected and prepared, and clerks may have no idea why they go through the routines. For the system to work well, you need to know both sides of the story.

Most people are cooperative if they feel that contributions they make are appreciated and valued. People like to have a part in creating changes that influence their lives and usually want to participate in planning a new work system. You need to nurture this willingness to cooperate by including the input of other users when you consider these changes, keep the others informed, and solicit advice. If you approach people in an arrogant or condescending manner, you cut off the free flow of information—and this information is vital for the successful conclusion of the system design and implementation.

The following list shows the main steps of a database management project:

1. Design the system
2. Write and document the application
3. Implement the system

In the following section, you look at some considerations these steps may entail, with an emphasis on the *human* aspects of the problem not covered elsewhere in this book.

Designing the System

The first step in system design is to determine the results you want this application to produce.

A previous section of this chapter concentrated on output—especially printed reports—to determine the results you want an application to produce for a good reason. Despite a basic desire to cooperate, getting people to tell you what they really want is often harder than pulling teeth.

You may encounter a million reasons why people do not or cannot tell you their needs. People may not know what is possible; may not know the job well enough to explain the needs of certain tasks; the discipline of communicating needs in the detail required by a project of this nature may seem too *hard*; some may just not care; others may be afraid to tell you what they want in case they don't get it (or in case they *do* get it and are then committed to the results of the change); a few may occasionally withhold information to exercise power over you or over their surroundings; some may even consciously or unconsciously try to sabotage the project, either out of malice or because they feel threatened; others may believe their needs may sound stupid; and so on.

Communicating needs to others may be work, a risk, and a commitment. People often avoid work, risk, and commitment.

To get the information you need, listen closely to what the people who use the applications are saying (and what these people are not saying). Become sensitive to the situations and possible motives of others. Become a combination interviewer and therapist! Because you are (or soon may become) the database expert, you can help those with limited vision comprehend the possibilities of the system's design and application. You can draw on your previous experience in similar situations to point out alternative results that others may find useful.

Concentrating on output is a useful approach because data in this form isn't particularly threatening or personal. A report also is tangible and real: you and others can pick up, look at, react to, review, and analyze the material. People don't have to think hard to describe what they do if they can simply hand you the end product of their work.

Collect specific examples of desired output to help you analyze the systems in effect now, how and why they work—or how and why they do not work. When others are sure that you are listening to real needs and appreciating the importance of the work they presently produce, they feel encouraged to share with you their *wish lists* (such as reports these users don't currently get and the user tasks you can simplify).

How a system fits in place with all the other systems in an organization also is important. You cannot totally change over most organizations to a new system overnight, which means that the piece you are adding cannot disrupt other kinds of work that now function smoothly.

As you design the tables and the way the database fits together, remember to also design all required support systems. Remember that information is entered *into* a database system, is processed, and then is sent *out* of the database system in various ways. How, exactly, is the information going to be placed in the system? What forms are filled out? Can existing forms work, or do new forms need to be designed? Who collects, enters, and distributes information? What will the work flow be, and what schedules must be met? Are checklists planned to help perform the job or organize work flow? Who designs these checklists? When information comes out of the system, to whom does the information go, and when is the information needed? Are special forms, such as preprinted invoice forms, needed for output? Who designs these forms? How and when are the forms ordered? An appreciation of the importance of these details and a willingness to attend to or oversee a resolution to each detail is crucial to the acceptance of the people who use the system.

Writing and Documenting the Application

Throughout this book, you learn about creating the application as a process of designing menus, data-entry screens, and different kinds of output. As you design and produce these different elements, document your work, both for users and developers. Good, or at least adequate, documentation results in substantial savings in training and support over a system's lifetime. If written in concert with the writing of the application, documentation can assist measurably in refining the design of a system and in discovering potential problems.

Documentation is a strategic tool that pays off in the long term. Documentation helps you concentrate on the long-term needs and implications of the system as a whole, rather than just using the development process to remedy the most pressing and immediate needs.

Testing a system is another integral part of the development process, which you should perform at every step of development. When you consider an application complete, test the entire system again. Take the application through a complete cycle: installation, day-to-day operations, special month-end or year-end procedures, and maintenance procedures. If possible, use real data. Try to re-create the real operating environment as closely as possible. Besides seeing whether the system actually produces the desired results (for example, check the arithmetic in the reports), note how the menus and data-entry screens feel when used. Consider how the system may feel to a data entry clerk who must perform these tasks over and over again. Test the system on the equipment that will run it.

Good communication between you and the user of the system also must extend far beyond the development phase. If documentation and one-on-one assistance is not sufficient to instruct the participants in the use of the new system, develop training programs. Establish a system for monitoring and reporting program errors and suggestions for changes and enhancements. You can build into an application error-handling routines which can save details about the error and also give instructions to the user on how and what to report.

Encourage users to submit requests for improvements and added features. You may not be able to fulfill all the requests immediately, but you may find ways to incorporate improvements as you change the application for other reasons. Users appreciate a responsive attitude on your part and are usually excited about contributing to the improvement of the application. The more the users contribute, the more personally *invested* they feel in the work—and the more successful the system becomes.

Implementing the System

When you are ready to install the application, make sure that everyone involved in the system's use is ready. Make sure that all the forms are ready, that equipment is installed and running, and that all users are clear about the part they play in the system. Make sure that schedules are in place and that the flow of work is clear. Make sure that data to be entered into the system is ready and organized.

Now, you may need to hire temporary personnel to assist in entering a large volume of existing data. Be sure that the source data these temporaries are given is organized and ready and that the rules for data entry are clear. You may need to develop a *style sheet* for entering customer names and other data. Alternatively, mark the source data with the codes needed for the computer system.

If you already have information collected on a computer, such as with a word processing, spreadsheet, or other database program, you may be able to import this information directly into FoxPro and save some if not all the time required for data entry. If you are designing this system for use by you, the organization for which you work, or a specific client, you may be able to use this method easily. If, however, you are designing a relatively generic application that can be used by many organizations which collected data by any other computer programs, this method becomes less useful, or more expensive, to apply. You learn about the possibilities of this method in a following section of this chapter.

Run the system *in parallel*, while the old system is still operating. Check the results of the new system with the results of the old system and make sure that the new system produces accurate and complete results. This stage of the project is difficult for everybody; some people may have two full-time jobs collecting and entering data into two separate systems. A useful alternative to running parallel in real time, is to *run parallel backwards*—choose an earlier date (perhaps a month ago) and begin using the system as of this date. Because all the output from the earlier period is already available for cross-checking, you can usually enter a month's worth of data, and therefore verify the accuracy of the data (and the system) in a week or so.

When everyone is comfortable with the new system, and the design appears to work properly, somebody has to decide that the project is completed. The old system is abandoned, and the new system replaces the old.

Managing the Entire Project

Manage the design and implementation of a database system as you manage any other large project. Break down the entire project into specific goals and establish timetables. Assign responsibility to a specific person for each phase of the project and monitor results. Determine who has authority to approve the various aspects of the project. Who, for example, can approve the system design? Who determines that the project is truly complete?

In a database system project, concentrate specifically on the three main steps. Make sure that each step is completed before continuing to the next step.

Complete the design stage by making a presentation of the design in as much detail as possible. If you can, present a demonstration of the system that includes—at a minimum—the way menus and data-entry screens look and operate. Also, if possible, provide samples of all the reports the system generates. Try to get the approval, official or otherwise, of the people who use the system. As you see in following chapters of this book, FoxPro 2's design tools make the creation of a *mock up* system easier than you may think. Finally, get official final approval of the system design.

Complete the writing and documenting phase with thorough testing. Test both the program and the documentation.

Complete implementation with another official final approval. Then take everybody to lunch—they deserve it!

NOTE

No database management application is ever really *completed*. You may know this already if you have reached this stage in a project. As you write the application and the documentation, you may see ways to improve the design of the system. As you write the application, you often may feel that you can do something more efficiently, but that you lack the time needed to implement the change. Both you and the application's users also may see ways to improve areas while implementing the system, and beyond. Depending on the circumstances, you may improve some areas and not others, some areas right away and some areas later, but you soon learn that the refinement process is always a trade-off.

Importing Available Data

The preceding section explains that you can import existing computer data into a FoxPro application. You also can export data from the FoxPro table format to other programs.

Again, being close to the environment in which the program operates makes a difference when you use the import and export capabilities of FoxPro. Even if you are remote, however, this feature can enhance an application to include importing and exporting capabilities that support the most popular word processing, spreadsheet, and database programs.

You are still at an early stage in your FoxPro education to be introduced to all the possibilities and complexities of importing and exporting data, but you may find a broad outline of some of the available features useful.

In Chapter 3, you learn that you can export text to a disk file, which then can be read in any word processor with FoxPro's LIST TO command or the Print to File option of FoxPro's File menu. FoxPro provides a number of these kinds of utilities, including the SET PRINTER TO <*filename*> command, which sends the results of printing statements to a file and the COPY MEMO <*memo fieldname*> TO <*filename*> command that sends the contents of a memo field to a separate file on disk.

Although the language FoxPro uses is rich with text creation and export features, exporting text files that include the internal formatting commands of specific word processing programs can get a little complicated. Although creating a preformatted WordPerfect—or another word processor file—is difficult, creating fully formatted files for desktop publishing programs, such as Ventura Publisher (which uses embedded character codes for formatting purposes), is relatively easy.

Importing and exporting data, as opposed to text, is an entirely different story. FoxPro can import information from word processing, spreadsheet, and other database programs.

Importing data from a word processing program requires the text to be formatted in one of two ways, either delimited with a special character (usually a comma or tab) or in a fixed field length (known as *SDF* format). If you understand how to create these files with a word processor, you can import data by using FoxPro's command APPEND FROM—either APPEND FROM <*filename*> DELIMITED with <*character*> or APPEND FROM <*filename*> TYPE SDF. First, you create a FoxPro table into which to import this data. The table must contain fields long enough to accept the imported data, and the fields must be physically able to accept the data one field at a time.

Perhaps the easiest way to see how this process works is to export an existing FoxPro table to two separate text files, using the COPY TO command with first the delimited and then the SDF option. To reverse the process, you need a text file that looks like the results of either of these COPY TO procedures and APPEND FROM.

NOTE

FoxPro can APPEND character data to character fields (in the delimited option, you usually need to enclose the data in quotes to distinguish these characters from numbers) and numeric data into numeric fields. However, date fields can import only data that matches FoxPro's internal date structure of YYYYMMDD. If you cannot easily change the source data to reflect this convention, import the dates into a character field and then process the table to convert this character data into a date-type field by using CTOD( ) and other date functions FoxPro provides for this purpose. Refer to Chapter 19 for more information about conversion of data from one type to another.

The APPEND FROM... DELIMITED command has a keyword (WITH) that is confusing to many people. A delimited file actually contains *field separators* and also *delimiters*. In the following default format, the commas are field separators, and the quotation marks are delimiters:

```
"Bob","ones","Suite 140, 123 ElmStreet","Omaha"
```

In the street address, the comma is properly interpreted as data because it is placed between paired quotation marks. Sometimes, however, the data also may contain quotation marks, as well as commas. You can use the DELIMITED WITH *<character>* option or (where convenient) WITH TAB or WITH BLANK to specify another field separator other than commas. Although field separators are commonly used, these characters aren't required in FoxPro except where no delimiters at all are used.

APPENDing data FROM spreadsheets and other database programs and COPYing data TO these applications is more simple in FoxPro 2 than in previous versions of FoxPro. FoxPro 2's new IMPORT and EXPORT commands further refine the process. Many popular file formats are now supported directly, including Lotus, Excel, Paradox, Multiplan, Rapidfile, Symphony, and Framework formats. Of course, FoxPro also transparently reads all xBase data files, including files created on Macintosh computers.

When you import data, the difference between APPEND FROM and IMPORT is that the first requires an existing FoxPro table into which the data is added, and the second creates a brand new table. To combine these approaches, you can use the IMPORT command to create a table (in FoxPro format) and then use APPEND FROM or other FoxPro commands to transfer specific records and fields from the new table into an existing table. Using IMPORT also may give you information you need as you try to design a table that can efficiently append data thereafter.

When importing data from spreadsheets, FoxPro imports columns as fields and rows as records. FoxPro imports the data from the spreadsheets, but not the underlying formulas. If you are fairly sophisticated in using spreadsheets and use different regions of the spreadsheet for look-up tables or sub-tables that feed information into the main table, you may encounter unpredictable results when you import spreadsheet data into FoxPro. For this reason, before you import spreadsheet data, make sure that the spreadsheets you import are as simple (row- and column-wise) as possible. This may require that you extract and copy portions of the spreadsheet into a temporary spreadsheet for the purpose of exporting this data to a table.

Finally, as you learned in Chapter 3, FoxPro memo fields can contain any data you can store on a computer, including graphics files (pictures, photos, and so on), tables, programs, digitized sound, and so on. Presently, you can't use FoxPro to do much with nontext memo fields, such as pictures and sound, although you can export the contents of memo fields intact to the hard disk and therefore make this information available to programs that can import this information. FoxPro also can run external programs that use either sound or pictures (or both), which enables you to access the contents of these memo fields as part of FoxPro's applications.

FoxPro uses the APPEND MEMO <*memo fieldname*> FROM <*filename*> to place this kind of information into a FoxPro memo field and the COPY MEMO <*memo fieldname*> TO <*filename*> to send a file to the hard disk for use by other programs. The external programs are run either directly by DOS (using FoxPro's RUN command), as binary modules (using FoxPro's LOAD and CALL commands), or through use of the API and FoxPro 2's SET LIBRARY command. The use of these external programs is briefly discussed in the section on third-party products in Chapter 15.

Chapter Summary

In this chapter, you learned how to approach the job of designing a database system, with an emphasis on the tasks you want the system to handle and how to put the system together so that you accomplish your goals.

You saw the importance of broadening and refining your approach to information systems, and how constantly having both the big picture and the details before you can help you design and implement a superior system.

You learned how the elements of FoxPro—fields, records, tables, and databases—are created and work together.

You also began to consider the implications of the real world, in which every person is different and every operating environment has an *ecology*, and the way database information systems must fit gracefully, efficiently, and usefully into these constraints.

With so many constraints and goals to consider, you're probably wondering how you can ever take care of everything. In the next part of this book, you start using the unique FoxPro 2 productivity tools that help you perform this job.

Getting Productive with FoxPro 2 Databases

OUTLINE

5

CHAPTER

Using the RQBE as the Gateway to Queries

After you set up the tables and enter the data, you want the capability of extracting information from the tables. Finding some information can be a straightforward operation; you can search by BROWSing the tables. Eventually, however, you may need to extract more complex answers from the data than BROWSing allows. Here, the RQBE, or *Relational Query By Example*, comes into play. *RQBE* is an interactive tool that enables you to extract and organize the data in tables. With RQBE, you can derive answers that, prior to FoxPro 2.0, required you to write complex programs.

As you venture into FoxPro's RQBE, you may find the available choices overwhelming. Don't worry—after looking at each section individually, you find that the RQBE is a productive and easily-used tool.

In this chapter, you examine the different sections of the RQBE and learn how to use each section to create some simple queries.

Before you get into the RQBE, make sure that the Budget table is open in the current work area. From the File New dialog, open a Query type file. You now see the RQBE screen with the `Budget` table selected, as shown in figure 5.1.

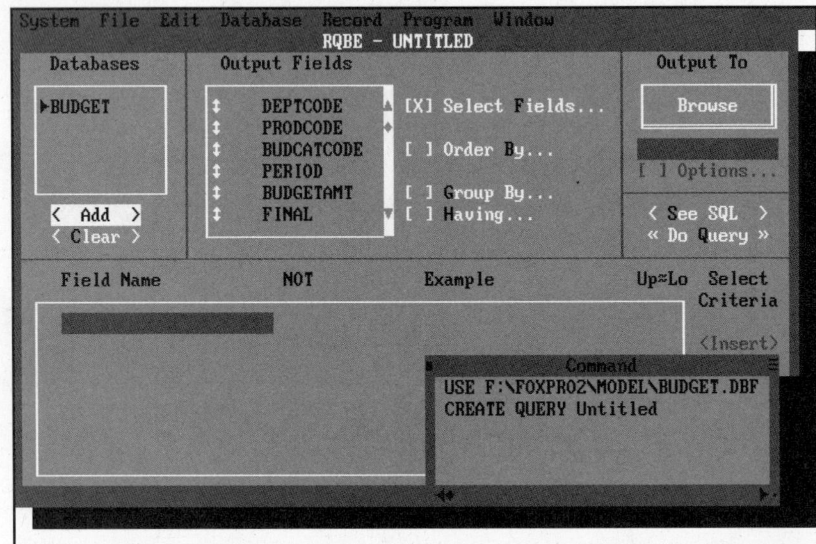

FIG. 5.1

The basic RQBE screen with the Budget table selected.

TIP In the RQBE and at any other time, you can press the F1 key to call up FoxPro's context-sensitive help system. The RQBE help entry gives you a quick refresher course on the different features of the RQBE window.

To create the first query, you can click the `<<Do Query>>` text button, press Ctrl-Enter or use the Do Query hot key combination, CTRL-Q. The result may look like the screen in figure 5.2.

Congratulations! You created and executed your first query. The BROWSE window you see is not too different from all the other views of the data you previously used. You may be impressed, however, by how easily you can modify RQBE's default values to create valuable results.

You can control the Browse window that you created by a query in the same way you control other windows. The Zoom, Size, Split, and Close controls all are visible and active. You also can reposition the Browse window. The query-created Browse, however, is unusual in an important way: Browse is a *read only* option (you cannot change the data that appears on-screen). For now, just close the Browse window—either by clicking the Close control or by pressing Esc—so that you can continue exploring the RQBE.

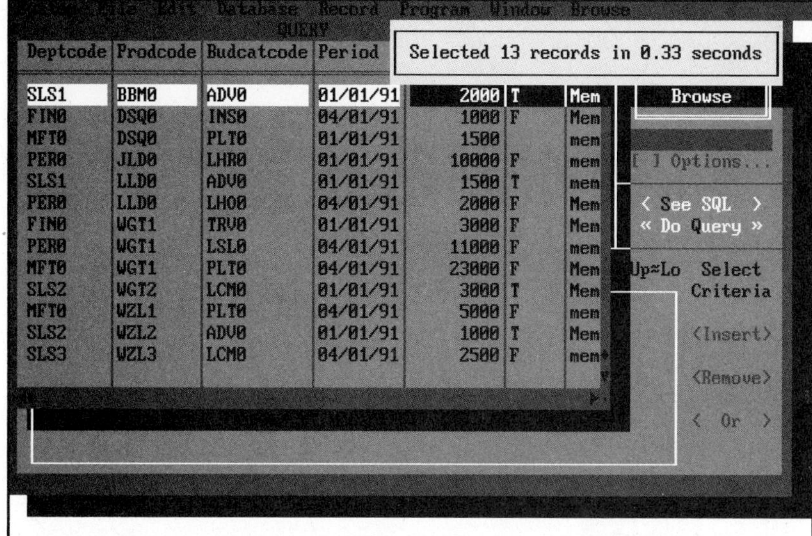

FIG. 5.2

A simple query.

Major Components and Default Values of a Query

The RQBE Window is divided into five main areas that control the following information:

- The tables involved in the query
- The information that becomes the query's results
- Where this information is sent by the query to become output
- The relationships between the tables in the query
- The final action of generating the query (executing or just checking the query before execution)

The Databases list, found in the upper left section of the RQBE window, lists all the tables currently used by a query. In this example, only the Budget table is displayed. You can add more tables with the `<Add>` text button, and you can remove tables one at a time with the `<Clear>` button.

After you open the RQBE window to create a query, you are presented by default with one table. If no tables are open in the current work area when you enter the RQBE, FoxPro asks you to select a table with the

Open File dialog. When selected, a file becomes the default table for this query. If you choose `<Cancel>` in the dialog, you still are allowed in the RQBE but no tables are selected. You must use `<Add>` to add the tables.

The Selected Output section is found in the upper center section of the RQBE screen. A list shows the fields currently selected for output. You can change the order of the fields in this list, and the order in the query output changes to match. Several check boxes to the right of the list of the output fields enable you make further adjustments to the fields and records.

If you select the Select Fields check box at the top of the group, you can control the fields that appear in the output. The Order By dialog, where you can set the sort Order for the data, is the next control, followed by a third check box for the Group By dialog, which controls groupings and subtotals. Finally, the bottom check box provides access to the Having dialog, where you can set criteria by which records are chosen for output.

The defaults here are no Order, no Grouping, and no Having. As you saw in the first query, if a table was open when you first entered RQBE, all fields in that table are selected for output, in the natural order.

You see the `Output To` popup control in the upper right section of the RQBE window. With this control, you can choose where to send the results of the RQBE. You can send the results to a Browse window (as you did with the simple query, by using the default), a Report/Label, a Table/Dbf, a Cursor, or a Graph.

The Selection Criteria section takes up the bottom half of the RQBE screen. This section has two purposes, to tell RQBE which records to include/exclude and to tell RQBE how to link multiple tables, when applicable. By default, nothing shows here. When this box is empty, all records in the table are included with the query.

The small box below the Output To section contains two buttons: `<See SQL>` and `<<Do Query>>`. Because the real output of the RQBE is a SQL SELECT statement that FoxPro executes to produce the output you see, clicking the `<See SQL>` button shows you the SQL SELECT statement that RQBE uses. You can look at this statement at any time while you are building the query, although you cannot edit the statement at this point. The statement helps you learn SQL and also helps you understand how the RQBE works.

You can pronounce SQL as "Sequel." *SQL* stands for "Structured Query Language," and is the name for a language entirely separate from FoxPro. SQL is available for many different hardware platforms and is specifically designed to query databases, just as you are doing here. The implementation in FoxPro 2, however, is a specially-enhanced subset of the SQL language that you don't need to leave FoxPro—or go into a special mode—to access.

You can use a SQL statement in any FoxPro program, and you can enter this statement directly into the *Command Window* as you enter any other command. When you save the statement, the query is saved as a normal text file (with a QPR extension), ready to edit or to add to a program you are writing.

The `<<Do Query>>` button executes the query. You can choose this button when an open table is available and at least one Output Field is selected.

You also can choose most of the RQBE options from the RQBE menu pad, which appears on the system menu when a RQBE window is active. As you see in figure 5.3, however, the RQBE menu popup contains Comments, a menu option not found elsewhere in the RQBE. *Comments* are notes of unlimited length, which are for reference only and are saved with the query file in the same way other program comments are saved (in lines that begin with asterisks, which are ignored by FoxPro) and can be viewed at any time (see fig. 5.4).

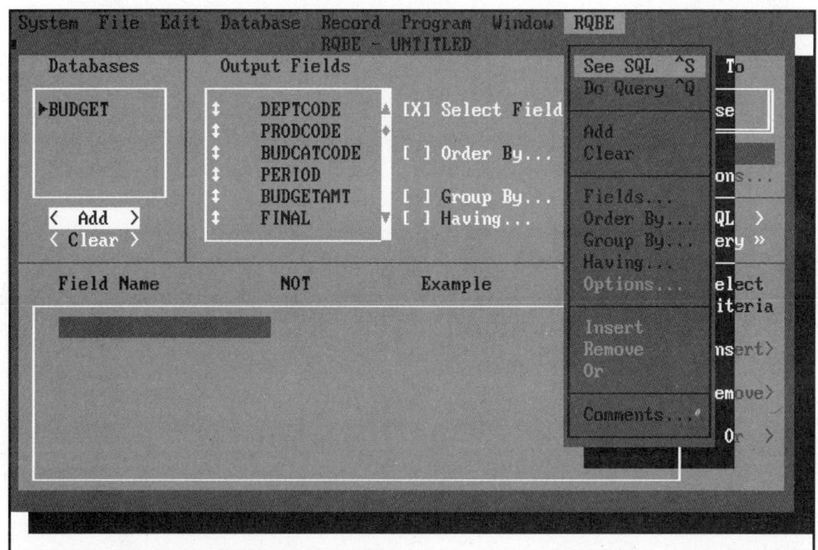

FIG. 5.3

The RQBE Menu popup.

Details, Details

Now that you have looked around the RQBE, the various options may no longer seem particularly mysterious. You already learned methods of selecting and ordering records, and in previous chapters you learned the way tables are linked together by using SET RELATION. In the following sections, you select each of these options to see the way to use these processes in the RQBE.

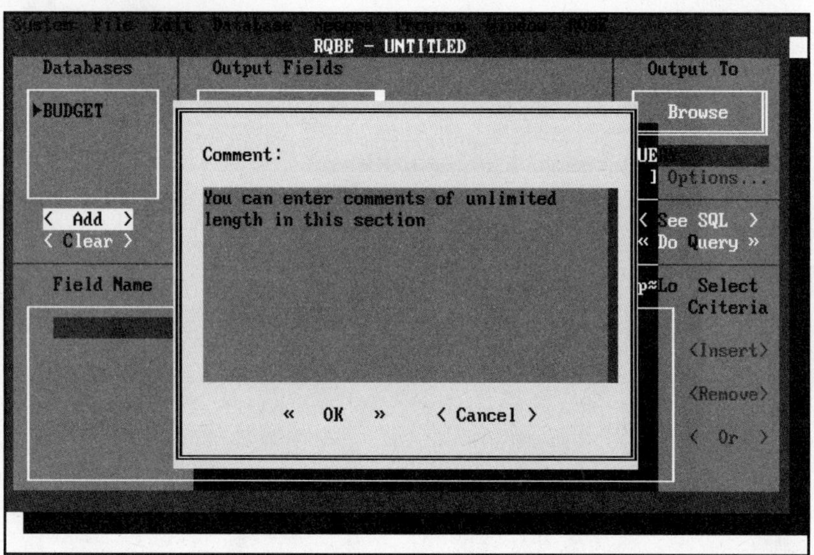

FIG. 5.4

The Comments text entry box.

Selecting Fields

You probably don't need all the fields in the Budget table to appear in the query output. Mark the `Select Fields` check box in the Selected Output section of the RQBE to see the dialog in figure 5.5.

On the Selected Output screen, the Database Fields list on the left side of the screen contains all the potential fields you can chose. If you select multiple tables in the Databases section, this list shows all the fields from all the selected tables. The Selected Output list on the right side of the screen shows all fields you choose for output by the query.

NOTE The fields previously selected as output are disabled from the list on the left. You also can see that the field names are preceded by the table name `Budget`, which is necessary when multiple tables are involved.

You can remove any or all fields from the selected Output list. If you use a mouse, double-clicking on a field name moves the file from selected Output to the Database Fields list. With the keyboard, highlight the field you want to move and press Enter or press the space bar rapidly twice (FoxPro's keyboard equivalent of double-clicking a mouse). You also can mark multiple field names by using the Shift key and the space bar—or by using mouse clicks—and then selecting Remove to remove all the marked fields at one time. You also can remove all the fields at one time without marking if you click the `<Remove All>` text button. Fields are moved to the Selected Output list in a similar way, by clicking `<Move →>` instead of `<Remove>` and `<All →>` instead of `<Remove All>`.

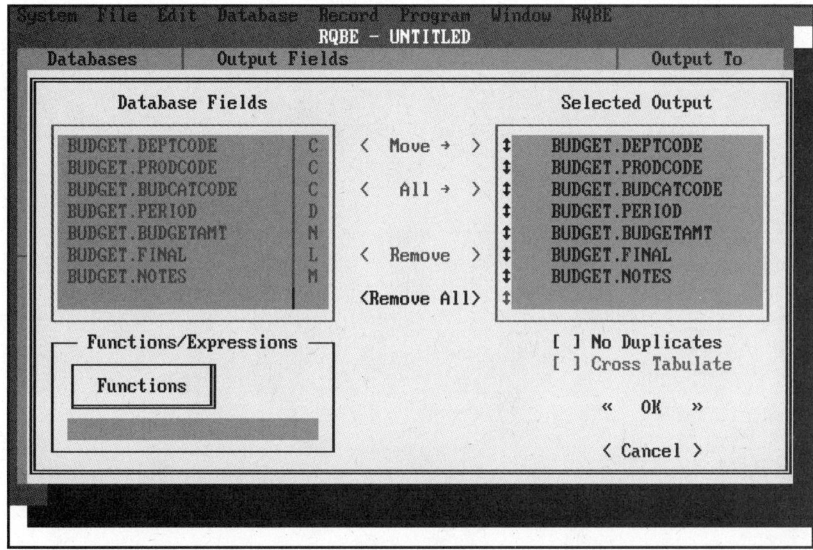

FIG. 5.5

The Select Fields dialog.

In the following example, you want to see only a few fields. Often, a quicker method is to use `<Remove All>` to remove the fields and then choose the few fields you want rather than to remove the fields you do not want individually. Using either method, select the following fields:

BUDGET.DEPTCODE

BUDGET.PERIOD

BUDGET.BUDGETAMT

Press the `<<OK>>` button to confirm the selection. Do the Query. The Browse displays only the fields you choose, as shown in figure 5.6. When you finish marveling at the query, close the Browse window.

If you don't like the order in which the fields are displayed, several ways are available for you to change the current order. You can alter a field's relative position in the Selected Output list of the Select Fields dialog. Moving items in this list is done the same way you learned to move items in the Setup dialog of the View window, when you created the Budget table. You soon notice that all FoxPro lists of this kind behave in the same way. You have another opportunity to reshuffle the output fields in the main RQBE window's Selected Output list, using the same keystrokes. If you just want to alter the order in which you see the output columns temporarily, a third alternative is to change their sequence in the Browse window produced by the query, as you learn in Chapter 8.

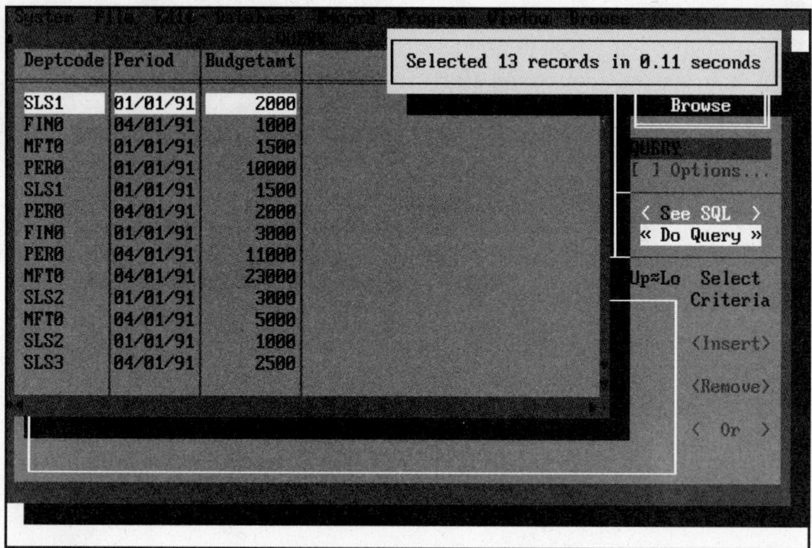

FIG. 5.6

A query with selected fields.

NOTE The multiple alternative selections are an example of the freedom provided by FoxPro's event-driven environment. You aren't restricted to making every decision in a precise, rigid order. You can improvise changes, one or two at a time, as you work until you get exactly what you want.

You now convert the dates displayed on-screen in this Browse to Calendar Quarters. To perform this step, you add an expression to the Selected Output list. Returning to the Select Fields dialog, access the Function/Expression text box in the lower left corner of the screen.

To convert these dates to the calendar quarter, you use FoxPro's CEILING( ) function, which rounds numbers *up* to the nearest whole number, and the MONTH( ) function, which extracts the number of the month in a date you supply. You learn more about FoxPro expressions and functions as you progress in this book. The following expression is the key to the conversion you need:

```
CEILING( MONTH( date ) / 3 )
```

If the date you supply is *5/15/91*, the preceding expression returns the number 2 for the second quarter. To display this number with the year, however, you must convert the number into a string of characters. As you create reports and labels in Chapters 9 and 10, you see many more conversions of this kind, and the conversions are more thoroughly discussed as you go along. For now, however, type the following expression in the Function/Expression text box. FoxPro scrolls as you type to allow more characters to fit; do not press Enter until you finish typing the following expression:

```
'Q' +STR(CEILING(MONTH(Budget.Period)/3),1) + ' ' +
    STR(YEAR(Budget.Period),4)
```

(If you read the preceding string from left to right, you can interpret the expression to mean "Add the letter **Q** to the character equivalent of the number you calculated as the calendar quarter of the date field **Budget.Period**, add a space to the end of this string, and then add the characters of the year for the field **Budget.Period**.")

Now press Enter twice or select the `<Move →>` text button. Select `<<OK>>` to exit the dialog. After you Do the Query, you see a more meaningful representation of the Period field.

If you see an error message when you Do the Query, you probably typed the preceding expression incorrectly. Check the expression for accuracy and Do the Query again.

TIP

By selecting Save from the File pad of the menu bar, you can save a query any time you are in the RQBE window. As you learned when you opened new files of other kinds, if the query is still UNTITLED, FoxPro prompts you for a file name. For the query name, type **CHAP5001** (FoxPro adds the extension QPR). You can exit the RQBE at any time by pressing Esc. If the most current version of the query on which you are working is not saved when you press Esc, FoxPro gives you an opportunity to save the current query before you exit the RQBE.

To open a previously saved query, choose Open from the File menu popup and select Query for the file type. You see a list of the available queries. Pick the query with which you want to work, and you return to the RQBE screen, where you left off.

To tidy up the display, go back to the Select Fields dialog and remove the BUDGET.PERIOD field from the output because this field is redundant now that you can see the calendar quarter. Also, remove the BUDGET.DEPTCODE field and add the BUDGET.PRODCODE field. (Besides giving you more practice, this change is necessary for the following exercise because you filled the Product table with data in Chapter 1.) You also can move the order of the fields so that the date expression is the second field displayed on-screen.

After you format the fields, select `<<OK>>` to exit the Select Fields dialog. Do the Query to see the results of the work.

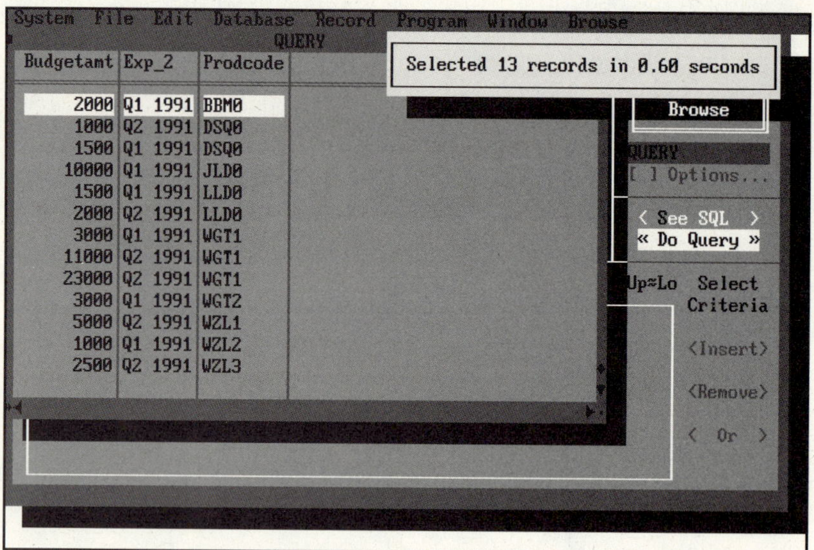

FIG. 5.7

A query that shows calendar quarters.

Adding More Tables

With this query, you are forced to try to understand the rather cryptic product codes. Displaying the product *names* on-screen is definitely a better way to understand the screen. With FoxPro's RQBE, you only need to join the Budget table with the table of product descriptions.

The first step of the join process is to add the Product table to the query. To add the Product table, select `<Add>` under the Databases section of the RQBE. You see the Open File dialog, in which you choose the `PRODUCT.DBF` table. Choosing PRODUCT.DBF triggers the RQBE Join

Condition dialog. The RQBE needs to know how the PRODUCT table relates to the BUDGET table. Both the tables hold a field that contains the product code. You need to tell RQBE that this relationship exists. The RQBE Join Condition dialog, similar to the Relations button in the View window, is the place to link these two fields.

Select the empty popup control on the left side of the screen. A popup appears with the names of the fields in the newly added table, `PRODUCT`, as shown in figure 5.8. You want to *join* the tables based on Product code, so select PRODUCT.PRODCODE. Next, select the empty popup control on the right side of the RQBE Join Condition dialog. You see the popup list of all the fields in the Budget table; choose BUDGET.PRODCODE from this list.

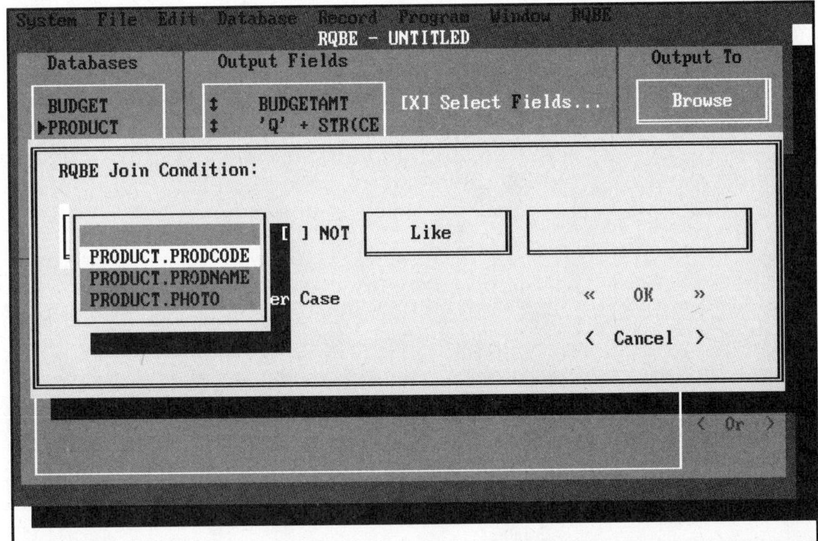

FIG. 5.8

The RQBE Join Condition dialog.

After you press the <<`Ok`>> button to confirm the selection, the Join Condition dialog disappears, and you return to the RQBE screen, which now looks a bit different. On the lower half of the RQBE window you see the same phrase you just typed in the Join Condition dialog. To the left of this phrase, you see a small `\backslash\` character that indicates a join condition.

WARNING

If you have more than one table and do *not* specify a join condition for each table, Doing the Query attempts to *join every record of every table with every record of every other table*. If you have two tables with 100 records each, this combination produces meaningless output of 10,000 records. If you have three tables with 100 records each, the output has a *million* records! Not only is this step not useful, if you send these joined tables to the printer for a report, you need to plant many trees to replace the paper you waste! Better ways are available to give a computer some exercise.

Now that you have linked the two tables, you can choose output fields from both tables as if you are working with one combined table. Return to the Select Fields dialog. Notice that the list on the left contains fields from both the Budget and Product tables (see fig. 5.9). Now add the product description field, PRODUCT.PRODNAME. With the product name present, the code becomes redundant, so you can remove the code field from the output list. Finally, move the Prodname field to the top of the list. The screen now looks like the one in figure 5.9. Select <<OK>> to exit this dialog.

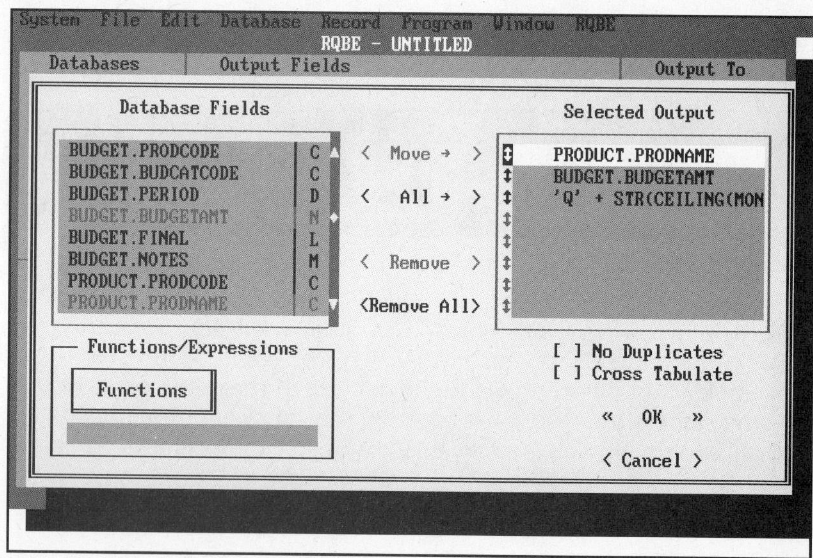

FIG. 5.9

Expanding the Available Field List.

Do the Query and notice that the Browse feature has become much more informative. After exiting from the Browse, use the Save As dialog to save this query as **CHAP5001**. (Remember that you do not need to type QPR—FoxPro adds this extension).

Sorting Your Output Records

Presenting information in a sorted order makes the output of a query more readable. In this example, you order the output by product name and descending order. To bring up the Order By dialog, mark the `Order By` check box (see fig. 5.10).

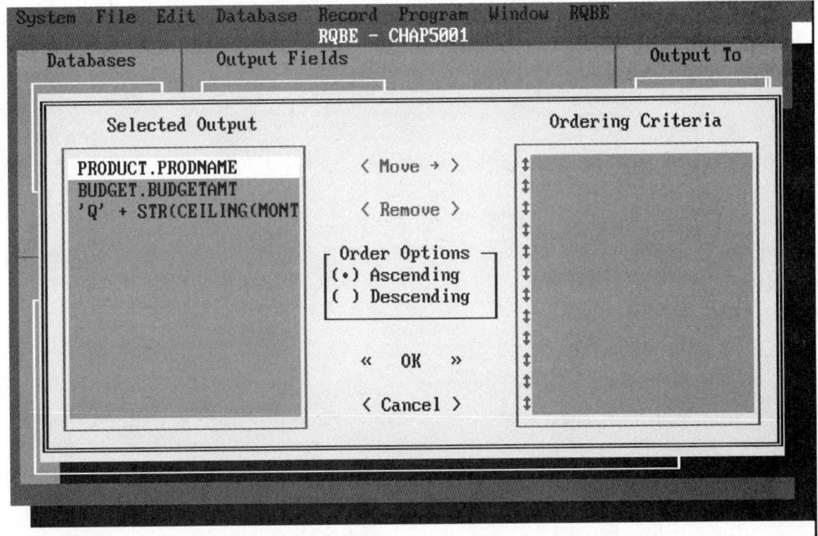

FIG. 5.10

The Order By dialog.

With FoxPro, you can sort output by each output field in ascending or descending order. You are limited by the RQBE to the fields selected for output. (For advanced queries, you can use SQL to sort by fields *not* selected for output. You learn more about using SQL in Chapter 7.)

You want to sort the output by the PRODNAME field in ascending order, and the calendar quarter expression, which you created earlier, in descending order. To perform this process, move the PRODUCT.PRODNAME field from the Select Output list to the Ordering Criteria list. The Ordering Criteria list works in the same way the Select Fields dialog does—and much like the index-creation procedures you learn about in Chapters 3 and 4. You see the `PRODUCT.PRODNAME` field appear with a (↑) to the left of the field. The ↑ indicates that the order is *ascending* (product names beginning with A appear first, and names beginning with Z appear last). Now change the Ascending/Descending radio button to `Descending` and move the calendar quarter expression field over. This expression appears in the Ordering Criteria list with a ↓ to its left.

TIP

When you change the ascending/descending order status, you must understand which objects are affected. Any tagged item is affected by the ascending/descending radio button status. (Tagged bars are marked with a triangle to the left of the item). As tagged selections in the Selected Output list are moved to the Ordering Criteria list, the selections are set to the ascending/descending status in effect at the time. If any current ordering criteria are tagged, their ascending/descending status change if the Ascending/Descending radio button is changed.

Select `<<Ok>>` to return to the RQBE screen. Before you run the query, notice the `1` ↑ beside `PRODNAME`, and the `2` ↓ beside `"Q"+STR(CEIL` in the Selected Output list. These notations tell you that the data is sorted in ascending order by PRODNAME and descending order by quarter within PRODNAME.

This compact representation of an increasingly complex query can be a powerful tool. A great deal of credit should go to the people at Fox Software who designed the RQBE (see fig. 5.11)!

Now, Do the Query, and see the results of your work. As you see in figure 5.12, the product names are in ascending alphabetical order, and the quarters (labeled `Exp_3`) are in descending order within product. Exp_3 is a rather cryptic name for the field. RQBE assigns field names similar to these names to all the expressions you create. You can use Output To to send data to the report generator, where you can manipulate the format in almost any way imaginable, which is discussed in a following section of this chapter.

After closing the BROWSE, save this query as **CHAP5002**. (You can do this with the Save As dialog from the File menu. Remember that the QPR extension is provided by default.)

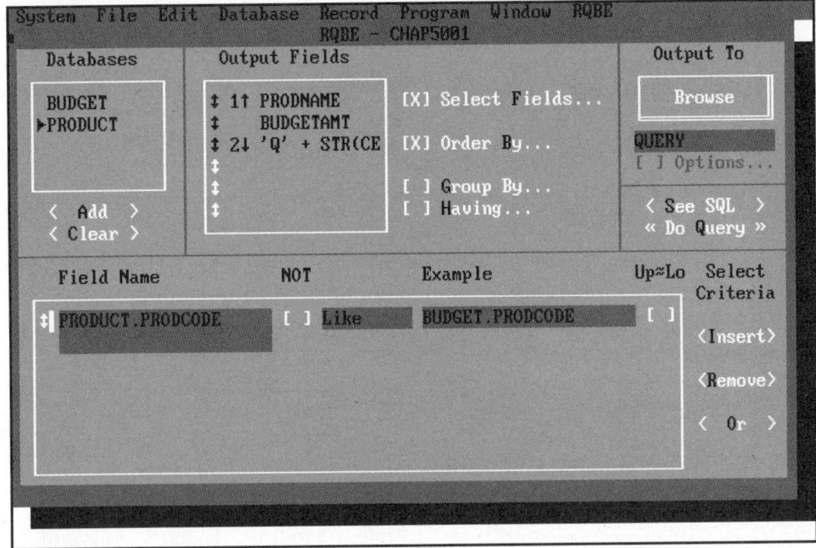

FIG. 5.11

The elegant design of the RQBE allows a compact representation of the complex index conditions.

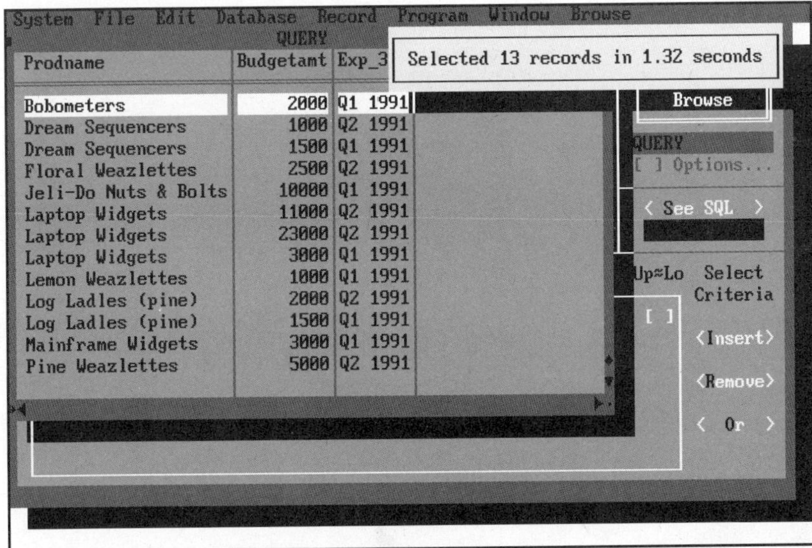

FIG. 5.12

The ordered query.

Grouping Your Data into Summaries

When analyzing data, you occasionally want only a summary of the information. You may not want to see every budget entry for each product; you may want to see only the total budgeted amount—by product—which is where the Group By operation comes into play. To see how Group By works, you first create a query. If you have not already done so, close the CHAP5002 query and close all open tables. From the File menu pad, select the New menu option and click the `Query` radio button. When the file dialog asks for a table, choose BUDGET.DBF.

Go to the Select Fields dialog and deselect all fields except the BUDGET.PRODCODE. (Remember that you may find that using `<Remove All>` is easier than removing fields one by one and then moving `Move` → over the `BUDGET.PRODCODE` field). For this example, you want the SUM of the amount budgeted for each product. To perform this step, select the Functions popup button (in the Functions/Expressions section of the dialog in the lower left corner of the screen). You see an extensive list of the available functions, as shown in table 5.1, but because you want to sum only the budgeted amounts at present, select SUM( ). The dialog produces another menu popup with all numeric fields in the selected tables highlighted, as shown in figure 5.13. In the current list, the only numeric field is BUDGET.BUDGETAMT. Because BUDGET.BUDGETAMT is the only field that can use this function, all other fields on the list are unselectable. To select this field, press Enter.

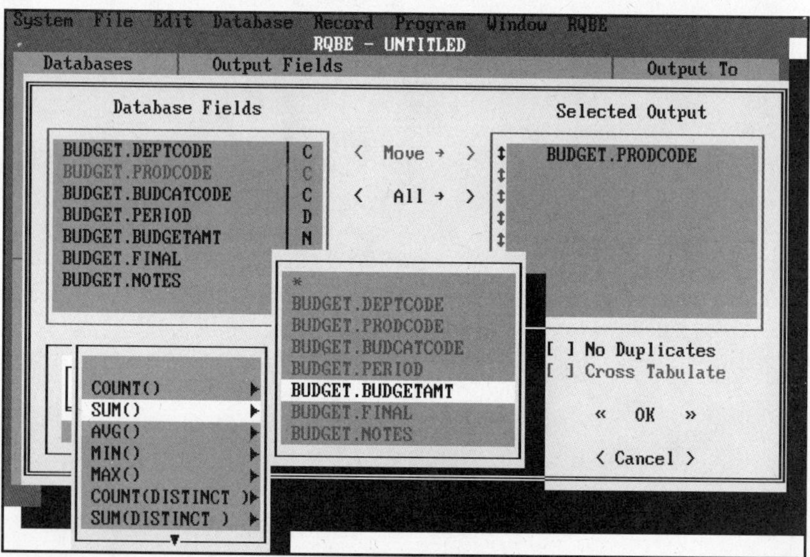

FIG. 5.13

Creating a Function expression.

NOTE Each function in the following table is calculated separately for each Group if you specify any Groupings of the data.

Table 5.1 RQBE Functions

Function	Definition
Count( )	Counts the number of records processed
SUM( )	Sums a numeric field
AVG( )	Calculates the arithmetic average of a numeric field
MIN( )	Returns the lowest value of a field
MAX( )	The opposite of MIN( ); returns the largest value of a field
COUNT(DISTINCT)	Counts the number of unique values found in a field (if you have COUNT(DISTINCT STATE), you probably never get a value larger than 51, including DC, unless Puerto Rico is added as a state.)
SUM(DISTINCT)	Sums values, similar to the SUM( ) function, except SUM(DISTINCT) sums only one occurrence of each value. If the values in the table are 1, 2, 3, 3, and 4, the result of SUM(DISTINCT) is 10.
AVG(DISTINCT)	Works like SUM(DISTINCT), except AVG(DISTINCT) computes an average, not a sum.

The expression `SUM(BUDGET.BUDGETAMT)` appears in the text box just below the Function popup. Note that the `<Move →>` button at the top also is enabled. You now can use `<Move →>` to place this expression in the Selected Output list and click `<<Ok>>` to leave the dialog.

If you forget to move the expression to the output list and then try to select OK, FoxPro senses that you have an incomplete expression and asks whether you want to include this expression in the output list.

If you were to Do the Query at this point, you only get one output record, which has the name of the last Prodcode in the table and the sum of all the budgeted amounts for all products. This query is not at all meaningful.

You want the RQBE to subtotal on—or Group By—the product code. To do this, mark the `Group By` check box. The Group By dialog (see fig. 5.14) looks and acts like the Order By dialog, without the ascending/descending radio buttons.

The BUDGET.NOTES and SUM(BUDGETAMT) fields are not selectable because NOTES is a memo field, and SUM(BUDGETAMT) is an expression. You cannot Group By memo fields or expressions. Using SQL commands directly, rather than through the RQBE, you can group by expressions and functions, which is discussed in chapter 7.

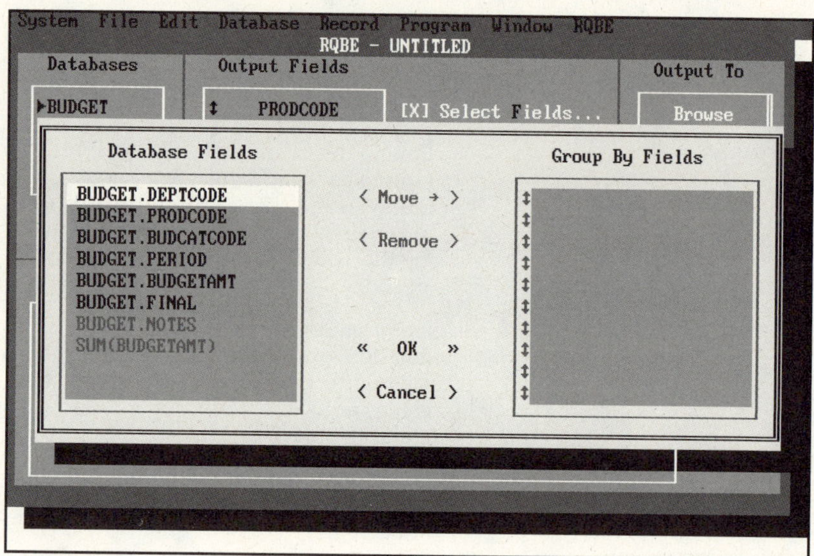

FIG. 5.14

The Group By dialog.

Use Move → to move the Prodcode field to the Group By Fields list because this field is one you want to subtotal. Return to the main RQBE window by selecting <<OK>>. When you Do the Query, you can see a list of unique product codes with the total budget for each product.

An easier way to perform this process is to have the actual product names displayed instead of the codes. You can perform this as you did in the CHAP5002 query. Doing so again now helps you to become familiar with the *joining* process. Again, you perform this procedure in the following manner: select the <Add> button from the Databases section of the RQBE and select the PRODUCT.DBF table. For the RQBE Join Condition, join the PRODUCT.PRODCODE field with the BUDGET.PRODCODE field. Next, return to the Select Fields dialog, add the field PRODUCT.PRODNAME to the Selected Output, and remove the field BUDGET.PRODCODE. Exchange the position of the two selected fields so that the PRODUCT.PRODNAME is first and select <<OK>> to return the RQBE. After you Do the Query, you receive some useful information! Save the query by typing **CHAP5003.QPR** and then exit the RQBE.

Filtering Your Data

Another major feature of the RQBE is the capability of filtering tables so that the only records appearing in output are records that meet a criteria you set. For an example of this filtering, look at the data for just one product.

Open the query CHAP5001.QPR, which you saved previously.

Filtering conditions are entered either in the Having dialog or by using the Select Criteria section, located in the lower half of the RQBE Window. The Having options are discussed in detail in the following chapter. The conditions you place here are processed in a query after other conditions in the Select Criteria section are satisfied. Select the blank text region below the box that contains PRODUCT.PRODCODE. This action triggers a popup with the list of fields, shown in figure 5.15. Note that the fields from each table are separated by a bar. Select the field PRODUCT.PRODNAME.

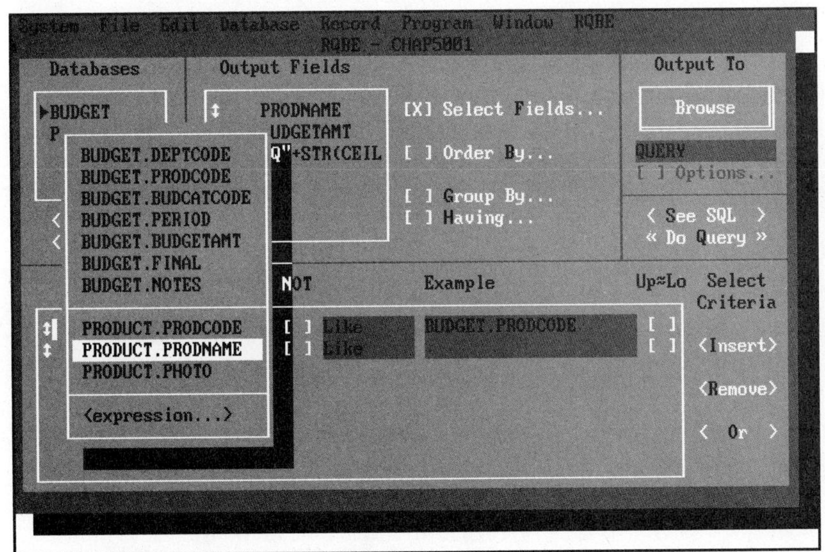

FIG. 5.15 Choosing fields for a Filter Criterion.

If you used the keyboard to select PRODUCT.PRODNAME, you are placed in the NOT check box. This check box works with the text field to the right to specify how the filter discriminates between records. For now, leave `NOT` unchecked. Select the text box on this line with the word `Like` in it. The popup that appears contains a list of available connectors, described in table 5.2.

Table 5.2 RQBE Join/Filter Conditions

Like	Like is affected by the setting of ANSI. ANSI, unlike most other SETtings in FoxPro, can only be changed from the Command window, with the SET ANSI ON and SET ANSI OFF commands. The default for SET ANSI is OFF. With ANSI set OFF, Like checks to see whether the beginning of a shorter character field matches the longer and continues to compare characters until one of the strings is exhausted. For example: "JIM" **Like** "JIMMY" "JIMMY" **Like** "JIM" "JIM " **Like** "JIM" "JIM" **Like** "JIM" The preceding comparisons are all considered matches but "JIM " **Like** "JIMMY" is not a match. With SET ANSI ON, FoxPro adds spaces to the shorter field to make this field the same length as the longer string before comparing. For example, with "JIM" **Like** "JIMMY" FoxPro actually compares "JIM " **Like** "JIMMY" ... and this comparison is not considered a match.
Exactly Like	Checks for exact matches
More Than	Checks to see whether the field on the left is greater than the field on the right
Less Than	Checks to see whether the field on the left is less than the field on the right
Between	Checks to see whether the field on the left is between two values, separated by commas, on the right
In	Checks to see whether the field on the left is in the list of values supplied on the right

You are only interested in records where the product name is the same as, or Like, the text "Dream Sequencers." Select Like from the popup and type **Dream Sequencers** in the Example text box. Be careful whether you type the text in upper- or lowercase, because RQBE performs a *case-sensitive* search by default. To carry out a case-insensitive search so that (in this example) all entries of DREAM SEQUENCERS are found, check the check box below the on-screen heading `Up≈Lo`.

You also can type only the first part of the string for which you are searching. If you type **Dre**, RQBE finds *Dream Sequencers*. RQBE, however, also finds *Dreadnoughts* if Omnipresent Widgets makes them! You can disable this feature by using Exactly Like rather than Like.

If the screen looks like figure 5.16, you are ready to Do the Query. You may see is a message box with the message `Invalid BROWSE setup — default setup used` as FoxPro tries to use the setup from the prior Browse window displayed from the RQBE. Press Enter to get rid of the message box, and the query appears.

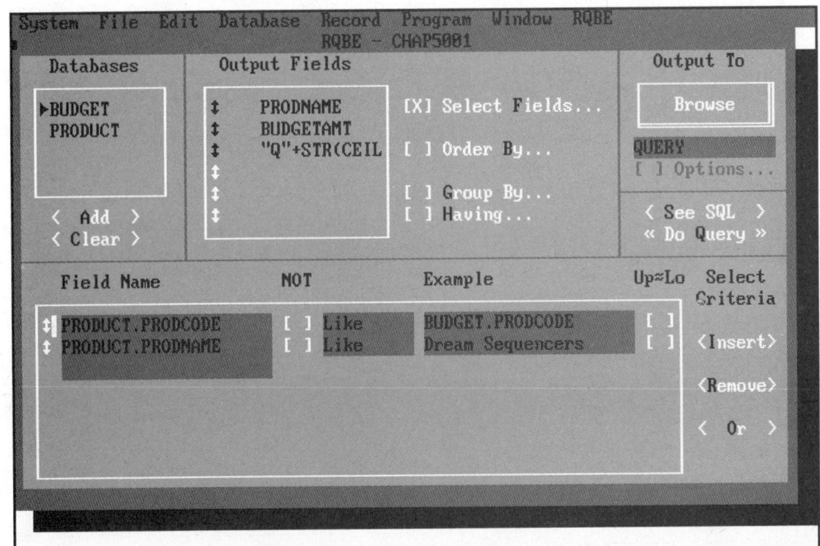

FIG. 5.16

A completed Filter Example (note the absence of a symbol because this condition is not a join condition).

Suppose that you want to see records for both Dream Sequencers and Bobometers. Just change the Like to In. Edit the field that contains the words Dream Sequencers by typing a comma after the string and then the word *Bobometers*. This corresponds to the English instructions "Select all products in the list Dream Sequencers, Bobometers." To see the records for all products *except* Dream Sequencers and Bobometers, check the `Not` box. When you Do this Query, you see records for Log Ladles, Weazlettes, and so on, but no records appear for Dream Sequencers and Bobometers.

Continue to experiment by adding more complex filtering conditions. When you are satisfied with the selected conditions, save this query as **CHAP5004.QPR**.

Directing Your Query Output

Until now, all the query output was directed to a BROWSE window. You can now get fancy with RQBE output. Sending query results to a printed report is easy because the Report Writer is integrated into the RQBE window. Using the **Output To** popup control, choose `Report/Label` as the output type. This choice enables the Options check box beneath the **Output To** control.

Now select the Options box. The RQBE displays the RQBE Display Options dialog you see in figure 5.17.

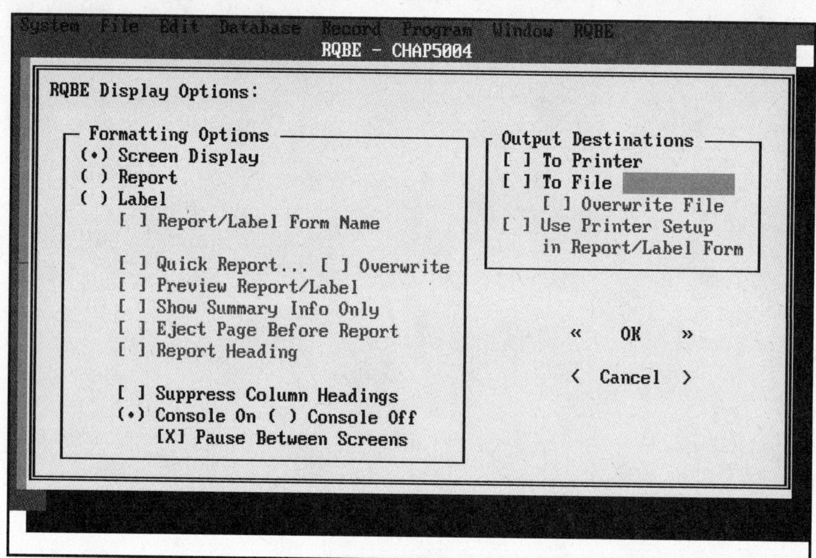

FIG. 5.17

The RQBE Display Options dialog.

The RQBE Display Options dialog presents a wealth of options. To produce a printed report, select the `Report` radio button. Now most of the options in the Formatting Options section of the dialog are available. Select the `Quick Report` check box. You now see the RQBE Quick Report dialog (see fig. 5.18). This dialog enables you to format the report by using either the `Column` or `Form` radio button. Selecting either button updates the layout guide picture on the right side of the RQBE Quick Report dialog. For this example, leave the default `Column Layout` radio button pressed. You also can specify the Report Width but leave this setting at 80 columns. The last item in the dialog is the Save As, which defaults to the same name as the query. To exit the Quick Report dialog, select <<OK>>, and you return to the Display Options dialog.

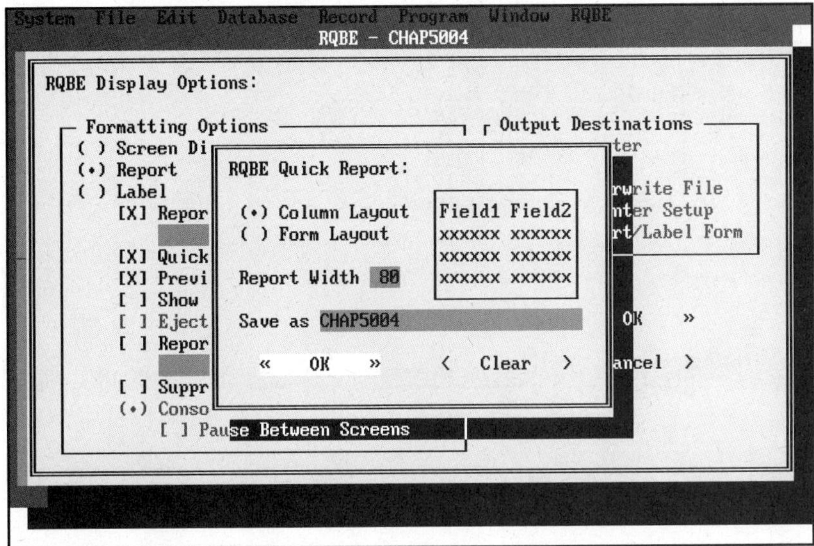

FIG. 5.18

The RQBE Quick Report dialog—(Column Layout).

Notice that the Preview Report/Label check box is checked. This check box enables you to see the report on-screen before you print. Select the <<OK>> text button to exit the dialog, then Do the Query to preview the report (see fig. 5.19).

You are now in the Report Writer's Page Preview mode. You have now created a report from a query that you can edit, add headings, totals, and so on from the Report Writer. Report Writer is covered in Chapter 10, "Using the Report Writer and Label Designer." All changes made in the report writer are reflected when you run the query again.

To print the report, return to the Display Options dialog and deselect the Preview Report/Label check box. Doing so enables you to check the To Printer check box. Now mark the `Report Heading` check box; the Expression Builder dialog appears on-screen. This complex dialog enables you to choose a field or variable or to type a report title, which will be in use throughout FoxPro 2. You learn more about the Expression Builder in the following chapters. For now, just type **"Budgets by Product and Quarter"** (include the quotation marks), as shown in figure 5.20.

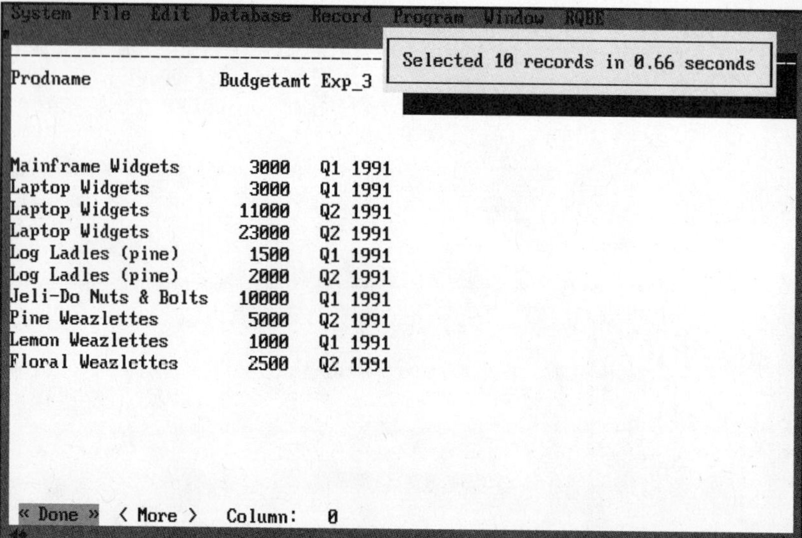

FIG. 5.19

The Report Preview from a query.

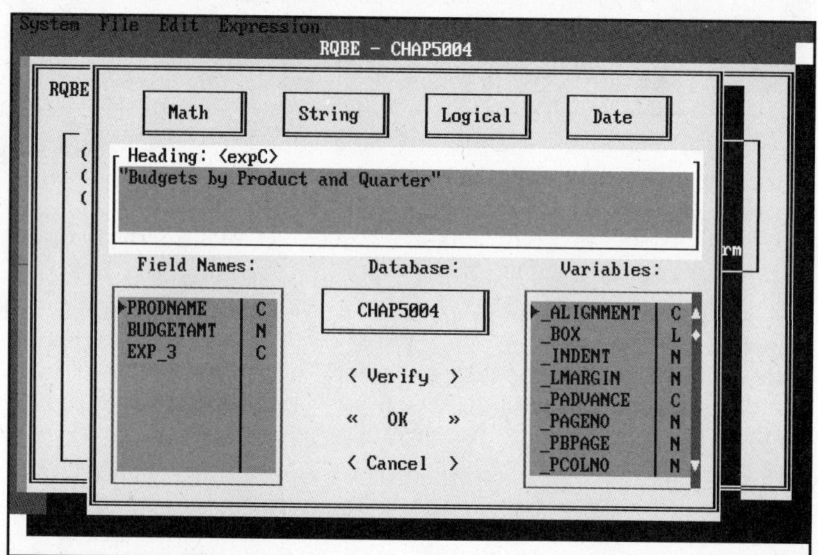

FIG. 5.20

Creating the Heading with the Expression Builder.

Select <<OK>> to leave the Expression Builder. (You can first click the <Verify> text button to ensure that you typed a valid expression. If a message appears that says the expression is not valid, you may have forgotten to add quotation marks.) To print the report, mark the

`To Printer` check box. Click <<OK>> to leave the dialog. Do the Query, and the report is sent to the printer.

As you learn in Chapters 9 and 10, labels—although similar to reports in FoxPro—use a simpler set of options. Therefore, you have fewer options from which to choose in the RQBE Display Options dialog. Because no Quick Label feature is available in FoxPro, you cannot create labels until you are introduced to the Label Designer in Chapter 9. Then you can specify the name of a pre-existing label as your query output.

When you specify the name of a pre-existing label or report as your query destination, be sure that any alias referenced in the label or report form is removed or edited to be appropriate for the temporary table, or cursor, used by the RQBE as an interim place to store the results. (This problem is presented in greater detail in Chapter 7.)

Screen Display, the default Report option, is just the DISPLAY or LIST command that shows the query results on-screen or directs output to a file or the printer. This operation is similar to the way you used LIST and DISPLAY to show records in Chapters 3 and 4.

If you haven't already done so, use Save to place this query on disk in the present form, as **CHAP5005.QPR**. If you also want to save a copy of the data that results from this table, you can send the data to another table on the disk. Select Table/DBF. A File Save dialog appears with various naming options available. For now, accept the default. When you return to the main RQBE dialog, note that the text box just above the Options check box changes from CHAP5005 to CHAP5005.DBF.

By selecting Cursor as the output type, you can send the results to a temporary read-only file. Cursors are deleted when closed.

If you own FoxGraph, you also can send the query results directly to a graph by selecting Graph and running the query. If you have another graphics package, you also may be able to link this software to FoxPro's RQBE. FoxPro 2's new API (Application Programming Interface) makes writing the necessary routines possible, as is discussed briefly in Chapter 15.

Chapter Summary

With the RQBE, you can create complex queries to extract information from tables in a matter of minutes. Before FoxPro 2.0, experienced programmers took many hours to create hundreds of lines of program code to accomplish the results that one FoxPro query can provide. For complex queries, the most sophisticated program code does not execute as fast as the SQL-Select created from FoxPro's RQBE—largely because of SQL's use of the *Rushmore* technology, which is discussed in greater detail in Chapter 7.

In this chapter, you learned to manipulate the RQBE as a tool. Now that you know how to use this feature, you are ready to take on some real work. In the following chapter, you learn about the more intricate queries and more detailed uses of the various clauses of the SQL SELECT command.

6

CHAPTER

Investigating Your Data with Advanced Queries

In Chapter 5, you learn about most of the simple tools of FoxPro's RQBE. You have seen only a sliver of its potential, however. In this chapter, you begin to see the power of the RQBE by learning how to use its tools to create complex queries.

Because the Budget and Prodcode tables you use in Chapter 5 are not sufficient to demonstrate some of the more powerful capabilities of the RQBE, you use some of the sample tables provided with FoxPro. These tables are located in the Tutorial directory, under the main FoxPro directory.

If you did not install the Tutorial files when you installed FoxPro, you need to install them now if you want to use the sample tables in this chapter.

To install the Tutorial files, move to the FoxPro directory and complete the INSTALL program in one of the following ways:

- Type the DOS command, **FOXPRO INSTALL**
- Choose DO INSTALL from the command window
- Choose INSTALL.APP from the Program Do dialog

Because you already installed FoxPro, you do not proceed exactly as you did during initial installation. Choose No when asked whether you want to overwrite your Fox user file. Choose the tutorial files from the Supplemental Product list. You then are prompted to insert the correct disk.

Creating Complex Filter Conditions

More often than not, you want to filter data from your tables by using more than one criterion. In Chapter 5, for example, you filter records by using one criterion: product code. The queries selected all records with one or more products, or all records without those products. In this section, you learn how to be more selective with your filtering.

Asking Questions with AND and OR

To begin, open a new query (from the File New dialog), and select the CUSTOMER.DBF table from the Tutorial directory. Don't use the CUSTOMER.DBF table in the Model directory. Use the Directory popup of the Open File dialog to move back to the FoxPro2 directory, and then select Tutorial from the directory list. Select the CUSTOMER.DBF table from this list.

You can look in the RQBE's Select Fields dialog or the Setup panel of the View window to understand the structure of this and other tables from the Tutorial directory that you use in this book. To get a good sense of the entire Tutorial database and the way its tables are interrelated, refer to the chart at the beginning of the "SQL Quiz" section in your Developer's Guide.

The first thing you want to do is eliminate some of the fields from the Output Fields list. (This step will probably be true for most of your queries). From the Select Fields dialog, select the following fields for output:

CUSTOMER.COMPANY

CUSTOMER.STATE

CUSTOMER.YTDPURCH

If you do not see these fields on your Select Fields list, you are using the wrong Customer table. Go back to the main RQBE dialog, `Clear` this table, and `Add` the correct one from the Tutorial directory.

Suppose that you are interested only in customers based in New York. To select those customers, set a filter in the Select Criteria section of the RQBE window, select the popup underneath the Field Name heading, and select CUSTOMER.STATE from the popup. Leave the NOT box empty and retain Like in the joiner box. Underneath the Example heading, type **NY**. Do the Query, and the result shows a Browse of all customers in New York. Your screen should look like figure 6.1.

Perhaps you want to see only your best customers from New York, with year-to-date purchases of $5,000 or more. To see these customers, add another filter beneath the one you just entered, specifying that CUSTOMER.YTDPURCH is Not Less Than 5000.

When you are finished, your screen should look like the one in figure 6.2.

Notice that even though you are interested in customers with year-to-date purchases of $5,000 or more, you selected customers in New York with year-to-date purchases of not Less Than $5,000. This procedure may seem a bit backward; however, had you selected customers with purchases of More Than $5,000, you would have missed customers whose purchases were exactly $5,000.

If you Do the Query now, your browse contains only those customers you want, as shown in figure 6.3.

System File Edit Database Record Program Window Browse
▸CUSTOMER
COMPANY
STATE
YTDPURCH
[X] Select Fields...
[ ] Order By...
[ ] Group By...
[ ] Having...
Browse
[ ] Options...
< Add >
< Clear >
< See SQL >
« Do Query »
Field Name NOT Example Up≈Lo Select Criteria
CUSTOMER.STATE [ ] Like NY [ ]
<Insert>
<Remove>
< Or >
QUERY

Company	State	Ytdpurch
Ansari Produce	NY	4403.71
B-J Astra	NY	1347.19
Bedford Office Solutions	NY	8165.48
Blue Solutions	NY	3325.99
COB Companies of Design	NY	516.28
Citco Ltd	NY	1625.05

FIG. 6.1

All customers in New York.

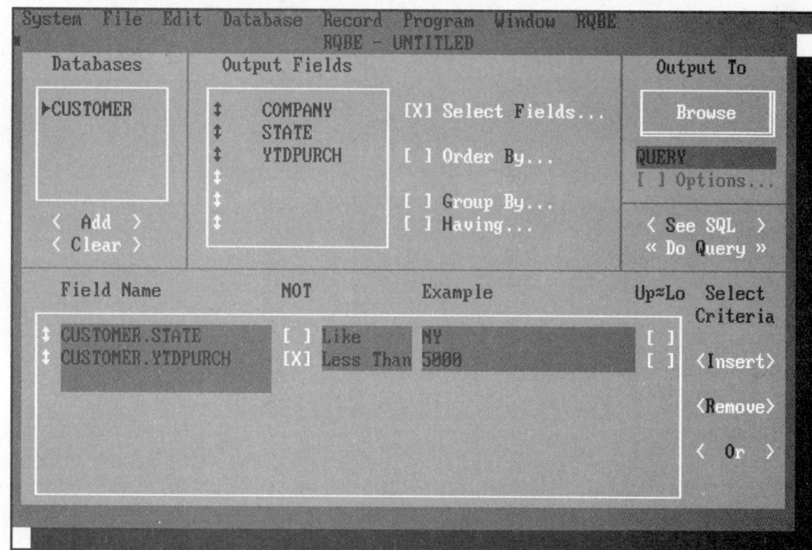

FIG. 6.2

Filtering by state and year-to-date purchases.

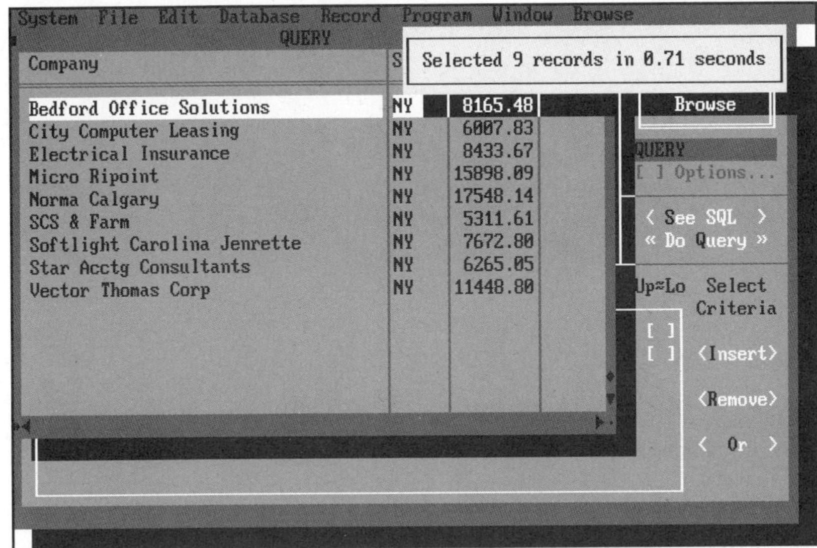

FIG. 6.3

The best customers in New York.

Perhaps you want to see your best customers (those with $5,000 or more in year-to-date sales) and your worst customers (those with less than $100 in year-to-date sales). This query seems pretty straightforward. Just add another filter, specifying CUSTOMER.YTDPURCH Less Than 100, and your screen should look like figure 6.4.

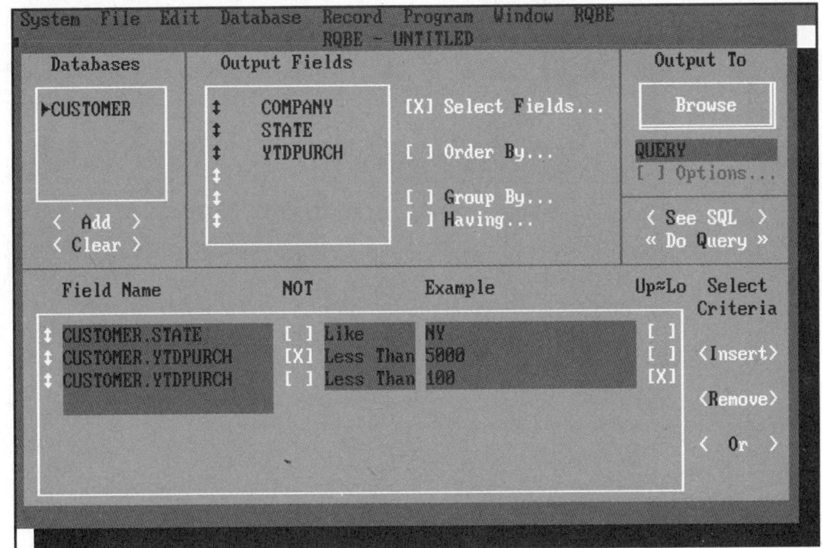

FIG. 6.4

The best and worst customer filter.

If you make this query exactly as written, it doesn't work—no output records are produced even though you know from the previous example that you have nine good customers. The problem here is that the RQBE is doing exactly what you told it to do, not what you want it to do. The following shows how the computer translated the query:

> Select all customers whose state is New York, AND whose year-to-date purchases are not less than $5,000, AND whose year-to-date purchases are less than $100.

The trick is knowing that the computer asks this three-part question of every customer. For any given customer, all three parts cannot be true.

What you really want to ask the computer is the following:

> Show me all customers from New York whose sales were $5,000 or more, OR whose sales were less than $100.

To make the query work, you need to add *OR*. Select the OR button (its hot key is O [zero]). The RQBE places a line underneath the CUSTOMER.YTDPURCH filter with the word OR in it, as shown in figure 6.5.

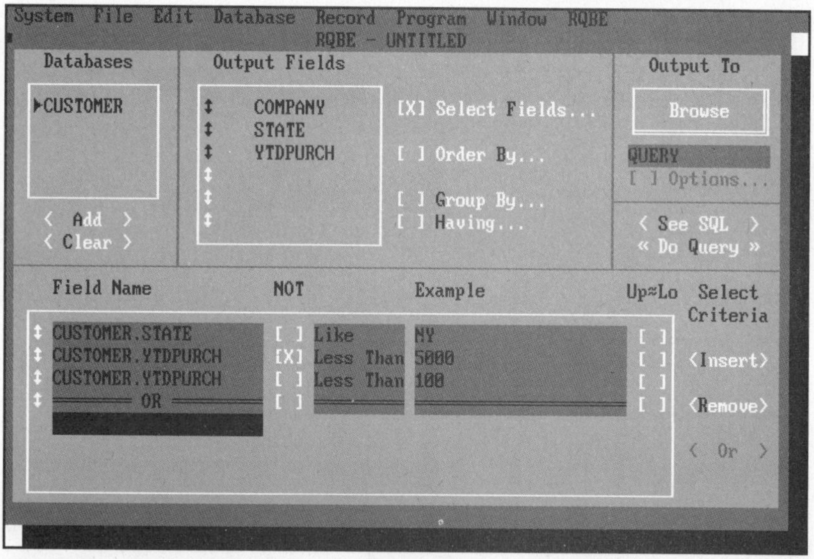

FIG. 6.5

The OR line.

Move the OR line so that it is between the two YTDPURCH filters. The OR line can be moved by using the Ctrl-PgUp and Ctrl-PgDn keys, or by clicking the mouse on the doubled-headed arrow character at the far left. Fields are moved the same way in the Output Fields, and in other, similar, lists. After you have moved the OR line, your screen should look like figure 6.6.

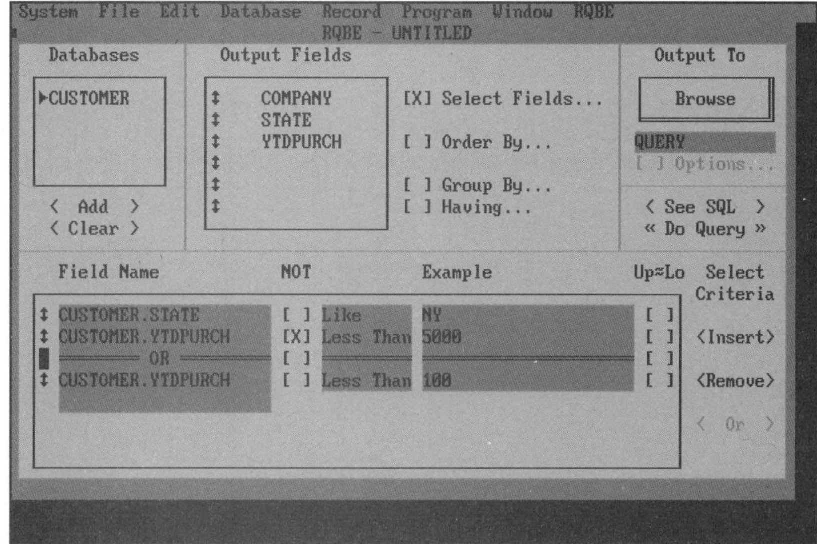

FIG. 6.6

The OR line moved.

Now, Do the Query again, and you see your best and worst New York customers in the same Browse—almost what you want. The RQBE is connecting filters on both sides of the OR line. For all customers, RQBE made sure that they were in NY AND had sales of $5,000 or more. If this test failed, it did so because RQBE checked to see whether the sales were less than $100. The second test knew nothing about NY. To correct this problem, add a new filter condition at the bottom exactly like the first filter condition. After adding the filter, your screen should look like figure 6.7.

You should see the exact information you are looking for. If the information is still hard to read, then Order By CUSTOMER.YTDPURCH, Do the Query, and you can better distinguish between the best and worst customers, as shown in figure 6.8.

At this point, you should save your query. Saving this file is not as simple as before, however, because you used tables outside the current directory. When you bring up the File Save dialog, you see that the Directory is Tutorial, because the table you used is in the Tutorial directory. Because you want to save your query in the Model directory, change Tutorial in the Directory popup by going up one level to the main FoxPro 2 directory and then select Model from the list. After that, type in the name for your query: **CHAP6001**. (FoxPro adds the default extension, QPR.)

WARNING

If you do not get the results you are expecting, then the RQBE may be ignoring some of your filter conditions. The first-release versions of FoxPro 2 are inconsistent in the way they handle different instructions to Do a Query. If you use a mouse click, hot key, or press Ctrl-Enter to confirm that you are ready to Do your Query and your results do not show that all your criteria are being met, then use the Tab key to move to the Do Query option and press Enter while it is highlighted.

Continue these steps throughout your work in the RQBE, and contact Fox Software to receive the latest version of the program (information on updating your software is included in Appendix H, "Finding Available Help").

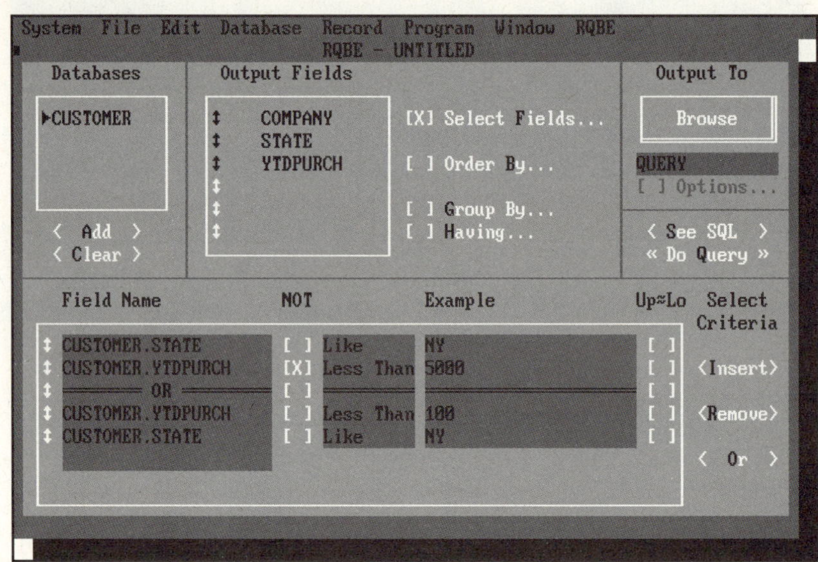

FIG. 6.7

Duplicating filters to determine your best and worst customers.

WARNING

The RQBE does not save the directory name of the tables with the query file. Consequently, if you close a query and its associated files, and then try to reopen it, FoxPro will not be able to find the proper tables. Instead, FoxPro opens the CUSTOMER table in the Model directory. Because this table does not have the correct fields, FoxPro gives you an error, and you can't access your query. Whenever your tables are in a different directory than the query file, you have to open the tables yourself before you open or execute the query.

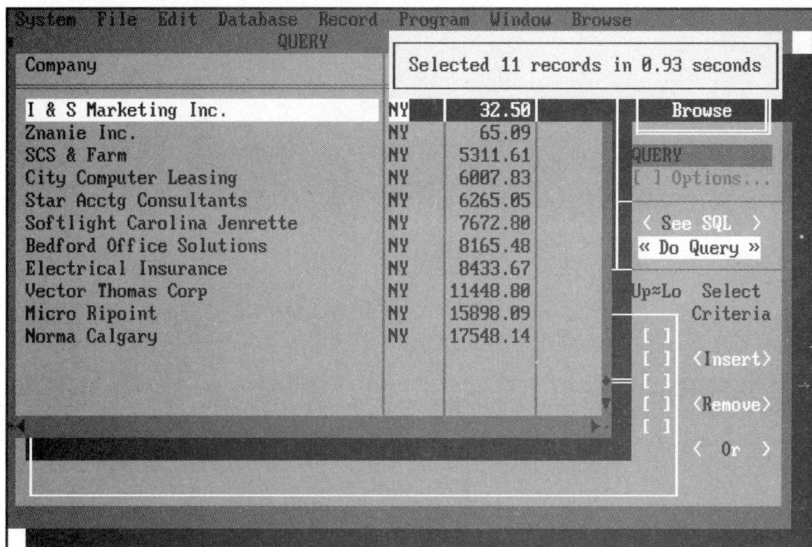

FIG. 6.8

The worst and best NY customers in sales order.

Deciphering AND, OR, and NOT

AND, OR, and NOT are simple words in English sentences, but using them properly can be confusing when you're working with computers. Look closely at the way they are used to correct expressions.

Filters are made up of *Logical Expressions*. In other words, the expressions can either be *TRUE* or *FALSE*. The filter expressions are evaluated for every record. If a filter expression is TRUE, then its record will be included. If it is FALSE, then its record will be excluded. Table 6.1 shows how TRUE and FALSE conditions work with AND, OR, and NOT.

Table 6.1 AND, OR, and NOT logic

AND	When two items are joined by AND, both must be true to obtain a result of TRUE.
	TRUE AND TRUE = TRUE
	TRUE AND FALSE = FALSE
	FALSE AND TRUE = FALSE
	FALSE AND FALSE = FALSE
OR	When two items are joined by OR, only one must be true to obtain a result of TRUE.

continues

Table 6.1 Continued

	TRUE OR TRUE = TRUE
	TRUE OR FALSE = TRUE
	FALSE OR TRUE = TRUE
	FALSE OR FALSE = FALSE
	NOT The NOT function (check box in RQBE) reverses a TRUE or FALSE.
	NOT TRUE = FALSE
	NOT FALSE = TRUE

In mathematics, similar types of expressions are evaluated from left to right; that is, in their order of appearance. In RQBE, logical filter expressions are evaluated from top to bottom. In the last example, your final filter looked like the following:

```
CUSTOMER.STATE          Like              "NY"
CUSTOMER.YTDPURCH       NOT Less Than     5000
=========OR======= =====  ===========      =======
CUSTOMER.YTDPURCH       Less Than         100
CUSTOMER.STATE          Like              "NY"
```

Each record in the customer table was tested with the preceding filter rules. The items immediately next to each other were joined with AND. The OR separator separated two sets of AND clauses. If either of the two AND sections resulted in TRUE, then the entire expression was considered TRUE.

No matter how many filter expressions are used, all can be broken into sets of AND clauses, separated by OR clauses. By using the preceding table, you can pick apart the filters to figure out exactly what is going on. Often, in complex situations, studying the SQL that FoxPro uses (by selecting the See SQL button) helps you figure out just what your query will do.

If you are experienced in earlier database dialects, you will notice that the words AND, NOT, and OR are not written with surrounding periods (.AND., .OR., and .NOT.) as they would be in other database syntax. The periods are not required with these operators in FoxPro 2, although the logical values True and False still require them (.T. and .F.).

NOTE

You can use the See SQL button at any point to see the SQL Select statement FoxPro uses to execute the query, and any other FoxPro commands used to output the query, such as BROWSE. This way, you can use the RQBE to learn the syntax of the SQL SELECT command and see how simple FoxPro commands are used to enhance the basic SQL SELECT. Remember that the QPR file created by the RQBE is just a regular program, composed of normal FoxPro statements, which you can issue singly from the command window or in programs in combination with any other commands you wish. In FoxPro, SQL is not a separate mode; it is completely integrated into the language.

Along with helping you get accustomed to SQL syntax, a quick look at See SQL every now and then helps you understand how the different controls on the RQBE work. You can use the RQBE tools to learn SQL, and in turn, SQL commands can help you learn about the RQBE.

Filtering Groups with the Having Clause

In Chapter 5, you learn how to set groupings. You also learn how to filter your data by entering selection criteria. This filtering eliminated the unwanted data before any other work or grouping was done on it.

On some occasions, you may want to do the filtering after the grouping has taken place. For example, using the same customer file you used in the last example, you may want to get a listing of the year-to-date purchases by state, where the total purchases in each state exceeds $50,000. Because you need to base the filter on the state *grouping*, you need to use the Having dialog. Create this query to see how it works.

If you have not already done so, close the CHAP6001.QPR query. Make certain that the CUSTOMER.DBF table from the Tutorial directory, the same one you used before, is open and in the current work area. Next, from the File New dialog, open a new query.

Because you are interested in year-to-date purchases by state, most of the fields in the customer file don't need to be output. From the Select Fields dialog, adjust the Selected Output so that the following fields are selected:

CUSTOMER.STATE

SUM(CUSTOMER.YTDPURCH)

NOTE Remember, to get the SUM( ) expression, use the Functions popup in the lower left section of the Select Fields dialog.

Next, from the Group By dialog, move CUSTOMER.STATE into the Group By Fields list. The current query should list each state and its year-to-date purchases. Do this Query to make sure. Your screen should look like the one in figure 6.9. FoxPro makes it easy to Do the Query at any time to make sure that you are on the right path.

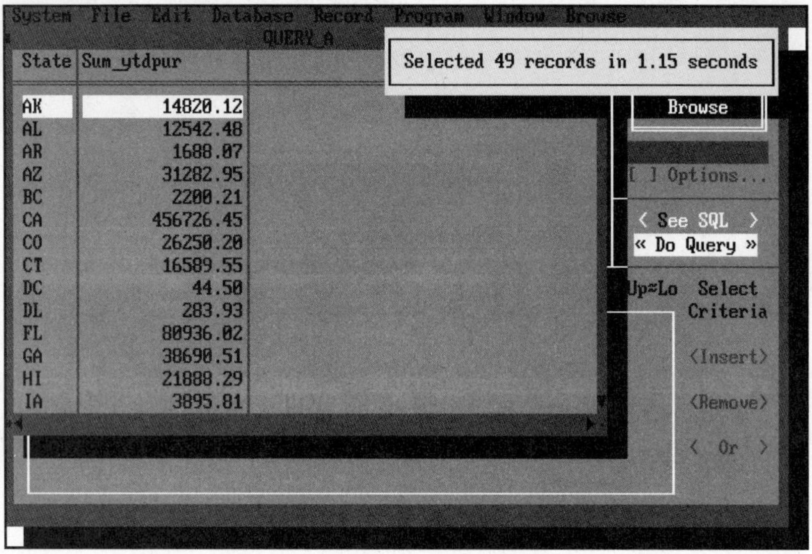

FIG. 6.9

Year-to-date purchases by state.

So far, this query is doing exactly what you want. Next, rule out states where the year-to-date purchases are less than $50,000. Exclude these states by using the Having dialog, as you see in figure 6.10. To get to the Having dialog, select the Having check box (use its hot key, H).

The Having dialog works much like the Join Condition dialog. When you are in the Having dialog, select the highlighted bar under the word Fields, and you produce a list of expressions and fields that can be used in filters. You want to limit the output based on the sum of the year-to-date purchases, so select SUM(), which produces a popup of the numeric fields. Select CUSTOMER.YTDPURCH as the field to SUM(). Check the NOT box, change Like to Less Than, and then enter 50000 in the Example text box. As before, you want all records *not less than 50,000.* If you select *more than 50,000,* you miss any states with exactly $50,000 in purchases.

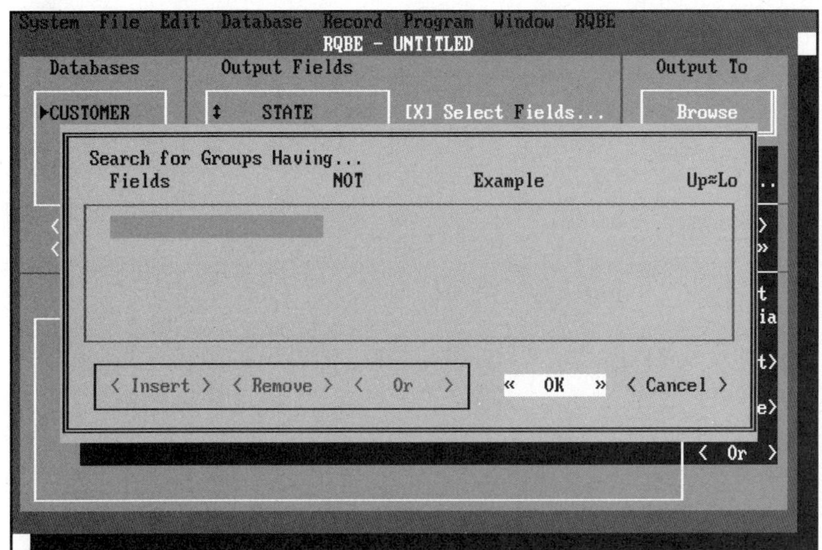

FIG. 6.10

The Having dialog.

Also notice that you can have multiple Having criteria, connected with implicit ANDs. You can also connect the criteria with OR lines. These conditions are logically connected the same way as you saw earlier in the Select Criteria section of the RQBE window.

Your screen should look like the one in figure 6.11.

Now, select « OK » to leave the Having dialog, and Do the Query. Your output should look like figure 6.12.

Based on this query, you may want to move your headquarters to California, which would reduce costs immensely.

Save this query as CHAP6002.QPR. Make sure that it is saved in the Model subdirectory and not in the Tutorial subdirectory.

Joining More than Two Tables

For this example, you want to determine how many of each part was purchased by each customer who purchased five or more of that part.

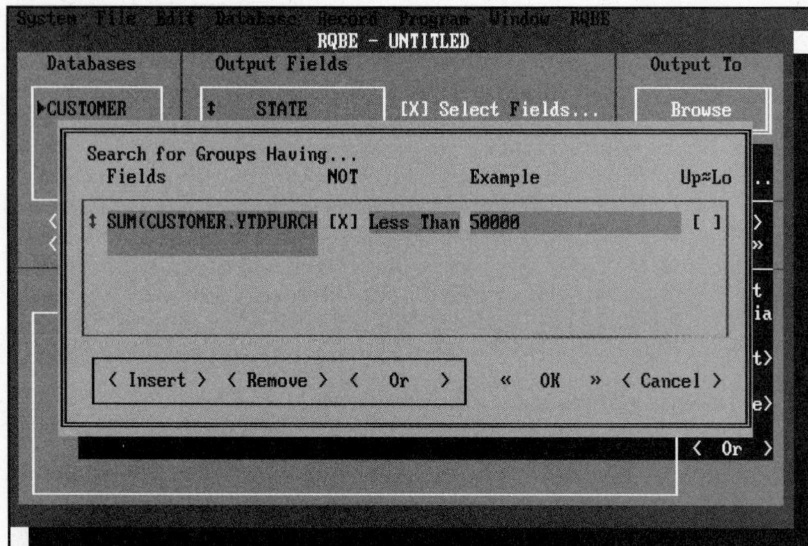

FIG. 6.11

Having the sum of year-to-date purchases of 50,000 or more.

Selected 8 records in 1.32 seconds

State	Sum_ytdpur
CA	456726.45
FL	80936.02
IL	78386.02
NC	55356.25
NY	166896.89
OH	58053.23
PA	58600.16
TX	114293.11

Browse
QUERY_A
[ ] Options...
< See SQL >
« Do Query »
Up≈Lo Select Criteria
<Insert>
<Remove>
< Or >

FIG. 6.12

All states with year-to-date sales of $50,000 or more.

You need to join the Customer table with the Parts table, because you are looking for parts per customer. Because no common fields exist between the Customer table and the Parts table, the tables cannot be joined directly. However, they can be indirectly joined. To do so, join the Customer table with the Invoices table (by CNO). Then join the Invoices table to the Detail table (by INO). Finally, join the Detail table with the Parts table (by PNO).

By using the SET RELATION command, you can express the same type of indirect relationship in a series of commands, such as the following:

```
SELECT 4
USE parts
INDEX ON pno TAG pno
SELECT 3
USE detail
INDEX ON ino TAG ino
SET RELATION TO pno INTO parts
SELECT 2
USE invoices
INDEX ON cno TAG cno
SET RELATION TO ino INTO detail
SELECT 1
USE customer
SET RELATION TO cno INTO invoices
SET SKIP TO invoices, detail, parts
BROWSE FIELDS CUSTOMER.COMPANY, PARTS.DESCRIPT
```

In the RQBE, however, you can make it a much simpler problem. If you have not already done so, then exit from the RQBE and close any open tables. Now open a new query. FoxPro prompts you for a table. If the listed directory is not Tutorial, then change it to Tutorial, as before, and select the CUSTOMER.DBF table.

Now add the other tables you need. Select < `Add` > and select the INVOICES.DBF table. RQBE brings up the Join Condition dialog. Join the tables with the following command:

```
INVOICES.CNO      Like      CUSTOMER.CNO
```

After you join the tables, select « OK ». Next, add the DETAIL.DBF table and join it to the invoices table with the following command:

```
DETAIL.INO        Like      INVOICES.INO
```

After you join these tables, select « OK ». Next, add the PARTS.DBF table and join it to the detail table with the following command:

```
PARTS.PNO         Like      DETAIL.PNO
```

After these tables are joined, select « OK ».

After you have finished and returned to the main RQBE screen, your screen should look like the one in figure 6.13. Now you should understand why the table name must be placed in front of the field name in the RQBE popups. When multiple tables are used, the table reference makes it clear which fields are referenced—even if the field names are exactly the same.

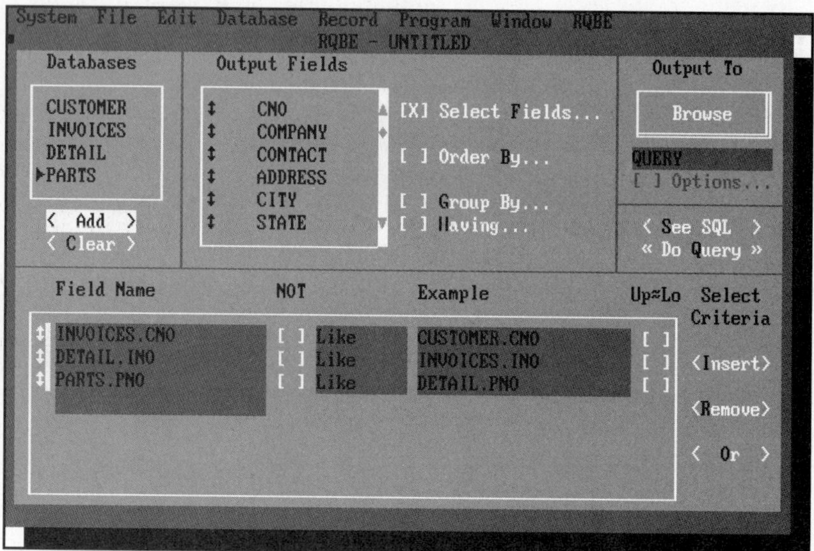

FIG. 6.13

A four-table join.

Before you Do the Query, you may want to choose Select Fields for output. Because RQBE is still in its default state at the moment, it would just output every field from the Customer table, and none from the other tables. This step would make the other three tables superfluous; you wouldn't learn anything from them. Go to the Select Fields dialog and select the following fields for output:

CUSTOMER.COMPANY

PARTS.DESCRIPT

Now Do the Query; your results should match figure 6.14. You may notice that this query takes longer than those in the previous exercises. It takes longer because, by default, no indexes exist in the Tutorial tables, so you have forced SQL to create them. (In the equivalent example using RELATIONs, from the View or Command window, you had to create those indexes as well.) You discuss fine-tuning your queries for the best possible performance in Chapter 7.

Save this query as CHAP6003.QPR, in the Model directory. The query has produced one line of output for each part each customer purchased and is useful as it is; however, it would be even more useful if it showed how many of each part each customer purchased. That determination is your next step.

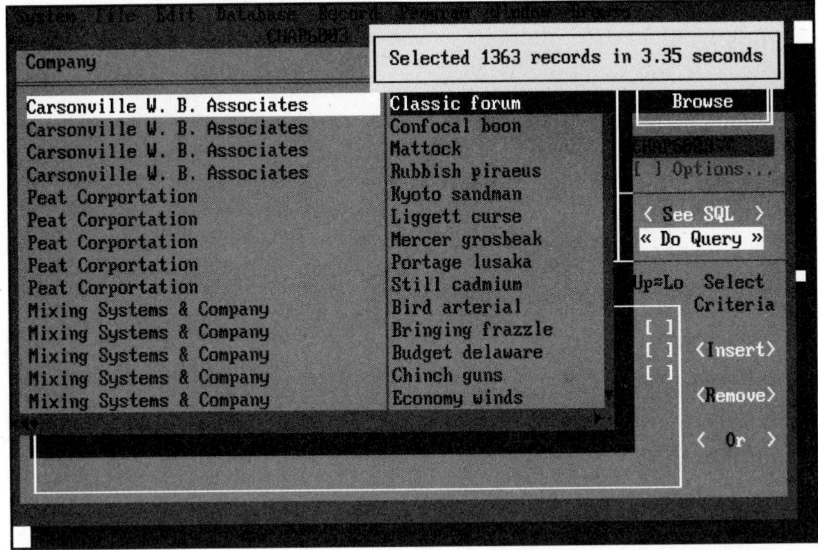

FIG. 6.14

The results of a four-table join.

You want to subtotal (group) the DETAIL.QTY field by customer, then by part, which requires two groupings. Go to the Group By dialog and add the following groupings:

CUSTOMER.COMPANY

PARTS.PNO

After you add the groups, select « OK ».

You also can group by DETAIL.PNO, instead of PARTS.PNO, which would produce the same result because you have only one matching part record for each detail record. Although changes like this may not alter the output, often they can have performance implications. In this case, however, it doesn't seem to matter.

This step tells the RQBE to break on part number (PNO) within company, enabling you to calculate a separate SUM(DETAIL.QTY) on each part number for each company. Thus, you are asking the question, "How many of each part did each customer purchase?"

Now you want to add a field to the output to display the summed quantity field. Go to the Select Fields dialog. You want a SUM of the QTY field for each grouping, so go to the Functions popup and select SUM(), which will produce the popup of fields, with the Numeric field available for selecting. Select the DETAIL.QTY field and leave the Select Fields dialog.

Now Do the Query. One of the things you may notice is that the output is too wide to fit into the default Browse window. You can use the Tab key to see the hidden fields, or you can resize the Browse window to fit the fields. If you resize your Browse window, your output looks something like figure 6.15.

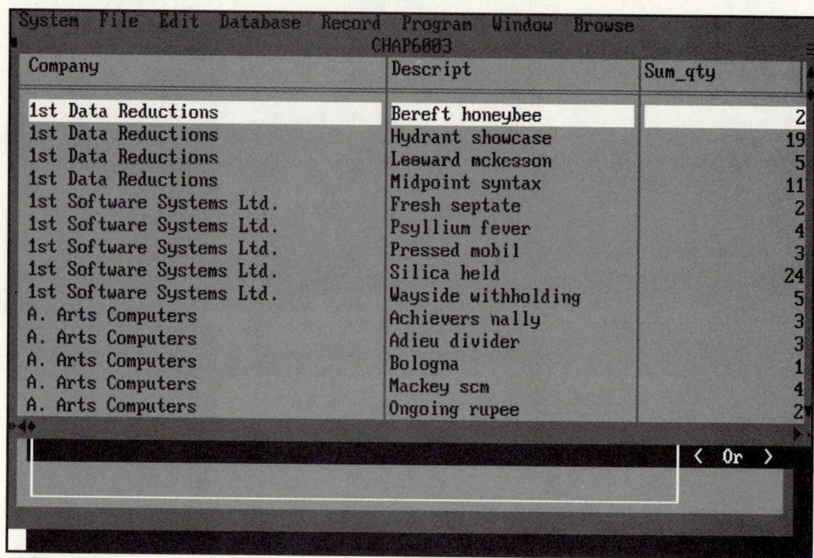

Company	Descript	Sum_qty
1st Data Reductions	Bereft honeybee	2
1st Data Reductions	Hydrant showcase	19
1st Data Reductions	Leeward mckesson	5
1st Data Reductions	Midpoint syntax	11
1st Software Systems Ltd.	Fresh septate	2
1st Software Systems Ltd.	Psyllium fever	4
1st Software Systems Ltd.	Pressed mobil	3
1st Software Systems Ltd.	Silica held	24
1st Software Systems Ltd.	Wayside withholding	5
A. Arts Computers	Achievers nally	3
A. Arts Computers	Adieu divider	3
A. Arts Computers	Bologna	1
A. Arts Computers	Mackey scm	4
A. Arts Computers	Ongoing rupee	2

FIG. 6.15

How many of each part each customer purchased.

The last thing you must do to satisfy your original question is to limit the output to five or more parts purchased per customer. This step is a job for Having, because Having works on Groupings instead of on individual records. Go to the Having dialog and add the following criteria:

```
SUM(DETAIL.QTY)      More Than       4
```

You can also specify *not less than 5*, but because the QTY field does not hold fractions, you don't need to do this. Select « OK » to leave the Having dialog. Now, Do the Query again, and your output should look like figure 6.16.

You have now met your original goal. You did it in simple, discrete steps, and were able to check yourself every so often by Doing the Query. Save this query as CHAP6004.QPR, in the Model subdirectory.

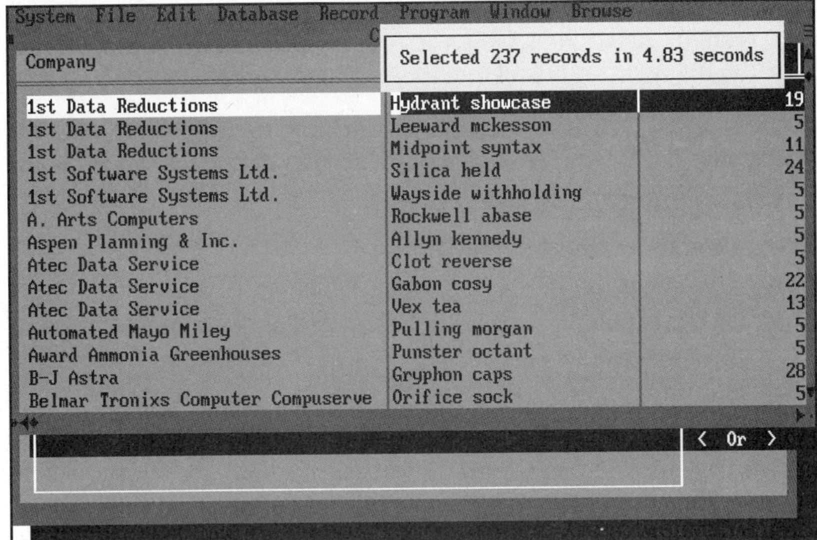

FIG. 6.16

Parts popular with particular customers.

Creating One-to-Many Relations with RQBE

You created *one-to-many* views of your data by using the SET RELATION, and SET SKIP commands in Chapter 4. You also can create one-to-many relations with the RQBE, with a little less work. You cannot get the intuitive *look* of the integrated one-to-many Browses that FoxPro creates from direct commands—with shaded blocks indicating the extent of each parent's child records. With RQBE, however, you can get the same information in fewer steps by enabling FoxPro and SQL to do some of the work for you. Also, with RQBE, you need not have any indexes on the tables, as you did with the SET RELATION method, although the presence of indexes improves the speed of queries.

To see a short example of one-to-many views, create a new query. If you have not already done so, then close the CHAP6004 query, and close any open tables. Next, create a new query. When FoxPro prompts you for a file, move to the Tutorial directory, if it is not current, and select the CUSTOMER.DBF table.

In this example, you look at all customers and all their invoices. Each customer will have one or more invoices: the one-to-many relation.

You now have a query with the customer table open. Because you want to relate the customer table with the invoices table, you need to < Add > the invoices table and join them with the following:

```
INVOICES.CNO    Like     CUSTOMER.CNO
```

Next, to get useful output, go to the Select Fields dialog and select the following fields:

CUSTOMER.COMPANY

INVOICES.IDATE

INVOICES.ITOTAL

If you were to do the query now, you would get a list of companies and their invoices. The companies would be in random order, and you would not be able to see how many invoices a particular company had. Ordering by company will put all the invoices for each company next to each other. Go to the Order By dialog, move CUSTOMER.COMPANY to the Ordering Criteria list, and return to the RQBE screen. Do the Query now, and your output should look like figure 6.17. Save this query as CHAP6005.QPR, in the Model directory.

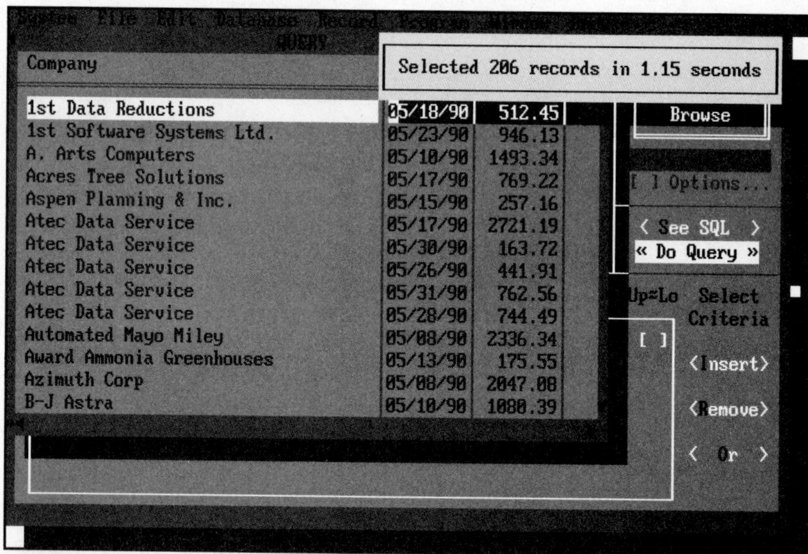

FIG. 6.17

A one-to-many query.

Adding a Dimension to Your Output with Crosstabs

The query you created in the previous example listed customers, their invoice amount, and invoice date. This kind of data is usually provided by spreadsheets. The useful format of spreadsheets is a major reason for their popularity. FoxPro offers a spreadsheet format that lists customers down the side, invoice dates across the top, and invoice amounts at the intersecting cells. This format is called a *crosstab table* and is part of a FoxPro program called GENXTAB.PRG. You don't have to know anything about the GENXTAB program, or how it works, although you may enjoy studying it. GENXTAB has an interface to it built into the RQBE. Give it a try.

If you have not closed the CHAP6005.QPR query, you're all set. Otherwise, reopen it. (Remember, you must *first* open the CUSTOMER.DBF and INVOICES.DBF tables from the Tutorial directory, because they are not in the Model directory with the query file.)

A spreadsheet with invoice dates across the top could result in a tremendous number of columns, unless the columns were months. To make your columns months, first tell RQBE you want crosstabs, then go to the Select Fields dialog.

Notice that the Cross Tabulate check box, underneath the Selected Output list, is enabled. Remove INVOICES.IDATE from the Selected Output list. After you do this, you see the Cross Tabulate check box become disabled. The box becomes disabled because crosstabs are only available when exactly three fields are selected for output; one each for the COLUMN headings, ROW headings, and the data. None of these fields should be a memo field.

Go to the Functions/Expressions text box and enter the following expression:

```
MONTH(INVOICES.IDATE)
```

After you enter the expression, move it to the Selected Output list.

NOTE Whenever you see a field name, it has been preceded by its table name. This feature is to prevent FoxPro (or you) from getting confused if more than one table has the same field name. If you are referencing a field name unique to a particular table, you need not specify the table name. In this example, the MONTH(IDATE) expression is valid. You can save some typing this way, but including the table name is a good habit to get into.

Now, rearrange the Selected Output list so that the fields are in the following order:

> CUSTOMER.COMPANY
>
> MONTH(INVOICES.IDATE)
>
> INVOICES.ITOTAL

Now there are three fields again, so the Cross Tabulate check box is enabled. Check it now and then select « OK » to exit from this dialog.

The first thing you may notice when returning to the RQBE screen is that the Order By and Group By check boxes have been checked and disabled. To do crosstabs, the table must be ordered by the ROW, then COLUMN, and must be grouped on them. RQBE does this automatically, which is why the controls are disabled.

Now, Do the Query, and your screen should look like the one in figure 6.18.

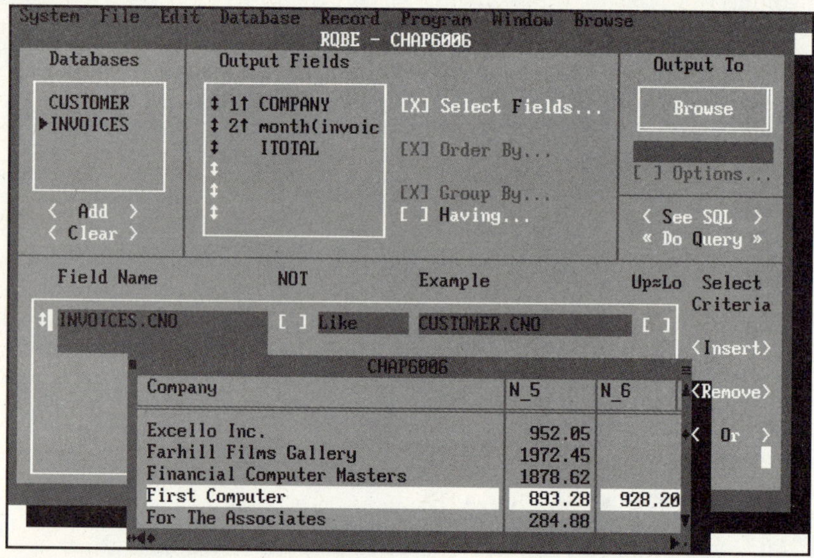

FIG. 6.18

FoxPro becomes a spreadsheet with crosstabs.

The column headings are N_5, and N_6. The N indicates a numeric field, and the number is its value. In this case, the column headings represent May and June. If you scroll down the Browse, you see some data in the June (N_6) column. If there had been data from other months, columns would have been included for them also.

Save this query as CHAP6006.QPR, in the Model directory.

Using User-Defined Functions with RQBE

A *user-defined function* is a FoxPro procedure that returns a value of any data type. Although UDFs are not built into the language, they can be used in almost any place that built-in FoxPro functions can be used. You learn more about UDFs as you continue in this book. For now, however, just know that UDFs, like other FoxPro functions, can be entered into queries, from the Functions/Expressions text box of the Select Fields dialog, and that you should be cautious about using them with queries.

From within a UDF, you can use any FoxPro command. Among other features, you can open tables, close tables, change record pointers, and change the data in fields. However, doing anything of this sort in a UDF called from a Query, or an SQL-SELECT statement, can cause disastrous results. Because FoxPro determines the best way to perform a query when it is executed, no way exists to determine how doing such things will affect the outcome of a query.

You can write a UDF that changes the currently selected work area. Although this query can work perfectly forever, it also can give completely incorrect results at any time. FoxPro keeps detailed information about your data, and based on this information determines the best way to perform the query, every time you do it. If you add, remove, or change the data in any of the tables, FoxPro can change how it builds and optimizes the query. This feature could cause a query that had worked in the past to give incorrect results, because of an errant UDF.

CAUTION: The only thing you can assume about the FoxPro environment and how it is altered by queries, whether for the purpose of adding a UDF or for any other reason, is that you can assume nothing.

When you begin to write your own UDFs, especially when you're designing a report or a screen, you can manipulate your FoxPro environment with impunity from within functions that you write. Just remember that, because the internal optimizer used by FoxPro to process the query operates with relative autonomy, you do not have the same freedom in a query.

Doing a Query from within a Program

After you have saved a query, you can Do it from within a program by entering the following syntax:

DO *QUERYNAME*.QPR

QUERYNAME is the name you assigned to your query. In other words, you could, from within a program, enter the following command:

DO CHAP6002.QPR

To make this an even more useful feature, you can use *variables* in a query. For example, you can add a filter to a query, such as in the following command:

```
CUSTOMER.STATE    Like     StateVar
```

Then, in a program, you can produce something like the following:

```
StateVar = "NC"
DO StateQry.QPR
```

With this command, the query would look only at customers in North Carolina.

You must have the variable *StateVar* created when you put the filter in the query, or RQBE will think you are looking for a state called *StateVar*.

As discussed in the last section, queries can change your environment. You should therefore *save* your environment before you execute a query, and *restore* your environment afterward. You learn more about these features in Chapter 16, "Understanding Program Structure."

Using the RQBE Wisely

You have seen a sampling of what the RQBE can do to select, group, subtotal, and order information. Following are a few suggestions to help you get the most out of the RQBE and some warnings to help keep you out of trouble.

Create Query Skeletons

You can save much time by creating query skeletons. A query skeleton is a query that can be used repeatedly, with only minor changes. For example, you may have a query with a filter that restricts the output to customers in a particular state. This query can be brought up at any time; the state changed; and the query reexecuted. Other filters can be added or removed. You can add expressions and fields to the output and use Save As to save your modified query, which leaves the skeleton intact for further use.

Use Variable Names in Filters

You can put variable names in query filters, which can be useful for queries called from within a FoxPro program. You can take the example query, CHAP6002.QPR, where you listed states with year-to-date sales of $50,000 or more, and make it more general. You can replace the Having filter of 50000 with a variable name. You can then have your program prompt the user for the preferred dollar limit of record, store the answer into the variable the query is using, and Do the query.

Use Queries To See the Forest AND the Trees

When you use a query to gather and summarize information from your tables, the output is usually summary information. What is missing at the end of these summary lines is a TOTAL line. If you send the output of a query to a report, then you can add totals and other calculations from Report Writer. The Report Writer is discussed in detail in Chapters 9 and 10.

See Double with Multiple Queries

FoxPro enables you to have multiple RQBE windows open at the same time. Sometimes it's useful to compare the results from different queries.

If you send your query to a Browse window, and try to select an item outside the Browse window, then the Browse window will be closed. It can be reopened from the View window, or the Command window (with the command BROWSE). You can open your first query, Do it, and then close the Browse window—and reopen it immediately. Then open a second RQBE file, Do it, and see the two results on the same screen.

If your hardware supports one of the extended screen modes, then using it can be helpful. Check the on-line help for the command SET DISPLAY and see whether any of the allowable modes work for you.

Keep Your Records in Order

You may notice that grouping a table automatically structures the table in ascending order of the grouped fields. On rare occasions, this grouping will not be true, often depending on how FoxPro optimized the query. If you want to be sure that your output is ordered, then you must use the Order By dialog.

Get Your Queries Out Fast

You can do a few things to help make sure that your queries run quickly. The single most effective measure you can take is to have the indexes necessary for *Rushmore optimization* present when you Do the Query. Rushmore optimization requires that the comparisons used in filter conditions have exact counterparts in index expressions. You already learned to create indexes in Chapters 3 and 4; in Chapter 7, you learn to be certain that Rushmore can use them.

If you have a slow query that uses UDFs, you might try to redesign the query to work without the UDFs. Many times UDFs do not noticeably affect the performance of a query. However, at times they slow down a query greatly.

Leave RQBE's Tables Open

Never close a table used in a query, while the RQBE is open. Doing so can cause you to lose your query.

Clean Up after Yourself

If you output to a Cursor (discussed in the next chapter), then you don't have to worry about cleaning up after yourself. Although a Cursor acts like a read only table (in reality it is much different), when a cursor is closed, it is removed from the disk. It won't sit around taking up valuable space.

If you choose to output to Browse, a Report/Label, or a Graph, the RQBE actually sends the output to a Cursor, then Browses, Reports on, or Graphs the cursor. If you send your output to Report/Label but have it display to the screen, then the output is not saved, so you don't have to worry about it.

If you output to a Table/DBF, then that is another story. The table created by the query stays on your hard disk until it is either overwritten, or deleted. If you don't want it sitting around, you may have to delete it yourself.

Clean Up after the RQBE

After working in the RQBE and doing several queries, take a look at the View window. You see that the RQBE leaves some files behind, as shown in figure 6.19. These files are usually Cursors, but they look and act like regular tables. When you do an *untitled* query, the Cursor name is usually query; otherwise it is usually the name of your query. If you do many different queries without closing these files, FoxPro may run out of work areas, because only 25 are available. Closing Cursors removes them from the hard disk, making them easy to clean up.

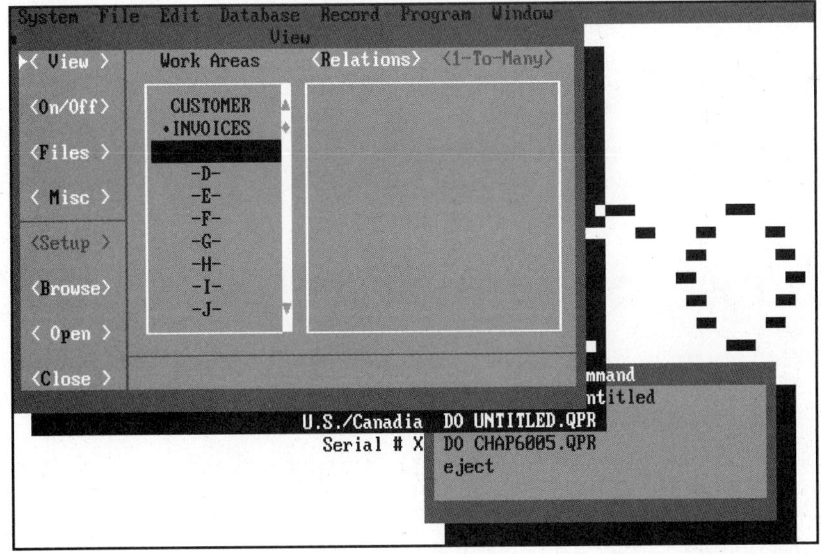

FIG. 6.19

Left over files from RQBE.

Query One Step at a Time

Often complex queries can be easier to design as multiple simple queries. This procedure can be easily done if the first query outputs to a Table/DBF. Unlike a Cursor, Tables are permanent, and can be used by subsequent queries. Of course, if you do this, remember to delete the temporary tables when you're done, so you don't clutter up your disk.

Keep Expressions Consistent

When using expressions and UDFs that return character data for output fields in a query, make sure that they always return values of the same length. For example, if you want to produce the name of a month, you use the following expression:

```
CMONTH(SomeDate)
```

This function returns months such as `January`, `February`, and `March`. This function returns between three characters (May), and nine characters (September). Depending on how your data is organized and how FoxPro optimizes the query, you may get only three or four characters for this field in your output. If four characters are assigned to the field, for example, then the user sees months such as Octo, Janu, and Febr. In this case, you can use the PADR() function, which PADS spaces to the right of an expression. The syntax is as follows:

PADR(CMONTH(*SomeDate*), 9)

This syntax tells FoxPro to pad the cmonth expression to nine characters by placing spaces on the right.

Chapter Summary

In this chapter, you joined several tables together and got results from them based on information from each of them at the record level and at the summary level.

In Chapter 7, you discuss the SQL SELECT command, the single FoxPro command that the RQBE uses to do the queries you design. You also discuss the Rushmore technology and various performance optimization techniques, especially for queries.

7

CHAPTER

Querying with SQL and Searching with Rushmore

In Chapters 5 and 6, you work with FoxPro's Relational Query By Example, which is an interface between you and the SQL command, SELECT. SQL, or *Structured Query Language*, is a concise and powerful language developed to maintain databases. The SELECT command is the main tool SQL uses for database queries. In this chapter, you learn more about the SELECT command, how this command's components relate to the RQBE, and how to use SELECT to exceed the RQBE's capabilities. A special subset of the SELECT command is included in FoxPro 2 and is one of FoxPro's most versatile new features.

You also look at FoxPro's *Rushmore* technology, which can accelerate database and table searches. Rushmore, which you can use in many native FoxPro commands to boost performance, is the key to the lightning speed of FoxPro 2's implementation of the SQL command.

Asking Questions with SQL

When you use the RQBE to create a query, you are indirectly using SQL, or at least the version of SQL's SELECT command, which is built into FoxPro 2. SELECT is an important part of FoxPro's capability of handling fast and flexible database searches. You expand the SQL SELECT options when you issue the command directly instead of building a query through the RQBE. In this section, you examine the clauses available with SQL SELECT that contribute to this command's flexibility. Following is the full syntax of the SQL SELECT command:

```
SELECT [ALL | DISTINCT]
   [<alias>.]<select_item> [AS <column name>]
   [,[<alias>.]<select_item> [AS <column name>]... ]
FROM <table>[<local_alias>] [, <table>[<local_alias>]...]
[[INTO <destination>]
   |[TO FILE <file>[ADDITIVE] | TO PRINTER]]
[NOCONSOLE]
[PLAIN]
[NOWAIT]
[WHERE <join_condition>[AND <join_condition>...]
   [AND | OR <filter_condition>[AND | OR
   <filter_condition>...]]]
[GROUP BY <group_column>[, <group_column>...]]
[HAVING <filter_condition>]
[UNION [ALL] <SELECT command>]
[ORDER BY <order_item> [ASC | DESC]
   [,<order_item> [ASC | DESC]...]]
```

Table 7.1 gives you a summary of the use for each clause of the command.

Table 7.1 Summary of SQL SELECT Clauses

Clause	Use
ALL |	Include duplicate rows or records
DISTINCT	Eliminate duplicate rows or records
[<*alias*>.]<*item*>[AS <*column_name*>]	Specify output columns (usually a field list) in a list separated by commas and for each one, optionally specify the name the column is given
FROM<*table*> [*local_alias*]...	Specify the source tables in a list separated by commas, and for each one, optionally specify a local name that refers to the table in the rest of the SELECT command

Clause	Use
INTO ARRAY | INTO CURSOR | INTO DBF/TABLE | TO FILE<*name*> [ADDITIVE] | TO PRINTER	Specifies the destination of output. DBF and TABLE are used interchangeably.
NOCONSOLE	Prevents output from appearing on-screen
PLAIN	Omits column headings in output
NOWAIT	Omits pauses between screens of output
WHERE <*conditions*>	Specify join conditions (such as SET RELATION commands) and filters records to further specify which is used for output. Multiple WHERE conditions are separated by AND or OR.
GROUP BY <*column*>...	Specify columns of output, used to summarize or group the records, in a list separated by commas
HAVING <*condition*>	Specify filters to be used to eliminate some groups from the output
UNION [ALL] <*SELECT*>	Combine the results of one SELECT command with another. Eliminates duplicates by default; if duplicates are desired, include the optional ALL keyword.
ORDER BY <*item*>[ASC | DESC] ...	Sort the output based on information from one or more columns, which are specified in a list separated by commas. For each column indicated, the data in ASCending order is sorted by default, but DESCending order may be specified.

You now examine each component of the command separately and learn how to use each clause, beginning with the following clause:

```
SELECT [ALL | DISTINCT]
   [<alias>.]<select_item> [AS <column name>]
   [,[<alias>.]<select_item> [AS <column name>]... ]
```

SELECT commands begin by specifying OUTPUT fields and expressions, usually in a list. You don't always see a BROWSE as a result of the SQL SELECT statement, and a SELECT doesn't always produce a new table. But you can always think of the output specifications as the columns of the query results. The rows are the selected output records that meet the query conditions, as specified by other, filtering, clauses of the SELECT command.

Each [<*alias*>.]<*selected_item*> in the list can be a field name from one of the tables included in the query, optionally preceded by the file's alias name. If the same field name is used in more than one of the involved tables, then the alias must be specified. Placing the *DISTINCT* clause first tells SQL to eliminate duplicate rows from the output. *ALL*, which is the default, includes duplicates instead. You can use the optional *AS* clause to specify the column headings, which become the field names of the output in the case of a cursor or table. Be sure that the AS-specified column name is a valid field name or a variable or name expression that contains a valid field name.

You also can include constant values for output. When a column is added to the output, for example, all rows contain the same constant in the column. Some good uses for constant values are covered in a following section about the UNION clause.

You can use an asterisk (*) as shorthand to tell SQL SELECT to include all fields in the output list, rather than specifying a fields list. All fields from a particular table are included if you specify <*alias*>. *.

The output list also can include the following functions:

AVG(<*select_item*>)

COUNT(<*select_item*>)

MIN(<*select_item*>)

MAX(<*select_item*>)

SUM(<*select_item*>)

As in the RQBE, the values that will be output in columns using these functions are reset based on any data Group By you use in the query.

The next clause is as follows:

FROM <*table*>[<*local_alias*>] [,<*table*>[<*local_alias*>]...]

This clause tells SQL what tables to include. You can specify tables already open either by file name or alias name. If any tables you specify in the SQL list are not open, SQL must be able to find the tables in the current directory or on the FoxPro search path. You cannot specify a path to the tables by including the path in the SELECT command.

Whether you specify open or closed tables, and whether you specify tables by alias or name, you have the option to assign a special *local alias* for use in this SELECT command. A local alias doesn't change the way you refer to tables elsewhere. If you need to refer to a table several times in a long SELECT command, a local alias of two or three characters can be very convenient. If, however, you decide to use a local alias, make sure that you use the alias consistently every time you refer to the assigned table throughout the SELECT command.

The following clause tells SQL where to send the output:

[[INTO <*destination*>] | [TO FILE <*file*>[ADDITIVE] | TO PRINTER]]

The destination can be CURSOR <*cursor_name*>, ARRAY <*array_name*>, TABLE <*table_name*>, or DATABASE <*table_name*>.

Specifying CURSOR as the destination is usually quicker than outputting to a TABLE. *Cursors* are temporary tables removed from the disk when closed. The values in a CURSOR can be affected if the data in the source-tables is changed (which can be a significant consideration in multi-user situations), but they are not directly editable. (In Chapter 19, you learn about another SQL command, CREATE CURSOR, included as part of FoxPro's SQL implementation. Cursors created through this command, rather than through a SELECT, can be edited.)

You can send the output of a SQL SELECT to a FoxPro memory array by specifying ARRAY <*array_name*> as the destination. Remember the following points when you use an ARRAY as a destination:

- If the array exists before the SELECT is executed, then any information the array held before the SELECT is lost when the SELECT re-creates the array.
- If the array does not exist before the SELECT is executed, and no output is generated from the SELECT (such as when no records in the database match the filter conditions), then the array is not created. You can check the system memory variable _TALLY to see if the query produces any output. If no records are selected, this variable contains the value 0 immediately after the SELECT is executed.
- If the array previously existed and the SELECT produced no output, then the array was not deleted. Again, you must check _TALLY to determine whether the SELECT produces output.

The keywords TABLE and DATABASE are interchangeable and are used to store the results of a query to a table on the disk. If the table name already exists and if SAFETY is set ON, then FoxPro asks you to confirm that you want to overwrite the file before proceeding.

Using the TO FILE syntax creates a text file with the output of the query. With the ADDITIVE clause specified, the results are appended to the end of the text file, if the file already exists; if ADDITIVE isn't used, the existing file is overwritten. TO PRINTER sends the output to the printer.

If both TO and INTO are specified, the INTO is honored, and the TO is ignored. Usually, when you specify a TO destination—or no destination—the output of the SQL SELECT is echoed to the screen. Including the NOCONSOLE clause prevents the output of the SELECT from appearing on-screen.

Including the PLAIN clause prevents SELECT from showing the field headings on the output. This keyword and NOCONSOLE do not apply for queries output to a TABLE, CURSOR, or ARRAY destinations, but are meant for use when the TO clause is specified, or when no destination clause is specified.

Unless the NOWAIT clause is included when output is directed to the screen, you are prompted to press a key before data scrolls off-screen.

[WHERE *<join_condition>*[AND *<join_condition>*...]
[AND | OR *<filter_condition>*[AND | OR
<filter_condition>...]]]

The WHERE clause serves two purposes with SELECT. WHERE *joins* multiple tables together and specifies *filter conditions*.

You can have multiple join conditions and filters. You must connect these options with ANDs.

To create a join condition with WHERE, you use an expression of the form *fieldname_1 operator fieldname_2*. *Fieldname_1* and *fieldname_2* are the related field names of the tables being joined, and the operator is any of the following words or characters:

=
Like
<> or != or #
==
>
>=
<

String comparisons respect ANSI conventions when ANSI is SET ON, although with ANSI SET OFF these conventions work in the same way as all other FoxPro commands. (For an explanation of ANSI string comparisons, see the LIKE condition listing in table 5.2).

The LIKE comparison is new to FoxPro and is usable only with the SQL SELECT command. Almost the same as =, LIKE also can use the % and _ wildcards. (The % and _ characters are treated as normal text when a comparison uses other operators.)

When the SQL SELECT queries include comparisons of character strings with the LIKE operator, the characters _ and % serve as *wildcards*, similar to the characters ? and * in MS-DOS commands.

The _ (underline character) represents a single character, and the % (percent) represents any number of characters. The following expressions all evaluate to TRUE:

```
'Bobometer' Like 'Bobometer'

'Bobometer' Like '___omet__'

'Bobometer' Like 'Bob%'

'Bobometer' Like '__b%'
```

You can type a string of characters surrounded by two % characters (**%obo%**) to find the string no matter where the string is positioned in another string. Looking for a character string inside another string, field, or expression is known as a *substring search*. You can use the wildcard characters to perform substring searches in the LIKE conditions you create in the RQBE and in queries you write directly with SQL SELECT commands.

Filter conditions also are entered with the WHERE command. The following line shows the simplest form of filter conditions:

WHERE <*field1*> *operator* <*field2*> | <*expression1*>

Field1 and *field2* are database fields and *expression1* is any valid FoxPro expression, including user-defined functions (UDFs). (From the discussion of UDFs in Chapter 6, remember that you must use care when invoking UDFs in a SQL SELECT statement.) A filter condition may be similar to the following:

```
WHERE STATE = 'NY'
```

You can connect filter conditions with AND and OR, as in the following command:

```
WHERE STATE = 'NY' AND YTDPURCH >= 15000 OR YTDPURCH <=
20000
```

You can include the BETWEEN clause in a filter condition to specify a range by using the following syntax:

WHERE <*field*> BETWEEN <*low_value*> AND <*high_value*>

Using BETWEEN, the preceding filter condition changes to the following:

```
WHERE STATE = 'NY' AND YTDPURCH BETWEEN 15000 AND 20000
```

You can use the IN clause to search a list for a value, as in the following command:

```
WHERE PRODUCT.PRODNAME IN ("Dream Sequencers","Bobometers")
```

This clause finds all products named *Dream Sequencers* or *Bobometers*.

You can nest one SELECT statement inside another. The results of the *inner* SELECT query form a set which is then processed by the *outer* select. The clauses used with these kinds of nested SELECTs are *ALL*, *ANY / SOME*, *EXISTS*, and *IN*. These filter conditions are best explained with the following examples.

The following filter condition finds all customers whose year-to-date purchases are greater than the sales volume of any salesperson:

```
WHERE CUSTOMER.YTDPURCH > ALL ;
                 (SELECT YTDSALES FROM SALESMAN)
```

The following filter condition finds all customers whose year-to-date purchases are greater than the dollar amount of goods that any one salesperson sold during the year:

```
    WHERE CUSTOMER.YTDPURCH > ANY ;
                 (SELECT YTDSALES FROM SALESMAN)
```

EXISTS returns a true if any rows are returned by the sub-query; otherwise EXISTS returns a false. Therefore, the following filter condition finds all salespersons with a customer within the salesperson's ZIP code.

```
SELECT * ;
  FROM SALESMAN ;
  WHERE EXISTS ;
  (SELECT * FROM CUSTOMER ;
         WHERE CUSTOMER.ZIP = SALESMAN.ZIP)
```

You can use the IN clause to see whether a value is in a sub-query.

The following query finds all products which have a record in the budget table. You return to examine this query more closely in a following section of this chapter:

```
SELECT PRODUCT.PRODNAME ;
          FROM PRODUCT ;
          WHERE PRODUCT.PRODCODE IN ;
                 (SELECT BUDGET.PRODCODE FROM BUDGET)
```

You use the [GROUP BY <*group_column*>[, <*group_column*>...]] clause to specify groupings. The *group_column* variable can be any field name in the selected tables. The grouping fields do not have to be—but usually are—included in the output. You cannot GROUP BY an expression with the following syntax:

GROUP BY <*expression*>

If an expression is included in the output, however, you can group on the expression by specifying the column number. The following query groups by the expression being output as the third column, PADR(CMONTH(BUDGET.PERIOD), 9):

```
SELECT PRODUCT.PRODNAME, SUM(BUDGET.BUDGETAMT),
            PADR(CMONTH(BUDGET.PERIOD), 9) ;
         FROM BUDGET, PRODUCT ;
         WHERE BUDGET.PRODCODE = PRODUCT.PRODCODE ;
         GROUP BY 3, PRODUCT.PRODNAME ;
         ORDER BY BUDGET.PERIOD, PRODNAME
```

Similarly, although you cannot use an expression directly in the grouping, if you used the optional AS clause to give this column a new name, you can specify the column by name as well as number.

The [HAVING <*filter_condition*>] clause is used to specify filters on groupings. The *filter_condition* here usually is based on one of the groupings, as in the following example:

```
SELECT company, COUNT(*) ;
  FROM Customer ;
  GROUP BY company ;
  HAVING COUNT(*) > 1
```

This clause finds all company names that appear in more than one record.

The [UNION [ALL] <SELECT *command*>] clause links multiple SQL SELECT commands. Without the [ALL] clause, duplicate records from the two SELECT statements are discarded. You must use the following rules for UNION to work:

- SELECTs linked with UNION must have identical format for the output expressions of both statements.
- Only the last SELECT can have an ORDER BY clause.
- UNION cannot join nested SELECTs.

You return to a discussion of the UNION clause and the meaning of these restrictions in the following section, "Surpassing RQBE with Direct Use of SQL SELECT."

You use the [ORDER BY <*order_item*> [ASC | DESC][,<*order_item*> [ASC | DESC]...]] clause to tell SQL SELECT the order in which you want the output. The <*order_item*> variable can be a field name in one of the selected tables or the position number of one of the output fields, just as in the GROUP BY clause.

Going from Theory to Practice

Now you look at the SELECT statements produced by some of the RQBE examples to see how SQL SELECT really works.

You start with the query you saved as CHAP5003.QPR. Remember that, although generated by the RQBE, the QPR files are normal text files. You can open the file from the File Open dialog, either as a Program or as a File.

You also can use the commands MODIFY COMMAND CHAP5003.QPR or MODIFY FILE CHAP5003.QPR in the Command window. If you type **MODIFY QUERYCHAP5003** or use the File Open menu option to open the file as a Query, you find that FoxPro reads and then uses the text file to open the RQBE. Be careful if you edit QPR files directly as text files—if you want to use these files in the RQBE later—to maintain the files as valid queries and to use only clauses and features the RQBE can handle.

This query used the Budget and Product tables in the MODEL directory and produced the total amount budgeted for each product. The SQL SELECT that RQBE produces (as it appears in the `<See SQL>` of the RQBE—line numbers are added for reference, but otherwise is exactly as the RQBE creates it, including the uppercase letters) is shown in the following list:

1. SELECT PRODUCT.PRODNAME, SUM(BUDGET.BUDGETAMT) ;
2. FROM BUDGET, PRODUCT ;
3. WHERE PRODUCT.PRODCODE = BUDGET.PRODCODE ;
4. GROUP BY BUDGET.PRODCODE ;
5. INTO CURSOR QUERY
6. BROWSE NOMODIFY PREFERENCE QUERY

Except for the Browse command on line 6, this example is just one SQL SELECT statement. The semicolons that end each line tell FoxPro that more statement follows. Without semicolons, FoxPro tries to interpret each line as a separate command.

The first line tells FoxPro to perform a SQL query, outputting the PRODUCT.PRODNAME field and the SUM of the BUDGET.BUDGETAMT field. This information was the data entered in the Select Fields dialog of the RQBE.

The second line of the command tells SQL which tables to include. The tables do not need to be open to be used by SQL; if the tables are in the current directory or FoxPro's search path, SQL opens the tables. If the tables are open, SQL senses this condition.

Line 3 contains the Join Condition for the two tables, which is created with a WHERE clause, and tells SQL how the tables are related. This process corresponds to the information you entered into the Join Condition dialog of the RQBE.

Line 4 is the GROUP BY line, which was accessed via the Group By dialog of the RQBE. This query tells SQL to group by and produce subtotals of BUDGETAMT by the BUDGET.PRODCODE field. SQL produces 1 output record for each Grouping. For each output record, line 4 reports any accumulating calculations—here, the SUM(...) function. The GROUP BY line then restarts these calculations for the next group.

Line 5 tells SQL to send the output of this SELECT to a CURSOR named QUERY. Remember that a CURSOR is like a temporary file; when closed, all traces of the file are deleted from the disk. Because line 5 is the end of the SELECT statement, you see no semi-colon at the end of this line.

The last line—not part of the SQL SELECT—has nothing to do with the SQL language. This line is a regular FoxPro BROWSE command. The NOMODIFY clause makes the Browse Read-Only and is displayed onscreen by using the BROWSE preference named QUERY, if RESOURCE is set ON. (BROWSE is a FoxPro command with a rich variety of features and a clause list even more varied than the clause lists you are learning about here. In Chapter 8, you learn about BROWSE preferences and more about this powerful command. Chapter 15 discusses how you maintain and use the FoxPro Resource file.)

Look at the RQBE query you saved as CHAP5005.QPR, in which you used a wider selection of SQL options:

1. SELECT PRODUCT.PRODNAME, BUDGET.BUDGETAMT, ;
2. "Q" + STR(CEILING(MONTH(BUDGET.PERIOD)/3,1) + " " + STR(YEAR(BUDGET.PERIOD), 4)
3. FROM BUDGET, PRODUCT ;
4. WHERE PRODUCT.PRODCODE = BUDGET.PRODCODE ;
5. AND PRODUCT.PRODNAME NOT IN ("Dream Sequencers","Bobometers") ;
6. INTO CURSOR CHAP5005
7. CREATE REPORT CHAP5005.FRX FROM CHAP5005 WIDTH 80 COLUMN NOOVERWRITE
8. REPORT FORM CHAP5005.FRX TO PRINTER NOCONSOLE HEADING "Budgets by Product and Quarter"

This query gathers products and the budgeted amounts for all products—except Dream Sequencers and Bobometers—and sends the output to a FoxPro report. The query starts with the same clauses (output fields and expressions, tables to use) as the first example used. Line 2 holds the Quarter Expression entered in the Functions text box of the Select Output dialog of the RQBE. You can enter all valid FoxPro expressions, including UDFs, in the output list of a SQL query.

Line 4 contains the Join condition between the two tables in this query, and line 5 contains a filter condition. Notice that filter conditions and Join conditions are both entered in the same WHERE clause. If both sides of a WHERE expression are field names from the currently used tables, the WHERE expression is treated as a Join condition; otherwise, the WHERE is treated as a filter. Here, you are clearly looking for product records where PRODNAME is not Dream Sequencer or Bobometer.

Line 7 is a FoxPro command to create a quick report in column format. The NOOVERWRITE clause tells FoxPro to use a report named CHAP5005 (if this report already exists) rather than over-writing the file. This clause enables you to modify the report from the Report Writer without worrying about losing the changes when the query is rerun.

The last line is a standard FoxPro command that executes the report.

Surpassing RQBE with Direct Use of SQL SELECT

The SQL SELECT command has several capabilities that you cannot tap from the RQBE. The following list shows some of the commands:

- The capability of ordering the output by fields not selected for output
- The use of a nested SELECT
- The capability of specifying output field names
- SQL Unions

Suppose that you want to list the products and the products' total budgeted amounts for each month, ordered by month. The following SELECT command shows the procedure:

```
SELECT PRODUCT.PRODNAME, SUM(BUDGET.BUDGETAMT),
       PADR(CMONTH(BUDGET.PERIOD), 9) ;
    FROM BUDGET, PRODUCT ;
```

```
WHERE BUDGET.PRODCODE = PRODUCT.PRODCODE ;
GROUP BY 3, PRODUCT.PRODNAME ;
ORDER BY BUDGET.PERIOD, PRODNAME
```

Note that the first ORDER BY field, BUDGET.PERIOD, does *not* directly appear in the output list. Using a direct ORDER BY here is not possible with the RQBE; with the RQBE, you are forced to order by PADR(CMONTH(BUDGET.PERIOD, 9), which orders the months alphabetically instead of by calendar order.

In another query, you also may prefer to show calendar quarters based on the BUDGET.PERIOD field and yet have the individual entries in strict date order. Here, entries for 01/01/91 and 03/30/91 show the same output (the quarter expression); however, you must order the entries directly, by the BUDGET.PERIOD field.

Examine, for similar reasons, the GROUP BY line:

```
GROUP BY 3, PRODUCT.PRODNAME
```

The first item you are grouping by is 3, which tells SQL to group by the third output field. Foxpro 2.0's SQL SELECT does not enable you to directly GROUP BY expressions, although you can use GROUP BY in this way by referring to the expression by column position. If the line is GROUP BY PADR(CMONTH(BUDGET.PERIOD), 9) the query produces an error message and is not executed.

The *PADR(...)* function (which adds characters to an output expression until the expression reaches the length you specify) was placed around the CMONTH function to make sure that the output has enough columns for the longest month names.

If you try this SELECT statement, you may notice that the column headings are not entirely helpful. These heading names are PRODNAME, SUM_BUDGET, and EXP_3. Although the first two names are not pretty, they are at least understandable. EXP_3, however, has no real meaning. Fortunately, you can use the AS clause to customize column headings. Change the output fields portion of the SELECT statement to the following:

```
SELECT PRODUCT.PRODNAME AS 'PRODUCT',
SUM(BUDGET.BUDGETAMT) ;
AS 'BUDGETED', PADR(CMONTH(BUDGET.PERIOD), 9) AS 'MONTH' ;
```

The output headings are now changed to PRODUCT, BUDGETED, and MONTH. Because you can direct a SELECT to a CURSOR or a TABLE, the field name specified with the AS clause must comply with the field name rules for tables—the field name cannot contain spaces or other characters not allowed in field names, must begin with an alphabetic character, and cannot exceed 10 characters in length.

Although Foxpro 2 only allows one nested SELECT, in all but the most complicated situations, one nested SELECT is sufficient. To get a list of all the products which are not in the Budget file, you can use a nested SELECT statement to do the job:

```
SELECT PRODUCT.PRODNAME ;
       FROM PRODUCT ;
WHERE PRODUCT.PRODCODE NOT IN ;
       (SELECT BUDGET.PRODCODE FROM BUDGET)
```

Although at first cryptic looking, you can read this expression as "List all products in the product file where the product is not in the Budget file." The inner (nested) SELECT, (SELECT BUDGET.PRODCODE FROM BUDGET) builds a list of all the prodcodes found in the Budget table. Then the first SELECT searches the Product table for records whose prodcode is NOT IN the list the second SELECT created.

Removing the word NOT produces a list of all products for which Budget records *exist.*

FoxPro's SQL also enables you to link multiple SQL SELECT statements with the UNION clause. UNION works only if the output from all linked SELECT statements is in exactly the same format.

If you have both a Customer and an Employee table and want to print mailing labels for all records in both tables, you can use the following SELECT:

```
SELECT CUSTOMER.NAME, CUSTOMER.ADDRESS, CUSTOMER.CITY, ;
        CUSTOMER.STATE, CUSTOMER.ZIP, CUSTOMER.COUNTRY ;
FROM CUSTOMER ;
UNION ;
        SELECT EMPLOYEE.NAME, EMPLOYEE.ADDRESS, EMPLOYEE.CITY, ;
               EMPLOYEE.STATE, EMPLOYEE.ZIP, EMPLOYEE.COUNTRY ;
        FROM EMPLOYEE ;
INTO CURSOR MAILLIST
```

This statement produces a CURSOR with the names and addresses of all customers and employees. If duplicates exist, the duplicates are eliminated. You then can print the labels with the FoxPro label generator.

Remember that this procedure works only if the field types and lengths for the fields specified as output are the same in both tables. Occasionally, a field from one table isn't available in the other table, (such as EMPLOYEE tables, which don't have a COUNTRY field—too much of a commute if you are based in Toledo!), you still can use the union by replacing the expression EMPLOYEE.COUNTRY with a literal expression that contains the same number of spaces as the country field in the customer table. If the field CUSTOMER.COUNTRY is 10 characters long, then revise the second SELECT to look like the following lines:

```
SELECT EMPLOYEE.NAME, EMPLOYEE.ADDRESS, EMPLOYEE.CITY, ;
        EMPLOYEE.STATE, EMPLOYEE.ZIP, "          " ;
```

You can replace numeric fields with numbers. If the numeric field being matched has more than one position to the left of the decimal point, you must use numbers, such as *100*, *1000*, and *10000.00* to achieve the appropriate width. This replacement can cause confusing output and must be used carefully. Logical fields can be simulated with *.F.* and date fields with *{}*.

The preceding situation is common in mailing applications and addresses the problem of needing to "merge/purge" two parallel lists of duplicate entries. If, however, you do not want the duplicates eliminated, you can use UNION ALL.

No limit exists to the number of UNIONs you can place in one SELECT statement.

When two tables are joined, records in either table that have no corresponding record in the other table are ignored. *Outer Joins* is a method available in some other SQL dialects that permits you to include these records. Although not directly available in FoxPro's SQL SELECT, Outer Joins can be simulated in FoxPro by using the UNION clause, as shown by the following query:

```
SELECT PRODUCT.PRODNAME, BUDGET.BUDGETAMT ;
     FROM BUDGET, PRODUCT ;
     WHERE PRODUCT.PRODCODE = BUDGET.PRODCODE
```

This query doesn't output a record for the product *Unscented Weazlettes*, which appears in the Product table but not the Budget table. To make sure that all products are listed—even if no Budget records are prepared for these products—you can simulate an outer join with a UNION clause by using a second SELECT, shown in the following listing:

```
SELECT PRODUCT.PRODNAME, BUDGET.BUDGETAMT ;
     FROM BUDGET, PRODUCT ;
     WHERE PRODUCT.PRODCODE = BUDGET.PRODCODE ;
UNION
     SELECT PRODUCT.PRODNAME, 10000000 ;
     FROM PRODUCT ;
     WHERE PRODUCT.PRODCODE NOT IN ;
       (SELECT BUDGET.PRODCODE FROM BUDGET)
```

The original specification was added to another one by the UNION. In the second SELECT, all products *not listed* in the Budget table are specified. Three drawbacks exist with this method:

1. The method is complicated to write and conceptualize, which increases the chance of making mistakes and achieving results that may not be what you want.

2. The method is not executed quickly (although quicker than the task is otherwise accomplished).

3. All products not in the budget table appear to have a budget amount of $1,000,000. The reason the 1000000 was entered in the output scope for the second select was to force the output fields to exactly match the output fields of the first SELECT. This step is required by the UNION clause.

Any number that matches the number of digits and decimal places matching the BUDGET.BUDGETAMT can be used; perhaps 9999999 is a better choice to point out items as non-budgeted. (You can use a character string, a logical .T. or .F., or a dummy date as a placeholder where necessary to simulate output fields of other types.) The Report Writer provides the flexibility to check for these non-budgeted records. You can specify all records that show a 999999 BUDGETAMT, that also show the budgeted amount as 0, and that are flagged as non-budgeted items. You learn how to perform this procedure in Chapter 10.

Going Places with the Results

The SQL SELECT statement can send the output to the screen, the printer, a CURSOR, a TABLE, a TEXT FILE, or an ARRAY. Usually, you send the output of the SELECTs to a CURSOR or an ARRAY. CURSORs are useful because they can be used to report on, display, graph, browse, create cross tabs, print labels—anything that you can do with a regular table—and then can be disposed of when you are finished. Because the cursor contains a preselected set of fields and records, possibly joined from several related tables and formatted exactly the way you need for a single use, getting the output to look exactly the way you want is often more convenient if you first create the cursor, rather than try to output directly from the table or tables.

Sending SELECTs to an array is generally done in programs. You learn more about the use of arrays later in this book. All arrays created through a SQL SELECT command have the proper number of rows and columns to hold the query's output (unless no records are SELECTed by the query, as explained in the description of ARRAY as a query destination, in the section "Asking Questions with SQL").

Unlike reports, labels cannot be created by the RQBE because FoxPro has no Quick Label feature to generate a generic label format. However, you can send the output of a SQL SELECT to pre-existing label forms (you learn how to create these forms in Chapters 9 and 10). Just put the command LABEL FORM *<labelname>* after a SELECT statement whose output was sent to a CURSOR or TABLE. Immediate after the SELECT is executed, this CURSOR or TABLE becomes the current work area, and the labels are processed on this basis.

You also can send SELECT output to labels from the RQBE (using the Report/Label Options dialog). The RQBE does not run the query unless you specify an existing label form name.

CAUTION: When you use the RQBE or issue a SELECT directly to send output from a table to a report or a label form, remember that the SELECT statement sends results to a cursor first and then issues a REPORT FORM or LABEL FORM statement. If you specify a pre-existing report or label for the output, then you probably created the report or label by using the original table as a model. If the report or label form includes the alias of this table in the references to fields, then the output is incorrect when you try to use the report or label with the cursor, even though the field names are the same.

After the SELECT statement, the original table is opened in another work area and information from the current record in the original table is repeated for each record in the cursor, while the report or record moves the pointer through the cursor to generate output.

You can easily fix this problem by removing the alias from the field expressions in the report or label. Because you cannot know in advance the alias that may be used for a cursor created by the SELECT statement, make sure that all reports and labels designed to work with queries do not include aliases.

Rarely, you may create a report or label that uses a cursor in a work area other than the current area. Because here, you need to reference the fields with an alias, check the cursor's ALIAS() before you issue the REPORT or LABEL FORM command and store the alias to the variable. Use this variable as part of the field reference.

In Chapter 6, you create a *crosstab* report by using an option in the RQBE. You can create a crosstab, however, by using all the complex SQL SELECT options not allowed directly by the RQBE and by calling the GENXTAB.APP program after the SQL SELECT produces an appropriate table or cursor. Crosstab is just a FoxPro application like any other.

The table or cursor must have at least three fields. By default, the first field is used for Rows; the second field is used for Columns; the third field is used for the data for the intersecting Cells. The table must be ordered by the field to be used for the ROW. You also can change some of GENXTAB's default behavior by calling the command with some *parameters* to take more control of GENXTAB behavior than the RQBE allows.

The following list shows the complete syntax needed to call GENXTAB:

```
DO GENXTAB WITH     <out file name>, ;
                    [<cursor only>], ;
                    [<close input>], ;
                    [<show thermometer>], ;
                    [<row field>], ;
                    [<col field>], ;
                    [<cell field>], ;
                    [<xfoot>]
```

GENXTAB follows the rules of parameter passing used by all FoxPro programs, which you learn about in Chapters 16 and 17. The important information to remember here is that, to use the *last* parameter (*<xfoot>* in this case), you also must pass all prior parameters, specifying behavior otherwise used by default if parameters are omitted. To specify cross-foots, and use default behavior otherwise, use the following syntax:

DO GENXTAB WITH '*filename*',.T.,.F.,.T.,1,2,3,.T.

<out file name >, the first parameter, is the name of the file or cursor that you want GENXTAB to create. The default for this parameter is XTAB.DBF.

<cursor only> is a LOGICAL parameter. If the parameter is .F. or not specified, then the output becomes the same type as the input. If the input is a CURSOR, then the output is a CURSOR. If the input is a TABLE, then the output is a TABLE. Typing **.T.** here forces the output to be a CURSOR.

<close input> is a LOGICAL parameter. If the parameter is .T., the input table/cursor is closed when GENXTAB is finished.

<show thermometer> If the parameter is .T., a thermometer appears onscreen to show GENXTAB's progress. This result is the default behavior; set this parameter to .F. to turn off the thermometer.

<row field> is the field number in the input table/cursor that corresponds to the ROW. The row should be the first field in the input to GENXTAB, and the value of this field number should be 1. This result is the default.

<col field> represents the field number in the input of the COLUMN. The column is usually the second field in GENXTAB's input. The default value of this parameter is 2.

<cell field> is the field number of the data cell in the input to GENXTAB. This field is usually the third (and final) field. The default for this parameter is 3.

<xfoot> is a LOGICAL parameter, which defaults to .F. If you specify .F., then GENXTAB creates a column at the end of the crosstab table with a cross-foot total of each row. To specify cross-foots, and use default behavior otherwise, use the following syntax:

DO GENXTAB WITH '*filename*',.T.,.F.,.T.,1,2,3,.T.

The use of the row, column, and cell field designators (the fifth, sixth, and seventh parameters) is another FoxPro feature that may be limited by the build date of the version of the product. In previous release versions, the capability of specifying and ordering the fields—by using these parameters—appears planned but not completely implemented.

Unless you are sure that the build of GENXTAB uses the fifth, sixth, and seventh parameters correctly, call this procedure only for a table or cursor of three fields in the proper default order.

If you have a copy of *Foxgraph*, a graphing program available separately from Fox Software, you can send the output of the query to a GRAPH. At the end of the query, add a line that uses the following syntax:

DO F:\FOXPRO2\GENGRAPH WITH *<sub title>*, *<column title>*

You can send a SUBTITLE and Column Title to GENGRAPH as the first two parameters. By default, the program has no SUBTITLEs or COLUMN titles (these parameters are optional).

You can use Foxgraph to produce two- and three-dimensional graphs from data in xBase table format (Foxgraph is not just for use with GENGRAPH or SQL SELECTs, although GENGRAPH was written specifically to work with Foxgraph). You then can view these graphs onscreen or send the output to a printer or plotter.

Enhancing the Performance of SQL SELECTs

You noted some general do's and don'ts for wise RQBE use as you concluded the previous chapter. Similarly, keep in mind some principles as you continue to expand your understanding of—and explore new ways to use—SQL SELECT's potential. Do not consider the following principals as absolute constraints on the use of this powerful command; just use them to guide the course of your investigation.

Create Indexes SELECT Can Use

SQL SELECT statements, for the most part, are fast. More complex queries execute faster with SQL than are done with regular FoxPro code. The most significant step you can take to wring the best performance from SQL is to make sure that the appropriate indexes are available.

Usually, if you are joining multiple tables together, having indexes or index tags on the joining fields helps. Having indexes or index tags that correspond to fields used in filter conditions also helps considerably. Occasionally, SQL determines that building indexes on the fly and on its own is faster than processing a query without indexes. Even so, if the index is available, then the time taken to create the index is saved.

Structural indexes are particularly useful if you allow SQL to open the tables. If the indexes to a table are not structural and SQL opens the tables, SQL doesn't *see* the indexes and therefore doesn't *realize* the indexes are available.

Avoid Nested SELECTs When Possible

You can construct many queries in more than one way. If you have a query with a nested SELECT that also can be processed without a nested SELECT, then the latter method almost always executes faster. Practice with SQL SELECT syntax to look for similar alternatives.

Include UDFs Only When Necessary

You can include UDFs in the selected output list of a SELECT and in filter conditions specified in the WHERE clause. You also can GROUP By the conditions if you use the GROUP BY <*position*> syntax and use the UDF for output. This FoxPro SQL SELECT feature is powerful but tends to considerably slow down processing. A query done without a UDF almost always executes more efficiently than a query done with a UDF.

Monitor HAVING and WHERE Clauses

When you have no GROUP BY, you can use either HAVING or WHERE to get the same results, but a difference exists in speed of execution. On rare occasions, specifying filter conditions in the HAVING clause instead of the WHERE clause results in a faster query. However, this occurrence is rare and likely to change in future versions of FoxPro as the internal methods by which FoxPro optimizes the SQL processing are continuously improved. Use the WHERE clause by preference unless you are specifying filter conditions on a Grouping.

Optimize Indexes and Orders

You can more quickly complete SQL SELECTs that must be in a certain order by not specifying the ORDER BY in the SELECT command and INDEXing the result of the SELECT. Although you see the results of the query more quickly, processing the table is slower because the table no longer processes in the natural order. You discover the best way to handle a particular situation only by experimentation.

Searching with Rushmore

During the development of FoxPro's new and patentable data retrieval mechanism, Fox Software used the code name *Rushmore*, originally a tongue-in-cheek reference to the Alfred Hitchcock movie, *North by Northwest*. The name persists in FoxPro 2's official vocabulary, however, because the name is both appropriate and memorable.

Rushmore searches for sets of data by making intelligent use of all available indexes, including all FoxPro index types: standard IDX files, compact IDX files, and compound CDX files.

Prior to FoxPro 2.0, the SET FILTER, the LOCATE FOR/CONTINUE, COUNT FOR, SUM FOR, and similar commands were far too slow to use on large tables. These commands individually examined all the records in a table and consequently, indexes were of no help. With Rushmore, however, these commands become *very* useful with tables of any size—even tables with millions of records.

The first example uses the same CUSTOMER.DBF table you used in Chapter 6 (in the TUTORIAL directory, not the MODEL\CUSTOMER table). You see how Rushmore can help find all the customers in New York, with year-to-date purchases of $15,000 or more.

Using the sample tables, FoxPro 2 is already too fast to demonstrate the difference Rushmore can make. If you have spare disk space and want to see Rushmore in action (as opposed to just believing what you read), then you must create a larger table—which you can do in a few easy steps—and you learn a few new FoxPro commands along the way.

First, open the table \TUTORIAL\CUSTOMER, which you find under the main FoxPro 2 program directory. Make sure that the default directory remains the MODEL directory so that the example files are saved there. If you're not sure, type the following command in the Command window:

```
WAIT WINDOW SET("DEFAULT")+SYS(2003)
```

If the drive and directory for the MODEL files don't appear, substitute them and type the following command in the Command window:

```
SET DEFAULT TO C:\FOXPRO2\MODEL
```

Now use the Database menu popup Copy option or type the following instructions in the Command window to create a new file:

```
COPY TO Bigcust FIELDS COMPANY, STATE, YTDPURCH
```

You are copying the COMPANY, STATE, and YTDPURCH fields from the currently selected table (the TUTORIAL Customer table) to a new table, Bigcust.dbf in the MODEL directory. (Copy selected fields only to save disk space and to simplify the examples.)

Next, close the Customer table and open the Bigcust table you just created by using the View window. You can do the same thing by typing the following line in the Command window:

```
USE bigcust
```

Notice that the USE command closed the Customer table because the table was in the current work area. The Bigcust table holds 500 records, just like the Customer table. You can enlarge the table by appending more copies of the table to itself. Use the Append option on the Database menu popup or enter the following command in the Command window:

```
APPEND FROM bigcust
```

If you have the View window open, you see that the Bigcust table now has 1,000 records. You can enter the APPEND FROM Bigcust command as many times as you like—if you have enough disk space—and FoxPro continues to double the number of records each time you APPEND.

(In the Command window, just move the cursor to the line you typed and press Enter as many times as you want to repeat the command.)

The larger you make the table, the more noticeable is Rushmore's effect. Entering the command four times results in an 8,000 record Bigcust.dbf; if you have a fast computer, you may have to make the table this large, or even larger, to appreciate Rushmore.

If you are familiar with xBase, you may be surprised to learn that you can APPEND records from a table into itself. Because FoxPro 2 now can APPEND records FROM a table open in another work area, and because FoxPro also can open several instances of one table in different work areas (with the USE AGAIN command), this capability is not too surprising. APPENDing from a table into itself is a handy way to create large tables for other tests.

To create a Browse of all the customers whose year-to-date purchases are $15,000 or more, type the following command in the Command window:

```
BROWSE FOR ytdpurch >= 15000
```

After a few seconds, a FoxPro Browse screen appears with all the requested customers listed. (If the screen's appearance is nearly instantaneous on your computer, you may want to issue another APPEND FROM Bigcust command to increase the table size.)

This wait isn't too bothersome, but now limit the Browse to the customers from New York with $15,000 or more in purchases. To do this, type the following command:

```
BROWSE FOR state = 'NY' AND ytdpurch >= 15000
```

Remember that here, as usual, FoxPro *understands* commands regardless of the mixture of upper- and lowercase letters you type. The character data you type, **NY**, however, is searched with case sensitivity; be sure that you type the character data in uppercase.

This time, you probably waited a while before Rushmore completed the cycle. See the difference Rushmore makes if you make sure that indexes are available for use.

Add a structural index with two tags, a tag on the STATE field, and another tag on the YTDPURCH field. If you add these tags from the View window's Setup/Index Add dialog, the tags by default use the same name as the fields on which they are based. You also see the equivalent command echoed in the Command window. You can assign any other tag names; Rushmore finds the needed data based on the contents of the key expression, not on the tag names.

If you created the indexes from the View window, set the Order off. From the Command window, issue the equivalent SET ORDER TO command. The significance of having the table in natural order is explained when you use Rushmore in a following section of this chapter. Try the last BROWSE command again.

This time, the Browse popped up much more quickly. This enhanced speed is Rushmore in action. If the table holds a million records, a similar search may take hours without the indexes, but with the indexes, the search probably doesn't take noticeably longer than with an 8,000- or 16,000-record file!

The time Rushmore takes to retrieve a set of records depends more on how many records meet the searching criteria than on how many records are in the table. If 25 customers in New York exceed purchases of $15,000 and you have a million records in the Customer table, Rushmore can find the 25 good New York customers in a few seconds. The more customers that match the search criteria, the less effective Rushmore becomes. If the search criteria matches all records in the table, then Rushmore becomes virtually useless except for the purposes of a COUNT FOR.

Consequently, the more specific you make the search definition, the more accurate and more prompt is the response. This situation is almost opposite of the rules you have to use for other search techniques, in which you trade off benefits of a narrowly targeted search with the speed penalty this kind of search entails.

Now that you see what Rushmore does, you need to step back to understand some of the details you need to know to use the feature properly. Remember that any command or series of commands that you execute here as interactive instructions to FoxPro also can be used to enhance programs that you write in FoxPro.

When can you use the help provided by this technology (usually referred to as Rushmore *optimization*)? Rushmore is available any time a FoxPro command is issued by using a FOR condition for which a matching index or tag is available. The commands to which this apply are listed in table 7.2. Think of a FOR condition, again, as a request to FoxPro to check *all* the records in a table against the requirements you specify, which help you understand why SET FILTER is included even though no explicit FOR is issued. Commands that can take a FILTER into account as they move through a table also can benefit from Rushmore—even if the commands have no explicit FOR clause.

Table 7.2 Commands That Benefit from RUSHMORE Optimization

AVERAGE	DISPLAY	REPORT
BROWSE	EDIT	SCAN
CALCULATE	EXPORT	SET FILTER TO
CHANGE	LABEL	[SQL-]SELECT
COPY TO	LIST	SORT
COPY TO ARRAY	LOCATE	SUM
COUNT	RECALL	TOTAL
DELETE	REPLACE	

Working with Optimizable Expressions

Suppose that you have index tags only on STATE and YTDPURCH, but you want to find the records where COMPANY = 'Micro'. Because Rushmore works with indexes, you expect (correctly) that Rushmore doesn't help in this search. At other times, however, you may expect Rushmore to have an effect, but the effect doesn't occur. In this section, you examine the conditions under which optimization takes place.

A FOR expression can be Fully Optimizable, Partially Optimizable, or Not Optimizable. All fully optimizable expressions are made up of one or more Basic Optimizable Expressions, which are usually found in this form:

Index-Like Expression *<joining operator>* Search Expression

In this expression, the Index-Like Expression component is a field name or a concatenation of field names, exactly matching an index key; Operator is a FoxPro operator; and the Search Expression is a string for which you are searching. Table 7.3 shows you the FoxPro operators that you can use in optimizable expressions.

Table 7.3 Rushmore-Optimizable Operators

Operator	Description
<	Less than
>	Greater than
=	Equal to
<=	Less than or equal to
>=	Greater than or equal to
<>	Not equal
#	Not equal (same as above)
!=	Not equal (same as above)

If you are familiar with the FoxPro operators, you may notice the absence of == (*Exactly Equals*), which is not optimizable in the present version of FoxPro 2. Several other FoxPro operators exist that cannot be optimized (notably, the *$* for finding the incidence of one character string as a part, or *substring*, of another string).

Creating Fully Optimizable Expressions

The BIGCUST table you created currently has two index keys, on the fields STATE and YTDPURCH. Therefore, the following expressions are fully optimizable:

```
STATE = 'NY'

'NY' = STATE

STATE <> 'NY'

'NY'  <> 'NY'

STATE = 'NY' OR STATE = 'CA'

STATE = 'NY' AND YTDPURCH > 15000

STATE = 'NY' AND NOT (YTDPURCH > 15000)

STATE = 'NY' AND (YTDPURCH > 15000 AND YTDPURCH < 16000)

(STATE='NY' OR STATE='CA') AND (YTDPURCH > 50 AND YTDPURCH < 60)
```

Notice that the more complicated expressions are built from simpler, basic optimizable expressions. The last expression on the list is constructed from four basic optimizable expressions:

```
STATE = 'NY'

STATE = 'CA'

YTDPURCH > 15000

YTDPURCH < 16000
```

You can continue adding basic optimizable expressions without compromising Rushmore's capability of quickly finding the matching records, at even greater length. Notice that parentheses are used to indicate the expressions which are evaluated first.

Recognizing Nonoptimizable Expressions

Some expressions are not optimizable by using the file and tags described:

The following expression is not optimizable because the COMPANY field has no index:

```
COMPANY = 'Micro'
```

The following expression is intended to find all companies whose names begin with 'Micro' in the state of New Jersey. You already know that Rushmore needs a tag on the COMPANY field to be useful for a search of this field. However, even this tag cannot help you in this search.

```
STATE + COMPANY = 'NJ' + 'Micro'
```

With EXACT left at the default setting of OFF, this expression finds all the appropriate records, but Rushmore isn't available to speed up the search. For Rushmore to work, the expression must *exactly match* an index key. You can create another tag on STATE + company, if you want, but this step is unnecessary. With a tag on each of the fields involved, the expression STATE = 'N' AND COMPANY = 'Micro' is used and optimized. These separate tags provide more flexibility for other searches. You also can perform, for example, an optimized search for a company alone or companies with a particular YTDPURCH amount, as in the following line:

The following expression is not optimizable for the same reason as the other expressions; YTDPURCH * 1.10 has no index. If an index did exist, then the search for this criterion can be optimized.

The following case is unusual. The expression is optimizable when EXACT is set ON but not when EXACT is set OFF. When EXACT is OFF, the expression is guaranteed to *never* find a match, but with EXACT ON, the statement matches any record where the STATE field is equal to "N ".

```
YTDPURCH * 1.10 > 15000
'N' = STATE
```

To understand this limitation, you must understand how FoxPro compares character expressions in different cases. In Chapter 5, table 5.2 shows you the difference between LIKE and EXACTLY LIKE in the RQBE, as used to make comparisons in a SQL SELECT statement, and how LIKE is affected by SET ANSI ON/OFF.

Other (non-SQL) FoxPro commands compare character strings by using slightly different rules, in which both the order of the strings examined and the command SET EXACT ON/OFF play a role.

When EXACT is set OFF, FoxPro compares character expressions left to right until a character that does not match is found or until the expression on the *right* ends. This situation means that when EXACT is OFF, the following list applies:

"NJ"	=	"NJ"	is true
"NJB"	=	"NJ"	is true
"N"	=	"NJ"	is false

And

"N "	=	"NJ"	is false
"N "	=	"N"	is false

When EXACT is set ON, FoxPro returns FALSE if both character expressions are of different lengths, but ignores trailing spaces, as shown in the following examples:

"NJ"	=	"NJ"	is true
"NJB"	=	"NJ"	is false
"N"	=	"NJ"	is false
"N "	=	"NJ"	is false

But

"N "	=	"N"	is true

Notice that the last expression here is considered EQUAL with EXACT ON, but unequal with EXACT OFF. In this case, EXACT ON is less exact than EXACT OFF.

The == operator applies the most rigorous test. This operator considers two character expressions to be equal only if the expressions are identical, including trailing blanks.

> **CAUTION:** The preceding rules can be generalized to most comparisons you make in FoxPro (or in Xbase). The difference between the right and left side of an expression can be useful when you search tables. You must remember, however, that SQL SELECT is an exception to this rule. In SQL SELECT comparisons, the order in which two expressions surround the operator makes absolutely no difference.

To return to the previous example, in a non-SQL SELECT comparison and with SET EXACT OFF, STATE = 'N' matches any state that begins with the letter N; whereas 'N' = STATE finds no matches because STATE is a two-character field.

If you SET EXACT ON or (in SQL SELECT) SET ANSI ON so that the shorter string ('N') is padded with blanks to match the length of the other, however, then 'N' = state is optimized. Rushmore uses the tag on the STATE field and compares the tag to the character string you supply—of course, no records are found to match.

This example gives you a chance to explore the real subtleties of a FoxPro character search. You go on to look at other forms of comparisons that cannot be optimized, as in the following line:

```
UPPER(STATE) = 'NJ'
```

UPPER(STATE) = 'NJ' is not optimizable because the index does not contain the UPPER() function. Just as you can create a tag on YTDPURCH * 1.10, you can create a tag on UPPER(STATE). You then can perform optimizable, case-insensitive on STATEs.

```
STATE = 'NJ' OR COMPANY = 'Micro'
```

This expression is not optimizable because every record in the file still must be examined in the search. Although Rushmore can build a set of records that includes only records for which the first condition is satisfied, every record in the rest of the file still must be checked for the second condition.

Combining Fully Optimizable and Non-Optimizable Expressions

The preceding expression—where an optimizable expression is combined with a nonoptimizable expression with an OR—is not typical of the way that Rushmore handles complex expressions.

Often, combining fully optimizable expressions with non-optimizable expressions produces partially optimizable expressions. If you combine a partially optimizable expression with another partially or fully optimizable expression, you get another partially optimizable expression. Only when you connect a non-optimizable expression to others by an OR—or if all components of a complex expression are non-optimizable—is Rushmore completely ineffective.

Rushmore, upon encountering a partially optimizable expression, first searches the indexes for all the records that match the fully optimizable portion of the expression and then checks the records in the actual table against the nonoptimizable portion of the expression.

This section shows some examples of partially optimizable expressions, such as the following:

```
STATE = 'NY' AND COMPANY = 'Micro'
```

Based on the index, Rushmore finds all customers from NY and then looks at these NY customers to rule out customers whose companies do not begin with 'Micro'.

```
(STATE = 'NY' OR STATE = 'CA') AND YTDPURCH > 15000 AND
COMPANY = 'Micro'
```

In the preceding expression, Rushmore first finds all the NY and CA customers—based on the State index tag—and then uses the Ytdpurch index tag to find which of the NY and CA customers match. Thus far, the search is fully optimized. Without a tag to match the rest of the query, Rushmore then checks the actual records in the subset already collected to see which records have companies with names beginning with 'Micro'.

This sequence may not be exactly the way in which the expression is evaluated. Rushmore may determine that checking the Ytdpurch index is faster and proceed accordingly, but the idea and results are the same. Table 7.4 shows all the possible ways in which you can combine optimizable and non-optimizable expressions.

Table 7.4. Combining Basic Optimizable and Non-Optimizable Expressions

Basic Expression	Connector	Basic Expression	Optimization
Optimizable	AND	Optimizable	Full
Optimizable	AND	Non-optimizable	Partial
Optimizable	OR	Optimizable	Full
Optimizable	OR	Non-optimizable	None
Non-optimizable	AND	Non-optimizable	None
Non-optimizable	OR	Non-optimizable	None

Increasing the Performance of Rushmore

You can take several steps to help Rushmore deliver the best performance.

- Set order to 0 whenever possible.

  Commands that produce output either displayed, printed, or processed by other FoxPro commands, benefit more from Rushmore optimization when the table is left in the natural order and Rushmore is left to decide on which tags best suit a search. If the ORDER is SET to a particular index—perhaps because you are outputting a report in customer sequence or labels in ZIP code order—Rushmore must process the table in the order specified.

  FoxPro always processes a table faster in natural order when you are moving through all the records. This attribute, although not unique to Rushmore, can significantly affect your perception of Rushmore's value.

  Table 7.5 contains a list of commands that perform better when order is set to 0. This list is a subset of the commands in table 7.2.

  Note that SQL SELECT is omitted from this list. You can use SQL SELECT or the RQBE (which uses SQL) without concerning yourself with the current order of the table.

Table 7.5 Commands That Perform Better When ORDER Is Set to 0

BROWSE	LABEL
CHANGE	LIST
COPY TO	LOCATE
COPY TO ARRAY	REPORT
DISPLAY	SCAN
EDIT	SET FILTER TO
EXPORT	TOTAL

Note: This table applies whether or not Rushmore is involved.

- Use a DELETED() tag if you SET DELETE ON.

  SET DELETED ON tells FoxPro to ignore deleted records and acts just like a filter. Rushmore treats ANY operation as partially optimizable at best when SET DELETED is ON. This procedure occurs because FoxPro must look outside of the index, to the actual table to find out whether or not a record has been deleted. Fortunately, you have a way around this; if DELETED() has an index tag, then Rushmore uses the tag to optimize SET DELETED.

As explained at the beginning of this book, a number of FoxPro 2 features were in a state of flux in the early stages of the product's release. Rushmore's capability of using an index with DELETED() in conjunction with SET DELETED ON wasn't available in the first release of FoxPro 2. If necessary, refer to Appendix A for information about upgrading to a more recent version of FoxPro.

- Avoid using NOT and FOR in index tags.

  Rushmore doesn't recognize indexes that contain NOT or ! in an index key, such as in the following:

```
NOT DELETED()
NOT animal = "CAT"
```

  This kind of key is sometimes used to group together all records not matching the condition, followed by all records matching the condition (because these expressions always evaluate to FALSE or TRUE). If an index contains NOT, this index is not usable by Rushmore. If you create the indexes without NOT, Rushmore can use the indexes, and, when necessary, these indexes perform the same service for you (you can reverse the group that appears first in the index by using the DESCENDING keyword when you SET ORDER).

You know from Chapter 4 that you can create a conditional index by using the FOR clause, which will filter the records so that only a subset of the file appears in the index. People often create conditional index expressions, such as the following:

```
id_code FOR NOT DELETED()
zip FOR animal = "CAT"
```

Rushmore cannot use conditional indexes. Instead, create these filters by using FOR clauses on the table-manipulating commands or the SET FILTER command, by using a regular index tag, such as in the following clauses:

```
INDEX ON id_code TAG code
INDEX ON DELETED() TAG del
SET DELETED ON
SET FILTER TO id_code = "XYZ"

INDEX ON zip TAG zip
INDEX ON animal TAG animal
SET ORDER TO zip
REPORT FORM statusrpt FOR animal = "CAT"
```

In the second example, ORDER is not SET to 0 because the report is printed in ZIP-code order. Rushmore, however, still provides a benefit in selecting the "Cat" records to be processed.

- Use Rushmore with care.

Rushmore can speed up many operations in FoxPro, but relying too much on this technology may hurt performance. With a little work on your part, some procedures are done faster without Rushmore. The examples below use SCAN/ENDSCAN, a programming construct with which you may be unfamiliar. Review SCAN/ENDSCAN again, if necessary, after you read Chapter 16. You need to understand only that, when you SCAN records in a program, FoxPro moves through all the records in the table, performing the operations you specify for each record before moving to the next one.

Using the BIGCUST.DBF table, the following is much faster with Rushmore than without Rushmore:

```
SET ORDER TO
      SCAN FOR State = 'NY'
      ....
            do something with the record
      ....
ENDSCAN
```

The following is still faster, although you may not notice the difference unless you process very large files:

```
SET ORDER TO State
            SEEK 'NY'
            SCAN WHILE State = 'NY'
            ....
            do something with the record
      ....
ENDSCAN
```

However, change the line SCAN FOR State = 'NY' in the first code segment to **SCAN FOR State = 'NY' AND YTDPURCH >= 15000** and change the line SCAN WHILE State = 'NY' in the second code segment to **SCAN WHILE State = 'NY' FOR YTDPURCH >= 15000**, and you find the first method faster than the second method by a large margin.

With these kinds of elaborate conditions, Rushmore's advantage is most apparent because the SEEK can use only one index order at a time, and Rushmore uses multiple tags. Usually, if you are in a situation where you need to squeeze every last drop of speed from the code, then trying several different methods to see which works best for the situation may be worth the effort.

- Pick the right index format.

  Rushmore works with any of the three index types provided by FoxPro 2.0. Better performance usually results from using either the compact or compound indexes because these indexes are smaller (all compound indexes also are inherently compact). The more efficiently information is stored in an index, the more index information FoxPro can keep in memory at one time, which in turn reduces disk accesses. (Accessing the disk is one of the slowest parts of database operations; you learn more about this factor in Appendix C, which covers the relationship between FoxPro's performance and computer hardware.)

Rushmore works as quickly with noncompound compact indexes as with compound indexes, but as you already learned in Chapter 4, compound indexes offer other advantages and are probably the best choice, unless you are building a temporary index intended for one-time use.

Compound indexes also have a few disadvantages; the index file bloat phenomenon is mentioned in Chapter 4. Related to (and a partial cause of) this problem is *compound index fragmentation*. In standard and compact index files, all information concerning each *index key* is stored together. In compound indexes, this kind of storage, however, is not always the case. Information about an index key may be spewed all over the file. This scattering forces FoxPro to perform far more disk access than is otherwise necessary, which can slow operations considerably. You can reduce this problem by occasionally rebuilding the compound index files, either by REINDEXing or by deleting and rebuilding all the tags individually.

Working without Rushmore

You may think that you must do everything possible to optimize each search or filter condition. Sometimes, you must decide not to use Rushmore. When Rushmore encounters a command using FOR with an optimizable expression, Rushmore determines which records match the expression *only once*, when the FOR condition is first encountered. The command works only on the records Rushmore finds. If the data is changed while the Rushmore set is still in use, then the Rushmore set is inaccurate because the information is not updated, as are active indexes.

Be particularly careful of this condition when you use FoxPro on a network, where many people may be editing the table in which you are working at the same time.

The size of Rushmore-optimizable tables in the extended version is limited only by the amount of memory in the computer. When you use the standard version of FoxPro (either because you are running on a 286 or lesser machine, or because the 386 doesn't have sufficient memory for the extended version), however, Rushmore becomes unavailable when the tables include 500,000 or more records.

If Rushmore doesn't operate, either because you are using the Standard version of Foxpro or because of insufficient memory, a FoxPro message informs you that not enough memory is available for Rushmore optimization. FoxPro then executes the command (without Rushmore) while you take a coffee break.

If you encounter in this situation, then use a NOOPTIMIZE clause on the commands usually subject to optimization, or SET OPTIMIZE OFF for *all* operations until you issue another command to SET OPTIMIZE back to the default state of ON.

Chapter Summary

You looked closely at the effect Rushmore has on the SQL SELECT command and other FoxPro 2 search methods. When you ask FoxPro to present a set of records that satisfy criteria you set, think of each request as a series of comparisons of records against the criteria. You now know that the results of these comparisons, the format in which FoxPro presents them, and the speed with which FoxPro responds to requests to produce these comparisons can vary significantly—depending on how you phrase the request.

Working with SQL SELECT syntax represents an enormous increase in the search vocabulary and the fluency with which you can make these kinds of requests of FoxPro. You now have a working knowledge of some of the unique capabilities of FoxPro searches and you also learned about these capabilities' inherent limitations.

A significant limitation in FoxPro's implementation of SQL SELECT is a lack of direct support for outer joins. Outer joins are not part of the *ANSI SQL standard* but are included in many other SQL implementations.

ANSI, the *American National Standards Institute*, is an organization that sets standards for programming languages and other engineering disciplines. Currently, no ANSI standard exists to which FoxPro or the xBase dialects are held, although ANSI standards exist for other programming languages—such as C, Fortran, COBOL, and SQL—in use on personal computers and mainframes. Because most SQL implementations respect the ANSI SQL standard, you can write an SQL SELECT in any SQL implementation and then use the statement on another computer. Many FoxPro SELECT statements you used produce the same results in Oracle or other languages.

The FoxPro SQL SELECT, however, has some clauses that ANSI SQL doesn't support, such as INTO DBF and INTO ARRAY. These clauses were added to help make SQL easy to use with the rest of FoxPro.

This situation is probably not of great concern to you at the moment. As you explore SQL SELECT in FoxPro, however, you may become interested in the way SQL is used in the larger database management community.

In fact, at some point, this use of SQL SELECT may form an integral part of the way FoxPro uses information from—or communicates results to—other database systems. If you find yourself thinking about these issues, then you can consult some of the following sources. These books also help you to organize your thoughts and find new approaches as you use SQL SELECT from within FoxPro.

The Database Experts' Guide to SQL, Frank Lusardi. Intertext/McGraw-Hill, 1988.

Paradox Programmer's Reference, Steve Shepherd. Que Corporation, 1991.

The Practical SQL Handbook, Sandra L. Emerson, Marcy Darnovsky, and Judith S. Bowman. Addison-Wesley, 1989.

SQL: The Structured Query Language, Dr. Carolyn J. Hursch and Dr.Jack L. Hursch. TAB, 1988.

Using dBASE IV, Que Development Group. Que Corporation, 1991.

8

CHAPTER

Organizing the Answers with BROWSE

BROWSE is FoxPro 2's most useful command for viewing and editing records contained in a table or multiple tables in a database. You can display the records in a columnar, spreadsheet-style format, in a vertical format, or in both formats at the same time. You also can limit the display to certain records and fields and can rearrange the size and position of each field.

In this chapter, you learn how to use the FoxPro menu system and the Command window to access the power of BROWSE for interactive use. Then, in Parts III and IV of this book, you take a close look at the useful features and characteristics when BROWSE is included in a FoxPro program.

Opening and Closing a Browse Window

Figure 8.1 shows a Browse window in the default Browse format. You can use several methods to open a Browse window:

- Select Browse from the Database menu.
- Click the <Browse> push button in the View window.
- Output the results of a query to a Browse window.
- Type **BROWSE** in the Command window.

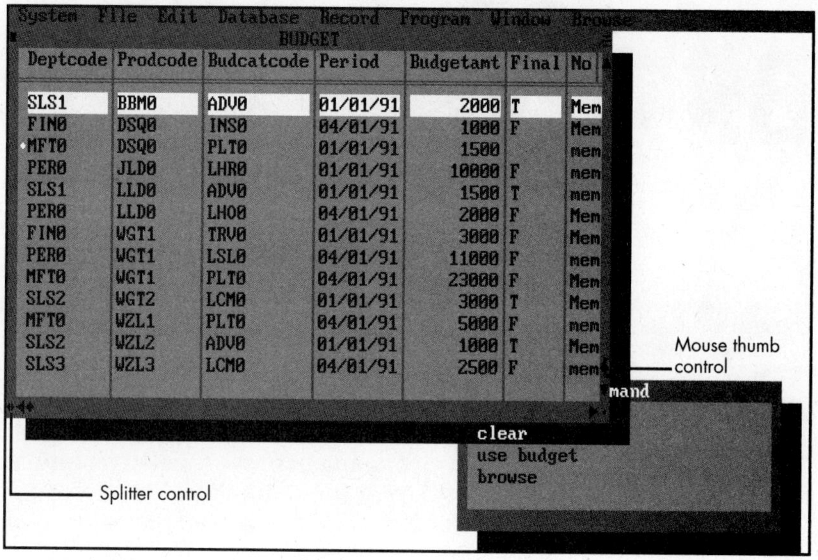

System File Edit Database Record Program Window Browse

BUDGET

Deptcode	Prodcode	Budcatcode	Period	Budgetamt	Final	No
SLS1	BBM0	ADV0	01/01/91	2000	T	Mem
FIN0	DSQ0	INS0	04/01/91	1000	F	Mem
MFT0	DSQ0	PLT0	01/01/91	1500		mem
PER0	JLD0	LHR0	01/01/91	10000	F	mem
SLS1	LLD0	ADV0	01/01/91	1500	T	mem
PER0	LLD0	LHO0	04/01/91	2000	F	Mem
FIN0	WGT1	TRV0	01/01/91	3000	F	Mem
PER0	WGT1	LSL0	04/01/91	11000	F	mem
MFT0	WGT1	PLT0	04/01/91	23000	F	Mem
SLS2	WGT2	LCM0	01/01/91	3000	T	Mem
MFT0	WZL1	PLT0	04/01/91	5000	F	mem
SLS2	WZL2	ADV0	01/01/91	1000	T	Mem
SLS3	WZL3	LCM0	04/01/91	2500	F	mem

mand

clear
use budget
browse

Mouse thumb control

Splitter control

FIG. 8.1

A Browse window in Browse format.

Selecting Browse from the Database menu issues a BROWSE LAST command, which opens a Browse window that hasn't changed since the last time you browsed the current table.

BROWSE LAST deals only with the current table. The BROWSE command, however, can display records from a table or tables (a database).

Clicking the <Browse> push button in the View window also issues a BROWSE LAST command but gives you more flexibility by enabling you to set a filter, specify a list of fields to appear, or use a format file to control the display format. If you need these options, click the <Setup> push button in the View window before selecting Browse. For more information on using the View window, see Chapter 3, "Exploring Databases and Tables."

As you learn in Chapter 5 "Using the RQBE as the Gateway to Queries," you can output the results of a query to a temporary Browse window. This method is a powerful way of limiting the display to those items that provide the answers you are after. Because a copy of some of the records is created in one or more tables, you can use RQBE to create multiple *views* of data and use BROWSE to switch from one view to the other without affecting the original tables.

Finally, you always can work directly from the Command window. This approach gives you the greatest degree of flexibility in specifying the exact combination of BROWSE options that result in the display format and editing criteria you want. Using this method also is the only way to create a *preference*, which permanently saves the configuration options and enables you to restore them later. Preferences are discussed later in this chapter.

BROWSE always works on the table in the current work area. If no table is currently open in this area, FoxPro asks you to select a table through the Open File dialog. After you make the selection, FoxPro opens the table.

You can have more than one Browse window open at one time. As you saw in Chapter 3, you can have a separate Browse window for each work area if the computer has sufficient memory. You can move from one window to another by clicking the one you want with a mouse or by using Ctrl-F1 to cycle among the open windows.

To close an active Browse window, press Esc or click the close box. Closing a Browse window does not close the related table.

Arranging the Browse Window's Appearance

Browse, a special kind of FoxPro window, has several unique options that enable you to change the way in which the data is displayed on-screen. You can access these configuration options through the Browse menu, which appears when a Browse window is active, or you can use the mouse and the window's several control objects.

In this section, you learn the ways in which you can create a customized look for Browse windows. In the following section, you learn how to save and restore this look in later Browse sessions with the same table.

Sizing and Rearranging Fields

In the default Browse format, each field is displayed as a separate column. The fields appear from left to right in the order in which they exist in the table. The width of each column is the same as the size of the associated field, unless more room is needed to show the name of the field.

You can change the order in which the fields appear so that the most important fields are grouped together and visible. With a mouse, just click-drag a field name to the new position and release the mouse button. From the keyboard, select Move Field from the Browse menu, use the left- and right-arrow keys to position the field, and press Enter to complete the move. (FoxPro assumes that you want to move the field in which the cursor is blinking. To select a different field, use Tab or Shift-Tab to select the field before pressing the arrow keys.)

You also can change a column's width so that more or fewer columns are visible together. This technique is useful when you are viewing wide fields that typically end in blank spaces, such as first and last names and want to bring additional information into view. With a mouse, click-drag the vertical line to the right of the field name, resize the column width by moving the mouse cursor to the left or the right, and release the mouse button. From the keyboard, select Size Field from the Browse menu, use the left- and right-arrow keys to decrease or increase the column's width, and press Enter to complete the operation.

Resizing a column affects only the display of the data. The actual field lengths and their contents remain the same.

Using Change To See the Whole Record

Browse's columnar format is great for displaying many records at once, but usually a table has more fields than are displayed on-screen horizontally. When you want to see all the information for a particular record, the Change Edit format is more useful.

FoxPro 2's Edit format displays on-screen each record in a vertical format, with each field on a separate row (see fig. 8.2). The last field of one record is followed by the first field of the next.

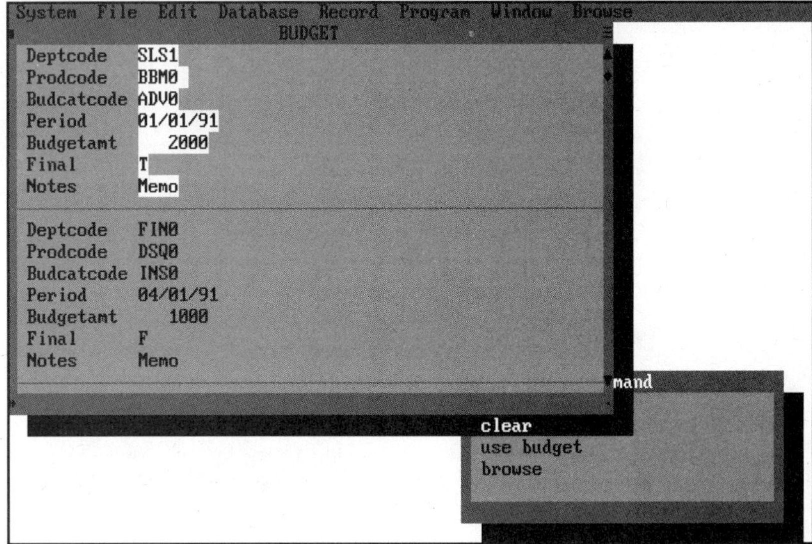

FIG. 8.2

Viewing records in Change/Edit format.

To switch the display format from Browse to Edit, select Change from the Browse menu. When you activate the menu the next time, you see that the Change option is replaced by Browse. This menu option toggles between Browse and Change, enabling you to switch from one format to the other. From the Command window, you can issue either the CHANGE or the EDIT command to use the vertical format; both are essentially identical.

Splitting a Browse Window

As you can see, both of Browse's display formats are useful at different times. You can use both of them together, however, by splitting the Browse window into two partitions.

To split a Browse window, you use the *splitter control*, which is located in the lower left corner of the Browse window. Activate the splitter with a mouse by click-dragging and moving splitter control to the right. From the keyboard, select Resize Partitions from the Browse menu and use the right-arrow key to move the splitter to the right. Moving the splitter changes the relative sizes of the two partitions in the window. As you move the splitter to the right, the middle bar (which is the left border of the right partition) moves with the splitter. When the partitions are sized the way you want them, release the mouse button or press Enter. Figure 8.3 shows a split Browse window.

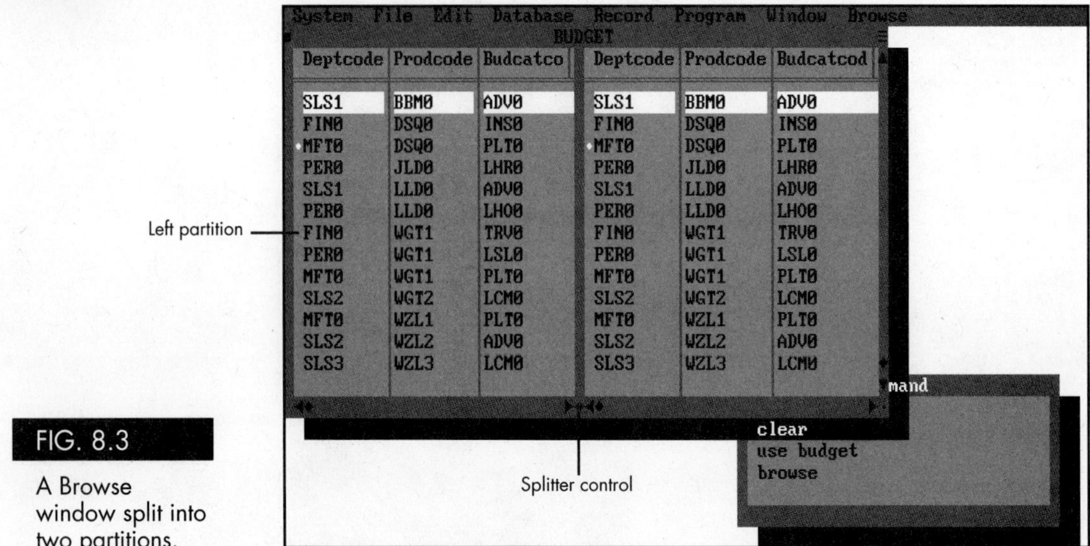

FIG. 8.3

A Browse window split into two partitions.

After you first split the window, both partitions have the same format (Browse or Edit), and the right partition is active. When you toggle the display format, the change affects only the currently active partition. Thus you can have one partition that uses the Browse format, and one that uses the Edit format, as shown in figure 8.4.

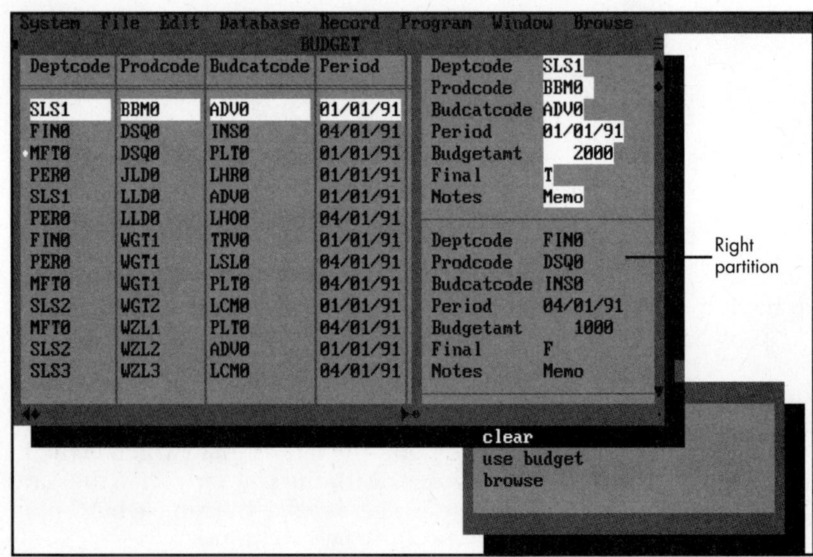

FIG. 8.4

A split browse window, with a different format for each partition

You switch from one partition to the other by clicking a field (*not* a field name) in the other partition, by selecting Change Partition from the Browse menu, or by using the control key shortcut, Ctrl-H.

Change the format of one of the partitions now so that one side uses Browse and the other uses Edit. Then activate the side currently in Browse mode. As you move the cursor from one record to another, notice that the highlight in the other partition moves in unison because the partitions are *linked*. Both parts of the window show the current record.

Unlink the partitions by selecting Unlink Partitions from the Browse menu. Notice that a *mouse thumb control* then appears in the scroll bar of each partition, indicating that the table may be scrolled independently in each partition. Understand, however, that a table has only one record pointer. The current record is always highlighted in the active partition. Unlinking the partitions just tells FoxPro not to update the inactive side of the window to display a different set of records. When you activate the other partition, the window is refreshed, and the current record is highlighted in both partitions.

Although each partition may display a different set of records, a change in a field's position on one side also is reflected on the other. In fact, the entire process of moving the field is shown in both partitions.

Saving a Browse Window's Look in a Preference

As easy as rearranging the appearance of a Browse window is, you still don't want to have to perform this step every time you browse a table. Fortunately, FoxPro 2 has two methods for restoring the look of a Browse session. Both methods use a special FoxPro table known as the *Resource file*.

Every time you exit a Browse window, FoxPro saves in a Resource file certain information about the status of the window. By default, the name of this file is FOXUSER.DBF. If FoxPro cannot find the Resource file, the file is created.

NOTE

FoxPro 2 has a built-in function that tells you the name of the Resource file in use. Type the following command in the Command window:

WAIT WINDOW SET("RESOURCE",1)

The full path name of the Resource file then appears in the upper right corner of the screen. Note the name of the file; then press any key to clear the message window.

You can tell FoxPro to use a different Resource file by using the SET RESOURCE TO *<filename>* command or to not use or update the Resource file settings by using the SET RESOURCE OFF command. Refer to Chapter 15 for more information on changing the Resource file.

After you select BROWSE from either the Database menu or click `<Browse>` in the View window, `BROWSE LAST` appears in the Command window, and the command is executed. LAST indicates that you want to use the same BROWSE settings you used the last time the currently SELECTed table was browsed. After you exit the Browse window, the Resource file is updated with the current settings.

To have more than one *view* of the table, or if more than one person uses the table and each user wants a different look, you can create a *preference* in which to store the BROWSE settings as a separate record in the Resource file. From the Command window, type a command that uses the following syntax:

BROWSE PREFERENCE *<preference name>*

Substitute the name of the preference for *<preference name>*, as in BROWSE PREFERENCE CUSTPREF1. A preference name can consist of up to 24 characters.

If the preference does not exist yet, FoxPro creates the file. Adjust the Browse window to look the way you want; then close the window, using any of these methods, *except* Esc or Ctrl-Q, to close a window. The preference is stored in the Resource file. When you tell FoxPro to use this preference, by again typing BROWSE PREFERENCE *<preference name>*, FoxPro restores the Browse window to the way this window looked when you last created or made changes to this preference.

One noteworthy exception is a *zoomed* Browse window. The size and shape of the window are saved in the Resource file only if you sized the window either by using its size control or by selecting Size from the Window menu.

Keep in mind that the Resource file is a table with a particular structure. You can view and edit the Resource file just as you can any other FoxPro 2 table. To view the contents of the Resource file, you first must close the file by typing, in the Command window, the following command:

```
SET RESOURCE OFF
```

After the file is closed, you can open the Resource file, just as you can open other tables. Try taking this step now.

Figure 8.5 shows the contents of a typical Resource file. Records that hold information about preferences created with Version 2 of FoxPro contain PREF2.0 in the Type field. Preferences created with previous versions of FoxPro have PREF in the Type field.

In Chapter 15, the Resource file is discussed in greater depth and explains that you can USE a Resource file with the AGAIN keyword while the file is active. As a rule, however, editing the currently active Resource file isn't a good idea.

System File Edit Database Record Program Window Browse

FOXUSER

Type	Id	Name	Readonly
PREF2.0	HELPPOS		F
PREF2.0	WINDBROW	CURRDBF	F
PREF2.0	GETEXPR		F
PREF2.0	WINDCMD		F
PREF2.0	WINDBROW	STUDIO	F
PREF2.0	REPORTPOS		F
PREF2.0	WINDBROW	FOXHELP	F
PREF2.0	FILERPOS		F
PREF2.0	MNBLDRPOS	UNTITLED.MNX	F
PREF2.0	WINDBROW	BIG	F
PREF2.0	VIEWPOS		F
PREF2.0	QBEPOS		F
PREF2.0	MODPRJPOS	FOXHUNT.PJX	F

Command

```
? set("resource",1)
set resource off
use d:\free\steve\foxuser
browse
```

FIG. 8.5

Browsing the FoxPro 2 Resource File.

FoxPro uses the Id field of the Resource file to distinguish among the different kinds of preferences that you can create. Browse window preferences contain WINDBROW in the Id field and either the table alias or the name of a user-created preference in the Name field.

The primary reason for examining the Resource file is to edit the READONLY field. This logical field usually is set to false (F), which indicates that the current settings for this preference may be updated at any time. After you create a preference and make all the adjustments you need, you can prevent accidentally overwriting the new preference by changing the READONLY value from false to true (T) by typing **I** in the field.

NOTE

One other reason exists for learning how to modify the Resource file's Browse preference records: you have no way to use and make changes to an existing preference, and to create a preference by saving the existing preference with a new name. To create small variations of the basic preference, you can copy the preference in the Resource file by following these steps:

1. Browse the Resource file and highlight a basic preference.

2. Activate the Command window.

3. Create memory variables that contain the current contents of this record by typing **SCATTER MEMVAR MEMO** in the Command window.

4. Create a record by typing the command **APPEND BLANK**.

5. Move the data from the memory variables into the record's fields by typing **GATHER MEMVAR MEMO**.

   You have now created a copy of the basic preference!

6. Create additional copies by using **APPEND BLANK** and **GATHER MEMVAR MEMO** for each one.

7. Browse the Resource file again and enter a unique preference name in the Name field for each new preference. You now can refer to each new preference by name, and you can use and modify all preferences separately.

8. Close and reactivate the table for use by typing the command **set resource on**.

You now have multiple, identical preferences that you can modify to fit your needs by browsing the table, using the name of each preference, modifying the table's appearance, and then closing the Browse window.

Creating a Subset of Records in Browse

A database can store a huge amount of information; however, a file cabinet can do the same. What makes a computerized database a better storage medium is the capability of creating, based on any combination of criteria, a subset of the data.

If you have a company-wide personnel file, you can easily tell FoxPro to show you only married people in San Francisco with two or more children. Try this sorting job with a file cabinet full of forms arranged in alphabetical order by last name!

You can restrict the table to certain records by using the SET FILTER TO command, but that filter affects *all* operations you perform on the table until you turn off the filter. Browse's filtering options remain in effect only as long as the Browse window is active.

BROWSE has two options, FOR and KEY, that enable you to restrict the records that you display. To use these options, you have to activate the Browse window from the Command window.

BROWSE FOR is more general in scope and doesn't require an active index, although FoxPro 2's new Rushmore technology uses one or more of them, if available, to optimize a search. (Rushmore is covered in depth in Chapter 7, "Querying with SQL and Searching with Rushmore.")

New to Version 2, BROWSE FOR enables you to specify any number of criteria that a record must satisfy to be included in the subset. The FOR condition is specified in the same manner as the FOR clause in the LIST command. FOR is a logical expression, which is evaluated as true or false for each record in the table.

You can display only records in the BUDGET table that have SLS1 in the DEPTCODE field. In the Command window, type the following lines:

```
SELECT BUDGET
BROWSE FOR DEPTCODE = "SLS1"
```

The Browse window shows only the data for department SLS1.

You can limit the subset even further. Activate the Command window and edit the BROWSE command to the following line:

```
BROWSE FOR DEPTCODE = "SLS1" AND BUDGETAMT > 1500
```

You can see that the subset is reduced further by adding another filter criterion. If no records in the table satisfy the FOR expression, an empty Browse window appears.

BROWSE KEY uses an active index file to find quickly the first record and last records that satisfy the filter expression. You can use a single value or a range of values. You can use BROWSE KEY to display the data for department SLS1, for example, by typing the following line in the Command window:

```
SET ORDER TO TAG DEPTCODE
BROWSE KEY "SLS1"
```

Now modify the command to include a range of values, as in the following example:

```
BROWSE KEY "SLS1", "SLS3"
```

The most important things to remember about KEY are that the table must be indexed on the field for which you are specifying a value or values and that index must be the current master index. If you are not getting the results you expected, use the Status option on the View window to check the table's index settings. Refer to Chapters 3 and 4, for more information on indexes.

In the examples given here, the entire command is typed in uppercase letters. Although the case of a command is not significant, the case of the filter expression *is* significant. That is, *BROWSE KEY "SLS1"* is equivalent to *browse key "SLS1"*, but *not* equivalent to *browse key "sls1"*.

When working with character data, such as first and last names, however, you usually don't care about the case of the entries. To see the data for everyone whose last name is Jones, you don't want to exclude a record because the operator typed in JONES. You can tell FoxPro to ignore the case of the data in a BROWSE FOR (*not* in a BROWSE KEY) command by converting the characters to a particular case for the purpose of performing the comparison to the filter expression. So, to ensure that you see all the Jones entries, you can use the UPPER( ) and LOWER( ) functions, like this:

```
BROWSE FOR UPPER(DEPTCODE) = "SLS1"
```

or

```
BROWSE FOR LOWER(DEPTCODE) = "sls1"
```

As FoxPro tests each record, the program converts the field contents to the specified case before comparing the field to the match criterion. This conversion does *not* change the table's data in any way. The conversion is done entirely in memory.

This technique works only with BROWSE FOR. BROWSE KEY uses an index, which you cannot change "on the fly" in this manner. If you know beforehand that you don't want the case to be significant, you should use the UPPER( ) or LOWER( ) function as part of the expression used to create the index, as in the following example:

```
INDEX ON LOWER(DEPTCODE) TO TAG DEPTCODE
```

Now, when you want to search the table or view only certain records, you must remember to use lowercase letters in the search or filter expression, because the index is composed of all lowercase letters:

```
BROWSE KEY "sls1", "sls3"
```

Again, if you are getting unexpected results, such as an empty Browse window when you know that some matching records should exist, use the View window to verify that the master index is the correct index and that the index expression matches the filter expression.

Taking Control with FIELDS

BROWSE has a FIELDS clause that enables you to specify exactly the fields with which you want to work, how you want the data to appear, and what kind of entries are allowed in each field.

The FIELDS clause always is followed by a field list name, which contains the name of each field you want displayed on-screen. The field names must be separated by a comma, as in the following example:

```
BROWSE FIELDS PRODCODE, BUDCATCODE FOR DEPTCODE = "SLS1"
```

Note that the last field name is not followed by a comma, even though that name is not the end of the command. Also, you don't need to include a space between field names, but spacing makes the command easier to read.

To each field in the list, you can attach one or more options that control the field's display format, column width, column heading, and range of acceptable entries. You also can use options that prevent any changes to the field or that accept changes only under certain conditions.

The multitude of FIELDS options—and the ways in which you can combine these options—may seem a little bewildering. Table 8.1 lists each of the options along with the required syntax and an example of how each is used. You may want to refer back to this table as each option is discussed in this chapter.

Table 8.1 The FIELDS Clause Options

Option	Name	Syntax	Example
:P	Picture	:P=<*exp*C>	:P="!!!!"
:H	Heading	:H=<*exp*C>	:H="Department"
:B	Boundaries	:B=<*exp*>,<exp>[:F]	:B=0,10000
:R	Read-Only	:R	:R
:<*n*>	Column Width	:<*n*>	:10
:V	Valid	:V=<*exp*>[:F][:E=<exp>]	:V=!EMPTY(DEPTCODE)
:W	When	:W=<*exp*L>	:W=!EMPTY(DEPTCODE)

Using :P (The Picture Option)

The :P option enables you to create an editing template for the field. You may want the field to contain only uppercase characters, for example, regardless of the case in which the characters are typed. In a telephone number, you may want to enclose the area code in parentheses, without having to type them. To save disk space, you may choose not to store the parentheses in the field, using them only for display purposes. These choices are but a few of the ways in which you can control the display and editing format of a field.

FoxPro 2 has two kinds of field formatting codes. *Function codes* act on all characters in the field and are preceded by the at (@) symbol. *Picture template codes* act on a single character.

You also can use all the picture and function codes available in the @ SAY/GET command, except for the M function code, with the :P option. A complete list of available picture template codes is given in table 8.2. Function codes are listed in table 8.3.

Table 8.4 shows some examples of picture clauses that you may find useful. Pay particular attention to the ways in which some clauses are combined to achieve precise formatting control.

Table 8.2 BROWSE Picture Template Codes

Code	Description
A	Allows letters only
L	Allows true (T or Y) or false (F or N) only; can be entered in upper- or lowercase
N	Allows letters and digits only
X	Allows any character to be entered
Y	Allows only true (Y or y) or false (N or n). Lowercase entries are converted to uppercase (Y or N).
9	If the data is of character type, only digits are allowed. If the data is numeric, digits and signs are allowed.
#	Allows digits, blanks, and signs
!	Converts lowercase letters to uppercase letters
$	Displays on-screen the current currency symbol. By default, the placement of the symbol is immediately before or after the field, depending on the placement required by the particular symbol. The currency symbol and its placement (SET CURRENCY), the separator character (SET SEPARATOR), and the decimal character (SET POINT), however, all can be changed.
*	Shows asterisks in front of a number
.	Shows a decimal point
,	Shows a comma

Table 8.3 BROWSE Function Codes

Code	Description
A	Allows letters only
B	Left-justifies numbers
C	Displays a CR (credit symbol) on-screen after a positive number
D	Uses the current SET DATE format (for example, BRITISH, GERMAN, and so on) to edit dates
E	Edits dates, using the European (BRITISH) date format
I	Centers text in the field

continues

Table 8.3 Continued

Code	Description
J	Right-justifies text in the field
L	Displays on-screen leading zeros rather than spaces in numeric values
R	When used with formatting characters, shows but does not store the extra characters in the field or memory variable; may be used only with character data
S<*n*>	Limits the display width to <*n*> characters, where <*n*> is a positive integer. After the end of the displayed field is reached, the characters scroll to the left to enable you to enter or display the remaining characters, up to the defined length of the field. May be used only with character data.
T	Trims leading and trailing blanks from the field
X	Displays a DB (debit symbol) on-screen after negative numbers
Z	If the value of a numeric field is 0, displays the field as blanks
(	Encloses negative numbers in parentheses. The left parenthesis is displayed in the first column of the field, and the right parenthesis is shown in the last column.
!	Converts letters to uppercase
^	Displays numbers, using scientific notation
$	Displays numbers in the current currency format. The currency symbol appears before or after the field value, depending on the current setting of SET CURRENCY.

Some of the examples shown in table 8.4 contain characters other than those that actively participate in the picture, such as the parentheses in "(999) 999-9999." These characters are *formatting characters*. Don't try to type these characters because FoxPro automatically skips over them. Formatting characters are stored along with an entry, so the field must be wide enough to hold both the formatting characters and the data. If you don't want to store the extra characters, use the @R function clause, as shown in the table.

Table 8.4 Some Examples of Using Picture Clauses in BROWSE

Picture/Function	Description
:P="@!"	Converts any and all lowercase letters to uppercase letters.
:P="AAA999"	In an invoice number field, requires that the first three characters be alphabetic, and that the last three characters be digits.
:P="@! AAA999"	Same as preceding example, but converts the alphabetic characters to uppercase.
:P="(999) 999-9999"	In a telephone number field, accepts only digits, and formats the display for easy viewing.
:P="@R (999) 999-9999"	For the same telephone number field, tells FoxPro not to store the formatting characters along with the data. Because the extra characters are not being stored, the field needs to be only ten characters in length.
:P="999,999.99"	In an invoice amount field, separates the thousands, hundreds, and cents.

The last example shown (`:P="999,999.99"`) works fine with existing data, because numbers are displayed right-justified in the field. Data entry always starts at the left of the field, however, even when the field is numeric. FoxPro inserts a comma after you type the third digit, even though the number you are entering may be less than one thousand. After you press Enter, the number is right justified, and the commas (if any) appear in the correct positions.

Some functions may be combined within a single picture clause as long as they don't conflict with each other. "@A!" is a permissible combination, for example, but "@IJ" is not, because you can't have data both centered and right-justified at the same time.

Using :H (The Column Heading Option)

By default, FoxPro uses the field name as the column heading. Because they are limited to ten characters, field names often don't tell you what kind of information the fields are supposed to contain. A Social Security number field, for example, may have SSNO as a name. You can replace the default column heading of SSNO with Soc. Sec. #, which is easier to read, by using this command:

```
BROWSE FIELDS SSNO :H="Soc. Sec. #"
```

Of course, you have to balance the desire to use descriptive headings with the need to not waste a great deal of screen space, because the column width is adjusted if the specified heading is longer than the field size. In the case of a Social Security number, the field must be at least nine characters long (you may choose not to store the dashes), so changing the field name to **Soc. Sec. #** increases the length of the column by two at most.

BROWSE has a separate WIDTH clause, which is used to limit the displayed width of all fields in the Browse window. FoxPro does not override the WIDTH clause to display a column heading that is longer than the specified value. The program does override WIDTH, however, if you attach the :<*n*> option to the field.

Using :B (The Boundaries Option)

:B enables you to specify a range of acceptable entries for the field. This option works the same way :V does but is much more limited in scope. You cannot have a user-defined function, for example, as part of a boundary condition.

When you press Enter, FoxPro enables you to type any value in the field and then check the entry against the specified range. If the entry doesn't fall within the range, the FoxPro message `Invalid input` appears, and you are forced to change the entry before you can move to the next field.

The data type of the boundaries must be the same as the data type of the field. Therefore, if you're entering data in a Social Security number field of date type, be sure that you enclose all literal boundary expressions within *curly braces* ({}), the delimiters for dates in FoxPro.

By default, the boundary conditions are checked only if you changed the contents of the field. If you previously typed data in the field, FoxPro doesn't force you to change this data. To force existing data to be checked for validity, include the :F (force) option. Note that the cursor has to enter into the field for the :F option to take effect.

Using :R (The Read-Only Option)

You can prevent changes to a field by using :R, to temporarily make the field a read-only field. The field is shown on-screen as usual, but you cannot edit the field, and FoxPro causes the computer to beep if you try to make a change.

The :R option is used most often within a FoxPro program but also is useful when you work from the Command window. If you're setting up a Browse window for others to use, you may want to ensure that certain information isn't changed inadvertently by someone who is typing from a form without realizing that the cursor is in the wrong field.

Using :<*n*> (The Column Width Option)

FoxPro uses the greater of the field's length and the column heading as the default column width. To use a different width, include the :<*n*> option, replacing <*n*> with the number of columns to be used.

The sample BUDGET table, for example, contains the BUDCATCODE field. The field's length is only four, but its field name is 10 characters. To reduce the column width from 10 to four, you can resize this setting from the Browse window, as previously discussed, or you can use the :<*n*> option, as in the following example:

```
BROWSE FIELDS DEPTCODE, PRODCODE, BUDCATCODE :4
```

Of course, making this change also truncates the column heading to BUDC, which may not be acceptable. As with the column heading option, you have to balance the need to conserve screen space with the need to use descriptive column headings.

Using :V (The Valid Option)

More than any other factor, the capability of validating entries is responsible for the adoption of BROWSE as a data-entry vehicle by people who program in the xBase language. The BROWSE command in dBASE III Plus and FoxBASE+ did not have this feature and generally was used only for interactive data entry and simple record displays.

The validation expression is any legal FoxPro expression that evaluates to true (.T.), false (.F.), or 0. This expression can be a simple test for whether the field was left blank or was a call to a *user-defined function* (UDF) that may perform hundreds of operations before returning to the Browse window.

If the expression is *true*, the cursor moves to the next field. If the expression is *false*, the cursor remains in the field, and an error message is displayed. If the expression evaluates to 0, the cursor remains in the field, but no error message appears.

The following paragraphs provide a few examples.

In the sample application, several of the tables have the DEPTCODE field in common. The entries in this field enable you to link the tables. If the DEPTCODE field were allowed to be blank, FoxPro cannot create the linkage.

Using a validation clause, you can prevent others from *blanking out* the DEPTCODE entries. Use a validation clause similar to one of the following:

```
BROWSE FIELDS DEPTCODE :V=!EMPTY(DEPTCODE)

BROWSE FIELDS DEPTCODE :V=(DEPTCODE != SPACE(LEN(DEPTCODE)))

BROWSE FIELDS DEPTCODE :V=(DEPTCODE != "     ")
```

All three of these commands say the same thing and differ only in the way the fact that DEPTCODE must not be blank is expressed. Of the three, the first command is both the easiest to read and the most general way of expressing the condition because the EMPTY( ) function works on all categories of data.

As with :B, the boundaries option, an entry that doesn't satisfy the validation expression causes an `Invalid input` message to appear. Because this message isn't very informative, you can attach a custom error message to the :V option. Use :E=*<character expression>*, replacing *<character expression>* with the text of the error message to appear, as in the following example:

```
BROWSE FIELDS DEPTCODE :V=!EMPTY(DEPTCODE) ;
   :E="Department may not be blank!"
```

Now, when the field is left blank, the user understands the problem and—after reading the message and pressing a key to remove the message window—knows how to make the correction.

You can force the validation expression to be evaluated, whether or not the data is changed, by including :F as part of the option. The validation is forced, however, only if the field is entered.

An in-depth discussion of commands and functions is not the subject of this chapter, but seeing an example of what you can do with a user-defined function attached to a BROWSE field validation option may whet your appetite.

What if, rather than leaving the DEPTCODE field blank, you typed **SSL1** rather than **SLS1**? Making this kind of error is as bad as leaving the field blank, because FoxPro is unable to find the matching records in the other tables.

What you really want to do is ensure that a *valid* department code is entered. All the valid department codes are contained in the DEPT table. The following paragraphs give you a look at a user-defined function that ensures that only valid entries are made in the DEPTCODE field.

Activate the Command window and type the following command:

```
MODIFY COMMAND VAL_DEPT.PRG
```

Now, type the following lines in the FoxPro editor window, just as they appear here:

```
FUNCTION val_dept
* This UDF ensures that only valid department
* codes are entered in the DEPTCODE field of any table.
PARAMETERS mdeptcode
RETURN SEEK(mdeptcode, "DEPT")
```

Save the program by clicking the window's close box, by selecting Save from the File menu, or by pressing Ctrl-W.

This simple UDF searches the DEPT table for a record with the same department code as the one you entered. This job is performed by FoxPro's built-in SEEK( ) function, which returns true if a match is found and false if one is not found. The communication between BROWSE and the UDF is handled by the PARAMETERS command, which accepts information from BROWSE, and RETURN, which passes information back to BROWSE. In this case, what is returned is the success or failure of the SEEK( ) function.

To use the UDF in a Browse window, you first must open both the DEPT and BUDGET tables. Then activate the Command window and type the following lines:

```
SELECT DEPT
SET ORDER TO TAG DEPTCODE
SELECT BUDGET
BROWSE ;
    FIELDS        DEPTCODE
:V=VAL_DEPT(DEPTCODE) ;
                    :E="No such Department Code!", ;
          PRODCODE, ;
          BUDCATCODE
```

Remember that you may type a single command on more than one line by placing a semicolon at the end of any line that should be continued onto the next line. Breaking up the command in this fashion makes reading the command easier and enables you to find errors more easily. This formatting style is used in the remainder of this chapter.

When an invalid entry is made in the DEPTCODE field, you should see the custom error message displayed in the upper right corner of the screen. Press any key to clear it. FoxPro does not enable you to exit the field until you either enter a valid code or press Esc to cancel the entry and close the Browse window.

Instead of displaying only an error message, you can display the valid choices in a pop-up window or in a separate Browse window. This method requires that you know a little bit about programming in FoxPro 2. More advanced validation techniques, such as the preceding technique, are covered in Parts III and IV of this book.

Using :W (The When Option)

The :W option works much like :V. Both options are followed by an expression that triggers an action, and the expression may include a call to a user-defined function. The When expression, however, is evaluated *before* the field is entered rather than *as* you're trying to exit it.

If the expression evaluates to false (.F.), the cursor skips over the field and moves to the next one. If every field has a :W expression that evaluates to false, the cursor appears in the first field, but you cannot enter or change anything.

The :W option enables you to add some intelligent behavior to the Browse window. When entering a customer's address, for example, skipping the second address line if the first was left blank makes sense. The following example shows how you can use the :W option to enact that rule:

```
BROWSE ;
    FIELDS              FIRSTNAME, ;
          LASTNAME, ;
          ADDRESS1, ;
          ADDRESS2      :W= !EMPTY(ADDRESS1), ;
          CITY, ;
          STATE, ;
          ZIP
```

If you leave the ADDRESS1 field blank, the cursor skips to the CITY field, bypassing the ADDRESS2 field.

As with :V, :W may include a UDF as part or all of the expression. You might use a UDF to present the available choices in a pop-up window and enable the user to select one. You then can *stuff* the choice into the field. This technique also requires some understanding of programming and is covered in Part IV of this book.

Using Calculated Fields

FoxPro can display the result of a calculation as if this result were a field in the table. You also can use this feature to verify the accuracy of entries or to mark certain records based on the value of one or more fields.

Suppose that you are entering invoices into the SALES table, working from handwritten order forms. The table has a QUANTITY field to hold the number of units ordered and a PRICE field to hold the price per unit.

Because the total charge for the item can be calculated by multiplying QUANTITY times PRICE, you don't need to store the total as a separate field in the table. The capability of comparing the calculated total to the total entered on the form by the salesperson, however, may be useful.

To create a calculated field, you have to assign to the field a name other than the name of a field in the table. For the invoice example, you can use TOTAL:

```
BROWSE ;
    FIELDS              INVOICE, ;
          PRODCODE, ;
          DATESOLD, ;
          QUANTITY, ;
          PRICE, ;
          TOTAL = QUANTITY * PRICE, ;
          SALESMAN, ;
          CUSTCODE
```

Figure 8.6 shows the results. When you make an entry into either the QUANTITY or PRICE field, the value of the calculated field TOTAL is redisplayed.

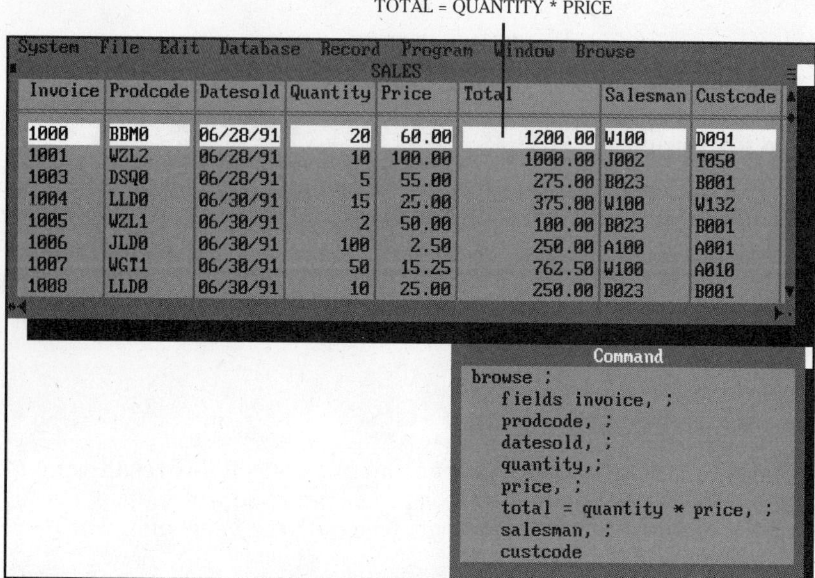

FIG. 8.6

Using a calculated field.

You also can use a calculated field to *flag* certain records. Figure 8.7 shows an example of how you can use a calculated field in the BUDGET table. In this example, the check-mark symbol (ASCII 251) is used as the flag character, but you can pick any character you prefer. A FoxPro 2 event-handling command (ON KEY LABEL) also is used to trap the keystroke used to mark the record. You learn more about this command and other similar techniques in upcoming chapters.

To set up this calculated field, open the BUDGET table and type the following lines in the Command window:

```
ON KEY LABEL CTRL-Z REPLACE FINAL WITH !FINAL
BROWSE ;
   FIELDS      DONE = IIF(FINAL, CHR(251), " "), ;
       DEPTCODE, ;
       PRODCODE, ;
       BUDGETAMT
```

FINAL is a logical field, meaning that the field can hold only one of two values, either true or false. DONE is a calculated field that gets its value from the current state of FINAL. If FINAL is true, a check mark appears in the DONE column; otherwise, the field is blank.

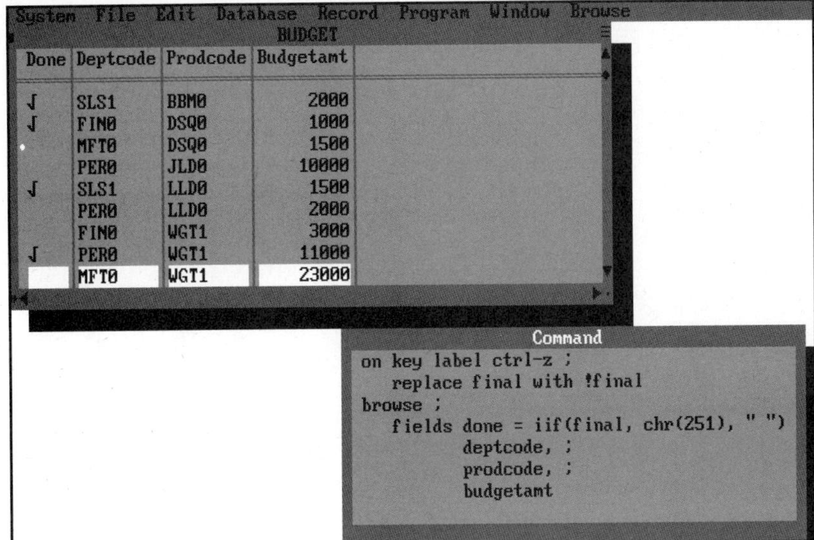

FIG. 8.7

Using a calculated field to flag records in a Browse window.

Two advanced techniques are in use here. One technique is the use of FoxPro's IIF( ), or *immediate if*, function. IIF( ) evaluates a condition (is FINAL true or false?) and returns one value (CHR(251), the check-mark character) if the condition is true, and another value (" ") if the condition is false. Using IIF( ) enables you to incorporate some simple IF...THEN...ELSE logic into a Browse window without using a user-defined function.

The second technique is the use of FoxPro 2's ON KEY LABEL command. Every time the specified key is pressed, FoxPro executes the command that follows. In the preceding example, when the Ctrl-Z key combination is pressed, FoxPro replaces the FINAL field with the opposite of its current value. Ctrl-Z therefore acts as a toggle. When you move the highlight bar to a different record, the contents of the DONE field change to reflect the current state of FINAL.

These kinds of techniques are explored in detail in Part IV of this book.

Using BROWSE To View Related Tables

FoxPro 2 is a relational database management system. Thus you can link a table to one or more other tables, using a field that each table has in common to create the linkage. The table from which the link, or *relation*, is created is known as the *parent* table. Each table related to the parent is referred to as a *child* table.

After you link tables, you can treat them as if they were part of a single table. You can create a single Browse window, for example, that shows fields from each of the related tables. You do so by preceding each of the field names with the alias of the work area in which the table is installed. The alias tells FoxPro from which table to take the data. If you don't specify an alias, FoxPro assumes that you're referring to the table in the currently active work area, which is usually the parent.

Using SET RELATION

An example may help to clarify some of this information about linking tables. Open the BUDGET and DEPT tables. Use the View window to open the tables so that you can use this window to link the tables. By linking BUDGET to DEPT through the common DEPTCODE field, you can display data from both tables in a single Browse window or in two related Browse windows.

If the View window is not active, make View the active window and select BUDGET as the parent table. Select the `<Relations>` push button and notice that `BUDGET` then appears in the Relations box beneath the push buttons. The ↳ symbol indicates that a relation is now formed between BUDGET and another table. To complete the link, select the DEPT table by double-clicking the table name with a mouse or by highlighting `DEPT` and pressing the space bar.

What happens next depends upon whether the index order for DEPT is set. If you opened the tables as part of this exercise, the index order probably isn't set. Here, the Set Index Order dialog appears. Select the DEPTCODE index, and the Expression Builder appears, with DEPTCODE as the default expression. Accept this field as the link between the tables, as you accept any other default in FoxPro and notice that `DEPT` then appears next to the ↳ symbol in the Relations box of the View window, indicating that the two tables are related (see fig. 8.8).

If the index order for DEPT had been set, the Set Index Order dialog would have been bypassed. If the field on which the child table currently is ordered has the same name as a field in the parent, that field automatically becomes the default expression.

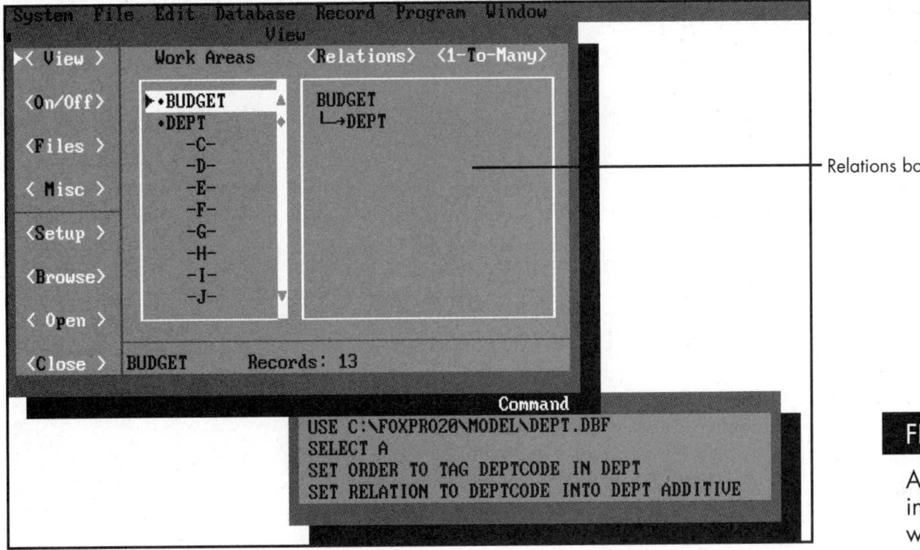

FIG. 8.8

A relation set in the View window.

Look at the commands FoxPro 2 used to create the relationship. Activate the Command window. You should see entries similar to these:

```
USE C:\FOXPRO20\MODEL\BUDGET.DBF
SELECT B
USE C:\FOXPRO20\MODEL\DEPT.DBF
SELECT A
SET ORDER TO TAG DEPTCODE IN DEPT
SET RELATION TO DEPTCODE INTO DEPT ADDITIVE
```

The relation was created by the SET RELATION command, which has the following syntax:

SET RELATION TO <*fieldname*> INTO <*alias*> [ADDITIVE]

The <*fieldname*> is the field that the two tables have in common and on which the relationship will be based. The child must be indexed on this field, and the index must be the child's master index. Setting the index to the proper tag was handled by the SET ORDER command. <*alias*> is the alias of the child, here, DEPT. ADDITIVE is optional and is required only when a parent has two or more children. When you link the parent to the second child, you have to use ADDITIVE to tell FoxPro to create an *additional* relation. Without ADDITIVE, all current relations are replaced by the new one.

Now that you set the relation, you can find out what this relation enables you to do. Open a separate Browse window and size each so that you can see both windows at the same time, as shown in figure 8.9.

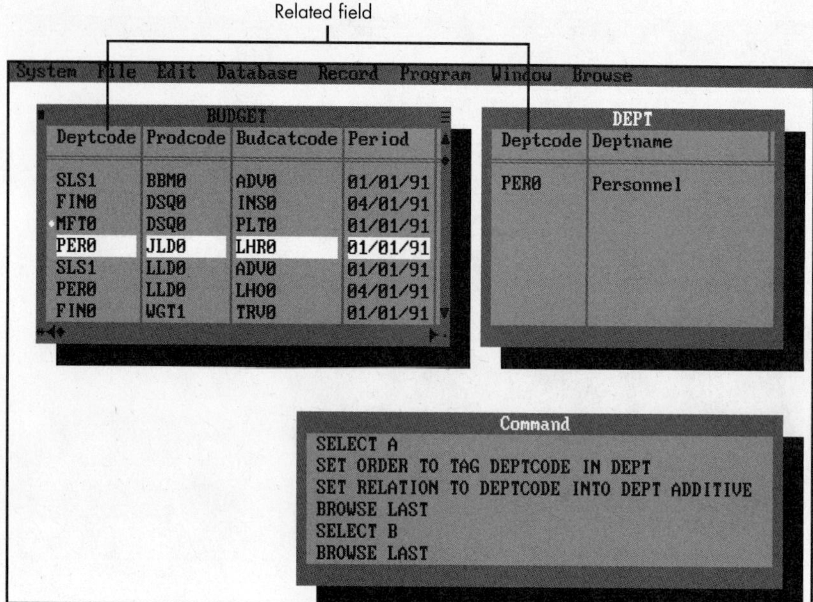

FIG. 8.9

Displaying related Browse windows.

Activate the BUDGET window and move the highlight bar from one record to another. As you move the record pointer in the parent table, the record pointer in the child table moves to the first record that contains the same value in the field on which they are related—here, the DEPTCODE field. Remember the way FoxPro operates here; this unusual feature is important to an upcoming part of this discussion.

If the child has no record of the same value in the related field, then the child's record pointer moves to the end of file (EOF) position, and the child's Browse window appears to be empty.

Now create a single Browse window that contains data from both tables. Close both Browse windows, activate the Command window, and type the following lines:

```
SELECT BUDGET
BROWSE ;
    FIELDS                    DEPTCODE, ;
          DEPT.DEPTNAME, ;
          PRODCODE, ;
          BUDGETAMT
```

Because BUDGET currently is active, you do not need to precede its field names with an alias, although you can . You do have to specify, however, that the DEPTNAME field is part of table DEPT in order for FoxPro to execute the command, because BUDGET has no such field.

The resulting Browse window, shown in figure 8.10, shows four fields: three from BUDGET (DEPTCODE, PRODCODE, and BUDGETAMT) and one from DEPT (DEPTNAME).

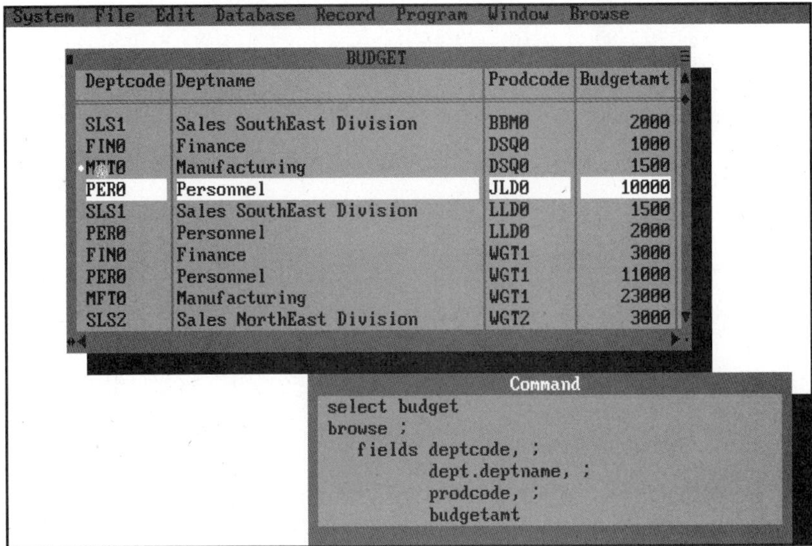

FIG. 8.10

A single Browse window with fields from two tables.

As you can see, the name of each department has been pulled from the DEPT table and is displayed next to the related department code.

You should understand that displaying data from more than one table in a Browse window really has nothing to do with setting relations. FoxPro happily pulls in the value of the current record in any open table if you tell the program which table you want to access. The difference here is that because you have linked the tables, the record pointer in the child always is updated as FoxPro moves through the parent to display the records.

TIP

If the field values pulled from a child table into the Browse window are the same, the tables probably aren't linked. The relation may not have been created properly, or perhaps the relation was inadvertently broken. Use the View window to verify this situation and, if needed, to re-create the relation.

The relation that you just created between BUDGET and DEPT is a *many-to-one relationship*. That is, the parent (BUDGET) may have many records that use a particular department code, but the child (DEPT) has only one department code.

A more natural way to think of the data is as a series of *one-to-many relationships*. A report showing sales by customer code, for example, is more informative than a listing in simple invoice number order. To create a report by customer, you need the capability to relate each unique customer code in the CUSTOMER table to those invoices in the SALES table with that customer code.

Using SET SKIP

FoxPro 2 gives you this capability with the SET SKIP command. Using SET SKIP, you can create Browse windows and reports that show a unique parent table value, followed by any number of related child table records, for each record in the parent table. A one-to-many relationship is created either from the View window or the Command window. Because FoxPro types the appropriate SET SKIP command in the Command window when you set the relationship from the View window, this chapter uses the View window to produce an example. After you're done, you can look at the command that FoxPro constructed in the Command window.

Activate the View window. Open the CUSTOMER table in work area A and the SALES table in area B. Select and then link CUSTOMER to SALES on the CUSTCODE field. (As with any relation, the child must be indexed on the field that relates the two tables. If necessary, index SALES on the CUSTCODE field before trying to link the tables.)

Notice that the `<1-To-Many>` push button is enabled. When selected, the 1-To-Many dialog appears. The list on the left shows the alias names of any child tables. In this case, only one exists: SALES. To create the one-to-many relationship, simply move SALES from the Child Aliases list to the Selected Aliases list on the right by selecting the `<All>` button. Then confirm the choices to exit the dialog.

The square box to the right of CUSTOMER indicates that the table is a parent involved in a one-to-many relationship with one or more of this table's children.

Close the View window and activate the Command window. The last line should be `SET SKIP TO SALES`. SET SKIP is the FoxPro 2 command that transforms a many-to-one relationship into a one-to-many relationship. What the command does is tell FoxPro to process your keystrokes in the Browse window as if the child rather than the parent were the controlling table. The record pointer in the parent table moves in sync with the current record in the child rather than vice-versa.

Take a look at what this feature does for you. To open a Browse window that pulls data from both CUSTOMER and SALES, type the following lines in the Command window:

```
BROWSE ;
   FIELDS            CUSTOMER.CUSTCODE, ;
        CUSTOMER.COMPANY, ;
        SALES.INVOICE, ;
        AMOUNT = SALES.QUANTITY * SALES.PRICE
```

The records now appear as *record blocks* (see fig. 8.11). Each block consists of a single record from the parent and one or more records from the child. If the child has more than one related record, the parent's records are separated from each other by a hash pattern that fills the fields taken from the parent. You can move from one block to the next by pressing Ctrl-down arrow and to the previous one with Ctrl-up arrow.

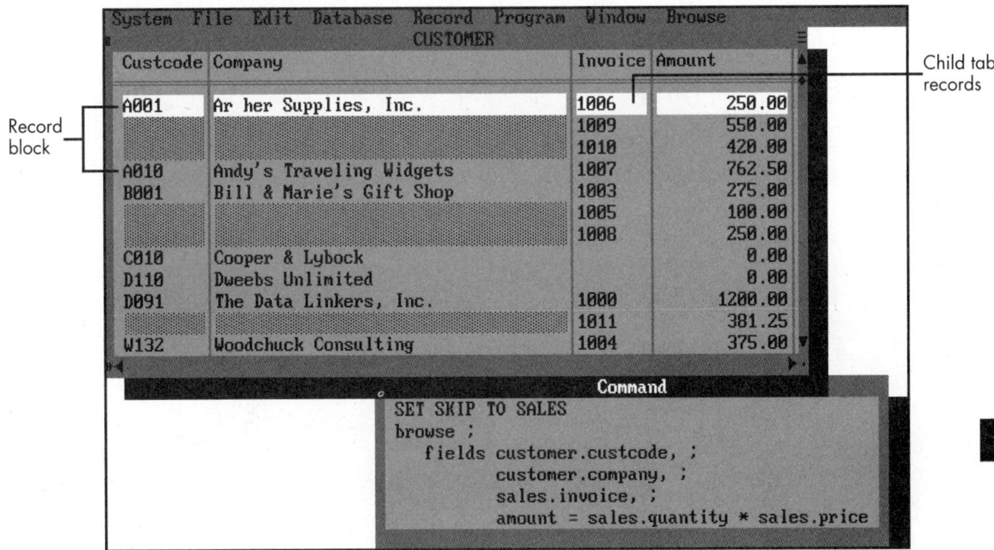

FIG. 8.11

Browsing with a one-to-many relationship.

You can break up these happy romances as easily as you created them. Select the parent table and type the following lines in the Command window:

```
SET RELATION OFF INTO <child alias>
```

Now activate the View window. Notice that table names no longer appear in the Relations box. You also can dissolve this relationship from the View window by modifying the relation and then deleting the linking field name from the Expression Builder.

You also can use relations to replace the user-defined function you used in the :V part of the FIELDS clause earlier in this chapter. Remember that the purpose of the UDF was to ensure that only valid entries were made in the DEPTCODE field of the BUDGET table. The UDF was used the SEEK( ) function to move the record pointer in the DEPT table. If the entry was invalid, the record pointer moved to the end-of-file (EOF) position.

Remember that the child's record pointer also moves to EOF when the child does not contain a record that matches the current record in the parent. You can use this fact to rewrite the BROWSE validation command in the following way:

```
BROWSE ;
    FIELDS               DEPTCODE      :V= !EOF("DEPT") ;
                         :E="No such Department Code!", ;
          PRODCODE, ;
          BUDCATCODE
```

Rather than calling a UDF to perform the validation, you can use FoxPro 2's EOF( ) function to tell whether the record pointer in the child (DEPT) is positioned at the end-of-file position. If the pointer is at this position, then the entry doesn't exist in the child and therefore must be invalid.

The lesson to learn from this example is that you often have more than one way to perform a task in FoxPro 2. If you find yourself working too hard, step back from the problem and make sure that you haven't overlooked an easier way to accomplish this objective.

Exploring Other BROWSE Options

BROWSE has a few other options of which you should be aware. Most of these options are used more often from within FoxPro programs than from the Command window or the menus, but you may find some of these options useful. Other than Format, all the options are saved in a preference when you exit the Browse window.

Using BROWSE FORMAT

The FORMAT option enables you to use a separate file known as a *format file* to control the format of the Browse window's display. The format file contains a series of @ SAY and @ GET commands and can include VALID, WHEN, PICTURE, and RANGE clauses for each field.

Although you can use a format file with BROWSE, this file originally was designed to control the display and editing format of a full-screen edit, using the READ command. As such, the format file contains screen positioning instructions (@ *<row>*, *<column>*) for each field. BROWSE ignores these instructions, but you must include them to use the format file successfully.

Look at a format file that you can use with the sample BUDGET table:

```
@ 0,0 GET DEPTCODE VALID !EMPTY(DEPTCODE) PICTURE "@!"
@ 0,0 GET PRODCODE PICTURE "@! AAA9"
@ 0,0 GET BUDCATCODE PICTURE "@! AAA9" WHEN !EMPTY(PRODCODE)
@ 0,0 GET BUDGETAMT PICTURE "9,999,999" RANGE 0, 1000000
@ 0,0 SAY IIF(FINAL, CHR(251), " ")
```

When you include @ SAY in a format file, BROWSE treats this expression as a calculated field and shows on-screen the result of the next expression. All GET statements' validation and formatting clauses are respected by the corresponding BROWSEd fields.

Format files don't provide the same power of expression and control available with the FIELDS clause, but they do provide backward compatibility for anyone who made use of them in dBASE III Plus or FoxBASE+.

In Chapters 12 and 13, you learn how to use FoxPro 2's Screen Builder to *generate* @ SAY...GET statements through the Screen Builder's *template* program, GENSCRN.PRG. GENSCRN doesn't create files that you can use as default Format files. Because GENSCRN is a program written in FoxPro, however, you can create an alternate version that, if desired, can generate Format files. In Chapter 17, you learn about the *textmerge* commands used by GENSCRN and how to edit a template program.

Using BROWSE LOCK

You may at times need to keep in view certain information, such as a person's first and last names, while moving the other fields in and out of view. You can control the view in this way with the LOCK option. You simply specify how many of the left-most fields should be placed in their own partition.

To see how LOCK works, open the CUSTOMER table and type the following lines in the Command window:

```
BROWSE ;
    FIELDS                FIRSTNAME, ;
          LASTNAME, ;
          CUSTCODE, ;
          COMPANY, ;
          CITY, ;
          STATE, ;
          ZIP ;
    LOCK 2
```

The LOCK 2 option tells FoxPro that you want the first two fields in the list, FIRSTNAME and LASTNAME, to appear by themselves in the left partition of a split Browse window. The right partition is active. These two fields also appear in the right partition so that you can still edit the fields without switching partitions.

Although this technique is useful in an interactive editing session, moving the fields around and creating the partitions by using a mouse or the menus is almost always easier than typing all this information in the Command window. Unless the fields that you want to keep in view are the first ones in the table field order, you have to use the FIELDS clause to *put* them together and at the left of the Browse window, which means that you have to type the name of every field you want to view.

As with the FORMAT clause, LOCK has been superseded largely by more powerful and flexible methods of achieving its goal. Because compatibility with earlier versions is an important consideration, however, LOCK will probably be here for some time to come.

The FREEZE clause is another BROWSE option retained from earlier xBase dialects. FREEZE is often used with LOCK and is handy for quick interactive editing. FREEZE is followed by a single specified field name and permits editing only on the specified field, no matter how many fields are displayed in the BROWSE.

Using BROWSE TITLE

Just as each field name is used as the default for column headings, the table's alias is used as the default for the title of the Browse window. You can create a title by using the TITLE clause.

Just follow the TITLE key word with a character expression or any expression that evaluates to a character string. You can, for example, create a more descriptive title for the BUDGET table by using these lines:

```
BROWSE ;
  TITLE "Budget For Fiscal Year Ended December 31,1991"
```

or

```
BROWSE ;
  TITLE "1991 Budget As Of " + DTOC(DATE())
```

Figure 8.12 shows the BUDGET table with a new title. As you can see, DTOC(DATE( )) results in the current date.

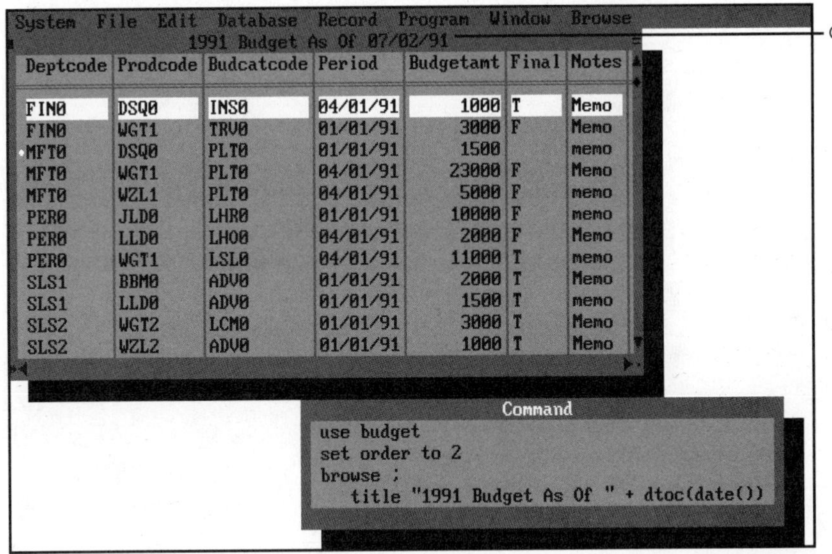

FIG. 8.12

A custom Browse window title showing today's date.

In the first example, the title is a simple character string, which must be enclosed in single or double quotes. In the second example, you use a character expression formed by concatenating the result of the DTOC( ) function and the character string `"1991 Budget As Of "`. If you always use BROWSE LAST, or if you save the title information in a preference, the Browse window always shows the current date as part of the title.

Using BROWSE WIDTH

FoxPro 2 uses the greater of a field's name and physical length to determine how many columns to use when displaying each field's contents. The WIDTH clause enables you to specify a maximum width for each column in the Browse window. This feature is useful when you want to view many fields at once without having to type a field list.

The CUSTOMER table, for example, contains many wide fields, such as COMPANY and ADDRESS1, that greatly limit the amount of information you can view at once. Figure 8.13 shows the view of the CUSTOMER table in the Browse window.

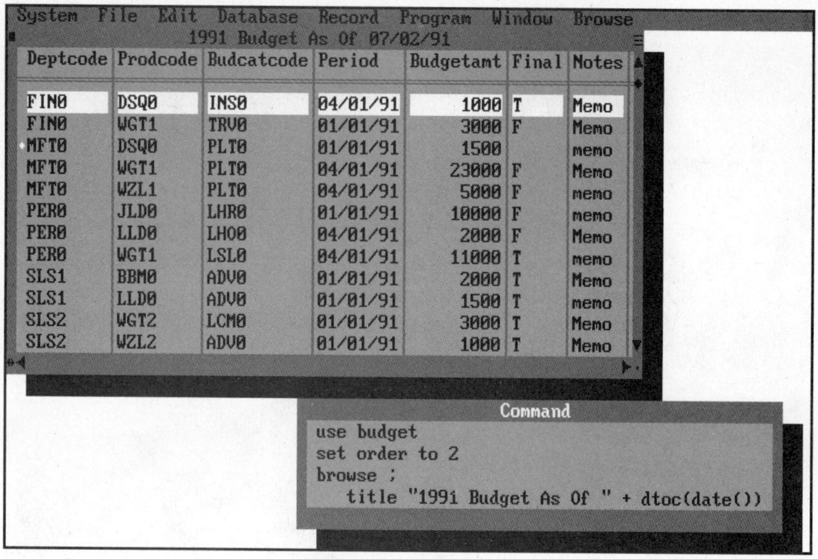

FIG. 8.13

Browsing the CUSTOMER table with default column widths.

Because you usually can identify a company name without seeing the entire field, you may want to limit each column's width to something less than its maximum. You can use this command, for example, to limit each column's width to 15 characters:

```
BROWSE ;
   WIDTH 15
```

Figure 8.14 shows the results in the Browse window. Now you can see enough of each field to identify it, and more of the information is visible at once.

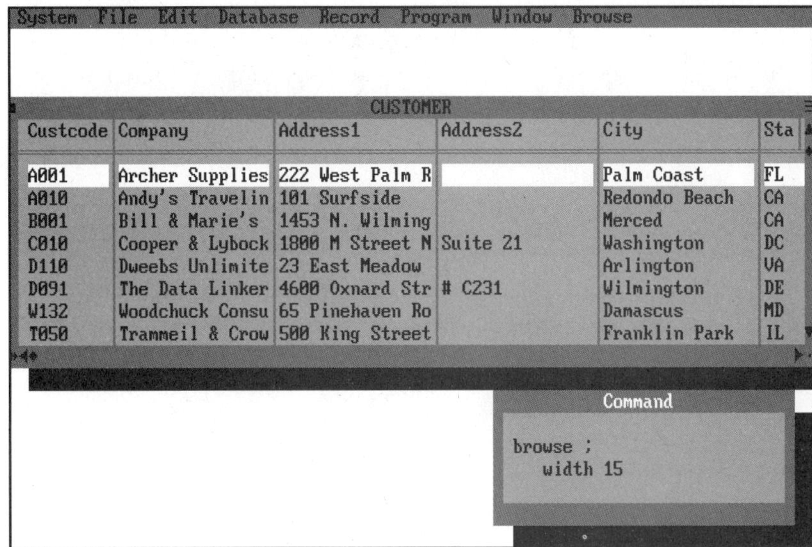

FIG. 8.14

Using the WIDTH clause to limit column widths.

Notice that the CUSTCODE column is still only nine characters wide (eight for the title plus one to show the "deleted" marker in column one). The WIDTH clause specifies a *maximum* width. If the default width is less than the maximum, the default is used.

Remember also that if you are using the :W option of the FIELDS clause to specify a width for a particular field, that width overrides a global column width set with the WIDTH clause.

Using BROWSE COLOR or BROWSE COLOR SCHEME

FoxPro 2 makes intelligent use of colors to distinguish among the different elements of the Browse window. The most obvious example is the highlight bar, which must use distinct foreground and background colors so that you can tell which record you're currently working on.

Each kind of FoxPro window has a default *color scheme*. BROWSE takes its colors from Color Scheme 10 unless you use the COLOR or COLOR SCHEME clause to use a different set of colors.

Color schemes and the *color picker*, which enables you to create and edit color schemes interactively, are the subject of a discussion in Chapter 15. For now, just be aware that you're not stuck with the colors shown so far in the BROWSE command.

You can see some of the color combinations that make up the various color schemes by using the COLOR SCHEME clause with different numbers. Try Color Scheme 8, for example, with any of the tables that you currently have open. Type the following command:

```
BROWSE ;
    COLOR SCHEME 8
```

The results look much like the default Color Scheme 10 except that the highlight bar uses a different color pair.

To use a particular color pair for a particular window element, you can use a *color pair list* rather than a color scheme. A color pair list can have up to ten color pairs. Each pair is separated from the others by a comma. To take advantage of this feature, you first have to know which color pair affects which window element. Not every interface object uses all ten available pairs. As you see here (in table 8.5, which lists the color pair positions and shows the window element that each pair controls), BROWSE doesn't use the last two pairs.

Table 8.5 The Browse Window Color Pairs

Pair No.	Affected Browse Window Element
1	All records other than the current record. The second color is the grid background.
2	The current field of the current record
3	The window border. The second color is the grid foreground.
4	The window title when the window is active
5	The window title when the window is inactive
6	Selected text in the window
7	Fields of the current record other than the current field. The second color is the delete marker.
8	The window's shadow (if any)
9	Not used
10	Not used

A color pair consists of a foreground color and a background color. This coloring works the same way here as you see with printed text. The text you're reading right now, for example, uses a black foreground (the letters) on a white background (the paper on which the letters are printed).

You don't have to specify all the color pairs in the color pair list. You have to specify only the pairs you want to change from the defaults. Commas are used as placeholders for any color pairs that you skip, however, so that FoxPro applies only the pairs that you change to the proper window elements.

To change only the colors of the highlight bar in fields other than the current field, for example, type this command:

```
BROWSE ;
   COLOR ,,,,,,W+/R
```

FoxPro then uses bright white letters on a red background for the highlight bar. The + means bright or high intensity and may be used with any color.

You can use only four *colors* on monochrome monitors: white, black, underlined (U), and inverse video (I).

In Chapter 15's section on color control (table 15.1), you see a listing of all the colors (and the related codes) available in FoxPro.

Chapter Summary

In this chapter, you have learned to use FoxPro 2's BROWSE command to view tables, restrict the display to certain fields and groups of records, validate data input, create and save customized Browse window "looks," and link one or more tables. In the process, you also learned a great deal about using the View window and the Command window together, and you now have a good understanding of which window is appropriate for the task at hand.

Setting relations among tables is a powerful tool. Getting relations right requires a little experience with manipulating tables and a good understanding of database design principles. The time you spend planning the database layouts pay handsome dividends in the form of easy access to all the information through inter-table relationships.

After you achieve a satisfactory database design, you can use BROWSE to display the information on-screen in any way you choose.

9

CHAPTER

Putting the Answers To Work in Reports and Labels

In Chapter 8, you learn how to use Browse to review data on-screen, which can differ greatly in appearance from the contents of the records in the tables. Now that you are familiar with the flexible capabilities of FoxPro 2, you may want a more permanent kind of output to help you evaluate, use, and share the information in the data files.

You previously learned that the LIST command can send quick snapshots of the tables to the printer or a file, but you begin to tap the real power of FoxPro 2 for output when you use the Report Writer and Label Designer. These two tools give you the same flexibility in the creation of printed results as FoxPro provides, with Browse for the screen.

Typically, a *report* is output composed of many records in a format that lists the records down and the fields across, one record per line.

A *label*, however, usually contains information about only one record and is formatted more as a Change/Edit. Because labels are meant to accommodate mailing labels you can buy in sheets or rolls, you can designate the number of labels you want to print across the page, and FoxPro moves to the next record for each label.

No hard-and-fast rules exist for report and label formatting; you can format a report exactly like a label (in *form* rather than in *column* layout), and each report can contain information about only one record. You may find this feature useful for printing mail-merge letters or even to format addresses for continuous-form envelopes. You also can use a label design on normal paper to print information about many records, when information about multiple records on each line is desirable.

The following two chapters describe ways to create and use labels and reports so that you can experiment with the differences of each procedure as you learn the techniques shared by these two versatile FoxPro tools.

This chapter concentrates on the Label and Report Writer *as* tools because using these applications may differ from other kinds of editing you learned on a computer. If, however, you previously used desktop publishing programs on the PC or the Macintosh computer—which take a similar editing approach to the Label and Report Writer—you may become comfortable right away with these tools. You manipulate the elements of labels and reports as objects, which you can move, size, and attach to each other.

First you create a Quick Report, in which you use the Report Writer as a learning tool to introduce you to these objects. Next, you learn about the different kinds of objects you can use, you learn to manipulate these objects in a Report layout, and you learn ways to change the layout report as a whole.

After becoming familiar with these options, you look at the file formats that FoxPro uses to make the options available. Finally, you apply the same techniques and principles in creating labels in the Label Designer.

Designing a Quick Report

FoxPro 2 makes designing a first report easy—without knowing anything about the way the Report Writer works—if you use the Quick Report feature. After you create this report, you can examine and alter the components to suit your needs.

If you have not already done so, open the Budget table. (In the following chapter, you also use the Product table with the relation set to the PRODCODE field as you learn in Chapter 3, "Exploring Databases and Tables.") If you created a View with these two files related, you can access View now (by using either SET VIEW TO *<viewname>* or the File Open dialog), and the Budget table is opened as part of the View.

By using the File New dialog, open a Report file. You see a new kind of window, the Report Layout screen. The window shows that you have created a new and unnamed file, UNTITLED; in the case of a Report, the file's extension is FRX. You also see that you have a new pad, Report, on the menu bar. Choose this pad, and you see the options listed in figure 9.1.

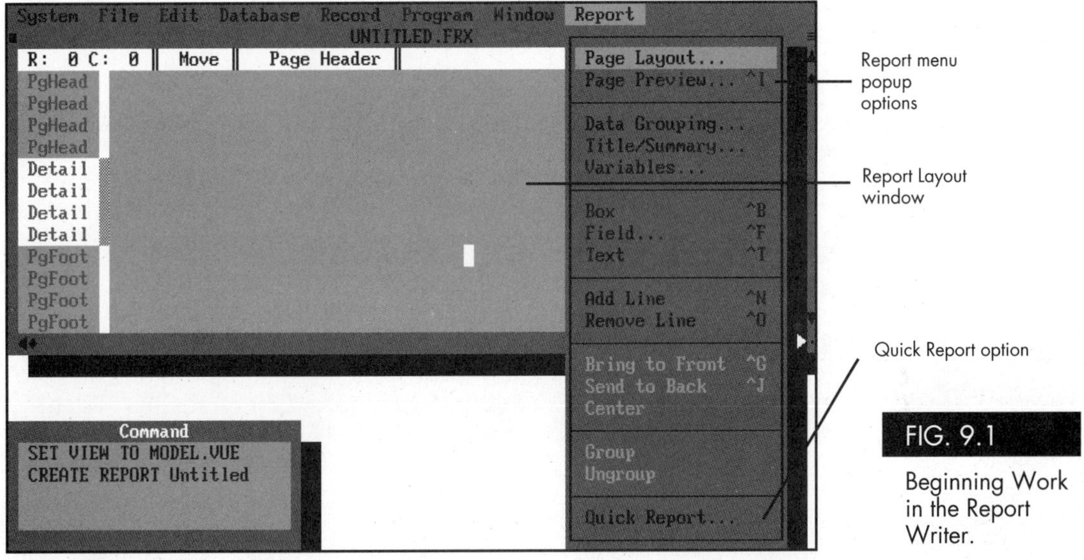

FIG. 9.1

Beginning Work in the Report Writer.

Choose the `Quick Report` option, listed at the bottom of the popup. (You can use the Quick Report feature only when you are working with a blank report.)

The dialog you see (on the left) in figure 9.2 has two radio buttons that enable you to specify a `Column` or `Form` layout. Select the `Form` button, and the diagram to the right of the radio buttons changes to show you the layout you have chosen; then return the layout to the default of Column.

The `Titles` check box enables you to specify whether you want the columns to have headings. Quick Report supplies headings by using field names. If you mark the `Add Alias` check box, the Report Writer adds a reference to the appropriate table when reference is made to data contained in fields. Leave both of these options at the default setting.

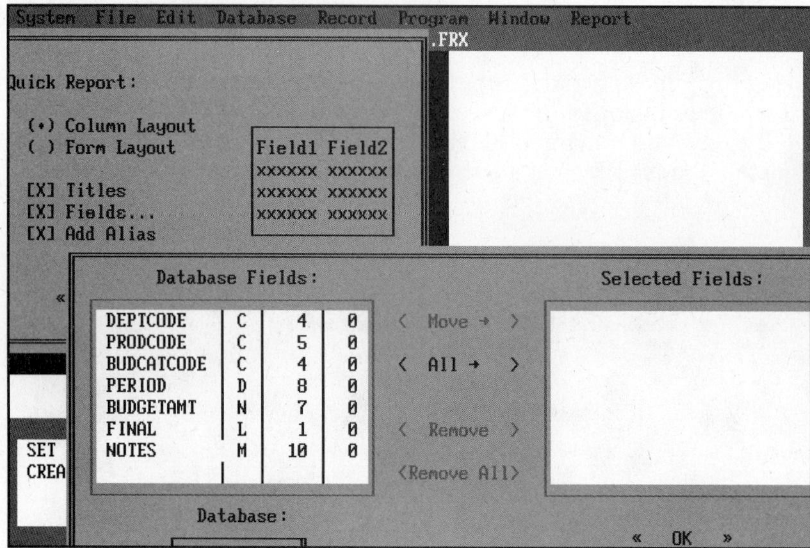

FIG. 9.2

The Quick Report dialogs.

Mark the Fields check box to see the dialog (lower down and to the right) active in figure 9.2. Choose the <All →> text button and all the fields from the Database Fields, or Field Picker, list on the left side of the dialog appear in the Selected Fields list to the right. This list is the default fields list that you get by using Quick Report if you did not select the Fields check box. Notice that each item is prefaced by *Budget*, the current alias by which you can refer to the file from where these fields come, followed by a period (.) to separate the alias from the field name.

Here, you may want to eliminate or rearrange the order of some fields. Mark the fields that appear on the list by clicking the mouse button or pressing the space bar and holding down the Shift key for additional fields if you want to mark more than one field at a time. A character appears to the left of all selected fields. Click the <Remove> button to delete these marked fields; the fields again become available for use in the Field Picker list on the left. Now mark the fields on the left and click the <Move →> button to move the fields, one at a time, back to the rightmost box in the order you want the fields to appear (left to right) in the report. For this sample report, make sure that all fields are selected (all files are selected when no files are visible on the left side).

Besides using the <Move →> button while fields are selected, you can press Enter, double-click, or press the space bar twice to move any field into the Selected Fields list. (If more than one field is currently selected, you need to hold down the Shift key as you double-click the space bar.)

Confirm the choices in both dialogs, and the report is laid out. If what you see makes no sense, look at the output produced by using the Page Preview option (or by pressing Ctrl-I) from the Report menu popup, as shown in figure 9.3.

You may want to use Page Preview repeatedly during the following exercises and while designing any report to check the results of each action you take.

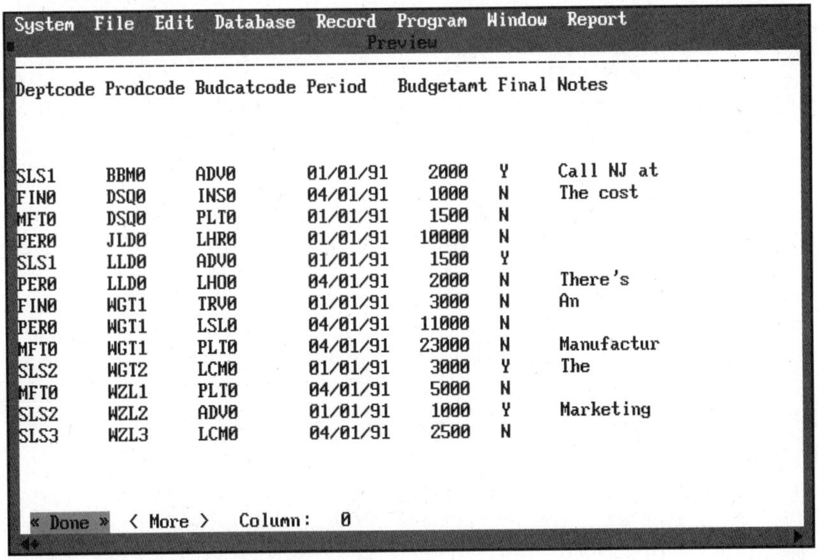

```
System  File  Edit  Database  Record  Program  Window  Report
                              Preview
------------------------------------------------------------------
Deptcode Prodcode Budcatcode Period    Budgetamt Final Notes



SLS1     BBM0     ADV0       01/01/91     2000   Y     Call NJ at
FIN0     DSQ0     INS0       04/01/91     1000   N     The cost
MFT0     DSQ0     PLT0       01/01/91     1500   N
PER0     JLD0     LHR0       01/01/91    10000   N
SLS1     LLD0     ADV0       01/01/91     1500   Y
PER0     LLD0     LHO0       04/01/91     2000   N     There's
FIN0     WGT1     TRV0       01/01/91     3000   N     An
PER0     WGT1     LSL0       04/01/91    11000   N
MFT0     WGT1     PLT0       04/01/91    23000   N     Manufactur
SLS2     WGT2     LCM0       01/01/91     3000   Y     The
MFT0     WZL1     PLT0       04/01/91     5000   N
SLS2     WZL2     ADV0       01/01/91     1000   Y     Marketing
SLS3     WZL3     LCM0       04/01/91     2500   N


 « Done »  < More >   Column:   0
```

FIG. 9.3

Page Preview of a Quick Report.

Examining the Report Layout Screen

The Quick Report is a good way to get started, but several other ways are available to improve this report. To use these ways, you must understand and learn to edit the components of a FoxPro 2 report.

In a FoxPro 2 report, each horizontal line (or row), belongs to one of several kinds of *report bands*. Each band represents a part of the report page (see fig. 9.4).

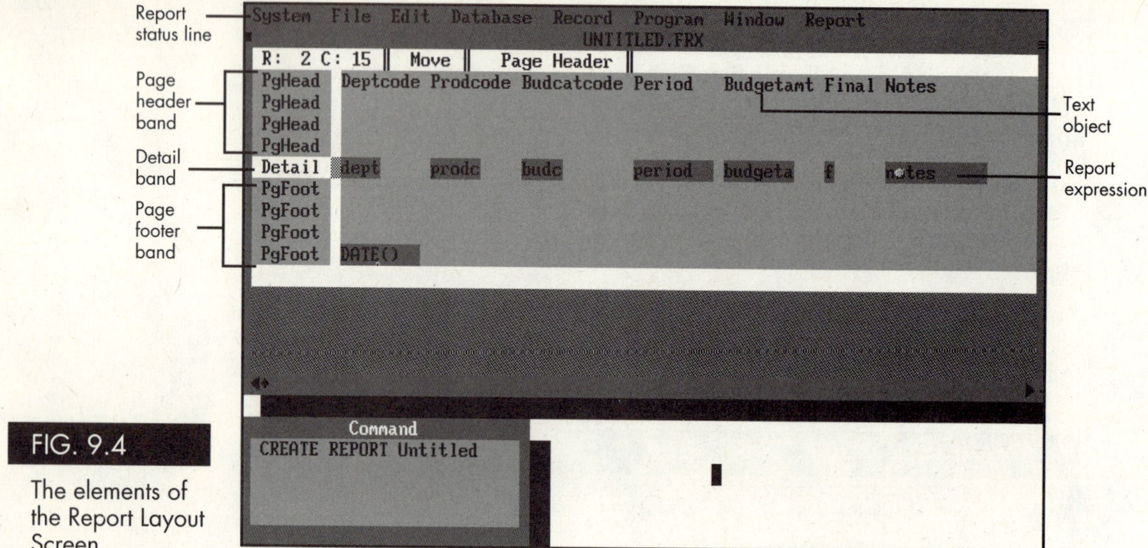

FIG. 9.4

The elements of the Report Layout Screen.

On the left side of the Report Layout screen, you see that each row is designated as a line in a `PgHead` (page header), a `Detail`, or a `PgFoot` (page footer) band. Lines in the page header and footer bands appear at the top and bottom of each page. By using the appropriate Report menu options, you also can add `Title` and `Summary` bands that appear only at the beginning and end of each report. (Other band designations, indicating data *groupings*, also may appear as you work. These designations are discussed in the following chapter.)

In the middle of the Report Layout screen is the `Detail` band. Although you currently see only the one line, this band actually generates most of the lines in the page preview shown in figure 9.4. When you produce a report, the Report Writer moves through a table, record by record, and generates a set of items for the detail band for *each* record. By default, the Report Writer leaves room for the page footer band on each page, starts a new page by reprinting the page header lines, and then continues with the next available record until the end of the table is reached (or until the scope you supplied is exhausted).

A detail band can hold more than one line. As many as 255 distinct detail lines can exist in a report. The Report Writer prints all the detail lines for one record and then prints a new detail band (or set of detail lines) for the next record.

Report bands contain three different kinds of *report objects*: *field*, *text*, or *box*, as described in this chapter. Each object is a self-contained unit that you can edit or alter. Each band can contain objects of any kind or, if you desire, objects of all three kinds.

Look at the report layout, to the right of the band designations. Notice that the items in the page header (the field names supplied by the Quick Report as column headings) are shown in different colors or intensities than the detail band items or the item in the footer. The Report Writer is differentiating between *text objects*, which appear exactly as typed, and *report expression objects*, which Report Writer evaluates. When FoxPro *evaluates* an expression, the results of this expression, rather than the expression itself, is placed in the report.

You can see that the report expression in the page footer is the FoxPro function DATE(). If you look in the help file, you see that the result of this function is the current system date and what the Report Writer shows in the report where this expression is positioned. (This function is formatted according to the current default as set either in the View Misc panel options or by using the SET DATE command in the Command window.)

Each report expression in the detail band is the name of a field in the Budget table. For each detail line, the Report Writer evaluates each expression by asking: “What is the current value of this expression?” The Report Writer places at the appropriate position the contents of the field for the current record in the report.

Don’t be alarmed if only a few letters of each field name appear in the report expressions listed in the detail band. The Report Writer is showing you how much space the results of the report expression need to occupy within the report (here, the width of each field in the Budget table). The actual expression may be much longer.

The sample page header band, however, contains some *text* objects that Report Writer literally copied into the report rather than evaluated. Each text object appears on-screen as it prints out in the report.

An object of box type, such as text objects and in contrast to report expressions, appear in the layout exactly as the object appears in the report. *Box* objects consist of lines and boxes that you can draw to enhance a report. In the report layout, box objects are shown in the same colors or intensities as text objects.

NOTE The top line in the Report Writer is the *status line*. On the left, the status line tracks the current cursor position, which is useful as you decide where to fit a new item in the layout. The next item in the status line tells you the action you are currently performing. Here, `Move` is displayed on-screen, but `Box` (when you draw a line or box object), `Text` (when you type a text object into the layout), or `Field` (when you manipulate report expressions) also may appear. The final status line item is a reminder of which report band the current action is going to affect.

Making Simple Layout Adjustments

The first thing you may want to change in the sample report is to remove the empty lines in the page header and footer bands. Place the cursor in an empty line in the page header band and use the Report menu option to Remove Line (or press Ctrl-O) until only one line, with the field names, is left. (If you make a mistake and try to remove a line that contains data, the Report Writer asks you to confirm the choice.) You can do the same in the footer band.

Perhaps you may decide that the empty line between the data and the date in the page footer is a good idea. To insert an empty line, place the cursor in the line that contains the DATE() expression and choose the Add Line menu option or press Ctrl-N. A blank line appears above the cursor.

You also may want to separate the column headings in the page header band from the data with at least one blank line, or perhaps draw a line between the two bands. To do so, place the cursor on the line that contains the page headings, press Shift while you access the Report menu or press Ctrl-N. On-screen, the option changes to `Add Line After`.

Mouse users have an alternative way to add and remove lines. Place the mouse cursor in the area to the left, where the band titles are located. Click-drag the mouse down to add lines to the band in which you are located, or up to take empty lines away, much like unrolling or rolling up a window shade. Hold Shift down while click-dragging up or down to affect the band *above* the band in which the cursor is located.

Now draw a line between the column headings and the data. Place the cursor in the middle of the blank line you added to the page header and select the `Box` option from the menu popup (or press Ctrl-B). You see a small flashing box appear. Although invisible, the cursor is now at the lower right corner of this box. You make the box wider by moving the cursor to the right and taller by moving the cursor down (use the arrow keys or click-drag the mouse). You can make the box narrower by moving the cursor to the left and shorter by moving the cursor up. When you move the cursor to the *same row* on which you began the box-drawing, the box becomes a horizontal line. When you move the cursor to the *same column* on which you started drawing, the box becomes a vertical line. The box continues to change, as shown by the flashing, until you press Enter, click the mouse, or press the space bar.

Notice that you cannot draw the line or box either above or to the left of the original cursor position. When you *size* the box you use a technique known in FoxPro—and in other programs—as *rubberbanding* or *stretching*. In FoxPro, you usually stretch an object down and to the right.

Suppose that the line you drew didn't start far enough to the left (under the `Deptcode` heading). You can select this line (or any other object in the Report Layout screen) by clicking on the line with the mouse or pressing the space bar while the cursor is on the line. After selection, you can move an object with the cursor keys or by click-dragging with the mouse. Now move the line further to the left. When the object is positioned as desired, press Enter or the space bar, or click elsewhere in the layout to unselect the line. When no object is selected, click the mouse, use the cursor keys, or press Tab to move to other objects in the layout.

Because you moved the line to the left, perhaps the line no longer extends far enough to the right. You can resize—by pressing Ctrl at the same time you select the box with the space bar or the mouse. After the object begins to flash, you can use the cursor keys for the resize operation.

Continue moving the cursor to the right, stretching the box, and you notice that the movement does not end at the window border. You can stretch the line until you reach the right margin of the page, which by default is wider than the report layout window can show at one time. (You learn how to change the report margins in the following section.) You now are accustomed to the scrolling that takes place (and to the movement of the thumb in the scroll bar in the border) as you continue to the right or down in the layout window.

After you reach the right margin of the report, you see two more objects in the page footer, which were previously invisible. One object is the text object *Page*, and beside Page you see a report expression that holds the system variable, *_PAGENO*, which FoxPro uses to internally track the page count for the report you are running. The DATE() expression to the far left and this page numbering pair of expressions to the right are inserted by the Quick Report option. For this report, perhaps you want to place the page number in the page header (you may want to add a page header line for this procedure). You already know how to select one object; you select multiple objects by holding down the Shift key as you select additional objects with mouse clicks or presses of the space bar. (Hold down Shift and click again or press the space bar again to unselect a particular item while you keep the other items selected.) Now you can move the two objects at one time to the top of the report.

You may want to move these objects often, and you also may always want to move these objects *together*. After selection, you can use the Report menu option to Group the objects. The next time you select one of these objects, both objects are selected by default.

Mouse users have an alternative method to select multiple objects. Place the mouse cursor in the report, but *do not touch* any report object, and click and drag. You see a box with dotted lines, which you also can stretch and size. This box is a *selection marquee*. Because you cannot touch any report object when you begin to size the selection marquee (otherwise the click selects only the object you touch), you can stretch this box in all directions, rather than only to the right and down.

When you release the mouse button, all objects (even objects partially within this box) are selected. Figure 9.5 shows a selection marquee in the act of selecting multiple objects. You can unselect inadvertently selected objects by holding down the Shift key and clicking or pressing the space bar on them. You can then choose to Group the selected objects as before.

You also can remove from the layout any object or group in the report just by selecting the object or group and pressing Backspace or Delete. You can copy, cut, or paste all objects by using the usual editing shortcuts (Ctrl-C, Ctrl-X, and Ctrl-V). Any formatting and other attributes that you previously defined for an object are included when you paste the object in the new location. Practice moving the DATE( ) expression to different places on the page and then return the expression to the page footer band.

You can open several report layout windows at one time, just as you can open several text editing windows. You may want to copy a report object, or several, from one report to another. You can easily copy a standard page heading for your company from layout to layout.

As you practice selecting different objects, occasionally check the Report and Edit menu popups. Depending on whether an object is currently selected, you see various items become available or unavailable on the menus in a similar way to when you edit a text file.

With the DATE() expression selected, you may want to try an additional option on the Report menu: Center. (No shortcuts or mouse equivalents exist for this option.) Grouping takes on a special significance with the centering option; if you select more than one object, each object is centered individually, relative to the central character in the line. This step means that if two or more objects are in the same row, all objects are overlaid on top of each other. All the objects are present, and print over each other, although you cannot see all of them in the Page Preview. If you want these objects to be centered together on the line, however, group the objects before you choose the Center menu option. (The order in which you select the objects before grouping does not affect the order in which they appear on the line after centering; the objects remain in the same right-to-left order. The distance *between* the items also remains the same as before centering.)

Another example in which grouping objects has a special significance occurs when box or line objects touch each other: you can change the characters at the connection points so that the boxes or lines are joined. The difference is shown in figure 9.5. If you need to edit only one object from a group, you must first Ungroup the objects by using the Report menu.

If you frequently check the Page Preview, you may see a number of improvements you can make. The column headings, for example, are still raw field names that you can edit to English words with the usual text-editing strokes. With the cursor directly on a text object, press Ctrl-T. You see `Move` change to `Text` in the status line. You can continue to edit text until you press Enter to return to Move status. Edit the first column headings to read `Dept #`, `Product`, and `Budget Code`. You may want to shift the Product and Budget category columns and headings to the right or left as you change the width of the headings.

The next column, Period, is already an understandable heading. Suppose that, however, you want to show all four digits of the year in the date? Use the Window View Misc panel to check off the `Century` option. Now return to the Report Layout window and do another preview. The change, although made, was not completely successful; the dates read 01/01/19 and 04/01/19 instead of showing the year. You have to make room for the extra digits in the Period report expression. Luckily, you can resize a report expression in the same way you resized the box object. As necessary, move other objects to the right side of the screen to make room.

Place the cursor inside the Period report expression and select the expression with the Ctrl key pressed. You notice that the column indicator on the status line immediately shows the *last* column occupied by this object, regardless of where the cursor was when you selected. Watching the status line indicator, resize the object to two columns wider. For the same reason and by the same method, resize the DATE() expression in the page footer. Now perform a Page Preview to see the results.

You may want to make other change to the NOTES field. If you typed new entries into the NOTES memofield, you see that they are cut off after only a few words. Although you can resize the NOTES field a few characters, a memofield is unlimited in length so you cannot possibly provide for all the memofields in this manner.

Because you have limited room to expand horizontally, the solution is to stretch vertically this report expression. Before you accomplish this expansion, make the problem a little more interesting by adding a box around the NOTES field. Add two detail lines and move the current detail expressions to the middle line of the three, either by selecting the expressions in the usual way or by using the selection marquee shown in figure 9.5. The extra detail lines enable you to draw the box object around the Notes report expression. Resize the NOTES field to take as much room as you have within the margin, without overwriting the box.

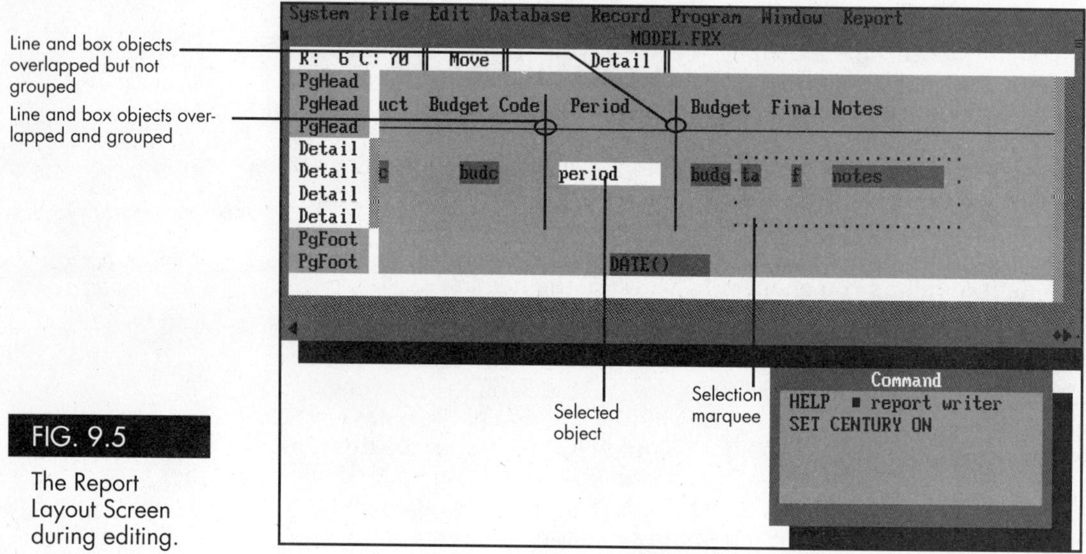

FIG. 9.5

The Report Layout Screen during editing.

Now double-click on the NOTES field or place the cursor on the field and either press the space bar twice or press Enter. You see the Report Expression dialog as shown in figure 9.6; you cover this feature more fully in the following chapter. For now, mark the `Stretch Vertically` check box, which tells the Report Writer that you want this field to continue for as many lines as necessary to contain the Notes for each record.

To coordinate with this change, you need to tell the Report Writer that the box that surrounds the Notes must adjust for the NOTES field length. You bring up a dialog for styling box objects by using the same techniques on the box object that you used on the field object. This dialog enables you to make an object `Float as Band Stretches`, which means that FoxPro places the field one line below the last line of the stretched character field (see fig. 9.7). If you don't select this option, the field is placed on the report as defined on the Layout view; if the character field stretches, the data overwrites the bottom field and makes a mess.

You also see options to modify the *style* of the box object; you have radio buttons that enable you to pick a double line or panel for the box as opposed to the default single line, and an opportunity to form the box from any character from a version of the ASCII character list that appears. (Fig. 9.7 shows the results you can achieve with the `Character` radio button; remember that if a box is formed from a character in this list, the box has no true corner characters, as do all of the other three radio buttons.)

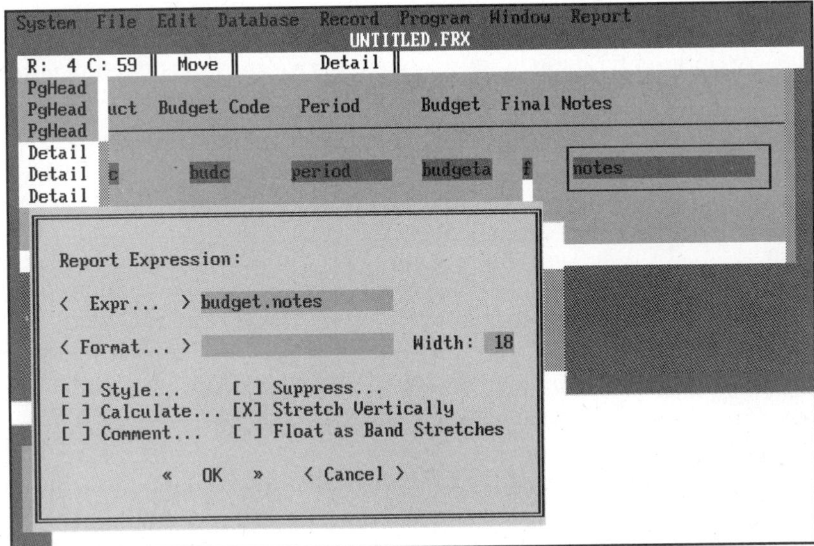

FIG. 9.6

The Report Expression dialog.

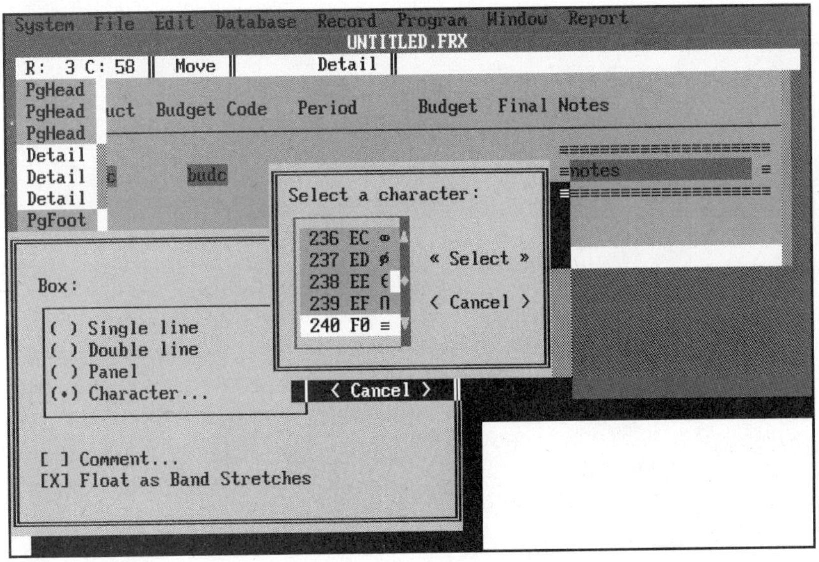

FIG. 9.7

The box object dialog and the associated ASCII Character List.

You may want to add a text object, under the box, to indicate that this box can include hand-written memos jotted down in the empty space the box contains if no notes are added to this record's memofield. If you perform this process, you can double-click on this object, press Enter, or press the space bar twice as you can for the other object types, and you see a dialog that affects the style and position of text objects, as shown in figure 9.8. Mark the `Float as Band Stretches` check box because this object also must move relative to the NOTES field. (The options to Stretch and Float are active only in the detail and page header bands of a report.)

If you also mark the `Style` button, you can select printer enhancements, subject to the printer driver you previously installed. The enhancements you check from the Style list on the left and the Alignment list on the right appear as codes underneath, to which you can add custom codes if you have written or use a printer driver that can handle these style and alignment options. (You find information on printer drivers in Chapter 15, "Discovering More FoxPro 2 Productivity Features.")

NOTE

Style dialog enhancements differ from other formatting changes you can make because these enhancements are specific to printed output, which includes printing to a file for later use with a printer. Style enhancements are ignored when you send a report to the screen, and you cannot see the results of these changes in this dialog when you perform a Page Preview.

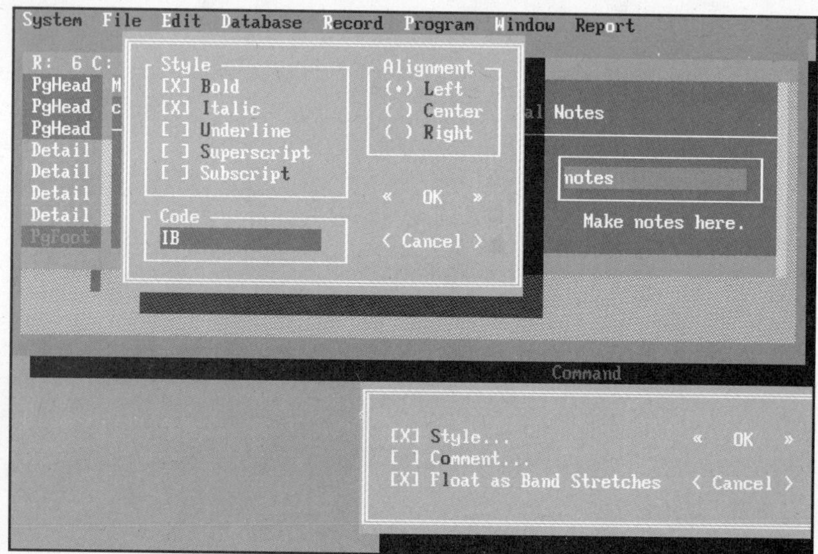

FIG. 9.8

The Text Object and Style dialogs.

All three kinds of object dialogs have an additional `Comment` check box. If you select this box, a text editing window appears. Whatever you type in the window serves as notes on the creation and use of this report object; this information does not appear in output. The Comment feature is especially useful if you are copying objects between two reports.

Making Changes That Affect the Entire Report

So far, you altered different kinds of individual report objects. You may want to make some global changes, however, that affect the report as a whole. You can find these selections under the Page Layout option of the Report menu popup.

Figure 9.9 shows the Page Layout dialog and the associated Options dialog. Except for the Environment text buttons, discussed elsewhere in this chapter, the items you can choose here are mostly self-explanatory. Here, you can affect the page margins by typing **132** as a right margin for a report in standard compressed pitch type.

The Suppress blank lines check box in the Options dialog enables you to specify that all *completely blank* lines in the detail band do not appear. (This step doesn't include lines with numeric fields in which 0 prints or lines that hold no objects. You learn more about suppressing blank lines in reports and labels in the following chapter.) The Summary report check box suppresses *all* detail lines, which is useful if you grouped the data and want information only on each group. Usually, however, you get more flexibility if you do not mark this box; you always can make a given incidence of a report a summary report by choosing the appropriate Report dialog check box.

When the Page Layout settings are as you want them, save this report in any of the ways you previously learned to close and save a text file window. FoxPro requests a file name and assigns the extension FRX to the name you choose. Save the file as *MODEL.FRX*. (You return to this report in the following chapter and show the final results of the work performed here.)

When you save a report for the first time, you get an alert that reminds you to save the work before exiting. This alert also asks whether you want to save the report environment.

A report's *environment* is a special way of saving the information required to run the report (the files that must be open, the relations that must be set, and the order in which you want to see the data). Unlike an independent VUE file, this information is saved directly in the report file.

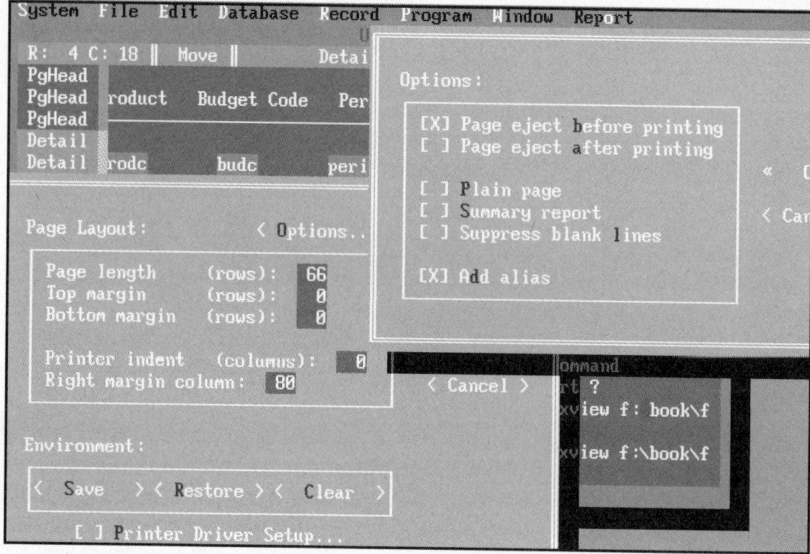

FIG. 9.9

The Page Layout dialog and the associated Options dialog that shows default settings.

You normally choose to save this information when you first create a report. If you save the environment, you can later edit the report, and each time the appropriate files are opened when you open the report. Then you may decide that another file is required, or a different index is useful. Here, you can use the Page Layout dialog to `<Save>` the new environment information to the report form or you can decide that the new information is only temporary. You use the other Page Layout options to `<Restore>` the original environment information, or `<Clear>` the environment information attached to the report form.

Note that when you use the Page Layout option to `<Save>` the environment, you affect only the report form *currently loaded in memory*; the environment is saved to disk *when you save the entire report* or else discarded if you cancel the entire editing session.

Rather than separately SETting VIEW before you run the report, you can mark the `<Restore>` environment check box in the Report dialog. The options to MODIFY REPORT or run the REPORT FORM from the Command window also include clauses you use to restore the environment. (Open the MODEL.FRX file from the File Open dialog without the `<Restore>` Environment box checked, and you see that the `MODIFY REPORT MODEL.FRX` line echoed in the Command window includes the keyword `NOENVIRONMENT`.)

The Printer Driver Setup option brings you to the same Printer Driver Setup dialog available throughout FoxPro 2. If you want the Report Writer to use any style enhancement to report objects (or if you want Report Writer to issue other printer-specific instructions), you must have a currently active printer driver. In Chapter 15, you learn how to ensure that the printer driver you load supports the enhancements you select.

When you load a printer driver, you make a special change in the FoxPro environment. The Report Writer saves this information with the current report (similar to how View information is saved), and when you are ready to print a report, you can choose to load the printer driver with which the report was saved—rather than the currently active driver, or no driver at all—by using the PDSETUP keyword.

Looking Closely at Report and Label Files

NOTE

Eventually, you may settle on several standard features for the reports you produce: you may never want a page to eject before the report begins to print; you may use the same heading on all reports; and you may save report environment information for all (or none of) the reports. The printer also may use a standard number of lines that differs from FoxPro's default, especially if you have a laser printer; or, you may want to set standard margins to other than the defaults.

In all these cases, you may want to set up and save a *blank* report with a special name. When you are ready to start designing a new report, you can open and then save this *template* report to a new file name. To avoid overwriting this special report file, you can set the file attributes to *read only*. (Use FoxPro's Filer, described in Chapter 15, to set the file attributes.)

You already observed that reports are composed of various kinds of objects and that you can assign each object different attributes, which are carried with the object as the object is moved or copied from one location to another.

FoxPro 2 stores the objects and assigned attributes by saving information about a report or a label in a *database table*. This table is like other tables you design and use, with the following exceptions:

- The extension FRX is used by default, and the associated memo field uses the extension FRT (the extensions are LBX and LBT for a table that stores information about a label).
- A required structure is internally set by FoxPro.

As you work in the Report Writer or the Label Designer, FoxPro 2 stores a copy of this table in memory. As you add and delete objects and the assigned attributes, FoxPro adds and deletes records in the table and fills out the table fields.

By opening MODEL.FRX, you can examine the structure of the FRX like any other table. Choose File Open, select Database type files, and mark the `All Files` check box. When you browse this table, you see that the first field is OBJTYPE. If you examine the contents of each record, you soon realize that the different OBJTYPE fields correspond to the report objects you are examining. The first record, OBJTYPE 1, holds the report's global information; notice that the record's HEIGHT and WIDTH fields hold the report dimensions. Each record has a number of memofields used to store an object's expression, styles, and other attributes—including the associated Comments you may have added. Not all fields are in use for all kinds of objects, of course.

NOTE The structure of the FRX/FRT and the LBX/LBT tables are available in the FoxPro 2 documentation. As you learn to manipulate FoxPro tables, you become comfortable altering or directly viewing the information in the FRX or LBX. You may find creating a report to access the information in the FRX and LBX tables useful. Because the file structure of these tables never varies, you can use such reports to keep records of all the reports or labels you created—and what these reports and labels contain.

Although so far in this chapter, report forms were discussed, many of the features you learned in the preceding sections also are important when you design and use labels. You can edit and style label lines by using procedures similar to those used for report objects. You may find that storing a master label form that saves the general attributes your company wants for all the labels a good idea. You can open several label layout windows and move expressions between the windows. Labels share the reports' capability of containing environment information without using a View file.

That FoxPro 2 labels are internally maintained as tables, similar to report form tables, is a key to this process. In following chapters, you learn that other FoxPro 2 tools maintain information in a similar way.

Designing Basic Labels

The FoxPro 2 Label Designer is a tool similar to the Report Writer but contains far fewer options. Perhaps for this reason, no analog of the Quick Report feature is available in the Label Designer. Still, if you use the skills you already have, standard mailing labels are simple to prepare.

For this exercise, you need a standard address file. The Organize application supplied as a sample with FoxPro 2 contains addresses in a Clients table. The example label in this section uses the Clients table structure.

If, however, you created all the tables in the model database by using the structures found in Appendix I, you may want to use the Customer table it includes. You also may have previously constructed a FoxPro address table by using the procedure you learned in Chapter 4. You also may have imported address information from another data format. Practice with any table of address data that you prefer and follow along in the exercise, substituting new field names as necessary.

First, open the address file you plan to use. Then use the File New dialog to open an UNTITLED file of Label type and LBX extension by default. You see the Label Layout window, as shown in figure 9.10.

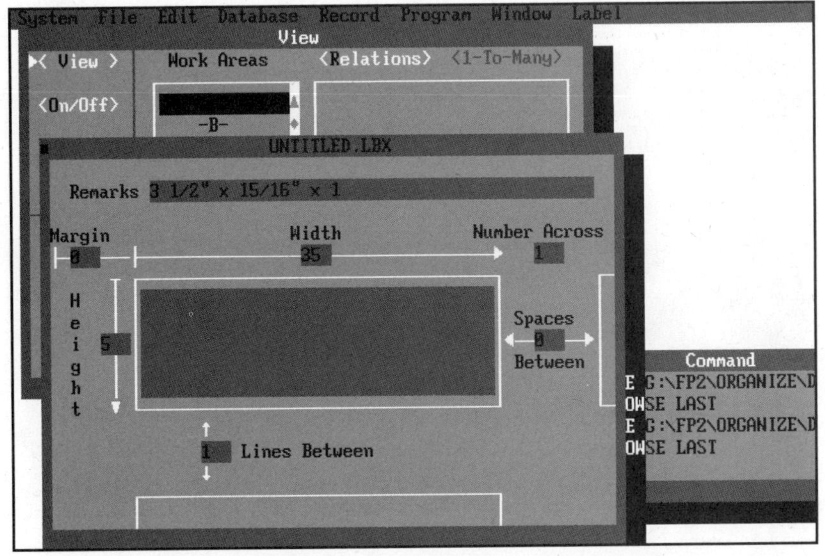

FIG. 9.10

The Label Layout window.

The first thing you need to do when designing a label is to figure out the label's dimensions according to the following limits:

- The number of labels you print across the page
- The size of each label
- The number of lines between the bottom of one label and the top of the next
- The number of characters between labels on each side

These dimensions are usually decided by the kind of labels the printer can handle and the kind of labels you purchase. You can, however, tremendously vary label dimensions in FoxPro 2. A single label can be 255 lines long and 255 characters across. You also can place up to 120 labels across the page. These capabilities come in handy if you use the Label Designer to create special report forms.

As shown in figure 9.11, the Label menu popup that appears when you open a label layout window seems a much simpler version of the Report popup options, but three options are available that enable you to select, save, and delete standard label Layouts.

Because Label Layouts options are designed to handle the dimensions so basic to label output, these options are handled separately from the label environment and printer setup information. The Environment option on the Label menu popup handles these two features.

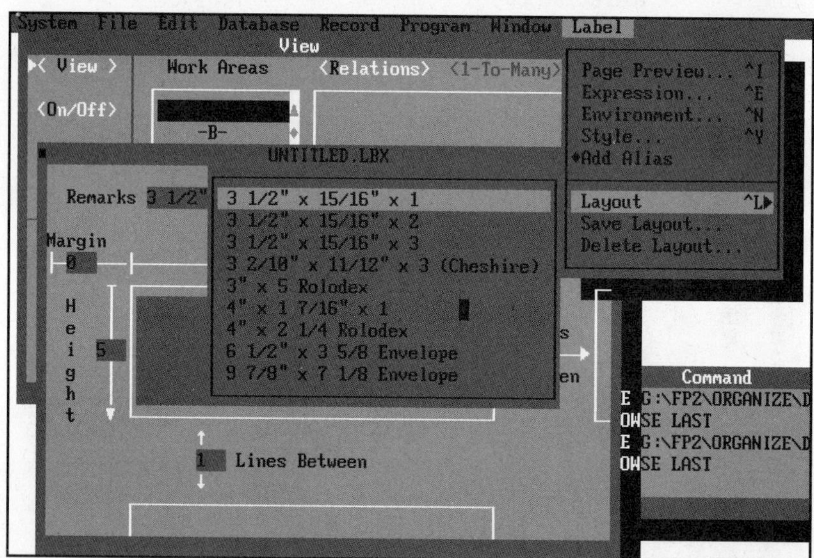

FIG. 9.11

The Label menu options and Sample Layout popup menu.

If you choose the Layout option from the menu (or press Ctrl-L), you see a popup list of standard layouts. Choose a few items from this list and watch the changes that occur in the label layout window, to the various dimension assignments and to the Remarks box that reminds you of the current label type. You may want to edit the Remarks information to include a stock number after you find a label type you use regularly. You also can edit the dimension-assignment boxes to fit another standard label type, edit the Remarks box to describe the label, and then use the Save Layout option to add the label to the available layouts.

You note that the standard label layouts and the label dimensioning process, are meant for printers that handle labels in rolls, or continuous form. (You can use the envelope layouts either with continuous form envelopes or with single envelopes sent through the printer from special envelope feeders.) Each label must be exactly the same distance from the next label; no direct provision is available for the top and bottom margins for the group of labels almost universally required by label sheets used in laser printers.

In FoxPro 2, however, you can use a printer driver (described in Chapter 15) to tell the printer the top and bottom margins to use to fit these laser labels. You then design the label layout to fit the dimensions of the label you are using, including a number for Lines Between labels that matches the distance between labels *within one label sheet*. The printer takes care of ejecting the sheets.

In Chapter 15, you also read about the existing ways to use the printer drivers to create setups appropriate to Hewlett-Packard LaserJet and compatible printers with commonly used label stock and tips on creating setups for other printers and special needs.

Placing Your Label Expressions

Unlike the Report Writer, the Label Designer has no provisions for text or box objects. Each label line is evaluated by FoxPro as an expression in its entirety. Because FoxPro doesn't need to distinguish between expressions and other kinds of objects in labels, you can type the expressions directly into the label lines.

In the following chapter, you learn how to construct and verify complex expressions, but for now, you use the fields in the address table as expressions. Place a Browse of the address table on-screen so that you can more easily refer to the field names, as shown in figure 9.12, then type the field names in the label layout.

Look at the line in which you typed *City, State, Zip*. Because each label line must be an expression that FoxPro can evaluate, if you want to place more than one field on a line, you must *concatenate*—or add together—the fields in some way to form a valid expression. In FoxPro, you usually concatenate fields or expressions by typing *plus signs* between the fields or expressions, such as *CITY* + *STATE* + *ZIP*. The Label Designer, however, also enables you to use *commas* to concatenate with special convenience; each comma tells FoxPro to eliminate blank spaces from the *right end* of the expression before you add the first expression to the following expression, with exactly *one* space between the two expressions.

Note that you also place *TO:* in the first line of the labels. This word is not a valid expression, but the quotation marks around the word tell FoxPro to report data enclosed in quotatation marks as a *literal*, or a *string* of characters that require no further evaluation.

After you type the label layout, use Page Preview—as you did in the Report Writer—to check the work. Depending on the address data with which you are working, you see a screen similar to the example in figure 9.13.

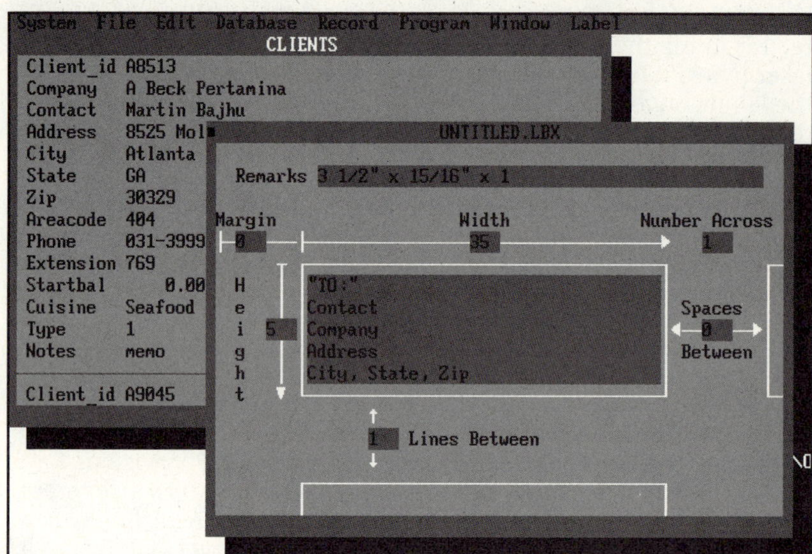

FIG. 9.12

Editing a label.

Try the first and last label lines without the quotation marks and commas to see the difference. Experiment by moving items around in the layout (you can cut and paste selected expressions). Because each label line is an expression, where you type the expression within the line doesn't matter. FoxPro ignores spaces typed before the field name just as it ignores spaces in a command typed in the Command window. To indent the Company line, you must create an expression that indents (perhaps by adding two spaces between the quotation marks), such as the following line:

```
".."+Company
```

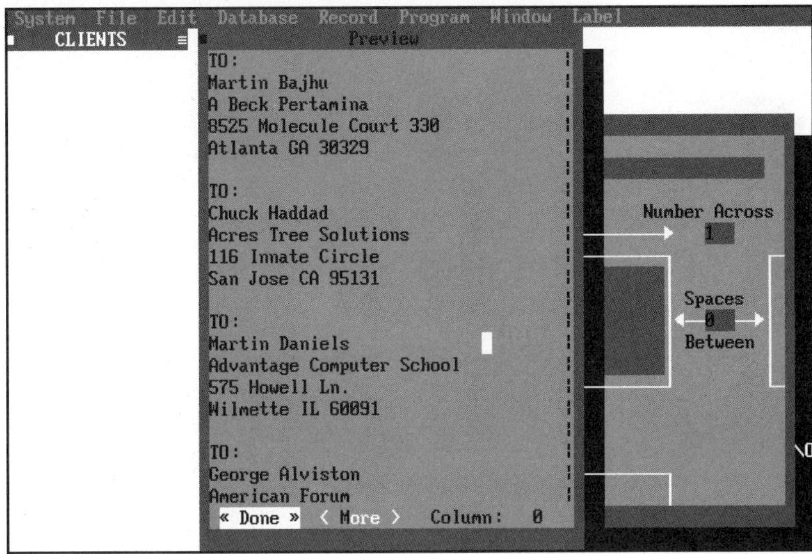

FIG. 9.13

Previewing Label Layout.

Another effect that occurs when each complete label line is an expression is that you use the Label menu option or press Ctrl-Y to choose a Style for each label line as a single object. Otherwise, the Style options and Alignment options and the procedures for saving label files and the associated environment and setup information are familiar from working with reports.

Sending Labels and Reports Out

Now that you can create simple labels and reports, you need a way to deliver these items.

The Database menu pad contains two options, Report and Label, which have associated dialogs for this purpose. You already were introduced to the Report dialog in Chapter 2, "Understanding the FoxPro 2 Interface." You also learned ways to specify records to be considered (the Scope) and the conditions for which a command should act (FOR and WHILE clauses and the capability of SETting FILTERs), when you used the LIST command in the Chapter 3. Now you can use these dialogs to good purpose. Remember that you can use the `<Form>` button to specify the name of the report or label and use the Environment option to open all required files with no further commands.

Notice that the Preview option also gives you the same capability as the Page Preview options of the Label and Report menu popups. If you need to check the scope or conditions you selected, or need to verify that you identified the correct report or label file, this option is useful.

> **NOTE** To view the report or labels on-screen with more flexibility, use the `To File` check box and specify a file name. You can then open the file you created (which has a TXT extension by default). You can scroll through, search through, and even edit or import the file into a word processor, just like all other text files. Usually, you want to choose `Edit Preferences` when you open a text file created in this manner to turn word wrap off. If desired, just open the file as a program (and not as a text file), and word wrap is turned off by default.

As shown in figure 9.14, the Label dialog offers another option to print `Sample` labels. Continuous-form labels usually must be positioned very carefully in a printer, both horizontally and vertically. FoxPro provides this option so that you can run a sample label, or as many samples as needed, which are composed of lines of asterisks that match the full dimensions of the label you specified. (In fig. 9.14, you also see three sample labels echoed to the console behind the dialogs.) You can adjust the label stock in the printer and print more samples until the asterisks are completely contained within the label. Each time you print a sample, you may be asked whether you need more samples, whether you want to Do labels, or whether you prefer to Cancel. Start the print run after you are satisfied with the position of the stock.

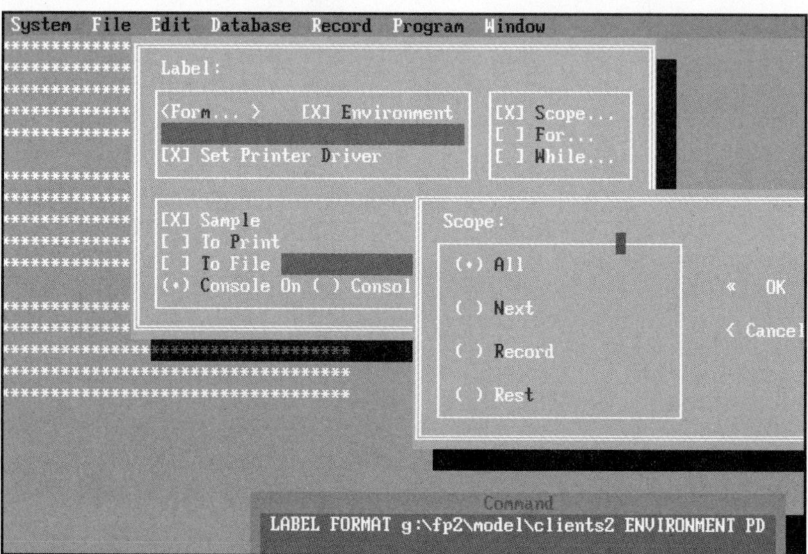

FIG. 9.14

The Label and Associated Scope dialogs.

Chapter Summary

Reports and labels are the true representatives of your database management skills. By using the Report Writer and the Label Designer, you can quickly create, test, and rearrange countless formats in which you can present database information on-screen and on paper.

Creating this kind of output—even on the rudimentary level you have achieved so far—once required many hours of tedious programming. In the following chapter, you learn to produce more sophisticated label and report formats by using these two powerful tools and a little more effort.

10

CHAPTER

Using the Report Writer and Label Designer

As you continue exploring FoxPro 2 output, you need to draw on all you have learned about database systems (related tables, data order, and so on). Although the data sets available to you are still relatively limited, by using the Report Writer and Label Designer, the options for displaying on-screen and printing these data sets are almost unlimited.

Using Related Tables in a Report or Label

Reopen the Model.FRX report form so that you can continue to make changes. Open the tables with the View file or use the View window to verify that the Budget and Product files are open. Because you are examining budget items in relation to the model product line in this session, set the PRODUCT file order to PRODCODE and set a relation to PRODCODE in the Product file. This step ensures that, as you learn in Chapter 4, the record pointer in the Product file moves to information appropriate to the current record in the selected (Budget) file.

Because you are creating a report that concentrates on the Products and the associated budget lines, add a few page header lines and use Ctrl-T or just start typing in an empty space to add a Text Object with a title that indicates the purpose of this report. If the title doesn't end up on the right line, move and, if you prefer, center the title.

Remove the information about departments (because this data isn't useful in the report) and move the Product field expression and heading to the left. Presently, the product code isn't too informative, but you have the PRODNAME field available in the Product table. You can add a new report expression under the product code by using the Report Field menu option or by pressing Ctrl-F. The Report Expression dialog you saw in the preceding chapter appears as shown in figure 10.1. Select the `<Expr>` (Expression) push button and the Expression Builder dialog appears (see fig. 10.2).

You first encountered the Expression Builder while building FOR and WHILE conditions for a LIST command or for report and label output. You also saw that this dialog is available to SET a FILTER on the records that you plan to display or use—for any command—from a table. The Expression Builder is used throughout FoxPro as a way to create complex expressions for all purposes. The popup controls at the top of the window are labeled with the different kinds of functions and operations available to act on each data type. In the left bottom corner is a Field Picker list, enabling you to add database fields to an expression. Use the `<Database>` push button to see fields from any currently open tables. To the right, you see a list of the variables currently in memory, including the system variables FoxPro creates (these variables begin with the _, underscore character) and all variable names to which you assigned values.

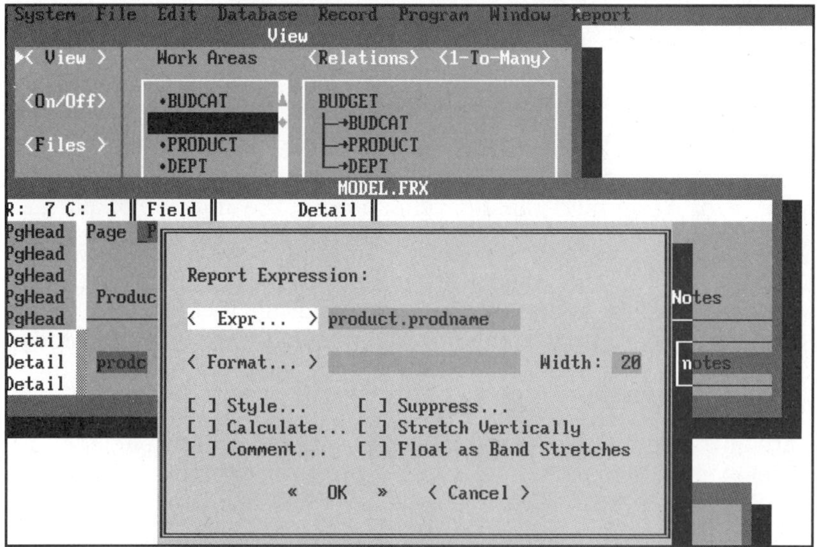

FIG. 10.1

A report expression from a second table shows in the Report Expression dialog.

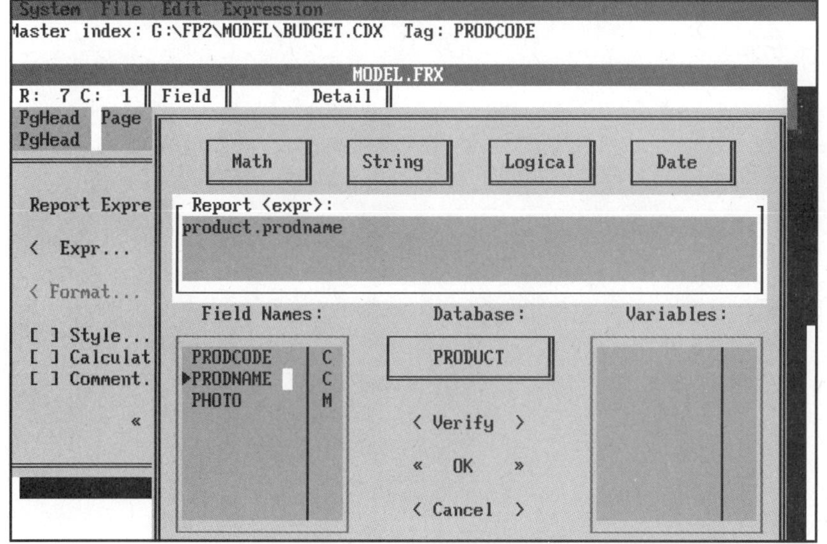

FIG. 10.2

Creating the report expression in the Expression Builder.

You can select items from all of these sources, which then appear in the *expression box* in the middle, where the expression is built. You also can type directly into this box, and you can edit the contents in the same way you can edit other FoxPro text.

You use the Expression Builder extensively in this chapter to create increasingly sophisticated expressions for reports and labels. For now, select the Product Table and place the PRODNAME field in the expression box, as shown in figure 10.2.

Notice that the file alias, *product*, is placed in the expression box with the field name, separated by a period. When you are forming expressions or creating output from different sources, the addition of aliases is essential so that FoxPro knows from where to find each item.

Confirm this choice, and you are returned to the Report Expression dialog, with the expression box filled out. (You can, if you prefer, type the information directly into the box.) Notice that the expression *width* also is filled out; by default, this number is the length of the field you chose. Confirm this choice as well.

You are now returned to the report layout window, where a new report expression object appears. If necessary, move the expression to a position under the PRODCODE expression. The result may look something like figure 10.3.

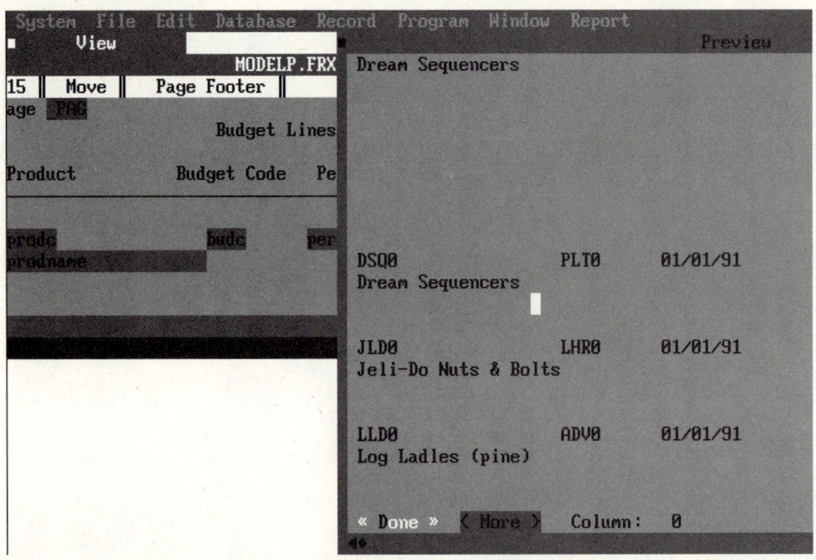

FIG. 10.3

A Report that uses Related tables.

Save the report to a new name to preserve the original report if you want to return to the original version at a later date. Be sure to save its new environment along with the report.

You can easily see how you may reproduce the same situation in a label form. A Customer address table can hold a code that indicates a contact's position within the customer company. A second Position table may contain the same codes, along with the actual titles corresponding to each one. These kinds of tables are related by the code field, with the customer table selected. If the first label line reads *Customer.contact*, the second label line may read *Position.title*, and the rest of the label is filled out with information from the Customer table as before.

Using One-to-Many Relationships in a Report

The situations described in the preceding section are commonly known as *lookups*, or many-to-one relationships, in which one table is used to store information that otherwise would be entered repeatedly in another table. Lookups avoid wasting both valuable disk space and data-entry time, and you can retrieve the information in labels, reports, and other output only when needed. Other cases may exist, however, where the relationship between the tables in a report or label is not quite so straightforward.

Suppose that you have a Customer table in which one customer record may be related to many Order records, each of which may be related in turn to many line item records. You need to generate an invoice for each customer, but the record pointers in the related files must move many times for each customer record. Perhaps you have a Customer account table related to an address table with several possible addresses for each account (for shipping, billing, and home office purposes). When you generate mailing labels for a marketing release, you may want to send each customer a flyer at each address you have on record.

You know that FoxPro 2 can handle this kind of situation by using the SET SKIP command, which you can execute by defining a one-to-many relationship between files in the View window. The files you currently use can handle a one-to-many relationship between products and the associated budget entries, so you can use this for the following example.

In the View window, first eliminate the current relationship between the Budget and Product tables (leaving this relationship in place can cause a *cyclical relation* error because only one of two tables at a time can control the relationship between the tables). In the Relations box of the View window, select the Product table (currently *pointed to* by a relation from the Budget table). The Expression Builder appears with the field PRODCODE, on which the relation was set, appearing in the expression box. The field is already selected, as indicated by the highlight, so just press the backspace or Delete key so that the expression box is empty. Confirm the choice, and when the Expression Builder disappears, the relation between the Budget and Product tables is no longer set.

Now make the Product table the current work area (a ▶ appears next to its name in the Work Areas list), press R or select the `<Relations>` push button, and set a new relationship *from* the Product table *into* the Budget table. You need to set the order of the Budget table on the PRODCODE field and accept the default of PRODCODE when the Expression Builder asks on which expression the relation is to be set.

When you return to the View window, press T or select the `<1-To-Many>` push button. If you have several files open and other relationships set, as shown in figure 10.4, you are asked for a related table (or tables) to which you want the one-to-many relationship set; designate the Budget table here. In the Work Areas list, a ■ symbol appears to the right of the Product table entry, indicating that this action was taken.

Now generate a Quick Report for the Product table, using the PRODCODE and PRODNAME fields. As you learned to do in the last section, add a detail entry (and a heading, if you prefer), for a field from the related Budget database (BUDGET.BUDGETAMT is used in the example).

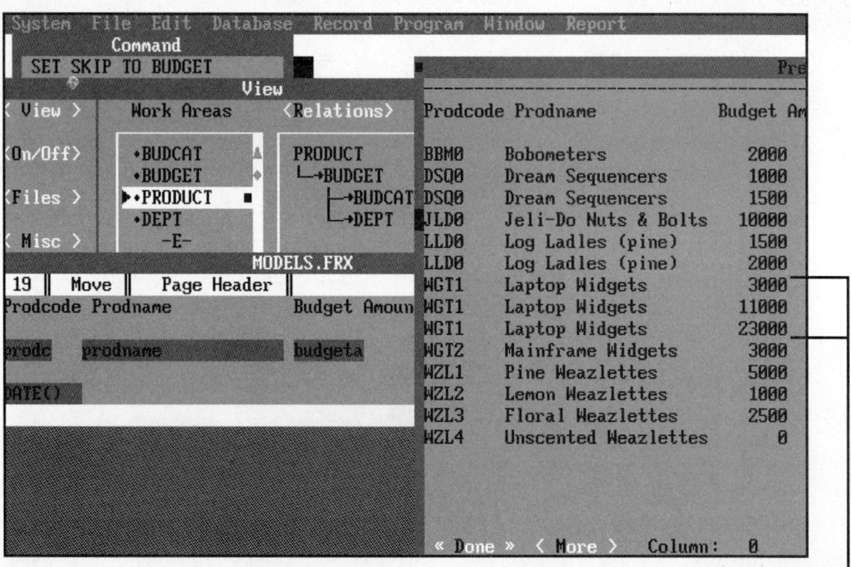

FIG. 10.4

A 1-To-Many Relationship in a report.

As you see in figure 10.4, with the one-to-many relationship set, as many detail entries exist for each Product table record as Budget table entries exist for the product. Remove the one-to-many relationship from the View window, preview the report again, and you see the difference. Replace the one-to-many relationship and save this report to a new name, using the File Save As menu option.

Adding Complex Label and Report Expressions

Now you return to the model Budget report with the product lookup information saved earlier in this chapter to explore more ways of refining the report expressions you can produce. Make sure that you restore the environment to the File Setup and relationships this report requires, including the many-to-one relationship. (To avoid a "cyclical relation" warning, you can CLOSE DATABASES from the command window so that the Budget and Product tables are re-opened using your saved report environment.)

Formatting Expressions in the Report Writer

After you Select the Product.prodname expression for editing (either with a double-click or two presses of the space bar), the report expression dialog reappears. Below the `<Exprs>` button and text box, you see another set for expression `<Format>`. Select this button, and you see a wide range of possibilities (see fig. 10.5).

Because PRODNAME is a character-type field, FoxPro assumes that the expression you are building is a character-type expression and gives you choices appropriate to character data. As you build more complicated expressions, you find that FoxPro takes a *best guess* at the kind of data the expression eventually returns. This guess, however, isn't always correct, so radio buttons are provided to enable you to specify the kind of expression you are creating. Change this radio button selection, and you also see the formatting options change.

In figure 10.5, the format check box `To Upper Case` is selected. When you return to the report expression dialog, you see the appropriate codes, added to the Format text box. You also can type these format codes directly in the text box or in the Format dialog. By typing these *picture* and *format templates* in the Format dialog, you can make more formatting decisions about the way the expression looks than are available when you can create from the check box choices. If you access the help file while in the Format dialog, you see a convenient list, which you recognize from the formatting functions and pictures available for BROWSE fields discussed in Chapter 8.

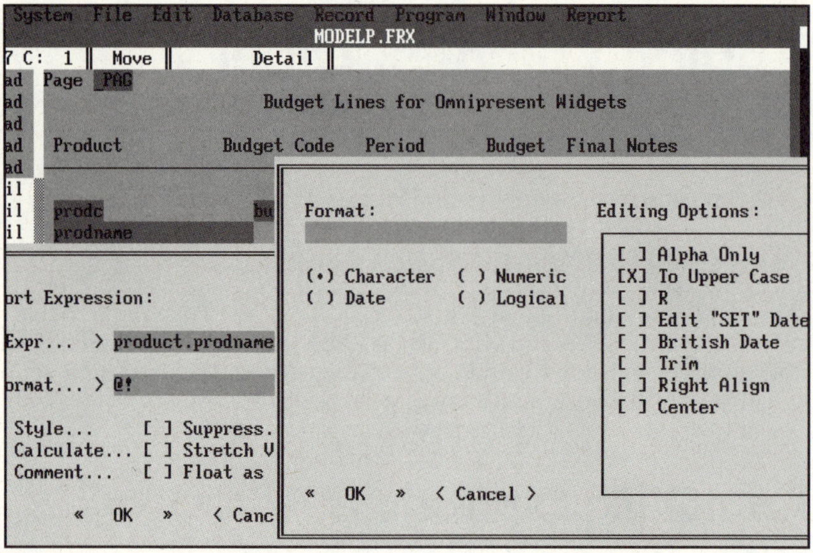

FIG. 10.5

The Format dialog for a character-type expression.

Practice using the format options available by clicking the check boxes for each data type. Because you altered a character expression (PRODUCT.PRODCODE), choose fields of other types—BUDGET.PERIOD for date, BUDGET.BUDGETAMT for numeric, and BUDGET.FINAL for logical—to see all the options.

TIP

The `Right Align` format option is not equivalent to the `Right Alignment` style you encounter in Chapter 9. Styles affect only printer drivers, not the formatting of the object when the report is run. If you use the `Right Alignment` style for any object, be sure that you also select Right Align in the Format dialog for the same object so that it appears right-justified whether or not a printer driver setup is used.

No check boxes exist that make format options directly available to you for a logical-type report expression. The BUDGET.FINAL expression, however, shows a format template—the letter `Y`. When this letter is used, logical data appears as either `Y` for *yes* or `N` for *no*, rather than the `.T.` for *true* and `.F.` for *false* that otherwise appears.

The Quick Report creates this format for logical data without your intervention. Remove the format and use the Page Preview option to see the difference. You see only a period showing in each detail line under the Final heading! Often, when you create custom expressions or adjust the format for an expression, you need to adjust the expression Width to match by using the option provided in the Report Expression dialog. To make room for the expression, type **3** in the BUDGET.FINAL Width box.

If the model report is arranged like the report in figure 10.5, you also may want to adjust the width of the PRODUCT.PRODNAME field so that the field's right edge does not come all the way under the BUDGET.BUDCATCODE beside it, which makes the report look sloppy. You can shorten the field by a few characters and lose any whole word that doesn't fit, or you can use the option to `Stretch vertically`, and the expression wraps to the next line. Here, the latter idea is better because you know the memo field in the report often adds a number of detail lines to each report entry.

So far, you still are adjusting the look of a single field, but both the Report Writer and the Label Designer handle more sophisticated expressions as report objects. These tools use the Expression Builder to handle this task.

Using the Expression Builder in the Label Designer and the Report Writer

In the Expression Builder, you use database fields, constant values, values stored in memory variables, and the functions and operators of the FoxPro 2 language to literally build an expression, which is evaluated by FoxPro. You then can *return* the result of this evaluation as the report or label object you want to print.

In Part V of this book, "Getting To Know FoxPro 2 Commands and Functions," you develop a better sense of the wide variety of actions you can take to manipulate different kinds of data. As previously stated, the four popup controls divide the available functions by data type for easy reference (see fig. 10.6). You can select these controls from the popups or type the function names directly in the expression box in the following quick practice samples.

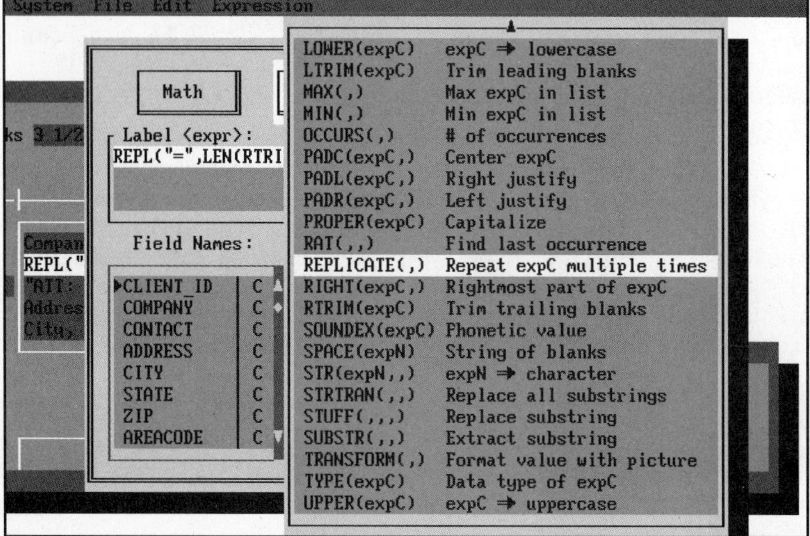

FIG. 10.6

One of the Expression Builder's popup controls provides the functions available for use on character-type data.

Usually, a FoxPro *function* consists of a *keyword* (a word with a special meaning in the FoxPro language) followed by a set of *parentheses*. These parentheses can enclose one, more than one, or no *parameters* (items of data or other instructions you give the function). If more than one parameter exists, the parameters must be separated by *commas*. Using these instructions, each function performs a particular action and then *returns* a value. The value is then used for output or examined by still other functions until you have the desired result. If more than one function exists in an expression, the function in the *innermost* set of parentheses is acted on first, followed by the next innermost, until the outermost level is reached, and the expression returns a value. When an expression includes other expressions, the expressions are *nested*.

Consider the somewhat alarming-looking expression in figure 10.7. The expression is really simple when you examine what the expression does.

The object here is to draw a graphics line in the Label Designer, which doesn't share the box and line-drawing capabilities of the Report Writer. The label you created in the previous chapter is adjusted; the company name is now first. The string `ATT:` and the contact name are now placed in the third line; these items are concatenated with the + sign to form a valid expression. In the second line, a line was added beneath the company name. You want this line to vary in length to match the company name entry. You opened the Label Expression Builder by using the Expression option of the Label menu or pressing

Ctrl-E. (To edit any label expression after you create the expression, select the expression and access the Label Expression builder again, as shown in the example.)

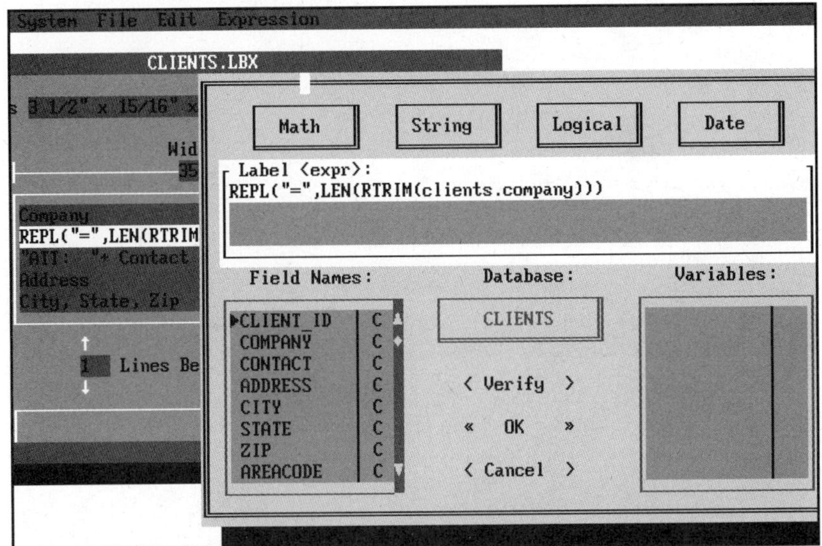

FIG. 10.7

The Expression Builder at work in the Label Designer.

As the innermost function, you type the following expression:

RTRIM(CLIENTS.COMPANY)

The RTRIM() function removes trailing blanks from the expression passed to it, so this expression takes the CLIENTS.COMPANY field and removes all blank spaces that may exist after the company name.

The LEN() function then takes the character expression passed to it (the result of the RTRIM() function) and returns the *number* of characters in the expression. Now, you know how long the line should be.

The REPLICATE() function takes all characters received as the first parameter and repeats this passed information a number of times, according to the second parameter, the result of the LEN() function. (Note that you use the graphics character "=", using the quotation marks so that FoxPro interprets the character literally. But you also can express this character as an ASCII value by using the CHR() function; type **CHR(205)** to represent this double-line character.)

In figure 10.8, you see the results of the expression in the Label Page Preview.

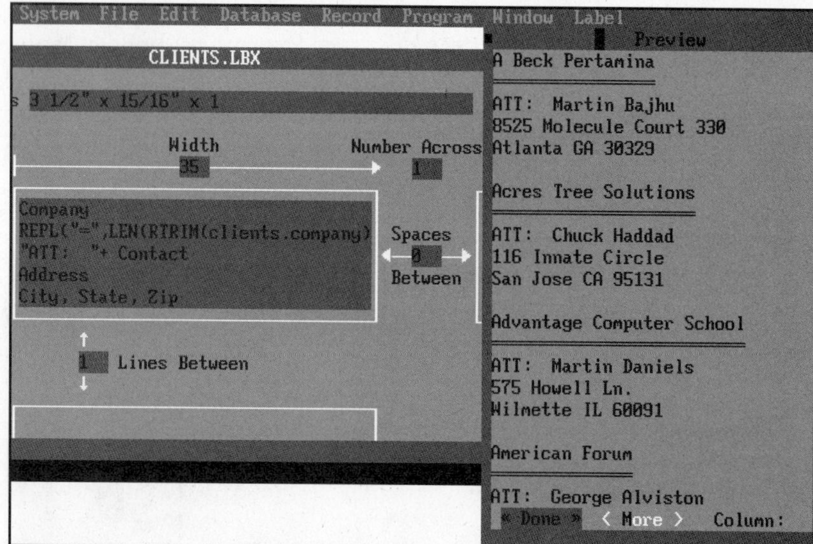

FIG. 10.8

The Expression Builder's results in the Label Preview.

T I P As you followed along in the Expression Builder, you may have easily made at least one typing mistake, such as leaving out one of a pair of parentheses. Click the `<Verify>` push button in the Expression Builder to check the work. Verify's error messages are not especially enlightening, but you still can save a great deal of time if you make sure that FoxPro can *understand* what you previously expressed before you continue with the report or label design session.

For another example of the Expression Builder at work, return to the model report (use any version). If you pay attention to the page number in the header when you Preview, you notice that an unsightly gap exists between the word `Page` and the actual number provided by the system variable _PAGENO. As created by the Quick Report feature, `Page` is a text object, and the page number is a numeric report expression that defaults to a width of 4. This expression enables you to easily prepare a Quick Report of up to 9999 pages, but the resulting page number in the report is not very attractive.

As a quick fix, you can use the `<Left Justify>` formatting option on the _PAGENO object. The Expression Builder, however, gives you greater flexibility.

First, remove the text object Page. (You may need to Ungroup the two objects first, if the objects were grouped when you previously edited the report.) Now select and edit the report expression that contains the _PAGENO variable. Create an expression that *includes* the word **Page** (or **P.**, **Pg.**, or another word or abbreviation you like) with a single following space. Concatenate the expression with the _PAGENO *expressed as a string of characters*, by using the following expression:

```
"Page " + ALLTRIM(STR(_PAGENO))
```

The STR() function converts the number you pass as the parameter to a string of characters, and the ALLTRIM() function that surrounds the string removes all leading and trailing blanks. Now change the Width of the expression to allow for quite a few more characters. Now that this expression is charactertype, the digits are left-justified by default. Any extra characters in the expression width are placed on the right side, where they don't interfere with the expression's appearance. You are now ensured a well-formatted page number whether you are on page 1, page 100, or page 1000 (up to the *ten digits* that STR() uses by default), and you did so with *one* report object that you can easily reposition on the page without grouping.

NOTE The preceding technique—changing a number to a character format—is extremely useful for solving a wide variety of output problems. Investigate the TRANSFORM() function, and also STR(), to get a better idea of all the possibilities.

A fundamental rule for creating valid expressions that you concatenated from several parts, as is done in the Expression Builder, is that all the elements added together *must be the same data type*. Often, you must convert parts of an expression to match the other parts, as you did here.

A good use of the Expression Builder is to format dates for display and in reports. In the model report, the date the report prepares is used in the page footer with the DATE() function, which checks the system clock. FoxPro has a function you can use simply, to show the date in a more legible way. To create a more readable date, use the following expression:

```
MDY(DATE( ))
```

In this expression, the MDY() function evaluates the system date and produces a *Month-day-year* format, which may not provide exactly what you need. Single-digit days of the month, for example, appear like the following line:

June 06, 1991

With the following expression, you can produce a much more attractive *dateline* for the reports:

```
CDOW(DATE())+", "+CMONTH(DATE())+" "
+ ALLTRIM(STR(DAY(DATE()))) + ", "
+ STR(YEAR(DATE()),4,0)
```

FoxPro evaluates this expression, reading the associated elements from left to right, in the following way:

- Returns the day of the week, followed by a comma and a space
- Adds the month of the system date, expressed as a string of characters (another function, MONTH(), is available that returns the *number* of the month for the date evaluated), followed by a space
- Adds the day of the system date, converted to a string and with all leading and trailing spaces removed, followed by another comma and a space
- Adds the year of the system date, converted to a string and including four characters with no decimal places

As an added advantage, the final STR(YEAR(DATE()),4,0) element of this expression correctly includes all four digits of the year, regardless of the current state of the SET CENTURY switch previously discussed.

Notice that you used no semicolons to type this long line, as you usually do to make the line manageable in the Command window (and as you subsequently do when you write programs). In the Expression Builder, an expression too long to fit on one line wraps, and all lines in the expression box are part of the same expression even if you use carriage returns.

This expression obviously has a variable length, depending on the system date. Make sure that you use a Width that includes as many spaces as the longest possible date would occupy. When you mark the `Center` check box for this kind of variable length expression, centering the report object in the layout is not really sufficient because what FoxPro returns isn't always the same number of characters as the full width of the object. If you select the `Format` check box to `Center` the expression, you are centering the actual expression *within the width of the report object*. You then can properly center the resulting object in the layout using the `Center` menu option.

So far, you have dealt mostly with character and numeric data in expressions, using care to convert some elements to different data types to make sure that you can concatenate all the elements into one expression. You told FoxPro to accept a literal string of characters, such as a comma and a space, by *delimiting* (or enclosing) the characters with quotation marks. You also can delimit character data with single quotes (by typing the right single quote character, ', only) or brackets ([]). You can use a literal date in an expression by enclosing the date in curly braces ({}), as the following example shows:

```
MDY({12/01/91})
```

Be careful that you express the date according to the current DATE format, which you learned to check and adjust in the View Misc panel.

In a similar way, you delimit logical data by using a period on either side so that FoxPro *sees* the .T. as *the value True*, rather than as *the letter T*.

A valuable function in the Expression Builder is the *IIF()* (or "Immediate If") function. These parentheses must enclose the following three parameters:

- The first parameter checks a condition and evaluates to a logical value (true or false).
- The second parameter is returned if the condition is true.
- The third parameter is returned if the condition is false.

In the model report, the instruction `Make notes here.` is included under the box that holds the Notes memofield data. This instruction, however, isn't really useful if the box is filled with text. Delete and replace this text object with the following report expression:

```
IIF(EMPTY(BUDGET.NOTES),"Make notes here","")
```

This expression tells the Report Writer: `If the Notes field has nothing in it for this record, print some instructions. Otherwise, don't print anything.` Here, `nothing` is expressed in the third parameter with the *null string* (""). An important fact illustrated here is that a Report Writer or Label Designer expression doesn't need to return anything to be printed; the expression can simply evaluate a condition or do other work, including issuing printer instructions, without creating visible results.

Always be careful that you adjust the Width of any expression that returns different widths under different conditions because FoxPro cannot guess the eventual width. An expression must have *some* width, so if you know the expression never returns anything as output, type a width of **1**. This step, although seemingly unnecessary or annoying, is actually highly convenient because you now can see and manipulate this expression object within the report layout.

Perhaps you are interested only in reading the Notes field (and taking up a correspondingly large number of lines in your report) if the budget item concerns a significant amount of money. You can use the following for the IIF() function in the model report:

```
IIF(BUDGET.BUDGETAMT > 2000, BUDGET.NOTES,
"Minor budget item.")
```

You can decide how significant the item has to be for NOTES to be included when you run the report, if you replace the literal **2000** in this expression with a *variable*, such as the following change:

IIF(BUDGET.BUDGETAMT > *big_item*, BUDGET.NOTES,

"Minor budget item.")

In the Command window and before running the report, you assign a value to this variable, such as the following example:

```
big_item = 1500
```

As needed, you can adjust the assigned value for every report you run. If you forget to assign this variable a value, the FoxPro 2 error message `Variable 'big_item' not found` appears in an alert window when you try to run the report. (Later in this chapter, you will learn a trick to avoid this error by using report variables.) If, however, you assign the variable in the Command window before inclusion in the expression, before or while you design the report, notice that you can select big_item from the Variables list in the Expression Builder, as shown in figure 10.9. You also can Preview the report and Verify the expression.

Figure 10.9 shows another IIF() expression being designed; an asterisk is placed in front of the same significant budget items. Notice that this expression returns a character string (the `"* "` concatenated with a converted BUDGET.BUDGETAMT field) in one case, and a number (the BUDGETAMT field value) in the other. Having an expression return values of different types at different times is perfectly proper; usually, however, you need to be careful that you assign a width and all needed formatting to the return value.

Figure 10.10 shows the result of some suggested changes you made in this report.

This Preview was created with the screen set to 50 lines, using the command **SET DISPLAY TO VGA50**, available on systems with VGA video monitors and boards.

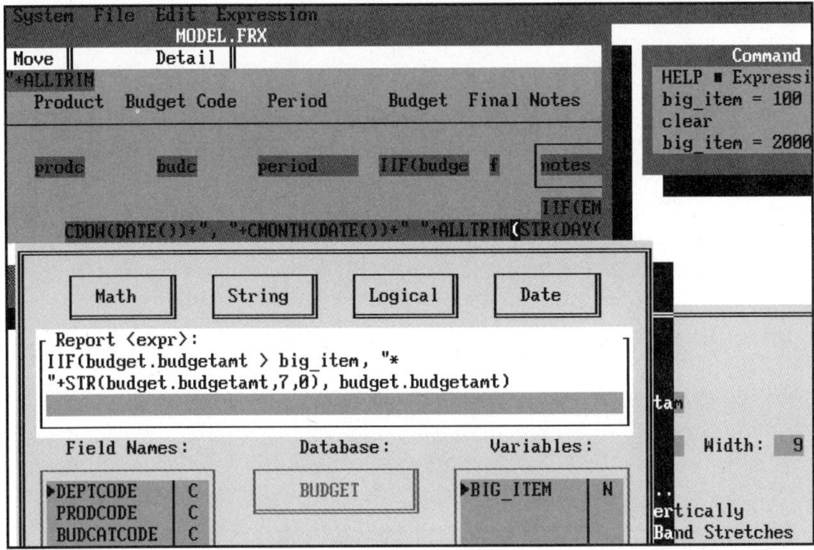

FIG. 10.9

Designing an expression with the IIF( ) function.

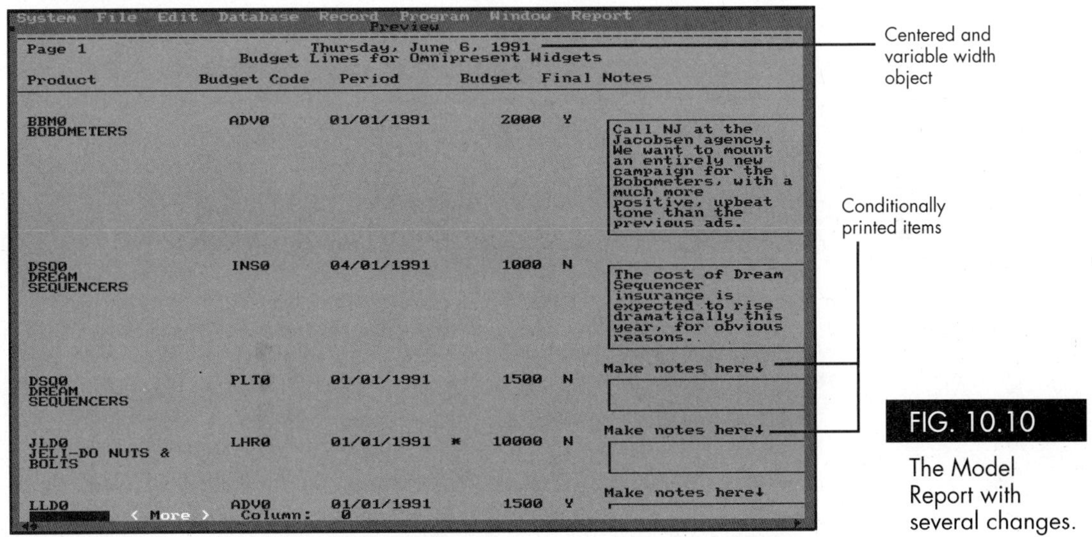

FIG. 10.10

The Model Report with several changes.

In Chapter 7, you create a SQLSELECT statement that uses the UNION clause to simulate an outer join. Recall that a placeholder value was added for all products that had no Budget table entry. For a report on the results of this query, you can replace the placeholder item with a more meaningful entry, as follows:

```
IIF(budgetamt=9999999,"Unbudgeted!",budgetamt)
```

Remember that using the Expression Builder can be equally varied in the Label Designer, and a common use of the IIF() function is for addressing purposes. Suppose that you have an address table that enables you to store the full names of two different individuals. To address a label properly, you need to format the names differently when two individuals are listed, and you also may need to check whether both individuals use the same last name. The following expression uses two nested IIF() functions to accomplish both these checks; as usual, the innermost element is evaluated first:

```
IIF(EMPTY(fname2),
  ALLTRIM(fname1),
     IIF(ALLTRIM(lname2) = ALLTRIM(lname1),
        ALLTRIM(fname1) + " & " + ALLTRIM(fname2),
        ALLTRIM(fname2) + " " + ALLTRIM(lname2)+ " & " +
        ALLTRIM(fname1))) + " " + lname1
```

No matter how complicated this expression looks, you can evaluate one section at a time, just as FoxPro does, and just as you did with simpler expressions. You return to the IIF() expression for further tricks in following sections of this chapter.

Using User-Defined Functions

In spite of the bewildering variety of tools available to you at the touch of a popup control in the Expression Builder, you still may want to perform some actions or to manipulate data in ways not directly available with FoxPro functions.

You can, however, write short programs or procedures that can be called in report or label expressions just as the internal FoxPro functions are called. These procedures are known as *user defined functions*, or *UDFs*.

If you previously used FoxPro Version 1, be aware that you have less need to create UDFs for reports in Version 2 than ever before because of FoxPro 2's new *report variables*, described in a following section of this chapter. Situations still exist in which you may want to call external functions that you design.

One reason to use UDFs is that the Expression Builder limits you to 254 characters for a given expression. You may possibly want to exceed this length as you evaluate data while you create a single item for output.

Another reason to use UDFs may be that you need to break down what you want to accomplish into several steps. In a UDF, you can issue a long sequence of commands before you return a result.

Designing and creating a UDF is covered more thoroughly in Chapter 16, "Understanding Program Structure." Here, you concentrate on the way you can include UDFs in reports and labels by using simple examples.

If the printer uses single sheets rather than continuous forms, or if you feed single letterhead sheets to a printer that otherwise uses a bin, the Report Writer has no internal provision for a pause until you insert each additional page. But this feature is easy to provide with a UDF.

In the Command window, type the following command:

```
WAIT WINDOW
```

Press Enter to issue the command. You then see a small system window in the upper right corner of the screen, similar to other notices you have received, which vanishes when you press any key or click the mouse. This window and the required keypress is FoxPro's way to provide the kind of pause you need. Now all you need to do is tell the report form to issue the pause.

From the File New menu option, choose the Program option to create a program. A text editing window opens that looks like any other (except that the UNTITLED file you are creating uses the default extension PRG), which appears as the window title.

In this editing window, type the same two words that you typed in the Command window a minute ago, followed by one more line:

```
WAIT WINDOW
RETURN " "
```

End each line by pressing Enter (programs are not word wrapped). Now save and close the file, typing **WAITPAGE.PRG** as the name.

You just wrote a program. If you haven't previously tried programming, you may think that the process is terribly complicated, but a program is just a text file that holds a sequence of actions you want to perform. Each action is like a command that you see generated in the Command window as you make menu choices or a command you type. When you are ready to run this sequence of actions, issue a command to DO the program, and FoxPro *reads* and then executes the commands, one after the other.

Position the cursor in the *first position of the first pageheader line* of the report and create a report expression object at this position. In the expression box type, as you type any function belonging to the FoxPro language, the following expression:

Waitpage()

Give this expression the width **1**. This UDF, Waitpage() function, which has no parameters, executes the WAIT WINDOW command and then RETURNs the null string to the report for output. Because you placed the function in the first position of the page, you caused the report to pause at this line while you take the printer off line and position a new sheet of paper. After you are ready to continue and the printer is back on line, press any key or click the mouse and the report continues printing the rest of the page. You can even see the process work in Page Preview mode.

Suppose that you sometimes feed single sheets to the printer, and at other times (perhaps when you use a different printer), you don't need the pause between pages. You can reopen the waitpage.prg and edit the file to read:

```
IF pause
  WAIT WINDOW
ENDIF
RETURN ""
```

Now all you need to do before running the report is to create a variable called *pause*, as you created the variable *big_item*, assigning the variable the value of *true* or *false*, as in the following:

```
pause = .T.
```

or

```
pause = .F.
```

Using the IF/ENDIF construct, which is explained in a following section, the revised Waitpage function checks whether or not to interrupt the report.

Before running a report, FoxPro must find all included UDFs. Here, you make Waitpage() available by saving the UDF as a separate file in the directory in which you are working (with the model reports and database). In Chapter 14, you find out how to include this separate file in a project, and in Chapter 16, you find other ways FoxPro can find UDFS within a larger program file.

You may want to rewrite as a UDF the previously created complicated nested IIF() expression that formats two individuals' names for a label line. Often, maintaining this kind of expression (or far more complex expressions) as a UDF is easier than as a report or label expression. You can create a program, NAMELINE.PRG, similar to the following example. The lines that begin with asterisks are *comments*—not part of the program—that help you understand what the program does. Lines beginning with this character are ignored by FoxPro as the program is interpreted:

```
mreturn = ""
* create a variable to hold the string
* the UDF will eventually RETURN to the label or report
IF EMPTY(fname2)
  * is there only one person at this address?
  mreturn = ALLTRIM(fname1)
  * put the one person's first name into the string
ELSE
  * two people exist
  IF ALLTRIM(lname2) = ALLTRIM(lname1)
        * do they share one last name?
        mreturn = ALLTRIM(fname1) + " & " + ;
                    ALLTRIM(fname2)
        * put the two first names into the string
  ELSE
        * two last names exist
        mreturn = ALLTRIM(fname2) + " " + ALLTRIM(lname2);
                    + " & " + ALLTRIM(fname1)
        * put the second person's whole name and
        * the first person's first name into the string
  ENDIF
ENDIF

* take the string we have created and add
* the first person's last name to the end
mreturn = mreturn + " " + lname1

* send the string back to the label
RETURN mreturn
```

Now, the label line expression simply becomes the following:

Nameline()

If you have other output involving this address table, you can use this UDF to format the output names properly in each case.

TIP When UDFs in a report do a lot of processing or evaluating of expressions as Nameline() does, you may sometimes see some of the intermediary results of these steps echoed in the report. SET TALK OFF and run the report again; this undesirable side effect of UDGs disappears. SET TALK determines whether or not command processing of any type is echoed by FoxPro, usually to a window or the screen. However, for the duration of a report, all output (including such command processing) is directed to the report destination, whether it is the screen, a file, or the printer.

Suppressing Blank Lines in Reports and Labels

One common problem in reports and labels is the need to suppress blank lines. Suppose that a household address table contains not only names for two individuals but also two fields for address information (to leave room for apartment numbers and so on to be entered separately from a street address). Where both address fields are not used, you want to *close* the label or the address portion of an invoice so that no blank line is left in the center of the address.

In the Label Designer, you accomplish this correction easily by using a semicolon at the end of all lines that may be left blank. In this example, the label definition looks like the following:

```
Nameline()
address1;
address2;
RTRIM(city)+", "+state+"     "+zip
```

These options, however, are more varied and more complicated in the Report Writer.

As mentioned in the preceding chapter, the FoxPro 2 check box option in the Page Layout Options dialog enables you to `Suppress blank lines`. For some kinds of reports, this option works well to suppress completely blank lines contained in the detail band.

Many users, however, frequently want to put address information in the page header band of a statement or invoice or want an address on the left side of a detail band and other information about the customer on the right side. In the former case, the Suppress blank lines option doesn't apply because the affected lines are not in the detail band; in the latter case, the lines aren't suppressed because there are additional (non-blank) expressions in the same line.

`Suppress blank lines` does not consider an expression consisting of only spaces to be completely blank—a useful fact when you want some blank lines in a report omitted and others left alone. This option also does not suppress a detail line in which you have placed *no* expressions. Therefore, you still can place completely blank lines in a report as visual separators when you want them.

The way to *close* this kind of blank, paradoxically, is to concatenate all the expressions involved into one long expression and *force line breaks* in this expression where needed. Type the special Format instructions @; to tell the Report Writer to *see* all semicolons enclosed in quotation marks as a request for a line break. When you use this format, the expression `Stretches Vertically` without you choosing this option. You, however, need to tell any other objects on the same or following detail lines to `Float as Band Stretches.`

The address information is reported as two, not four, report expression objects in the Report Writer. The first object contains the following expression:

```
Nameline( )+
  IIF(EMPTY(address1),"",";" + address1) +
  IIF(EMPTY(address2),"",";" + address2)
```

This object is given the width of the longest of the three possible lines and is assigned the Format @;. The second object contains the following expression:

```
RTRIM(city) + ", " + state + "      " + zip
```

This expression is identical to the last line of the label definition—but in the Report Writer, needs to `Float as Band Stretches` accommodate the changing size of the preceding object.

You also can take care of more complicated situations by a UDF that examines each part of the expression and decides where and when the line breaks occur. The UDF's name then appears in the expression box, and the same Format feature is used.

TIP In a twist on this problem, you can use the REPLICATE( ) function to return any number of ";" strings to the Report Writer if a situation exists in which you want to force extra line breaks or a page break. The system variable _PLINENO can tell you where on the page you are currently positioned. You can evaluate this information with a UDF and decide how many extra lines you need to move down the page at any point. After the semi-colons, be sure to add at least one space to the returned expression (i.e. REPL(";",nlines)+" "), or the Report Writer discounts all the extra line breaks.

Adding Groups and Totalling to Reports

Often, you want to examine data *grouped* on the basis of one or more criteria. You previously saw that, by putting data in a certain order, you can examine, for example, all Budget items for one product and then for the next product. If you change the order, you can report on Budget items one period or department at a time.

FoxPro, however, also enables you to perform certain actions relative to each group of items, setting up *group headers* that appear when a new group is reached and *footers* that follow the end of the group. As with page headers and footers, these group headers and footers contain information that concerns the whole group (not individual detail items) and can be formatted differently from the detail lines.

In the Report Writer, this kind of grouping is known as a *control break*. A control break literally tells FoxPro to stop printing detail lines and to do something else when the conditions are met.

You usually define a group or control break by using the same expression you used in the tag or index that controls the data order for this report. In the model database View order the Budget data by Product (use the View window's `<Setup>` push button, highlight BUDGET.PRODCODE on the index list, select the `Index` button to Set Order, and confirm the choice).

Choose the Data Grouping option from the Report menu popup. Opt to `<Add>` a group, and the Group Info dialog appears, as shown in figure 10.11.

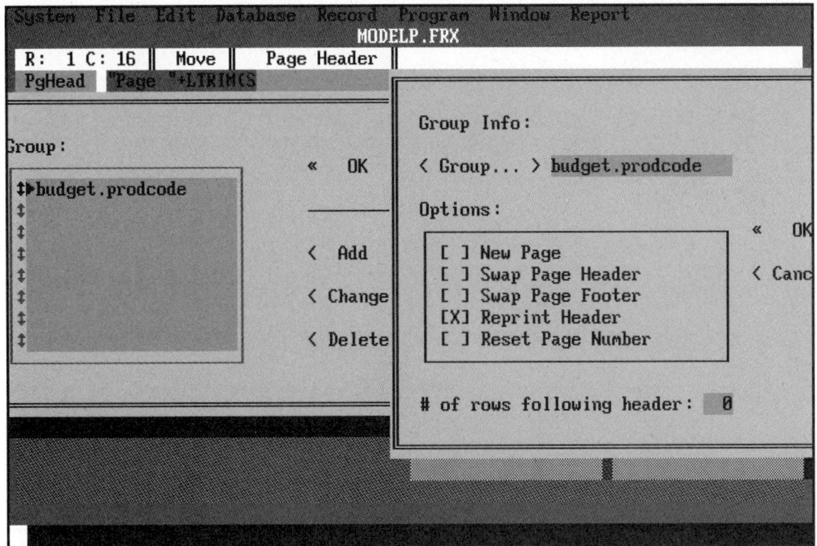

FIG. 10.11

The Group and Group Info dialogs.

You can type the same expression as is used in the current controlling index or tag, or you can click the `<Group>` button to select and edit the appropriate fields and other information in the Expression Builder.

Look at the Options list available in the Group Info dialog. Every time a new group is reached, you can tell FoxPro to begin a `New Page`. You can use the `Swap Page Header` or `Swap Page Footer` options to use the group headings instead of page headings when a new group is reached; this setting selects `New Page` by default because doing the swap makes no sense if the groups started mid-page.

You also can choose to `Reset Page Number` so that every new group begins with the page number `1` (this setting also forces, by default, groups to start new pages) or `Reprint` the group `Header` when a group spans two pages, as happened here. You also can use the # of Rows Following Header option to ensure that group headers are not *orphaned* at the bottom of a page, with no room left for detail without detail items.

When you return to the report layout, you see that new bands were added. You can now add lines that print to head and summarize information for this group.

Often, in the group header band, you may place information that displays on-screen the currently reporting group. Reporting the product name in each detail band is unnecessary, for example, when you know the name is the same for each item in the group. Using the

PRODUCT.PRODNAME field in the group header band, place an expression now. Remove this information from the detail band and move the other objects in the detail band to suit your needs.

A common procedure is to *calculate* data by group and show the results in a group footer band, which you perform by marking the `Calculate` check box in the Report Expression dialog, as shown in figure 10.12.

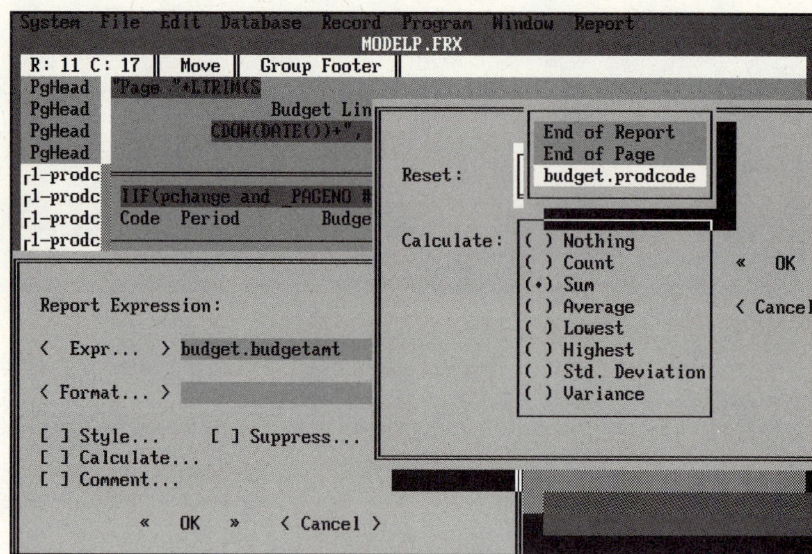

FIG. 10.12

The Calculate options for a Report Expression, choosing to Reset at the end of a group.

Because you may want a subtotal of the budget amounts for each group, the expression is the field BUDGET.BUDGETAMT. When you select the `Calculate` option, you choose to `Sum` this expression, using the `Reset` popup control to end the calculation on the group expression (BUDGET.PRODCODE here).

Place this expression with an appropriate defining text object in the group footer band. Select and copy the band by pressing Ctrl-C. Then, using the Title/Summary option from the Report menu, create a *summary band* for the end of the report. Paste a copy of this object in the summary band with Ctrl-V and edit the object to Reset on End of Report. You now also have a grand total of the budget. (The results of these changes are shown in figures 10.14 and 10.15, in the following section of this chapter.)

You probably noticed that you also can use any of the Calculate options to create page-level calculations, but you may want to use another similar object to put calculations even in the detail band. Paste another copy of the summary band object into the detail band (which, like the original version, still is set to reset on a group level). Do a Page Preview, and you see that this object keeps a running total of the budget amounts in a group or, if you change the Reset, throughout a report.

Calculate is handy for creating item numbers on a report, perhaps within a page. Define a report expression, which is the numeric value *1* (almost any other expression works), click the `Count` radio button, reset the value on a page, and place it in the detail band, formatted appropriately.

You even can coax the Calculate feature to give a conditional count. Suppose that you want to report the number of budget items that have a budgetamt higher than 1000. Define a report expression similar to the following:

```
IIF(Budget.budgetamt > 1000, 1, 0)
```

Mark the `Sum` radio button. You can place the expression in any of the footer bands, reset it appropriately, and produce an answer. Variations of this problem, and the resulting output, are shown in the following "Understanding Report Variables" section.

You aren't limited to one level of subtotals or other calculations in a FoxPro report; you can have as many as *20 nested group levels*. If you want to report on the budget by department and within each department by period, you can create an index or tag by using the following expression:

```
deptcode + DTOS(period)
```

The DTOS() function converts the date field, PERIOD, into a character form so that you can concatenate and properly order this field with the DEPTCODE field. Add one group level, the *outer* or more important level, by using the expression BUDGET.DEPTCODE, and have another, inner level to also cause FoxPro to start a new group within the department listing when a new period is reached. Again, assign headers and footers to each level of grouping.

Groupings do not necessarily have to take the form of database fields. In FoxPro 2 you can create an index expression that includes a UDF, which means that the ways you group data are almost unlimited.

On rare occasions, you may want to create groupings that have nothing to do with the index expression. In certain special cases, setting a group to start a new page is a good way to force a page break. A common reason to take this step is to avoid splitting up a long memofield between two pages. Use a UDF in the detail band of a report to evaluate these conditions and to change the value of a variable when the conditions are met. Create a group on the variable and have this grouping level start a new page. In FoxPro 2, this procedure is easy with report variables (see the following section).

Understanding Report Variables

So far, you have touched only on a few of the extensive settings allowed in the Calculate option. Besides the settings' usage with numeric values, you find that several settings (`Highest`, `Lowest`, and `Average`) also work capably with date-type expressions.

However, the Calculate feature of report expression objects has a major limitation: after you choose to use the feature, you cannot further manipulate the result before putting the result into the report. You cannot TRANSFORM() the result for special formatting, concatenate the result with other expressions, and—most important—perform several calculations and create another expression by doing a computation that involves the Calculated results.

To return to a previous example, suppose that you need to keep a certain amount of cash on hand, a percentage of all budget items. You know how to calculate and sum the amount, as shown in the following expression:

```
budgetamt * .15
```

You also know how to restrict the calculation if you are required to perform this calculation only for significant expenditures, as in the following expression:

```
IIF(budgetamt >= big_item, budgetamt * .15, 0)
```

Perhaps you want to compare this calculation's result to the amount of money you deposited in the bank (this information is derived from another table). You may want to print a line in the summary band of the report to reflect a shortfall. If the deposited money is sufficient to cover the requirements, a different message is printed.

In previous versions of FoxPro, you handled this kind of situation with a UDF in a group-, page- or report-level summary band. Rather than using the internal Calculate `Sum` feature, you wrote instructions to move through all the records of the file (or perhaps just through the records of one group), check certain criteria, and arrive at an answer. The UDF either returned the correct output directly to a report expression or placed the total into variables that you created before running the report, which was then used in other report expressions.

Besides being fairly complicated, this method is wasteful because you make at least one extra *pass* through the records in the file. FoxPro is already moving through the file to print the lines you see in the detail band in the report. In FoxPro 2, *report variables* do this kind of calculation along the way. The Report Writer performs operations that you designate, both on these variables and on the report objects, for each record in the report.

Choose the Report Variables menu popup option, and you access the dialogs shown in figure 10.13. As you see, you choose to Add a variable, give it a Name and an `<Initial Value>`, and tell FoxPro what you want to do with it (the `<Value to Store>`) for each record of the controlling table, as you usually create other report expressions. You also can choose the same Calculate options as you choose for regular report expressions, assigning a level on which the expressions are Reset to their initial values.

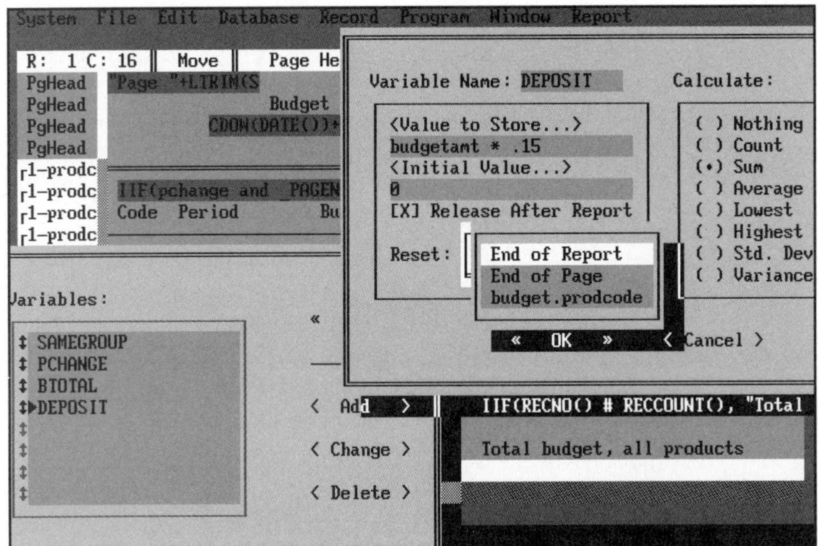

FIG. 10.13

The Report Variable dialogs.

The difference is that you can now *use* this created variable in another report expression, or even in the calculation of another report variable. In figure 10.13, you see how performing the task suggested in the example works—by creating the variable known as *deposit* to sum the budget amount percentages. Choose to Reset at the End of Report, because you intend to use this information in the summary band. Now you can create expressions, such as the following, in the summary band:

```
IIF(deposit > bankacct.deposit,
  "Additional deposit required: ", "")

IIF(deposit > bankacct.deposit,
  deposit - bankacct.deposit, "")
```

You can easily concatenate these two expressions, using STR() or TRANSFORM(), but keeping the two expressions separate in cases where you may have more than two possibilities is more convenient. You return to this example in a following section, "Overlaid Report Objects."

Report variables also can *persist* after a report is run. If you uncheck the default `Release After Report` option, you can send a message to the screen with the *results* after the report is run or use these values in other reports, store values to a table that stores information about report runs, and so on using a sequence of page numbers that is carried from one report to the next, as chapters in a larger report. An example of this process is included in Chapter 18.

Expanding Use of Report Variables

A calculation that involves other calculations is the most obvious reason to create report variables. If you return to the model reports, however, you find many other tricks to perform.

Previously, you used the option to `Reprint Header` for a group that spans two or more pages. When this occurs, you may want to add a message to the header and footer of the group that indicates that more information for that group is available than is showing on the current page. You don't want this message to print when switching groups but are still on the same page, and you don't want it printing when you switch pages and groups at the same time. This procedure requires a check to see exactly when pages and groups switch, which is a simple feat for report variables.

Create a variable, *samegroup*, with an initial value of .F. and store to the variable the value .T.. If this variable is Reset on the group level, you can check to find out when the group changes.

Create another variable, *pagechange*, with an initial value of *.T.*, storing the value *.F.* and choosing to Reset at End of Page.

The following expression creates a message when needed in the *group* header during a Reprint at the top of a page:

```
IIF(samegroup AND pagechange,
  ALLTRIM(product.prodname)+" details continued from
  the previous page... ",
  ALLTRIM(product.prodname))
```

The following expression creates a message when needed in the *page* footer:

```
IIF(samegroup,
  ALLTRIM(product.prodname)+" details continued
  next page...", "")
```

TIP

You also can use a similar technique to suppress certain page-level band information at the beginning or end of a report, where this information may be redundant because of title and summary band material. _PAGENO = 1 tells you when you are at the beginning of the report. If you output the results of a temporary table from a SQL SELECT statement, as you learned to do in Chapters 5 and 6, you can use the expression RECCOUNT() = RECNO() to see whether you are at the end of a report (when you reach the last record of the table). If, however, you are reporting on a table that may be ordered or filtered or if you are using FOR or WHILE conditions, you can check the record number of the last record you are selecting before you begin the report run by storing the number to a variable. Compare the RECNO() to this variable in an IIF() expression to decide when to suppress page-level information.

Figures 10.14, 10.15, and 10.16 show the resulting report, with the conditional page band objects implemented. In figures 10.15 and 10.16, the conditional page headers and footers are designed to continue groups across pages and to suppress redundant page information just before a summary band. To show the variation in page bands, the number of lines per page was reduced (using the appropriate Page Layout item).

The item labeled `Total of Budget Items So Far` in figure 10.16 is a report variable known as *btotal*, which stores the value of the BUDGETAMT field, uses the `Sum` option, and is set to Reset at the end of report. You can choose, however, to increment or otherwise calculate a report variable as a manual operation (rather than using the Calculate options). Here, rather than marking the `Sum` radio button, you use btotal+BUDGET.BUDGETAMT as the value to store.

This kind of expression gives you more flexibility to affect the value of the report variable. You can use a UDF in the expression that creates the value to store, as you did with report expressions. The expression Xtotal+Your_UDF(), for example, may increase the value of the report variable Xtotal by a different figure or percentage for each department or each product line.

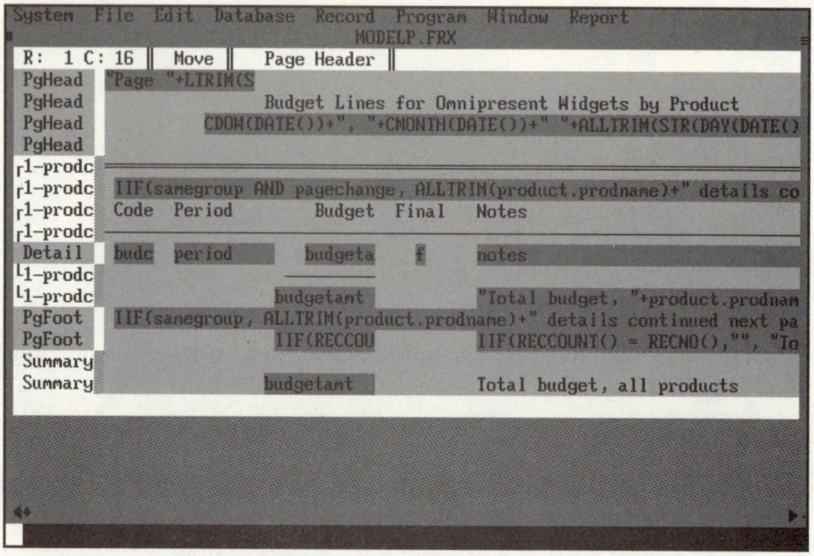

FIG. 10.14

Our Model Report Layout Revised.

For convenience, you can do all calculations on a report variable by using UDFs and letting FoxPro 2 initialize the variable.

Suppose that you want detail lines to show each budget item as a percentage of the total budget for the group. The report expression object may look like the following line:

```
STR(budgetamt/totalbudg * 100,3)+"%"
```

To evaluate this expression, you need the total budget figure for the group *before the detail items for the group are gone through*, and the only way you can get this figure is by using a UDF in the group header line. This procedure requires an extra pass through the table, which was previously mentioned as a practice to avoid; you *cannot* avoid this step here.

The UDF saves the current RECNO() (at the start of the group), to another variable, and then moves through the records of the group (using the command CALCULATE WHILE) to store the total of the BUDGETAMT fields to the totalbudg variable. Then the UDF returns the record pointer to the beginning of the group (using the GO command and the now-saved record number). The report now can process the detail lines.

In previous versions of FoxPro, you had to initialize the variable totalbudg before the report was run by typing the command **totalbudg = 0** either in the Command window or in the program that runs the report. If you didn't initialize the variable, the report generates the error `Variable not found`. By choosing to create totalbudg as a report variable, you ensure that this command is *bound* to the report, and you avoid the error.

```
System  File  Edit  Database  Record  Program  Window  Report
                              Preview
Page 1
                 Budget Lines for Omnipresent Widgets by Product
                        Sunday, June 9, 1991

Bobometers
Code  Period          Budget  Final    Notes
ADV0  01/01/91          2000    Y      Call NJ at the Jacobsen agency.  We want
                                       mount an entirely new campaign for the
                                       Bobometers, with a much more positive,
                                       upbeat tone than the previous ads.
                        2000           Total budget, Bobometers
Dream Sequencers
Code  Period          Budget  Final    Notes
INS0  04/01/91          1000    N      The cost of Dream Sequencer insurance is
                                       expected to rise dramatically this year,
                                       for obvious reasons.
PLT0  01/01/91          1500    N
                        2500           Total budget, Dream Sequencers

                        4500           Total of Budget Items So Far in this Repo
Page 2
                 Budget Lines for Omnipresent Widgets by Product
                        Sunday, June 9, 1991

Jeli-Do Nuts & Bolts
Code  Period          Budget  Final    Notes
LHR0  01/01/91         10000    N
                       10000           Total budget, Jeli-Do Nuts & Bolts
Log Ladles (pine)
Code  Period          Budget  Final    Notes
            < More >  Column:   0
```

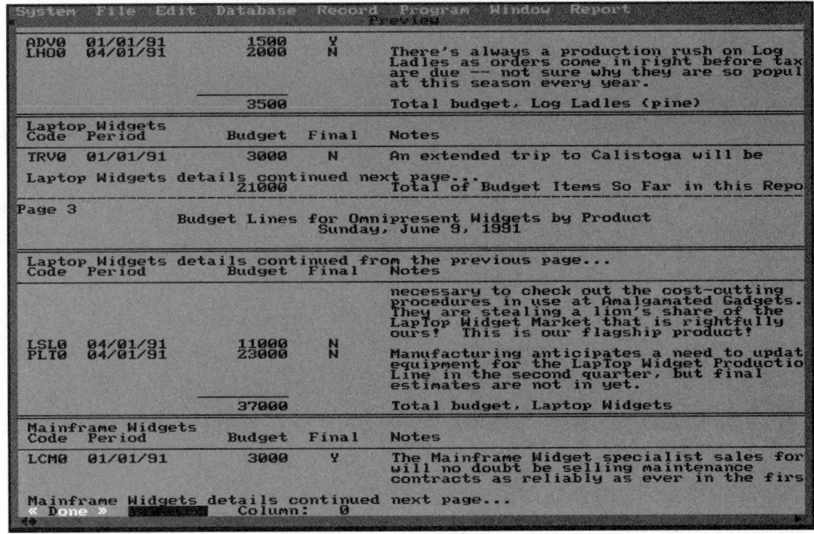

```
System  File  Edit  Database  Record  Program  Window  Report
                              Preview
ADV0  01/01/91          1500    Y
LHO0  04/01/91          2000    N      There's always a production rush on Log
                                       Ladles as orders come in right before tax
                                       are due -- not sure why they are so popul
                                       at this season every year.
                        3500           Total budget, Log Ladles (pine)
Laptop Widgets
Code  Period          Budget  Final    Notes
TRV0  01/01/91          3000    N      An extended trip to Calistoga will be
Laptop Widgets details continued next page...
                       21000           Total of Budget Items So Far in this Repo
Page 3
                 Budget Lines for Omnipresent Widgets by Product
                        Sunday, June 9, 1991

Laptop Widgets details continued from the previous page...
Code  Period          Budget  Final    Notes
                                       necessary to check out the cost-cutting
                                       procedures in use at Amalgamated Gadgets.
                                       They are stealing a lion's share of the
                                       LapTop Widget Market that is rightfully
                                       ours!  This is our flagship product!
LSL0  04/01/91         11000    N
PLT0  04/01/91         23000    N      Manufacturing anticipates a need to updat
                                       equipment for the LapTop Widget Productio
                                       Line in the second quarter, but final
                                       estimates are not in yet.
                       37000           Total budget, Laptop Widgets
Mainframe Widgets
Code  Period          Budget  Final    Notes
LCM0  01/01/91          3000    Y      The Mainframe Widget specialist sales for
                                       will no doubt be selling maintenance
                                       contracts as reliably as ever in the firs
Mainframe Widgets details continued next page...
 « Done »             Column:   0
```

FIGS. 10.15 AND 10.16

The revised report in Page Preview, using report variables.

You can use a similar trick to avoid an error even if the value of a variable is usually set by a calling program but may not be set during testing, by using the TYPE( ) function to determine whether or not this variable previously exists. For the *big_item* variable used to decide when to print Notes earlier in the chapter, create a report variable with the same name, initialized to the following value:

```
IIF(TYPE("big_item") = "N", big_item, 500)
```

When the TYPE( ) function returns `"N"` (for “Numeric data type”), this expression assigns *big_item* the value of the existing *big_item* variable. Otherwise, *big_item* is assigned the default value of 500.

You must realize, however, that FoxPro 2 usually expects to assign values to report variables; the program re-evaluates these variables every detail line, using the information you assigned as the `Value To Store`. When you don’t want FoxPro to interfere with manipulation of a report variable, such as *big_item* or *totalbudg*, use the variable’s own name as the `Value to Store`, and nothing is changed.

When used with UDFs, the IIF() function again comes in handy in report variable calculations. As discussed previously, you can use the `Count` option to give you line numbers or item numbers in a report, and you can use IIF() to give a conditional count based on certain factors. If you put together all these functions, you have an easy way to distinguish the parent records in a one-to-many relationship as you examine the detail lines of a report.

Return to the report you previously prepared in this chapter when you were using a one-to-many relationship. Add a report variable, *prec*, that has the initial value of *0* and stores the expression *RECNO("product")* (the record number of the controlling database). Add a second variable, *newrec*, also initialized to *0*, and FoxPro stores the following expression:

```
IIF(RECNO("product") = prec, 0, 1)
```

Choose the Calculate option to `Sum` this variable. Now *change the order of the report variables* in the list that appears in the dialog so that the variable known as *newrec* is first.

When you use report variables that reference each other, the order in which the variables appear in the list is important. Here, the Report Writer should be instructed to evaluate newrec *before* the value of prec changes. Putting the variable first in the list accomplishes this task.

Figure 10.17 shows the difference between a straight count of the detail items (under the heading `# Budget lines`) created in a report expression and a count of the parent records (under the heading `# Products`) created with the newrec and prec report variables. (Both the # Products and the Product Name columns use the option to Suppress Repeated Values here.) You find that this technique, which tells you when the parent record has changed, has many uses in reports.

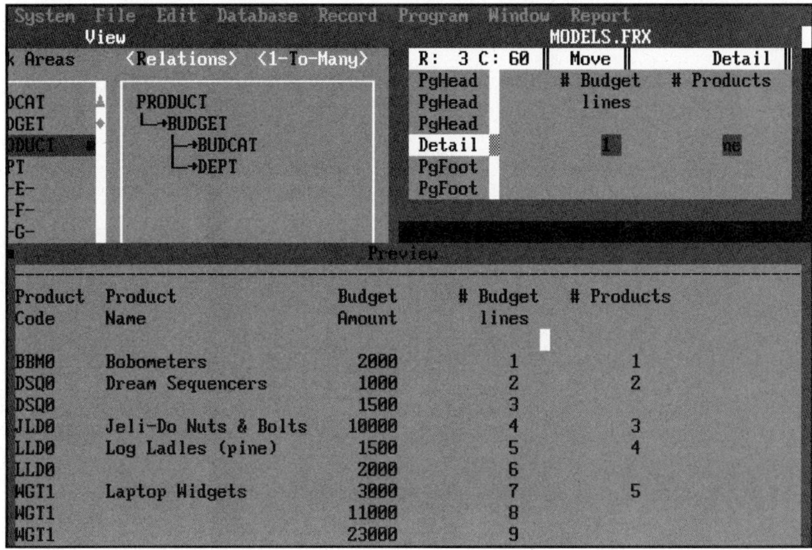

FIG. 10.17

Using Report Variables in a one-to-many relationship.

Overlaying Expressions

You made frequent use of the IIF() function, which is limited to two choices for any one expression. Using different, *overlaid* expressions in the same physical location of the report layout, however, you can easily accommodate more possibilities.

You may have noticed that, when moving objects around the layout, two or more objects can occupy the same physical space. When you print a report, you find that *all* the objects print, even though not all objects are visible at the same time in a Page Preview or when you send reports to the screen. Experiment with the Bring to Front (press Ctrl-G) and Send to Back (Ctrl-J) options of the Report menu, and you can designate the object that appears on-screen.

Recall the previous example of the budget figures that you compared to money on hand in a bank account. You may want to expand this example to have three overlaid objects, with these instructions at one position:

```
IIF(deposit > bankacct.deposit,
  "Additional deposit required: ", "")

IIF(deposit < bankacct.deposit,
  "Additional money available: ", "")

IIF(deposit = bankacct.deposit,
  "Bank deposit covers present requirements.", "")
```

Two overlaid objects at another position are expanded by using the following instructions:

```
IIF(deposit > bankacct.deposit,
  deposit - bankacct.deposit, "")

IIF(deposit < bankacct.deposit,
  bankacct.deposit - deposit, "")
```

Here, the IIF() expression evaluates the situation so that only the correct information prints in each report run.

At other times, you may want more than one item to print at one position, and the Report Writer will print each overlaid expression in turn. You can, for example, print a line of shaded blocks overlaid with a text heading as part of a form design. Use either a box object with the proper graphics character designated or use the REPLICATE() function, discussed previously in one of the label designs, to accommodate variable-width text. To create a shaded box for a memofield in a report, use REPLICATE() and the option to `Stretch Vertically`.

> **CAUTION:** When objects overlap in the same row, the object that begins in the *lowest column* is printed first. If two or more objects start at exactly the same position, all objects are sent to the printer with the one in the *back* first, in order, until the front most object is sent. This process is important if you use any of these objects to send printer instructions.

To do its page-pausing job at the right moment, the Waitpage() function, which introduced you to UDFs in this chapter, always must be in the first row and first column of a report, but you can now see that you can put another report object in the same position. Just use the Send to Back option on the Waitpage() object to ensure that this object prints first.

Chapter Summary

The two preceding chapters covered the features of FoxPro 2's Label Designer and Report Writer in some detail, but you have barely touched on the capabilities available.

As you practice with these tools, and as you learn more about FoxPro 2's special features in other parts of this book, consider the following possibilities to extend your reach:

- Use one report or label with different files, using an ALIAS. This chapter mentioned that you may want to set up a report in which you open a label or report database and examine the objects the file contains. You may create a second database as a *lookup* for report or label files, with expanded versions of the field names more meaningful to you. If you USE different FRX and LBX files with the same alias, the same report works for all files with one structure.
- Use an all-purpose alias, such as TEMP, for reports or labels designed to work with the results of SQL queries, and just output the results of queries to a temporary database with this name.
- Use labels to create columnar reports. Experiment with page headers and footers that surround a LABEL FORM command that uses a NEXT scope suitable to the number of labels you can fit on a page. Investigate the PRINTJOB/ENDPRINTJOB programming construct you find discussed in following chapters.
- Use reports for quick set-up and detailed formatting of information that you export to an SDF (columnar) format.
- Use labels to create merge files suited to various word processors, easily including any merge codes required, or investigate FoxPro 2's TEXTMERGE capabilities and use a report form to handle mailmerge completely within FoxPro.

You can accomplish these and many other specialized tasks with the Report Writer and Label Designer. As you develop dexterity with these tools, you practice skills equally valuable as you explore other important tools in FoxPro 2.

Building FoxPro 2 Applications

11

CHAPTER

Coordinating a FoxPro 2 Application

In the previous chapter on the Report Writer and the Label Designer, you found that you can add style and formatting enhancements—including boxes and other graphics elements—to database output. Remember that having these capabilities, however, is not the same as needing to use them in every report you create.

In fact, this kind of decoration may run counter to the real purpose of effectively communicating the information you derive from collected data. Without the benefit of thoughtful design, indiscriminately *gimmicky* reports can distract from the truly interesting content they are supposed to present.

Part III deliberately begins with a note of caution. You are about to encounter other tools in FoxPro 2 which are the building blocks of *applications*, systems that can include tailored data-entry screens, output procedures, and also the underlying tables that constitute a database. In this chapter, you investigate the following tools:

- The Screen and Menu Builders you use to accept entry from and give choices to the people who need to use and add to data

Although a triumph of gear ratios, the machines [mechanical representations of the solar system called orreries] did commit a grave sin of information design—Pridefully Obvious Presentation—by directing attention more toward miraculous contraptionary display than to planetary motion.

Edward R. Tufte,
Envisioning Information, p. 16

- The Project Manager you use to integrate all the entry, output, and utility tasks of a system into one structure
- The Distribution Kit you use to present the new FoxPro 2 application to the outside world
- A number of additional devices you can use to enhance and embellish applications.

Interface Design and FoxPro 2

In some ways, these FoxPro 2 tools make the business of *programming* applications more efficient and easier than ever. You are not, however, relieved of the responsibility to work hard on *designing* applications.

Like any owner of a sparkling new set of tools, you may be bewildered by the array of options in front of you. Because so many tools are available, you may find isolating and using the features to effectively help the user accomplish tasks difficult.

For this reason, the following section offers thoughts to help you approach the FoxPro 2 design tools with some discrimination. A full-scale discussion of the principles of application design is obviously beyond the scope of this book. However, in this short introduction, you find some helpful and provocative directions for a continued exploration of these topics. This chapter also attempts to provide a perspective on FoxPro 2's design tools.

This is the last time in Part III where you see the icon that indicates new FoxPro 2 Features. Although interface design in FoxPro 2 bears an evolutionary relationship to FoxPro 1.x and FoxBase Mac, the actual design tools, the way these tools are integrated, and the methods of programming the tools represent a fairly complete departure from previous versions.

Almost all the information in this part of the book is new to FoxPro 2 or is significantly enhanced over previous versions.

Developing Criteria for Interface Design

Return for a moment to the list of interface elements with which you began the chapter on the interface of FoxPro 2. In building the interface of applications you create, you need to work with the following components:

- The items you present on-screen
- The language and formats the program commonly uses to ask questions and give information
- The methods by which the program can accept responses
- The clues (such as colors, sounds, or positions on-screen) the program uses to indicate the current task and options

These items, formats, methods, and clues require you to make design decisions about the on-screen display, how best to display the different items, and how to establish effective two-way communications with a user that makes transparent what everything in the application means. You must evaluate the effectiveness of each decision by using a consistent set of standards. The following section suggests the standards of *comfort*, *clarity*, and *consistency* and attempts to describe the use of these standards in the interface design process.

Offering Comfortable Choices

Comfort, for anyone, is largely found in familiarity. You provide comfort for the users by providing situations, language, and objects to manipulate that the users already know and understand.

For example, the word *password* is often used in computer systems that require security clearance to access some or all functions. This word literally means a countersign spoken between two people before one of them can enter a specific area. In a computer system, the user is not actually entering a secure room, no word is spoken, and no second person is involved. Yet the *metaphor* of password is understood, and the user knows exactly what task is accomplished by *giving a password* to the computer. Think how much less comfortable you may become if, instead of a password, you were required to *enter a security identification #.*

Metaphors are often used in this way so that people can identify computer tasks with chores they already know how to perform. When you use metaphors, whether with a visual representation of a familiar object on-screen or with metaphoric language, think about how *suitable* the metaphor is to the task at hand. Does the metaphor help you imagine the necessary images and words, or is the concept that the metaphor represents too abstract or otherwise difficult to represent? If you need to add to this task later, is the metaphor easily extended to include possible new uses? What other connotations may the metaphor represent?

You must also make sure that whatever metaphor you choose is suitable to the potential audience, not just to you. This kind of correspondence is often heavily dependent on age or cultural background. For example, the *desktop* metaphor that FoxPro uses—with calculator, diary, and notes arranged and rearranged over a desk—may not be as comfortable for children using an application as a *toybox* that contains items that can be taken out, used, and then put back into the box.

Apart from metaphor, another easy way of maintaining a high level of comfort is to reproduce the exact language—and even exact representations—of existing manual systems. You can use the Report Writer and Screen Builder to precisely mimic standard manual order forms, and you can arrange tasks on an application menu exactly in the order in which they are performed in the office. Even if these tasks and forms are going to change in the system, you can continue using the same language to describe them wherever possible. In the preceding example, if the expression *security identification #* is presently in use, continuing to use this expression in the system can provide a higher level of comfort than creating *passwords*.

Where no possibility of familiarity with a task or a situation exists, you still can maintain comfort *if the user is aware that all actions they take are reversible*, or at least (where complete reversal can't be provided) that any harm done by choosing an action is minimal. You can maintain this high comfort level if you communicate clearly with the user about the choices available and make the results of a given action predictable and consistent. The steps you can take to provide and maintain comfort for the user are described in the following section.

Presenting Information Clearly

When you need to communicate information about the application to the user—either because you need to ask the user a question or because you want to answer a question—you may need to go beyond the bounds of the familiar. If the user needs to *understand* or *learn* something, your job is to make the information comprehensible.

Despite the current interest in graphical interfaces, icons, and other nonverbal methods of using a computer to communicate, effective use of language remains one of the best tools at your disposal to exchange information.

NOTE Although FoxPro is a text-based program in the current incarnation, you also can use symbols to communicate your intentions. *Be careful, however, when using symbols.* Like metaphors, symbols are open to interpretation and must be tested for clarity just as words must be. For a real-world example, consider the following symbols, which are found on the buttons in some elevators:

These symbols do not indicate the buttons' functions as clearly as do the words *close* and *open*—although apparently, in at least one elevator designer's mind, these symbols seem preferable and sufficient. Perhaps the best choice here is to use both the words and the symbols together, mutually reinforcing the meaning.

Use appropriate language in all communications, making sure that you provide the following information:

- Do not assign blame to the user. When a procedure fails, make sure that the *error messages* say that the *system*, not the user, made a mistake. `Cannot locate file` is better than `File specified does not exist`.
- Without assigning blame, try to suggest that the user is in control of the system whenever possible. `Enter filename when ready:` is better than `Filename required:`.
- Avoid computer jargon. Choose language with which the users of your application are comfortable, as described in the preceding section. Also, avoid unnecessarily harsh language (`Abort procedure`, `Kill history file`) that may alarm the user about what happens to the data!

Make all questions and answers for the user follow these principles. Moreover, when the user is expected to provide a response, the language must clearly indicate all possible choices and explain what results to expect from each choice.

Beyond questions and answers, make sure that your applications provide constant *feedback* messages to let the user know what the system is doing, especially during lengthy procedures. (In FoxPro 2, the SET TALK command is enhanced to make this process easy.)

You also need to use language appropriately to produce *help text* for the users' reference. In Chapter 18, "Enhancing the Applications You Program," you learn how to create help systems for applications, with the same format and functionality as the FoxPro 2 helpfile. For now, however, you only need to use words and to organize information in categories familiar and clear to the users.

By now, you are beginning to realize that building an application involves designing very frequent and even densely layered instances of communication. Many people think that software interfaces should avoid *information overload*, which they interpret as *too many* words or images. This confusion, however, is not directly proportional to the number of items a person must read or understand. Whether words or images are involved—and no matter how few or how many words or images appear—confusion occurs if these elements are not appropriately chosen by the designer.

Data also can be extremely complex. When you try to gather this data in an entry screen, to organize the data in a report, or to exhibit all the tasks required to maintain the data in a menu, communicating all this complexity is hard work. Simple reduction of the data, however, by eliminating a level of the detail or otherwise omitting some of the data's aspects, is not the answer. These techniques not only limit the value of the application by limiting the variety of tasks the application can handle, these omissions also show a disrespect for the abilities and intelligence of the users. A patronizing attitude inherent in the design is obvious to the users and can seriously damage their attitude toward your work.

Consider, therefore, offering some organizing structure in the design that gives the users a *macro-view* (a general impression) of the data if this information is all they want and a *micro-view* of all conceivable detail when needed.

In the Report Writer, you previously accomplished this task when you learned how to group data, providing up to 20 levels of summary, subtotal, and expanded detail. In the Screen Builder, you can group sections of data entry visually by enclosing the sections in boxes and then labeling the boxes, as you learned in the Organizer application screens. You also can separate sections of data into different windows, creating a *screen set*, with the initial window that holds the items that always need attention and with other windows, which are *brought forward* as the need for the subjects—or as the user's interest—arises. In the Menu Builder, you can organize options into menu pads with understandable titles and create subordinate menu popups that appear in a sequence logical to the user. When both menus and screens are unnecessary, you also can make items unselectable, further organizing the current task in the user's mind.

Using a Consistent Interface

When words that must be repeated and objects that look alike always mean the same thing and always produce similar results, the interface is known as *consistent.* Consistency is important because, besides performing comfortable, familiar actions, the users must develop confidence that a new, unfamiliar action proceeds according to past experience.

The more confident a user is that the system's meanings and responses follow a defined pattern, the more the users feel they are gaining skills and competence while they perform tasks. As a result, users are more open to exploring new features you may add to the system and are more willing to teach other users how to use the system.

Besides developing confidence, consistency has the added benefit of making users more sensitive to small variations. If you always use the same audible tone to indicate that the printer is not ready, and the user suddenly hears a different tone, the user is prepared for a different kind of alert.

The previous chapter suggested that you create a *master report*, with the defaults for your company by saving the format to a special name. If you also use particular style enhancements or other indications to indicate grand totals in one report, use the same enhancements in every report. If you use a particular column heading for certain kinds of information in one report, repeat the column heading for every report in which this information appears.

Similarly, if you create one format for error messages in the Screen Builder, use the same format for all alerts. The following sections show how easily you can edit the window dimensions or text while leaving the basic *style* of the window (colors, border type, title) intact and save the window to a new name. Create a different format for informative messages that are *not* alerts—use different colors, borders, or placement—and the user quickly learns that each kind of window requires a consistently appropriate response.

You also can make sure that language remains consistent from screen to screen. Make abbreviations, the style of capitalization, even the general sequence of movement through data-entry items relative to their placement on-screen, the same throughout all the screens. If choosing the word `<Cancel>` on one screen reverses all current changes, consistent design requires that `<Cancel>` produces the same effect wherever you place the word in the application.

Compared to the profusion of menu systems available in previous versions of FoxPro and in the other xBase dialects, the Menu Builder almost enforces a consistent interface style for the applications you create. Try, however, to extend this advantage by making shortcuts and hot keys behave consistently from one menu to the next. If Alt-D means *delete an entry* on one screen, Alt-D should never mean *enter the current date* on another screen!

You often can maintain this consistency across applications, although you must always consider the users for whom each system is designed. Besides a regard for the language and facts with which users are familiar, also make sure that you considered the method of input preferred by each user. Is a particular user, for example, more comfortable with a mouse or with the keyboard?

To be both safe and consistent, make sure that users can perform each task in the system with either device and that both key presses and mouse clicks give dependable results.

Sometimes you may need to depart from a consistent interface to make a major modification in an application. The users may tolerate new interface features and objects—in fact, the new objects and language can be boldly transformed, alerting users to the importance of the change and preparing them to learn these changes—if you have helped the user develop confidence during previous experiences with the application.

Pursuing Comfort, Clarity, and Consistency

All the preceding suggestions require that you, as a designer, remain *open to change* and are able to acknowledge some false starts. Just as the users need feedback as they use the system, you need feedback from the user as you work to create or revise the application.

In this process, known as *acceptance testing*, you can involve as many kinds of potential users as possible—users with different needs, expectations, levels of skill and even of physical ability. Try to maximize the comfort of the process for each of the users. Explain that you are testing the *system*, not the *user*, and that if something goes wrong, you make changes or corrections to the system, not to how the user works with the system.

You can make acceptance testing a creative part of the design process if you begin early in the design stage, and the users feel encouraged to share their perceptions and *wish lists* with you. Users also become more convinced of the value of the new system because they have a personal investment in the design. Far from a simple process of uncovering bugs, testing provides yet another way that empowers users and lets them know that they are *in control* of the system.

The FoxPro 2 tools encourage you to remain willing to change the design throughout the creation of an application. The ease with which you can make changes in a report, a menu, a screen, or a query, and also gather together all the necessary elements in projects, represents a high degree of compliance with the standards of good interface design that you see within FoxPro 2.

Introducing the FoxPro 2 Design Tools

The FoxPro 2 interface, however, occasionally does violate some of the design principles discussed in the preceding section. Perhaps you are bewildered by FoxPro error messages or have difficulty locating or understanding items in the Fox help file. Viewing the FoxPro interface (or a FoxApp-generated application or the sample applications) with a critical eye is a constructive exercise that helps you develop a strong *design sense*. Study helps you understand that no program is ever perfect, and every program can be improved. The process of design never really ends.

Learning to program has no more to do with designing interactive software than learning to touch-type has to do with writing poetry.

Ted Nelson, "The Right Way to Think About Software Design", *The Art of Human-Computer Interface Design*, p. 243

On the whole, however, the FoxPro 2 design tools provide a comfortable, clear, consistent working environment, and spectacular conditions under which you can create the same kind of environment for others.

The nature of the design tools enables nontechnical people to become involved in the design process. As you saw in the Report Writer, and as you are about to see again in the Screen Builder, page or screen layout in FoxPro 2 is similar to graphics design work in a desktop-publishing program; objects are *drawn*, *stretched*, *colored*, and *placed*. Encourage the appropriate design professionals to participate in this part of the work and to lend their talents to the application. This method is yet another way to cultivate a unique *design sense* as you work.

If you read the first chapter of this book, you had a glimpse of the Screen Builder and by now, you must realize that this feature is strikingly similar in design to the Report Writer. You also may have previously run DEMO.APP, which is found in the FoxPro 2 main program directory. Now is a good time to run DEMO.APP once more. Whether for the first time or as a repeat, DEMO's quick display of all the FoxPro 2 features can give you a panoramic view of the information presented in the following section (see fig. 11.1).

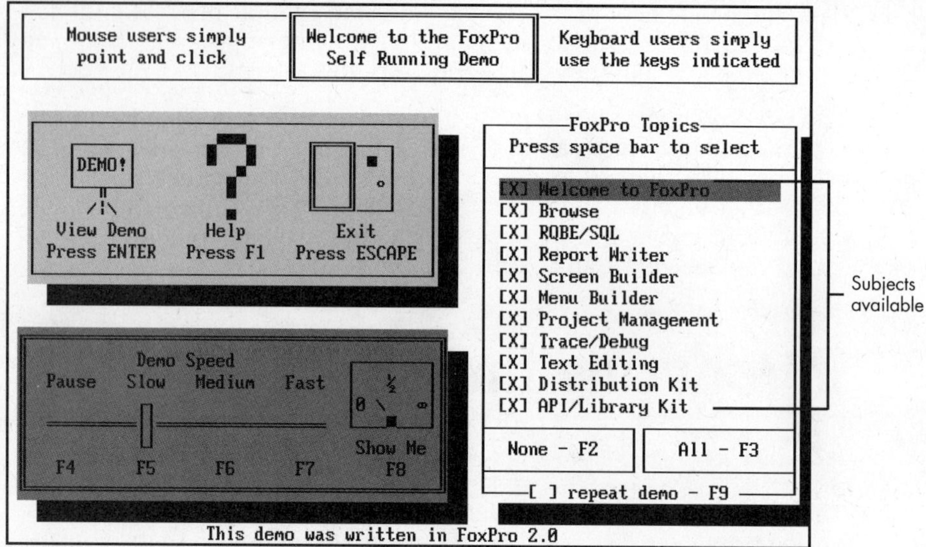

FIG. 11.1

The FoxPro 2 Self-Running Demo's initial screen.

Because the Menu Builder and the Screen Builder, like the Report Writer and Label Designer, make creating and altering interface objects easy, you are free to concentrate on design goals while you use these applications.

In Chapter 14, you see how the Project Manager plays a key role in overseeing the developer's environment. Take a moment now to look at any projects provided on the FoxPro 2 installation disks—even the PRODUCT.PJX project that FoxApp created for you in Chapter 1. To open a project, just use the File Open option from the menu and select files of Project type from the popup control or type **MODIFY PROJECT ?** in the Command Window and a PJX file.

The following figures show LASER3.PJX, a sample project that you find in the GOODIES\LASER directory below the main FoxPro 2 program directory.

After you open a project, move the highlight to different files in the list and choose `<Info>` to learn how a project maintains information on the contents and the history of the file (see fig. 11.3). Select `<Edit>` for any entry and learn that you can open the component screens, menus, programs, and databases of a project with this simple action. As you notice in figure 11.4, editing a screen set within a project enables you to make many choices about a project's use specific to this application. These choices enable you to use—over and over—screens, such as the *control panels* you saw in Chapter 1, but also to tailor a screen's use in each system you design.

TIP

When you first try to open a sample project, you may see a message like the one in figure 11.2. When you open a project you did not create, FoxPro gets ready to re-establish the locations of the component files in your disk's directory structure. Among the other housekeeping chores, a project tracks the location of all the project's files on the disk, navigating from what FoxPro calls the project *home directory*. When you open a project that was created by another person on a disk with a different directory structure than yours, you see this message as the project prepares to relocate the elements into the directory structure you selected. This talent of the Project Manager's is integral to the capability of coordinating the application when you distribute the completed application to users.

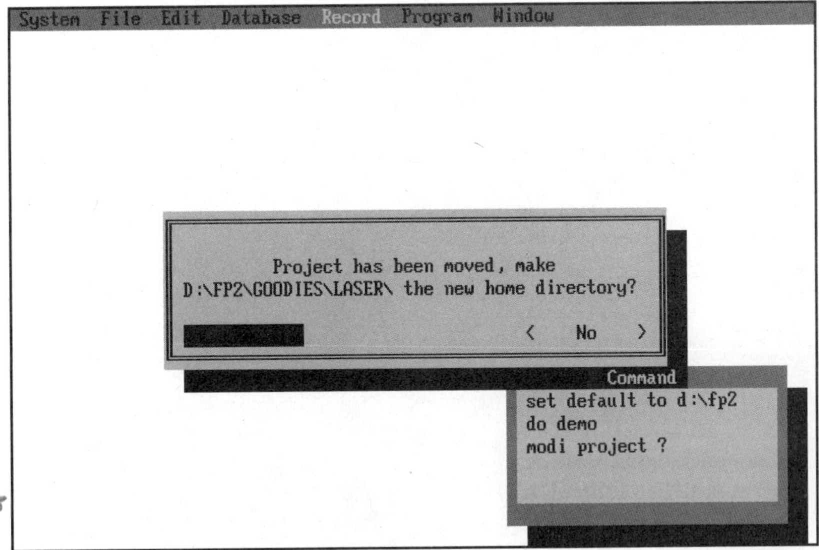

FIG. 11.2

The message that appears when you try to open a file you did not create.

Finally, select Build and access the dialog that is truly a project's *raison d'être* (see fig 11.5). A project *builds* applications by putting together all the component files to compile an APP file, such as the files you previously learned to DO to run applications or (with the addition of the Distribution Kit) to generate two kinds of *executable* files, which is covered in the Chapter 14, "Organizing and Packaging Your Applications."

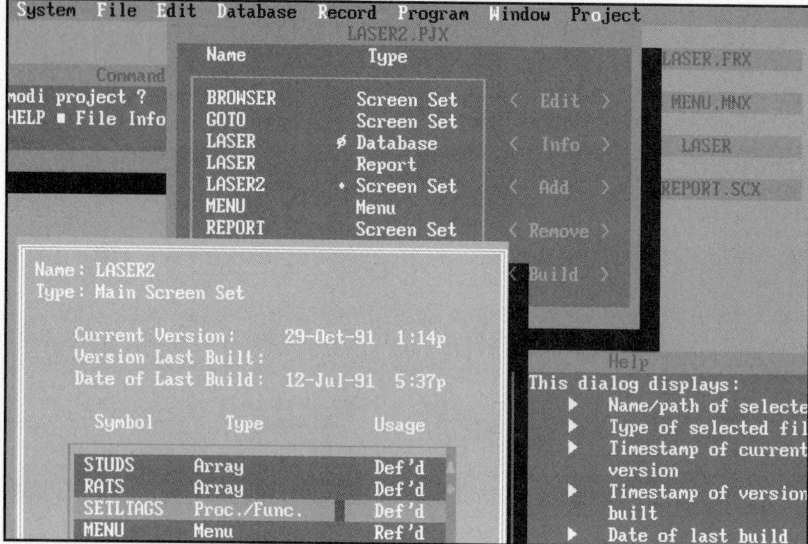

FIG. 11.3

The information on a file maintained in the project.

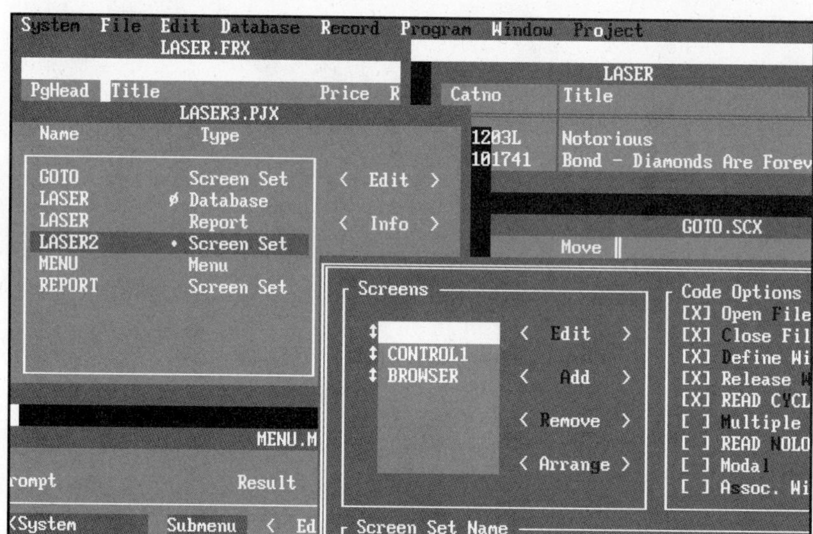

FIG. 11.4

Opening and editing different kinds of files in a project.

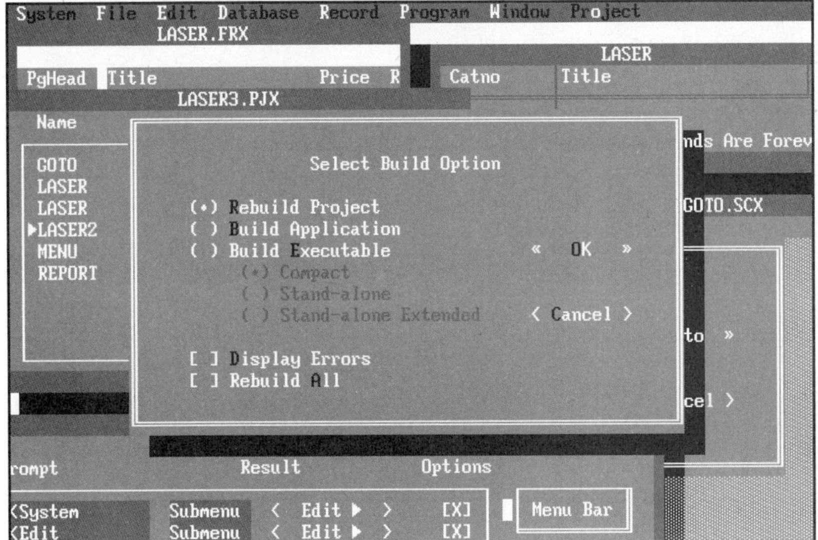

FIG. 11.5

The Project Manager's Build dialog.

Chapter Summary

Applications design is one of the most creative parts of using any database management system, and FoxPro 2 is no exception. You should go on to enjoy this aspect of working with FoxPro and continue to expand your thoughts on these issues as you explore the FoxPro 2 design tools in Part III of this book and beyond.

Sources for new design ideas are all around you in the real world. The books listed below, from which many of the recommendations in this section are drawn, are just one place to start.

**Interface Design Issues:
a Short Bibliography**

Apple Human Interface Guidelines: The Apple Desktop Interface. Addison-Wesley, Reading, MA, 1987 (and revised editions).

"The Ziggurat Zone," Peter C. Coffee, *PC Tech Journal*. October, 1988, pp. 147-152. (also see other issues that contain his "Outfitting the End User" column)

The Elements of Friendly Software Design, Paul Heckel, Warner, New York, 1984. (Besides the subject in the title, to which Heckel provides a good general introduction, this book contains among the best analyses of how software developers—and other creative people—work together in collaborative design processes.)

The Art of Human-Computer Interface Design, Brenda Laurel, ed., Addison-Wesley, Reading, MA, 1990. (An anthology of views from diverse sources.)

The Design of Everyday Things, Donald A. Norman, Doubleday, New York, 1990. (previously published in hardcover as *The Psychology of Everyday Things*)

Designing the User Interface: Strategies for Effective Human-Computer Interaction, Ben Shneiderman, Addison-Wesley, Reading, MA, 1987.

Envisioning Information, Edward R. Tufte, Graphics Press, Cheshire, CT, 1990. (also see Tufte, *The Visual Display of Quantitative Information*)

12

CHAPTER

Creating Application Elements

In the first chapters of this book, you learn a quick and easy way to enter data by using the BROWSE command to navigate in a table. In the next few chapters, you learn that BROWSE and a companion tool, EDIT/CHANGE, provide a powerful means to format and enter data. However, you also learn that data entry and other screen displays can take many forms in FoxPro.

The multifaceted READ command gives you almost unlimited access to the same interface objects for the data-entry designs that FoxPro uses. Chapter 2 introduces you to these objects, which you manipulate from the first action you take in the program. Now, you also learn how to use these interface objects as a developer, by using the versatile Screen Builder.

You use the Screen Builder to *paint* and arrange these objects on-screen so that you can concentrate on creating an ideal layout. Similar to the Report Writer, the Screen Builder requires careful study. Although initial efforts with the Builder may be useful and attractive, adding a few lines of programming instructions *attached* to some of these objects (just as you added UDFs to the reports), provides far greater control over both the content and the appearance of screens.

For data-entry screens, this control often involves some form of *data validation*. Data validation techniques make sure that information entered into a field or fields meets certain criteria that you set. You can make the information in one field, for example, dependent on the information contained in another field, or you can make sure that the field contains one of the choices stored in a *lookup* table, a concept you encountered when you worked with reports and labels.

Of course, the Screen Builder can produce other application elements that aren't strictly data-entry forms. For example, you can design logos and other background screens, informational displays, alerts, dialogs, database-managing *control panels*, and all other forms of communication a system needs.

This chapter introduces the Screen Builder as a tool. The experience you had with the Report Writer has prepared you for many of the features with which you are going to work here. Therefore, you can move quickly through the section on enhancing the screens with various forms of data validation, such as including more than one window and building the windows into a *screen set* like the one in PRODUCT.APP. This process continues in the following chapter, with examples of more-complex screen sets and data validation.

If you're new to program writing, several programming concepts introduced in this chapter may intimidate you. Take the time to work through these concepts; don't try to complete all the exercises in one sitting. Rather, practice creating the interface objects by using the techniques described in this and in the following chapter, without adding all the validation codes. To further help you understand the material, return to this section after you read the chapters on programming.

Even if you're well-versed in programming, you may have difficulty getting used to the Screen Builder. For many programmers, this tool represents a radical departure from standard methods of program design, creation, and maintenance. Expert programmers may find relinquishing their edge on experience and expertise to adapt to completely new working conditions especially difficult.

However, whether you are a novice or a veteran, if you give time and attention to the Screen Builder, the investment repays you many times over.

Using the Screen Builder Design Screen

As usual, start FoxPro 2 from the MODEL directory. However, if you are already working in the data directories, you can access the practice files by issuing the following command in the Command window:

```
SET DEFAULT TO C:\FP2\MODEL
```

Examine the screen that FoxApp built for you and that you edited slightly in Chapter 1. Open the MODEL.VUE file and use the View window to make the Product table the selected work area, or type the following command in the Command window:

```
USE PRODUCT
```

In the File Open dialog, open the screen-type file PRODUCT.SCX (note the default extension) or type the following in the Command window:

```
MODIFY SCREEN PRODUCT
```

The screen-designing window you see is similar to the Report Writer. The window includes some text items (here, the field names), and differently colored or highlighted field expressions (in this screen, the Product table fields). You can select and move objects around, resize objects, or use a selection marquee and group together objects.

If you select an object and access the Screen pad from the menu bar, you see the following groups of options on the Screen menu popup, as shown in figure 12.1:

- The first group contains a Screen Layout option, which presents a dialog in which you make decisions that influence the look and behavior of the screen as a whole. The Open All Snippets option gives you access to the *code snippets*, which are *attached* to this screen. Code snippets are lines of programming instructions that can *belong* to a single screen object or give you screen-wide control. As you see in a following section, snippets are similar to the UDFs you created for the reports, but are stored internally in the screen file.
- The second group on the menu popup are options for each kind of screen object that you can use. You are already familiar with Box and Text objects from reports, and you used all the other options as you explored the FoxPro 2 interface.

- The third group of options on the Screen menu popup influences the behavior of a selected object or objects (the items are enabled here because the text object Prodcode was selected). Although most of these options are familiar from the Report Writer, some options take on new significance when applied to screens.

- The fourth, or last, group has only one option, Quick Screen, which is disabled in figure 12.1 because a Quick Screen is generated only when you work with a completely empty screen. The original PRODUCT.SCX generated by FoxApp, before modification as shown, was a Quick Screen created by a programming command.

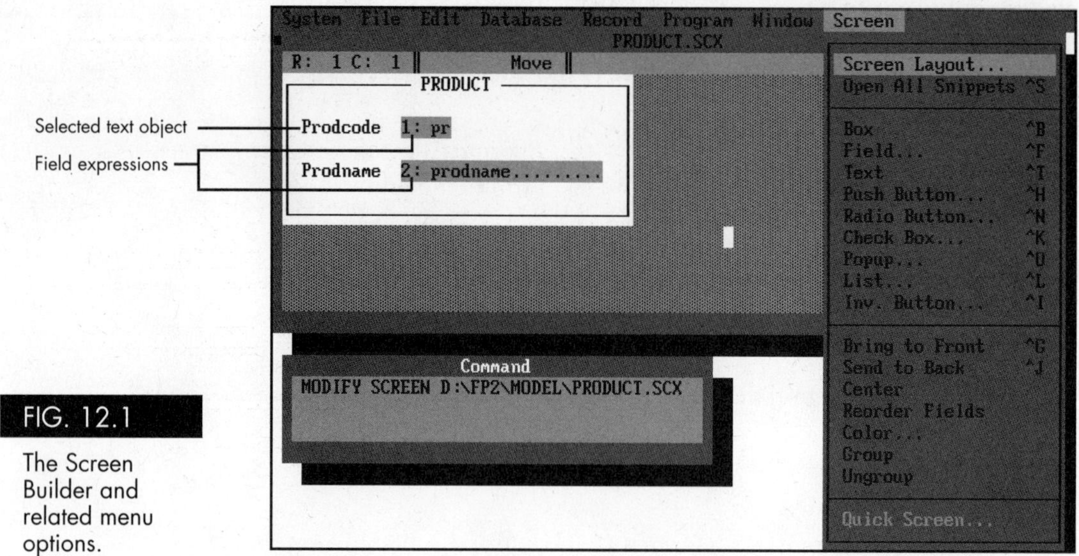

FIG. 12.1

The Screen Builder and related menu options.

Practice moving the objects around and perhaps changing the text objects to make them more understandable. Notice that pressing Ctrl-T or typing text on-screen, puts you into *text mode* as opposed to the default *move mode*. You see the difference in the screen's status line. Pressing Enter while creating a text object puts you back in *move mode* and *affixes* the text object in the screen.

If you like, you can add a Box object with Ctrl-B by selecting the style with a similar set of radio button options (`Single line`, `Double line`, `Panel`, or `Character`), as shown in figure 12.2. Notice that you see no Float option here because this option makes no sense in a screen. Instead, you can use the `<Fill Character>` push button to fill the box with any character you choose.

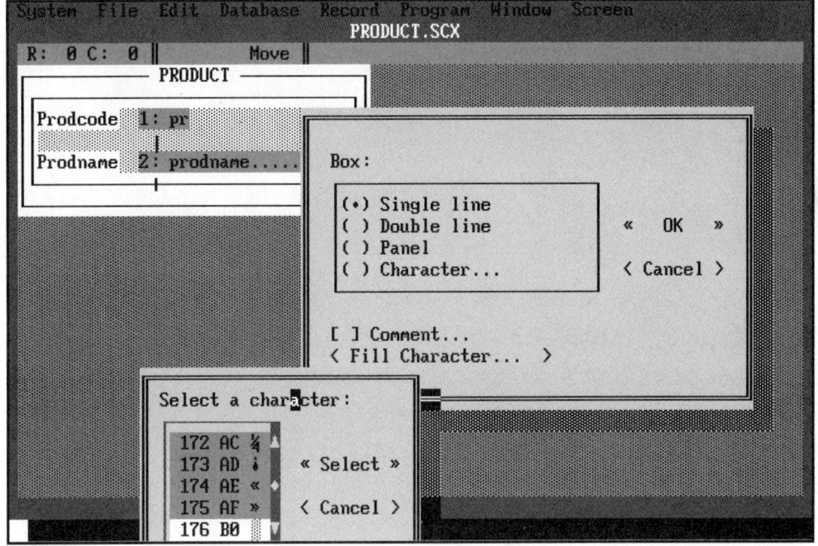

FIG. 12.2

A box filled with a graphics character is overlaid by text and field objects.

After you create and fill a box, you may have to select the box object and use the Send to Back option before you can see the text objects again. This concept, too, is familiar, although in reports you use Send to Back differently for printing effects.

You also may notice that, here, the box doesn't add significantly to the elegance of the screen display. Select the box again, press Delete, and the box disappears.

Using the Field Expression Dialog

Selecting the PRODCODE field expression for editing brings up a dialog with a few familiar features but, here, you begin to see the real differences between a report (which is entirely output) and a screen (where some objects are meant to be edited by the user).

As shown in figure 12.3, the top set of radio buttons in this dialog enables you to designate the field expression as a `Say`, a `Get` (shown here), or an `Edit`. In a screen, a Say is an expression that appears as a kind of label, similar to a column heading in a report. The Edit and Get expressions, in contrast, are the items into which the user places new information. Edit expressions are, like memo fields, variable in length, and Get expressions provide text boxes for data entry.

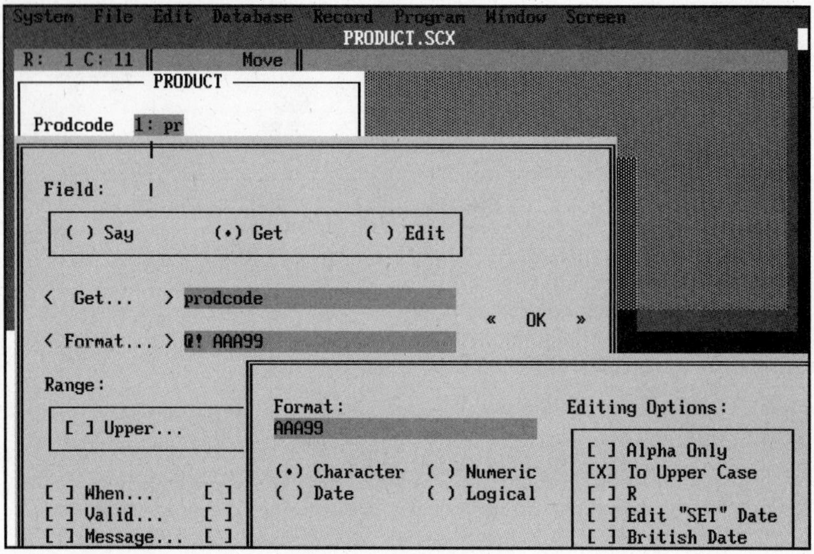

FIG. 12.3

Formatting the product code.

The other options in the Screen Layout dialog (`Push Button`, `Radio Button`, `Check Box`, `Popup`, `List`, and `Inv`—or invisible—`Button`) all are specialized forms of Get expressions. You know how these forms work from FoxPro's dialogs and system windows. In following sections of this and the following chapter, as you create examples of these specialized objects and explore the distinctive properties of each object, consider the actions that each option is best suited to perform.

If you change the radio button selection from `Get` to `Say` or `Edit`, the other options in the dialog become enabled or disabled, as appropriate for the different kinds of field expressions. You learn more about the other options in a following section of this chapter. For now, return the selection to GET.

Beginning To Validate GETs

The PRODCODE field expression currently enables you to enter any character, but the data-entry screen is more useful if two items are ensured:

- Every product code follows a particular format; the Omnipresent Widget product line uses three capitalized alphabetic characters followed by either one or two digits.
- Each product has a unique code to provide proper lookups for the Budget and other tables.

To provide the first kind of data validation, click the <Format> button. You see a new dialog, also shown in figure 12.3. Using the check box `To Upper Case` and typing the format *AAA99* gives you the Format shown in the Field Expression dialog's text box.

> **TIP**
> You can press F1 at any time to get context-sensitive help on a current action. You need not remember all the possible Formatting template characters. As you see when you access the help file, the template `AAA99` means that the first three characters must be letters and that the last two characters must be numbers.

The second problem is more complicated. To make sure that every product code you enter is unique and that every product name has a code, attach the first *code snippet* to the field expression by using the `Valid` check box.

A GET's VALID clause works the same way as a BROWSE field's :V switch, which you learn about in Chapter 8. The VALID clause is a logical expression evaluated when new data has been entered into that field and the user tries to leave the field. If the expression evaluates to False, the contents of the field are not valid, and the user remains in that field. If BELL is SET ON, which is the default, the bell sounds. If NOTIFY is SET ON (also the default), a window with an error message appears. The default message is `Invalid Entry`. You can provide more informative error messages by using the ERROR clause, like the BROWSE field's :E switch, for which you also see a check box.

As in a BROWSE, a VALID clause does not handle data entry in a field concluded with a press of the Esc key, which is treated as cancellation of the entry (the GET reverts back to the data the field held before editing). You should treat this kind of cancellation separately and consistently throughout the system.

Unlike a BROWSE field's :V switch, a VALID clause also can return a positive or negative number as well as a .T. or .F. result. A positive number advances the cursor that number of GETs forward, and a negative one forces the cursor backward. In a following section, you return to this way, and other ways, of influencing the order that GETs are entered.

A VALID clause can contain a simple expression, such as the following line:

```
! EMPTY(prodcode)
```

The clause also can contain a single UDF or more complicated expressions—such as the work you created by using the Expression Builder—that include multiple UDFs.

If you use the `Valid` check box to create an Expression (by marking the `Expression` check box), you can type the expression directly or use the Expression Builder. You also can use Valid to create a `Procedure` (see figs. 12.4 and 12.5). This process enables you to write a set of instructions, which you *attach* to this object, that FoxPro creates as a UDF (as you see when you examine the program you generate later). This method is a convenient way to avoid worrying about what you named, or where you stored, the UDF. Advantages exist in creating an Expression, however, which you see in the following sections.

NOTE

Screen files (tables with the default extension SCX) can hold procedures to be used in conjunction with these files' related elements, but report files (FRX tables) cannot. Screen files have this capability because they are sent through a *generating template*, which produces complete programs that you include with the applications you create. The attached procedures are generated as parts of these programs. The generated programs must then be *compiled*, like other programs that you can DO, so that FoxPro can interpret them.

Report files, however, do not produce programs to be used at runtime; FoxPro interprets reports directly in table form. All procedures run in conjunction with report files, therefore, must exist *outside* of the files so that FoxPro can compile them separately.

FRX tables cannot generate code but, although this limitation may seem a disadvantage, a compensatory benefit exists. Because reports need not be compiled, users can modify and create reports with applications that you create. This feature is covered in Chapter 14, where you explore various ways to distribute the applications you create and where the significance of this difference becomes clear.

When you mark the `Procedure` check box, you see a small text editing area in which you can type. However, you may prefer to mark the `Edit` check box, as shown in figure 12.4. `Edit` opens a full-scale editing window for the snippet and puts you back at the Field Expression dialog. Choose OK or press Ctrl-Enter and you enter the snippet editing window, shown in figure 12.5.

The instructions to validate the product code are relatively complex. These instructions, however, contain several tricks worth learning,

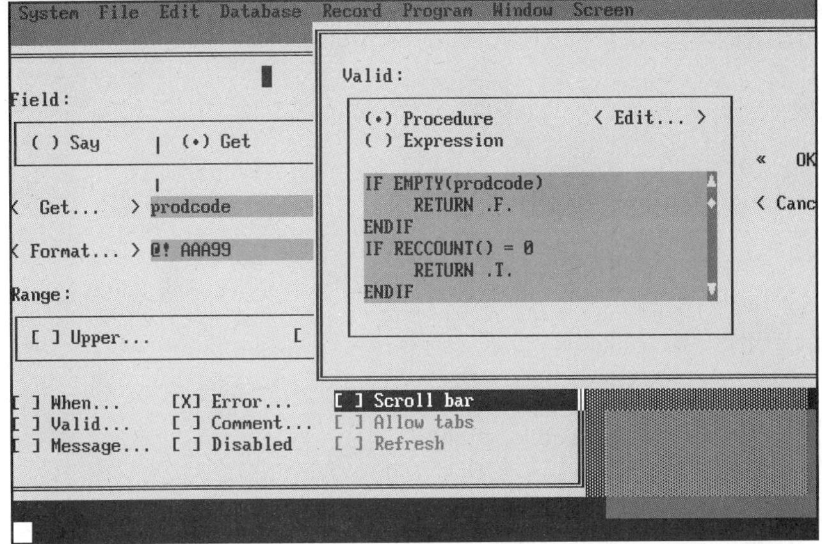

FIG. 12.4

Accessing the VALID clause and choosing to create a Procedure snippet.

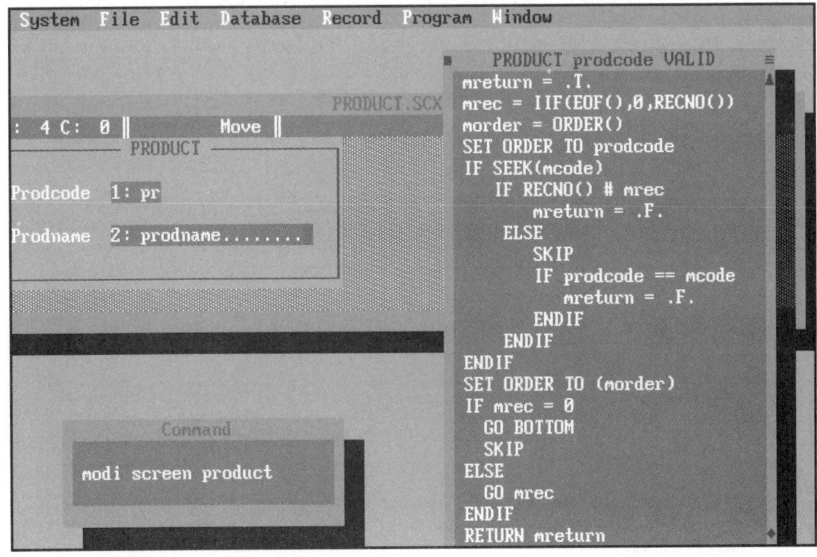

FIG. 12.5

The VALID clause Procedure snippet in an editing window.

because creating unique codes like these is a task required in almost every relational database system.

Remember that FoxPro ignores lines in a program that begin with an asterisk (*). These lines are used to provide *comments*. By using the comments in the following lines of code, and by checking the Commands and Functions documentation or the helpfile to understand the capitalized keywords with which you aren't familiar, you can follow and reproduce this procedure for programs you write:

```
IF EMPTY(prodcode)
   * it should not be blank
   RETURN .F.
ENDIF

IF RECCOUNT() = 0
   * there's no problem if you're adding
   * the first record in the table
   RETURN .T.
ENDIF

mcode = prodcode
* save the entered value into
* a variable, 'mcode', and
* set up a variable, 'mreturn',
* to hold the RETURN value

mrec = IIF(EOF(),0,RECNO())
* save the current record number
* so you can return to it after
* moving around in the table
* set it to 0 if you're at the end of
* the file

morder = ORDER()
SET ORDER TO prodcode
* save the current table order
* so you can set up the order the way you want to
* but restore it afterwards

mreturn = .T.
IF SEEK(mcode)
   IF RECNO() # mrec
     mreturn = .F.
   ELSE
     SKIP
     IF prodcode==mcode
       mreturn = .F.
     ENDIF
   ENDIF
   * can you find this code in the table?
   * and is it on a different record
   * than mrec, the record you are
   * currently editing?

ENDIF

* now put things back the way you found them
SET ORDER TO (morder)
```

```
IF mrec = 0
  * go to end of file

  GO BOTTOM
  SKIP
ELSE
  * go to original record

  GO mrec

ENDIF

RETURN mreturn
```

A simpler procedure, shown in figure 12.6, enables the two error conditions you identified to produce different error messages. Use the `Error` check box in the Field Expression dialog and choose to `Edit` a `Procedure`. Follow these steps with a colon in the editing window and enter the following code:

```
IF EMPTY(prodcode)
  RETURN "Product Code field cannot be empty."
ELSE
  RETURN "Product Code already in use."
ENDIF
```

Alternatively, because only two possible messages exist, you also can `Edit` an `Expression`. The Expression Builder appears, and you create the following expression, which is shown in figure 12.7:

```
IIF(EMPTY(prodcode)"Product Code field cannot be empty?",
    "Product Code field already in use.")
```

TIP

After at least one snippet is created, you can use the second option on the Screen menu pad to Open All Snippets at the same time as you work. (Use Ctrl-S as a shortcut). You may find that keeping all snippets open in docked form is convenient as you work with a screen. Remember that you can resize the layout window to make room on-screen, as shown in figure 12.6. If you save a screen with snippets open, these snippets remain open and ready for use when you are ready to modify the screen.

If the screen looks too cluttered, access the Screen popup menu with Shift-Alt-C or a shifted mouse click to change the option to Hide All Snippets. If you're in the Layout window, use Shift-Ctrl-S as a shortcut to hide all snippets.

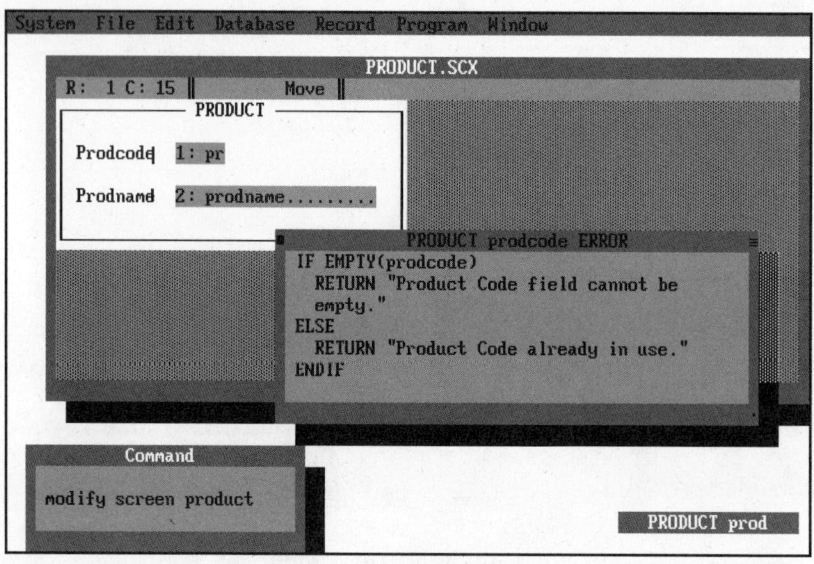

FIG. 12.6

The Screen Layout window with Prodcode Valid snippet docked and available and the Prodcode ERROR snippet being edited as a procedure.

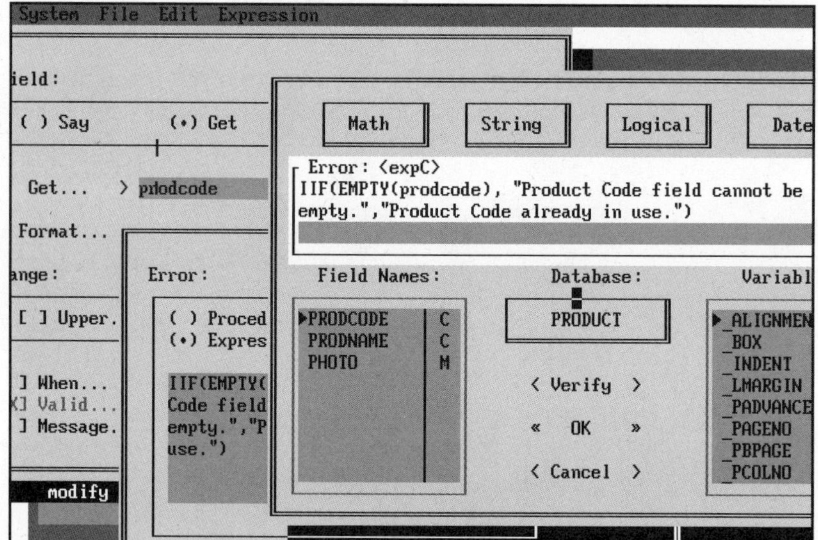

FIG. 12.7

The Prodcode Error snippet being edited as an expression.

Generating and Running the Screen Program

To see the results of the work, access the first option on the Screen menu pad to save the Environment. (If you are creating this screen from scratch, you are given an opportunity to save the environment the first time you saved the work. You see a similar message in figure 12.8. Because this screen was created by FoxApp with a command that CREATEs a Quick Screen, but doesn't save the environment in the screen file, you should now deliberately save the state of the files.)

When you work on this screen again, you can change the environment saved with the screen by using the option in the Screen Layout dialog. If you try to open the screen file at a later date and you are missing a necessary index or other part of the environment, you get an error message but you still can edit the screen. If this situation occurs, adjust and then resave the environment in the Screen Layout dialog.

With the active window as the screen on which you are working, access the Program menu pad and notice that the Generate option is now enabled. If you press Ctrl-F1 or otherwise activate the Command window or one of the other system windows, or any text file that you open in the usual way, you notice that the Generate option is disabled again. Activate the screen design window to reactivate the option. Choose the «Generate» option and, because you made changes since the last time you saved the screen, you now can fix the changes on-screen and save

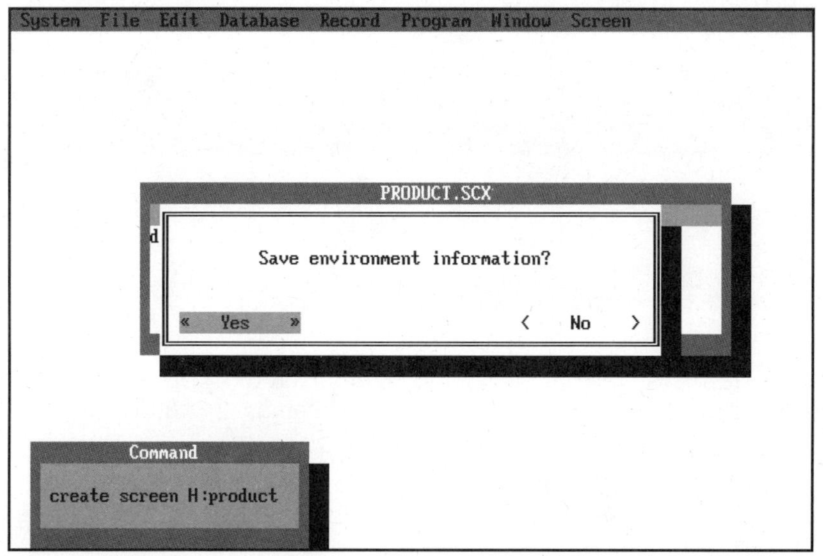

FIG. 12.8

Newly created screens give you the choice shown when you first try to save them to a file.

the screen. In response to the alert shown in figure 12.9, select «Yes». The screen saves, and the generation of the new screen program, PRODUCT.SPR, begins.

> **CAUTION:** If you want to DO the generated application again in the original state, and you do not choose another file name to which you save the screen, you see an error from FoxPro that indicates `Source code is out of date` when you try to DO PRODUCT.APP later. The Product project file needs to be rebuilt, a process you learn about in a following chapter. To continue using PRODUCT.APP, therefore, choose «No» when asked whether you want to overwrite, by using the File option Save as, which saves the screen as PRODUCT1. Use this name in the following instructions.

The first step is to choose from the bewildering range of options in figure 12.10. For now, just press Ctrl-Enter to accept all the defaults.

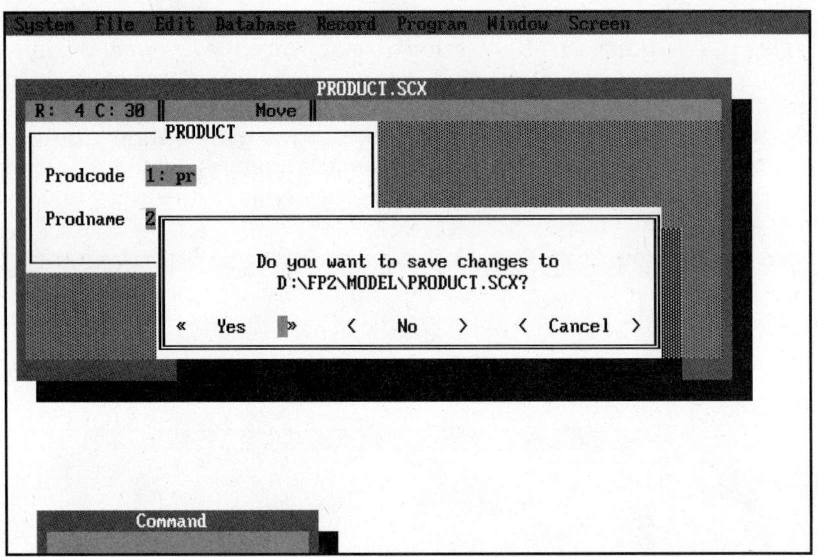

FIG. 12.9

Preparing to generate a screen file.

In figure 12.10, the Output file should be changed to PRODUCT1.SPR, with the drive and directory, if you want to keep using PRODUCT.APP.

You can decide whether you want to overwrite the old PRODUCT.SPR file (generated by FoxApp). If you saved the screen to PRODUCT1.SPR, you don't see this message because no previous PRODUCT1.SPR exists in the directory.

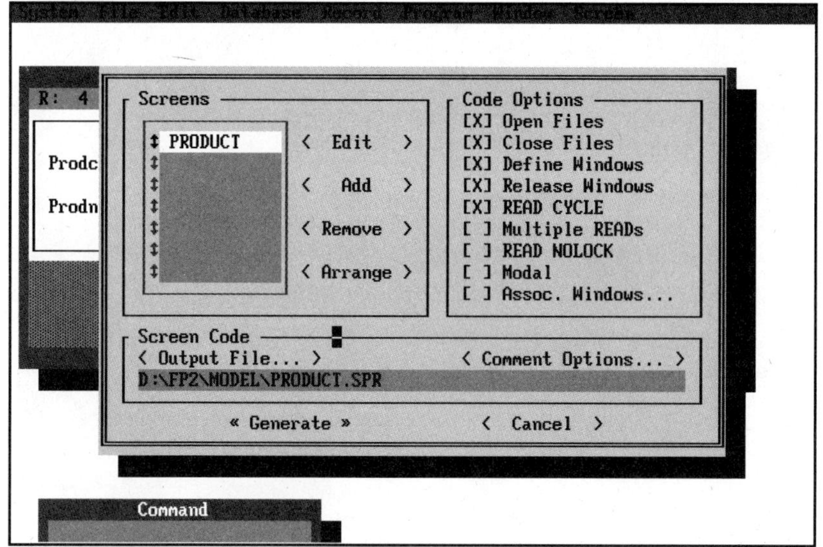

FIG. 12.10

The screen generation options dialog, showing default settings.

A *thermometer* appears that shows you FoxPro's progress as the program is generated. You saw a similar thermometer if you generated a crosstab report in the *Query* chapters or created an index on a large file. You also may have seen a similar thermometer during the FoxPro installation procedures (shown in the figures in Appendix A). If you are generating a screen for the first time since installing FoxPro, you see an additional thermometer as FoxPro *compiles* the program GENSCRN.PRG used to produce the screen code. (GENSCRN is a *template* or program-creating program, supplied with FoxPro 2. In a following chapter, you learn that GENSCRN is another set of FoxPro instructions that you must compile the first time the instructions are run so that FoxPro can interpret this template as a program.)

Don't be alarmed if the thermometer doesn't appear to progress at a constant rate. Some parts of screen program generation involve many more lines of code than others, so the indicator may seem to pause for a while.

Before you try to run PRODUCT.SPR, compile the generated program. By default, FoxPro compiles the program the first time you try the DO command, but compiling the program before a DO enables you to check for errors you may have made in typing the snippets when you edited the screen. After selecting the Compile option from the Program menu pad, highlight and select PRODUCT.SPR from the file list in the Compile dialog, and accept all other default settings as shown in figure 12.11. If typing errors exist, you see an error message similar to the message shown in figure 12.12.

System File Edit Database Record Program Window

Compile:

[..]
BROWSE.PRG
CREATET.PRG
CREATET2.PRG
PRODUCT.SPR
WAITPAGE.PRG

Drv. G

Dir. MODEL

< Tag All >

< Tag None >

[ ] All Files

Options
[ ] Encrypted
[X] Debugging Information
[ ] New and Updated files only

Output to
< Directory... >

Log Errors
( ) None
(•) To .ERRs
( ) To File [ ] Append
< File... >

« Compile » < Cancel >

FIG. 12.11

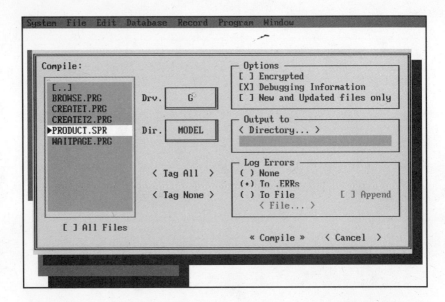

Compiling a screen file.

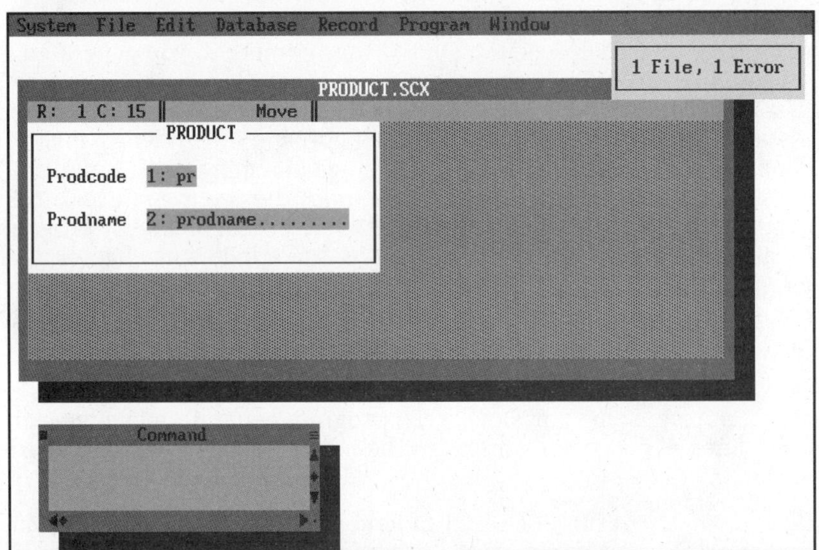

FIG. 12.12

A typical error message from the Compiler.

As you see in figure 12.13, you can then look for a file name with the extension ERR, either from the File Open menu option or (a faster way) by typing the following command in the Command window:

```
MODIFY FILE *.ERR
```

This command finds a file that contains the instruction or instructions that FoxPro wasn't able to interpret. The best thing to do here, as shown in figure 12.14, is to reactivate the screen you were building, open the snippets, and look for the error that caused the problem. (Don't forget to highlight and copy the error first and use the FoxPro editor to Find this text in the snippets.)

After you find and edit all errors, save, generate, and compile the program again. If no more errors are found, type the following command:

```
MODIFY FILE *.ERR
```

This command results in a `File does not exist` error message because FoxPro erases the old error file during the compilation process.

The process of finding and fixing errors in programs is known as *debugging* the code. FoxPro 2 has sophisticated tools, the *Debug* and *Trace* windows, which you learn about in Chapter 18, "Enhancing the Applications You Program." These tools are indispensable in large systems that contain many programs. For now, however, this simple error-correcting method suffices.

After all errors are corrected, you can use the Program Do option to run the PRODUCT.SPR program. As you can see in figure 12.15, attempting to edit the product code for the first record (Dream Sequencers) to a code already in use for another product (WGT1) results in a useful error message, as does an attempt to enter a blank code.

But something is missing. How do you add records? How do you move off the first record in the file?

In the FoxApp-generated program, you added new records by using a menu entry and moved around in the table with a second window, known as a *control panel*. You can provide both of these, and many other, capabilities in a control panel, placing the control panel with the data-entry screen in a *screen set*.

In the following section of this chapter, you create a more sophisticated data-entry screen for the Budget table, and you can try out all the tantalizing interface objects assembled in the Screen menu popup. First, however, create a few more simple screens by using some of the other lookup tables in the model database (Budcat and Dept). This process gives you a chance to explore these basic database management needs.

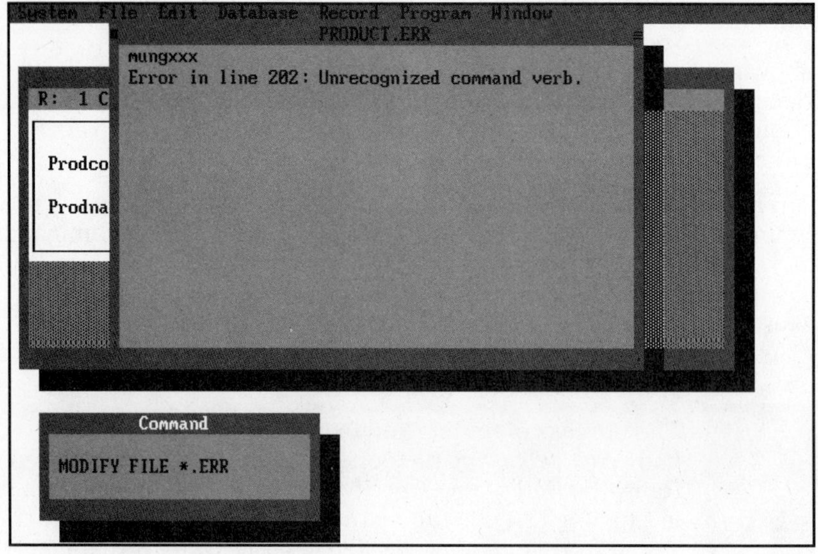

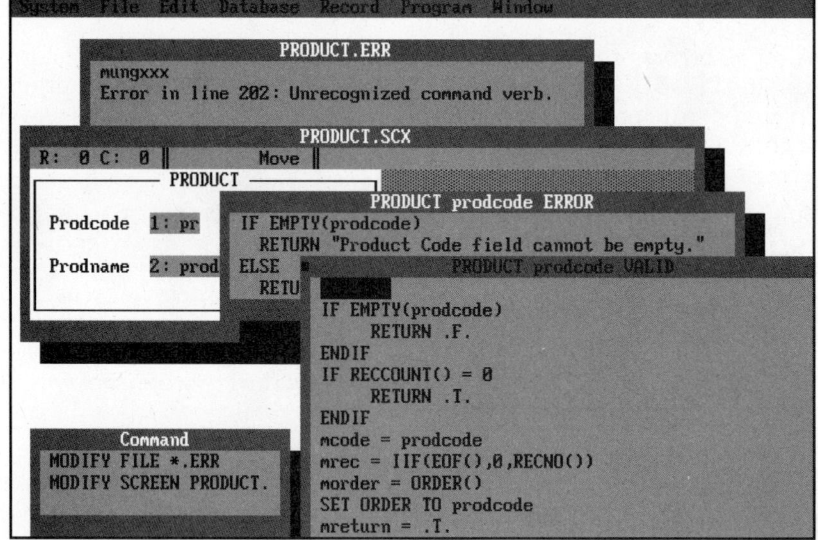

FIGS. 12.13 AND 12.14

Finding and fixing errors in the Screen file.

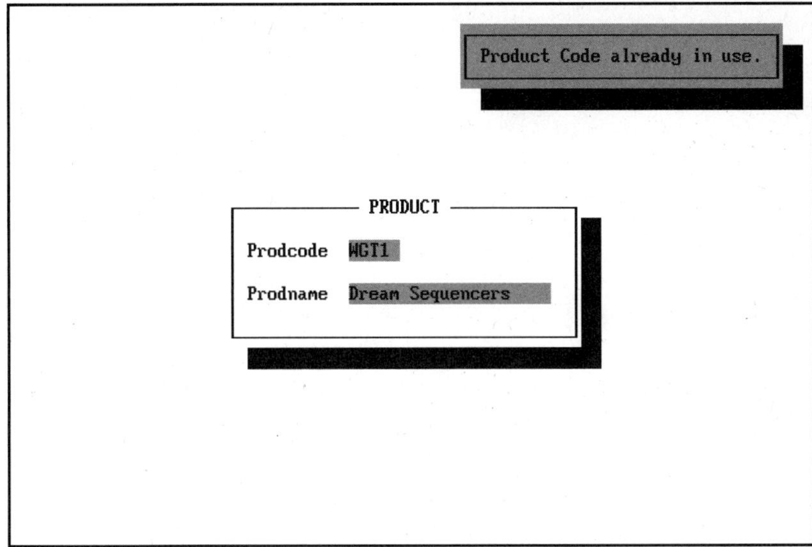

FIG. 12.15

Product table data entry with validation.

Gaining Proficiency in Screen Builder Use

You enter data in the Budget table in Chapter 3 and the Product table in Chapter 1. If you have not previously created or entered information in the Budgcat and Dept tables, however, do so now, so that you can use this information to perform data validation in the Budget data-entry screen. In the following section, the examples refer to the Dept table and DEPT.SCX, but you should repeat this process and create a screen set for the Budcat table when you finish with the Dept table.

Tables 12.1 and 12.2 give you structures and sample records that provide lookups for all the records you created previously in the Budget table.

Create the structures shown in table 12.1 as you created the Budget table (by using the View Window to select an unused work area, choosing `<Open>`, and then New when asked to select a file). Create tags on both fields in each table.

Select the new lookup table, DEPT, to begin the screen-creation process. Choose to Open a New screen file, by using the same name as the table, and then choose the Quick Screen option to see the dialog in figure 12.16.

Table 12.1 Structures for the Budcat and Dept Tables

BUDCAT.DBF

Field	Field Name	Type	Width	Index
1	Budcatcode	Character	4	Asc
2	Budcat	Character	20	Asc

DEPT.DBF

Field	Field Name	Type	Width	Index
1	Deptcode	Character	4	Asc
2	Deptname	Character	30	Asc

Table 12.2 Records for the Budcat and Dept Tables

Omnipresent Widget's Budget Categories (BUDCAT.DBF)

Record Number	Budget Code	Budget Category Name
1	INS0	Insurance
2	LHR0	Labor, Hourly Reg
3	LHO0	Labor, Hourly Over
4	LSL0	Labor, Salary
5	LCM0	Labor, Commission
6	TRV0	Travel
7	ADV0	Advertising
8	PLT0	Plant

Omnipresent Widget's Departments (DEPT.DBF)

Record Number	Dept Code	Department Name
1	SLS1	Sales Southeast Division
2	SLS2	Sales Northeast Division
3	SLS3	Sales Western Division
4	FIN0	Finance
5	MFT0	Manufacturing
6	PER0	Personnel

For data entry in a READ, rather than in a BROWSE/EDIT, you can provide a layer of protection in case the user decides to cancel editing changes. You have a choice of using GET to provide information directly to a record in a table, or into memory variables that can be created to represent a record. Either way, you create a *snapshot* of the original data, a set of variables with one variable having the same type and size as each of the fields in the record. FoxPro's SCATTER command is the usual method of creating this set of variables.

If you use GET to enter information directly in the record, you can replace the contents of the fields with this *snapshot* if editing is cancelled. If, however, you use GET to enter information to memory variables, you place the contents of the variables into the fields of the record when the editing changes have been confirmed. In either method, GATHER is the command used to bring the contents of the memory variables back into a record.

Both methods have advantages. FoxApp and the revised PRODUCT.SPR use direct editing of a record. This time, choose to edit memory variables instead and explore the way this protection works.

As shown in figure 12.16, you should use Quick Screen's check box labelled `Memory Variables`, which is not the default. (Notice that when Memory Variables is checked, the `Add Alias` check box becomes disabled.) Quick Screen now creates GETs that are memory variables rather than fields. These variables are referenced by the Screen Builder and by the procedures you write, by using the names of the fields prefaced by `m.` in each case. After choosing this option, you can accept the other defaults and create the Quick Screen.

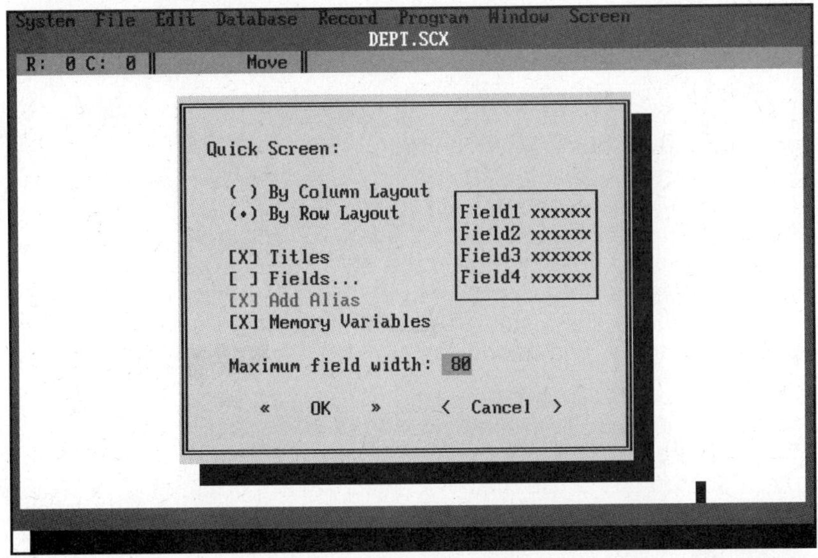

FIG. 12.16

The Quick Screen dialog, choosing to GET to Memory Variables.

As you did with the FoxApp-generated screen, you want to move the items around slightly, access the `Screen Layout` options next, and size the window more appropriately for the two-field table data entry.

First, notice in figure 12.17 that the radio buttons on the top row have defaulted to a `Desktop` screen, which means that the GETs and other items are placed directly on-screen. Click the `Window` radio button and you see the window Name, Title, Footer, and the `<Type>` options become enabled. Type a Title for the window's top border and a Footer if you like and use the `Height` and `Width` options to size the window more appropriately. Click on the `<Type>` button and look at the resulting dialog.

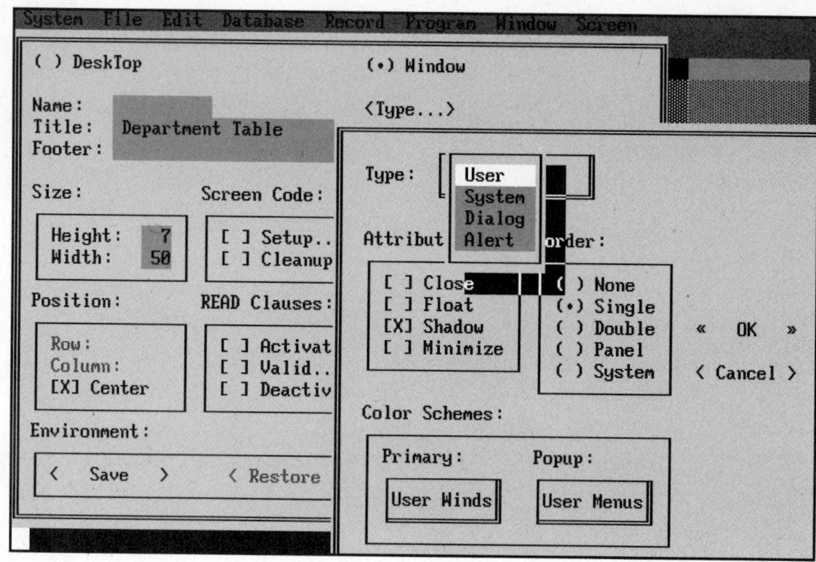

FIG. 12.17

Adjustments in the Screen Layout dialog and the Window Type dialog.

Although, for now, you do not change anything here, you can use this option to change the colors of the window as a whole or use the `Type` popup control to assign colors and other characteristics (Border and Attributes) to match the patterns you learned for System, dialog, and Alert windows in the FoxPro 2 interface. If you change from one type of window to another in this dialog, you see that not all attributes or borders are available for each kind of window. This feature is FoxPro's attempt to encourage you to become consistent in interface design.

Next, you need to attach the same kind of data validation to the Deptcode (or Budcatcode) as you used in the Product table. Bear in mind that you can have more than one screen open at once, open the PRODUCT screen file to use the `@! AAA99` formatting template. Activate and then paste the screen on which you are working into the Format text box of the field expression `m.deptcode`, changing the name to **@! AAA9**, as is appropriate for this four-character field.

Rather than copying an edited version of the VALID and ERROR clauses for each of the two other lookup tables, however, you can make the process more generic by creating a short UDF shared by many similar tables.

Each table can use the same validation scheme because the FoxPro functions VARREAD() and EVALUATE() give you the information you need. VARREAD() tells you the name of the current field or memory variable into which you are entering data. EVALUATE(), as the name suggests, evaluates a character-type expression and returns the result of the evaluation. If VARREAD() is currently deptcode, Evaluate (VARREAD()) is the *current value* of deptcode, which may be SLS1 or FIN0.

TIP

If you're experienced in other X-Base dialects, you may recognize EVALUATE() as something like a *macro-substitution*, which is another way to treat the contents of a variable as a character string literal and evaluate variable's contents at runtime. Tests show that this new EVALUATE() function is significantly faster in execution than macros in some circumstances. Rushmore optimization, discussed in Chapter 7, is unavailable when the conditions include EVALUATE(), so if you are collecting sets of records, use a macro. Usually, however, EVALUATE() is faster if the expression is to be expanded once, as in this example.

First, see how this process works with the simpler ERROR clause. After marking the `Error` check box in the Field Expression dialog for the m.deptcode object, enter the following UDF that you are evaluating as an Expression (not a Procedure):

errcode()

Now, create a program file by choosing New from File menu popup or by typing the following command in the Command window:

MODIFY COMMAND errcode

You can type the entire UDF into the text editing window, as shown in figure 12.18, by entering the following listing:

```
IF EMPTY(EVALUATE("m."+VARREAD()))
   * if the current contents of the variable
   * being READ is blank
```

```
        * note that you add the "m." to VARREAD() to
        * distinguish the variable deptcode
        * from the field deptcode

        RETURN PROPER(VARREAD())+;
                " field cannot be empty."

        * use a message with the name of the variable
        * that explains the problem
        * the PROPER() function capitalizes the name of
        * the variable appropriately for the message.

    ELSE

        * the error was that the code is already in use
        * you need an appropriate message for that, too:

        RETURN EVALUATE("m."+VARREAD())+;
                " already in use in "+;
                PROPER(VARREAD())+" field."
    ENDIF
```

Of course, you also use the code field's `Valid` check box, and the Expression it should hold is the name of another UDF, chkcode(). Following are the contents of CHKCODE.PRG, using VARREAD() and EVALUATE(), which also refers to a variable, *addmode*, that you use in the screen set to inform this UDF what you are currently trying to do.

Because chkcode() is almost the same as the procedure you used in PRODUCT.SCX, the following comments are limited to explaining the changes that make the code generic:

```
the_code = VARREAD()
* store the name of the variable being READ

IF EMPTY(EVALUATE("m."+the_code))
 * check to see if the variable is empty
 * using "m." again to distinguish the variable
 * from a field of the same name

 RETURN .F.
ENDIF

IF RECCOUNT() = 0
 RETURN .T.
ENDIF

mcode = EVALUATE("m."+the_code)
* store the contents of the variable

mreturn = .T.
```

```
mrec = IIF(EOF(),0,RECNO())
morder = ORDER()
SET ORDER TO (the_code)
* reference the name of the variable
* to set the order

IF SEEK(mcode) AND (addmode OR RECNO() # mrec)

 * if you are trying to add a record
 * NO record in the table should
 * have this code, regardless of what
 * record you're on in the table

 * when you're NOT adding, a record with
 * a different record number than mrec
 * represents a problem, as it did before

 mreturn = .F.

ENDIF

SET ORDER TO (morder)
IF mrec = 0
 * you're at the End-of-File marker, not a
 * regular record

 GO BOTTOM
 SKIP
ELSE
 GO mrec
ENDIF

RETURN mreturn
```

Now, you may begin to see why you want to create this kind of procedure as a UDF and why you want to call this procedure as an expression, rather than building the procedure as a snippet within a screen file (see fig. 12.18). Although complex, this program also can handle validation for most of the lookup codes in a system. *You need to write this program only once.* With few changes, the same UDF can handle the same kind of validation for direct READs rather than for memory variables.

In the past, you may have wanted to put a generic UDF like this into a *procedure* file to make the UDF available throughout an application. In FoxPro 2, you can create UDFs as little programs (which is covered in a few chapters) and the Project Manager takes care of building the application from all the procedures that you may reference, no matter where you keep them.

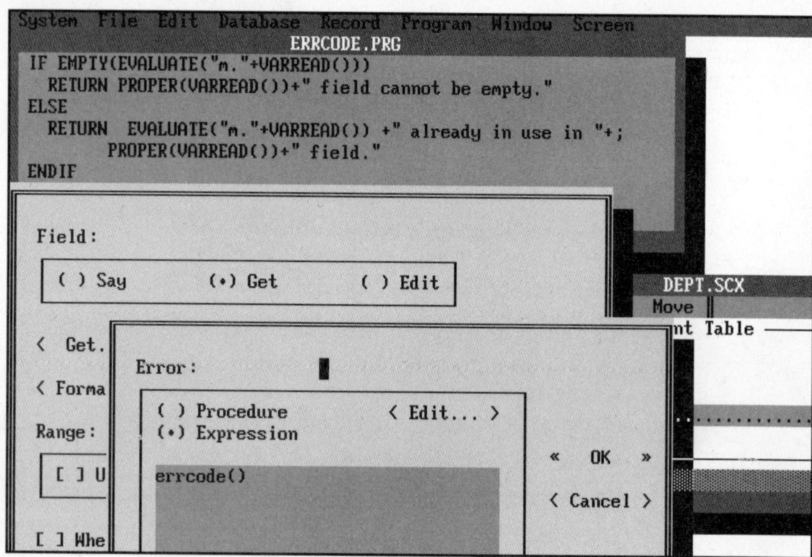

FIG. 12.18

ERRCODE.PRG being edited and used as a UDF in an ERROR clause expression.

The plan for data entry calls for the capability of moving through the table at will, adding and editing records and saving or canceling changes you make. This capability requires additional features to be added to this screen, which you return to after you incorporate a second screen—that contains a *control* panel based on the panels you already know from the sample programs that Fox supplies—with the first screen.

In the Command window, type **MODIFY SCREEN ?** or choose Open from the File menu popup and select screen-type files to look through the sample directories at the different screens available. Several directories use the name syntax CONTROL*?*.SCX, and all these directories follow the same basic principles. The screen you want to adapt for this example is CONTROL1.SCX, which is located in the GOODIES\LASER\SCREENS directory under the FoxPro root directory. Take the time to DO the three sample applications in the LASER directory (LASER1, LASER2, and LASER3) to learn more about how screen sets are put together. Then you are going to modify CONTROL1.SCX and save the file to a new name, CONTROLM.SCX, in the MODEL directory. Before you make the name change, however, you need to make a few adjustments.

As you see in figure 12.19, this control panel is a narrow rectangle with a group of push buttons that enables you to move through a table. You need to make this window longer to provide room for two more choices in the group. Use the Width and Height options in the Screen Layout dialog again, but don't worry about the Row and Col placement of the window on-screen. As you see in a following section, you can control the relative placement of the two windows when you bring together these windows in a screen set.

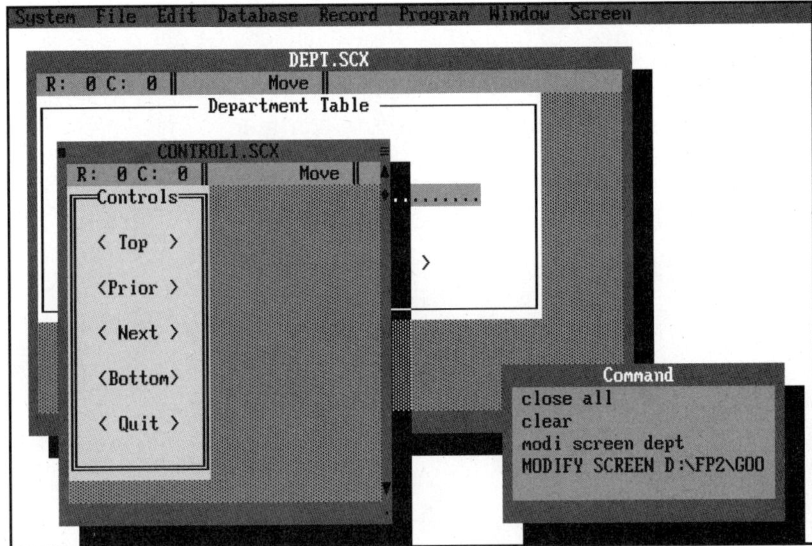

FIG. 12.19

The original CONTROL1.SCX control panel.

Use the Screen Layout dialog option to give this window a Name. You used the name Controls in the example. Notice that a window's *name* is not the same as the *title*, which appears in the top border, although in this case you have used the same word for both. A window name is used when you *DEFINE* the window, giving dimensions, colors, and attributes. As the term suggests, the Screen Builder uses DEFINE to define the window for you and generates a name for the window. However, because you refer to the window by name in some of the code snippets, give the window a name you can recognize easily.

After you lengthen the window by at least four lines, select the push button object. Because the buttons are a group, pressing the space bar twice—or double-clicking—on one button brings up the dialog shown in figure 12.20. As you can see in the dialog, the buttons are either Horizontal or Vertical radio buttons (as in this group). You control the <Spacing> between the buttons. You <Choose> a Variable in which to store a button choice (this option can bring up the Expression Builder if you want to see which variables are currently defined), or you can just type a variable name in the text box.

The on-screen heading Variable: is a little misleading. You can store the button choice to a variable, a field, or an *array element*. (You learn about arrays in following chapters.) In any case, you must store the choice as either a numeric or a character data type. If you allow FoxPro to create the variable for you, as you are doing here, as opposed to manually initializing the variable with a default choice, making the variable of numeric type is a good idea. A number corresponding to the number of the chosen button is stored to the variable. The variable for this button set happens to be `act2`. Buttons also can be designated as `Terminating`, which means that making a choice from this group terminates the READ. In the example, you do not want the buttons to terminate the READ; rather, you want the user to continue to make new choices and edit new records until choosing the `<Quit>` button.

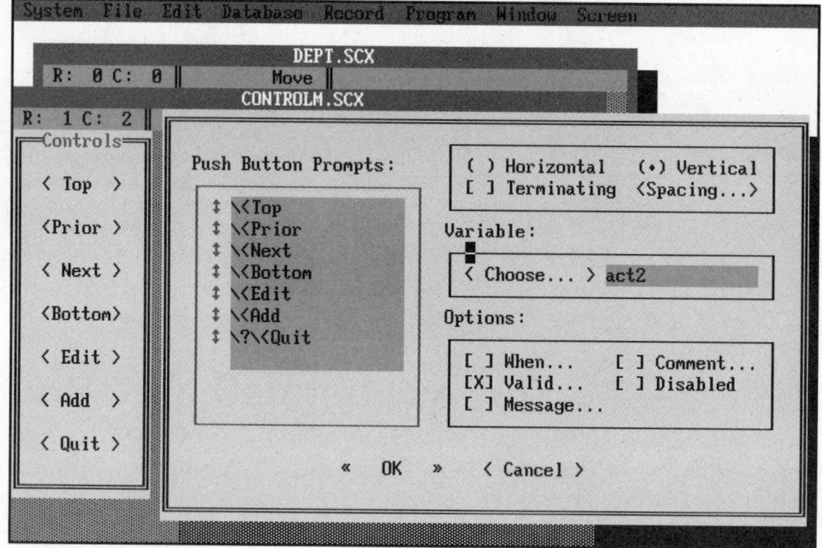

FIG. 12.20

The revised CONTROLM.SCX control panel, as you edit the push button.

Besides these options, you also see the check boxes `When`, `Valid`, `Message`, `Comment`, and `Disable` available for field expressions. Of course, the buttons also need to have *prompts*, which you create in the box on the left.

In figure 12.20, you edited the list of prompts to contain two new prompts, `<Edit>` and `<Add>`. (Type these new prompts at the bottom of the list and then select and move them as you usually move fields in structure-modifying dialogs.) You also placed the characters `\<` before the initial letters of each prompt, which highlights and designates the prompts as hotkeys. Note that the characters `\?` before the `<Quit>` prompt entry were maintained from the original Control screen and designate this prompt as an *escape button*. Choosing `<Quit>` is the same as pressing the Esc key. You can have only one escape button in a group.

Now is a good time to save the revised control panel screen file to a new name (the example uses CONTROLM.SCX) in the MODEL directory. After you save the file, you can return to editing this screen, knowing that you aren't overwriting the original CONTROL1.SCX needed by other programs.

Edit the VALID clause attached to the push button set.

TIP

If the `Valid` check box appears disabled, the related snippet is already opened in an editing window somewhere. As you learned previously, this situation can be true even if you haven't previously accessed it, if the screen file was saved with the editing window open. Check the list of windows from the Window menu popup list; the snippet may be docked or hidden behind the Screen Layout window.

By now, you probably have a good idea of what is happening in this procedure. The CASE structure, which you explore in Chapter 16, checks the value of the variable, *act2*, into which the button choice was placed. Depending on the choice, the procedure moves the record pointer in the file, issues a SHOW GETS command, which makes sure that information from the appropriate record appears on-screen. CASE ends the READ if the Quit choice is made and produces a RETURN 0 so that in other cases, you remain in the control panel rather than moving to another GET.

You need to add two more CASE structures to fit the two new push button choices. The new choices do not move the record pointer, but rather change the value of two variables, *addmode* and *editmode*, to tell you that a task is performing. Figure 12.21 shows this snippet and the two other snippets you create for this screen, with `CASEs act2 = 5` and `act2 = 6` storing `.T.` to *editmode* and *addmode*, respectively. The `<Quit>` button was moved to the end and is now `CASE act2 = 7`.

These two variables must be available to all the various parts of the screen program, because you check them frequently. You *initialize* these variables by creating another snippet from the Screen Layout dialog, in the option to create `Setup` code, in which you store the initial value .F. to both variables.

Two more snippets are needed. The SHOW GETS command that you issue in the button's VALID clause activates a procedure that you store in a *READ SHOW* clause. Like the Setup code, and like other clauses global to a READ rather than specific to one GET, the `Show` option is in the Screen Layout dialog. SHOW is a clause because you call this clause *when you issue the SHOW GETS command*, no matter how often or where you issue the command.

For the program, the SHOW clause uses the following instructions, commented to explain the tasks performed:

```
IF addmode
   * if you are adding a new record

   SCATTER MEMVAR BLANK
   * create memory variables with nothing
   * in them, but with the same characteristics
   * as a record in the current table

ELSE

   SCATTER MEMVAR
   * create memory variables holding the data
   * from the current record in the currently
   * selected table

ENDIF

* now when the GETs in the dept screen are shown, they
* have either blank memory variables if you're adding
* or show the data of the current record

IF editmode or addmode

   * if you're about to start editing or adding a record,

   SHOW GET act2 DISABLE
   * remove the ability to move around in the table
   * until you're through editing or adding

ELSE

   * you're not editing or adding when the SHOW GETS
   * is being called

   SHOW GET act2 ENABLE
ENDIF
```

The final snippet for this screen goes into the READ DEACTIVATE clause. The DEACTIVATE clause is called when the currently active window is changed, when you Tab through the fields, windows are cycled through with Ctrl-F1, or a new window is selected with the mouse or through the Window menu pad. If the DEACTIVATE clause issues a RETURN .T., the READ is terminated. You want this snippet to RETURN .F. at all times because the `<Quit>` button provides the only means of termination you need. Before the RETURN line is reached, however, the following DEACTIVATE clause gives you another chance to call the SHOW clause and make sure that options are appropriately displayed when the user switches windows:

```
IF UPPER(WONTOP()) = "CONTROLS"

  * WONTOP() tells you what window is
  * "on top" — which one has been activated.
  * Here's the reason you needed to know the
  * window's name!

  * it's always a good idea to use
  * the uppercase version of the window
  * name compared to the uppercase version
  * of what the window functions return,
  * just in case.

  * Now that you know you are in the control panel:

  addmode = .F.
  editmode = .F.
  * turn off both the record-changing tasks

ELSE
  * you're in a record-editing window
  IF ! addmode
        * in case you got here by switching windows,
        *  choose to edit by default
        editmode = .T.
  ENDIF
ENDIF

* now get a new set of memory variables and properly
* enable or disable the control panel, as before:

SHOW GETS

RETURN .F.
```

The snippet for the DEACTIVATE clause, the SHOW clause, the revised VALID clause for the buttons including the new choices, and the Setup code snippet are shown in figure 12.21.

Notice that all these instructions are completely generic, like the CHKCODE() function you wrote previously. After you decide on an approach for these data-entry screens, you can use the same approach over and over again without recreating the code. This feature is why you have chosen to attach the READ-level clauses to the control panel rather than DEPT.SCX, and check only to see whether Controls is the activated window; these instructions are now available and appropriate for any other data-entry screens using this control panel.

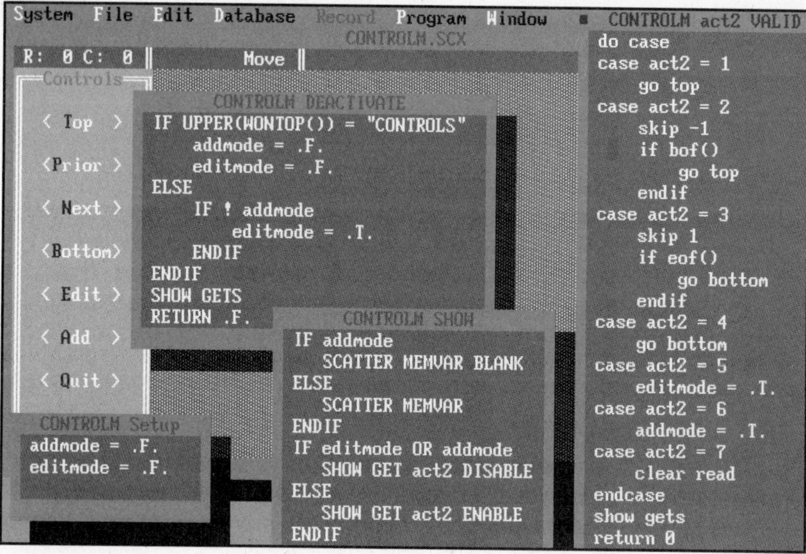

FIG. 12.21

The revised control panel snippets.

You still need to make a few more changes to the editing screen, DEPT.SCX. Resize the window slightly if necessary and add a push button set to this screen also (press Ctrl-H as a shortcut). The strategy here is to ask the user to confirm (Save) or Cancel the record in the process of being added or edited. Figure 12.22 shows the prompts and the VALID clause for this button set. Notice the `\?\!` before the `Cancel` prompt, which makes this push button the escape option and also the default.

The VALID clause for the new push buttons checks to see whether you got a confirmation of changes. If you did, and if the user is adding, you APPEND a BLANK record (which then becomes the current record). You then GATHER the contents of the memory variables into the current record, whether you are adding or editing. Resetting *addmode* and *editmode* and issuing a new SHOW GETS returns you to the control panel:

```
IF saveit = 2
  IF addmode
        APPEND BLANK
  ENDIF

addmode = .F.
editmode = .F.

SHOW GETS
```

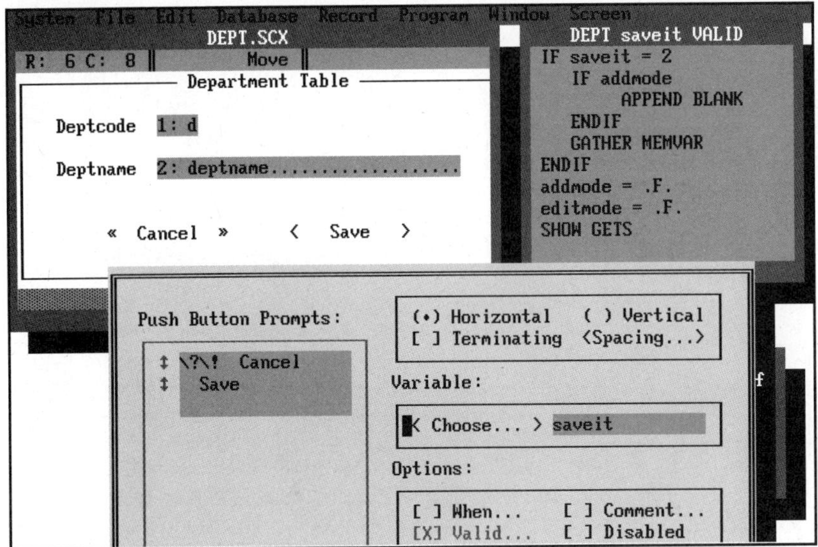

FIG. 12.22

Push Buttons in the data-entry screen enable you to save or cancel changes.

The VALID clause for the dept code field should be edited to hold the following expression:

LASTKEY() = 27 OR CHKCODE()

This expression enables a keypress of the Esc key, *seen* by the LASTKEY() function as 27, to get you out of the field. Otherwise, an Esc press while attempting to add a record doesn't take you out of the field because the current *m.deptcode* is empty. Of course, the ERROR clause should still hold the ERRCODE() UDF you designed previously.

Finally, you're ready to generate a screen set from the data-entry form and the control panel. Choosing the `Program Generate` option, this time, you want to `Add` the second screen to the `Screens` list on the upper left, as shown in figure 12.23. Make the control panel the first screen on the list, because you want this window to be the first window accessed during use. (Fig. 12.23 also shows the `Comments` options being filled out. Choose this dialog to affect the *look* of the generated program, which you examine more closely in the following chapter.)

You also must use the `Arrange` option in the screen-generating dialog to set the windows' relative positions. As shown in figure 12.24, the available options are simple, and the arrangement is easy to perform; just move the windows as you move other windows in FoxPro. Save the arrangement and then choose to Generate the program.

When you DO the resulting DEPT.SPR file, a simple way to use the data-entry system appears and provides valid entries for the lookup table. Notice the disabled controls that require you to complete or cancel editing one record before going on to affect any others (the disabled control panel is shown in fig. 12.25). Try pressing Esc at different points and switching windows with either the keyboard or the mouse to see what happens. Think about ways you may want to improve this system. Investigate the other control panels included in the sample applications, with Finding, Browsing, and Ordering capabilities, and design ways in which you can add those features to the control panel.

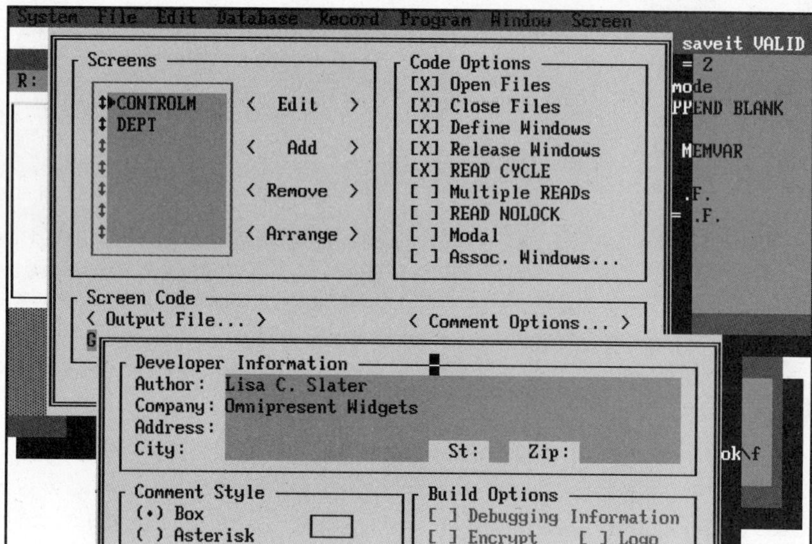

FIG. 12.23

Getting ready to generate screen code from multiple screens and using the Comment Options dialog.

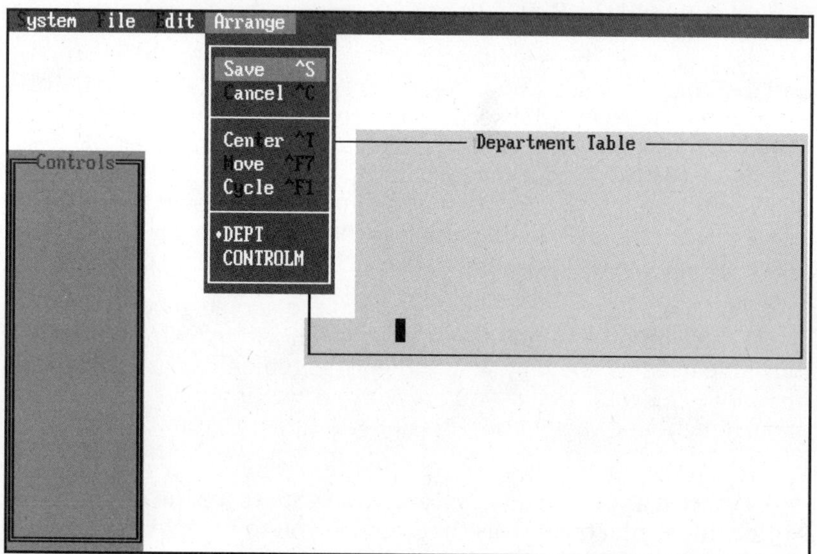

FIG. 12.24

The screen-arranging options.

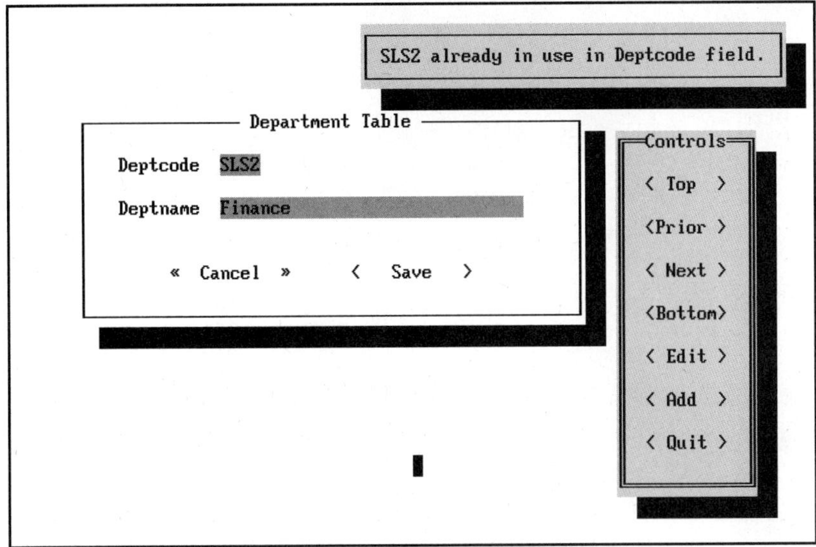

FIG. 12.25

The data-entry application in use.

If you like, continue to work with and to add features to the control panel. Generate mini-applications for each of the Budcat and Dept tables that use the custom controls. Use the new applications to enter the information shown in tables 12.1 and 12.2. Now, the lookup tables necessary for proper management of the Budget table are all completed.

After you enter this data, set the order of each of the three lookup tables to a tag on the respective code fields, select Budget, and set relationships to each of the three other tables on the code fields. The three lookup tables and the View window should then match figure 12.26. If the View file (MODEL.VUE) doesn't match this setup, you may want to use the File Save As option to resave the View to these specifications for further use. (Notice that knowing which file is in which work area is immaterial, if all the files are open and the relationships are set as shown.)

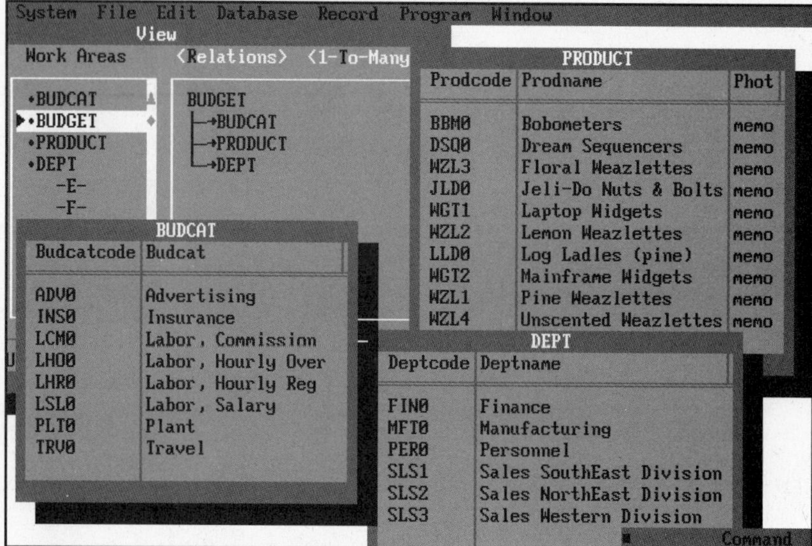

FIG. 12.26

The Model Application Environment and Lookup Tables as they are used in the Screen Builder work.

Chapter Summary

As you realize, through successive revisions and improvements to these data-entry systems, you have only just begun to tap the power of the Screen Builder. You learned a little about code snippets and other ways to attach procedures to GETs and other objects in a READ, and the difference between editing tables directly and editing memory variables. You developed some facility with the Screen Builder tool. You probably have begun to think about all the ways that you may like to validate and control the entry of data in the systems you design, and you also may be chafing at the bit to use radio buttons, scrolling lists, and all the other alluring features the Screen Builder puts within reach.

In the following chapter, you create a Budget table-entry screen that uses many more of the interface objects. You investigate the inclusion of BROWSE commands and memo-editing within a screen set and get a sense of the way the READ-level clauses interact with one another.

13

CHAPTER

Using Complex Screen Sets To Control Data Entry

In the preceding chapter, you built screens through the Screen Builder. As you built them, you became aware of an interim step: the template program *generated* screen programs, which were then *compiled* by FoxPro and interpreted when you executed the programs. Yet, you never actually wrote the programs.

In the past, writing screen programs was a programmer's most time-consuming and painstaking task. So far in this book, however, you have not been asked to look at the programs you created (the files with SPR extensions) with the Screen Builder's help. Fox Software doesn't recommend that you edit the generated programs in any way. Rather, you should make changes directly through the Screen Builder and regenerate the programs. You don't need to be proficient with the syntax for the different kinds of GET objects.

In the following section, however, you examine a generated program. Knowing the structure of a generated program can help you understand the relationship between the snippets and the different READ objects and clauses. You also see examples of window-defining commands and window-manipulating functions, which you use more and more as you develop intricate screen sets, such as the Budget data-entry system you create in the following section.

Understanding the Generated Screen Program

Type **MODIFY COMMAND DEPT.SPR** in the Command window or open the program DEPT.SPR from the File Open option. The first thing you see is a program *header*, created by GENSCRN. The header names and dates the program and provides a copyright notice, as specified in the Generate Comment options.

Following the header, you see several sections of setup code that follow a different order, depending on what you placed in the Setup code snippet. You can precede some or all of the Setup code snippet with a *generator directive* so that the snippet is placed ahead of all other lines in the program.

A generator directive is an instruction that GENSCRN uses as it creates a program. FoxPro doesn't use these directives in actual program execution. The appropriate generator directive to put setup code before all the other generated code is #SECTION1. You need to use this priority if, for example, you want to pass *parameters* (values or variables determined by a calling program) to the screen program. A PARAMETERS statement must be the first line in any program that receives values from a calling program.

Table 13.1, at the end of this section, lists the generator directives. You use these directives by placing them in the Setup snippet of a screen.

Following any code you create in the Setup snippet with the #SECTION1 directive is the *program environment code* that GENSCRN always creates. This code defines some *regional variables*, which save the state of the factors that GENSCRN is about to alter so that you can restore these factors at a later time.

Regional variables are specific to each window within a screen set. GENSCRN assigns a region number to each SCX included in a set and uses the number to distinguish the screen layout code and procedures that belong to each screen or window in the set when the SPR that includes all the procedures is generated. If you initialize any variables as REGIONAL, the compiler then generates variable names specific to each variable. These names tie the variables to the appropriate window. In this way, you can use the same variable names in code that belongs to different windows within each set, and the names don't conflict with each other.

The variables created by GENSCRN in the program environment code, however, are used by the entire screen set. GENSCRN precedes these variables with a #REGION 0 compiler directive to indicate this condition. You learn more about how regional variables work in Chapter 17.

Then, the *file-opening* code is generated only if you previously saved the environment with the screen and if you left this option checked in the Generate dialog. Next comes the *window-defining* code, also created only if you choose the appropriate option in the Generate dialog. Part of the window-defining code is visible in the fragment of DEPT.SPR shown in figure 13.1. Notice the `DEFINE WINDOW` command, which you use shortly, and the `WEXIST()` function, an example of a useful assortment of window-checking functions that FoxPro 2 provides.

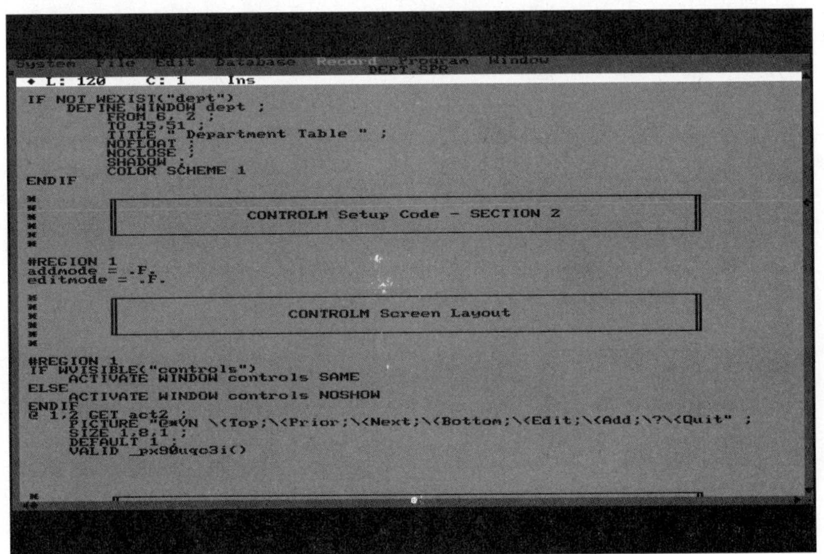

FIG. 13.1

A fragment of a generated screen program, showing part of the window definitions, setup code, and a screen layout.

As figure 13.1 shows, next comes any code you put in the Setup snippet if you did not use the #SECTION1 directive, or preceded by #SECTION2 if you used #SECTION1. Afterward, the windows are activated one at a time and filled with GETs. If you choose multiple READs in the Generate dialog, each expression has a specifically related READ command. Otherwise, after the final window in the set is ready, one READ command is issued for the entire set, as shown in figure 13.2. This READ command includes READ-level clauses and key words you created in the Screen Layout or by using the #READCLAUSES described in a following part of this section.

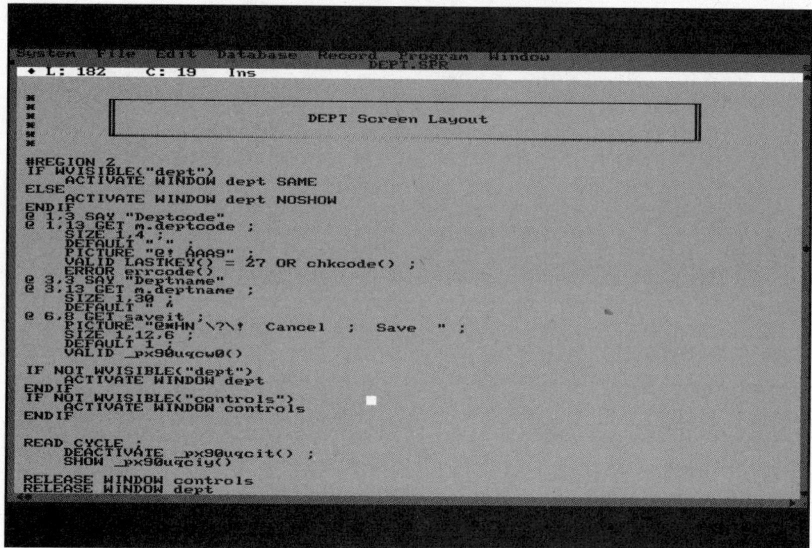

FIG. 13.2

Screen layout with READ command.

As you look at the code, notice the differences between the VALID and ERROR clauses you created for m.deptcode as expressions, the generated procedure names in the saveit VALID clause, and the READ DEACTIVATE and SHOW clauses.

The READ is followed by various kinds of cleanup code, as determined by the Generate dialog settings. First, you see *window-releasing* code, then *file-closing*, and finally the program environment is restored. All code that you added in the Cleanup code snippet, including UDFs that you attached to this screen set, comes next. (The DEPT.SPR doesn't include UDFs because you created CHKCODE.PRG and ERRCODE.PRG as stand-alone programs to make this code available to multiple screen sets.) Finally, the *generated* procedures (such as the saveit VALID) are put at the end.

Remember that all code that precedes the READ *is executed* before the user gets a data-entry screen and before the READ is activated. The code that follows the READ statement in the Cleanup snippet can contain commands that execute when you exit from the READ. The cleanup snippet, however, also can provide a convenient place to hold many subprocedures called before and during the READ, as the clauses on objects and the READ command are evaluated.

The clauses on each object are evaluated every time the user tries to alter the object. The clauses on the READ can be evaluated at any time, when the user does one of the following:

- Enters the READ (the READ-level WHEN, ACTIVATE, OBJECT, COLOR/COLOR SCHEME, LOCK/NOLOCK, NOMOUSE, TIMEOUT, and SHOW clauses)
- Attempts to move between windows (the ACTIVATE, DEACTIVATE, MODAL, and WITH clauses)
- Attempts to exit the READ (the READ-level VALID, DEACTIVATE, CYCLE, and SAVE clauses)

As shown in the preceding chapter, the READ SHOW clause also can be brought into play any time you issue a SHOW GETS command.

In the preceding example, you demonstrated how to use the SHOW and DEACTIVATE clauses, which are significant to the *control panel* approach to selecting and editing records. In the Budget table-entry screen, you use SHOW again and highlight the use of the ACTIVATE clause to provide integration of a BROWSE in a screen set for a different way to move through a table. Use the BROWSE WHEN clause and a number of tailored object-level procedures to assist in creating a graceful data-entry process.

Even with these two different techniques, you are not going to learn everything about the extensive READ options in this chapter. You have many more directions to go in, and you will want to experiment a great deal more.

Table 13.1 helps you gain a better understanding of GENSCRN. As you use the directives and other options of the Screen Builder, the Generator dialog, and READ, you may find that building a special practice screen that uses a trick can be valuable: put the WAIT WINDOW command, followed by the name of each clause and other valuable information, into each of the code snippets, as shown in the following line:

```
WAIT WINDOW "Deactivate Clause "+WONTOP()+" "+WLAST() NOWAIT
```

As you tinker with the screen and generate different versions to try out, the WAIT WINDOW helps you become familiar with the exact actions that initiate the various clauses, under exact circumstances, at any given time.

Table 13.1 The GENSCRN.PRG Generator Directive

<table>
<tr><th>Command</th><th>Action</th></tr>
<tr><td>#SECTION1</td><td>Place before setup code that must come before all other generated code</td></tr>
<tr><td>#SECTION2</td><td>Place before other setup code that can come in the usual position (after the “Program Environment” generated by GENSCRN)</td></tr>
<tr><td>#ITSEXPRESSION</td><td>Use this directive, followed by a single character, to indicate that picture clauses and window titles and footers are to be taken by GENSCRN as expressions, rather than as literal strings of characters. You may, for example, want to define the window with a title that you pass as a parameter from another program. Sometimes you may want to title this window “Confirm Your Work,” and other times you may want to call the window “Add an Entry.” The Setup snippet should contain the following code:

#SECTION1

PARAMETERS wintitle

#ITSEXPRESSION ~

#SECTION2

...

You use ~wintitle in the Screen Layout to represent the window title. Then you perform the following:

DO a_screen.spr WITH "Confirm Your Work," or DO a_screen.spr WITH "Add an Entry," as required.</td></tr>
<tr><td>#READCLAUSES</td><td>To add keywords to the READ statement for which no provisions exist in the Screen Builder. The following list shows these keywords:
<table>
<tr><td>COLOR or COLOR SCHEME</td><td>Change the color of the current GET from the default as specified by the SCHEME of the defined window or the other coloring options of the Screen Builder</td></tr>
<tr><td>NOMOUSE</td><td>Turn off the mouse for this screen, perhaps because you must have items entered in a precise manner</td></tr>
</table></td></tr>
</table>

Command	Action	
	OBJECT #	To specify, by number, which GET is initially selected for editing when the READ is issued. Individual buttons within a set have specific numbers.
	SAVE	Do not clear GETS after exiting from READ so you can reissue it without reissuing the GETs TIMEOUT #. End the READ after a specified number of seconds.
#REDEFINE	Makes GENSCRN generate window-defining program statements that do not check to see whether the window already exists	
#WNAME *<name>*	Enables you to assign a name for the window without using the Name option in Screen Layout (so that GENSCRN can generate a unique name for the window, yet you still can refer to the window name in code snippets)	

Improving Screen Design

To begin creating a Budget entry screen, you can generate a Quick Screen as you did in previous chapters. Because you are defining different kinds of objects and controls, however, the related vanilla GET objects may not be helpful. These objects are going to make data validation easier to arrange while providing a more attractive and simpler interface for the user. To start on the design, you need an easy reminder of the *structure* of the Budget table, which defines the information you want to GET. You create this reminder, similar to a notepad, with the first use of the DEFINE WINDOW command.

The DEFINE WINDOW command is not available from the FoxPro 2 menus. You may have noticed that, when you read the generated DEPT.SPR program, this command has many clauses you can use to create windows to mirror the windows FoxPro creates.

By using the following lines, create a short program called STRUCT.PRG:

```
IF ! WEXIST("struct")
  * no need to redefine window if you
  * created it previously
```

```
          DEFINE WINDOW struct FROM 1,1 TO 80,55;
                 SYSTEM FLOAT MINIMIZE CLOSE;
                 COLOR SCHEME 10;
                 TITLE "Structure"

     * You define the window by giving it a name,
     * coordinates, and other attributes

ENDIF

ACTIVATE WINDOW struct NOSHOW
* make this window the active-output window

LIST STRUCTURE
* list the structure of the SELECTed table

ZOOM WINDOW struct MIN AUTO
* place the window, docked, on-screen

SHOW WINDOW struct
* pop up window, filled and ready for use
```

Save this program and from the Command window or the menus, SET VIEW TO MODEL. (Refer to the last figure in the preceding chapter and make sure that the appropriate tables and relations are ready for the work you plan to do. The Budget table should be in the SELECTed work area.) From the Command window or from the Program menu's Do option, DO STRUCT.

You see the window docked and ready for reference. If you press Ctrl-F9 or double-click the window, you see something like the screen in figure 13.3.

TIP

This handy trick is included not only because it is useful during a screen design session but also because it shows normal window command usage. After you read the programming sections of this book, you may want to expand the idea by using a FOR/ENDFOR loop to check all tables open in FoxPro's work areas and list all the structures in a similar *notepad*. As a final hint, LIST STRUCTURES TO <*filename*> and then MODIFY FILE <*filename*> WINDOW STRUCT in the window.

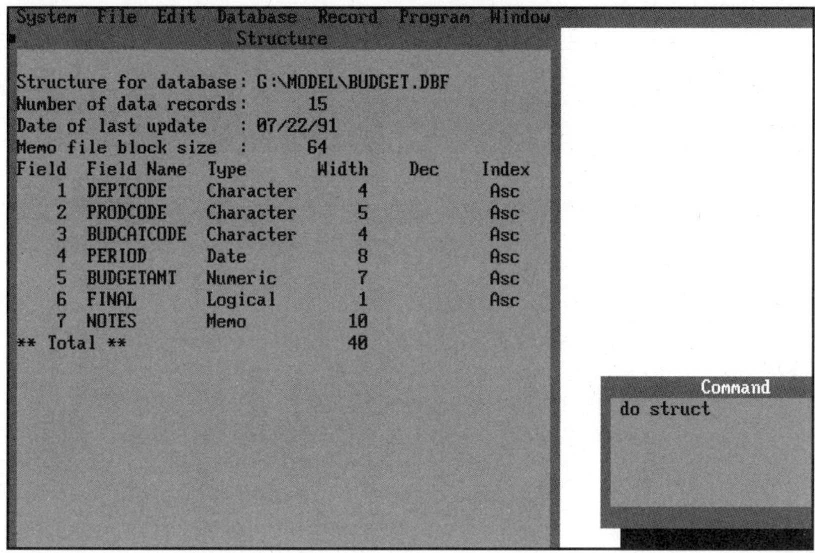

FIG. 13.3

The Budget Table Structure, ready for reference in a notepad.

Planning the Data-Entry Window

The following paragraphs define the strategy as you begin to design the Budget table entry screen.

This table structure includes three code fields (DEPTCODE, PROD-CODE, and BUDCATCODE) that should be restricted to information contained in the three lookup tables. Now that all three fields are complete with data, you can use them to make the budget entries.

This strategy calls for the FINAL field to provide you with an important criterion for the editing of the rest of the record. After a record is marked FINAL, the information contained in the record cannot be changed (although you can choose to allow editing of the NOTES field at any time). After a record's PERIOD date falls in a past quarter or within the present quarter, the record is automatically marked FINAL if the record was not already marked by the user. The Budget table records are used for projecting costs and cannot be altered after the quarter in which they fall has begun.

Blank entries are allowed in the BUDGETAMT, in case an event that causes no financial change requires NOTES of some kind, but you must assign a PERIOD date and department, product, and budget category codes to every added record.

You want to move through the table by using a BROWSE, but records are not editable except in the screen you design. You can GET information into memory variables again and GATHER the data to the current record if the editing is confirmed.

Editing the current record takes place on one portion of a relatively large data-entry window. This window, however, also holds several controls that enable you to change the order in which you view data and to query the data simply, so that you can see your progress as you carry out the budgeting process.

NOTE In the following example screen, you use three different methods of using lookups. Usually, you don't mix techniques in this way in one screen or in one system—this procedure is completely contrary to the rules of consistent design in Chapter 11, "Coordinating a FoxPro 2 Application."

Similarly, the Budget table data-entry screen contains almost every kind of interface object available in FoxPro 2. Again, you normally don't combine a screen like this with the radically different screens you designed earlier for the lookup tables' data entry. It is unusual for one database application to combine direct and indirect READs, as you did in the preceding chapter.

These demonstrations of different techniques are created only to introduce you to as many options as possible. You can, if you choose, continue with only some of these techniques, but consider all these techniques with this caveat in mind.

"Sketching" a Layout Screen

Start with the Screen Layout, accessible from the first choice on the Screen menu popup. As before, you need to click the top radio buttons to choose a `Window`, rather than `DeskTop`, layout (You want a movable window, not objects directly on-screen.) Because you have the Model view open, `<Save>` the Environment, which is previously set up as you want this screen set. Uncheck `Add Alias`, because you are READing to memory variables. Type the name **budget** for this window and add a title. The layout requires a Height of **18** and a Width of **78**. You can Position the layout at Row **1** and Column **1** after unchecking the default of `Center` (or you can choose to Arrange it in this position when you generate the code later). Next, choose the `Type` button. Although you maintain the default type of `User` window, change the Color Schemes, setting the Primary scheme to `Browse` and the scheme for Popups contained in this window to `Window Pop`. These two schemes coordinate well with each other and with the BROWSE you are using in the screen set. As shown in figure 13.4, add more Attributes to this window to include `Float` and `Minimize`, in case you want to devote attention at times to the BROWSE on the screen.

Return to the design window and draw a box to define the record-editing portion of the screen. Add an explanatory title for this box, as well. You can type the title wherever you want and then you can select and move the title to overlay the upper box line. You can use one of the techniques covered in Chapter 2 to add the graphics characters to the text object and window title (see fig. 13.5). Now is a good time to use the left quote character trick; the ▶ is displayed if you type **'P**, and the ◀ is displayed if you type **'Q**. With the object or title still selected, choose `Center` from the Screen menu popup, and the selected item is properly positioned on the line.

When you finish defining these characteristics, the Screen Builder design window should resemble figure 13.5.

Performing Actions with a Check Box

Now create a *Check Box* (use the Ctrl-K shortcut or choose the option on the menu popup). This object enables the user to indicate that a budget entry is Final; check boxes are best for logical, or *on-off*, fields. Because the Final designation determines whether the other fields in an entry are editable, you're putting the check box on the bottom boundary of the window box, centered directly under the title. As you see in figure 13.6, a check box has a *Prompt,* similar to a push button. You type **\<Finalize Entry?** as the prompt, and the \< characters indicate a hot key. You are going to GET to SCATTERed memory variables again; this variable is known as *m.final.*

Validating and Inter-Relating GETs

In the related VALID clause shown in the figure (if set to TRUE), you tell the user what is happening with a WAIT WINDOW and then a DO procedure known as *no_edit* that you call from several parts of the screen to DISABLE, or render uneditable, several of the GETs:

```
IF m.final
  WAIT WINDOW ;
        " Finalized Budget Entries are not editable. "
NOWAIT
  DO no_edit
ENDIF
```

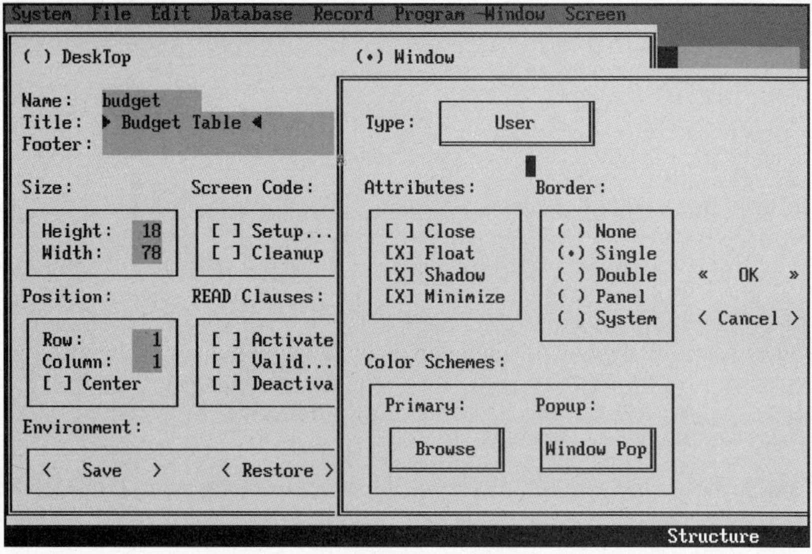

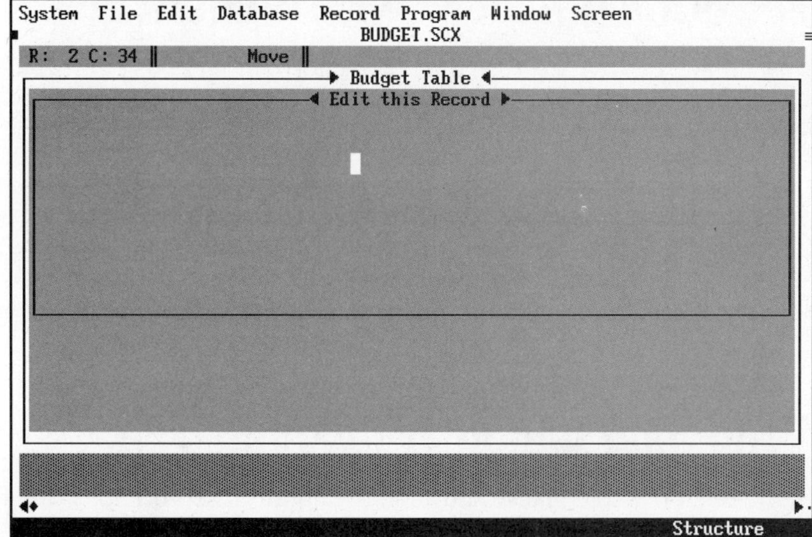

FIGS. 13.4 AND 13.5

Basic Screen Layout and Window Type for the Budget Table Entry Screen Set.

The no_edit procedure is placed in the Cleanup code section and looks like the following lines:

```
PROCEDURE no_edit
SHOW GET m.period DISABLE
SHOW GET m.budgetamt DISABLE
```

```
SHOW GET m.budcatcode DISABLE
SHOW GET m.product DISABLE
SHOW GET m.dept DISABLE
SHOW GET m.final DISABLE
_CUROBJ = OBJNUM(m.notes)
RETURN
```

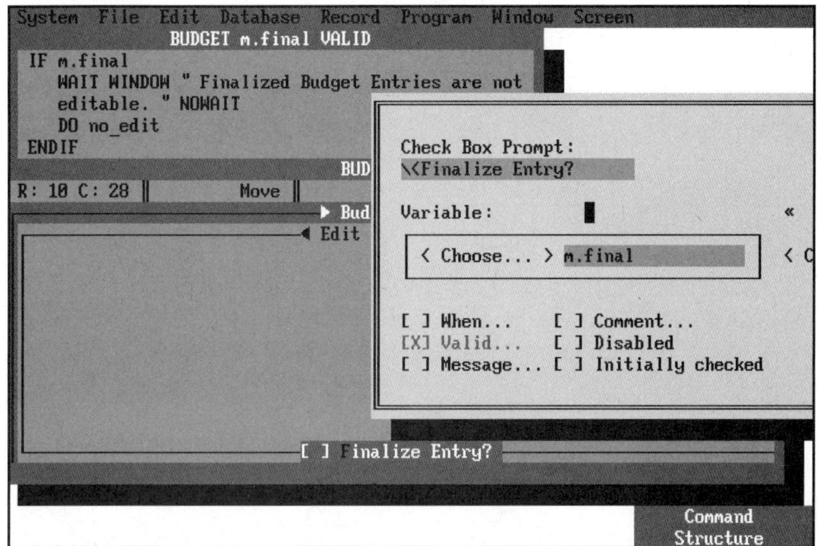

FIG. 13.6
Defining a Check Box and the related VALID clause.

The line preceding the RETURN line puts the cursor in the NOTES field. You may instead prefer to place the cursor in the Save/Cancel Edit object you create by using the following line:

```
_CUROBJ = OBJNUM(m.saveit)
```

Notice that _CUROBJ refers to GETs by number rather than by name. A GET's *number* is determined by the order in which GETs are accessed on-screen by using the keyboard, (the mouse also can access GETs in any order). You always can refer to GETs by number rather than by name by using the SHOWOBJECT command, which performs the same functions as a SHOW GET; for example, SHOW OBJECT OBJNUM (m.dept) DISABLE.

You can create some GETs as *sets* of objects, as you soon see when you add buttons to the Budget screen. Although the group of buttons has one GET variable, each button has a special object number. You can SHOW a group as a set by using SHOW GET <*the_variable*>, or you can redisplay any individual member of the group by using SHOW OBJECT <*number*> or SHOW GET <*the_variable*>,<*number*>. SHOW GET's second option, <*number*>, indicates the button's position within the group.

After you check the Structure notepad, you see that you need to define a GET for the date field, named *m.period*. This GET is a normal field expression, similar to expressions you created in the preceding chapter, but much of the other editing depends on this GET's contents. If you edit m.period to contain a date in the current or past quarters, you want to mark this entry as Final to prevent further editing.

The VALID clause, therefore, executes a UDF that you create and place in the Cleanup code, which checks the date and sees whether all requisite fields are filled out. If no necessary fields are blank and if the date is now in a current or a past quarter, this clause takes appropriate action. The UDF, named *to_final()*, is created as a function, rather than as a procedure because you can use the RETURN value (which tells you whether the entry is made Final). The procedure for the VALID is shown in the following listing:

```
IF ! to_final()
  DO can_final
ENDIF
RETURN .T.
```

This procedure first checks to see whether to_final( ) *automatically* makes the entry final. If not, this procedure runs another procedure known as *can_final* to see if all requisite fields are filled out. If these fields are filled out, can_final allows the user to make the entry final. Can_final is a simple procedure placed in Cleanup, as shown in the following listing:

```
PROCEDURE can_final
IF EMPTY(m.prodcode) OR EMPTY(m.deptcode) OR;
  EMPTY(m.budcatcode) OR EMPTY(m.period)

  SHOW GET m.final DISABLE
ELSE
  SHOW GET m.final ENABLE
ENDIF
RETURN
```

Following is the to_final( ) UDF for you to place in Cleanup:

```
FUNCTION to_final
mreturn = .F.
IF m.final

   * if the entry is already final,
   * as it will be in some circumstances
   * when this function is called
```

```
    DO no_edit
    * disable some GETs selectively

    mreturn = .T.
    * let the calling procedure know

  ELSE
    IF ! EMPTY(m.period) AND (m.period < DATE() OR ;
    (YEARm.period) = YEAR(DATE()) AND
     pd(m.period) = pd(DATE())))

    * if you got a date and it's either earlier than
    * today's date or it's in the same year and the
    * same quarter, which you determine with the
    * UDF PD(), you finalize the entry yourself:

    STORE .T. TO m.final
    WAIT WINDOW NOWAIT "Entry in past or present " ;
          +"Periods must be Final."

    * remember that users can still Cancel the
    * edit if this is unacceptable to them

    DO no_edit

    mreturn .T.
    * let the calling procedure know
    ENDIF

  ENDIF
  RETURN mreturn
```

The UDF Pd( ), which also goes in Cleanup and RETURNs the quarter in which a date occurs, is shown in the following listing:

```
FUNCTION pd
PARAMETERS the_date
* pass the date you want to check
RETURN CEILING(MONTH(the_date)/3)
```

The only step left to do for the GET object m.period is to give it the Format of Select on Entry, which appears as @K. When editing a date, you use the @K because having the entire original date wiped out by the new keystrokes is usually the most convenient method.

The @K is used when an edit to an entry usually entails a completely new entry. You see the way it works in the FoxPro System dialogs, wherever a default file name was supplied.

Position this GET and a text label that indicates what it is, in the upper left corner of the record-editing box. Put another one below the first, for the GET m.budgetamt. The second one will have a Numeric format, and you can choose to have it Selected on Entry as well. You also can choose a Currency format (choosing both appears as @K). No clauses are needed for this GET (no restrictions apply to this field.) Size it by referring to the Structure window and giving the same number of places (7) as the BUDGETAMT field. If you start by placing the object in Column 1, the status line column figure reflects the object's current length for easy resizing. Next, move the object to the desired position. The new object looks like figure 13.7.

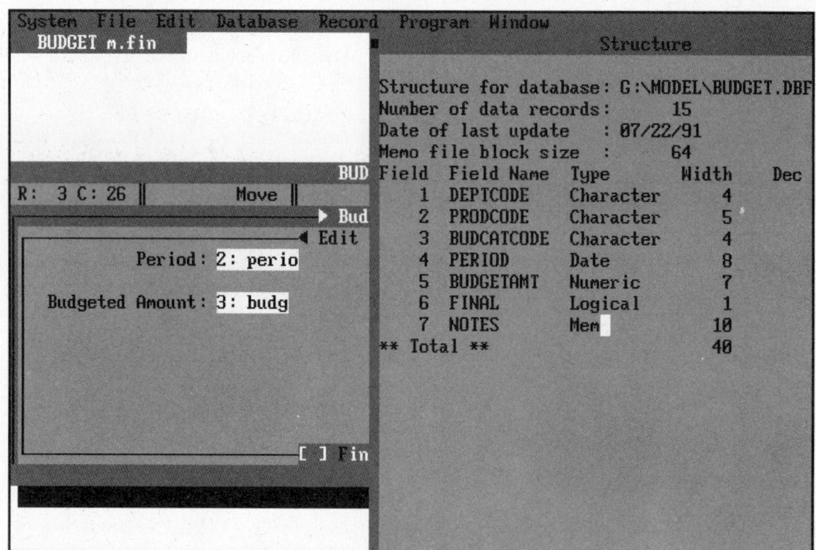

FIG. 13.7

Sizing GETs in accordance with the Budget Table Structure List.

Adding Lookups and Edits

Notice that this example sizes the *m.period* field with eight places. Although the PERIOD field, like all dates, also is eight places wide, the GET includes two extra characters for the *delimiters* between the month, day, and year (in the order you are currently presenting the date). You may want to explicitly SET CENTURY OFF in the Setup code to accommodate these extra characters or size the GET to 10 places. SET CENTURY ON if you want all four digits of the date to show.

The next GET is the first lookup. First, create a regular text label and field expression for *m.budcatcode*. You probably remember from the preceding chapter that the Format is *@! AAA9*. But now, you're checking both on the way into and the way out of the object (by using the WHEN and VALID clauses) to see whether the value held within also is found in the Budcat table. If not, *pop up* a list of values from the Budcat table and ask the user to pick a value. One UDF accomplishes this feat in both instances. The popup appears in the WHEN if the variable, *m.budcatcode*, is empty (if you are adding a record). The user, who may be familiar with the budget category codes, can edit the code manually or just to confirm the popup choice. If the user edits the code, either at this point or when subsequently re-editing the record, the VALID serves to ensure that the code still is a value in the Budcat table after the edit.

The WHEN clause contains the Expression valbudcat(). This UDF, which you can place in Cleanup with all the other UDFs, takes the following form:

```
FUNCTION valbudcat
IF EMPTY(m.budcatcode) OR;
  ! SEEK(m.budcatcode,"budcat")
  * if the variable is empty or if the value
  * can't be found in the budcat table

  ACTIVATE POPUP budcat

  * when the POPUP is DEACTIVATEd, code
  * execution continues here.
  * you place the value of the code
  * into the appropriate variable
  * and the NAME of the budget category
  * into another one created just to
  * provide visual confirmation of the choice

  SELECT budget
  STORE budcat.budcatcode TO m.budcatcode
  STORE budcat.budcat TO m.budcatname
  SHOW GET m.budcatname DISABLE
ENDIF
RETURN .T.
```

The VALID clause should contain the following snippet as a Procedure:

```
= valbudcat()
DO can_final
```

Again, the procedure can_final determines whether you have all requisite fields filled out and can make this entry final.

As noted in the comments in the code for FUNCTION valbudcat, you create another variable, *m.budcatname*, and put it in the data-entry window to show the name that goes with this code. As you can see in figure 13.8, you have placed this variable in the screen like other objects, although colored differently because you chose the Field Expression option to DISABLE the variable (this expression is never directly editable by the user). Figure 13.8 also shows part of the screen's Setup snippet. In the figure, the highlighted portion of the Setup code defines the popup activated by valbudcat() and determines the popup's behavior. The entire Setup code is reproduced near the end of this chapter.

The arrow between m.budcatcode and m.budcatname is actually four separate objects. First, you used Ctrl-B to create two short horizontal lines and one vertical line (in other words, two small 1-row boxes and one 1-column box). You then selected the objects, along with the option to Group Boxes, and smoothly joined the three into one. Then you pressed the Alt key and typed **17** on the keyboard to create the graphics character on-screen. (Alternately, type '**Q** by using the left quote method or the special characters or ASCII chart, as you did in Chapter 2.) Finally, you selected and moved the character and into position, overlaying the bottom left edge of the grouped box/line figure.

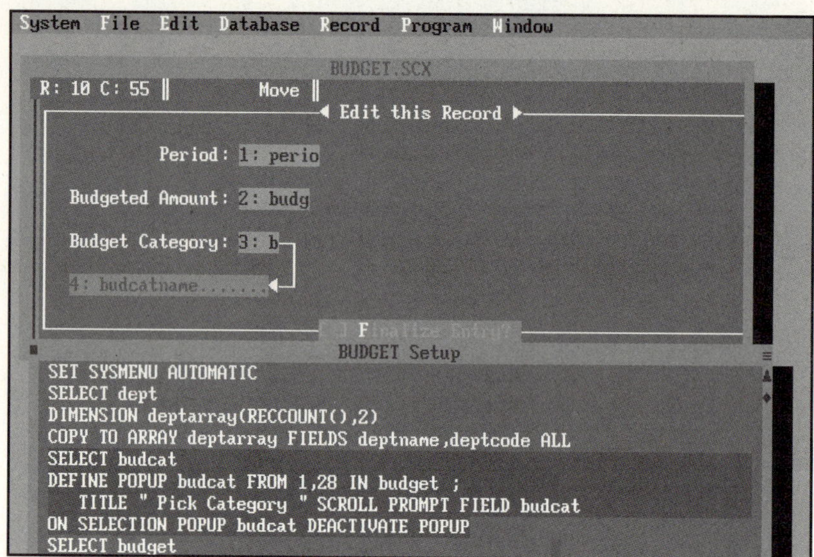

FIG. 13.8

The budget category field and the related text label, along with a disabled GET that holds the budget category name.

Next, you create a scrollable list (shortcut, Ctrl-L) to hold the Product choices. Here, you don't actually show the user the product codes. The list contains entries from the Product table's PRODNAME field. As shown in figure 13.9, this list's prompts are created. Choose the `Prompt Field` for a List Type and indicate that the field to be used is `product.prodname`. You store the results in a Variable named *m.product*. Then, putting a `Procedure` in the Valid snippet, check to see whether the user made a choice. If so, the record pointer in the Product table will have been moved to the appropriate record, and you can use the PRODCODE field to fill the m.prodcode with the right value. You then call can_final again, in case you want to allow this entry to be finalized. The following listing is the entire procedure for the snippet, also shown in figure 13.9:

```
IF ! EMPTY(m.product)
   STORE product.PRODCODE TO m.prodcode
   DO can_final
ENDIF
```

When you return to the design screen, size the list object until the box shows at least three entries and is wide enough to show the product names adequately.

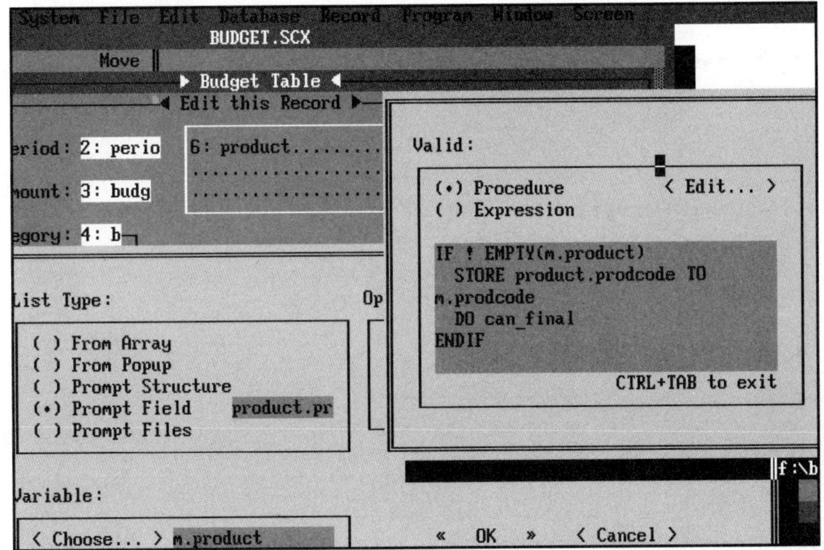

FIG. 13.9

Creating a Scrollable List.

You create the last lookup, *deptcode*, as a popup control (with the shortcut, Ctrl-0). You can create popup controls either as a List-type or as an Array-type. In a List-type popup, you type the prompts, as you do for a set of radio or push buttons. You chose an Array popup because you need not know the prompts to design the screen. An *array*, similar to a small table, has rows and columns of elements (although, like a table, an array also may have a single row or a single column). The array is a structured set of memory variables. FoxPro 2 contains a number of commands and functions designed expressly to manipulate arrays, which you learn about in Chapter 20. You create the array that fills this popup in the following sections of the Setup snippet:

```
SELECT dept
DIMENSION deptarray(RECCOUNT(),2)
* create an array that has as many rows as
* records in the Dept table
* and two columns wide

COPY TO ARRAY deptarray ;
  FIELDS deptname, deptcode ALL
* fill the array with the department names and codes
* in the first and second column, respectively
```

NOTE

You are using only one of many choices when you define the Product scrollable list with the `Prompt Field` option, as you can see in the list dialog shown in figure 13.9. Be aware that this may be the most flexible of the new GET objects available in FoxPro 2. The Prompt Field option used here can use an expression and a field name. The little text box in which you typed **product.prodname** scrolls, and you can type as many characters as you like for the list prompts. For example:

product.prodcode+": "+product.prodname

If, however, a list is created `From Array`, the list may hold almost anything you can imagine. You use an array for the next lookup you design in this screen, which is a popup control to designate a department for the Budget entry. If you chose a scrollable list popup, the `1st Element` and `# Elements` check boxes are enabled. In a two-dimensional array, like the *deptarray*, described in a following part of this section, the 1st Element is the column of the array you want to display in the list, and the # Elements is the number of rows, or items, to be included in the list. Among the sample files included with FoxPro 2 GETFILE.SCX and FLDLIST.SCX in the \GOODIES\SCREENS directory, which are good models for the use of this GET object. Written by Sherri Bruhn, these screens provide all the functionality of the FoxPro system file- and field-picking dialogs.

Now you need to tell the popup only the name of the array that you are using (deptarray) and the Variable in which you want to put the choice. The array popup prompts are taken from the first column of elements in this array. The variable is numeric and represents the number of the choice the user makes from the list of items the user sees. Choose to name the variable m.dept and, as shown in figure 13.10, you again create a VALID clause that evaluates the choice, fills the variable that stands in for an actual budget field, and checks to see whether you can make the entry final:

```
IF ! EMPTY(m.dept)

  STORE deptarray(m.dept,2) TO m.deptcode
  * m.dept tells you what choice was made
  * (i.e. what row)
  * the item in the second column of that
  * row is the appropriate department code

  DO can_final

ENDIF
```

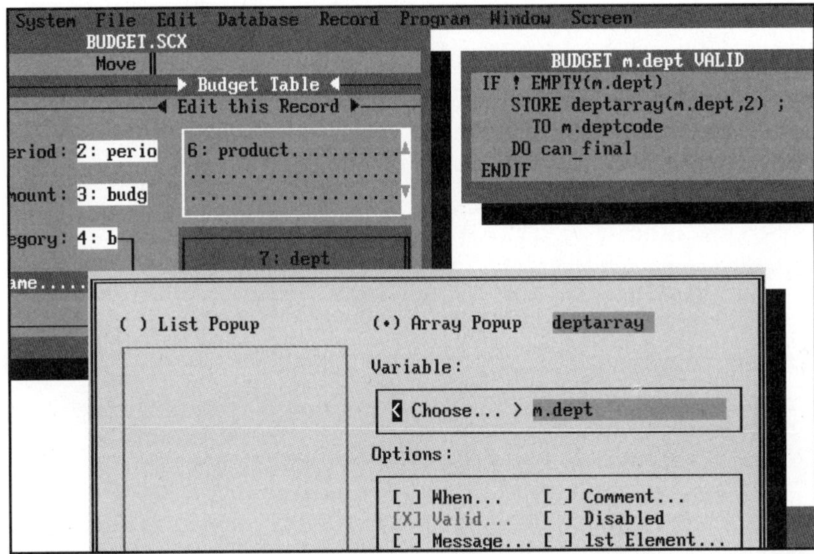

FIG. 13.10

Creating an Array Popup.

For the memo field, NOTES, use an `Edit` Field expression for the first time. Press Ctrl-F and choose the `Edit` radio button. Type **m.notes** as the variable to edit. Choose the option for a `Scroll bar` to have this familiar feature accompany this object, as shown in figure 13.11, and notice that you can use the `Length` option to limit the total length of the item you are editing. The option to `Allow tabs` is enabled for Edits because, by default, you can cycle through Edits with the Tab key just like all other screen objects. If you want to allow tabs within the Edit, choose to `Allow tabs` and then you can leave the field by pressing Shift-Tab or Ctrl-Tab, instead.

TIP Use the WHEN clause of an EDIT to KEYBOARD "{HOME}" if you want the user to see the beginning of the EDIT, no matter how long the EDIT is. Otherwise, the cursor is placed at the end of the current contents of the edit.

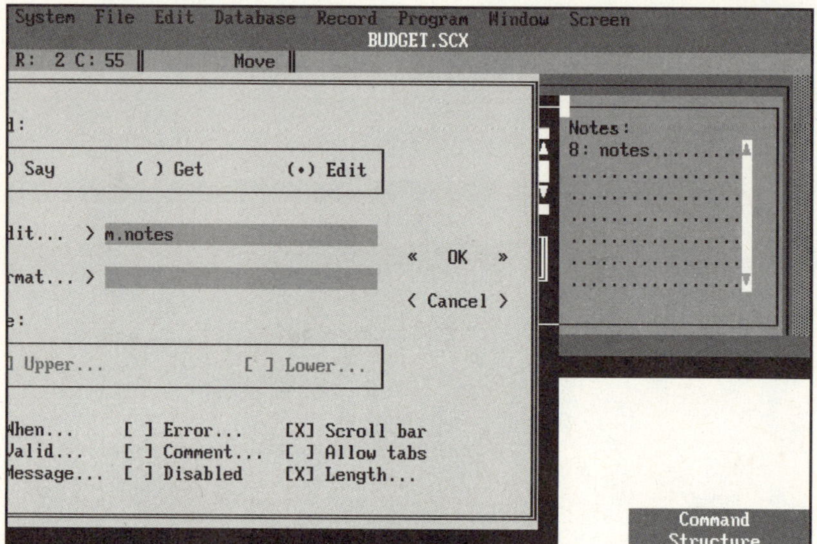

FIG. 13.11

Adding an Edit.

Using Buttons To Control Your Table

After you resize the Edit and, if necessary, the Department popup control, you have ended placement of the Budget table items to be edited. A few controls, however, still aren't yet created. The first control is composed of push buttons, with which you are familiar from the preceding chapter. As you see in the following figures, you create a similar set of Cancel/Save buttons to revoke or confirm editing changes. The buttons have slightly different prompts and are arranged vertically instead of horizontally. The real difference, however, is in the following VALID clause you use:

```
mreturn = .T.
IF m.saveit = 2
   * if they chose to confirm changes

   IF EMPTY(m.deptcode) OR EMPTY(m.budcatcode) ;
     OR EMPTY(m.period) OR EMPTY(m.prodcode)
         * you can't accept an incomplete record
```

```
        WAIT WINDOW " Fill out all information "+
              "before Saving, or Cancel Edit " NOWAIT

        * keep them here
        mreturn = .F.

  ELSE
        GATHER MEMVAR MEMO
        * notice the extra keyword to
        * account for the NOTES memo field

        SHOW GETS
        * will call the SHOW clause on the READ
        * which will SCATTER a new set of memory
        * variables and refresh all the GETs
  ENDIF
ELSE
  WAIT WINDOW " Editing Cancelled " NOWAIT
  SHOW GETS
  * see above comment
ENDIF

RETURN mreturn
```

Although you are choosing to RETURN .F. if the edit cannot be Saved because a requisite field wasn't filled out, you can send the user to the first field in the group of four still empty. Here, without GATHERing anything, you RETURN .T. from this procedure at all times. The following CASE statement determines the object that comes next:

```
* IF the user wants to save but
* you got an incomplete record,
* use the same WAIT WINDOW, and then
* check the important fields in order:

      DO CASE
      CASE EMPTY(m.period)
            _CUROBJ = OBJNUM(m.period)
      CASE EMPTY(m.budcatcode)
            _CUROBJ = OBJNUM(m.budcatcode)
      CASE EMPTY(m.prodcode)
            _CUROBJ = OBJNUM(m.product)
      CASE EMPTY(m.deptcode)
            _CUROBJ = OBJNUM(m.dept)
      ENDCASE

* continue as before with the
* ELSE
*     GATHER MEMVAR MEMO
```

TIP Rather than creating these two buttons as a set, you may prefer to create each button individually, each with a specific variable and VALID clause. This approach has an added benefit of making resizing individual buttons easier. If you prefer a set, you notice that you cannot size buttons by typing spaces at the beginning of prompts. Instead, use the *blank* character (created by holding down the Alt key and typing **255** on the numeric keypad).

Now, create a set of radio buttons (shortcut, Ctrl-N) to change the order in which you view the data at any time. Creating radio buttons is like creating a set of push buttons, as you can see in figure 13.12. Following is the Valid procedure snippet for these buttons:

```
DO CASE
CASE m.order = 1
   SET ORDER TO 0
CASE m.order = 2
   SET ORDER TO period
CASE m.order = 3
   SET ORDER TO deptcode
CASE m.order = 4
   SET ORDER TO budcatcode
ENDCASE
* Show the Browse again so that the new order shows
SHOW WINDOW "Pick" REFRESH
```

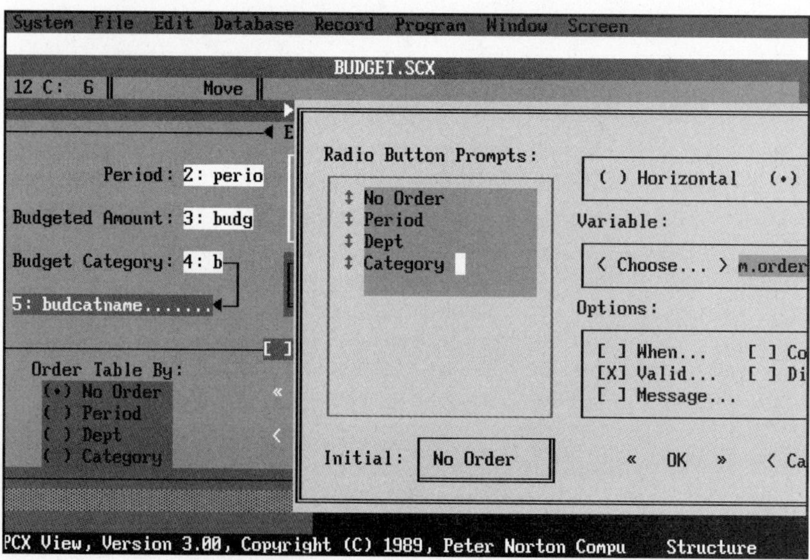

FIG. 13.12

Creating a Set of Radio Buttons.

The final controls on this screen are two Invisible buttons (shortcut, Ctrl-I). Invisible buttons are areas on-screen that you can size and select like other objects. Invisible buttons function like push buttons to initiate an action. In a graphical interface, you overlay these areas with an *icon* or other indicators that tell the user what happens when this area of the screen is clicked or selected by another means.

In FoxPro 2, you can devise this kind of representation with the graphics characters available, or you can overlay these areas with a text description of what the invisible buttons do, as you do here. With a text overlay, consider these Invisible buttons as push buttons—except that the prompts aren't required to have angle brackets. Because the prompts on push buttons can look unbalanced if you have a set with unequal-length prompts (because the angle brackets are the same distance apart on each button in a set, as required by the longest prompt), Invisible buttons can provide a handy alternative to other on-screen buttons.

Invisible buttons also can be used to arrange the user's choices in a visual display that uses the physical proximity of the elements in a meaningful way. These buttons, for example, can represent a *map* of locations about which reports are available, or underlay text in an embedded menu of helpfile subjects, which is described in Chapter 18.

The Invisible buttons on the Budget data-entry screen enable users to run two simple queries at any time. You create the buttons' overlaid text as Field expressions (SAYs), rather than as text objects, so that when the GETs are refreshed on-screen with a SHOW GETs command the buttons are not on top of the labels.

The SAYs expressions literally name the two queries the buttons process, which is not necessary. You can make these names "Query1" and "Query2" if you like and allow the users to substitute any queries they prefer for the sample queries you provide. You can even have each SAY contain a variable so that the users can provide labels for each of two queries they prefer. The queries themselves can be kept in a table and placed in a memo field, with a character field that holds the label for each one. In this way, users may draw two of their favorite questions from a bank of useful queries, to be immediately available on-screen as they work on the budget process.

The Invisible buttons are defined separately, although you can design them as a set of two, if you prefer. As shown in figure 13.13, you assign each button a variable (you used `m.query1` and `m.query2`). The `Valid` Procedure for each button is as follows:

```
DO budget1.qpr
* or budget2.qpr
SELECT budget
```

When you select the button, the query is executed. The VALID procedure must then reSELECT the Budget table because any query may leave you in a different work area.

If you define these buttons as a set, just assign one variable and use CASEs in the VALID to test the result and decide which query to run.

Whether you define the buttons singly or as a set, you should keep the button areas as large as you have room for and of consistent sizes, so the user does not have trouble clicking on them with the mouse.

Now create the SAYs expressions that overlay the buttons. The two SAYs are as shown in figure 13.14 (use ASCII 251 to type the first character, which often is used to represent a check mark):

"[√] Dept Totals for Pd"

and

"[√] Product Totals For Year"

Notice that you choose to Refresh the SAYs; as stated in the preceding instructions, this keeps them "on top" of the buttons when the GETs are refreshed. Notice, also, that you have surrounded each label with quotation marks, so that it can be seen as a literal character string. Just as in the Report Writer, where you built report expressions from a combination of functions, strings, variables, fields, and operators, you can use the Expression Builder to design any kind of SAY you want.

Build the queries run by these two buttons in the RQBE and save them as QPR files with the appropriate names. You can type these queries directly by using the command MODIFY COMMAND budget1.qpr and then MODIFY COMMAND budget2.qpr. You also can use these samples as an RQBE exercise—go backward, from the syntax, through the RQBE to achieve the same results.

The following listing is BUDGET1.QPR, as created by the RQBE:

```
SELECT DEPT.DEPTNAME, BUDGET.PERIOD, ;
        SUM(BUDGE.BUDGETAMT) ;
  FROM BUDGET,DEPT ;
  WHERE DEPT.DEPTCODE = BUDGET.DEPTCODE ;
  GROUP BY BUDGET.PERIOD, BUDGET.DEPTCODE ;
  HAVING BUDGET.PERIOD = m.period ;
  ORDER BY BUDGET.PERIOD ;
  INTO CURSOR BUDGET_A
BROWSE NOMODIFY PREFERENCE BUDGET_A
```

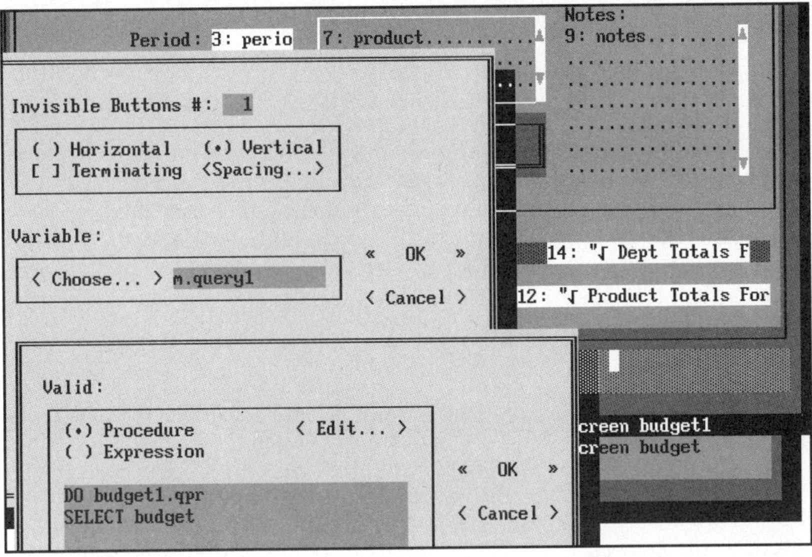

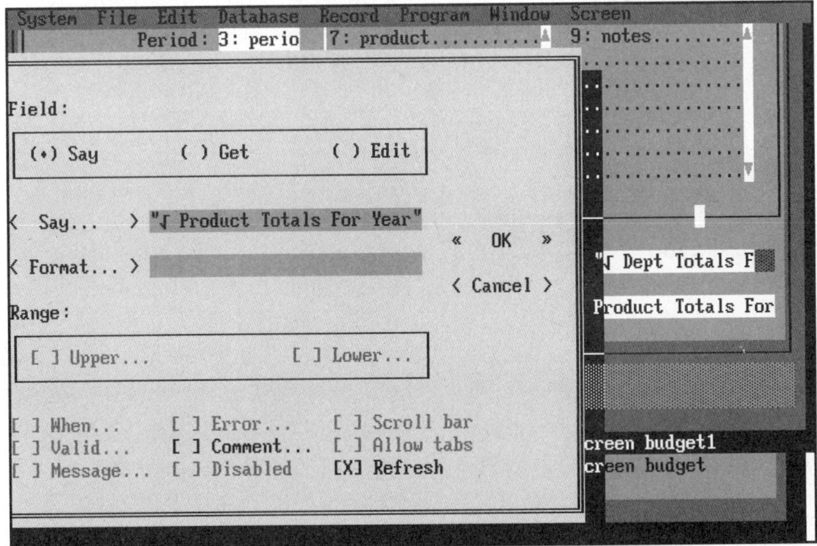

FIGS. 13.13 AND 13.14

Creating Invisible buttons and SAYs to label them.

The following listing shows BUDGET2.QPR:

```
SELECT PRODUCT.PRODNAME, BUDGET.PERIOD, ;
        SUM(BUDGET.BUDGETAMT) ;
  FROM BUDGET, PRODUCT ;
  WHERE PRODUCT.PRODCODE = BUDGET.PRODCODE ;
```

```
   GROUP BY BUDGET.PRODCODE, BUDGET.PERIOD ;
   HAVING YEAR(BUDGET.PERIOD) = YEAR(m.period) ;
   INTO CURSOR BUDGET_A
BROWSE NOMODIFY PREFERENCE BUDGET_A
```

Both of these queries use the variable *m.period*, which you must make available before designing the queries in the RQBE. Using the variable *m.period* in the query allows the user to type *any* date in the edit window and use the query processor to find out something about it (the user can always cancel the edit afterward). If you prefer instead, you can use the actual data from the Budget table (*budget.period* in place of *m.period* in each query).

Ordering Objects On-Screen

All the screen objects are now created. However, if you recall, you created the *Finalize* check box as the first GET. You certainly don't want this item to be the first entered by the user, so you need to *reorder* the objects in a more logical progression on-screen. To reorder, select all objects (hold down the Shift key) in the order you want the items accessed. (You may need to move the long text label "[√] Product Totals for Year" laterally so that you can select both the label and the related push button separately, although the order in which the two SAYs and the disabled m.budcatname GET are *accessed* isn't crucial.)

Starting from the m.period GET, choose the objects by going down the columns within the data-entry area and then across to the next column: m.period, m.budgetamt, m.budcatcode, m.budcatname, m.product, m.dept, m.notes. Next (still holding down the Shift key so everything remains selected), select the m.final GET and the m.saveit, for the controls that actually affect the data-entry process. Last, select m.order and the query objects.

Be careful that you don't move all the selected objects as you perform this procedure (although you can move them back when you finish). After objects are selected in the proper order, use the Screen menu popup option to Bring to Front (shortcut, Ctrl-G) and you see the assigned object numbers change. Use Send to Back (or Ctrl-J), and you can watch the object numbers change to a reverse order.

After you have reordered the objects (and repositioned the SAYs laterally, if you moved them during the reordering process), the completely designed screen should look like figure 13.15.

WARNING

You just reordered the fields in a sequence appropriate for data entry in the screen. In a screen, fields are initially ordered in the same sequence in which you define them. You can select all groups of objects on-screen and choose the option to Reorder Fields from the Screen menu to reorder the selected objects left-to-right and top-to-bottom, an order inappropriate here but possibly convenient at other times.

Grouping objects (which you can do to move or otherwise manipulate them as a set as you did in the Report Writer), however, also affects the objects' sequence. Grouped objects are by default reordered left-to-right and top-to-bottom within the group, with consequences you may not expect or desire. You can Ungroup all objects and then explicitly choose all objects and reorder these selections as you prefer when finish designing a screen.

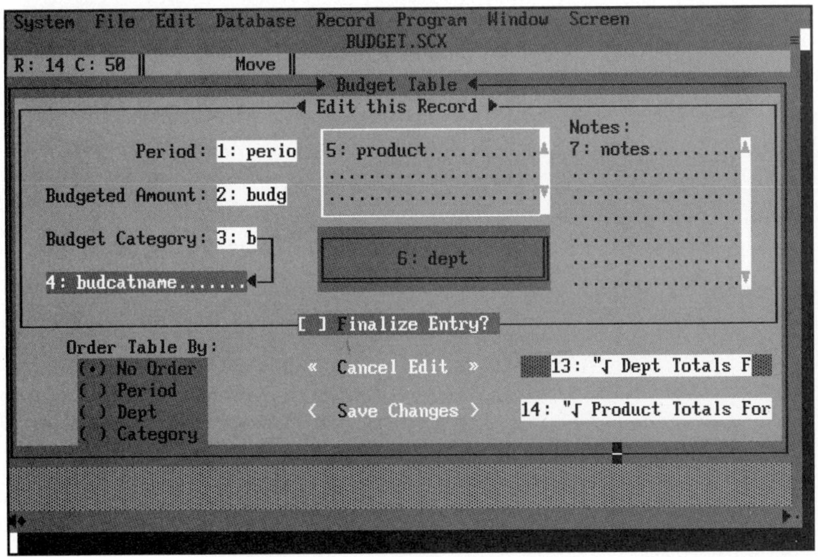

FIG. 13.15

The completely designed Budget screen.

Combining Objects into a Polished Screen Set

Although all the objects are created, you still have work to do before you can generate the BUDGET.SPR and run the code. Recall that you are going to have a BROWSE appear in this screen set; you take care of this feature in the Setup snippet of code, and you also need to add a few more screen-wide code sections by using the options in the Screen Layout dialog.

Setting Up the Screen

Although you have already seen much of the Setup snippet in previous sections of this chapter, the following listing reproduces the snippet in its entirety:

```
SET SYSMENU AUTOMATIC

* SYSMENU is ON by default but does not
* show on-screen during programs until the user
* presses ALT, F10, or double-clicks the
* right mouse button
* unless the preceding line is added.

* Remove the preceding line if you don't want
* SYSMENU showing at all times,
* and replace it by
* SET SYSMENU ON

* Look at the program environment code to see
* how you might save the old value of SYSMENU
* and restore it in Cleanup, too.

* Because this program uses SYSMENU shortcuts to
* add and delete records (from the BROWSE pad)
* do NOT SET SYSMENU OFF!

* You can choose to have the Screen Builder generate
* file-opening statements by using the
* environment saved with the screen, so everything
* should be set up for you to do the following:

SELECT dept
DIMENSION deptarray(RECCOUNT(),2)
COPY TO ARRAY deptarray ;
  FIELDS DEPTNAME, DEPTCODE ALL
* set up the array for the m.dept object
```

```
SELECT budcat
DEFINE POPUP budcat FROM 1,28 IN budget ;
  TITLE " Pick Category " ;
  SCROLL PROMPT FIELD BUDCAT
ON SELECTION POPUP budcat DEACTIVATE POPUP
* set up the popup for the m.budcatcode object

SELECT budget
SCATTER MEMVAR MEMO
* here, again, the extra MEMO keyword is used
* to account for the NOTES memo field
* You must initially set up these variables
* to be available to all parts
* of the program, although the SHOW routine
* refills them with the initial values.

* Do the same for the special object-variables
* below. If there is any chance of these
* variables reappearing in other screen sets
* that may be active at the same time as this one,
* you should declare the variables
* REGIONAL, as GENSCRN does with the variables
* it creates in the program environment section
* of the code before storing the initial values to them.

* If you're not on a blank record, use the
* RELATIONs that have been SET to get the
* budget category name from the Budcat table and the
* product name from the Product table, as follows:
m.budcatname = IIF(EMPTY(m.budcatcode), ;
                   SPACE(20),           ;
                   budcat.budcat)

m.product = IIF(EMPTY(m.prodcode),      ;
                   " ",                 ;
                   product.prodname)

* Get m.dept from the row number of the
* array deptarray in which m.deptcode can
* be found:
m.dept = IIF(EMPTY(m.deptcode),             ;
                  0,                        ;
                  ASUBSCRIPT("deptarray",
                       ASCAN("deptarray", ;
                             m.deptcode), ;
                  1) )
```

```
* Initialize the m.order variable
* and make it appropriate to the current order
DO CASE
CASE UPPER(ORDER()) = "PERIOD"
  m.order = 2
CASE UPPER(ORDER()) = "DEPTCODE"
  m.order = 3
CASE UPPER(ORDER()) = "BUDCATCODE"
  m.order = 4
OTHERWISE
  * order may not be set,
  * or it may be set to one you're not
  * allowing access to in this screen
  SET ORDER TO 0
  m.order = 1
ENDCASE

* Depending on the situations in which you
* call this program, you may want to
* save ORDER() in a variable first, so you
* can restore it in cleanup.

DEFINE WINDOW brow FROM 20,12 TO SROWS()-2,68;
  SYSTEM FLOAT GROW ZOOM COLOR SCHEME 10
* Define a window of appropriate attributes
* and size for the browse.
* Note the use of the SROWS() function, so that
* the browse stretches to the bottom of the
* screen regardless of which display mode you're in.

* comments on the BROWSE follows below

BROWSE SAVE NOWAIT NOEDIT WINDOW brow ;
  TITLE " Pick Budget Entry  " ;
  WHEN Do_Show()

RELEASE WINDOW brow
```

Using Browses in a Screen Set

At the bottom of the Setup snippet is the first time a programmatic use of a BROWSE command is used. The SAVE keyword means that it is kept open when you cycle through the windows in the READ. The NOEDIT keyword means, as you may expect, that the BROWSEd records are editable directly. The NOWAIT keyword means that the program does not remain in the BROWSE after creating it, but continues with the rest of the programmed instructions.

The WINDOW brow clause means "open this browse with the characteristics defined by the WINDOW named *brow*, which you previously defined."

TIP

The TITLE clause is important in this context—you can refer to a BROWSE window in a program by referring to the BROWSE window's title (or by the first word in the title, if the title includes non-alphabetic characters). If the window has no title, you can refer to the BROWSE window by the title given to the WINDOW (if you defined the WINDOW with a TITLE clause). Failing this, if the BROWSE was defined IN WINDOW (a separate clause you do not use here) and that window was defined with a title, you can use this window's title to refer to the BROWSE in window functions. If none of the above situations apply, you can refer to the BROWSE window by the alias of the controlling table.

If you find the preceding paragraph confusing, rest assured that you are not alone. Referring accurately to a BROWSE window is important, however, as you see in a the following paragraphs. The best way to get a sense of how this works is to use another WAIT WINDOW trick, similar to the trick you used to learn about READ clauses:

```
ON KEY LABEL F10 WAIT WINDOW WONTOP()+" "+WTITLE()
```

Using this command in the Command window, try defining, titling, and windowing the BROWSEs in different ways and issuing BROWSEs. While each BROWSE is active, press F10 and check the current status of these two functions, watching for the changes.

When you finish, issue the command ON KEY LABEL F10 (with nothing following it) to cancel the previous instruction. You learn more about ON KEY LABEL commands in the chapters that cover programming.

The BROWSE WHEN clause is evaluated when the user moves between records (or rows) in the BROWSE. With a SHOW GETS in the WHEN clause, the Budget table data-entry window is refreshed as the user changes the current record by using the BROWSE. Because it RETURNs .F., the record currently being *moved to* is unavailable for editing (this record is read-only). You need to take these steps, even with the NOEDIT keyword, because a BROWSE NOEDIT still can have records added to it with Ctrl-N, and these records still are editable. You are taking advantage of FoxPro's native method of appending (and also deleting) records in this program. You also can use the keywords NOAPPEND and NODELETE to make these options unavailable or even NOMENU to make all the native BROWSE menu options unavailable. You then can devise new menu options or ON KEY LABEL options for the users to add and delete records under your control. Records added in this way are uneditable, like all others, in a BROWSE NOEDIT.

Many reasons exist to prefer programmatic control over record-adding, rather than the simple method you chose here. You may want to add a unique identification number for each record as the record is added or to check for recyclable deleted records before you choose to add one. You also may want to allow the user to choose certain fields for automatic entry of particular values throughout one data-entry session (creating a custom version of the SET CARRY command).

You can use the NOMENU clause on a BROWSE to fain full control. You then replace the options on the menu popup that usually appears when a BROWSE is the active window, with similar options of your own. Adding records may be done by SCATTERing MEMVAR MEMO BLANK and APPENDing a BLANK when the edit is confirmed for a new record, as you did with the EDIT screen in the precious chapter. You still can allow adds only while in the BROWSE screen, using a check for IF WONTOP("Pick").

BROWSE has many other features you can explore. Besides the keywords and clauses that you learned about in Chapter 8, equally useful for interactive and programmatic use are the row-level Browse VALID clause and the various clauses that you can issue to determine a BROWSE's *look* in a program: LPARTITION/RPARTITION and PARTITION, NOLGRID/NORGRID, and NOLINK are among the new FoxPro 2 features.

Meanwhile, you are going to stow the simple WHEN clause UDF in the Cleanup snippet, as follows:

```
FUNCTION do_show
SHOW GETS
SHOW WINDOW "Pick" REFRESH
RETURN .F.
```

The SHOW WINDOW <*browse window*> REFRESH command makes sure that all new records added appear in the proper order.

The Setup of the Budget data-entry screen set shown here uses the technique recommended by Fox for integrating a BROWSE with READ windows. This approach, however, does not enable you to begin a data-entry session in the included BROWSE window. If you want to start the session by picking a record to edit or adding a new record, don't initiate a BROWSE... NOWAIT in the Setup. Instead, start the BROWSE without the NOWAIT clause when the entire screen first appears. Appendix I provides a generic sample program (STARTOFF.PRG) that demonstrates this alternative approach.

Another capability you want in many screen sets is a BROWSE of a related table. You can use the SET SKIP and SET RELATION commands you learned in Chapter 4 to provide a BROWSE of child records when you are editing the parent table or a BROWSE of parent records from which you decide which children to edit. Realizing that BROWSEs are not perfectly integrated within READs, however, is important. The techniques used in the following section to control windows do not work if you have more than one BROWSE in a READ, because these techniques depend on READ-level clauses (ACTIVATE, in this example) when the user moves between two windows (unless one is a "normal" READ window that contains GETs). You get the best results if you restrict each READ to include only one window of the BROWSE or MODIFY MEMO/FILE type along with the related GET windows. Of course, you can have multiple BROWSEs on the screen if these BROWSEs are attached to different screen sets (different READs).

Adding More READ-Level Clauses and Integrating the BROWSE

The Budget data-entry screen requires a simple but extremely significant READ ACTIVATE clause, which consists of the following lines:

```
IF ! WVISIBLE("Pick")
  CLEAR READ
ENDIF
```

The ACTIVATE clause is evaluated when a new window is chosen during a READ; the window, however, must be participating in the READ with normal GETs rather than a BROWSE, MODIFY MEMO, or desk accessory window. This procedure reads as "If the browse window is no longer visible"—remember that you are going to refer to the browse by the title—"end the READ."

You also can choose to make the opposite assumption. If the user closed the BROWSE, the closure was accidental and the READ should not be CLEARed. You may decide that you only want to allow an exit from the READ by using a Quit option that you included as a button in the data-entry window. Here, rather than using the preceding ACTIVATE clause, you may want to use the following code:

```
IF ! WVISIBLE("Pick")
    DEFINE WINDOW brow FROM 20,12 TO SROWS()-2,68 ;
          SYSTEM FLOAT GROW ZOOM COLOR SCHEME 10
    BROWSE SAVE NOWAIT NOEDIT WINDOW brow ;
                TITLE " Pick Budget Entry  " WHEN
Do_Show()
    RELEASE WINDOW brow
ENDIF
```

Here, you redefine and reissue the BROWSE if it no longer exists. The NOWAIT keyword is required even if you used the alternative method of starting up the BROWSE without referring to NOWAIT at the end of the last section.

In the BROWSE's WHEN clause, as before, the SHOW GETS calls the SHOW clause, which does the real work of giving the memory variables the correct values for the current record. The following lines show the entire SHOW clause:

```
IF ! budget.final AND ! EMPTY(budget.period) AND ;
   (budget.period < DATE() OR ;
   (YEAR(budget.period) = YEAR(DATE()) AND ;
    pd(budget.period) = pd(DATE())))

   * If the actual record has not been marked 'final'
   * yet, but the date is within the current or past
   * quarters:

   REPLACE budget.final WITH .T.
   WAIT WINDOW NOWAIT "Entry in past or "+  ;
         "present Periods must be Final. "

   * (change the value in the actual record).
   * This part of the procedure will be in use
   * when the SHOW GETS command is called by
   * the BROWSE WHEN. In fact, you should see
   * the message quite a bit the first time you
   * run the BUDGET.SPR and cursor through the
   * BROWSE, especially if you typed the dates
   * you indicated for the sample data and you
   * are using this book in 1992 or later!
   * A useful strategy is to add a button
   * to SET FILTER TO !final in this screen in case
   * the users want to see only editable records.

ENDIF
```

```
* Now create appropriate values for the current record
* for all the variables, as you did in the setup code.
* You don't need to reset m.order just because you
* are moving between records, however:

SCATTER MEMVAR MEMO

m.budcatname = IIF(EMPTY(m.budcatcode), ;
                    SPACE(20),          ;
                    budcat.budcat)

m.product = IIF(EMPTY(m.prodcode),      ;
                    " ",                ;
                    product.prodname)

m.dept = IIF(EMPTY(m.deptcode),                   ;
                    0,                            ;
                    ASUBSCRIPT("deptarray",
                         ASCAN("deptarray", ;
                               m.deptcode), ;
                         1) )

IF m.final
   DO no_edit
   * disable some GETs
ELSE
   DO can_edit
   * selectively enable GETs
ENDIF
```

The SHOW GETS command, besides calling the SHOW clause, also *refreshes* the GETs on-screen (which shows all the new values you may have given) by default. SHOW GETS is flexible, powerful, and has several optional keywords you can use to change default behavior. You previously saw the ENABLE/DISABLE keywords, which also are available for the single SHOW GET command. You also can use the LEVEL <Exp*N*> clause to SHOW GETS at a particular level if you have *nested* READs (you learn more about these READs in the following chapter) or—if you have more than one window—the WINDOW <*window name*> clause to SHOW GETS in a particular window. You may decide to SHOW GETS WINDOW Controlm DISABLE, for example, to prevent the user from moving to another record while you edit a record in the Dept screen set you designed in Chapter 12. The COLOR or COLOR SCHEME clause can SHOW GETS in any colors required to alert the user to a change in status, at any time.

You may want to call the SHOW clause at some point without refreshing the GETS, which you can do with the OFF keyword, or refresh the GETS and not execute the SHOW clause's commands, using SHOW

GETS ONLY. In a multiuser system, you use SHOW GETS LOCK when you have been browsing through the records with a READ NOLOCK and wish to secure a lock on the record you want to edit.

The Budget table screen set's SHOW clause uses one new procedure, can_edit, because, as you remember, the Budget table strategy for GETs to be enabled selectively according to some complex relations between them. Here is the can_edit procedure, the last one you need to place in the Cleanup snippet:

```
PROCEDURE can_edit
SHOW GET m.period ENABLE
SHOW GET m.budgetamt ENABLE
SHOW GET m.budcatcode ENABLE
SHOW GET m.product ENABLE
SHOW GET m.dept ENABLE
_CUROBJ = OBJNUM(m.notes)
DO can_final
* check to see whether the m.final
* GET can be entered yet
RETURN
```

Now, you only need to take care of the Cleanup snippet itself. This code should precede all the procedures and functions you typed into the Cleanup snippet. For clarity, you can end this code with a RETURN command (as shown in the following lines), although FoxPro 2 doesn't require this step. This RETURN statement is the RETURN from the SPR back to the calling program. The final cleanup code contains the following lines, to be executed after the READ:

```
RELEASE WINDOW "Pick"
* get rid of the BROWSE if you exited the
* READ from the data entry window
RELEASE POPUP budcat
RELEASE deptarray
* you don't need them and they don't need
* to continue taking up memory
RETURN
```

Following these lines, you should have (in any order) all the PROCEDUREs and FUNCTIONs you created above, to be used and called by different objects and clauses in the program. Here is a checklist; make sure that you have them all:

```
PROCEDURE no_edit
PROCEDURE can_edit
FUNCTION valbudcat
FUNCTION to_final
PROCEDURE can_final
```

```
FUNCTION pd
FUNCTION do_show
```

Using the Screen Set

Now, you are ready to generate the code (accepting all defaults in the Generate dialog once again) compile, check for errors, and DO BUDGET.SPR.

If you have followed closely in this chapter, what you see in the following section should look much like figures 13.16 through 13.19. In figure 13.16, the user has cursored into an old entry in the BROWSE, and the system informs him or her that the entry must be marked Final. Note the disabled GETs in the record-entry section, although queries still may be run; order still may be set; and notes still can be entered in the EDIT.

In figure 13.17, the user added a record and then changed the Order to Dept. After the file is put into Dept order, the new record is now positioned at the beginning of the BROWSE because a blank department code still exists. The GETs are now enabled, except for the capability of Finalizing the Entry. The Finalize GET remains unavailable until the required fields are no longer blank. For the same reason, when the user tries to `<Save Changes>`, the message displayed in the figure appears.

In figure 13.18, all fields were filled out, and Changes were Saved. The Finalize GET is now enabled. If the user chooses to mark the entry Final, all data entry GETs except for the NOTES field becomes disabled again. Notice that the information for this record now appears in the BROWSE, because the Changes were Saved.

In figure 13.19, a query was run against the data in the current entry. The results of the query, the total budgets for each department during this period, show in a separate BROWSE.

You have to play with this screen for a while to observe all the features of this system in action. Yet, again, it displays only a fraction of the abilities of the Screen Builder and screen sets.

System File Edit Database Record Program Window Browse

Entry in past or present Periods must be Final.

Period: 04/01/91

Budgeted Amount: $1000

Budget Category: INS0

Insurance

Bobometers
Dream Sequencers
Jeli-Do Nuts & Bolts

Finance

The cost of Dream Sequencer insurance is expected to rise dramatically this year, for obvious reasons.

[X] Finalize Entry?

Order Table By:
(•) No Order
( ) Period
( ) Dept
( ) Category

« Cancel Edit »

‹ Save Changes ›

√ Dept Totals For Pd

√ Product Totals For Year

Pick Budget Entry ↑↓

Deptcode	Prodcode	Budcatcode	Period	Budgetamt	Final
SLS1	BBM0	ADV0	01/01/91	2000	T
FIN0	DSQ0	INS0	04/01/91	1000	T

FIG. 13.16

The Budget Entry system, showing a "Finalized" record.

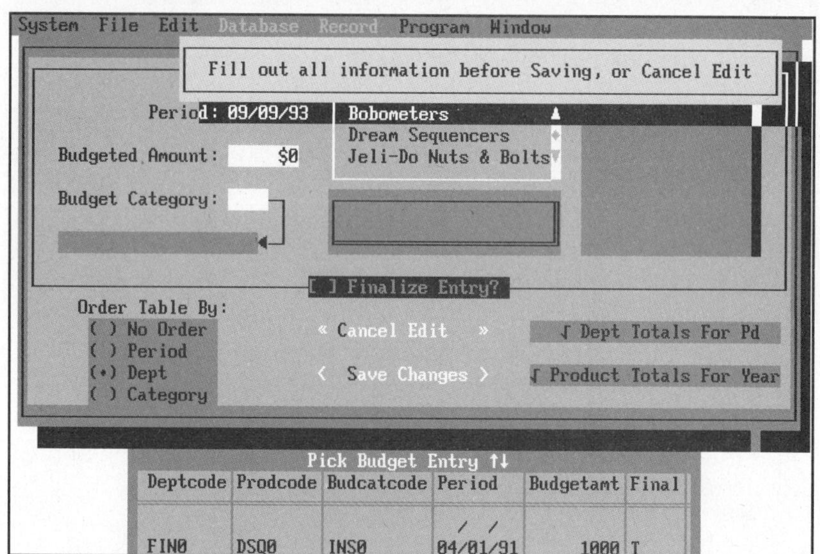

FIG. 13.17

The Budget Entry system. The user has tried to save an unfinished entry.

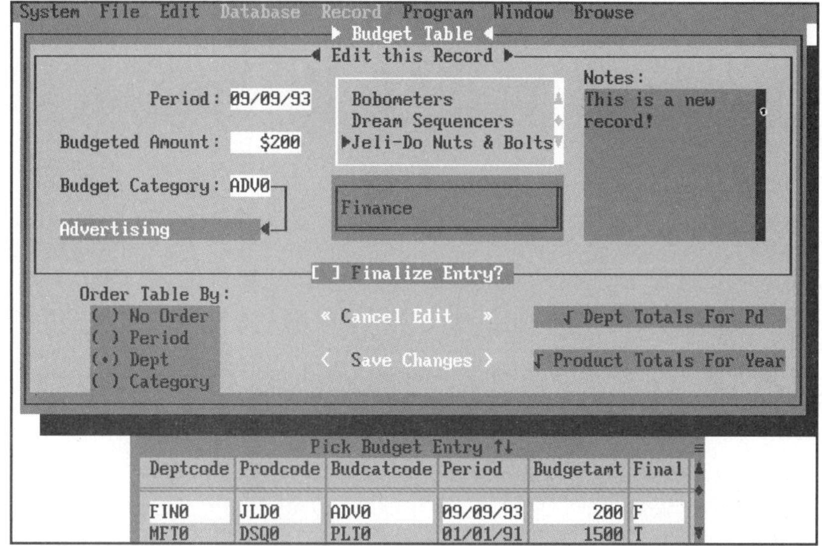

FIG. 13.18

The Budget Entry system, showing a record ready to be Finalized.

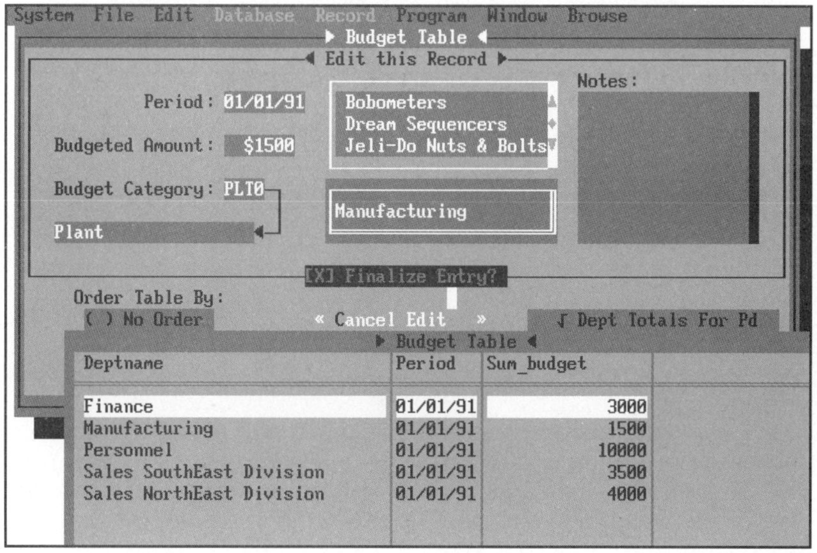

FIG. 13.19

The results of a query in the Budget Entry system.

Advancing Your Comprehension of FoxPro 2's READ Command

As you work with the practice system and build new systems, you can find many ways to incorporate existing window objects—including BROWSEs and MODIFY MEMOs, and also desk accessories, such as the calculator (a fixture on the System menu popup)—in screen sets. Occasionally, however, you may not want all windows equally available to users. You need to direct users to perform tasks in a certain sequence, keeping them in one *mode* of action at a time. The FoxPro interface contains *modal* dialogs, similar to the Report option on the Database menu popup. Modal dialogs are windows whose tasks you must finish before you can go on to choose the next action.

The opposite of *modal* systems are *modaless* or *nonmodal*, where you can move at will between activities the same way you cycled between the Filer, the Command Window, and text-editing windows in the first chapter. (Some Macintosh users and programmers prefer the term *modaless* to describe systems that behave in this manner.) So far, all the READs you have created have been nonmodal. But you may or may not have realized how careful you were to keep them that way; in the Setup snippet of the Budget screen, did you notice the last line, `RELEASE WINDOW brow`? Recall that this statement was the WINDOW you defined to set attributes and size for the Browse window. Had you not released it immediately, any user may have inadvertently moved into this window by choosing it from the Window menu popup.

At times, you need to communicate with users who have questions that the user must answer before work can proceed. You also may encounter times when you must limit users to a discrete set of windows, although you defined other windows needed for certain utility tasks. The READ keyword MODAL, together with the associated WITH clause, are provided to help you with this problem.

The MODAL command, when used alone, limits a READ to the windows in the particular screen set. Any attempt to bring other windows forward with a mouse results in a beep and no other change, just as when you try to click the Command window while still in the Report or Search dialog. You then can add the WITH clause (the word WITH, followed by a list of windows) to selectively enable certain other windows to be accessed without harm, as in the following example:

```
READ CYCLE MODAL WITH Brow, Calculator, Calendar
```

This command enables the three named windows (which includes two System pad desk accessories) to come forward.

Again, you see how important knowing how to make an exact reference to a window can be, especially with a BROWSE and the related, complicated window-referencing rules.

If you are building multiuser systems in FoxPro 2, besides knowing MODAL and WITH, you also want to know the LOCK and NOLOCK keywords on a READ. LOCK and NOLOCK specify whether MultiUser FoxPro tries to *lock* a record involved in any of the GETs in a READ, which means that other users are prevented from editing the record. LOCK, which allows edits, is the default, and NOLOCK makes the GETs read-only. The issues involved in record-locking, and whether you set locks explicitly or rely on FoxPro's automatic locking system, are among the key differences between reading directly to records and reading to memory variables. See Appendix B, "Using FoxPro 2 in a Network Environment," for a detailed discussion of these issues.

Apart from the READ-level options, you haven't fully explored all the object-level options for each kind of GET and the other screen elements. Some of these features are mentioned in following chapters, but this is another direction in which you should continue to experiment.

As you learn about the syntax used in creating GET and EDIT objects, you will see a DEFAULT clause in use. This option is not available in the Screen Builder and is, in the authors' opinion, of limited utility. In explanation, and so that you are not confused when you see the DEFAULT values in clauses GENSCRN inserts for each GET or EDIT in the generated SPR files, these values are used only to generate memory variables, if you include a GET or EDIT to an item that *does not already exist.*

If you GET directly to fields, or if you GET to memory variables and SCATTER MEMVAR (whether BLANK or filled with the contents of the current record), the DEFAULT clause is ignored. When you create GET controls that involve memory variables not directly related to a record, and therefore not created by a SCATTER, you should initialize them, as you initialized m.dept and m.product in the Setup code and in the SHOW clause of the Budget screen.

Although the example code initializes the variables to blanks if the user adds a new record, explicitly initializing these variables gives you a chance to indicate the default values you prefer. You can even maintain a table with each user's preferred defaults and RESTORE these memory variables from there if the user added a record.

Other GET-level options not directly supported by the Screen Builder are far more useful than DEFAULT. You may want to use the NOMODIFY keyword on an EDIT so that you can scroll and read, but not edit. You may want to use the COLOR clause, although, as you learn in Chapter 15, other ways are available to address color issues in FoxPro that may feel more natural in the Screen Builder.

Just as the #READCLAUSES generator directive enables you to add keywords and clauses to a READ that doesn't specify Screen Builder options, you can *attach* extra code on the object level. The easiest place to put this code is in the Format text box. Just use the #ITSEXPRESSION directive described in Table 13.1 to get GENSCRN to treat whatever you place in the text box as an expression instead of a literal string to be bounded by quotation marks. (Remember that you place the #ITSEXPRESSION directive, followed by the character of your choice, in the Setup snippet with any other generator directives you use.)

Because GENSCRN prefaces the information in the `Format` check box with the word `PICTURE`, just enclose the real format information within brackets or, if the GET or EDIT has no picture, add a pair of brackets with nothing between them. Suppose that the #ITSEXPRESSION character is ~, as shown in the example in Table 13.1, and you have a memo field that should be viewable but not edited in a certain screen. The Format text box should contain the following line:

```
~ [] NOMODIFY
```

GENSCRN then generates the following line of code:

```
@ r,c EDIT your_memo PICTURE [] NOMODIFY
```

If you have a password GET designed to accept only uppercase characters and you want the word displayed in black-on-black so that the password can not be read as typed, you can use the following Format:

```
~ [@!] COLOR ,N/N
```

GENSCRN generates the following code:

```
@ r,c GET your_pass PICTURE [@!] COLOR ,N/N
```

In this way, you can add to the generated code anything not directly included in the Screen Builder options.

Chapter Summary

With all these opportunities, mentioning that you still have other alternatives for screen design and generation in FoxPro 2 may seem almost cruel. If, however, you do not like the programs generated by the Screen Builder, you can change GENSCRN.PRG. To write screen programs, GENSCRN uses FoxPro 2's new *textmerge* commands, which are described in Chapter 17, "Using Advanced FoxProgramming Techniques." Textmerge commands are extremely powerful yet easy to use. You can customize GENSCRN or build as many special-purpose generator programs as you like with different names. When you are ready to generate a screen, just supply the appropriate generator program name to FoxPro by storing the name in the GENSCRN system variable.

Because the screen files are tables, you can easily investigate these files' structure to help you understand GENSCRN.PRG and also for other reasons. You can USE BUDGET.SCX like other tables and directly REPLACE ALL *<colorpair>* WITH a value you prefer FOR all objects of a certain kind. At times, this method may be quicker and more convenient than using the Screen Builder.

In the two previous chapters, you covered a great deal of ground in a short time. You moved from painting a few objects to the canvas of the Screen Builder to creating complicated multiple-window screen sets (using almost every feature of FoxPro 2) and learning and working with queries to arrays and many new programming instructions.

In the following chapter, you investigate other tools, including the Menu Builder and the Project Manager, that help you assemble full-fledged data management systems. You also are introduced to *foundation READs*, which you can use to maintain a system's tasks in a delicate balancing act, and other thoughts on ways to integrate, enhance, and share these various elements of FoxPro 2 applications.

14

CHAPTER

Organizing and Packaging Your Applications

Your exploration of the Screen Builder was productive but arduous. FoxPro 2's other new power tools that you approach in this chapter may loom in your imagination like a range of mountains you have yet to climb. These FoxPro components, however, are easier to master than the Screen Builder.

For some insight into the nature of the Screen Builder, in seven months of beta testing, the Screen Builder underwent a complex evolution. Testers struggled, much as you have, to master the Screen Builder, and to develop new programming procedures. These testers made numerous suggestions for new features. Fox Software responded both to the difficulties observed and to the requests for enhancements—and, as you have seen, Screen Builder emerged as both an intricate and an extremely powerful tool.

By contrast, the Menu Builder changed little in the same period. Although equally new, Menu Builder was adopted with relative ease by almost all the testers. The Menu Builder's features and options are limited in comparison to the features of the Screen Builder but still provide almost unlimited flexibility in handling the tasks for which this tool is designed.

The Project Manager also underwent relatively minor adjustments. At first, testers found the Project Manager's pivotal role in coordinating the pieces of an application somewhat perplexing. The Project Manager, however, is as simple to learn as the Menu Builder. This tool's advantages and purpose become obvious soon after you begin to use it and become increasingly apparent as time goes on.

The Distribution Kit, the third tool discussed in this chapter, is even simpler to use than the first two. The Distribution Kit is *not* sold with FoxPro 2 as part of the base product. You must purchase the Distribution Kit separately if you want to develop and distribute applications to people who do not own copies of FoxPro 2. The Project Manager alone is sufficient to *build applications* for distribution to other registered users of FoxPro 2. The Distribution Kit provides the capability of creating applications that work *without wires*; that is, without the underlying FoxPro 2 development tools. Because this tool's task is essentially subordinate to the Project Manager's, the Distribution Kit is treated as an option of the Project Manager in FoxPro 2; therefore, both tools are covered here together.

Building Your Own Menus

FoxPro's menu system is usually referred to as SYSMENU. In FoxPro 2, you can use SYSMENU's native pads and options (the System pads and menu names in the documentation) when creating new menus. You can remove all pads and options you don't like or need and add others you do want; SYSMENU is completely customizable in FoxPro 2 and in programs. Although all the menu systems and commands available in FoxPro 1 still are available to use, none of these items can remain active and accessible during a READ, as SYSMENU can. Because SYSMENU is so powerful and configurable, you may never need to resort to other menu systems in FoxPro 2.

By default, SYSMENU is ON in all programs, which means that the user can access SYSMENU by pressing F10 or Alt, or by double-clicking the right mouse button. If you decide not to use SYSMENU or to make SYSMENU temporarily unavailable, you can SET SYSMENU OFF. If, however, you want SYSMENU constantly available, as in the interactive environment, you SET SYSMENU AUTOMATIC. After you finish working on a particular task or in an application, you can return SYSMENU to the original set of pads and popups provided by FoxPro; just SET SYSMENU TO DEFAULT.

The Menu Builder is the design tool that enables you to customize SYSMENU. Like the Screen Builder, Menu Builder builds a table from options you designate. The template program GENMENU.PRG (similar to GENSCRN) then employs standard FoxPro procedures on the menu table (a file with the extension MNX). Menu Builder generates a program (with the extension MPR) that DEFINEs the MENU to specifications.

You DO the generated MPR program just as you can DO a SPR or PRG command file, or you can incorporate the program into a larger application, as is shown in the section of this chapter that deals with the Project Manager.

Menu Design Choices

A certain blurring of the distinction between *interactive* and *programmatic* use of FoxPro 2 results from the capability to tailor SYSMENU. Remember from Chapter 1 that the Organize application attached itself to the System menu pad, and you were returned to the Command window. Unlike conventional applications, Organize did not prevent you from continuing to issue interactive commands that USEd other databases, executed other programs, or performed other tasks—yet Organize always remained available as a discrete application.

After you chose an Organize option, SYSMENU became restricted to Organize-specific tasks and you were, in the conventional sense, definitely placed *inside* a running application.

If, however, you look at HELPTREE.MPR, you see a program that expands even further the envelope of what you may consider an application.

HELPTREE.MPR is a stand-alone menu program (found in the \GOODIES\HELPTREE directory, under the main FoxPro program directory). If this program was installed among the FoxPro optional files, use the Program Do menu option now to execute HELPTREE.MPR. As you see in figure 14.1, Helptree is an organizing tool for FoxPro's help file. Although installing this program on the SYSMENU bar adds a Help pad, just as Organize adds itself to the System pad, when you use Helptree you remain completely within the interactive environment. If you choose the Helptree Search option, shown in figure 14.2, you see a dialog similar to FoxPro's native dialogs. (This dialog is patterned exactly after the Filer's Find dialog, as you see when the Filer, one of FoxPro's additional productivity features, is discussed in Chapter 15.) Just as when you access the native dialogs, SYSMENU features inappropriate to the current task become unavailable, but otherwise, the environment remains unchanged.

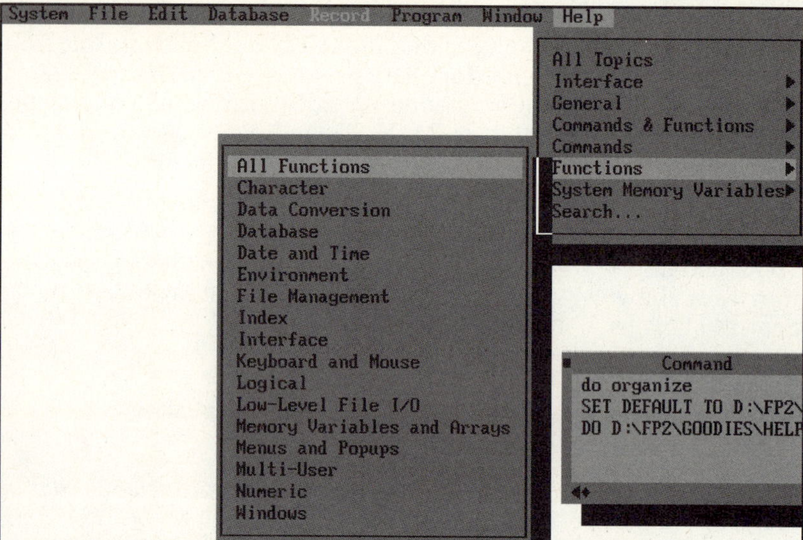

FIG. 14.1

HELPTREE.MPR in use.

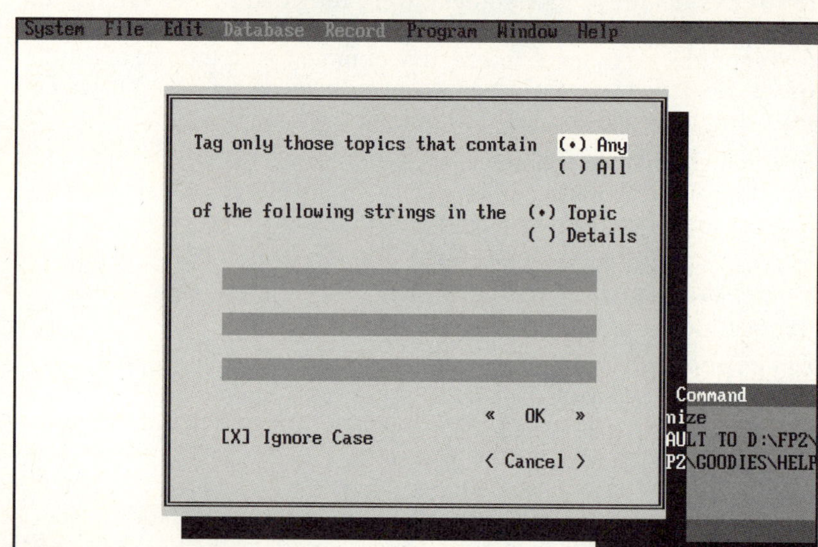

FIG. 14.2

Helptree's Search option, which is a model dialog like the native FoxPro dialogs.

The Command window still is available in the Helptree application (which functions in the interactive environment), although you can't execute a command until you exit the dialog.

At the other end of the spectrum (and as you also saw in Chapter 1) is the version of SYSMENU in use during a FoxApp-generated application, such as the PRODUCT.APP you created. All options are completely tailored to the needs of the currently executing program. The Command window is never available, and you can't USE other tables or perform any other interactive functions.

Deciding whether the menu is going to be part of the interactive environment or included in a self-contained program may be the most pivotal choice you make as you begin to design the interface of the program, but this choice is still only one of many choices. Because manipulating the Menu Builder is relatively easy, this section first discusses menu design in some depth. Determining the options to add to the menu and how to organize these options is one of the most difficult and most significant parts of the menu creation process.

Planning a menu in FoxPro or in any other computer software is a task that shares many attributes with the real-world object on which the *menu* metaphor is based. Whether an offering of hundreds of choices or a simple plan for a family dinner, a menu must be *balanced* (include everything necessary) and *inviting* (encourage people to try the items offered). The *courses* also must follow a progression that seems logical to onlookers.

If the *consumers* of this application don't like the menu, you don't necessarily have to throw out all the results of the *cooking*, but (as parents have said to children for time immemorial) how can you discover whether you like something if you won't try it?

As in Chapter 11's discussion of interface design, some guidelines are offered here for you to remember when you plan menus. Also remember the principles suggested there—consistency, clarity, and comfort.

All menu choices should be easy to follow. The Menu Builder enables you to build submenu upon submenu; a menu pad can lead to a popup, a choice from the popup can make another popup appear with further popups, and so on in a *cascade* of choices. Don't descend through more levels than you absolutely need. These kinds of hierarchies are difficult for users to remember, and making the users search unnecessarily to perform tasks isn't the best way to provide choices.

Whenever possible, avoid creating separate menu options that must be accomplished in a rigid sequence. You may need to post transactions before a certain month-end procedure can be executed. At the least, the application *must* provide an iron-clad check so that it refuses to run the month-end closing while transactions remain unposted. Users, however, get frustrated if, after choosing an option and setting up a printer with the appropriate forms and making other preparations, they are told that they cannot complete the job.

A second, somewhat better choice is to disable the month-end option while any unposted transactions remained in the files. However, the user may receive no immediate and obvious clues from the system about how to gain access to this option again.

The most suitable plan for this situation may be to have the month-end option look for unposted transactions, inform the user of the situation, and ask directly for further directions in a friendly manner, as in the following on-screen message: `Unposted transactions remain in the file. Do you want to post the transactions now, or continue later?` The posting option is then run directly from the month-end option if the user desires.

Occasionally a menu can present a single task in multiple ways, to give the user greater flexibility and control. When you consider which tasks to assign to menus, as opposed to control buttons in the screen sets, the advantages of a certain degree of redundancy become even more apparent.

FoxPro's documentation suggests using controls for reversible, commonly used options, reserving menu choices for less commonly used and more permanent changes. If you think about the standard SYSMENU Edit choices, which are reversible and commonly used, you see at once that you cannot possibly be consistent about this rule. (Implementing the Edit features through procedures you write is very difficult, whether for a menu option or a control button on a screen. Your versions of SYSMENU must almost certainly incorporate some of Edit's features by retaining the features in native form.)

A better rule-of-thumb is to restrict permanent and seldom-used choices to the menu while *repeating* the choices you want to make especially convenient as control buttons and menu options. The user then can select the choice instantly from the screen or use the hotkey a menu option affords.

How then do you decide what tasks belong on the menu? Resolving this decision is not too different from deciding what chapters belong in a book or—as is suggested in Chapter 16 where you start exploring programming in detail—from organizing the structure of a program. Usually, you begin by attempting to list all the jobs you want to accomplish in the application. You then rearrange and add to this list, noting which jobs are sub-procedures of others and which jobs must be split into separate actions. An outline format can help you here. You revise the outline as needed when new requirements must be met and new tasks are added to the system.

After you know what the tasks are, how do you physically arrange these tasks in a menu? The outline you prepared can serve as a basis for menu organization. Some attention to language also can provide you with an implicit organizing principle. Tasks in an application can be thought of as simple imperative sentences, much like FoxPro commands. Tasks start with a verb, the action to be taken (such as add, edit, or copy) and end with a predicate, or object, on which the verb's action impacts (usually files and records).

In most well-designed application menus, these verbs and objects are consistently placed. If a menu pad initiates an action, such as Report, the associated popup contains the objects available for use with the action (in this case, all the output formats available for reporting). If, however, the menu pad is a noun, such as Product, the associated popup contains all the actions you can take that involve the Product table.

Another possible approach is to create a menu pad name as a noun that represents a *group* of objects with all the popup options containing other nouns that are members of this group. For example, in the menu you design later in this chapter, you create a Tables menu pad that contains a popup bar for each table in the database. Each bar enables the user to perform the same action, data entry, for one table. Each bar's prompt is the name of the table to which it provides access.

When you design menu options to add to SYSMENU, these options should incorporate logic that disables and enables them appropriately, according to other tasks being performed. This feature also must appear consistent. If you disable the month-end procedure in the preceding description while the user is adding a transaction record, you may want to disable this procedure when records in the client file and other tables are being added, too, even if the disabling isn't equally crucial in all cases.

Previous experience with the default SYSMENU may have made you aware that no menu can be 100 percent faithful to these rules. Luckily, hunting through the choices in a menu is not an entirely unrewarding experience; on the occasions when you meandered around SYSMENU looking for a correct option for the task-at-hand, you probably discovered one or two handy features you had not previously seen. Users of your applications can enjoy this experience too, as long as they perceive the feeling of uncertainty as a momentary exception rather than as a rule.

Most database management systems include the following basic tasks:

- Input, in which records are added and edited to the basic tables or are incorporated from other computer file formats, or both
- Output, in which queries are processed and results are sent to reports, labels, summary tables, other computer file formats, and so on

- Setup and utilities, in which files, directories, and system parameters necessary to run the application are established, security passwords are recorded, and lookup files are filled
- System maintenance, in which files can be reinitialized and indexes can be rebuilt if necessary, error logs can be accessed (refer to Chapter 18 for information on error handling within an application)

Every application also takes care of housekeeping chores that the user does not initiate, such as opening the files needed for the application. These chores are discussed in Chapter 16, when you learn about program structure; you also see some ways you can integrate the chores into the application when you use the Project Manager in a following section of this chapter. Here, you see how the chores of which the user *is* aware—the application's *visible* responsibilities—become part of the System menu.

The Menu Builder Options

Begin the creation of a menu file, as usual, by choosing first the File and then the New option and choosing Menu as the type, or type the command **CREATE MENU** in the Command window. You also may notice, with some relief, that the number of available options on the Menu pad are fewer than you saw in the Screen Builder. As shown in figure 14.3, General Options are available that correspond to the Screen Layout, are menu-wide in their effect, and are available from the first menu popup choice. The second choice is labeled Menu Bar Options, which are instructions that affect this *menu level* as a whole.

This second choice changes as you define and edit different menu levels. The Menu Bar is SYSMENU's top level, the pads defined for the top row of the screen. A menu popup activated when a pad is chosen is the second level. A popup activated when a menu popup option is chosen is the third level. The second Menu popup choice enables each subsidiary level to have a procedure, a *mark* character, and a color scheme assigned to all the elements, as a group. *Each procedure, mark, or color scheme, however, can be superseded by instructions for individual elements at the next lower level.*

This hierarchy is simpler to manipulate and more useful than you may think. Figure 14.4 contains a rather frivolous example that graphically demonstrates the way these instruction changes work. The mark is turned on (SET to .T.) for the entire menu and set to the character ♪. This instruction is superseded for the File pad, which is set to the character ↨. The Window popup elements also are marked as a group but this instruction is superseded with individual instructions for the

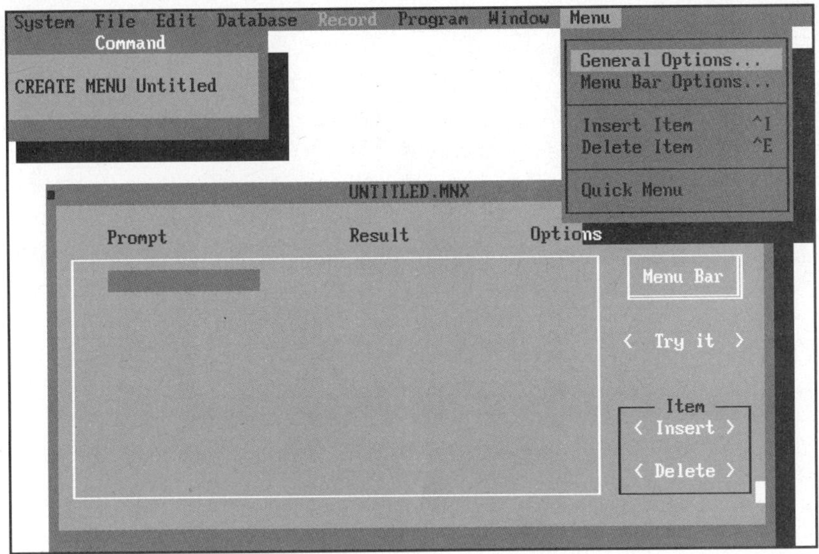

FIG. 14.3

Getting ready to create a menu by using the Menu pad options.

Hide bar (which has a different mark) and for the `Zoom ↑` bar (where the mark is turned off).

Similarly, you can activate one global procedure for every menu item or every option on a single popup and then *countermand* the procedure for specific elements assigned to each item's unique instructions. For convenience, you may want to create one such procedure to perform task routing for every menu option. This procedure examines the current status of the menu and determines what action to take. The status of the menu and the menu choice that called the procedure can be evaluated from a number of FoxPro functions, including PAD( ), PROMPT( ), PRMBAR( ), MRKBAR( ), and POPUP( ).

You start by using the Quick Menu option, which creates a duplicate of the default SYSMENU, complete in every respect. Like Quick Report and Quick Screen, this option is only available when the menu you're designing still is completely empty. Unlike these options, however, after you choose Quick Menu you are faced with no more choices or dialogs. The result you see is shown in figure 14.5. Does this result look familiar? It should—the items in the `Prompt` column are all the pads available on the default SYSMENU, with which you have worked since you first loaded FoxPro. The version created by Quick Menu is similar to the default SYSMENU, except for three differences: the File menu popup's Close All option and the Window menu popup's Hide All and Show All options. These three options are available on the default SYSMENU only when it is accessed with the Shift key but are provided by Quick Menu as standard options along with their non-shifted partners (Close and Hide).

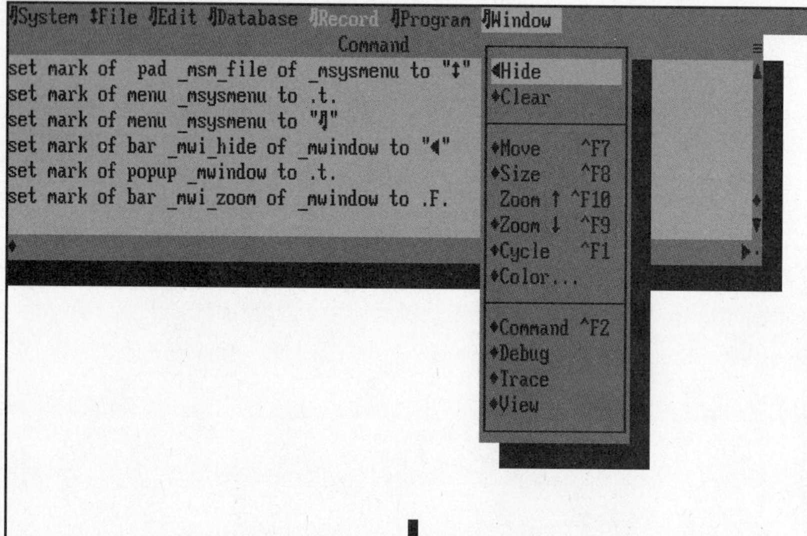

FIG. 14.4

The SYSMENU is marked as a whole, and individual pads, popups, and bars also received mark instructions.

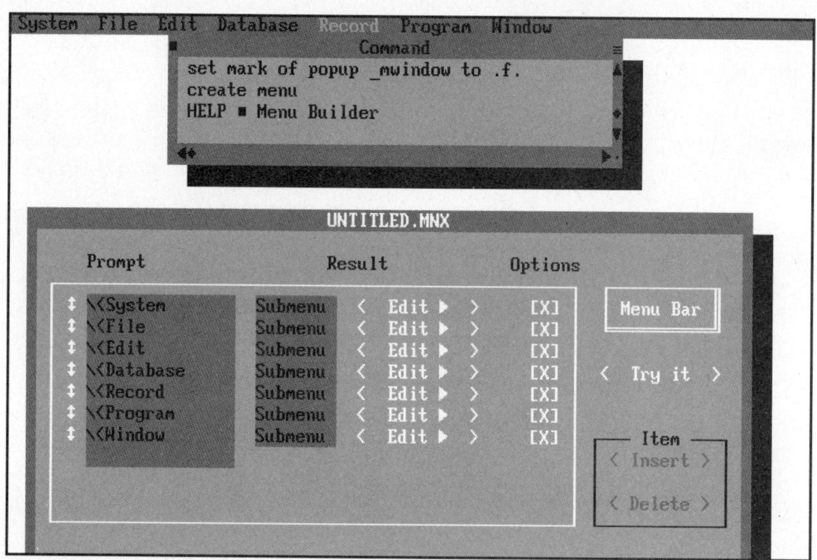

FIG. 14.5

The Quick Menu reproduces the System Menu.

The Prompt list may look familiar in another way: the \< characters are used here, as they were in prompts for control objects in a screen to highlight a letter in the prompt and indicate that this symbol is the hotkey for this option. You also can type **\-** alone in a Prompt when defining popup bars to separate the popup options into meaningful groups with dividing lines (although doing this on the menu bar makes little sense). You also can type \ at the beginning of any Prompt name to make the item unselectable, which is the equivalent of using the Disable option for an object you define in the Screen Builder. More convenient ways are available to disable a menu item conditionally, however, as you see in following sections.

Your menu requirements may include a need for variable menu prompts. Suppose that you want to enable the users of an application to change the prompts to any task titles that they find comfortable and easy to remember, rather than forcing them to use what you feel are appropriate designations for each choice. You can use the Menu Builder and GENMENU.

GENMENU surrounds any words you place in the Prompt text box with double quotation marks, as follows:

```
DEFINE PAD My_Pad OF _MSYSMENU PROMPT "My Prompt" COLOR SCHEME 3
```

To DEFINE a PROMPT using a variable, you have to concatenate your variable with an extra set of quotation marks so that the variable appears surrounded by null strings when the code is run. If your users' prompt choice for a particular bar is placed into the variable *barprmpt1*, you type the following into the Prompt text box:

"+barprmpt1+"

GENMENU generates the code to look as follows:

```
DEFINE PAD My_Pad OF _MSYSMENU PROMPT ""+barprmpt1+""
```

You can include literal strings along with your variable prompt. If you place the following in the Prompt text box:

"+"First option: "+barprmpt1+"

GENMENU generates

```
DEFINE PAD My_Pad OF _MSYSMENU PROMPT ""+"First option:  "+barprmpt1+""
```

All you have to do is make sure that the variable is properly initialized with the users' choice, and the menu prompt reads the way they want it to.

To the right of the `Prompt` column and its list of labels, you find the Menu Builder's `Result` column. Here, not surprisingly, you define the consequences that result from choosing any individual menu option. All the pads on the menu bar in the menu currently have `Submenu` as a result, because each default pad on SYSMENU leads to a menu popup.

Use the <`Insert`> push button or Menu option (the shortcut is <Ctrl-I>) anywhere you like in the list to create a new item. You see that the

Result is set to `Submenu` by default, but the pushbutton to the right of `Submenu` reads `Create` rather than `Edit` because you haven't yet assigned popup bars for this item. Press the Tab key or otherwise move the cursor into the text box that reads `Submenu` and select it to see the list of other possible Results, as shown in figure 14.6.

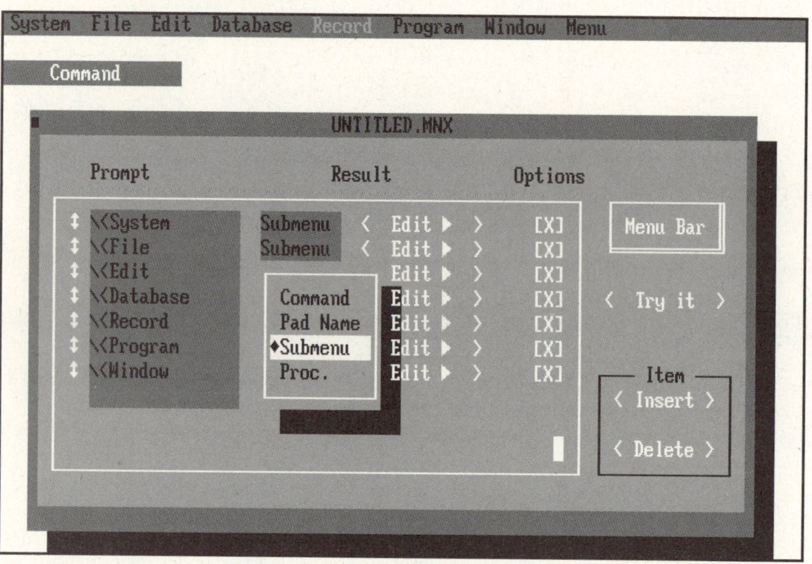

FIG. 14.6

The Menu Results selections available.

If you choose `Command` as the menu option result, the `Create` button changes to a text box. Here, you can type any FoxPro command you like, and the command is executed when this menu option is chosen. (Although this box appears limited, you have as much room as you need; as you type, the text scrolls.)

`Pad Name` is the Result selection that enables you to assign one of FoxPro 2's native system options to the new prompt. At lower menu levels, this result changes to `Bar Name`. You type the pad or bar name in a text box just as you might type a command.

If you look back for a moment at figure 14.4, you see the commands used to assign the various menu marks in the Command window, referring to the different bars and pads by special names. Each native element of SYSMENU is assigned a special *pad* or *bar name*, beginning with an underscore, that you and GENMENU.PRG can use to reference the element. All the bar names are available in the on-line help file under the topic Menu System Names, as well as a complete chart in the *Commands and Functions* manual under an entry of the same name. FoxPro's SYS(2013) also returns a complete list of these names, should you ever need to check them quickly or as part of a program. Nevertheless, if you generate a Quick Menu as you are doing here, these names are entered for you. You can cut and paste the names from the Quick Menu or from the help file without bothering to remember these names.

SYS(2013) does not provide bar, popup, and pad names for what is sometimes referred to as the *conditional* menu pads in FoxPro 2. These options appear and disappear from the default SYSMENU as you work, depending on the task in which you are engaged. When you are MODIFYing a LABEL, REPORT, SCREEN, MENU, PROJECT, or STRUCTURE, each of these tasks has an associated menu popup. When you use the Diary, a Browse window, the Filer, Expression Builder, or Macros, each of these interface elements has an associated menu popup with specialized choices.

FoxPro 2 does not offer any access to these menu popups or any way to remove them from your SYSMENU (short of SETting SYSMENU OFF) when you are performing one of these functions. The only partial exception is Browse, possibly because there are programmatic equivalents for the Browse menu options. You cannot access the bar names on the Browse menu, but you can issue a Browse with the NOMENU clause and then arrange the Browse any way you prefer, using the command's numerous clauses and switches. You can create your own Browse menu popup offering these options to your users.

The fourth Result selection is Proc. (or procedure). If you choose Proc., the rightmost column again reads `Create` in a push button. Select the button and the `Create` prompt changes to `Edit`, and a text editing window appears, as shown in figure 14.7. The editing window enables you to add a code snippet—just like the snippets in which you typed procedures for various objects and clauses in the Screen Builder—which is executed when you later choose this menu item.

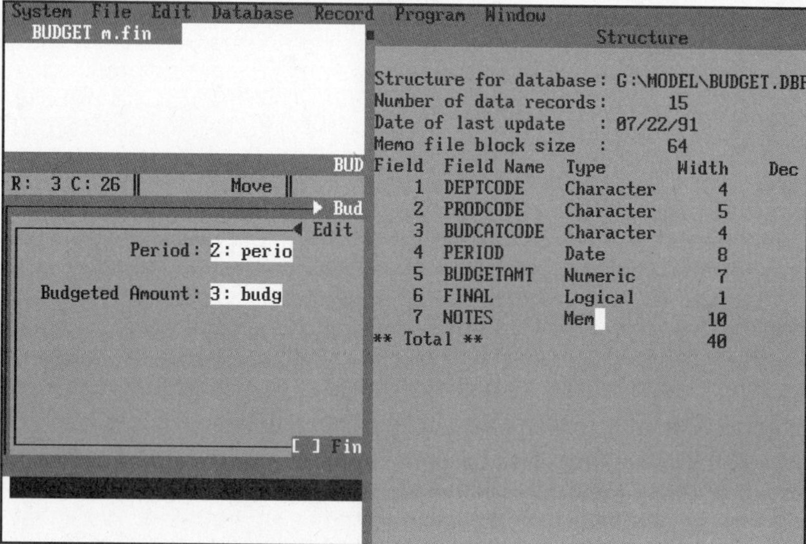

FIG. 14.7

Creating a procedure for a menu option.

At the far left of the Prompt column, you see double-headed arrows typical of a FoxPro 2 list that contains items you can shuffle. You may need to alter the relative positions of menu items many times before you are satisfied with the order. You can click-drag the arrows or press the Ctrl key with the up- or down- arrow key when the cursor rests in any column to move the menu items up and down in the list.

There is one more column, labeled `Options`, at the far right side of the screen. If you select a check box from this column, the Options dialog appears to enable you to assign more attributes to this menu choice.

A menu *shortcut* dialog is shown in figure 14.8, along with the Options dialog. Unlike menu hotkeys, which can be used only when the menu is currently active (after you pressed **Alt** or **F10**, or double-right-clicked the mouse so that FoxPro expects the next keystroke to *belong* to the menu), *shortcuts* are active all the time, as long as the menu choice to which they belong is not disabled. For this reason, you cannot use single letters and other keys as shortcuts. Shortcuts are always combination keypresses, such as Alt-S, the default for the System pad, or Ctrl-A, default shortcut for the Select All text option. (Imagine assigning the single keypress *A* as a shortcut and then trying to type in an Edit region!)

You press the combination of keys you want to assign, and the combinations appears in the Key Label text box. Then you can move the cursor into the Key Text box with the Tab key or the mouse and type the *remainder* of the shortcut that you want to appear in the menu popup next to the prompt.

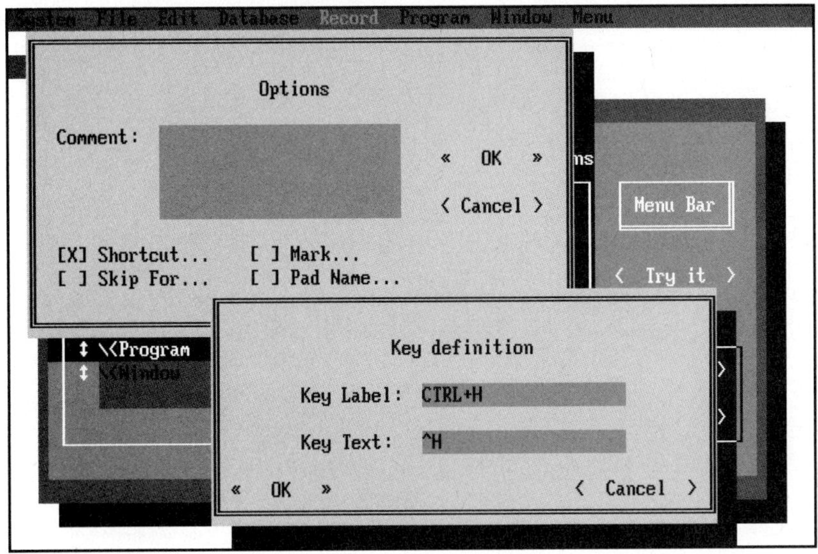

FIG. 14.8

The Menu Item Options and the subsidiary Shortcut dialogs.

Choosing Skip For from the Options dialog brings up the Expression Builder, with the Report Writer and Label Designer. This expression should evaluate to a *logical* value. When the expression evaluates to .T., the menu option becomes disabled, and when the expression evaluates to .F., the menu option becomes available for use. Many different ways are available to test for the suitability of a menu option. The window functions can be helpful here. For certain edit or dialog windows, you may disable some items if the WVISIBLE( ) function returns .T.. You may also disable an option if a test of RDLEVEL( ), the function that tells you how many nested READs are currently in progress, returns a result greater than a particular number. You also may disable an option if certain tables are either USED( ) or NOT USED( ). The important thing, as previously indicated, is to disable and enable options according to a logical pattern both discernible and predictable from the user's point of view.

The `Mark` check box was discussed in a previous section of this chapter. Use it to assign a character that appears on-screen when you SET MARK of this menu option TO .T.. Choosing this check box brings up the same modified ASCII table you used to pick special characters for Box objects in the Report Writer.

The Pad Name option (replaced by a Bar # option in other menu levels) is similar to the Window Name option in the Screen Builder. By default, GENMENU creates names for all the elements of the menu, just as GENSCRN creates window titles and procedure names, but the Menu and Screen Builders give you the opportunity to name the items if you want to refer to these names in procedures you write. If you chose Pad

Name or Bar # for the Result type (if you use the native SYSMENU elements), you do not see this option in the Options dialog because the pad or bar was already given a name now used by both GENMENU and the procedures you are designing.

Another option available for each single menu item is Comment, which functions in the same way here as it does in Reports, Labels, Queries, and Screens. You can keep notes to yourself here; as is seen in Chapter 18 when building a help system is discussed, these notes can become the basis of a custom-designed help file for your system. If you edit GENMENU to include new capabilities, the Comment text entry also can hold information for use in menu-generating procedures that you design.

Using the Comments field, you easily can extend GENMENU to generate MESSAGE clauses for your menu items, although the Menu Builder doesn't include an option to create them. This simple procedure is discussed in Chapter 17.

Return from the Options dialog to the main Menu Builder window and notice the popup control in the upper right. You use this control to move up a menu level if you are in a submenu. To move down, you also can select the `<Edit>` push button for any option that has a Submenu result. *Tour* the Quick Menu now and become acquainted with the structure, noticing the shortcuts in use, the hotkeys, and the hierarchy of items with which you are already familiar. If you check the `Menu` popup frequently, you see that the second choice changes to provide a level-wide set of options appropriate to each submenu you investigate. As previously indicated and as you see in figure 14.9, level-wide options include the assignment of a popup Name, a Procedure to be used for this entire popup (except for entries on it which have Results of their own assigned), a Color Scheme, and a Mark character.

TIP

So far, very little time has been spent discussing colors and the *color scheme* system in FoxPro. Chapter 15 discusses the basic concepts of the color scheme system, which you can apply throughout FoxPro. In the discussion of SYSMENU, however, just remember that you can choose a color scheme individually by submenu. This capability is a relatively arcane feature; different color schemes for different menu popups integrated into one SYSMENU is warranted only in special circumstances.

If you choose to alter the colors of all or part of your menu system, you may decide not to avail yourself of the Menu Builder's capability. You may want your menu or a particular popup to change colors dynamically in response to certain conditions. GENMENU is written to DEFINE each menu element with an explicit COLOR SCHEME clause. Each element's colors are fixed until that element is re-DEFINED. If you alter GENMENU not to issue the COLOR SCHEME clauses, you can use the FoxPro color control commands to alter the *color scheme* that governs the menu bar and menu popups (schemes 3 and 4), and the color of menu elements are altered immediately.

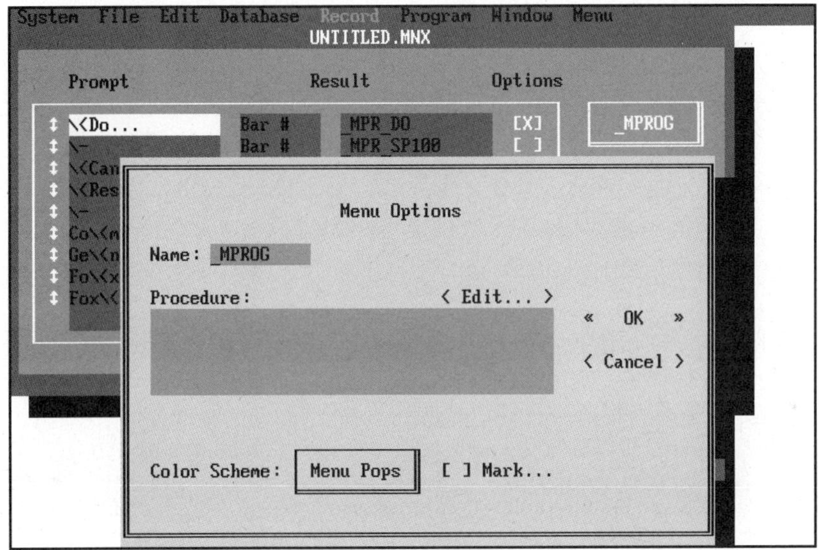

FIG. 14.9

Submenu-wide options in the Menu Builder.

The final options of the Menu Builder are contained in the General Options dialog. If you access this dialog now (which is available from any menu level) you find options only slightly more extensive than the choices available for submenus. Here, you can create the *Procedure* that executes for *all* menu options that have no set of instructions. You can set a `Mark` globally for the menu. You also can specify the *Location*—relative to the existing version of SYSMENU—of the menu options you are defining. The default is a complete `Replace` of the current SYSMENU. All other choices enable you to alter the existing SYSMENU instead. You saw how `Append` works when ORGANIZE and HELPTREE attached themselves to the SYSMENU. If you choose `Before` or `After`, as you did in figure 14.10, a list of the native SYSMENU pads appears so you can place all new options exactly where you want them.

The General Options dialog also uses check boxes that enable you to create `Setup` and `Cleanup` snippets for the SYSMENU. The setup code for a menu can be similar to the code of a screen or screen set; you can initialize values and set up conditions that force various menu options to be enabled or disabled. (Remember that you cannot reference and alter menu elements in the setup code because these elements aren't defined at this point of the generated program.)

The cleanup code, however, does not function in quite the way you may expect. In screens, all the action takes place at a READ command that precedes the cleanup code. UDFs tacked on the end of cleanup are available as subroutines of the SPR program, which continues to be active for a long time. Menu code, in contrast, DEFINEs the components of the new SYSMENU and the action taken when any of the components are chosen. Then the cleanup code *is immediately executed*, and in most cases the MPR program is no longer active. Control returns to the calling program or the interactive environment. Therefore, if you have a menu option with a Command result and if the command is to DO a procedure that you placed in the cleanup code for the menu, you need to issue the command in the following manner:

```
DO my_proc IN my_menu.mpr
```

Now, FoxPro can find the procedure when it is called by the menu option, although the program MY_MENU.MPR ceased to be active as soon as the menu was DEFINEd.

If your application changes the default directory from the directory in which MY_MENU.PRG is kept, or if your menu items are meant to be added to an interactive environment, your menu commands must provide some help for FoxPro to find this program again. The LOCFILE( ) function has been provided to enable your programs to ask the user to find files when they are not found where expected.

Look at LOCFILE( )'s syntax in the file-opening code generated by GENSCRN in Chapter 13. You should use this syntax in commands you use as Results in menu code. In the preceding example, your command would be as follows:

```
DO my_proc IN LOCFILE
        ("my_menu.mpr","mpr|mpx|app","Where is my_menu?")
```

All LOCFILE( )'s parameters are enclosed in quotation marks. The first one is the file that should be used. The other parameters are optional. The second is the list of extensions that should be checked by FoxPro for files to be displayed in the LOCFILE( ) dialog. The third parameter is a question that can appear in the dialog to help prompt the user as she attempts to locate the appropriate file.

If you are distributing applications to other users, as you learn to do using the Project Manager and Distribution Kit later in this chapter, you include the APP extension as one of the choices in LOCFILE( )'s second parameter. However, for FoxPro 2 to find a procedure in an APP file, *the procedure must be contained in the project's main file*. Keep this restriction in mind as you build menus and decide where to position the procedures they require.

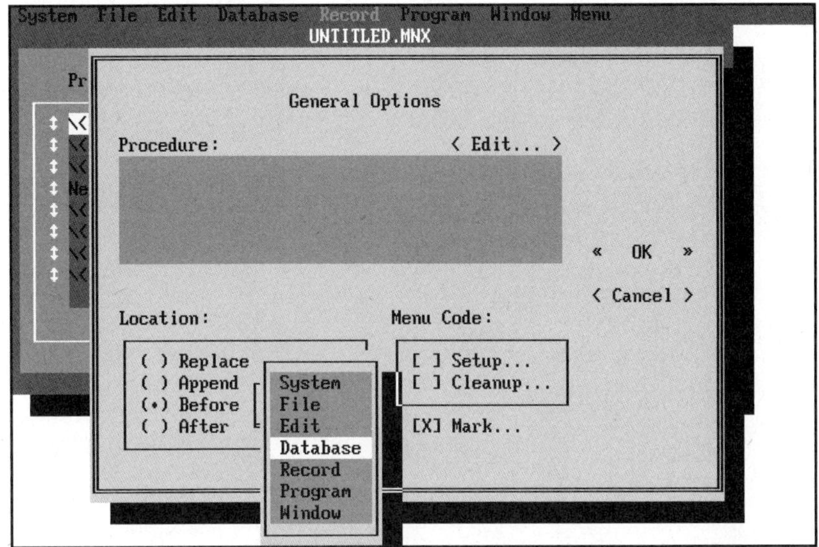

FIG. 14.10

General Options dialog in the Menu Builder.

Had enough touring? You have looked at all the options and facilities of the Menu Builder now. Exit the General Options and return to the main Menu window, where you are going to quickly build a rudimentary menu for the Omnipresent Widgets application. To start with a clean slate, use the `<Delete>` push button or the Menu popup option (the shortcut is Ctrl-E) to remove the New Item practice pad from the main menu bar.

Beginning with the System menu popup, you do not use the internal bar name _MST_HELP for Omnipresent Widget's help system. The reasons for this step are discussed in Chapter 18 but at the moment you don't yet *have* a help file written for this application. Change the Help option's Result to a Command and, as the command to be run, type the following line:

```
WAIT WINDOW "Help System not yet available." NOWAIT
```

NOTE Besides providing an example of a menu option that executes a command, you just demonstrated a typical technique used when designing menus for large systems. Although not all features are finished and available when the first changes are implemented, *fleshing out* the menu as fully as possible right from the beginning is helpful for both developers and users. Developers use these *mock-ups* to provide reminders of tasks not yet accomplished, but more importantly, the mock-ups help to determine the general flow of the application. Users become aware of the jobs they can eventually expect to be able to do and can provide early feedback if they spot missing pieces or task-grouping that seems to make no sense.

Because you made the first real adjustment to this menu, save the adjusted menu now, to the name WIDGET.MNX.

Move to the File menu popup, where you are going to eliminate all the options here except the last three options, Printer Setup, Print, and Quit (most of these File options become disabled while an application runs anyway). Although you are temporarily running the application menu in the interactive environment, in the Project Manager section you are going to integrate this menu into a larger program. Removing SYSMENU options that you never plan to enable is a good idea because users otherwise find these options perplexing. These options also confuse the issue for you when you are concentrating on the menu design process.

Highlight the `\<Quit` and press Ctrl-C to copy it. Go back to the end of the System popup list and press Ctrl-V to paste a copy of the `Quit` there. Notice that the Bar # and name are *not* pasted along with the prompt; any connected options also are lost in the copying process. Unlike attributes of report and screen objects, you must copy these menu attributes separately (they are not *attached* to the prompt).

Here, you're not going to use the default Result of Command, nor are you going to use the Bar # associated with FoxPro's native Quit option. Choose Procedure for the result and enter the following code snippet:

```
IF "Support Library" $ VERSION(1)
   * DO any necessary cleanup
   QUIT
ELSE
   SET SYSMENU TO DEFAULT
   ACTIVATE WINDOW Command IN SCREEN
   * DO other cleanup
   CANCEL
ENDIF
```

If you type **WAIT WINDOW VERSION(1)**, this command (as shown in figure 14.11 along with the code snippet you are creating) returns the version and serial number of the FoxPro versions you are currently running. This simple test looks for identification “Support Library,” which is found in all VERSION(1) returns under FoxPro’s Distribution Kit, discussed in a following section of this chapter. If this menu is run under any of the Distribution Kit facilities, rather than under the development version of FoxPro you are now using, a **Quit** command takes the user directly to DOS. (The comment in the code reminds you to do any necessary cleanup first; you learn more about the kinds of chores likely to be included in following sections of this chapter and in Chapter 16.) The Distribution Kit options enable users to run pre-created and compiled programs, and no interactive environment exists here to *drop back* into.

TIP

Although for the moment, the menu may not do much good outside the development version environment, providing for distributed applications separately is a good habit to form. A common approach is to create *two* Quit options; an *Exit to Fox* choice and a *Quit to DOS* choice. You can add **"Support Library" $ VERSION(1)** as the Skip For condition of the *Exit to Fox* option, which disables this choice when the menu is executed under a distributed application.

If, however, the user has the development version of FoxPro, as you are doing now, an *extremely important* provision you must make is to provide at least a minimal recovery path after you edit SYSMENU. Without explicitly restoring the Command window, as you do in the ELSE portion of the preceding example procedure, you may lose access to the Command window if you remove references to this window in SYSMENU! Fox’s documentation suggests that you set up a special hotkey procedure as a *panic button*, by typing the following command in the Command window before you start testing the revised window:

```
ON KEY LABEL Alt-F9 SET SYSMENU TO DEFAULT
```

(Substitute any key combination you prefer.) The Quit option may suffice, and you can set up a Shortcut to perform the same function as the previous ON KEY LABEL command.

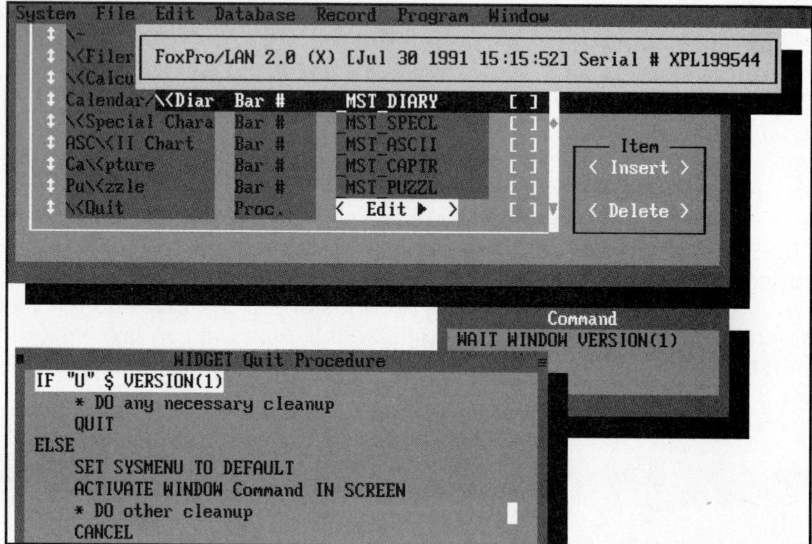

FIG. 14.11

Creating a Quit procedure in the menu.

Always separate the Quit option from other menu choices; `<Insert>` another bar before it and type \- as the Prompt. You only need to make this change; the default Result of Command provides a separator bar as long as you type no command in the text box.

Returning to the File popup option, highlight and copy the Bar # for the Print... option (_MFI_PRINT). You also are going to move this option to a new position on the menu, and now that you know the entire line is not pasted together, you may as well save yourself the trouble of remembering the Bar designation because the prompt is easier. On the main menu bar, `<Insert>` a new pad. Type the prompt **\<Utilities** and accept the default Result for a main menu pad, Submenu. Use the Options dialog to assign a Shortcut of Alt-U to this pad (it doesn't matter what the key text says, because the *reminders* won't show on the main menu bar). Now Edit this submenu by providing the submenu with the first bar: type **\<Print...** for the prompt, assign a Result of Bar #, and finally press Ctrl-V to paste the bar name into the accompanying text box. Repeat the procedure to add a **\<Printer Setup...** bar to this popup.

You now can `<Delete>` the File pad from the menu bar. Eliminate the Program pad completely, too, but keep the Edit popup unchanged because you may be editing memo fields and other text in the application, and most of the Edit options are valuable during any text editing.

On the Record pad, you want to keep all the entries that *search* for data, because you provided no mechanisms for this procedure in these programs. You can eliminate the entries that *edit* data (Append, Change, Replace, Delete, and Recall). You can add the Pack and Reindex options from the Database pad in the same way you moved Print. Perhaps you also should make a change in the Prompt of this pad to make it plural; *Records* describes the function a little better. Make the same change to the Window pad. But here you want to change more than the prompt; you also want to change the way in which FoxPro refers to the Windows pad. Choose to Edit the submenu and delete the Name in the Options dialog. This new version will behave differently from the native Window; it will not provide the names of all the active windows on the popup. (You may not want the user switching windows using the menu.) A menu name is required, but any name will do for this pad, except the native system name.

You must be getting a little anxious for a look at the revised menu. In the Menu Builder, you are not looking at a *canvas* on which you are arranging the objects as you do in the Screen Builder and Report Writer. The Menu Builder's format does not permit you to see the results of the work as you proceed, and visualizing the effects of each change you make is crucial in the design process. Fortunately, you don't have to regenerate a menu program file whenever you want to check the work. Notice the `<Try it>` push button in the main menu design window. If you select `<Try it>` now or at any time, the current SYSMENU appears to become the menu you are building. You can click on all options and see all the submenus. If you select an option with a Command result, the Try It dialog displays the associated command. *These are images only*; you cannot run this altered SYSMENU until you generate and install this new menu in place of the default. When you choose `«Done»` from the Try It dialog, the real SYSMENU reappears, and you are placed in the Menu window again (see fig. 14.12).

As you probably figured out, you need a menu pad that enables you to access the screen sets and perform data entry in this system. `<Insert>` a pad between Edit and Database, typing **\<Tables** as the Prompt. As the first entry in the submenu, type **\<Budget Entries** and assign it the Command result **DO budget.spr**. You separate it from data entry for the lookup tables with a separator bar and then add similar entries for **\<Products**, **Budget \<Categories**, **\<Departments**, and all the other tables in the database (you can find a list of these tables in Appendix I). Type the appropriate command for the tables that have screen sets already built for them. Assigning a WAIT WINDOW command to each bar that doesn't have an associated screen set would be silly, however; just edit the Table Menu Options as a whole to supply a Procedure (type **WAIT WINDOW "Data Entry not yet available for this Table."**) for this menu level, and you make the change for all the tables. Remember that any individual bar instructions supersede this procedure.

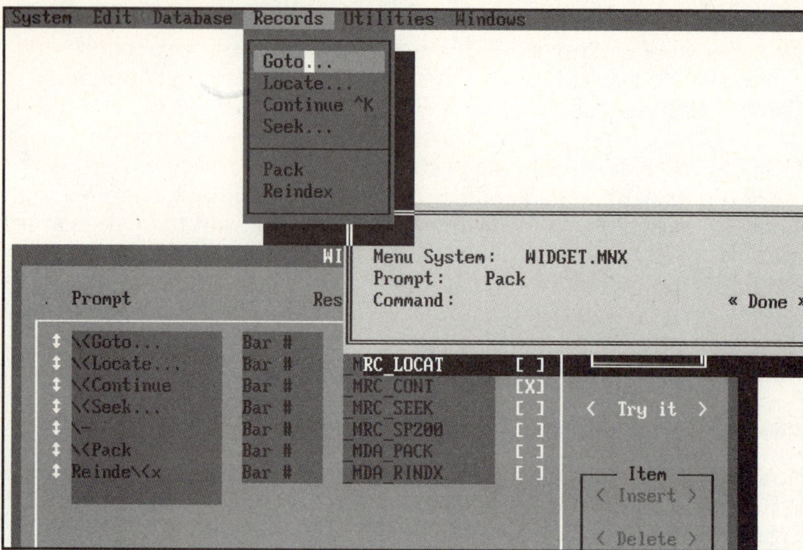

FIG. 14.12

Using the `Try it` option in the Menu Builder, you can check your work.

Returning to the top level of the menu, use the Options dialog for the Tables pad to provide a shortcut by pressing **<ALT-T>**. You also use this dialog's option to supply a Skip For condition; when the Expression Builder appears, type the expression **RDLEVEL( ) > 0**.

NOTE

This expression prevents more than one screen set from being active at a time. With more sophisticated methods, you can edit multiple screen sets at the same time. For now, you need a safeguard to prevent multiple READs of edit from causing a problem.

Now move the Database pad to the place between the Records and Utilities items and rename this pad to **Resu\<lts** because you are going to retain the pad options that may properly be considered output and you are adding the other forms of output here. Notice that the letter *L* is used as the highlighted shortcut key because you already used the initial letter—and all the other letters found in the word *Result.* Giving two different menu options the same shortcut name is bad program design. Don't forget to add the shortcut Alt-L in the Options; just designating the highlighted letter doesn't work. Change the Pad Name here, too, so that the behavior is controlled by you and not by the internal system definition.

From the Database options, you keep Browse, Average, Count, Sum, and Calculate. Note that these options are available only when you are not currently involved in a READ operation. If no table is open, the native Browse option enables you to open one of these options but gives you no mechanism for choosing another, so you must add a **Close \<Table** bar immediately below Browse that performs a simple USE command. This choice is not automatically disabled when you are in a READ because the choice isn't a native System option, so add a Skip For condition of **RDLEVEL( ) > 0** as well.

NOTE Because having an active BROWSE doesn't increase RDLEVEL( ) and doesn't prevent accessing the **Tables** pad—and because of the way you named the windows—a slight *bug* exists in the menu as currently set up. If you are BROWSing the Budget table and then choose to enter Budget data, BUDGET.SPR will *crash*. The application already *sees* a window defined with the name *Budget*, because this name also is the title of the system-created BROWSE window and doesn't DEFINE a new window. You can easily remedy this problem by regenerating the BUDGET.SPR file after adding the following lines at the beginning of BUDGET.SCX's the Setup snippet:

```
#SECTION1
#REDEFINE
#SECTION2
```

Refer to table 13.1, on the Screen Builder generator directives, if you need help.

Setting an order in the table you were BROWSing, without going to a great deal of trouble about it, might be a nice choice. You may remember a choice like this in FoxApp-generated applications. This feature was produced by a screen named GETORDER, which you can find in the \GOODIES\FOXAPP\SCREENS directory under the main FoxPro program directory. You can type **MODIFY SCREEN ?** in the Command window to find and then use the screen now to generate a GETORDER.SPR—be careful when you name the output file that you specify the MODEL directory in which you keep the application!

Add a new option to the Records popup by typing **\<Order...** for the prompt and **DO GETORDER.SPR** for the command, and you're finished. You gave the users a quick way to check any table in the system and use the other (calculation) options on the pad while the table is active.

Ordinarily, you also want to offer a Reports option similar to FoxApp's, which can specify an output device, enable reports to be chosen and enable the user to indicate whether or not to use the associated printer driver setup, no setup, or a different setup when the output is sent to the printer. You can look at FoxApp's screens GTDEST, PRTOPTS, and

PRTSETUP for some examples of how to do this. You also may want to think about creating a special table that holds all the report, label and query names, and perhaps even holds the model report and label files in memo fields so that users can edit these files and add new entries. You can use a *description* field as the PROMPT FIELD for a POPUP that can be ACTIVATEd to enable the users to choose available entries.

Many other additional items exist that you can put on the application menu; you can create a *Filter-builder* like the one in the BROWSER.SCX in the LASER sample application. Other Utilities pad entries can also be made, enabling you to create files in a user-specified data directory and to perform other tasks previously suggested. You have already built a great deal of flexibility into the application menu, and you practiced with all the options the Menu Builder offers. You can gradually expand your knowledge by using it.

For now, just put one Budget report on the Results menu and opt to send the results to the screen. Add a **\<Report on Budget** prompt to the bottom of the Results submenu. If the last-saved MODEL.FRX contains the variable big_item, which you initialized outside the report to *mark* certain items, make sure that the feature is available as part of the reporting Procedure, as shown in the following example:

```
* first find out if the variable exists; they
* may have already created one and you don't want
* to override the current value if they have
IF TYPE("big_item") = "U"
  big_item = 0
ENDIF

* Now find out what value they want to use; this
* screen file is a generic "question"-asker to which
* you pass a question, the name of the variable to
* hold the answer (which you initialize first), and
* a PICTURE clause if you want to use one to format
* the answer. It can look like anything you want,
* and you'll find the simple snippets it requires listed
* in Appendix I.
DO ask.spr WITH "Smallest entry to mark:", ;
  big_item,"99999"

REPORT FORM Model PREVIEW ENVIRONMENT
```

You now are ready to generate and install the menu code. If you're in the main Menu window, the «Generate» push button should be active on the Program menu popup. Select «Generate», and the dialog in figure 14.13 appears. (The last code snipped—the procedure for the Budget Report option—shows at the bottom of the screen.) Again, fewer choices are available to make here than you have with the Screen Builder; after making sure that the output file is going to the appropriate directory and specifying Comments style as you did before (if you want this capability), go ahead and generate the menu code.

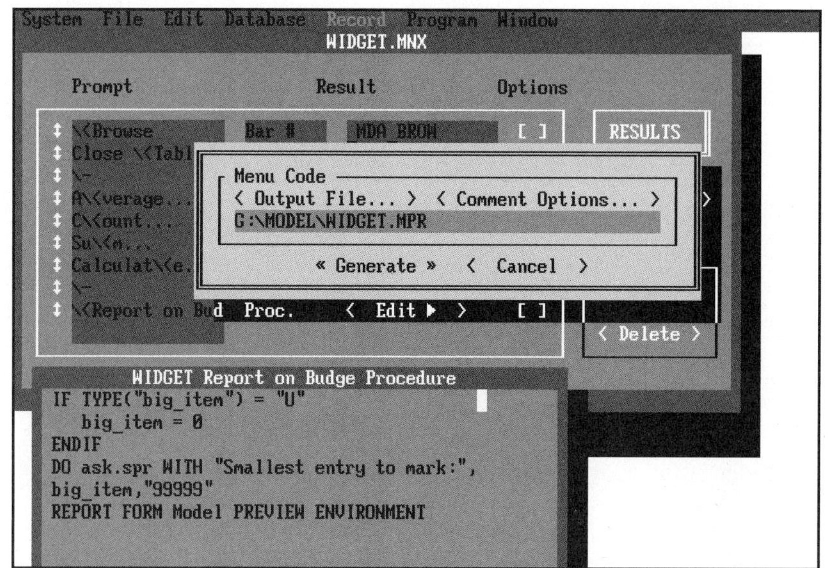

FIG. 14.13

GENMENU's option dialog.

You can type the command **MODIFY COMMAND widget.mpr** to look at the structure of a generated menu program. This code is straightforward, although SYSMENU's *component menu* approach requires quite a few different commands. Helptree has a sub-option that enables you to peruse, as a group, all the Menus And Popups commands and functions.

For now, however, you probably want to **DO widget.mpr** instead and see what happens.

You still have access to the Command window, but this altered SYSMENU makes some options accessible and inaccessible, depending on the current action. In figure 14.14, the Tables menu pad is disabled because you are currently involved in a READ, and the two options on the Utilities pad also, by default, are disabled. The Command window looks as though you can use it—you can click and type in the Command window—but no commands are executed while the READ is in progress.

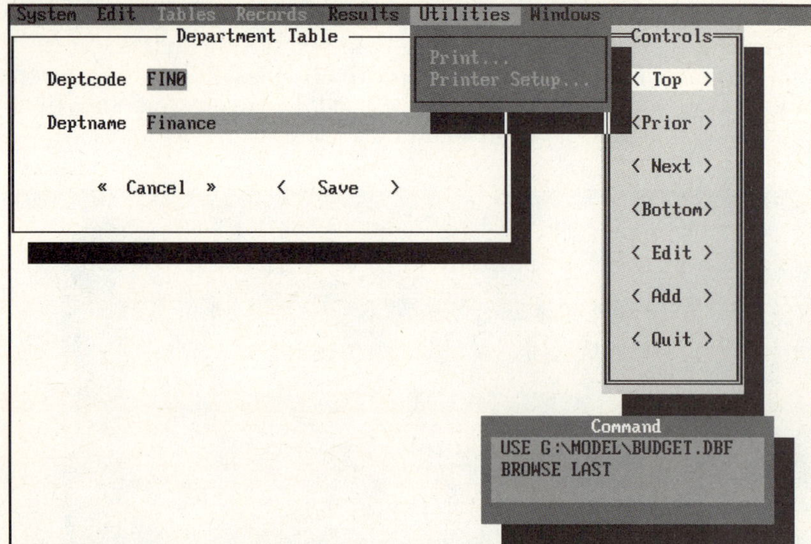

FIG. 14.14

Data Entry in the Revised SYSMENU. Note that the Utilities options are unavailable because a READ is in progress.

As you try out the menu options, you probably notice that the Product table's data-entry system should be redesigned to match the two lookup tables, Budcat and Dept, whose screen sets you designed last, so that you can add records in the tables data-entry system. (None of these screen sets are designed with deletion of records available because lookup codes should rarely be removed from a system. To add this capability, always be sure that none of the related tables contain records that use the lookup code you are removing.)

In figure 14.15, however, you chose to BROWSE the Budget table, and the Print option is available (as the figure shows, you even can print the contents of the current memo field, because the field is open in a window). The Command window also is perfectly usable, except when a dialog is active (this behavior is normal). While you BROWSE, you can choose the Order option or any other option from the Records pad, or the calculation options, which are part of the Results. You may like to try using the Average option to store the average of the BUDGET.BUDGETAMT field values to the variable name big_item. As shown in figure 14.16, you then can run the Report on Budget entry with this figure as the default amount; all budget items greater-than-or-equal-to the average amount are marked on the report.

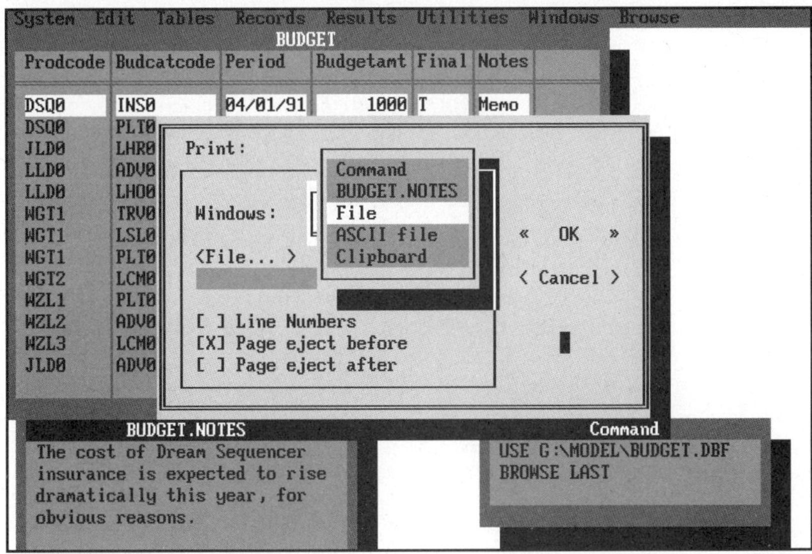

FIG. 14.15

Choosing the Print option while a Browse is in progress.

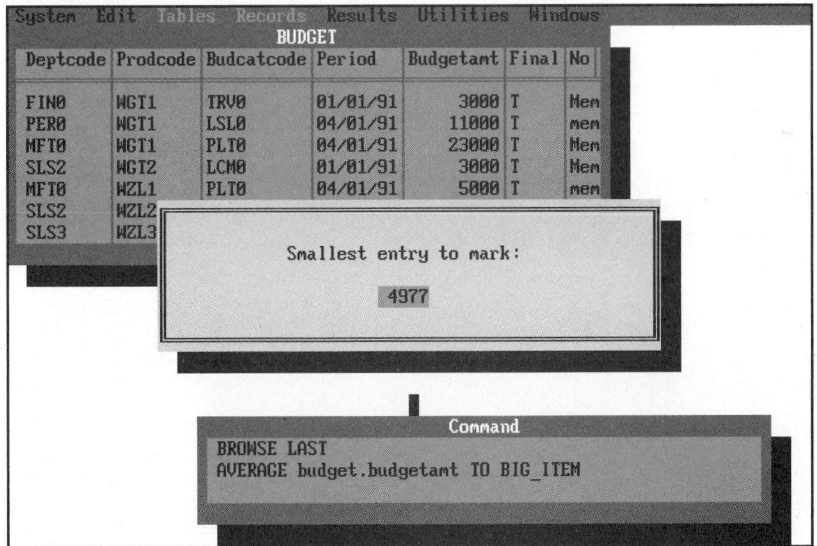

FIG. 14.16

Preparing to print the report.

When you use the Browse menu option, you note (by its behavior as well as by the commands echoed to the Command window) that the system option _MDA_BROW issues a BROWSE LAST command. In your Widget application menu, the native BROWSE option offers capabilities unavailable through any option you can design—most notably, access to the native record-locating options. Yet BROWSE LAST can be inconvenient; if you BROWSE the Budget table after running the Tables Budget option, the BROWSE LAST attempts to use the Do_Show.PRG required by BUDGET.SPR's BROWSE WHEN clause.

For your practice with this menu, you can avoid this problem by SETting RESOURCE OFF, so the Budget BROWSE has no *memory* of its previous incarnation. You also can write a simple standalone Do_Show.PRG available to any Budget BROWSE (all it has to do is RETURN .T.). This second solution, however, still creates your Budget BROWSE in the restricted size used for the BUDGET.SPR BROWSE. In a real application designed to work with interactive features as this one is, you probably would design all your programmed BROWSEs (such as the one in BUDGET.SPR) to use browse preferences, which you learned about in Chapter 8. A named PREFERENCE in the BUDGET.SPR BROWSE command prevents it from interfering with BROWSE LAST.

Techniques for Making an Altered Menu Available

You may need a little time to get used to which System options are disabled during a READ, which additional options you created *ought* to be disabled, and which options can safely work together. You already noted that a *modal* dialog or READ requires a conclusion before further work can be done. All other choices in the FoxPro interface are disabled. You also may find a need to create modal READs in your own programs.

SYSMENU is disabled when you issue the READ MODAL command. However, you can re-enable SYSMENU deliberately by executing the MPR program again *in the WHEN clause of the modal READ.* If you take this step, you must make sure that no inappropriate actions can be taken by disabling menu items selectively.

If you defined the SYSMENU as an additional set of pads or bars to be appended to an existing menu structure, rather than to be replaced as the default and as you did here, you face another problem. Re-executing the menu program gives you a second set of everything you define! The solution is to release the additional pads and bars before re-executing the menu program. When you want to edit any components of the menu currently active—for this reason or any other—you first must use the PUSH MENU command to place the menu on a *stack* in memory. DEFINE and RELEASE as needed and then re-activate the menu (bring it back from the stack with the POP MENU command).

This last point is about as complicated as FoxPro 2 menus get. After you create one or two menus and develop a personal style, not even this point can pose much of a problem. Generating a menu in the Menu Builder makes one of the most tedious and time-consuming parts of developing an application an enjoyable exercise.

You move on now to the Project Manager, to learn how to acquire control over other kinds of details during the development cycle.

Keeping Files Together with the Project Manager

When you look back over this investigation of the other tools, you realize that you created a motley collection of small files with all kinds of extensions and all kinds of formats. How on earth can you know which files you need to create a transportable application that you can share with others?

The Project Manager does this for you, and so easily that you're probably going to laugh out loud the first time you try it.

One or two tricks are available that you cover in following chapters but you can build the first project right now, before you learn more new techniques or the meaning of a single Project Manager control or option.

Create a new file of Project type, as you previously created menus, screens, and other files.

In figure 14.17, you see the window, which really isn't much to see except an empty box ready to display the Name and Type of this application's files, after you add them. The `<Add>` button is the only button available at the moment. The shortcut is Ctrl-A, (usually the Select All keypress, but you can't edit anything right now). Choose either the button or the shortcut to add a file.

A file dialog appears. From the files of Menu type, select the file WIDGET.MNX and confirm the choice. The name `WIDGET` and the type `Menu` appear in the main Project window. A character between these words indicates that this file is currently the *main file* for the project (see fig. 14.18).

You are, for all intents, done. You may think you still have to tell the Project Manager about all the other files but this program *finds out* about these other files by checking the references to other files in the menu file. Select the `<Build>` push button, and the Build dialog appears. You return to this dialog later; for now however, just accept the default choice (Build Project). You are asked to supply a name for the file. The name **WIDGET** is fine, and the Project Manager supplies the default extension of PJX.

Confirm the choice and watch the Project Manager begin to work.

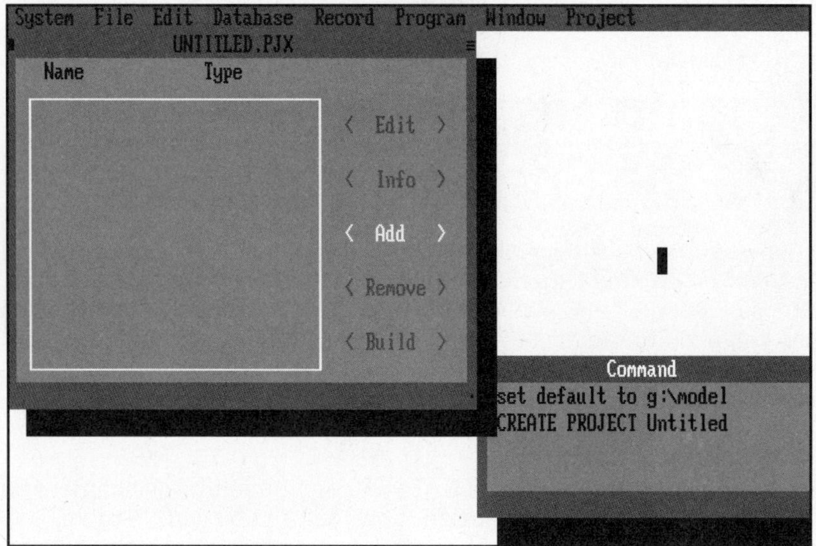

FIG. 14.17

Beginning work in the Project Manager.

When the Project Manager finds a reference to GETORDER (the screen you *borrowed* from FoxApp), it gets *stuck*. The Project Manager needs access to the original source files, which are tables in the case of menus and screens, *not* the generated programs. You added GETORDER.SPR to the MODEL directory but the Project Manager needs to find the SCX file so that this file can be checked later. The Project Manager regenerates the SPR anytime you have made changes to it—*without* your needing to do it yourself.

When you see the screen in figure 14.18, choose the `«Locate»` option. You have an opportunity to point the Project Manager *towards* GETORDER.SCX in the \GOODIES\FOXAPP\SCREENS directory.

After you find the GETORDER.SCX file, the Project Manager continues the Build process. As you see in figure 14.19, all the files are here—even the UDFs in the screen code snippets and reports! Figure 14.19 also shows a screen of Project Information (with the shortcut Ctrl-J) available from the Project menu pad, which provides a handy summary of the kinds and the status of files you are using in this application. Using the shortcut (Ctrl-I) or the information push button (`<Info>`) also displays on-screen detailed information on any file that you highlight in the project.

NOTE

If you ever move files around in the directory structure, you need to repeat the «Locate» process. Fortunately, after you locate *one* file in a previously-unknown directory during a Build process, the Project Manager is smart enough to check in this directory for other files as it works (you won't need to do use the «Locate» push button for each file in the directory.)

If you take over a project from another developer, you may need to go through the same process. The Project Manager has a *home directory* feature which makes the search slightly more automatic, which is discussed in a following section.

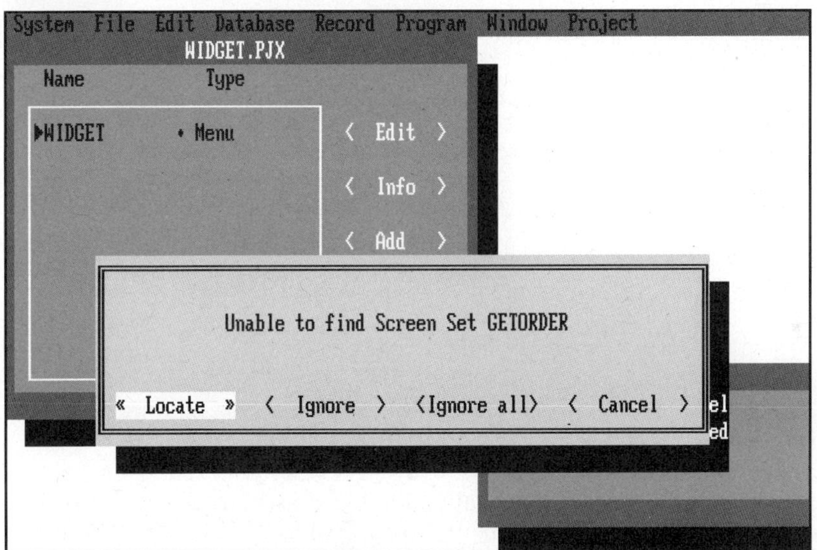

FIG. 14.18

The Project Manager needs you to «Locate» the GETORDER.SCX file in the FOXAPP subdirectory.

Selecting the highlighted file (double-click or press Enter), however, enables you to edit the file regardless of the type, from within the Project Manager. Editing files in this manner has several advantages, including the overview and perspective you can maintain on the application's development. Another important benefit of editing while in the Project Manager is that screen set options are saved through the Project Manager. You may remember that, although you used default settings for the screen options (Define Windows, Open Files, and so on), you had to re-Arrange the windows in their relative positions and *remind* GENSCRN that you wanted to add the control panel as a second screen in the set each time you regenerated the SPRs by using the

Generate option of the Program menu. Screen files do not save settings because a given SCX file may be used with many different applications. Each *project* saves these settings instead and generates the appropriate SPR code.

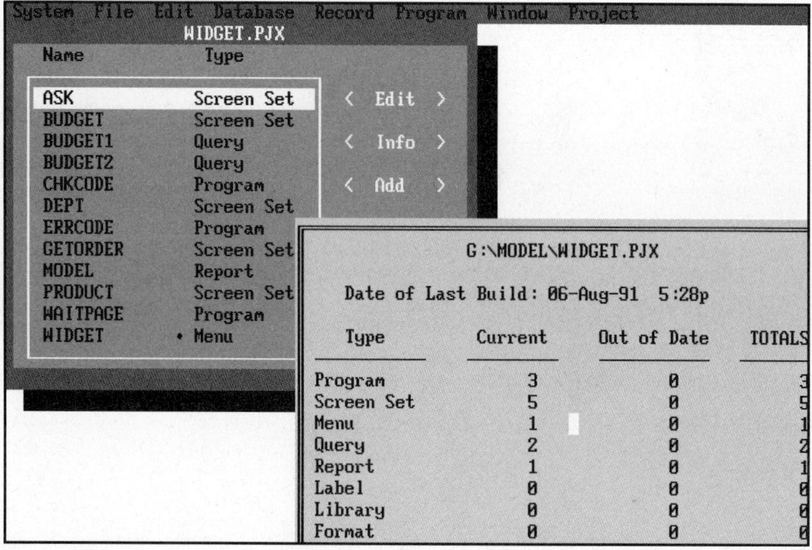

FIG. 14.19

The Build process is completed, and the Project contains the files needed to execute the Widget application.

Do this now for the DEPT.SCX and BUDCAT.SCX files, making sure that the screen lists appear as shown in figure 14.20. This means that the CONTROLM screen should appear first in the list, followed by the Code Options `Open Files`, `Close Files`, `Define Windows`, `Release Windows`, and `Read Cycle`. `<Arrange>` the screens to your liking, as well. Isn't knowing that you never again have to perform these steps for this particular screen set a reassuring thought? In figure 14.20, you can alter the actual screens by choosing the `<Edit>` option.

For the BUDGET.SCX file, make sure that the same Code Options are in effect. If you did not add the extra lines of code suggested previously for the Setup snippet, you can edit the screen now.

After you finish editing the screens, Rebuild Project again. You see that the Project Manager is very selective in the files chosen to regenerate. This option generates only the SPR files because you performed no edits of the menu.

Now go a step further. As you see in figure 14.21, the second radio button in the Project Build dialog is `Build Application`.

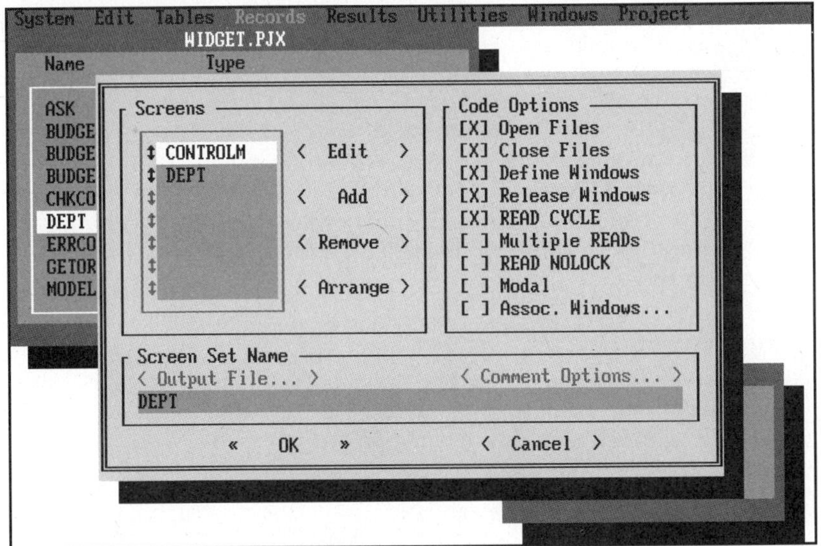

FIG. 14.20

By creating Screen Set options through the Project Manager, you save them permanently.

This option is where the APP files you used among the FoxPro 2 sample applications and the FoxApp-generated application are created. An APP file is a compiled version of all the programs necessary to run an application. You need to distribute only this file—as opposed to a collection of compiled SPXs (compiled screen files), FXPs (compiled programs), MPXs (compiled menus), and so on—to the users of this application.

When you `Build` an `Application`, you see a request for a filename. You can accept the default (which is the name of the project accompanied by the APP extension), and the build process begins. Building an application is all you need to do!

CAUTION: You can BUILD PROJECT *<project name>* in a program or in the Command window, giving the Project Manager the main file name to start with and any others you want to explicitly include. If you perform this step, *all the screen settings and all other options you previously set for this project will be lost!* Use this command when you really want to build a project from scratch or when you are in a low-memory situation. If you get an error message when you try to Rebuild Project in the Project Manager dialog, you can issue a BUILD PROJECT command instead. You then re-enter your screen settings and options. If necessary because of limited memory, USE the project as a table and edit your settings directly in its records.

`Building` an `Application` incorporates all the file regeneration required by any editing you have done since your last Build. Just like Rebuild Project, `Build Application` is selective and never regenerates files that have not changed. It is more convenient to go directly to Build Application and omit the Project Rebuild step entirely. Also, the BUILD APPLICATION command, which can be issued from the Command window, does not destroy your project setting as the BUILD PROJECT command does. You can BUILD APP <*filename*> FROM <*project filename*> from the Command window, for a safe, convenient way to re-build a Project at any time.

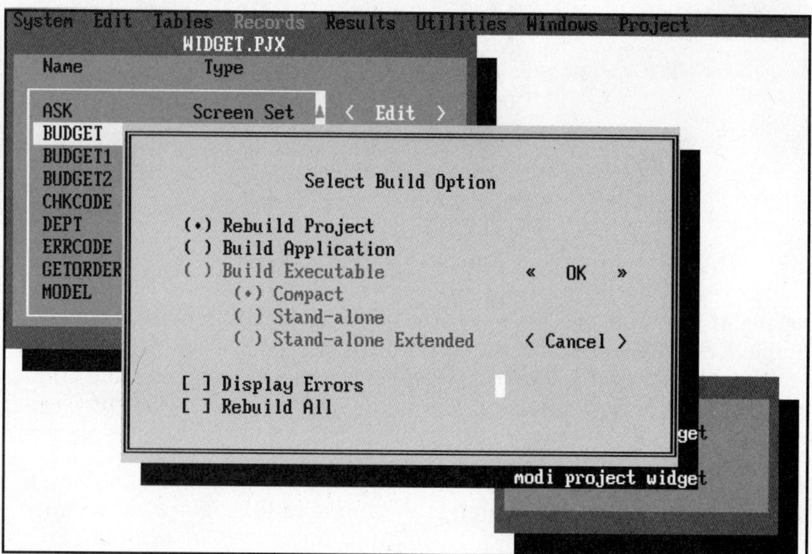

FIG. 14.21

The Project Build dialog.

Project Options and Alternatives

Although the preceding section implies that Project contains *all* the files needed for the application, this statement is, in two senses, not strictly true.

First, the Project does not actually contain the source code (the SCXs, PRGs, and so on), but contains *references* to the code, when the code was last edited and where the code is kept, so that the code can be used for version comparisons and application generation. If you want others to work with your project and have the capability of editing the source code, you must supply the source files along with the PJX/PJT.

Second, you may notice that the Project does not even contain references to the data files. By default, a Project is concerned with the *read-only* files used to build the APP file. You can hardly compile editable files into the APP file as if these files were programs because the APP file cannot be modified by the user. You need to give users copies of all editable files, separately, along with the APP file.

The Project Manager *guesses* at which files are read-only and which are editable when the project is being built, omitting tables and indexes, and including just about everything else. If you happen to have a read-only table, or a modifiable report form, just overrule the program's judgment! Use the Add (Ctrl-A) option to explicitly include the read-only table. Don't, however, be too quick to use the Remove (Ctrl-V) option to take out the FRX file; remember that this file is very convenient for keeping tabs on an application's requirements by storing information about all the necessary files in the Project table. You can incorporate the editable files into a Project *and* prevent these files from becoming a read-only part of the APP by using the Exclude option for any file. If you mistakenly Exclude a file, just Include the file again. Press Ctrl-C to toggle a file's status between Include and Exclude. You may find it convenient to Add all the data files to a project and mark them as Excluded.

TIP

Although the Project Manager usually is considered a developer's tool, its capability to manage all the files needed for one task or database can make it valuable—even if you never compile an application. Because you can select any files (including data tables) for editing from the Project Manager's file list, a Project can be thought of as a super View window, not restricted to table setup. If you have worked in early versions of xBase, you may be familiar with the SET CATALOG command, a close cousin to SET VIEW. FoxPro 2's Projects perform the same function as Catalogs, in a much more sophisticated way.

Whether you use the Project Manager to organize your own personal database tasks or to distribute applications, you find an added bonus in that the PJX files it uses are just ordinary FoxPro tables, like SCXs and FRXs. If you list all files (including editable tables and indexes) in your Project, you can use it to help you figure out what files are required if you need to move your database to another computer. You can USE the PJX and read from it to get a list of the files you need and where they are currently located. Then create a DOS batch file (using the low-level file functions and techniques described in Chapter 20) that create a compressed file (or perhaps one file per directory) from them all, using a file utility such as PkZip or Lharc. Be sure to add any associated memo files (FPTs) for the tables in your Project. Then add your Project's PJX and PJT to this file, and you are ready to move.

Figure 14.22 shows the project with the tables and index files added. You see that Excluded files are shown with the mark Φ (phi) immediately to the left of the file name.

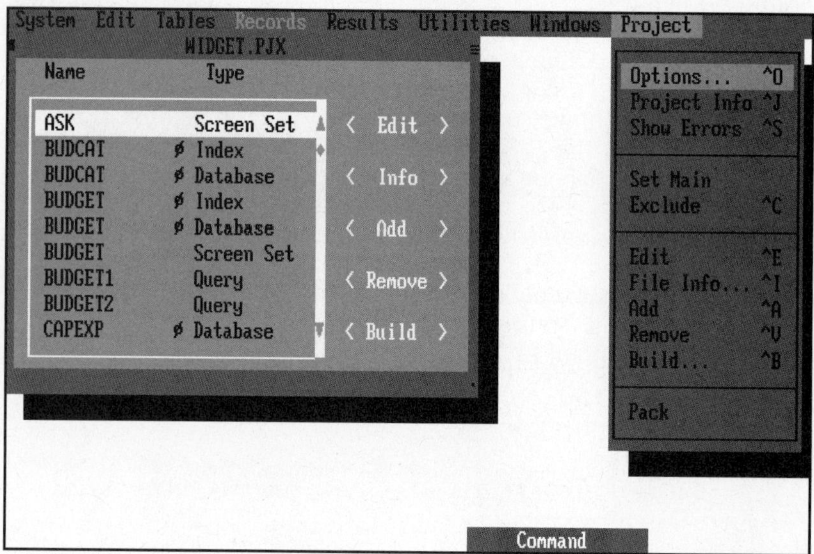

FIG. 14.22

The WIDGET.PJX project file with tables and index files added and marked Excluded.

Rather than distributing these editable files separately with the APP file, you also can include read-only *copies* of the editable application files. This application's installation process can then reproduce these files in editable versions on the user's disks. Unless these files should start out populated with default sets of data, however, using the commands CREATE TABLE and INDEX is an easier way to create the editable files during installation. This approach has the added benefit of helping to document, directly in the code, the structure of the application.

The Project Manager can become confused during the Build process if you use *indirect references* or *macro expressions* to refer to files in the code. You can tell the Project Manager to `<Ignore>` the problem and continue to build without resolving the reference, but an EXTERNAL command also exists, used only by the Project Manager, to *point* towards the real name of the file being referenced. EXTERNAL is used with a second keyword that describes the kind of file you want to reference, as in the following example:

```
* set up a variable
mreport = "Budget"

* here's the generic "question" screen again:
DO ask.spr WITH ;
  "Choose a <B>udget or <P>roduct Report?", ;
  mreport,"@M Budget, Product"

* tell the Project Manager about the choices
EXTERNAL REPORT budget
EXTERNAL REPORT product

REPORT FORM (mreport)
```

The EXTERNAL ARRAY command is used in a similar manner to point the Project Manager towards needed elements, which is necessary when an array is passed to a subprocedure. Here, the *calling* procedure should have an EXTERNAL ARRAY statement that shows what the array is to be named when referenced as a parameter. EXTERNAL ARRAY also is used when an array is referenced in a procedure that did not create the array. Here, the *called* procedure needs an EXTERNAL ARRAY statement that shows the array name used when the array was created. You can read more about these procedures in the *Commands and Functions* manual in the entry on the EXTERNAL command. You may want to wait before you try to use this command until you read the programming sections of this book, in which you learn more about the ways arrays are used.

The Project Manager has few additional options. As in any other table, entries that you Remove (Ctrl-V) are not really removed from the file, but simply marked deleted. A Pack option is provided on the Project menu popup to remove the unwanted entries completely from the table and to control the size of the associated memo file. A Show Errors (Ctrl-S) option displays on-screen all errors the Project Manager finds during the previous Build procedure (similar to when you compiled program files directly, you also can find these errors written to a file of the same name as the project and having an ERR extension). A Set Main option enables you to designate the main file on which the other files in a project *depend*, either because you are adding the files to a project manually (rather than letting the Project Manager perform an initial Build), or because you changed the structure of the application in some way.

Before you continue with the application structure discussion, finish this investigation of Project options by looking at the Project Options dialog, which has the shortcut Ctrl-O, as shown in figure 14.23.

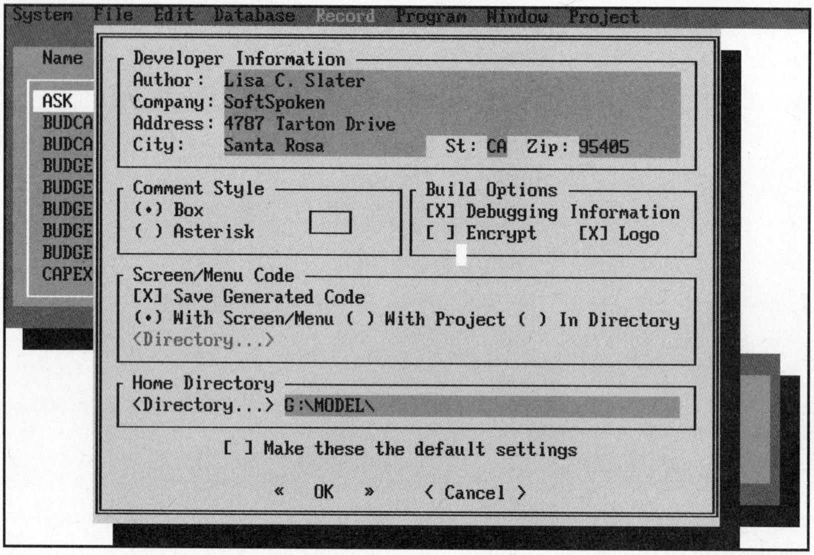

FIG. 14.23

The Project Options dialog.

Many of these items, such as Comment Style, Developer Information, and the opportunity to `Make these the default settings`, are the same as the items you previously saw when you generated programs by using the Program menu option. Now you can apply these options to the project as a whole. The Project Manager, however, also allows additional decisions about the way the code is generated, as shown in the following list:

- The code can have the `Debugging Information` removed (by clicking the check box of the same name). FoxPro compiled code contains a few extra bytes of information per line that enable line information to be provided if an error is found and also enable the Trace window to display on-screen and highlighted, each line as the code runs. (You learn about the Trace window in Chapter 18.) If you are distributing the application and do not need this information, you can make the compiled file a little smaller by choosing this option.

- The code can be encrypted (by marking the `Encrypt` check box). Figure 14.24 shows the same program compiled with and without encryption. As you see, without encryption, some messages and variables remain readable. It also is possible for someone to *decompile* a compiled file. Decompiling an encrypted compiled file is a much more difficult, if not impossible, task. If security is an important issue, you can protect the source by using this option.

- The Fox Logo can be suppressed when FoxPro is loaded by marking the `Logo` check box. If you always Do the application from *inside* FoxPro, this option may not matter to you, but if you use the Distribution Kit or if you or the users start Fox with the application file name as a parameter at the DOS command line, you can control the display of the Fox Software sign-on screen and `Normal Shut Down` message when you Quit with this option. This option is equivalent to the -t command line switch discussed in Appendix E.
- You can choose whether and where to Save the Generated menu and screen code by marking first the `Save Generated Code` check box and then toggling one of the `With Screen/Menu`, `With Project`, or `In Directory` radio buttons. When you generate APP files, the MPR files and SPR files aren't needed to run the application; these files' compiled versions are contained in the APP file and are displayed merely as an interim step. However, it can be convenient to occasionally check snippets and other elements of screen and menu code by typing **MODIFY COMMAND *.spr or *.mpr** instead of going through the Screen or Menu Builder for a quick look. You can use this option to save the generated file wherever the screen/menu resides (the default), wherever the project is located on-disk, in another directory that you specify, or not at all.

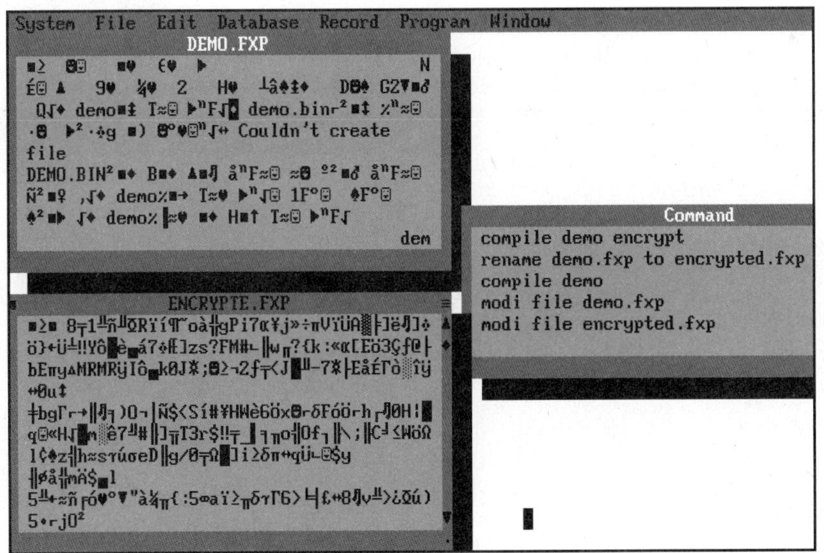

FIG. 14.24

A comparison between two compiled versions of the same program shows the effect of the `Encryption` option.

Closely related to the last choice you can make about code generation is the final decision you can make in the Projects Options dialog: the project's *home directory*. Although you saved all the practice files in one directory, you probably noticed that each sample project was installed by Fox with the project file in one directory and in separate subdirectories for screens, programs, menus, reports, and underlying database files. A project *remembers* the *relative path*, or the files' location in subdirectories relative to the directory in which the project is placed, for all the component files. If you move these files to the hard disk of another developer and use the same *relative* subdirectories for the subsidiary files, that the project is in a new directory, or even on a different drive doesn't matter. The Project Manager can find all the pieces after the new home directory is confirmed.

Project Structure for Different Types of Applications

You just explored the Project Manager as thoroughly as this tool can be explored. Like the Menu Builder, the Project Manager is simple to learn; the real challenge comes when you try to *structure* a project to maximum effect.

With the Project Manager, this structure is no less than the actual structure of the application. The Omnipresent Widget application, with a menu program as the main file, is simple and fairly typical of applications designed to be available alongside interactive work in FoxPro 2.

Using a menu program as the main file in an application designed to be run as a stand-alone application, however, is unusual because menu code DEFINEs and ACTIVATEs the menu and then—having no more work to do—returns you to interactive mode. A far more typical design for a self-contained program uses a PRG file as the main file. This main program includes the following four steps:

```
*** Setup Code
    DO SETUP.PRG
```

First, the program calls a *setup procedure* to open files and establish various system-wide parameters. The kinds of chores you do at this point in the program are discussed in Chapter 16, when you examine program structure more thoroughly. In the current WIDGET.APP, you may just SET VIEW to an appropriate file, but sometimes more elaborate setup procedures are required.

In your setup program or directly in your main program, you initialized the variables needed globally (throughout your application). If they are initialized in the SETUP.PRG rather than in the main program, they must be declared PUBLIC. Among these global variables should be one that indicates when the user wants to leave the application: `m.quitting = .F.`

```
***   Define a Menu
      DO WIDGET.MPR
```

Second, the main program calls a *menu program* to set up the options for the application.

```
***   Wait For the User To Take An Action
      READ VALID handler()
      * or
      DO FNDATION.SPR
```

The third, and most crucial, step is that a READ is initiated. READ can be in an SPR file that establishes the logo or a password screen for this application or just the READ command issued directly in the main program. Either way, this READ is the application's *foundation READ*, which remains in force until the application is ready to shut down. The VALID clause, or sometimes the DEACTIVATE clause, contains a UDF that launches all the other tasks of the application in response to *requests* made by menu options or other events, checking the tasks in progress and handling all adjustments that must be made. The foundation READ's managing clause continues to RETURN .F. until a *quit* command of some kind is received.

A foundation READ is a far more flexible and complicated management scheme than the RDLEVEL( ) check supplied in the current WIDGET.APP. Be sure that you investigate the applications in the \GOODIES\FNDATION sample file directory—and the GETLESS.TXT and GETANS.TXT files contained there, which summarizes Fox Software's ideas about event handling and the reasons for creating foundation READs.

When you read GETLESS.TXT and GETANS.TXT, you may get the impression that foundation READs are difficult to use and shouldn't be attempted without a great deal of preparation. Foundation READs are just an efficient method of placing users in a "wait state" at the menu between menu choices.

The examples provided by Fox Software in the \GOODIES\FNDATION directory, especially EX2, can seem bewildering. Keep in mind that they were designed to suggest ways to handle *event-driven* programming in FoxPro 2. In event-driven programming, the program responds gracefully to every action of the user, no matter in what sequence the user decides to make his choices. You can think of it as a completely modeless interface. In FoxPro, event-driven programming requires a great deal of backstage management to provide what looks like an effortless performance.

The VALID clause in EX2 has to assess the current state of any READs in progress and shut them down intelligently before initiating another one. It does this while preserving the illusion that an unlimited number of READs are taking place at the same time, even though FoxPro is currently limited to only five READ levels.

If your application provides mostly modal activities (and many common computer tasks, such as accounting, have inherently modal aspects), you can use a foundation READ in a far simpler way than is shown by the example applications. You can use a SKIP FOR clause on your menu options (using a RDLEVEL( ) > 1, allowing 1 level for the foundation READ this time, or checking the current windows available with WONTOP( ) and WVISIBLE( )) to decide when it isn't safe to bring another READ or task forward.

When an option is not disabled, it can DO a procedure directly (they don't have to be initiated in the READ VALID clause). During any specific editing activity, you can provide some nested modal READs (perhaps a "Confirm Edit?" dialog or a print setup dialog) without worrying that you will run out of available READ levels. Meanwhile, your READ VALID handler( ) function keeps checking the *m.quitting* variable. You have a Quit option on your menu that is a little different from the WIDGET.MPR version:

```
m.quitting = .T.
* Handle any GATHERing or confirming quit.
* Check the current activity and
* do other chores necessary to close up the
* current activity smoothly.
CLEAR READ
RETURN
```

Your READ VALID then is called. In this example, the expression does not even have to call a UDF; it can be as simple as the following:

```
READ VALID m.quitting
```

Keep in mind that this sequence of events (a CLEAR READ invoking a READ VALID clause) is specific to a *getless*, or foundation READ. If you issue a CLEAR READ during one of your *getful* (or normal editing) READs, the VALID clause on that READ is not called. If you are in the middle of an editing session that is a nested READ of a foundation READ, both READs are cleared when the CLEAR READ is issued. Therefore, the VALID clause on the foundation READ is the first item to be evaluated after the CLEAR READ statement.

More than two levels of READ nesting work differently, however. Presumably you are in a modal dialog of some sort when you test RDLEVEL( ) > 2. When you issue a CLEAR READ, you don't CLEAR the other READs of which this one is a "grandchild;" you only leave the dialog.

```
***   Cleanup and Leave
      DO CLEANUP.PRG
```

Finally, when the foundation READ ends, another procedure is called to properly end the application. You find a number of suggestions for appropriate cleanup procedures in Chapter 16. You also can look at the simple setup and cleanup routines included as part of ORGANIZE.APP, in the program UTILITY.PRG. In this program, you check for the version of FoxPro under which the application is running, as your Quit option did in WIDGET.MPR, and decide whether to QUIT or CANCEL.

Using a menu program as the main file in an application that includes a foundation READ is certainly possible. You add the foundation READ to the menu program in the Cleanup snippet, followed by all the other cleanup code and procedures. The order is unimportant. You place the setup code in the menu program's Setup snippet.

You also can specify a screen program as the main file. Here, the setup and a call to the menu program are made in the screen's Setup snippet; the screen program's READ is the foundation READ; and all cleanup is placed in—or called from—the screen's Cleanup snippet. Although no rules exist against *burying* in snippets the foundation READ and surrounding main components of the application, doing so can make the program structure difficult to comprehend and maintain. A PRG file that contains the preceding elements seems to work best.

Using a PRG as the main file can have a minor side effect that you may want to counter if you distribute source along with programs. Remember that FoxPro 1, FoxBASE+, and other xBase dialects all use PRGs just as FoxPro 2 does. If the main program uses an obvious name (MAIN.PRG or STARTUP.PRG, for example), users running other xBase software may begin to run your program and then crash when they come up against the first FoxPro 2-specific instruction. Adding the following test to the very beginning of the program is a good idea:

```
IF .NOT. checkver(PROGRAM())
  CANCEL
ENDIF
************************************************
```

```
FUNCTION checkver

PARAMETERS this_prog

IF .NOT. ("2.0" $ VERSION(1) .AND. ;
        "FOX" $ UPPER(VERSION(1)))

        WAIT "CAN'T CONTINUE: This version of "+;
         this_prog+" requires FoxPro 2.0!"

RETURN .F.

ENDIF

RETURN .T.
```

If you are using a dialect that does not support UDFs or the VERSION(1) command, this program still crashes, but before anything important happens! (Purists may note that other FoxPro-specific amenities, such as COLOR SCHEMEs, WAIT WINDOWs, or the capability of using NOT and AND without surrounding periods, were avoided in this function.)

Packaging Options with the Distribution Kit

After you become comfortable with the FoxPro 2 tools, develop a good sense of program structure and learn to assemble stand-alone applications that you feel are polished and complete enough to share with others, you may want to create programs that do not rely on the FoxPro 2 development files. If so, you can purchase the *Distribution Kit*, which Fox Software created for this purpose.

When you look at figure 14.21, you see that several options appear dimmed. These dimmed areas are the Distribution Kit options that become available when you install the Distribution Kit files along with the development files.

The options that become enabled are determined by the Distribution files you install. See Appendix A, "Installing FoxPro 2," for more information about this process. For now, concentrate on the different distribution options the kit offers.

The simplest option, and the only option not new in FoxPro 2, is the *runtime* application. To distribute a runtime program, you need to supply users with the APP file, all editable files not created by the program, and the *runtime support* library files. The support library files

FOXPRO.ESL and FOXPRO.ESO for the standard version of FoxPro and FOXPROX.ESL for the Extended version are the same whether you distribute single- or multi-user programs. You also need to distribute the runtime *loader* program, which is a small file named FOXR.EXE. (Appendix F provides more information about this file and the other Fox loaders.)

If you decide to create *compact executable files*, the Project Manager creates EXE files, which are very similar in content and size to APP files and require the same support library files to be distributed. You can start the EXE files, however, directly from the DOS command line, without the aid of FOXR.EXE.

Both compact executables and runtime applications can determine whether they are loading in an environment appropriate to the extended version of FoxPro 2 and use this environment if both support libraries are present. If you know the environment the application uses, you need to distribute only the support library files for the appropriate version of FoxPro.

Compact executables and runtime applications share another important feature: the license to distribute these creations is unlimited if you distribute the applications in your organization. Fox, however, requires you to charge a fee of some kind—even if the fee is nominal—if you distribute the support library files to users outside your organization. This requirement is not an onerous one but read the small *Distribution Kit* handbook carefully to be sure that you understand the rules.

The other distribution mechanism, *stand-alone* or *monolithic executables*, differs a great deal from a runtime application. You need to specify the standard or extended version when you generate the file, and you may find that this distribution mechanism creates a large file even for a simple program. The file is large because it contains *all* the parts of FoxPro needed to run the program. No secondary support files are required.

The compiler works with a certain degree of *granularity*, which means that if certain broad areas of FoxPro are not used by the program, the compiler doesn't incorporate these areas into the executable file. However, most of the sophisticated commands and features in FoxPro are supported by a number of other files, so the compiler cannot pick and choose among the necessary capabilities with a high degree of precision. The compiler's attempts to discriminate also can, in some circumstances, cause features you are actually using to be omitted. Suppose that all the SQL SELECT statements in an application were contained in macro expressions, as shown in the following examples:

```
DO CASE
```

```
CASE PROMPT() = "Query"
         do_action = "SELECT "+from_tables + ;
                have_cond   + ;
                group_cond     && etc
CASE PROMPT() = "Execute"

                do_action = "DO "+prog_name

CASE PROMPT() = "Report"

                do_action = "REPORT FORM "+rept_name  && etc

ENDCASE

&do_action

* the above line executes your command by
* expanding the macro expression at run time
```

If the compiler cannot *see* an instance of the SQL SELECT command, the compiler may omit the capability of using SQL SELECT. In this example, the command is invisible.

If the executable file returns the error message `Feature not available`, and you know the line that causes this error is not one of the unsupported commands for a distributable application, place a line of code in the program to *trick* the compiler into noticing that this feature is incorporated, as shown in the following example:

```
IF DATE() = {01/01/1800}
      SELECT ...
ENDIF
```

This code can never execute but is sufficient to make sure that the SELECT command is *seen* when the executable file is built.

You can reduce the size of a stand-alone executable file to a certain extent, if some of its sections are contained in supporting APP or compact EXE files. These files need to be distributed along with the main standalone EXE; they serve as *overlays* to the main file.

However, separating your program into modules in this manner can lead to a similar problem as macro expansion. To make sure that the compiler links in the appropriate FoxPro capabilities needed to support the features used in your subsidiary APPs or EXEs, you must add these APPs and EXEs to your Project. They are marked as `Excluded` by the Project Manager, but their presence serves to alert the compiler of the features they use, which may not be needed anywhere else in your application.

pile, and are easier to transport if you need to supply updates for the program. Stand-alone files, however, carry a certain connotation of professionalism for many developers. Because these files require no support files, you can't mistakenly run stand-alone files with support files that carry a different VERSION(1) from the development files.

Although EXE files are meant to be executed from the DOS command line, you also can run these files while in FoxPro by typing the command **DO *your_program*** in the Command window. By preference, FoxPro runs the executable application—if an executable application is found—then the APP file or, finally, an FXP file of the same name.

> **CAUTION:** FoxPro cannot execute EXE files not created in this way, however; use the RUN command. If the distributed application uses the RUN command's /N switch (FoxPro's RUN command) to specify the amount of memory (in bytes or kilobytes) FoxPro makes available for external programs, be aware that you need to distribute the file FOXSWAP.COM with the application. This file is found in the main FoxPro program directory.

All the distribution mechanisms share some limitations when compared to the development version of FoxPro. Only part of FoxPro 2's SYSMENU, for example, is available in a distributed application. Except for the Filer option, the System menu pad is available; the Edit pad is completely available; and the Window and File options appropriate to a noninteractive environment are available. (You can see that the WIDGET.MPR requires some revision for distribution.)

Many development commands have no meaning in a distribution application, so—besides not appearing on SYSMENU—attempts to invoke these commands in distributed programs are ignored. You cannot, for example, ACTIVATE WINDOW COMMAND or BUILD PROJECT in a distributed application. Check the *Distribution Kit* handbook for a complete list of commands and features not supported by Distribution Kit.

The most striking absences, however, are the Screen Builder, the Menu Builder, and the RQBE. Although you can create and modify labels and reports in a distributed application, the other power tools cannot be used because these tools generate and compile code, which is impossible without a full development version of FoxPro 2.

Of the three omissions, only the lack of the RQBE is likely to be important in a distributed application. You can create dialogs that give your users wide latitude in the queries they issue. SELECT statements can include variables that are *macro-expanded* at run time. Your query dialogs fill these variables with values based on the user's responses and include variables that are *macro-expanded* at run time. Your query dialogs fill these variables with values based on the user's responses and then executes the custom query.

You must balance these omissions against the control a distributed application provides (in comparison with a program run under the development version), over exactly what is done with the data the program is collecting. An important point to note here is that you must think carefully about each user's level of sophistication, with regards to the user's understanding of database management, before you recommend (to anyone) either a distributed application *or* the powerful development version of FoxPro.

When you decide to share applications that you have written for yourself with other people, no matter which distribution mechanism you choose, you face some new development problems. Procedures that work for you on your computer may fail on someone else's. If another user has the full FoxPro 2 package, he may have his own default macro sets that conflict with your application's. Perhaps he uses a different monitor type or keyboard or has limited disk space or memory.

Chapter 20 presents a sample procedure to be used as part of your application's installation process and examines any existing CONFIG.SYS file to make sure that its `FILES` and `BUFFERS` settings enable your program and FoxPro to run. This is only one of many such factors that must be considered when you distribute an application—the wider your distribution, the more possibilities—and the suggested approach is not foolproof. (For example, if the user has a memory manager such as Quarterdeck's QEMM installed, these settings in the CONFIG.SYS file can be deceptive.) You cannot anticipate, much less successfully guard against, problems of this kind.

In Chapter 18, you learn about recovering gracefully from errors you cannot always predict and how to keep your users informed at all times. These capabilities are just as crucial to the distribution of your application as the Distribution Kit.

Creating Demonstration Editions of Your Applications

As explained in Appendix A, you install the Distribution Kit by using the Developer's Activation key. You can use the *demonstration key* from outside the Developer's activation key envelope and install Distribution kit files that create distributable demo applications. Like FoxPro in the demo version, the demo applications you create in this way can contain up to 120 records. (You can contact Fox directly and get additional demo keys for your serial number that also enable you to generate applications with an upper limit of 30 records or 240 records.)

If you use the demo activation key, you find that, besides the normal limitations of a distributable application, this demo distributable program shares the limitations of the development files when installed with the demo key: the text files that you can create are limited in size, and the Calendar/Diary allows only a limited number of entries. More important, the RUN command that enables a DOS program to execute inside FoxPro cannot be used in a demo.

If any of these limitations poses a problem, consider the alternative—installing a similar *check* on table sizes of your own, but use the *live* activation key on the Distribution Kit. You can check for a total limit of records in any single file (as Fox does), or you can create a special variable or other condition and selectively use a `SKIP FOR demo` clause on the menu options. Remember that, because applications you create in this way are not demos by Fox's standards, you are required to charge a nominal fee at distribution time.

A third possibility is the creation of a *self-running demonstration program*. This kind of demo does not really enable the user to work with or edit files, but rather takes the user on a *tour* of the system of which keystrokes, system responses, and output are simulated. If you execute DEMO.APP, you see the self-running demo supplied with FoxPro. This demo is an attractive showcase for the features of the application. In the following chapter, you learn about *macros*, or recorded keystrokes, and the ways you can use macros in programs to create this kind of demo.

Chapter Summary

This chapter concludes the investigation of the principal FoxPro 2 *power tools*. Next, Chapter 15 discusses a number of other supporting features unique to FoxPro and which can add significantly to the functionality and the style of applications you create.

You now move out of the exploration of the FoxPro 2 interface agents. In Part IV, you begin a focussed study of the FoxPro *programming language*, a powerful and extensive set of commands and functions that provided the support and the vehicle for all you accomplished so far.

15

CHAPTER

Discovering More FoxPro 2 Productivity Features

As you practiced with FoxPro 2's application-building power tools described in the previous chapters, you rearranged the screen *desk* to your liking. Some people prefer to stack the files and code snippets they are editing, similar to pending documents in an *In file* basket. Other users prefer these packets of data in a tiled arrangement, as if the papers were spread across a desk. Still others keep open but inactive windows docked in a corner, like folders pulled from a file cabinet, closed but ready for use.

You may want the Command window to stay in the default position onscreen, or you may prefer a Command window that stretches the entire width but sits on the bottom of the screen—approximating the *dot prompt* command interface used by older xBase dialects.

How does FoxPro keep track of the elements and arrangement of the desktop? A special table, the *Resource file*, stores information about what Fox sensibly and literally labels *preferences* for differing work habits and tool use.

In Chapter 8, you learned about Browse preferences, which enable you to save an intricate Browse arrangement of fields and formatting to use again at a later date, without reissuing the same complex Browse command. You investigated the Resource file itself, to see the way FoxPro stores these preferences. You also BROWSEd and edited the Resource file as you do other tables.

In this chapter, you investigate the other preferences and related records maintained in a Resource file. You also discuss the following FoxPro features, many of which use Resource preferences and all of which provide enhanced personal productivity as you work in FoxPro:

- The *Filer* helps you manage files and directories without exiting from FoxPro.
- The *Color System* provides almost unlimited control over the colors you see for FoxPro system interface objects and the objects you design for applications.
- *Macros* enable you to store and replay complex sequences of keystrokes to automate tasks.
- The *Calculator*, *Diary*, and *Special Characters* and *ASCII charts* form a package of *desk accessories* with the same functions as the physical desk accessories with the same names. The *Capture* utility is an analog to a copy machine, completing this group of minor but helpful tools.
- *Printer Drivers*, and the *printer driver setups* that you store for individual printers as preferences in the Resource file, provide printer-specific information as FoxPro creates output from files and data.
- The *API* (Application Program Interface) serves as a gateway to special capabilities not directly available in FoxPro. You can use routines written in C and assembly language just as if these routines were native FoxPro functions.

All these special-purpose tools have implications for work in FoxPro 2's interactive environment, and many also can be used to enhance the applications you distribute to other users.

The Resource File

As with almost everything else in FoxPro, you can customize a Resource file and even SET RESOURCE OFF, closing the file. However, if you installed FoxPro and the program is still in the default state, the SETting of RESOURCE is ON, and the Resource file you use, FOXUSER.DBF, is found in the main FoxPro directory.

If you are not sure what Resource file is in use on a system, or wonder if RESOURCE may even have been SET OFF by another user, use the Files panel of the View window to check. In figure 15.1, you see a View window showing that RESOURCE is ON (the Resource box is checked) but is set to a different file name (H:\Q_USER.DBF).

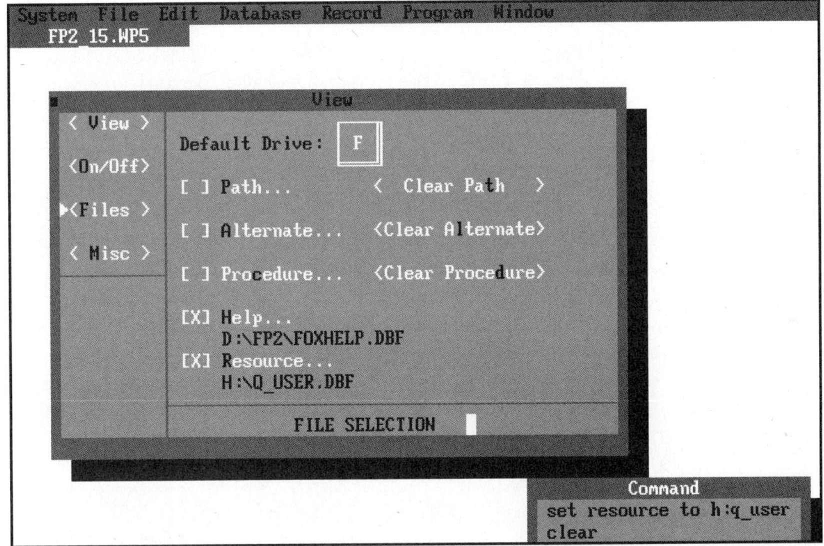

FIG. 15.1

The Files Panel of the View window.

As you perform the following exercises, you use the file that was, until now, the Resource file. If Resource was previously SET OFF in the system, look for a FoxUser file in the main FoxPro directory or in the directory from which you started FoxPro. In the unlikely event that you have no Resource file on the disk, the SETting of OFF may have been specified for RESOURCE in the CONFIG.FP file with the RESOURCE=OFF line, as described in Appendix D. Without this instruction, if you start up FoxPro and a Resource file cannot be found, FoxPro automatically creates a new FoxUser file in the current directory.

You also can create an empty Resource file at any time, with the following command in the Command window:

```
CREATE TABLE <filename> (Type       C(12),;
                         Id         C(12),;
                         Name       C(24),;
                         Readonly   L,    ;
                         Ckval      N(6), ;
                         Data       M,    ;
                         Updated    D)
```

You also can create a Resource table with this structure through the FoxPro interface, by using the View window or the *File New* dialog. A Resource file may have any legal file name, but the structure and field names must be in this exact form. You cannot add extra fields for new comments, for example, and have FoxPro *recognize* this file for Resource use.

As you may remember from Chapter 8, RESOURCE should be SET OFF or SET TO another file name before you can open the Resource table. You can use the On/Off panel of the View window to SET RESOURCE OFF or type **SET RESOURCE OFF** directly into the Command window.

Using the Resource check box in the Files panel of the View window will enable you to SET RESOURCE TO a different file name instead. This method only works if you have another Resource file already available on-disk; you cannot use the Open File dialog to generate a new Resource file "on the spot." If you specify a file name in this dialog but the file you choose is not a valid Resource file, no error message will appear, but the Resource file does not close or change.

Similarly, the SET RESOURCE TO *<filename>* command in a program or the Command window requires that the named file be available and of the correct format. When the command is issued unsuccessfully, you get an error message.

When you have SET RESOURCE OFF or TO another file, you can USE Foxuser (or whatever the original Resource file was called).

By typing the following commands, you can use the Command window and some FoxPro functions to open the current Resource file at the same time you learn of the file's name and location:

```
SET RESOURCE OFF
USE SET("RESOURCE",1)
* SET("RESOURCE",1), like SYS(2005), tells the name of the
* current Resource file even if RESOURCE is OFF.
* The USE command takes this information as a reference to
* a file name and opens the file.
BROWSE TITLE FULLPATH(DBF())
* The browse window title tells you
* exactly what file you are in.
```

TIP

In figure 15.1 you also see the file currently in use as Fox's Help file. As you learn in Chapter 18, investigating the FoxPro Help file calls for techniques similar to those you use with Resource files. Both can be SET OFF or TO any FoxPro table with the appropriate file structure. Neither one of them appears in a work area when in use, and neither one uses a structural index file while performing the specialized task (although in FoxPro 1.02 the Resource file did use an index).

Both can be opened while in use with the USE AGAIN syntax. The Help file is not editable when opened in this manner. Although the active Resource file does appear to be editable when USEd AGAIN, you might experience inconsistent results if you attempt to edit the file. Always SET RESOURCE OFF or TO another file before attempting to modify a Resource file.

On the other hand, you can USE the active Resource file AGAIN (include the NOUPDATE keyword for safety) and keep a BROWSE NOEDIT open while you work. You can learn a lot about Resource files by watching the active file's records change in the Browse while you interact with FoxPro.

However you decide to open the file, look carefully at the contents of the Resource file in a Browse. As you can see in figure 15.2, records are specified, by using the Type field, as either a preference (PREF) or a DATA type record. Within each Type, the Id field tells you the use of each record. PREFerences can have Ids that contain the letters `POS`, which denote records that hold position and size information for individual Menu Layouts, Projects, and Screen Layouts for different files (including the state of attached code snippets). Other POS records hold position and size for the Report and Label windows, the desk accessories, and other system windows.

Other records exist that use the Id of WINDBROW to hold characteristics used for a default BROWSE LAST for all files you BROWSed in the past and also all special BROWSE PREFERENCEs you previously designed and saved. WINDMODIFY records save preferences for editing a particular file or files with a particular extension. WINDMEMO records hold preferences for editing a particular memo or all memo fields. Each COLORSET record holds one complete set of references to colors for all the objects that make up the FoxPro interface.

The Preferences dialog discussed in Chapter 2, which affects Text Editing defaults, is where you give FoxPro the information stored in a WINDMODIFY record or records. The related Preferences dialog for Text Editing in memo fields creates WINDMEMO records. When you use the Expression Builder and the Calculator, the Preferences option on the Edit menu popup also is enabled and presents a specialized group of Preference options for these two tools. The two dialogs are shown in figures 15.3 and 15.4; each box has a separate record in the Resource file to store the selections you make.

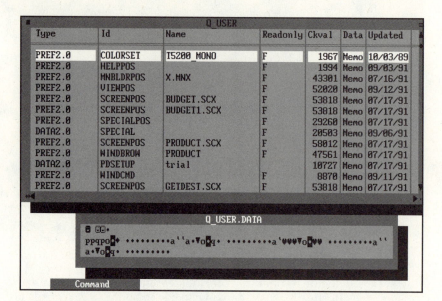

Q_USER

Type	Id	Name	Readonly	Ckval	Data	Updated
PREF2.0	COLORSET	T5200_MONO	F	1967	Memo	10/03/89
PREF2.0	HELPPOS		F	1994	Memo	09/03/91
PREF2.0	MNBLDRPOS	X.MNX	F	43301	Memo	07/16/91
PREF2.0	VIEWPOS		F	52020	Memo	09/12/91
PREF2.0	SCREENPOS	BUDGET.SCX	F	53818	Memo	07/17/91
PREF2.0	SCREENPOS	BUDGET1.SCX	F	53818	Memo	07/17/91
PREF2.0	SPECIALPOS		F	29260	Memo	07/17/91
DATA2.0	SPECIAL		F	20503	Memo	09/06/91
PREF2.0	SCREENPOS	PRODUCT.SCX	F	58012	Memo	07/17/91
PREF2.0	WINDBROW	PRODUCT	F	47561	Memo	07/17/91
DATA2.0	PDSETUP	trial		10727	Memo	07/17/91
PREF2.0	WINDCMD		F	8870	Memo	09/11/91
PREF2.0	SCREENPOS	GETDEST.SCX	F	53818	Memo	07/17/91

Q_USER.DATA

Command

FIG. 15.2

Using BROWSE on the contents of a Resource file.

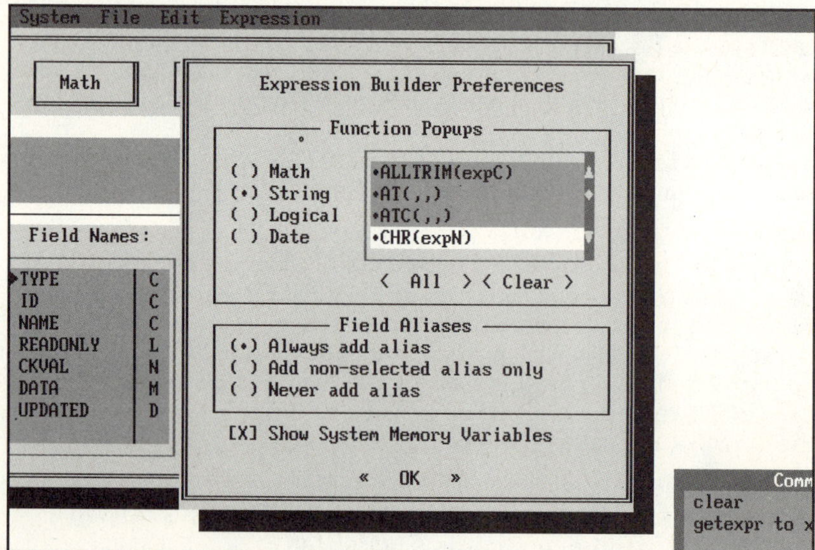

FIG. 15.3

The Expression Builder Preferences dialog.

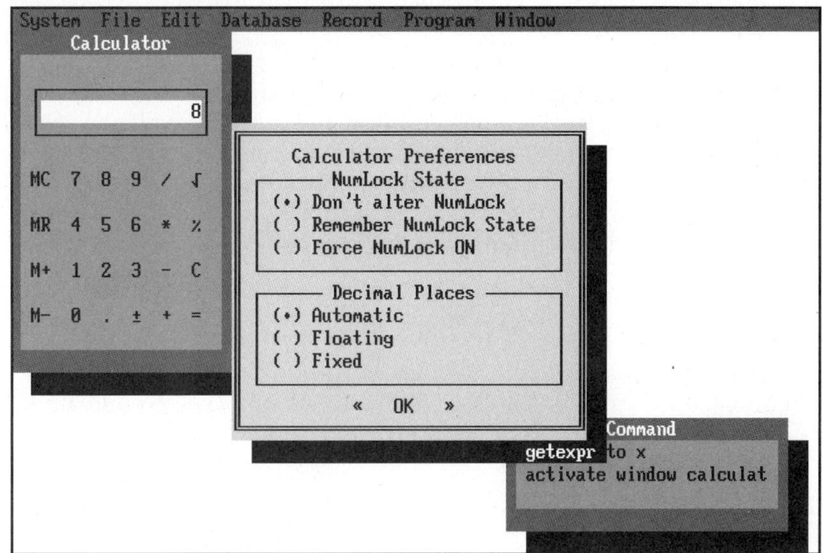

FIG. 15.4

The Calculator Preferences dialog.

Where a PREF or DATA record has an Id that can be shared by many records (such as SCREENPOS or WINDBROW), the Name field is used to identify each specific record. For example, DATA records with the Id PDSETUP hold printer setups you previously defined; the name you give to each setup shows in the Name field.

Other DATA-Type records store information obtained by each of the desk accessories. The most recent value displayed by the Calculator, the value held in Calculator *memory*, the most recently chosen item from the ASCII and Special Character charts, and the entries you make in the FoxPro Diary all are stored in the Resource file to which you can return in this and in future FoxPro sessions. All Label Layouts you define, and also the default labels available, are stored in DATA-Type records with the Id LBLLAYOUT.

Along with Name, the remaining fields in the Resource file structure are used in the same way by both PREF and DATA records. You can edit the logical Readonly field by changing the value to .T. as you did in Chapter 8, to make sure that a BROWSE setup, a Label Layout, or the position of a particular window is always the same when invoked, no matter how where you move the window on-screen or otherwise alter the window during use.

FoxPro uses the Ckval (checkvalue) field to make sure that the information in this record is accurate before the field is used to supply information about an interface element. With one exception (described in the following section), you should never have a reason to modify this field directly. The Updated field indicates the date of the last change made to this entry.

The Data memo field contains the instructions that FoxPro uses to store the PREFerence or DATA information. In figure 15.2 you can see that, in the memo editing window at the bottom right of the figure, this memo field can contain a binary, rather than an ASCII text, entry. Except for DIARYDATA, all Resource records store their data in a format you should not modify directly using the text editor.

If the Resource file was in use under both FoxPro 1 and FoxPro 2, you see records of Type PREF and DATA from FoxPro 1, along with the PREF2.0 and DATA2.0 records that belong to FoxPro 2. The formats of the Data memo fields for these records are not interchangeable. If you created COLORSET records under FoxPro 1, you can create equivalent PREF2.0 records by using the FIXUSER program (under the main FoxPro directory in \GOODIES\MISC). You must recreate and resave other FoxPro 1 preferences and Resource data in the new format.

Diary entries are the only exception to this rule. The Data memo fields for Diary entries are regular ASCII text, like all other memo fields you can edit. The Type continues to be DATA (rather than DATA2.0) and needs no conversion (records created under 1.02 are usable under 2.0). If you choose to edit these memo fields directly, however, you must ensure that the Ckval fields continue to match by using the following formula:

```
REPLACE ckval WITH VAL(SYS(2007, data))
* use a scope appropriate to the scope of records whose
* data field you have edited
```

Fox documentation is inconsistent about the proper value to use for the CKVAL field. The manual gives the preceding formula, and the help file uses VAL(SYS(2007, SUBSTR (data,3))). This second formula is correct for non-DIARYDATA Resource file entries (as stated earlier, you have no reason to edit these entries) but does not appear to work with diary entries. The formulas differ, perhaps, because the other Resource items' version information is stored in the first two characters of the Data field.

Managing Your Resource File

If you have been doing the exercises in this book and did not SET RESOURCE OFF, the Resource file contains more records than when you last examined the file in Chapter 8. FoxPro stores preferences for every window that appears on the desktop, even if you use the associated file only once.

For this reason, Resource files are subject to *bloat*. If you always use the same Resource file, you constantly add new records. After a time, printer setups you created for a test, preferences for text files with an extension you never use, BROWSE LAST setup for every sample table you investigate, and even old 1.02 Resource records remain in the file. This practice not only wastes disk space but also causes FoxPro to perform more slowly as it wades through the Resource file to find needed data.

Regularly SET RESOURCE OFF, USE the Resource file, and delete all unnecessary records. As always, in a BROWSE you can delete records by clicking the mouse in the extreme left column or by pressing Ctrl-T. Be careful not to delete default or saved label layouts or other needed DATA records you laboriously constructed. You may find that deleting all records of a certain Type and Id you no longer need is convenient, either from the Delete option of the Record menu popup or in the Command window. To perform this kind of group deletion, use the following formula:

```
DELETE ALL FOR Id = "MODPRJPOS"
* get rid of MODIFY PROJECT positions
```

After you are sure that you deleted all records you no longer need, PACK the file to reduce the size and to speed FoxPro operations.

Although you probably don't want to delete diary entries as you do other Resource records, from time to time you may archive these records to trim the Resource file. Suppose that you want to archive all diary information for dates older than two months. Assuming that you have no other deleted Resource entries now, you can perform the following:

```
olddate = DTOS(GOMONTH(DATE(), -2))
* The Name field stores the diary date for the entry
* in string form.

DELETE FOR Id = "DIARYDATA" AND Name < olddate
* Notice that you don't use the Updated field, which stores
* information about when the editing was done and not
* about the date to which the entry pertains.

COPY TO OLDDIARY FOR DELETED()
PACK
```

To perform the same process for the following month, however, you want to add to OLDDIARY rather than to replace the file with the next archival set of records. Instead of COPY TO Oldiary, add the following extra steps and a few SQL SELECT tricks:

```
SELECT Foxuser
olddate = DTOS(GOMONTH(DATE(),-2))
DELETE FOR Id = "DIARYDATA" AND Name < olddate
SELECT *, .T.;
  FROM Foxuser ;
  WHERE DELETED() ;
  INTO CURSOR Temp

tempdbf = DBF()           && Store the DBF name
                          && of the cursor
SELECT Olddiary           && Open the archive file

APPEND FROM (tempdbf)     && You use the DBF name
                          && in APPEND FROM
SELECT Temp               && You use the ALIAS name
                          && in the SELECT command

USE                       && Get rid of the cursor
SELECT Foxuser
PACK                      && Get rid of the old records
```

In this procedure, you added an extra field (the .T.) to the field list in the SQL SELECT command. When you perform a SQL SELECT using only one table as the source (the FROM clause), the resultant cursor has the name you specify with the INTO CURSOR clause as its ALIAS(). It does not have a different DBF() name from the original source table. FoxPro is saving time and diskspace by creating a *map* to the matching records in the original table, rather than creating a table on disk. Because the APPEND FROM command uses the DBF() name of the table for its source file, you are APPENDing FROM the original file and getting *all* of the records from the source Foxuser table, rather than just the ones marked `DELETED()`.

The addition of any constant to the end of the field list solves the problem. This addition forces SELECT to treat the cursor as a table with a new structure, requiring a temporary table on disk. This temporary table receives its own DBF(), which you store to a variable and then indirectly reference (using parentheses) in the APPEND FROM command. (The temporary table's DBF() is usually similar to `F:\QUE\58599707.TMP`, but you use the variable instead.) The extra field is ignored during the APPEND FROM; because the Olddiary table has the same structure as your real Resource file, it has no room for this information. After the APPEND FROM is accomplished, you close the cursor, and FoxPro disposes of the temporary table.

After you are satisfied that the Resource file is *clean*, save a copy of the file to a separate name in the main FoxPro directory. Use the COPY TO <*a new filename*> command to create this *template* Resource file, and then use the SCATTER MEMVAR MEMO, APPEND BLANK, and GATHER

MEMVAR MEMO commands to add new *permanent* records to the file from time to time, as you develop color sets, printer setups, and other Resources. By taking this step, you provide an extra layer of security for the FoxPro working environment and also a starting point from which you can create program- and user-specific Resource files for application and network use.

Another way to stop a Resource file from bloating is to make the entire file (rather than specific entries) read-only. In the following section of this chapter, you learn how to mark files read-only directly in FoxPro by using the Filer to reset the file's DOS attributes. You also can make a Resource file read-only for the application you create by including the file in the new APP file (as you may recall from Chapter 14 and from working with the Project Manager, all tables contained in the APP are read-only).

If a Resource file is read-only, you get the advantages of the material saved in it (color sets, label layouts, editing preferences, and printer setups) but you cannot add to it. As you work with FoxPro, your use of the interface and tools matures. You continue to do regular maintenance on the Resource file but eventually find that you no longer need to add new permanent records to the special template copy. You can then SET RESOURCE TO a read-only copy of this template file and eliminate the need for future maintenance.

In FoxPro 2, read-only Resource files also can be shared by many people on a network. Editable Resource files must be used by only one person at a time, which means that each user must have a separate copy of the file.

Each approach has advantages and disadvantages. Read-only Resource files are especially good in situations where disk space is at a premium or when you need tight control over the configuration in which multiple BROWSEs and other windows appear in an application. Editable Resource files give users the greatest degree of flexibility.

Sometimes a combination approach works best, especially if you plan to make diary entries. You can use an editable Resource file but mark many records as read-only by using the logical field provided. To maintain this file, you can enter the following:

```
DELETE FOR ! Readonly AND ! (Id = "DIARYDATA")
BROWSE FOR DELETED() ;
      FIELDS Readonly, Id, Name, Updated ;
      FREEZE Readonly
* The FREEZE allows only the Readonly field to be changed,
* so you can quickly change this field for the one or two
* new records that you really want to keep.
* You can RECALL other DELETED() records individually
* during the BROWSE, also to preserve some editable records
```

```
RECALL FOR Readonly
PACK
* get rid of the rest
```

On a network, a combination approach allows all users common access to a read-only Resource file, yet SETs RESOURCE TO separate editable files when editing diaries. A maintenance routine, performed by the network administrator, can update the DIARYDATA entries in the Common file on a daily basis by using the procedure described in the following listing:

- The user first can make an editable copy of the Common file (so that the user can continue to access the Common file while maintenance is performed). Each user Resource file is USEd AGAIN, and the records are checked for Updated entries with the ID DIARYDATA. The Name field of the copy of the Common file is checked for corresponding diary date entries, to which new records are added where no current entry for this date is FOUND( ), by using SCATTER MEMVAR MEMO from the user file and GATHERing MEMVAR MEMO into the Common file.
- REPLACE *common.data* WITH *user_a.data* ADDITIVE is used to create the cumulative diary entry if a record for this date already exists. (A comment line between entries can indicate each user's contribution to a given diary entry.) REPLACE Updated WITH DATE( ) marks each change. Finally, the Common file copy has the edited records completed by REPLACing the related CHKVAL field WITH VAL(SYS(2007, data)).
- The new copy of the Common file then can be rotated into active, read-only Resource status on the network.

This procedure is useful even in single-user FoxPro, if you maintain separate Resource files for all the people who use FoxPro on a computer but want to share a common calendar. You can work out a marking system for personal diary entries with symbols indicating that you can add certain entries to the common file while others are kept private.

You describe this process in general terms, rather than just reproducing the program, because a key detail (opening and selecting user Resource files) changes depending on how you keep records of users and user Resource files. After you finish reading about programming structures in the following chapter, you may decide this procedure is a worthwhile exercise to attempt.

Creating Application-Specific Resource Files

Whether you plan to make the Resource file editable or read-only, provide a copy of the file in the APP file of any application you distribute. You can make an editable copy of this read-only file during the installation routine. The read-only copy in the APP can provide backup in case the editable copy is destroyed or lost. This backup file also provides the template Resource file copy as new users of a system are added.

A Resource file for a custom-designed application is usually much smaller than the file you use for development. This file doesn't need all the available color sets or Label Layouts if you have settled on one or two settings for the program. A vertical market application Resource file (an application meant for sale in a particular industry, rather than custom-designed for one location), however, may need dozens of color sets and specialized printer setups to handle as many different hardware configurations as possible.

As always, you gauge the sophistication and the needs of users when deciding how many options to make available in a Resource file. Can 20 color sets make finding at least one set that *shows* well on every laptop screen easier, or will these users find so much choice bewildering?

Pay particular attention to the Calculator preferences, if the program you are creating allows access to this FoxPro feature. You may set Decimal Places to `Fixed` for an accounting application but change to `Floating` for a program that handles statistical surveys. You may want to set the Calculator to `Force Numlock ON` for some keyboards but prefer not to alter the state of Numlock for others.

Similarly, if the application uses the GETEXPR command to get user input for queries or other output, you must use the Expression Builder preferences to tailor this complex dialog appropriately. Do users need to see the System Variables, or if you included this information, and the users don't know what these variables are, will this addition only confuse them? Do you remove some functions offered on the data popups to direct users toward other, more useful functions for the kinds of information they want to derive? Do you allow users to edit Resource files? You must consider these individual design decisions for each application.

The Filer

In the preceding section, you archived diary data from the Resource file by using a COPY command, which is unlike the equivalent DOS command. This command copies a table to a new name, including the FPT memo file and main table file if necessary and accepts a scope and conditions. Other optional clauses of this command create data files in non-DBF file formats. You find COPY on the Database menu popup.

However, the FoxPro command COPY FILE performs the same function as a DOS command. In the same diary archiving procedure, you use the FoxPro ERASE command, which also is similar to DOS's ERASE or DEL. A RENAME TO, similar to DOS's RENAME, also is available.

Although these commands offer limited file management, the Filer is a tool expressly provided to enable you to conveniently perform more extensive file and disk management tasks within FoxPro.

The Filer is only available for interactive FoxPro use. If you include the FILER command or attempt to ACTIVATE WINDOW FILER in an application created and distributed by using the Distribution Kit, a `Feature Not Available` message appears on-screen.

Nevertheless, the Filer is useful when you work in FoxPro. The Filer displays information about the files on-disk and enables you to perform DOS functions with a handy visual representation of file maintenance tasks as they are performed. You also can mark (or tag) both files and directories to perform these tasks on groups of files efficiently. You can use file masks to display only files that match certain criteria or in a particular order. You can display and edit the contents of any file on-disk.

No menu shortcut exists for opening the Filer, although if you use Filer frequently, you can add a shortcut to a developer's version of SYSMENU. You also can dock the Filer on the *desktop* at all times, as suggested in Chapter 2. For now, open the Filer by using the System menu popup option or by typing the **FILER** command in the Command Window. The Filer window appears, as shown in figure 15.5.

Most of the Filer window is taken up by a file list similar to file lists you see in Open File and other dialogs. This list, however, gives you far more information about each file than other lists give. The information is the same you see if you issue a DIR command to DOS, and the list also indicates the DOS attribute setting for each file. As in all FoxPro file lists, an entry of brackets with two periods (`[..]`) indicates that you are in a subdirectory and can move up a level in the disk's directory tree by choosing this entry. To the right, the familiar drive and directory popup controls enable you to investigate other files in the system.

Below the popup controls, you see an indication of the file mask that applies to the file list you see. By default, the indication reads `*.*`, which means that you see all files. You can change the mask to look at only program files by typing ***.PRG** or at all files that pertain to the Budget table by typing **Budget.***.

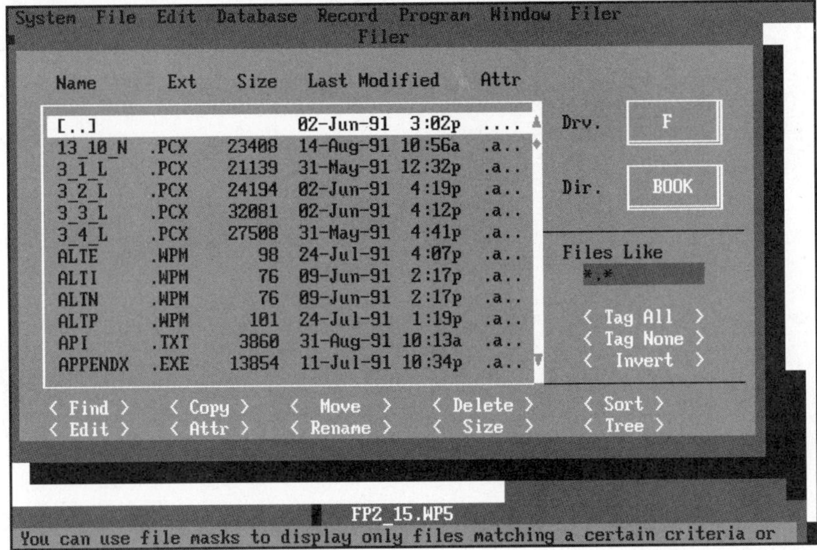

FIG. 15.5

The Filer in Files view.

As usual in a FoxPro list, you can tag entries singly or in groups and then perform actions on the tagged entries. In the file list, you toggle the tag by clicking or using the arrow keys to highlight a file and then pressing the space bar. The familiar ▶ mark appears as you select and tag entries. Use Shift-click or Shift-space bar to tag multiple entries. Below the file mask you see three push buttons that enable you to tag and untag the files in the listing as a group. Try changing the file mask to ***.PRG** and select the `<Tag All>` push button. Then change the file mask back to ***.***; all PRG files remain tagged. Select the `<Invert>` button, and all files except the PRG files are tagged. Select the `<Tag None>` button and all tags disappear.

TIP

You can activate the Filer from the Command window with a file mask already in place, by using the FILER LIKE <file mask> clause. A file mask created in this way or in the Filer Files Like text box may contain more than one skeleton, separated by semicolons, such as the following:

```
FILER LIKE *.txt; C*.; str???.fxp
```

In this example, the Filer displays all files with a TXT extension, all files that begin with C and have no extension, and all files with five-character names beginning with STR and ending with an FXP extension.

Below the file list, a double row of action buttons enables you to manage files. Most of these buttons are designed for use when files are tagged. Now that you used the `<Tag None>` button, for example, select the `<Edit>` button and the message `No files are tagged` appears. If a file (or files) is tagged, selecting the `<Edit>` button brings up one FoxPro text editing window for each tagged file.

The `<Size>` push button shows statistics on the files you tagged so that you can decide, for example, whether the file can fit on a floppy disk before you try to Move or Copy the file.

> **CAUTION:** In the FoxPro Filer, you may not always see all the files you tagged (unlike many other file-management programs you may have used). Tags persist even after you change drives and directories. Always use the `<Tag None>` button before you change directories or check tagged file statistics with the `<Size>` button before choosing to perform file management operations. With the `<Edit>` button, the worst that can happen is that you run out of memory before FoxPro can open editing windows for all the tagged files. However, if you are deleting files, you can lose a great deal of valuable information quickly.

As shown in figure 15.6, you can use the `<Attr>` push button to change the DOS file attributes for a file or files. The capability of marking a file as read-only makes this option especially useful for Resource file maintenance. The Filer cannot perform this action or any other on a file currently open in FoxPro.

Along with the capability of limiting the files you see provided by the file mask, the Sort button enables you to view files in different orders. In figure 15.7, you see the Filer Sort dialog, specifying a `Date Descending` order. This particular order is handy to see files on which you recently worked.

The `<Find>` button can help you locate, and tag for editing, any text string in files of any format. Recall that you used a variable named *big_item* in a report in Chapter 10. Suppose that you want to see all procedures that make a reference to this variable. As shown in figure 15.8, the Find dialog tools enable you to specify up to three text strings and whether any, or all, of the strings must be found for a file to be tagged. As usual, in a FoxPro Find dialog, you can specify case sensitivity.

Initiating the search as shown in figure 15.8 in the MODEL directory, you find that several files are tagged. If you select the `<Edit>` button, all tagged files open in edit windows, with the first instance of the search string highlighted. Here, you do not want to edit the files directly because these files are not ASCII text files, but you still can view the files to provide enough clues for you to open the relevant files with a MODIFY SCREEN or MODIFY MENU command and quickly locate the changes that you need to make.

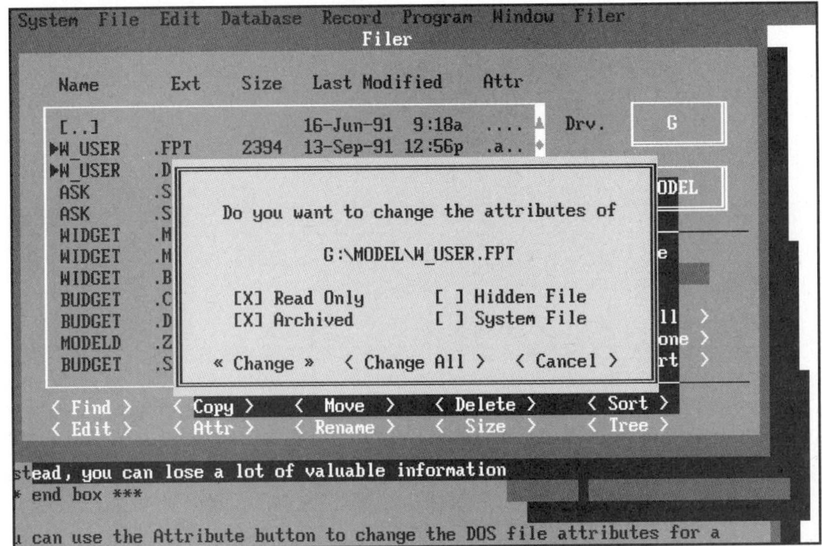

FIG. 15.6

The Filer Attributes dialog.

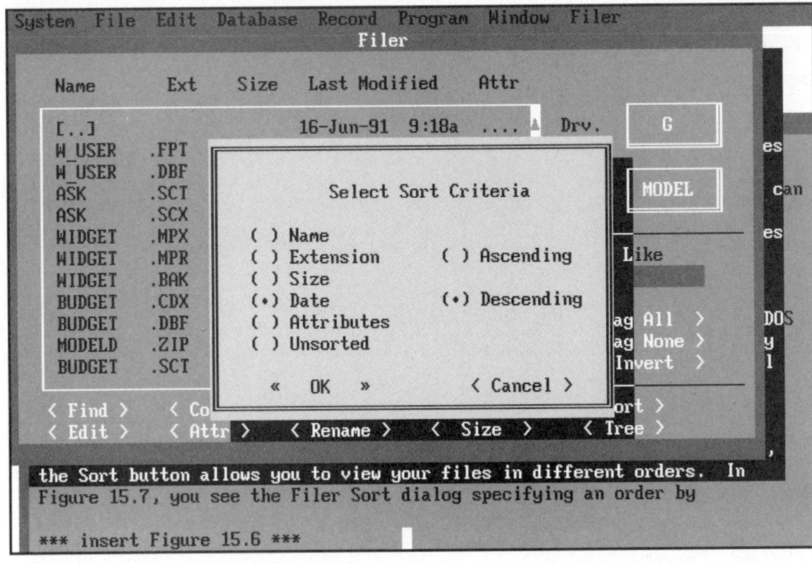

FIG. 15.7

The Filer Sort dialog.

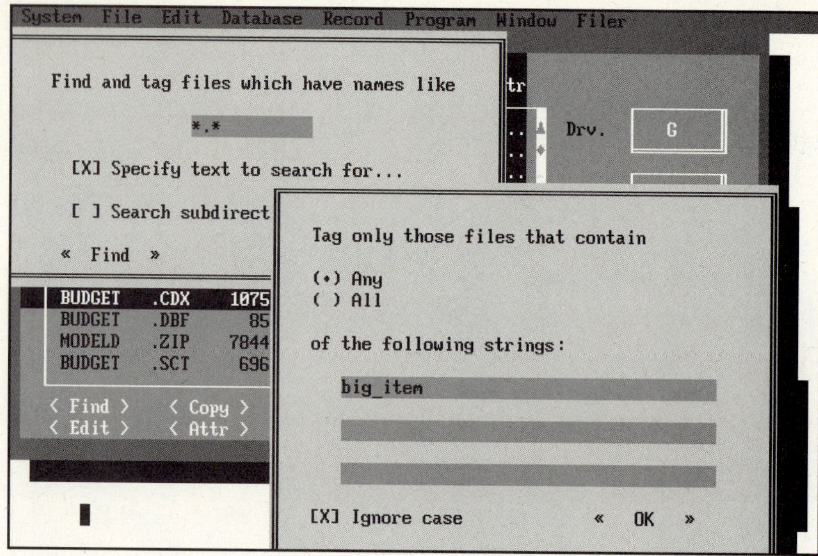

FIG. 15.8

The Filer Find dialogs.

Using the <Find> push button in the Filer changes the current search string in the Find dialog you access from the Edit menu popup, so finding other instances of the target in any file you open is easy. You open files for editing by pressing Ctrl-F.

The <Find> button has a separate file mask, which you can maintain separately from the file mask used to display files in the Filer list. You can even tag files not currently displayed. If you `Search subdirectories`, a small arrow appears to the left of a subdirectory name in which files were tagged in a search.

The Filer window is crowded, and maneuvering among the buttons with the Tab or arrow keys may be awkward. Fortunately, although the buttons do not have hot keys, menu shortcuts are provided in the Filer menu popup for *all* button options. Press Ctrl-L now, (the equivalent to selecting the <Tree> push button), to switch from a Files display to a Tree display.

Figure 15.9 shows the Tree and the Filer menu popup. Notice the menu shortcuts, which make the Filer much easier to navigate by keyboard. Also notice that, while in the Tree display, the buttons at the bottom change to a set appropriate to directory management. Many options in the menu popup also are disabled. In Tree mode, you can tag a directory or directories just as you previously tagged files. You can perform operations on entire directories, including any subdirectories just as you did on files. You also can create new directories and move whole directories of files to the new directory, preserving subdirectory structure as you do so. The <Size> button gives you at-a-glance information about whole directories.

A small dot indicates the current directory on the drive in view. You can use the <Chdir> push button to change the current directory on this drive. If you SET DEFAULT TO this drive, the chosen directory becomes the default FoxPro directory.

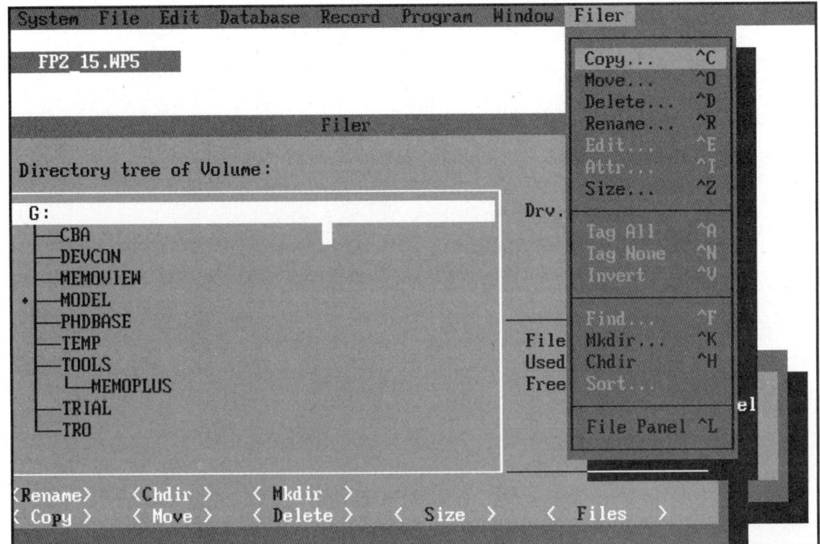

FIG. 15.9

The Filer in Tree view and the Filer menu popup options.

FoxPro Color Control

Most people who are familiar with DOS feel comfortable in the Filer, because the screen is similar in feel and operation to other utility programs available outside of FoxPro. The advantage is that you don't have to leave FoxPro to use the Filer.

On the other hand, the FoxPro color system, which has no obvious analogs in other computer programs, is a world unto itself because the system is designed specifically to handle the FoxPro interface. The color system gives you complete control over the colors used to display every element of each interface object. For this reason, newcomers to FoxPro often consider the color system an arcane subject suitable only for experts.

You may never need to adjust FoxPro's default colors. The use of color in programs, however, is a subject that affects every user at every moment; therefore, this system is worth study. This section starts with a few notes on color's effect on interface design. Then you learn to implement these principles by using the FoxPro color system. Because each interface element can have colors specified separately, you find that manipulating the color system requires patience and exacting syntax—but the system is not very complicated to use.

Understanding Color's Effect on the Interface

Paul Klee, whose art achieved a rare level of communication using simple forms and images, once airily described his work by saying, "To paint well is simply this: to put the right color in the right place." Although putting this much emphasis on color—either in painting or in computer interface design—may be an exaggeration, color has a significant role in keeping people happy. When you decide on the colors you want to use for different screen objects in a program, you may think you are making a highly personal decision. You, however, can apply a few basic standards and principles to ensure that other people are as pleased with the colors as you are.

Use strong colors sparingly, and always on dull background tones. Striking colors can provide annotation to the general content of a screen, highlighting important facts while the muted background keeps the screen calm and harmonious. In large doses, strong colors can confuse the eye; the viewer or user cannot spot what is important.

Never rely on color alone for communication. Remember that some users are color blind and that other users may see certain colors, but not respond well to this particular cue. To avoid relying on color to present a message, develop the interface with the understanding that some users have only monochrome or gray-scale monitors.

As in all other elements of interface design, make the colors consistent. If a particular color is reserved for the background of memo editing windows in all modules, the users get used to memo editing conventions (keystrokes, preferences, and closing methods) when they see this color.

Look around you (not just at computer screens) for color selections that you find pleasing and take note of color combinations that displease. Edward R. Tufte's, *Envisioning Information*, cited in Chapter 11, includes many examples of distinctive and extraordinarily beautiful color combinations. He also provides other examples that show how color can inflict active damage when used carelessly. Be warned, as he notes, that "some color applied to display screens has made what should be a straightforward tool into something that looks like a grim parody of a video machine." His examples of color usage to avoid include a screen shot used in a FoxPro 1 advertisement.

Learning About Color Assignments

As you think about color assignments, remember that this subject also affects users of monochrome monitors. In monochrome systems, FoxPro provides fewer choices with which to work but the same principles apply. You can set an object in reverse video; you can intensify the brightness; the object can be made to blink; or text can be underlined. You can use these differences in the same way that you use colors in color systems.

To use colors in a computer program interface, you assign colors to different interface elements. The FoxPro color system enables you to assign colors on three levels: color pair, color scheme, and color set.

The most basic unit in this system is the *color pair.* A color pair consists of two colors, the foreground and background colors for a single element of a single display object, such as the clock, the hot keys on a menu, or the border of a window.

The middle level unit is the *color scheme*, which consists of the color pairs required to display a single screen object. A color scheme consists of 10 numbered color pairs, although you don't need to use all 10 pairs with a given screen object. In Chapter 8, for example, you learned that the color scheme for the object "Browse," uses these 10 pairs in the following way:

- The first color pair is used for displayed records, and this background color provides the background color of the Browse grid.
- The second pair is used for the current field.
- The third pair is used for the border, and this background color provides the foreground color of the Browse grid.
- The fourth and fifth pair create the title (in active and inactive states).
- The sixth pair is used for any text selected with text-editing methods.
- The seventh pair is used for the current record, and this background color provides the color for the DELETE bullet.
- The eighth pair provides the shadow color.
- The ninth and tenth pairs are unused.

The object, *Menu Popup*, uses the 10 color pairs in this scheme to handle these completely different elements:

- The first pair is used for disabled options.
- The second pair displays enabled options, and so on.

A chapter in the *Developer's Guide* volume of the manuals contains charts that list the way each major interface object uses a color scheme. Various entries in the *Commands and Functions* manual that pertain to the definition of particular interface objects, such as the ones for @ GET controls, supplement these charts with more information.

Whenever you work in FoxPro, you have 24 color schemes available for use, each with the 10 pairs. These 24 schemes comprise a single color set. A *color set*, therefore, is the upper level of the color system, a collection of all the color schemes necessary to define the use of color in one application.

NOTE When you load FoxPro, a default color set is loaded. The default color set is determined by a COLORSET-Type record with the Name DEFAULT in the active Resource file. One of the standard COLORSET records was given this Name when you installed FoxPro and chose a Monitor Type, as described in Appendix A. If your CONFIG.FP contains the line `RESOURCE=OFF` or `RESOURCE= <filename>`, naming a particular Resource file that does not have a DEFAULT record, FoxPro checks your video hardware to determine whether a basic color or monochrome set should be used. You can create a color set with the name DEFAULT at any time—and if it is contained in the Resource file active at startup, the color set is loaded along with FoxPro.

Just as color pairs of a scheme are assigned numbers within the scheme, the available schemes also are numbered within the set. Each interface object is assigned a default scheme, using the first 12 schemes of the set By default. Browses take colors from Scheme 10, and Menu Popups use Scheme 4.

Although only one color set is active at a time, you can change the default assignments for the color pairs of any of the schemes in the active set. You can save new assignments as completely separate color sets. Each saved color set has a unique name and an entry in the FoxPro Resource file.

When you DEFINE an interface object, such as a WINDOW, if you do not issue specific color instructions, the object is given the default colors for the related object type, using the default scheme number and the color scheme currently loaded. You can change these defaults by performing one of the following steps:

- Changing the color pairs in its default scheme
- Defining the object with instructions to use a different color scheme or with an explicit list of color pairs
- Loading a different color set (normally not done within an application, except during setup procedures)

Editing, Saving, and Restoring Color Sets

You may think you must memorize the various color scheme and pair assignments or use cryptic codes to refer to the sets. The FoxPro interface, however, provides several ways to choose colors without remembering which pairs and which schemes go with each object. The following sections discuss these methods and cover the color codes, and the way you assign these codes in programs.

The FoxPro Color Picker

The Color Picker is the FoxPro's native dialog for making color changes. In Chapter 2, you used the Color Picker briefly. As you return to this tool, you certainly recognize many more of the interface objects to which the Color Picker refers.

The Color Picker, like the Filer, has no menu shortcut. No command exists to invoke this tool; the Window menu popup option is the only way you can access the Color Picker, so use this option now. Notice that the popup control in the upper right corner enables you to specify the scheme for which you want to pick color pairs. Select the scheme, and you see the screen shown in figure 15.10.

As you see in this dialog, FoxPro doesn't really expect or even encourage you to remember the number of schemes to which each interface object defaults. Rather than scheme numbers, you choose a scheme by the name of the related characteristic object. When you invoke the Color Picker, the popup control is preset to the type of object currently in the active output window. If you select the popup control and choose a different object, the list of radio buttons displays the pair assigned for this scheme, as applied to the scheme's default object.

Numbered schemes follow Alert Pops (Schemes 13 through 24), which do not have interface objects assigned to them by default. Of these, Fox Software indicates that, in the future, Schemes 13 through 17 may be assigned to new interface objects. When you create custom schemes, therefore, use Schemes 18 and higher.

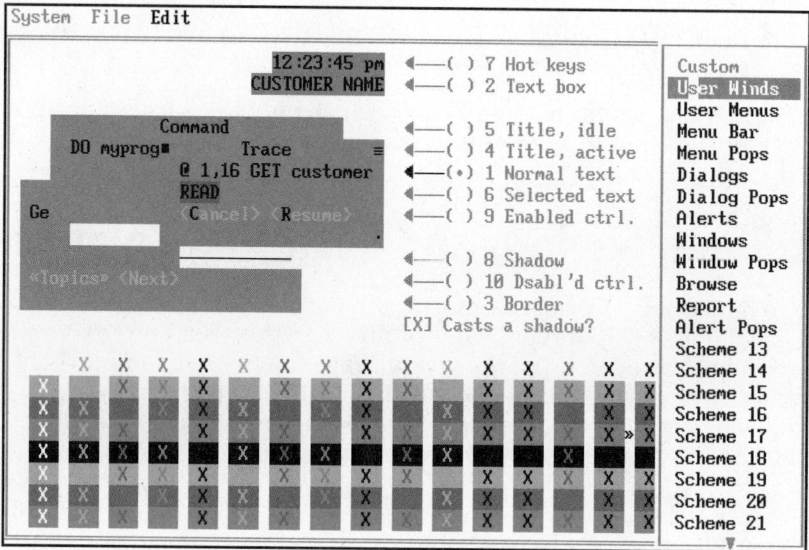

FIG. 15.10

The Color Picker, choosing a Scheme from the popup control list.

All the unused schemes (13 through 24) are presently set by default to the same colors as Scheme 1 (User Windows). Select User Windows from the popup control and look at the colors used in the sample windows on the left. These colors are what you see if you DEFINE a WINDOW without setting colors.

You also see a scheme labeled `Custom`, above the first (User Windows) Scheme in the popup control. This scheme is disabled unless you have DEFINEd one or more WINDOW. If you have, while you are working interactively, this scheme can be used to reference it. The `Custom` label in the popup control changes to a user window's DEFINEd name whenever that window is the active output window. When a different object is active, the Custom scheme is disabled again. You cannot use this Custom scheme in a program, and you cannot refer to it in any way by using a FoxPro command.

Look at the two check boxes in this dialog. The `Casts a Shadow` box applies to the scheme as a whole and indicates whether objects DEFINEd with this COLOR SCHEME cast a shadow by default. You can override this option with the SHADOW/NOSHADOW keywords when you DEFINE the object. The `Blink/Bright` check box applies to color pair in the scheme. If BLINK is SET ON (the default setting), you can make the object that uses any color pair blink on and off. If BLINK is OFF and you are using an EGA or VGA monitor, you can change the intensity of the background color of any pair to a brighter version of the same color. Use these two options sparingly because bright backgrounds and blinking objects can be tiring to view.

Start by changing the colors of one color pair in Scheme 1. Most people prefer to set the clock colors differently from the default. As you see from the radio button list in the middle of the dialog, the clock colors are determined by color pair 7 of this scheme (the first selection on the list).

Use the mouse to select the radio button for the clock (or press the Tab key to move to the button and then press the space bar). You can now use the color pair grid at the bottom of the display to choose new colors for the clock. The chevrons »« indicate the current color pair. Click the mouse on the desired color pair. With the keyboard, use the cursor keys to move the chevrons (after you pressed the space bar, while a selection is highlighted) to different color combinations on the grid and press Enter when you are satisfied.

This change represents an alteration on the first (color pair) level of the color system.

But as you change the color of the sample clock object, you notice that the hot keys for the `Enabled Ctrl.` radio button (otherwise controlled by color pair 9) also change. Color pair 7 actually controls more than one element of the interface in this scheme.

Suppose that you want to DEFINE a WINDOW in default User Window colors, either by yourself or through the Screen Builder and you want the clock to show, but you don't want the push button hot keys to reflect the same colors as the clock. You can assign new colors for the push button object directly from the Screen Builder (which is covered in the following paragraphs), but a more typical method is to make this change by using the middle level of the color system, which changes the SCHEME responsible for this window. You can perform this change easily through the Color Picker.

You see what looks like a modified version of SYSMENU at the top of this dialog. If you try to access the menu popups, the only options available are Copy and Paste from the Edit menu (and Paste is disabled until you use Copy in the Color Picker). Press Ctrl-C or select the Copy option to copy the color assignments for this scheme. Use the popup control to select Scheme 18 and press Ctrl-V (Paste). The colors in the sample objects, including the clock colors, change to the colors you picked for Scheme 1. Now select color pair 7 in this scheme, and change to a color pair that looks better as push button hot keys.

If you issue the following commands and have a READ with push buttons in this window, all button hot keys change to the colors you want while the clock continues to respond to the instructions of Scheme 1:

```
SET CLOCK ON
DEFINE WINDOW <window name> ;
FROM <row1,col1> TO <rol2, col2> COLOR SCHEME 18
ACTIVATE WINDOW <window name>
```

Use the <Save> push button to change the third level of the color system: save the edited schemes to a color set. After the list of available color set names appears, you can overwrite an existing set or save these changes to a color set with a new name. As previously explained, you create or edit an entry in the Resource file when you perform this procedure. To access a custom color set later, or in other FoxPro 2 sessions, the same Resource file entry must be available. You can use the Load button in the Color Picker and select this color set, or you can use the following command in a program or the Command window:

SET COLOR SET TO *<your set name>*

FoxPro contains many commands kept for compatibility with older xBase dialects that set colors of items of the interface as a separate step. You can SET COLOR TO or SET COLOR OF TITLES or INFORMATION TO explicitly named color pairs. When you do this, however, you change the colors in the active color set and you end up changing the colors of other elements in the interface you didn't mean to affect. Use the Scheme system directly rather than these older commands.

ProColor: an Application Alternative

The Color Picker is unavailable in applications you build and distribute with the Distribution Kit. A sample application included with FoxPro, ProColor, written by C. Blaise Mitsutama of Shared Resource Associates provides an example of ways you can give users these same capabilities.

ProColor's premise is more suitable for a distributed application than is the Color Picker. ProColor checks the Resource file you designate for available color sets and lists these sets. You select the color set you want to edit. Using a standard FoxPro 2 dialog approach, ProColor provides complete examples of different interface objects, each in a related default scheme, as shown in figure 15.11. Each object's elements are clearly labeled. Without worrying about the number scheme or pair at which you are looking, you choose an object with colors you want to change. After you choose an object, you see a list of attributes, such as the list in figure 15.12. After you select an attribute, a modified version of the color pair grid appears, with the name of the item you are preparing to change.

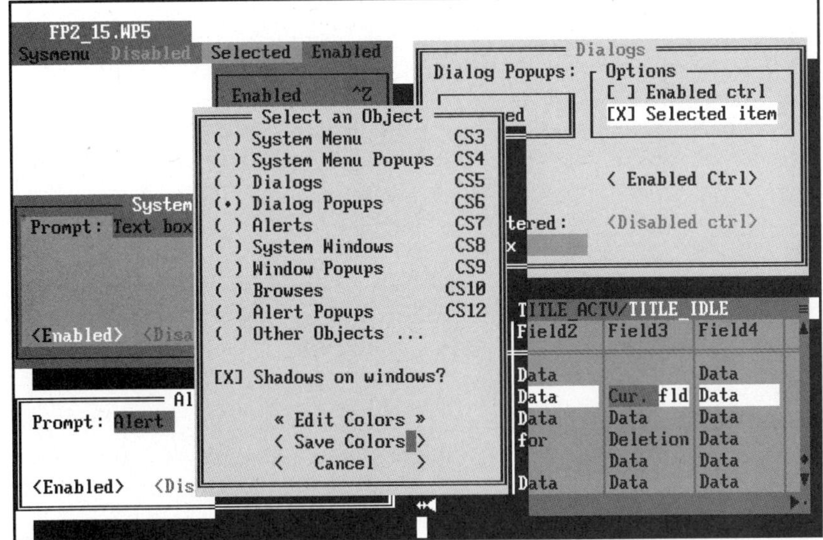

FIG. 15.11

Choosing an Interface Object to color-design in ProColor.

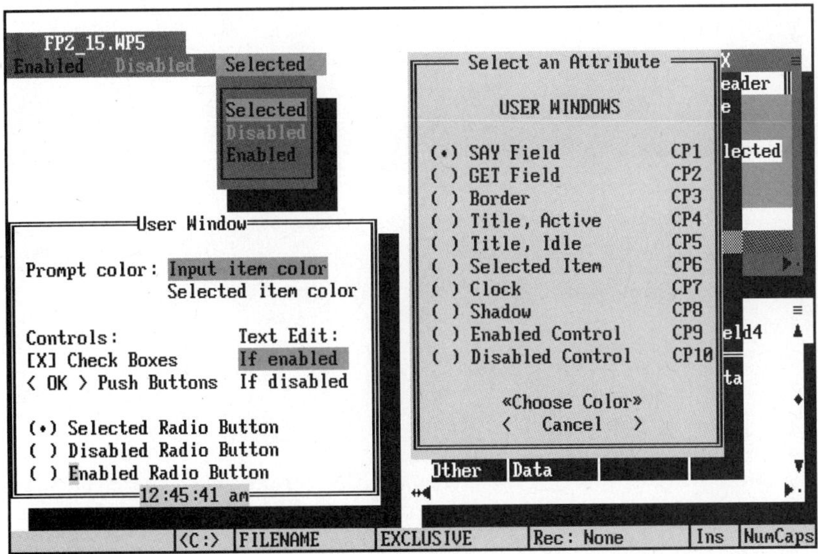

FIG. 15.12

Choosing color Attributes for an Interface Object in ProColor.

ProColor's help file includes the complete listings of the color pairs, the pair schemes, and relationships to interface objects. You can use the file while you run ProColor (as part of the APP) or investigate the file, and the rest of ProColor's source code, in the \GOODIES\PROCOLOR directory, under the main FoxPro directory. You will find these listings a useful reference, even if you do not use ProColor.

You may not want to give users the sweeping control ProColor provides; this tool is intended for developers who work on color sets for programs. However, ProColor provides a good model to use in simplified form: present users with a selection of usable and familiar objects, in the current default colors and ranged together so that the users can see how the entire interface works together. Give users a chance to make decisions about each object, but make sure that the objects continue to appear together so that the users can judge the effects of these changes. After the users are satisfied, use the CREATE COLOR SET command to save the results to a Resource file entry.

TIP

At start up, FoxPro checks the video board in the system to see whether colors are supported. When you create setup procedures for new applications, you have access to the same kinds of checks by using the ISCOLOR( ) and SYS(2006) functions. FoxPro, however, may see the system's *video board* as supporting color, while the *monitor* displays in monochrome or gray scale. If this situation occurs, you may not see all interface elements. Use the Color Picker or ProColor to choose one of the nondefault color sets immediately or tinker with the color pairs for various objects until all objects are visible.

Programs you create may have trouble setting default color sets for the same reason. Rely on ISCOLOR( ) and SYS(2006) only long enough to ask the users some setup questions. These setup questions can use the same approach that ProColor uses: create sample objects and make sure that all elements are clearly visible to the user.

Color Use in the Application-Building Tools

When you studied the Screen Builder in Chapter 13, you learned how to give color instructions within a screen so that GENSCRN generates the proper color clauses. You DEFINE a WINDOW with COLOR SCHEME instructions by using the Type dialog available as a Screen Layout option. This dialog enables you to specify both a general scheme and one for all popups contained in this screen.

When you select a GET or GETs, the Color option is enabled on the screen menu popup. You can generate a COLOR SCHEME clause to make an object responsive to color instructions in a scheme other than the one you specified for the screen as a whole. You also can select multiple objects, or group objects, and assign colors to all the objects at the same time.

Remember that no matter what scheme you specify, a GET or other interface object always uses the same color pair within the scheme. A selected option in a dialog popup, for example, always responds to color pair 6, in whatever color scheme is used.

When you select a SAY, a text object, or a box object in a screen you have the added option of selecting a color pair directly. Figure 15.13 shows the modified Color Picker that appears if you use the `Color pair` check box in the Color dialog (a box object was selected in the screen).

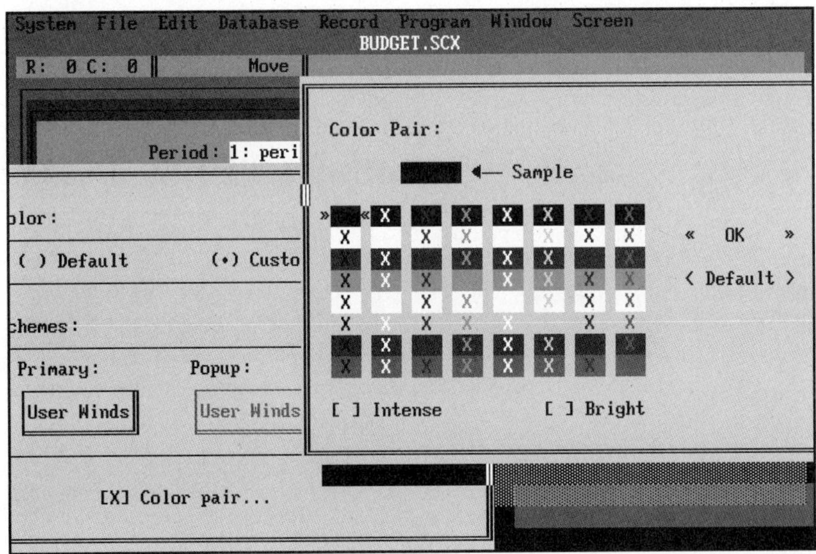

FIG. 15.13

Screen Object Color dialogs.

You may wonder why you cannot choose color pairs directly for other screen objects. Two good reasons explain why this option is not supplied:

- A single color pair is insufficient for most screen objects. You usually need to pick several pairs to define all the various attributes, and the scheme system is expressly designed to handle this procedure.

- Defining color pairs directly is not recommended under most circumstances because the effect—depending on the current hardware and color set in use—may be different than what you expect. Always define colors relatively, rather than explicitly, so that the selections coordinate with other colors in use. You explore ways to define colors in the following section.

You can use the generator directive #READCLAUSES (described in Chapter 13), to add a COLOR clause to a READ statement for a screen file. This clause changes the colors of the current GET object as you move through the objects in the screen. The COLOR clause, like single object color assignments, can be either a COLOR SCHEME or a list of color pairs, as described in the next section. Only the second pair (used for GETs) of the scheme or list is used for the READ-level COLOR clause.

In rare cases where you must attach a color clause to a GET or EDIT, you can use the ~ITSEXPRESSION trick described in Chapter 13 to include this clause in the Format text box, or you can use similar tricks to include it in any GET clause you want, assigning that clause an Expression (rather than Procedure) type. For example, a WHEN clause expression may read `your_when()COLOR SCHEME 3` or even `.T. COLOR g/b`.

The Menu Builder offers you access to color control by scheme for the menu bar and also for each associated menu popup. You specify the color scheme you want to use in the Menu Option of the Menu popup (the second bar, which gives you options specific to the particular level you are editing). Take care if you change the scheme for one or more popups in a menu; click the `<Try It>` push button several times to make sure that you like the effect produced. Chapter 14 gives you additional hints on color definition and redefinition for menus.

Although the Report Writer and Label Designer don't support color schemes directly, you can create special Style codes that issue printer-specific instructions for color printers. You need to edit DRIVER.PRG, which is a part of the printer driver application GENPD.APP or create a new driver to handle the style codes. Printer Drivers and GENPD.APP are discussed in a section near the end of this chapter.

Program Instructions To Alter Colors

As previously stated, setting color pairs explicitly is not recommended in FoxPro programs because users can't adjust colors, and you cannot use the same instructions to fit different hardware. Use relative color instructions to set a single pair or a scheme. The keys to this process are the SCHEME( ) function and the SET COLOR OF SCHEME command.

To match another scheme, you can use the following command:

SET COLOR OF SCHEME <*scheme number*> TO <*scheme number*>

This step is the same as using the copy and paste options in the Color Picker, but the SCHEME( ) function also enables you to adjust each color pair individually.

With one numeric parameter, the SCHEME( ) function returns a string of all the color pairs in the scheme that correspond to the number in the active color set. If you are using a color system and the color set is in the default state, you can use the following command:

WAIT WINDOW SCHEME(8)

The altered window contains the following string of characters:

```
W+/BG,W+/W,GR+/W,GR+/W,N+/W,W+/GR,BG+/BG,N+/N,B/BG,W/BG,+
```

This string is composed of the scheme's 10 color pairs, separated by commas, in numerical order from left to right. Scheme 8 provides the default colors for system windows, such as the command window and text-editing windows that appear after you use MODIFY COMMAND or MODIFY FILE.

With two numeric parameters SCHEME( ) returns information for a specific color pair. Issue the following instruction:

WAIT WINDOW SCHEME(8,3)

This instruction shows the foreground and background colors of the third color pair in Scheme 8, used for the following borders:

GR+/W

FoxPro uses the designations shown in table 15.1 for different colors available in the interface.

Table 15.1 FoxPro Color Codes

Code	Color	Used By
N	Black	Color and Monochrome
X	Blank	Color and Monochrome (used for passwords)
W	White	Color and Monochrome
U	Underline	Monochrome
I	Inverse	Monochrome
B	Blue	Color
GR	Brown	Color

continues

Table 15.1 Continued

Code	Color	Used By
BG	Cyan	Color
G	Green	Color
RB	Magenta	Color
R	Red	Color
GR+	Yellow	Color

Notice the plus sign (+) after the code GR in the table, used for Yellow. In a FoxPro color code, the + symbol denotes intensity for a foreground color (yellow is considered an intense brown). On a color monitor, after SET BLINK is OFF, you can use an asterisk (*) to brighten or intensify a background color. After SET BLINK is ON, the asterisk makes the object or element that uses this color pair blink.

On monochrome monitors, an asterisk used with a color pair always makes the foreground blink and a plus sign always makes the foreground bright, regardless of how you SET BLINK.

Foreground and background colors in the pair are always separated by a slash, and pairs are always separated by commas. Where you place the asterisk in relation to the color pair really doesn't matter. On a color monitor, for example, all the following codes—and any other variations you try—produce the same effect:

```
*+W/G
*W/G+
+W/G*
W/G*+
W*/+G
```

In the default SCHEME(8) string, you also see an extra plus sign after the 10th color pair and comma. This sign indicates that objects defined with this scheme cast a shadow if no SHADOW/NOSHADOW instructions are issued. Although officially you have only 10 pairs, you can use SCHEME(<*scheme number*>,11) to get this information.

How do you use what you learn from SCHEME( ) to edit a color set in a program? Suppose that you have a SAY in a screen that indicates whether the current record was deleted. This SAY expression may look like the following:

```
IIF(DELETED(),"Deleted Record",SPACE(14))
```

The SAY is marked Refresh so that when you issue a SHOW GETS command as you change records, either the "Deleted Record" comment or nothing appears in the appropriate position.

This window is designed in User Window colors but you want this comment to be noticed, rather than being the same colors as other SAYs. Because this window contains a *warning* comment, you may want to give the windows colors you normally reserve for Alerts.

If you decide to use the normal text colors from an Alert for this SAY, use the Color popup control to assign this SAY object to the Alert scheme. This step just tells FoxPro to use the same color pair (color pair 1) from Scheme 7 instead of the Scheme 1 colors used for the rest of the screen.

Suppose that you want to use the Alert enabled control colors for this SAY. You have a special control in the window that you can use to toggle the DELETED( ) state, and you want both states to have the same colors. You also want the "Deleted" warning to blink. If you explicitly set these colors for the SAY, you cannot edit—or enable users to edit—these Alert colors without destroying the subliminal connection between this "Deleted" warning and the other Alert messages.

Instead, determine the current colors for an Alert control in the setup snippet for the screen and place the changes into a *memvar* variable. Notice that pairs are separated by commas, and that commas are added between pairs to act as *placeholders* for the pairs not changed:

```
PRIVATE colorvar
* set up the memory variable to hold the information

* Then set up a string to represent this information,
* using the Alert color pair 9 and a "blink" asterisk for
* color pair 1 (the SAY), adding Alert button colors for
* pairs 6,7,9, and 10, which is used by the related button

colorvar = SCHEME(7,9)+"*"+    ;
           REPLICATE(",",5)+   ;
           SCHEME(7,6)+","+    ;
           SCHEME(7,7)+","+    ;
           ","             +   ;
           SCHEME(7,9)+","+    ;
           SCHEME(7,10)
* string colorvar now holds: W+/R*,,,,,W+/N,GR+/R,,W+/R,W/R

* store it to a scheme with an indirect reference

SET COLOR OF SCHEME 18 TO (colorvar)
SET BLINK ON
* so the SAY will blink rather than be bright
```

Now you can designate Scheme 18 for this one SAY and for the one related button through the Screen Builder. No matter what Alert colors you change, if the colors are consistently defined with Scheme 7, they match.

You aren't even restricted to using the information provided by SCHEME( ) one complete pair at a time; you can separate out a color pair into its foreground, background, and attribute components. You may have occasion to use an *invisible GET* that doesn't appear on the background of a screen; perhaps the related WHEN clause performs a check of some kind, or you are entering passwords. You can use the "X" (blank) color code instead, but this selection provides the same effect on color monitors as N/N (black). By using the color schemes, you can create a completely invisible GET without knowing the colors you are using in the surrounding screen.

First, find out the current color used for the background of the current window. Assuming that you are still working in a window DEFINEd with COLOR SCHEME 1, you find it using the following:

```
backcolor = SCHEME(1,1)
* get the first pair, used for normal
* text and the general window background —
* by default, this would be W+/B

backcolor = SUBSTR(backcolor,AT("/",backcolor)+1)
* find the position of the slash and
* take only what comes after it (B is the default)

* build a new pair using only this color
backcolor = backcolor+"/"+backcolor
* new pair is B/B in the default
```

Now you can put this new color pair to work:

```
* add a comma in front, so you can represent the
* second pair in a scheme, used by GETs
backcolor = ","+backcolor

* set up a scheme that will be designated for
* your dummy GET to use
SET COLOR OF SCHEME 19 to (backcolor)
* same as saying SET COLOR OF SCHEME 19 to ,B/B
* scheme 19 now holds:
* W+/B,B/B,GR+/B,GR+/B,R+/B,W+/GR,GR+/RB,N+/N,GR+/B,R+/B,+
```

After you designate Scheme 19 for this GET through the Screen Builder, the GET becomes invisible.

One inconsistency exists between user-defined objects and system objects, such as FoxPro error message alerts, dialogs, or the Command window: any change you make to an active color scheme affects the next appearance of a system object in the interface. A user object, however, receives the color instructions at the time you DEFINE the object. The user object doesn't change colors if you adjust the color scheme to which it responds unless you reDEFINE the user object, which sets new color instructions.

As a result, if you adjust a color scheme to handle a particular user window, as you learned to do in this section, you don't need to leave this scheme in the same state as long as you use the window. Unless you subsequently redefine this window, you can SET COLOR OF SCHEME <*scheme number*> TO, with no instructions following, to reset the scheme to the default state in the color set. You can use the same scheme to give other objects default or different instructions at any time.

Macros

Compared to the FoxPro color system, FoxPro macros are similar to utilities you may know from other computer programs. Macros are sequences of keystrokes produced in response to a single key combination. Macros are useful to automate repetitive tasks and to simulate keyboard input in an application.

You can store up to 1,024 keystrokes in one FoxPro macro, and macros can call other macros to produce even longer sequences. You cannot, however, repeat mouse clicks and mouse movements in a macro. When you define a macro, always use the keyboard equivalent for actions that you usually perform with a mouse.

To think about ways in which macros can be useful, consider the status line, a new feature of the FoxPro 2 editor. Windows opened for editing (either FILE or PROGRAM) do not include the status line by default. You can save a preference for the status line to appear for all files of a certain extension, but you may want to open and edit files of many extensions. A macro can make repeating this sequence unnecessary every time you start editing files with a new extension.

You define, or record, a macro by pressing the exact keystrokes you want replayed when the macro is run. Create the exact same situation that will exist when the macro is replayed so that these keystrokes have the proper effect. To create the proper environment, open a text file for editing. Press Shift-F10 to begin defining a macro. The dialog in figure 15.14 appears. Press a key combination you want to use for this macro, and the macro name appears in the Defined Key text box.

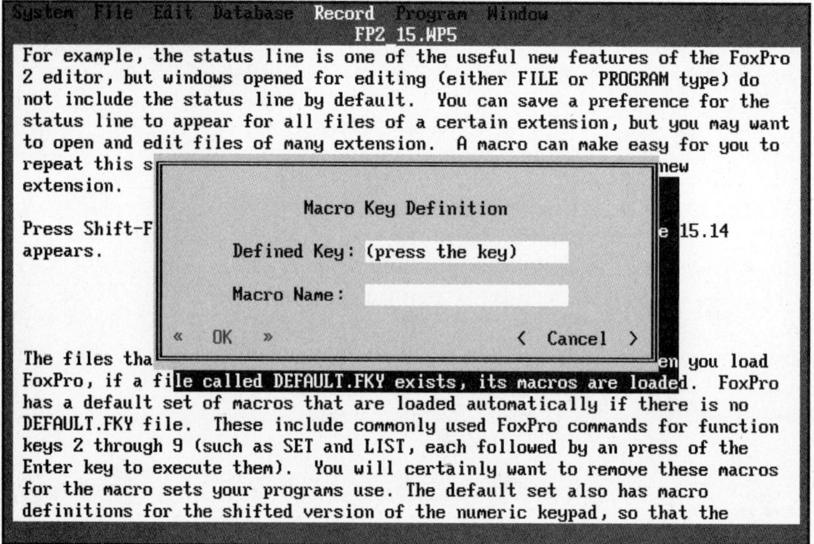

FIG. 15.14

The Macro Key Definition dialog.

You can use the Ctrl or the Alt key in combination with most keys, plus multiple shift combinations (Shift-Ctrl, Shift-Alt, Shift-Ctrl-Alt) with the alphabetic keys and function keys. You can use Alt-F10 with the alphabetic keys. You also can use certain non-alphanumeric keys as macros without shift combinations. In the *Interface Guide* volume of the documentation, you see a list of key presses valid for macros. All invalid key presses for macros are not accepted in the Defined Key text box.

Use multiple shift combinations for macros because so many single-shift combinations are already used by the standard SYSMENU.

If you want an easily remembered macro for *Status Line*, a good choice may be Ctrl-Alt-S, or Shift-Ctrl-S. Alt-S invokes the System menu popup, and Ctrl-S is a menu shortcut in a number of the conditional menu popups. (In Appendix F, you find a list of the single-shift combinations, with notes on how each combination is used in the FoxPro interface.)

After you press Ctrl-Alt-S, Ctrl_Alt_S appears as a default name for this macro in the Macro name text box. Because you use the macro name as a reminder of what the macro performs, change this name to something understandable. Use the mouse to click on, or tab to, the Macro name text box. (No other key works; if you try the down-arrow key, you define a macro for the DNARROW key. You cannot define macros for the Tab or Shift-Tab key, although these keystrokes can be used within a macro sequence of keystrokes.)

Macro names can be up to 19 characters long but may not contain spaces. Macro names are saved in all capital letters, no matter how the name is typed. Type **STATUS_LINE** as a macro name and press Ctrl-Enter to confirm the choice (or Tab to the «OK» button and press Enter). A message window indicates that you are now recording a macro.

Now type the exact keystrokes you want used in the macro. To create a macro for status lines in the editor, press Alt-E (for the Edit menu popup) and N (for the Preferences dialog).

As you see while recording, the Preferences object highlighted is, initially, the number of spaces per Tab. Press the Tab key and the space bar to check the box that indicates you want to use these preferences for all files with the current extension. Then press Tab and the space bar to mark the Save Preference check box. Press several more Tabs and a space bar to mark the Status line check box.

Having made these changes, add a pause to the macro so that you can check to make sure that the structure is exactly the way you want. You don't know whether these space bar presses haven't *unchecked*, rather than checked, the boxes; perhaps this macro was previously run for this file extension, or perhaps the change was made manually. To include the pause, press Shift-F10 again. The dialog in figure 15.15 appears. Choose P or click the <Insert Pause> push button. In the default state (Key to Resume), a FoxPro macro pauses here to enable you to make manual adjustments until you press Shift-F10 again.

The Pause\Key to Resume option is a useful feature for data entry, enabling you to combine boilerplate phrases in a macro with inserted keystrokes or words unique to each entry. The other Pause alternative (Pause\Seconds), which pauses the macro for a specified amount of time and then continues, is often used for creating self-running demonstration programs. A Pause\Seconds also can make sure that a keystroke that takes a moment to conclude (such as a Ctrl-A which is highlighting all of a file or memo field that may be lengthy) is finished before the next macro keystroke takes place.

A final choice available in the Stop Macro Recording dialog is Insert Literal. This choice enables you to record the literal keystrokes of the next key press, rather than playing the keystrokes of another macro assigned to this key press. The choice is similar to the PLAIN option on the KEYBOARD command, about which you learn in the programming chapters of this book.

Returning to complete the macro after the pause, record a press of Ctrl-Enter to save the editing preference. Press Shift-F10 again and choose «OK» to stop recording the macro.

To test the macro, open a new editing file with a different extension and press Ctrl-Alt-S.

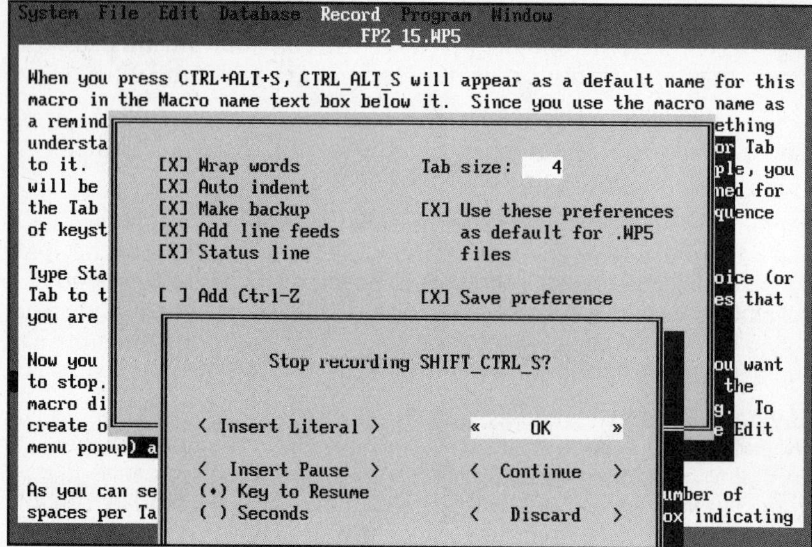

FIG. 15.15

The Stop Macro Recording dialog.

Does the macro work the way you expected? If not, you can edit the macro, rather than re-recording from the beginning. Use the System menu popup Macros option to access the Macros dialog you see at the upper left in figure 15.16. Select the `STATUS_LINE` macro from the list and click the `<Edit>` push button. The Macro Edit dialog at the bottom right of figure 15.16 appears.

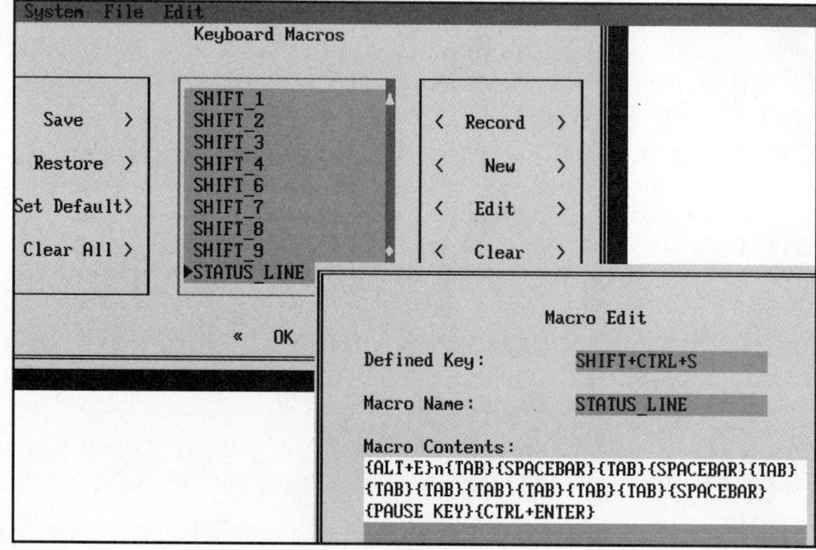

FIG. 15.16

The Macros dialog and the Macro Edit dialog.

The Macro Edit dialog enables you to change the key press, name, or recorded sequence to which the macro is assigned, that appears in the large text box, such as in the following example:

```
{ALT+E}n{TAB}{SPACEBAR}{TAB}{SPACEBAR}{TAB}
{TAB}{TAB}{TAB}{TAB}{TAB}{TAB}{SPACEBAR}
{PAUSE KEY}{CTRL+ENTER}
```

As you see, special key labels (such as the Alt+E key press you used to access the Edit menu popup) appear in curly braces; whereas regular key presses (such as the lowercase `n` you used to access the Preferences dialog from the menu popup) are shown alone. Special instructions, such as the PAUSE KEY, also are shown in curly braces. A Pause\Seconds looks like this: `{PAUSE 0.25}`. The Insert Literal looks like this: `{LITERAL+CTRL+C}`.

You can edit the macro sequence in the same way you edit other text in FoxPro, adding and deleting key presses by using key labels, special instructions, and regular keystrokes as needed. The key labels and special instructions are case-insensitive like Foxpro commands, but the regular key presses that represent straight typing are played back exactly as typed.

Key labels for all the special keys are shown in the chart in Appendix F. Note that the curly braces are given key labels ({LBRACE} and {RBRACE}) so that you can type these braces and not have them understood by FoxPro as key label delimiters.

After you are satisfied with this and other macros, you can save the current macro set for later use. Returning to the Macros dialog from the System menu popup, you can click the `<Save>` button to save these macros to a new name. If you look quickly at the rest of this dialog, you see options to `<Restore>` a macro set from an existing file. `<Restore>` macros is an *additive* option in FoxPro; although older macros are overwritten by new ones assigned to the same key presses, when you use restore, the existing macro set is added to, rather than cleared out. To remove all existing macros, use the `<Clear All>` button.

The `<Clear>` button in the Macros dialog enables you to delete one macro at a time. The `<New>` button enables you to directly type (rather than recording) a new macro sequence. As in the Filer, this dialog uses no hot keys but the Macros menu popup has menu shortcuts for all the options.

The Macros dialog isn't available in distributed applications, but the Record and Stop Recording Macros dialogs are available. You can, if you want, change the Shift-F10 key press to invoke these dialogs to a different combination by using the SET MACKEY TO <*key label*> command. You can turn off the macro capability by using the SET MACKEY TO command, followed by no key label. The Macros dialog is replaced programmatically by the RESTORE MACROS FROM, CLEAR MACROS, and SAVE MACROS TO commands. You can store macros in both a memo field and a file.

If you allow the users to restore personal sets of macros from memo fields or files, you can CLEAR MACROS, RESTORE MACROS FROM these personal sets, and then RESTORE MACROS FROM the application's default set. Because of the additive nature of the RESTORE MACROS command, this order ensures that the macros the application needs are available and that no required macros have been overwritten by new macros defined by the users.

The files that store FoxPro macros use the extension FKY. When you load FoxPro, if a file called DEFAULT.FKY exists, the related macros load. FoxPro has a default set of macros loaded if no DEFAULT.FKY file exists. These macros include common FoxPro commands for function keys 2 through 9 (such as SET and LIST, each followed by a press of the Enter key to execute the macros). You can easily remove these macros for the macro sets used by programs you create. The default set also has macro definitions for the shifted version of the numeric keypad so that you can use the shifted cursor keys to select text in the FoxPro editor. If you use the shifted numeric keypad to type numbers or if you have separate cursor and numeric keypads, you also need to remove these macros. Use the SAVE MACROS command or the Set Default option in the Macros dialog to save the preferred set to the file name DEFAULT.FKY.

DEFAULT.FKY is saved to the same directory as the current Resource file. This approach is carried over from FoxPro 1, in which each user on a network had a Resource file in a different personal directory. However, this setup can be problematic with the new shared Resource files; different users will overwrite each others' default macro sets.

If you share a Resource file in an application, the Macros option is not available on SYSMENU. The menu option you create to set default macro sets for individual users must create FKY files with names tied to individual users or store macro sets in memo fields in a table that holds records for each user.

But if you use FoxPro 2 interactively on a network and share a Resource file, consider altering the default version of SYSMENU to omit the Macros dialog. Users still have the option of creating macros, and the new version of SYSMENU includes options to save new macro sets to individual default files.

A convenient way to safeguard each user's default macros is to assign each a separate user directory that contains his CONFIG.FP file. You can use the -C switch or a DOS environmental variable to specify this CONFIG.FP file for each user. Although FoxPro does not automatically load a DEFAULT.FKY file in the same location as the active CONFIG.FP, you can use the CONFIG.FP's COMMAND = option, described in Appendix D, to indicate a startup program that runs as soon as FoxPro loads:

COMMAND = DO STARTUP

The STARTUP.PRG can be kept in your main FoxPro directory, because it is the same for every user. This program contains the following lines, along with any others you want to add for additional customizing of your FoxPro environment:

```
IF FILE(LEFT(SYS(2019),;
  RAT("\",SYS(2019)))+"DEFAULT.FKY")
       * Use the SYS(2019) function to find the
       * name and location of the active CONFIG.FP
       * file. Add the filename DEFAULT.FKY to
       * the same filepath and use the FILE()
       * function to see if such a file exist.
       * If so:
       CLEAR MACROS
       RESTORE MACROS FROM ;
                 LEFT(SYS(2019), ;
                        RAT("\",SYS(2019)))+"DEFAULT.FKY"
  * Use that file as the macro default file.
ENDIF
* Complete with a command to DO an MPR file,
* which customizes your SYSMENU to SAVE MACROS
* to the same SYS(2019) directory when the
* user chooses to save default macros.
* The MPR program may be the same for all users,
* in which case it too can reside in your main
* FoxPro directory, or you can have personal
* SYSMENUs designed for each user, stored and
* launched with the same SYS(2019) trick.
```

Always supply a generic DEFAULT.FKY file in your main FoxPro program directory; this file is loaded if no personal DEFAULT.FKY exists in the user's directory.

Macros can be used to make FoxPro's interface, especially the text editor, more closely resemble keystrokes with which users are comfortable. This default set can include, for example, editing keystrokes. A special macro file, FOXPLUS.FKY, is provided in the \GOODIES\MISC directory to change the editing keystrokes in FoxPro to match the editing keystrokes in FoxBASE+. If you use programs written in FoxBASE+ that check for these keystrokes, use this set of macros as the default set.

FoxPro 2's DEMO.APP has a Browse module that shows another common way to use macros in a program: it creates a self-running demonstration that looks as though a user is running the program directly. You use the PLAY MACRO <*macro name*> command in programs you created to run macros without a user keypress. You can use the TIME <*expN*> clause to create delays between the keystrokes for a demo, where *expN* is a number of seconds from 0 to 10 (you can include fractions in decimal form).

The following example shows an interactive use of the PLAY MACRO command, which allows any word under the cursor to be *looked up* in the current help file, without the word being highlighted. You can run this procedure from an ON KEY LABEL assignment or a menu option with a shortcut key combination. You learn more about adjusting the FoxPro help system in Chapter 18.

```
PROCEDURE Lookhelp

PRIVATE oldclip
oldclip = _CLIPTEXT
* store old value of clipboard

PLAY MACRO Helpfind

* This macro marks to the end of the word, copies the
* contents of the word into the clipboard.
* Then it presses the help key.

* Here are the contents of the macro:
* {SHIFT+CTRL+RIGHTARROW}{PAUSE 0.25}{CTRL+C}
* {PAUSE 0.25}{F1}

* The pauses may not be necessary on all equipment
* and the {F1} should be adjusted if you change
* this menu shortcut in your system.

* restore old value
_CLIPTEXT = oldclip

RETURN
```

If you use the PLAY MACRO command to execute several macros in a row, realize that no macros are played until FoxPro is in a *wait state* (in a READ, BROWSE, or memo- or text-editing window, or at a menu). PLAY MACRO statements issued in a VALID clause UDF, for example, are all considered *pending* until the UDF returns to the READ. If several pending PLAY MACRO statements exist, the last statement is executed first, and the others execute in reverse order until the first statement is played.

You also need to know that if you define a macro for a key combination, the macro definition takes precedence over the same key combination assignment as a menu or popup shortcut. Be careful not to repeat combinations.

The Desk Accessories

Macros also are useful general-purpose tools. To macros, FoxPro adds several features commonly found in computer programs—*desk accessories*. In Chapter 2, you learned about ASCII and Special Character charts. You know that you can mark, copy, and paste from either of these charts to add graphics characters and control characters when you are in a Browse.

Along with the other FoxPro methods for adding the characters described in Chapter 2 (Alt+ the numeric keypad, left-quote method for control characters, and pressing Enter on the desired character in either character chart), however, pasting special characters that use low ASCII values may not work in a Browse. You still can set up a hot key to paste these characters into the Browse by temporarily storing the characters as literal strings or as ASCII values to _CLIPTEXT and then pressing Ctrl-V to paste the characters to the BROWSE field. This method is useful when editing printer escape codes, which (as you see in the section on Printer Drivers in this chapter) you can store in a table.

The Capture utility, FoxPro's *copy machine*, helps you save all or a portion of a screen to the FoxPro Clipboard (_CLIPTEXT). When you access Capture from the System menu popup, you can choose to save the upper left corner of the area by using the cursor keys. After you press Enter to anchor the corner of the box, you can choose the corner of the box diagonally opposite. Press Enter again, and the area bounded by the corners is saved to _CLIPTEXT. A message window confirms that you captured the screen or partial screen and that _CLIPTEXT now contains the information.

You may find Capture useful as you create documentation for programs. You can go through the entire process of using an application, saving screens as you go, as *notes*. These notes provide a natural order in which to document the application's tasks. A hot key after each screen capture stores successive screens to a text file, by using the following procedure:

```
PROCEDURE capscreen
STORE SET("memowidth") TO oldwidth
SET MEMOWIDTH TO 80
* it's very important to set memowidth to the same number
* of columns as your screen
SET PRINTER TO screens.txt ADDITIVE
SET PRINTER ON
```

```
SET CONSOLE OFF
? _CLIPTEXT
SET CONSOLE ON
SET PRINTER OFF
SET PRINTER TO
SET MEMOWIDTH TO oldwidth

RETURN
```

The FoxPro Calculator is similar to many other *popup* calculators available for computer programs. Calculator retains a single value in memory and can perform basic calculation functions. Calculator, along with the Preference options, is covered in a previous section of this chapter.

The Calculator has no menu popup or shortcuts, but the related functions all have single-letter keyboard equivalents, as shown in table 15.2.

Table 15.2 Calculator Keystrokes

Press on the Keyboard:	Task in the Calculator:	
Q	_	(square root)
R	MR	(value showing restored to memory value)
N	±	(plus or minus)
A	M+	(add value showing to memory value)
Z	MC	(clear memory value)
S	M-	(subtract value showing from memory)
C	C	(erase current displayed value)
CC	CC	(erase current value and operator)

The Calendar/Diary is another tool used in a straightforward manner. You can use the cursor keys, the mouse, or hot keys to move through the dates on the calendar, or use the Tab key to move to the diary to write notes for a selected date. In the section on the Resource file, you learned how diary entries are stored and maintained and how you can archive old diary information. As you see in figure 15.17, you also can use a special option on the Diary menu popup to delete diary entries. If you select a date on the calendar and choose this option, you can delete all diary entries prior to the selected date.

Using the desk accessories within programs usually is a matter of including these programs on the application's version of SYSMENU. As explained in Chapters 13 and 14, however, a READ MODAL needs special help to allow access to menu options. Accessories must be made available on the version of SYSMENU executed in the WHEN clause of a MODAL READ. If you are creating a special, limited version of SYSMENU for this READ, make sure that the SYSMENU contains all desk accessories you want to provide. The READ MODAL also must have a WITH clause that lists the names of the windows for these desk accessories so that the accessories are included in the windows brought forward during this READ.

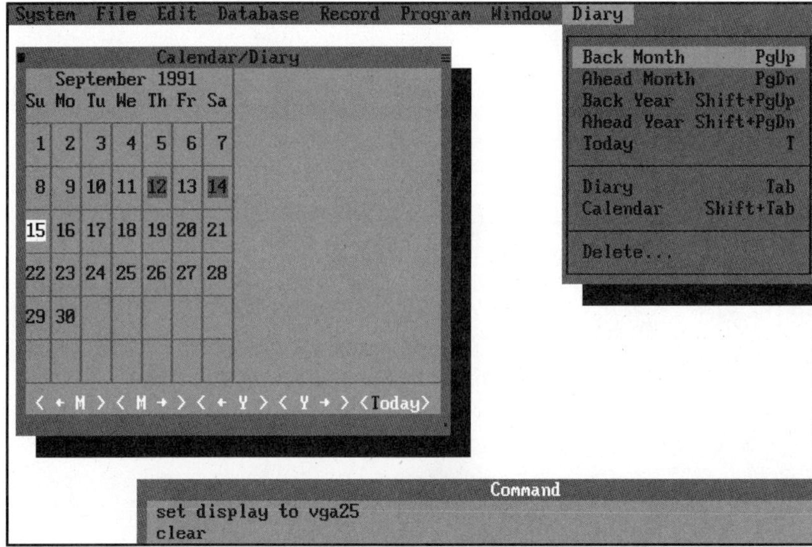

FIG. 15.17

The Calendar/Diary and the menu popup options.

Table 15.3 shows a list of window names for these accessories, exactly as returned by the WONTOP( ) and WTITLE( ) functions. For the READ MODAL WITH clause, use only the characters before the first non-alphanumeric character in the window name or enclose the entire name in quotation marks. The window references are not case sensitive.

Table 15.3 Window Names for the Desk Accessories

ASCII Chart	Calendar/Diary
Calculator	Special Characters
Filer	Puzzle

Besides allowing access to the desk accessories through options that invoke the related system bar names on SYSMENU, you can use the ACTIVATE WINDOW <*window name*> command to access these accessories as part of a hot key procedure during a READ.

To ACTIVATE the desk accessories by default, as part of a VALID procedure, rather than giving the user an option to ACTIVATE by key press, you may need to use a special nested READ to *hold* the user at this point. Otherwise, the user is returned immediately to the READ in progress. The following procedure demonstrates this kind of nested READ:

```
* thanks to super betatester Barry Chertov
* for help refining this one

CLEAR
ACTIVATE SCREEN
SET TALK OFF
this_date = {}
@ 1,1 GET this_date VALID vdate(this_date) ;
  ERROR "This date can't be blank!"
READ

FUNCTION vDate
PARAMETERS tempdate
mreturn = .T.
IF EMPTY(tempdate)
  PUSH KEY CLEAR

  ON KEY LABEL ESCAPE DO getdate
  ON KEY LABEL CTRL-W DO getdate
  ON KEY LABEL CTRL-Q DO getdate
  ON KEY LABEL CTRL-END DO getdate
  ON KEY LABEL F2 DO getdate
  ON KEY LABEL LEFTMOUSE DO chkmouse ;
     WITH MROW(""), MCOL("")

  * F2 is our chosen "quit-key";
  * all the other ones are other FoxPro ways to
  * close a window that must be controlled

  WAIT WINDOW ;
        " Press F2 to select a date. " NOWAIT

  ACTIVATE WINDOW Calendar
  mquit = .F.
  READ MODAL WITH "Calendar" VALID mquit
  * this READ is limited to the Calendar window
```

```
    WAIT CLEAR
    * just in case they closed calendar without
    * moving to a different diary entry first

    ON KEY
    POP KEY
    IF LASTKEY() # 27
       * 27 is value of ESCAPE press

       this_date = _DIARYDATE
       * store the new date to the GET

    ELSE
       * ESCAPE here will cancel
       mreturn = .F.
    ENDIF
  ENDIF
  RETURN mreturn

  PROCEDURE getdate
  * here's how we leave the special READ
  mquit = .t.
  DEACTIVATE WINDOW Calendar
  CLEAR READ
  RETURN

  PROCEDURE chkmouse
  PARAMETERS mouserow, mousecol
  IF mouserow = WLROW("Calendar") ;
     AND mousecol = WLCOL("Calendar")
    * was mouse positioned on close icon?
    DO getdate
  ENDIF && otherwise, just pass the mouse click on
        && to be used in the calendar —
        && a mouse click does not get "used up"
        && when it is trapped by an ON KEY LABEL
        && command as all other keystrokes are
  RETURN
```

Note that you use the same method of referencing the desk accessory windows when you ACTIVATE or DEACTIVATE the windows that you used in the READ MODAL WITH clause. Use only the characters before a non-alphanumeric character or enclose the entire name in quotation marks. The same names are used in the HIDE and SHOW WINDOW commands. Do not HIDE or SHOW any desk accessory windows before explicitly using the ACTIVATE WINDOW command for the window.

The preceding procedure uses a system variable, _DIARYDATE, to determine the user-selected date. FoxPro includes two system variables for the values obtained in the Calculator (_CALCVALUE and _CALCMEM) and _DIARYDATE for the Calendar/Diary. You can use these variables to transfer information from the accessories into a program's data-entry objects. The variables always hold information from the most recent use of the accessories.

You can use a procedure to assign a hot key or menu option, which pastes the Calculator value into a current GET if the current GET is appropriate. You also can call the procedure by default after an ACTIVATE WINDOW Calculator statement, in the same way as you just used _DIARYDATE, with the following example:

```
ON KEY LABEL ALT-Z DO Pastecalc WITH VARREAD()
* or make this a menu option

* this procedure only uses 2 decimal places of _CALCVALUE
PROCEDURE Pastecalc
PARAMETERS thisvar
PUSH KEY CLEAR
* remove OKLs while this procedure is running, prevent
* interruption and recursion
calcno = IIF(_CALCVALUE = INT(_CALCVALUE),;
ALLTRIM(STR(_CALCVALUE,25,0)),ALLTRIM(STR(_CALCVALUE,25,2)))

private toolong
toolong = .F.
* check the data type of the current VARREAD()
DO CASE
CASE TYPE(thisvar) = "N"
       IF LEN(calcno)  <= FSIZE(thisvar)
          REPLACE (thisvar) WITH _CALCVALUE
       ELSE
          toolong = .T.
       ENDIF
CASE TYPE(thisvar) = "C"
       IF LEN(calcno)  <= FSIZE(thisvar)
          REPLACE (thisvar) WITH calcno
       ELSE
          toolong = .T.
       ENDIF
CASE TYPE(thisvar) = "M"
       REPLACE (thisvar) with calcno ADDITIVE
OTHERWISE
       * date or logical field or maybe no VARREAD() at all
       WAIT WINDOW NOWAIT ;
        "Sorry -- Calculator value can't be pasted here."
ENDCASE
IF toolong
```

```
        WAIT WINDOW NOWAIT ;
         "Calculator value is too long for this field: "+calcno
ENDIF
POP KEY
* bring back key assignments
RETURN
```

Printer Drivers

The printer driver system in FoxPro 2 is somewhat paradoxical; the system is both more extensive and powerful in capability than most people ever need and yet less immediately flexible and comprehensive *out of the box* than most people may prefer. Similar to FoxPro's power tools, the printer driver system requires an effort to learn—but after you make this effort, you can accomplish almost anything you can imagine.

The default system is based on the use of a table, P_Codes.DBF, which contains one record for each printer. Each record holds character fields that contain the codes needed to give the printer particular instructions, such as enabling or disabling a particular print style or changing the page orientation. A second table, Fonts.DBF, holds information specific to Postscript printers, with one record that describes each font the printer recognizes.

Of course, you can add records to P_Codes.DBF and Fonts.DBF for all printers or fonts not included in these tables in the installed form. You discuss the procedure for adding these kinds of records in a following part of this section.

Each printer entry in P_Codes.DBF or font entry in Fonts.DBF does not, however, constitute instructions to the printer that FoxPro automatically interprets. A FoxPro program instead provides an interface with which the user selects entries and printer attributes. The same program manipulates, in the active Resource file, both the entries and all related information. Another program sends the results, through FoxPro, to the printer. FoxPro's internal participation in this process is limited to calling the relevant procedures in this second program at appropriate moments during printing.

FoxPro 2 is shipped with a sample application to perform the necessary tasks. GENPD.APP provides the interface that enables you to specify the printer record you want to access, and which characteristics you use from this record for a particular printing situation. GENPD.APP uses P_Codes.DBF or Fonts.Dbf to store printer information in a special system array named _PDPARMS. This array also stores the specifications you selected to a record in the active Resource file.

Within GENPD.APP and the GENPD project, DRIVER.PRG and PS.PRG show you how to write FoxPro programs to hold the procedures with special names called by FoxPro during printing. These procedures use the elements of _PDPARMS to build strings of control characters sent directly to the printer at different moments. For example, PROCEDURE PdDocst returns a string used to initialize the printer at the beginning of a document.

DRIVER.PRG and PS.PRG are not really used by GENPD.APP; rather, this application uses API library versions of these files, written in C language. If you look in the GENPD project in the \GOODIES\PDRIVERS directory, you see these libraries (DRIVER2.PLB and PSAPI.PLB) included in the Project file list. Library files are discussed in a following section of this chapter.

Just as you can replace GENSCRN.PRG and GENMENU.PRG custom template programs, with the associated names stored to the system variables _GENSCRN and _GENMENU, you can replace GENPD.APP by an application you write. You store an application's name to the system variable _GENPD, which provides an interface for the user. You set up the array _PDPARMS to use all the elements you need and fill the array with the information in P_Codes.DBF and Fonts.DBF (or replacement tables that you design) using any system you prefer. You GENPD replacement can add records to the Resource file, as GENPD.APP does, or to a separate "printer preferences table" that you design.

Your printer driver application specifies a program that you write to replace the actual printer-code-passing procedures in GENPD.APP's driver programs, by storing the program's name to the system variable _PDRIVER. The _PDRIVER program uses this version of _PDPARMS to find and return the correct codes to FoxPro during printing.

Although not used directly by GENPD.APP, DRIVER.PRG and PS.PRG are provided solely for use as models for _PDRIVER programs you create. If you decide to use GEN_PD.PRG, the part of GENPD.APP that provides the interface, but you want to change the driver programs from the API versions to edited version of DRIVER.PRG and PS.PRG or to new programs, you must edit GEN_PD.PRG to store the custom driver program's name to _PDRIVER. Search for _PDRIVER in GEN_PD.PRG; concise comments in the code tell you how to make this change.

The version of _GENPD you create is mostly unrestricted, except that you must include a PARAMETERS statement in the form expected by the command SET PDSETUP and the `Printer Driver Setup` check box. Consider the check box option only if you make the Printer Setup option using system bar _MFI_SETUP, the Report Writer, or the Label Designer available in the application you are creating; the command SET PDSETUP represents the programmatic alternative for access to the printer driver system.

FoxPro passes two parameters to any program specified in _GENPD. The first parameter indicates the conditions under which the program was called, and the second parameter indicates the name of a specific printer driver setup (as shown in the Resource file) with which the program was called. If you write a printer driver interface and generation program to use as the custom _GENPD, read about these parameters and related information in the special *Printer Drivers* booklet provided as part of the FoxPro documentation. Also read Part IV of this book, or otherwise be sure that you are familiar and comfortable with programming in FoxPro.

Most people don't want to spend a great deal of time creating printer drivers. People want to designate a printer driver and want this driver to work. Now that you see Fox's conception of—and the way you can extend—the printer driver system, look at the default behavior under the sample programs, and consider ways in which you can use the existing system provided by GENPD.APP. The following discussion refers to a sequence of events that can be completely different if you create a different application and store the application's name to the _GENPD variable.

NOTE

Because the default programs are FoxPro applications, Fox Software can decide to change the behavior in different release builds, just as you write programs to replace them. (The following information is current as of the November 1991 release of FoxPro 2.)

If you receive different results and VERSION(1) returns an earlier date for your copy of FoxPro, contact Fox for an update. If the results don't match what you read here and you have a later version, read the relevant Foxhelp entries. You will find a special topic on printer driver hints and another one with information about the latest changes to the product.

Specifying a Printer Driver Setup

The File menu popup lets you access a Printer Setup dialog. This dialog, and the Label Environment dialog and Report Layout dialog, has a check box option that enables you to choose a `Printer Driver Setup`. Each printer setup consists of specifications for a particular printer, the appropriate information from the related P_Codes.DBF entry or (for a Postscript printer) the Fonts.DBF entry for a particular printing situation.

You can create many printer driver setups for one printer, each setup giving instructions for different kinds of output. You may use one setup to generate 12-pitch print in Portrait orientation and another setup for compressed print in Landscape.

If you have a Resource file open, after you use the check box, you see a list of the previously saved printer driver setups (see fig. 15.18). If you create a `<New>` setup or decide to `<Edit>` an existing setup, the Printer Driver Setup dialog, shown in figure 15.19, appears. (If no Resource file is open, this dialog appears without the intermediary dialog shown in figure 15.18. Here, you can specify—but you cannot save for future use—a printer driver setup for the current session.)

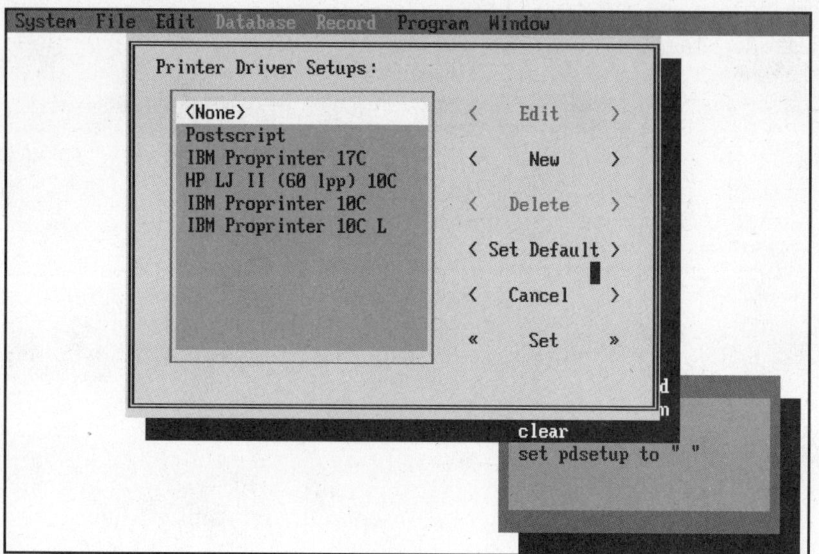

FIG. 15.18

Choosing a Printer Setup.

From the Command window or within a program, you can set a printer driver with the command SET PDSETUP TO. Follow this command with the name of the printer driver setup you want in a string. Follow the command with nothing to release the printer driver setup without installing a new driver. If you use a printer driver setup name unavailable in the present Resource file, you see the available list of drivers (see fig. 15.18) so that you can choose an existing or create a new driver. You can invoke this list deliberately during a program or from the Command window, by using the following command:

```
SET PDSETUP TO " "
```

If you issue the SET PDSETUP TO " " command and no active Resource file is available, you see figure 15.19 without the intermediary list, just as if you accessed the Printer Driver Setup options from the menu option.

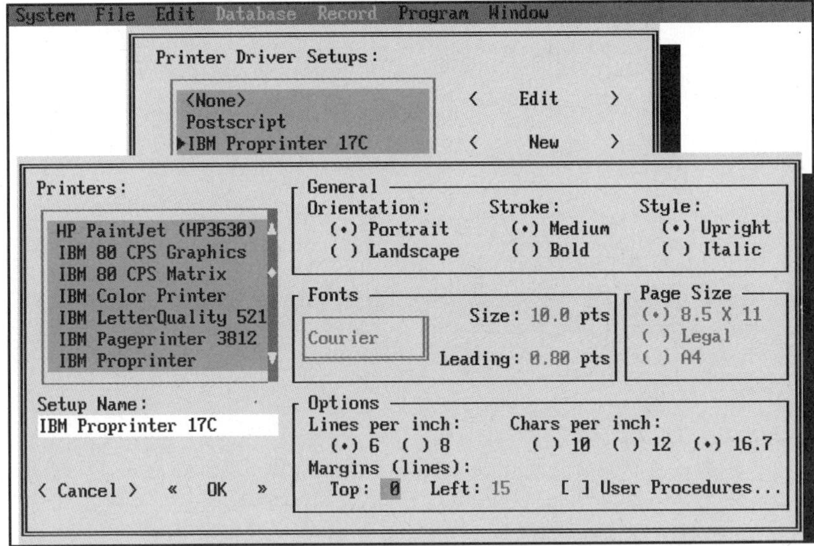

FIG. 15.19

The Printer Driver Setup dialog.

Using the SET PDSETUP TO command or specifying a printer driver setup through the menu option fills the array _PDPARMS with the appropriate values, as you see if you DISPLAY MEMORY LIKE _PDPARMS from the Command window. This command also puts the printer driver setup name in the system variable _PDSETUP. (When you remove the printer driver without specifying a new driver, _PDPARMS is released from memory, and _PDSETUP contains the null string, "".)

You can use the printer setup dialog's `<Set Default>` button to specify a default printer driver to load when you load FoxPro. Making a printer driver setup the default doesn't change the related version of _PDPARMS. If you open the related Resource file, you see the default printer driver setup has a hyphen (-) included as the first character of the name entry. When loaded along with FoxPro, GENPD.APP looks for and uses this character to set the default. The default printer driver setup isn't changed when you change Resource files. (Remember that this behavior is specific to GENPD.APP and that you can replace this behavior with new default-setting procedures by editing or replacing GENPD.APP.)

Although no comparable command exists to designate a default printer driver setup, you can edit a Resource file directly with FoxPro commands to provide the same results, as shown in the following expression:

```
LOCATE FOR Id = "PDSETUP" and LEFT(Name,1) = "-"
* find a current default, if any
IF FOUND()
   REPLACE Name WITH SUBSTR(Name,2)
   * remove the first character
ENDIF
* now locate or create the record you prefer
* as a default setup and in this record:
REPLACE Name WITH "-"+Name
```

TIP If you do not have a default printer driver setup, you can place the following line in your CONFIG.FP file to prevent FoxPro from searching for one. This line makes FoxPro load more quickly:

```
PDSETUP = "-"
```

Just as a shared Resource file can create conflicts if many people want different DEFAULT.FKY files (macro sets), a shared Resource file on the network can contain only one default printer driver setup for everyone. You, however, can override the default printer driver setup as designated by the Resource file by typing the line **PDSETUP** = "*your setup name*" to the CONFIG.FP file. Each user can have a separate CONFIG.FP file.

Even if you use the default GENPD.APP program to create a printer driver setup interface and _PDPARMS, you still can provide different driver procedures to send the control strings to the printer. In GENPD.APP's printer driver setup dialog, you can specify custom procedures for a printer driver setup on an individual basis. Click the `User Procedures` check box (see fig. 15.20). You can use this dialog to specify procedures that you write for each event during printing that cause FoxPro to call the driver program. (You don't need to specify user procedures for all the choices in this dialog. Often, you need only one or two user procedures.)

GENPD.APP stores procedure names you specify to elements in _PDPARMS, along with the other printer driver setup information (see fig. 15.20). During printing, the driver program builds special control code strings for each printing event. If the appropriate _PDPARMS element contains the name of a custom procedure, the driver passes the created string to the custom procedure. You can write anything you want to rewrite or to add to this string. The driver program passes the edited string back to FoxPro, which sends the string to the printer.

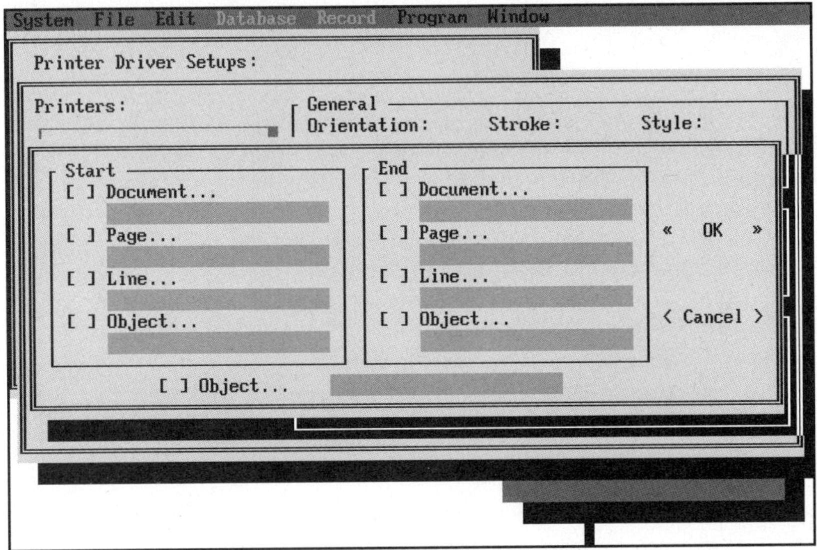

FIG. 15.20

The User Procedures dialog.

Using Printer Driver Setups Effectively

When a printer driver setup is loaded, you affect FoxPro's instructions to the printer in many different situations. These changes are shown in the following list:

- Issuing a REPORT or LABEL FORM command TO PRINT or TO a file, or causing a report of label to print by using the Database menu popup Report and Label options
- Using the TYPE command TO PRINT or TO a file
- Using DISPLAY or LIST commands, in all forms, TO PRINT or TO a file
- Using the ? and ?? commands to display output if PRINT is SET ON and the STYLE clause is used
- Using all choices in the File menu popup's Print option (the contents of a file, an open window, or the Clipboard), except for the ASCII file option

You may override the active printer driver setup with instructions stored in a label or report form. If you use the Printer Driver Setup option in the Report Layout dialog or the Label Environment dialog, you can access the same dialogs you see in figures 15.18, 15.19, and 15.20 while you edit a report or label. When you save the form, the name of the printer driver setup you specify is saved in the LBX or FRX table.

(To see the results, USE an LBX or FRX table and LOCATE a record with OBJTYPE 21 (the printer driver record). The name of this setup is stored in the related NAME field.)

To use this stored setup instead of the active setup, when you output labels or reports, use the PDSETUP keyword on the REPORT or LABEL FORM command or the Set Printer Driver option in the Database menu popup's Report or Label dialog. This step is the equivalent of issuing a SET PDSETUP TO <*setupname*> command separately. If the Resource file is not open or does not contain the setup whose name is stored with the table, the printer driver dialogs appear so that you can recreate the setup before output is sent to the printer.

When you use the RQBE to send results of a query to a report or label, the RQBE Display Options dialog has a check box to `Use Printer Setup` in Report/Label Form. This option adds the PDSETUP keyword to the REPORT or LABEL FORM command generated in the QPR.

> **CAUTION:** Be aware that the PDSETUP keyword or Set Printer Driver option loads a new printer driver without regard for the previously active setup, just like a SET PDSETUP command. You are responsible for restoring the old setup, if needed, afterward. You can store the contents of _PDSETUP to a variable before creating output and then SET PDSETUP TO <*your variable name*> after the output command is executed.

After a _PDPARMS array is filled by the active printer driver setup, all the preceding printing techniques cause FoxPro to call the _PDRIVER program's special procedures and any user procedures you added, in the process. You also can use the elements of _PDPARMS, however, for other kinds of control.

In the preceding list of printing techniques to which printer drivers apply, you see the *?* and *??* commands. The ?? command sends an expression to the current output device; ? sends the expression preceded by a carriage return and line feed. These commands' use of printer driver setups is limited to the STYLE clause; the document initialization and ending strings and other procedures are not triggered by ? and ?? commands. Suppose that you switch on the printer, SET PRINT ON, and SET PDRIVER TO a 12-pitch type setup, and the printer's default is 10-pitch. Use the following command:

```
? "This is a test"
```

If you use this command, the printer still uses a 10-pitch. You may also use the following command:

```
? "This is a test" STYLE "B"
```

If you use this command, the printer honors the STYLE clause (this example prints in 10-pitch bold type) because the instructions for 12-pitch type are sent as part of document initialization, not available to a ? command.

Suppose that you want to print the output with ? and ?? commands, but you want to use the active printer setup. You can use the *???* command, which sends instructions directly to the current PRINT device, to send the proper initialization string because the string is stored in _PDPARMS.

To find out which element of _PDPARMS to use, look at the program GEN_PD.PRG. As you can see in figure 15.21, the file contains lines of comments that explain exactly how _PDPARMS is used by this program.

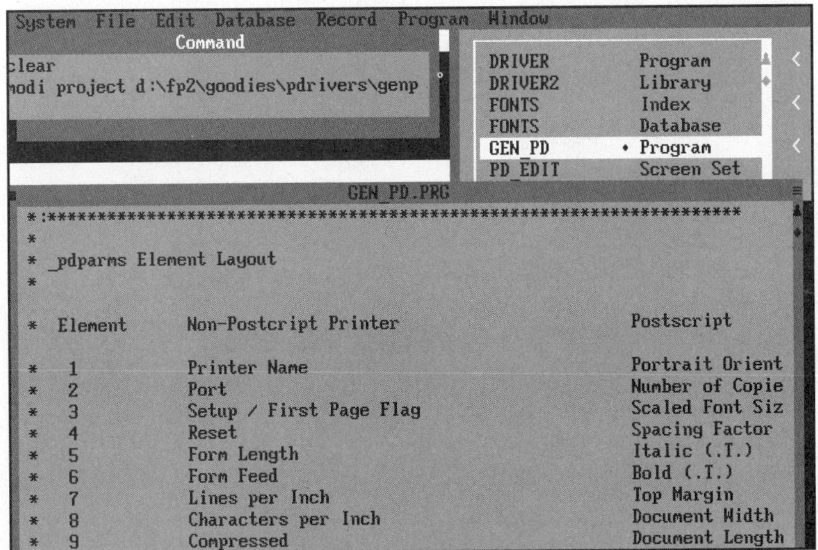

FIG. 15.21

Comments in GEN_PD.PRG show you the default _PDPARMS array used for both nonPostscript and Postscript printers.

If you look at DRIVER.PRG, also in the project, and check the procedure PdDocSt, you see that the document initialization string sent by PdDocSt uses all these elements of _PDPARMS:

_PDPARMS(3)	First page flag
_PDPARMS(10)	Portrait, landscape orientation
_PDPARMS(7)	Lines per inch
_PDPARMS(8)	Characters per inch
_PDPARMS(25)	Style code for whole document

_PDPARMS(26)	Stroke weight for whole document
_PDPARMS(40) OR _PDPARMS(41)	Top margin
_PDPARMS(22) OR CHR(13)+CHR(10)	Instructions to move to new line

You can combine all these instructions as PdDocSt does, if needed, to send to the printer with ???. In the preceding example, however, and in most cases, you use simpler instructions:

```
??? _PDPARMS(8)
   * set pitch according to current printer driver setup
```

You can even USE P_Codes.dbf and get the instructions directly from the fields, bypassing the current driver entirely except to check the printer currently specified, as shown in the following expression:

```
SELECT P_codes
IF TYPE(_PDPARMS(1)) = "C"
        * make sure that a printer setup is active
        * see note on Postscript use below
        LOCATE FOR P_name = _PDPARMS(1)
        * the first element of _PDPARMS holds printer name
        ??? P_setup+P_reset+P_12cpi
        * use P_codes information to initialize the printer and
        * send instructions to print in 12-pitch.
ENDIF
```

Just as you send _PDPARMS elements or P_codes fields directly to the printer by using ???, you can add these items to a report or label as expressions. In a label, concatenate the additions with other information on the same line, making sure that you have P_codes open in some nonselected work area:

```
"Normaltext"+P_codes.P_boldon+"Boldtext"+P_codes.P_boldoff+"Etc"
```

Or use the following line:

```
"Normaltext"+_PDPARMS(11)+"Boldtext"+_PDPARMS(12)+"Etc"
```

In a report, create a report expression wide enough to hold all the characters of the control codes that may be sent and insert the codes at appropriate positions in the report layout. Recall that you can overlay report expressions so that the instructions do not interfere with the positions of the expressions you want on the output. (Refer to Chapter 10 to determine the order in which expressions are evaluated and sent to the printer when overlaid.)

Although using this technique enables you to apply styles separately to different items on the same line of a label, ordinarily, you need not use the technique for reports. Assign styles to report objects individually. You can extend the P_Codes table, however, to store information about other styles not included by default, such as double-wide printing. Rather than bother changing _PDRIVER to an edited version of DRIVER.PRG that handles the new enhancements, you can pull these codes directly out of the added P_Code fields at printing time, while the default driver takes care of other styles.

TIP

All the preceding examples refer only to non-Postscript printers. Look at PS.PRG for equivalent Postscript printer information on elements of _PDPARMS and which elements are used by which printer procedures. Before you use _PDPARMS or P_codes.DBF directly, check TYPE(_PDPARMS(1)), as you did prior to the LOCATE statement in the preceding code example. This command returns a "U" (Unknown) if no printer driver setup is active. If a Postscript driver is active, you see an "L" (Logical), because the Postscript driver uses _PDPARMS(1) to store .T. for Portrait and .F. for Landscape orientation, rather than a printer name (printer names are irrelevant to Postscript).

Postscript document initialization requires a long *header*, or Prolog, of instructions, which are sent to the printer, as you see in PS.PRG in PROCEDURE PdDocSt. If you initialize a Postscript printer, copy the Prolog instructions and follow the rest of the procedure closely. If you change fonts for single objects, follow the additional procedures in PS.PRG for the instructions you pass to the printer with ???.

You can even store new information to various elements of _PDPARMS, which you can then use during FoxPro's default use of the printer driver setup and also instructions to the printer you send. This practice, however, doesn't work with the default _PDRIVER program (the library program DRIVER2.PLB), which loads the array only once; use DRIVER.PRG and PS.PRG as the _PDRIVER programs. Remember that you need to edit GEN_PD.PRG to coordinate this change, as previously explained.

If you plan to distribute an application as a standalone executable file and want to give the users access to the GENPD.APP dialogs and drivers, add GENPD.APP to the project. As an APP file, GENPD.APP is by default excluded by the Project Manager, but adding this file to the project ensures that all FoxPro features it uses are contained in the executable. Also, add the Resource file that contains the printer driver setups you want to supply with an application you create, excluded if you want the Resource file to be editable.

When you distribute the application, along with the executable file you must supply, and locate in the same directory, some additional files. GENPD.APP is required, and you should include a copy of the Resource file as well, if the file is not read-only and if you don't create an editable copy during the installation procedures. If you are distributing an Extended version standalone executable, add PROAPI16.EXE. You find this support file in the main FoxPro 2 program directory.

On occasion, you may want to bypass the printer driver system for a particular printing need. FoxPro 2 continues to support an assortment of FoxPro 1 printing system variables, which were added to the language before printer drivers were implemented. You can see these variables if you DISPLAY MEMORY (all these variables begin with _P). These variables also are listed in the *Commands and Functions* manual.

Some of these system variables must be used within a PRINTJOB/ENDPRINTJOB loop, which is indicated by a See Also reference to PRINTJOB/ENDPRINTJOB in their Commands and Function entries, but you can use other system variables at any time. Although these variables don't permit precise control of individual printers, as the printer drivers do, you don't always need to make adjustments printer-specific, and the system variables often do the job well.

Suppose that you want a report that uses a nonstandard page length. Many continuous-form invoices used by dot-matrix printers are 7 inches long rather than 11 inches. Continuous-form checks may be other lengths. If you create a report form 42 lines long (rather than 66 lines) by using the Report Layout option, you see that the printer still advances 11 inches at the end of each page where the printer expects to find the top-of-form. The unwanted advance occurs because, by default, a report form sends EJECT commands to the printer as a *form feed*, and the printer isn't instructed that the top-of-form has changed.

You can send the instructions through the printer drivers, of course, but you first must create these instructions for each applicable printer. This step may require a number of additional printer driver setups, or even separate printer entries, which you can add as described in the following section. You can, however, avoid adding setups or printer entries and instruct FoxPro to handle the job generically with the following commands:

```
_PLENGTH = 42
* default is 66
_PADVANCE = "LINEFEED"
* default is "FORMFEED"
```

Set the page length as before to 42 in the Report Layout option, but now, FoxPro sends *line feeds* to the printer until the line counter reaches 42 lines at the bottom of each report page or when an EJECT or EJECT PAGE command is encountered in the program.

Creating Printer Entries

Whether you distribute applications or only maintain a single-user printer driver system, you may need to create new printer entries in P_Codes.DBF or add extra fonts to Fonts.DBF. Perhaps you own an unusual printer not on the available list and not compatible with other printers on the list. Perhaps the printer was introduced to the market after the list was created. Perhaps the Postscript printer you own is capable of handling a far larger assortment of fonts than is contained in the default set.

You may want to add another entry for the printer, with different instructions, even if the printer is on the list. If you look on the list, you see two entries for the Hewlett Packard LaserJet II. One entry includes the phrase (60 lpp), which is default for the LaserJet. The other entry includes a nonstandard set of instructions in the P_6lpi field of P_codes, which reduces the amount of vertical space between lines to force the number of lines per page to 66.

This latter setup enables you to create a report form that works equally well with both dot matrix and laser printers because dot matrix printers usually default to 66 lines per page. The former setup is usually better for standard laser label formats, which were developed for the LaserJet's default vertical spacing. (Use this printer entry with a top margin that matches the label forms as the basis for a special printer driver setup with a name that indicates you intend to use the driver for labels.)

NOTE

If you have an early release copy of FoxPro 2, your copy of P_codes.dbf may not have the second (60 lpp) LaserJet entry. You can create this entry by adding a printer entry exactly the same as the existing LaserJet entry except that you edit the P_6LPI field to contain 8 instead of 7.27.

Some versions of P_codes.dbf may contain LaserJet entries but do not include the correct information in the P_8LPI field. For the 66 lpp record, the P_8LPI field should contain 5.45, and the 60 lpp record should contain a 6.

Even with two setups available, you may want to edit the LaserJet entries in P_codes. The LaserJet is shipped with a default character set that includes no line-drawing characters. To get the same graphics characters shown in the Report Layout when you draw box and line objects or use special characters, you can change the default character set by using instructions found in the LaserJet manual. However, you may have other applications that depend on the original default set, and you may prefer to change the printer's behavior only for FoxPro. If so, edit the two LaserJet entries in P_codes to give these instructions by changing the P_SETUP field. At the end of the default entry, type **(10U** to instruct the printer to choose the proper character set.

If the printer is not on the list of supported printers, and you want to add a new entry, try to find a record similar to start with. An earlier model of the printer, or another printer with which this printer is compatible for most purposes, may be on the list. If a similar printer is listed, SCATTER MEMVAR, APPEND a BLANK record, and then GATHER MEMVAR. Edit the P_NAME field and all other fields that must be changed. If you can't find a similar entry, just APPEND BLANK and add information to all the fields.

Before you use the new or edited printer entries in P_codes.DBF or font entries you have added to Fonts.DBF, remember that these tables are included in GENPD.APP as read-only files. (If the files were not, you would need to distribute them as separate files along with GENPD.APP when you distributed an application.) For entries to be *recognized* by GENPD.APP, therefore, you must rebuild GENPD.APP from the GENPD project. Only then is the new version of the P_codes and Fonts tables contained in the project.

External Libraries and the Application Program Interface

The FoxPro programming language contains more than 600 commands and functions, which provide more functionality than most users need in a database management system. However, you may discover certain facilities that you either need or may want available from within FoxPro, but which were not provided by Fox Software. To address these needs, FoxPro 2 provides the capability of using external API libraries and binary routines (BIN files).

Previous versions of FoxPro, and also FoxBASE+, enabled you to LOAD and CALL binary routines to perform tasks, such as checking for the presence of a disk in a floppy disk drive. Functions contained in an API library do the same things as binary files but have the advantage of working just like FoxPro's functions. You can use a library function as part of an index expression or as the test condition in an IF statement.

In this section, you discuss the API from the perspective of using external libraries created by third-party vendors, rather than from the perspective of creating external libraries. The creation of an external library is a complex subject, beyond the scope of this book.

You also learn how to use binary routines, as the recent introduction of the API means that relatively few third-party libraries are available. If a library routine cannot be found to meet a need, perhaps a binary routine can do the job.

Defining the Application Program Interface

The *External Routine Application Program Interface*, or *API*, is an interface definition that enables C and assembly language programmers to extend FoxPro 2's native capabilities by creating function libraries. These functions can be used in the same manner as built-in FoxPro commands and functions.

The API enables a programmer to access FoxPro 2's internal *engine* or the FoxPro internal routines that handle memory management, file input/output, window management, error trapping, etc. A library function usually executes faster than an equivalent FoxPro program, especially when the function performs an operation that may require the FoxPro program to call numerous different FoxPro functions.

The API is part of the Library Construction Kit, a separate product that, like the Distribution Kit described in Chapter 14, is not included with the FoxPro 2 base product. The Library Construction Kit contains library files with which you link C or assembly language program, the *include* files (PRO_EXT.H for C, PRO_EXT.INC for assembly) that contain the function prototypes, macros and structure definitions, a manual of instructions and API library routine documentation, and a modified version of the Watcom C compiler.

NOTE Fox Software maintains that only the Watcom C compiler can be used to create external libraries in C. The actual FoxPro program is compiled with Watcom C and uses Watcom's calling conventions, which are different from the calling conventions of Microsoft C and Borland's C compilers. However, some C programmers have successfully created libraries with Microsoft C by writing *bridge* functions (which translate Microsoft function calls to the format required by Watcom). Whether these libraries work under all circumstances is not proven, and Fox Software remains skeptical.

Using External Library Routines

How may you use an external library, and how do you actually execute the library's functions?

Suppose that PRODUCTS.DBF contains a memo field called PHOTO, where you intend to place a scanned image of a product. FoxPro, although capable of storing binary data in a memo field, has no built-in functions for translating the data into an image and displaying the image on-screen. This application is perfect for a third-party library.

To use a library, you need to know the name of the library file, how to load the library, the names of the functions the library contains, and how to use these functions. Suppose that you purchased a library to display product pictures within FoxPro. The library is a file with a PLB extension, like the DRIVER2.PLB and PSAPI.PLB files used by the default printer driver system. If you see a PLB file on the library disk, you can load this kind of file, such as IMAGES.PLB, by typing the following command in the Command window:

```
SET LIBRARY TO IMAGES
```

This command replaces IMAGES with the name of the library file.

If no PLB file exists, the library is probably bound into an application (APP) or executable (EXE) file. Naturally, if you purchased a library, the vendor also provides you with instructions on how to use the package.

With the library loaded, you can use the DISPLAY STATUS command to see the names of the library's functions. After all the other information is shown, FoxPro displays the API library status information, which appears as shown in figure 15.22.

Each name shown under the Function column is a library function that you can use wherever you can use a FoxPro command or function, with the exception of functions marked `Call on load` or `Call on unload`. These marked functions, such as PDONLOAD and PDONUNLOAD (see fig. 15.22), are special internal library routines executed only when the library is loaded and unloaded, respectively. These routines are not intended for your use.

You need to know the proper use of each of the functions. As with FoxPro, each function expects to receive zero or more arguments, and all arguments passed to the function usually are a particular data type (character, numeric, and so on). Each function also returns a value, also a particular data type.

To return to the example, the fictional Images library may consist of the following two functions:

SHOWIMAGE(<*memo field*> [, <*window name*>])
CLEARIMAGE([<*window name*>])

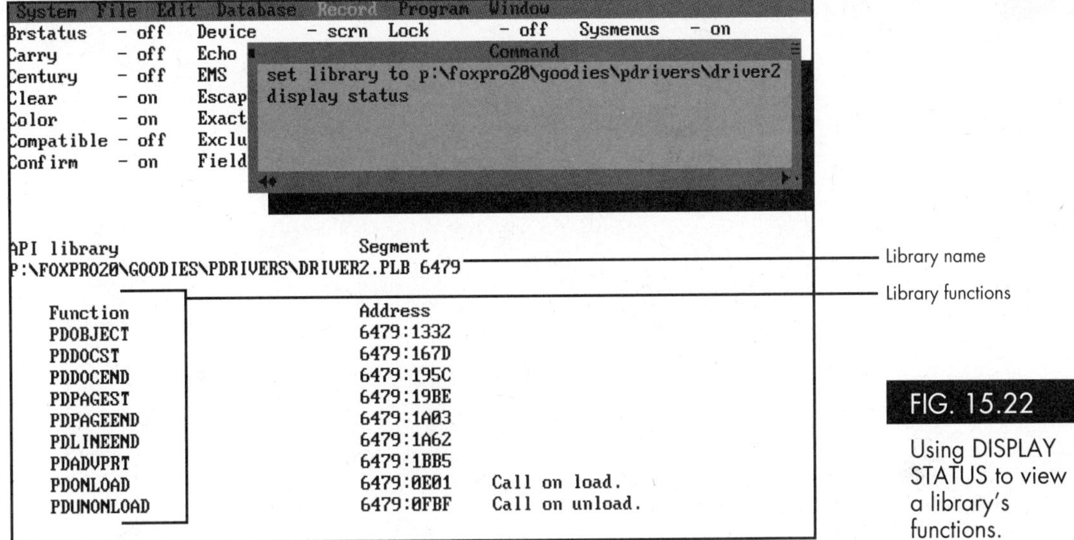

FIG. 15.22

Using DISPLAY STATUS to view a library's functions.

Remember that arguments enclosed in brackets ([]) are optional. You may tell SHOWIMAGE to display the image in a particular window by supplying the name of the window as the second argument or on-screen by excluding a second argument. The name of the memo field that contains the data to be translated into an image is required.

CLEARIMAGE can restore the screen or window to the previous display by using screen information that SHOWIMAGE saved before displaying the picture.

Examine the following FoxPro program that first loads the Images library and then uses related functions to display a picture of the products on-screen from within a Browse window. This program provides you with examples of proper use of libraries, with attention paid to the possible need to search for the library file and the possible existence of other libraries that you may load at the same time.

```
* PROGRAM viewprod
*

* This program is an example of how you might use a
* fictional third-party library called IMAGES.PLB.
*
* The program displays the PRODUCTS records in a Browse
* window and lets the user display a picture of the current
* product by pressing the F2 function key.
*
private old_f2, mchoice
```

```
* if the Images library is not loaded, load it
if ! "IMAGES.PLB" $ SET("LIBRARY")
   if !load_lib("IMAGES", "Please find IMAGES.PLB")
         * library was not loaded
         RETURN
   endif
endif

* make sure you're working with the PRODUCTS table
if used('PRODUCTS')
   select PRODUCTS
else
   select 0
   use PRODUCTS
endif

* save the current macro setting of the F2 key, then set it
* to display the picture by calling SHOWPICT
old_f2 = on('key', 'F2')
on key label F2 do SHOWPICT with PHOTO

* tell the user how to see the picture, and browse
* the PRODUCTS table

wait window ;
   "Press F2 to see a picture of the product" nowait
browse last

* restore the F2 key to its previous state
on key label f2 &old_f2

* let the user unload the Images library
wait window "Unload the Images library? (Y/N)" to mchoice
if upper(mchoice) = "Y"
   do unload with "IMAGES.PLB"
endif

return

PROCEDURE loadlib
   *
   * Load an external function library. Return True if
   * the library was found & loaded, otherwise return .F.
   *
   parameters lib_name, loc_msg
   private on_error, got_lib, full_name

   ** make sure you can find IMAGES.PLB
```

```
  * you have to trap for an error if LOCFILE can't find
  * the library, and the user selects Cancel or presses
  * Escape in the Open File dialog
  on_error = on('ERROR')
  got_lib = .T.
  on error got_lib = .F.

  * store the fully qualified file name in full_name
  full_name = locfile(lib_name, "PLB", loc_msg)

  * reset the previous ON ERROR routine, if any
  on error &on_error

  if got_lib
         * either LOCFILE found the .PLB,
         * or the user selected it;
         * load the library, without releasing
         * any other libraries
         set library to (full_name) additive
  endif

return got_lib (True if library loaded, otherwise False)

PROCEDURE showpict
  *
  * translate contents of memo field pict_memo into an
  * image, and display it on-screen
  *
  parameters pict_memo

  * turn off the F2 key
  on key label F2 *

  * display the picture; you use "=" because you're not
  * interested in the return value of the function
  = showimage(pict_memo)

  * wait until the user is done
  wait window "Press any key when done"

  * restore the previous screen
  = clearimage()

  * turn the F2 key back on
  on key label F2 do SHOWPICT with PHOTO

return

PROCEDURE unload
  *
  * Unload an external library and reload any other
  * libraries which are currently in use.
  *
```

```
* Note that there is currently no way to selectively
* unload an external library. If other libraries are
* loaded, you must close all of them, and then reload
* the other libraries.
*
parameters lib_name
* pass the name of the .plb to be closed

private lib_list, other_libs, curr_lib

* make sure the library name is in uppercase
lib_name = upper(lib_name)

* Save list of currently-loaded libraries; list is
* comma delimited, and contains the fully-qualified
* library file names.
* (e.g. C:\FOXPRO2\LIB1.PLB, C:\FOXPRO2\LIB2.PLB)
lib_list = upper(set('library'))

* close all libraries
set library to

other_libs = occurs(",", lib_list)

if other_libs > 0
* need to reload other libraries

lib_list = lib_list + ", "
* extra space needed below

do while "" != trim(lib_list)
      * get the name of the next library
      * in the list
      curr_lib = left(lib_list, ;
                          at(",", lib_list)-1)

      if at(lib_name, curr_lib) = 0
            * curr_lib is not the name of the
            * library that you don't want any more,
* so reload it
            set library to (curr_lib) additive
      endif

      * remove curr_lib and the comma delimiter
      * that follows
      * it from the beginning of the list
      lib_list = substr(lib_list, ;
                              at(",",lib_list)+1)

      * if curr_lib was last in lib_list,
      * lib_list is now " "
```

```
enddo
endif

return
```

Other likely uses for third-party libraries include providing access from within FoxPro to external devices, such as image scanners, and providing communications facilities, such as automated file transfers between a corporate headquarters and production sites.

Using Binary Routines

Because of the API's capability of making external functions work seamlessly with FoxPro 2, it seems likely that most capabilities provided by binary routines (or BIN files, as they are usually called) will eventually be replaced by external libraries. This, however, may take some time. Meanwhile, you may still need the functionality provided by the numerous BIN files written to supplement the capabilities of FoxPro and the other xBase dialects, so you need to know how to load, unload, and use a BIN file.

BIN files are loaded with LOAD, used with CALL, and unloaded with RELEASE MODULE. If the fictional Images library was a BIN file, you may have loaded the library by typing the following command in the Command Window, or by including the line in a program:

```
LOAD IMAGES [SAVE | NOSAVE]
```

The optional SAVE keyword (NOSAVE is the default) tells FoxPro to save the current contents of the video RAM in the FoxPro desktop upon return from a CALL to the binary routine. This step is important only if the binary routine modifies the screen. If the routine does (and assuming that the routine writes directly to video RAM), FoxPro treats what was written by the binary routine as though FoxPro had written the information and can therefore protect the routine from erasure by objects you may subsequently move or drag across the screen. This occurs, however, only if you use the SAVE keyword with either the LOAD or the CALL command.

The fictional external library contains two functions, SHOWIMAGE and CLEARIMAGE. Binary routines cannot contain separately addressable functions. You can CALL a binary routine only. You can, however, pass a parameter to a binary routine, and this parameter can contain code that tells the binary routine your intentions. You can, for example, tell IMAGES.BIN to display an image as follows:

```
CALL IMAGES WITH ".S" + PHOTO
```

Of course, the binary routine needs to know that ".S" at the beginning of the string means *show the image*. Likewise, you can type the following command to invoke the *clear image* routine in the binary file:

```
CALL IMAGES WITH ".C"
```

A CALL command also can contain the optional SAVE | NOSAVE keywords. If you use one or the other command, the default setting established when you LOADed the binary routine is overridden.

Finally, you unload a BIN file by using the RELEASE MODULE command. Unlike external libraries, BIN files are released by name, one at a time, so that releasing one binary file from memory disturbs no other files. To remove the Images file from memory, type the following command in the Command window:

```
RELEASE MODULE IMAGES
```

Chapter Summary

This chapter concludes the study of FoxPro's powerful interface-driven tools. Beginning with Part II and your investigation of the RQBE, you were gradually introduced to the concepts and statements of the FoxPro command language.

You have executed many FoxPro commands in the Command window. The lines you typed in the Command window also may have been executed from a program. As a *program*, or procedure, these lines are saved to a file so that they can be executed at a later time in the order you specify as a deliberate and repeatable sequence of instructions.

You learned to write short procedures to provide support for the screens, menus, and output you produced, mostly in the form Fox refers to as code snippets (short sequences attached to a menu or screen file). In this chapter, you provided more examples of these kinds of procedures.

When you learned about the Project Manager, you glimpsed the way you can combine these procedures to create an entire application. In the following part of this book, you begin an examination of programming structure and the FoxPro language in detail. You learn to use various groups of commands and functions that perform a wide range of database management tasks. The language you learn in the next part of *Using FoxPro 2* provides the true power and depth of capability of FoxPro 2.

PART

IV

FoxProgramming: Enhanced Use of the Design Tools and Beyond

OUTLINE

16

CHAPTER

Understanding Program Structure

In most books about database management programs that contain a command language, this section would be your first introduction to the programming language. Because FoxPro 2 allows you to attach user-defined functions and code snippets to objects, such as fields defined in the Report Writer and the Screen Builder, you already have done a fair amount of programming in FoxPro 2. However, most of the programs that you have written so far have had a limited scope and have been designed to accomplish a narrowly defined task, such as validating the data entered into a field.

This section explores the FoxPro 2 programming language in depth. This chapter covers many of FoxPro 2's more than 500 built-in commands and functions but does not discuss them all.

Rather than provide you with a simple reference guide, which would repeat much of the material contained in the FoxPro 2 manuals, this discussion focuses on *how to use* the language to achieve your database management goals.

This chapter introduces you to programming concepts, program design, and some of the author's opinions concerning programming style (a heated topic if ever there was one!). Along the way, you learn to control program execution and branching and to create subroutines that break tasks into manageable pieces.

Later chapters in this section present more advanced programming techniques. Part IV divides some of FoxPro 2's commands and functions by category and explores the ways in which you can use them—from the Command window and from within programs.

Learning What a Program Does

At its most basic level, a computer program is a combination of words and other symbols that can be "read" by a computer. A computer program is written in a specific language. Each language has its own rules and conventions, which enable the computer to understand your words and symbols and perform the tasks that you intend it to perform.

The FoxPro 2 language uses English-like words. The commands do what you would expect them to do if you understand the English language. For example, STORE saves a value somewhere, and REPLACE replaces the current contents of a field with another value. The FoxPro language, therefore, is very readable. Even if you don't know how to manipulate the commands, you often can read a FoxPro program written by someone else and understand what that program does.

Throughout this chapter, and those that follow, the discussion emphasizes the *readability* of the programs that you will write. Always keep in mind that writing a computer program is a form of *communication*, not only between you and the computer, but also between you and those who later will read your program to understand, enhance, and maintain your program.

Moving Commands You Type Repeatedly into a Program

You can think of typing a command in the Command window as creating a program that has one line and that is executed by pressing Enter. Each command may be part of a series of commands that have one objective, like finding and displaying the records for a particular customer in an orders table.

If you understand the sequence of events required to produce a certain result, you can design and write a program. For example, enter a few commands in the Command window and then use the FoxPro editor's cut and paste feature to move the commands into a program (PRG) file.

Activate the Command window and type the following commands:

```
USE SALES IN 1
SET ORDER TO CUSTCODE
BROWSE KEY "A001"
```

This series of commands opens the Sales table, orders the entries by customer code, and displays the orders for the customer whose code is `A001` in a Browse window. Now move these commands into a program file by typing the following in the Command window:

```
MODIFY COMMAND SHOWORDS
```

A blank window titled `SHOWORDS.PRG` appears on-screen. Without closing the new program's window, activate the Command window. Select the three lines that will make up the program and paste them into the SHOWORDS.PRG window. (Refer to the discussion of the FoxPro editor in Chapter 2, "Understanding the FoxPro 2 Interface," if you don't know how to do this.) Save the program (press Ctrl-W or select Save from the File Menu) and return to the Command window.

Now that you have transferred your command sequence from the Command window to a program file, you can run the program:

```
DO SHOWORDS
```

This program is not very useful, because it always displays only the records for customer A001. Working from the Command window, you can view other customers' records by modifying the BROWSE command to use a different customer code. You can accomplish the same thing in a program, but first you need to learn more about the structure of a program.

Examining a Program for Structure and Style

Take a look at APPSHELL.PRG, part of the FoxApp utility explored briefly in Chapter 1, "Understanding FoxPro Fundamentals." (This program is located in the \GOODIES\FOXAPP\PRGS subdirectory under your main FoxPro 2 directory.)

```
* APPSHELL is part of the FoxApp system.
* This is a routine to display a list of APP files
* and prompt the user for the one to run.
* It does not display the list of files if a file
* name is passed as a parameter.

PARAMETERS fname
SET TALK OFF
IF PARAMETERS() = 1
   DO (fname)
ENDIF

more = .T.
DO WHILE more
   fname = GETFILE('APP','Application to run')
   IF !EMPTY(fname)
    DO (fname)
    CLEAR PROGRAM
    more = .T.
   ELSE
    more = .F.
   ENDIF
ENDDO
```

Although short, this program contains features that you use in every application you write:

- A `PARAMETERS` statement that accepts information from another program
- An environment modifier (`SET TALK ON`)
- An assignment statement (`more = .T.`)
- A conditional branching construct (`IF...ELSE...ENDIF`)
- A conditional looping construct (`DO WHILE...ENDDO`)

Using just these few tools, you can write many useful programs. The following discussion examines what the program does and how the structure and style make reading and understanding the program easier.

The first thing you should notice is that lines following a conditional statement such as IF or DO WHILE are indented to make the program easier to read. The computer doesn't care whether these lines begin in column 1 or in column 100, but people require reading aids. Just as each new thought in a book begins with a new sentence, each set of statements to be executed under a certain condition should be set off from those executed under a different condition. Programmers define statement blocks by indenting them at the same level. Although you may not yet understand the following commands, you easily can see that they are executed if the memory variable fname contains a value:

```
DO (fname)
CLEAR PROGRAM
more = .T.
```

If you don't know what a memory variable is, don't worry. This chapter explains memory variables in detail. For now, just understand that memory variables are names that you can use to hold values and that you can compare those stored values to constants (like the number 2) and other variables to determine whether or not to take an action.

Just as related thoughts are grouped into paragraphs, related statements in a program usually are separated from other statements by one or more blank lines. The computer ignores blank lines. In fact, when FoxPro compiles your program, it removes all blank lines and spaces not required to separate one command from the next.

Using Pseudocode To Clarify Your Approach

Programs that proceed in a straight-line fashion in performing a simple task, such as the SHOWORDS program, usually can be written from start to finish without a separate planning stage. More ambitious, and complicated, programs require that you gain a good understanding of the steps that the program will take in achieving its objective—before you find yourself mired in the intricate details of writing the actual code.

To effectively plan a program, you need to use a *high-level language*, one in which a few words can convey your objectives. Spoken languages, such as English, are high-level languages, because a few well-chosen words quickly can convey a wealth of meaning and information. Spoken language, however, often introduces an unwelcome amount of ambiguity. Because computers do what we say rather than what we mean, ambiguity must be avoided.

What you need to express your ideas for creating the program is a pseudo-language, one that combines the expressiveness of a spoken language with the precision of a programming language, like FoxPro's command language.

Pseudocode (as the term is used here) is a language with no rules. You invent your own version. You mix and match English words and phrases with those of the FoxPro language to clearly express the steps that your program needs to take to achieve your goal. If you are a beginner, your first attempts at using pseudocode will consist mostly of English. As your knowledge of FoxPro increases, you will use a greater percentage of commands in place of English words and phrases.

The following example of pseudocode uses APPSHELL.PRG and presents the program in only English:

Purpose: Runs application programs (those ending in APP). Lets the user specify the name of the first one to be run. If no application is specified, displays a list of application (APP) files and prompts the user for the one to run. Continues running applications until the user chooses to stop.

Steps:

```
accept the name of an application to run
from the calling program

make sure that the TALK feature is off

if the user specified an application to run,
  run it now

if an application was not specified, or after it was
completed
  let the user specify one / another one

if the user selected an application
  run it
  go back and get another one to be run
otherwise
  end the program and return to the calling program
```

Now try to rephrase this pseudocode so that you get a little closer to the actual FoxPro commands that you need to use in your program—without losing the expressiveness of your original ideas:

Steps:

```
store the name of an application to run in a variable
called fname

set TALK off
```

```
if the fname variable is not empty
  run the application whose name is stored in fname now

until the user chooses to stop
  get the name of an application to run and store it in fname

  if fname is not empty
     run the application and then clear it from memory
  else
     s/he wants to stop

end the program and return to the calling program
```

The final step in the process is to write the program. Rather than start from scratch, use your pseudocode to create the program as follows:

- Convert each line of pseudocode *that represents a single FoxPro command or function* into the actual code.
- Use the remaining lines as **comments** for the sequence of commands or functions required to complete the task.

```
* A modified version of APPSHELL.PRG
parameters fname
set talk off

if !empty(fname)
   do (fname)
endif

do while .t.
   fname = getfile('APP','Application to run')
   if "" != fname
     * run the application, and then clear it from
     * memory
     do (fname)
     clear program
   else
     EXIT
   endif
enddo

return
```

Wait a minute! That's not the same as APPSHELL!

It's not the same because the programming style that is used differs from that of the person who wrote the APPSHELL program. The two programs are *functionally* identical. The difference is in the appearance of the code (mostly lowercase here, instead of mostly uppercase in APPSHELL.PRG) and the precise commands, functions, and techniques used.

TIP

Programming style is largely a matter of personal preference. Some programmers will tell you that the EXIT command (which causes the program to break out of an enclosing DO WHILE, SCAN, or FOR loop) is to be strictly avoided. Others (including the author of this chapter) find the use of flags, such as the variable *more*, to be inelegant and to add little to the readability of the program.

Which style you choose is not important. What *is* important is that you be *consistent* in your usage of a style. If you use uppercase letters for commands and lowercase letters for variable names in one program, be sure that they are used in the same fashion throughout your program. If you use different styles within the same program, you will not only confuse others who read your code, but you also will find your own programs difficult to read six months from now.

When properly used, pseudocode almost always decreases the amount of time required to design, write, and debug an application. Although it's often not easy, you *must* avoid the temptation to start coding before you have mapped out the logic of any non-trivial program.

Organizing the Tasks of a Program

The first step the authors took in the task of writing this book was to prepare an outline. They listed all of the topics they felt were needed to help you learn to use FoxPro 2, divided the topics into chapters, and then grouped related chapters into separate sections.

Developing an application requires the same amount of planning and structuring. The overall task is broken down into sub-tasks, and the related ones are grouped together into modules.

The medium used to provide access to the different modules is the *menu*. Just as FoxPro's features are organized into different menu pads, so should the features of your application.

If you didn't skip the chapter on the Menu Builder, you should be aware that you now can incorporate your own menu options into the FoxPro system menu, along with as many of FoxPro 2's menu options as you want the users of your application to be able to access.

FoxPro 2 has introduced a new way of accessing the tasks of an application. Central to this new philosophy is the READ command, which now enables you to do the following:

- Have GETs active simultaneously in more than one window;
- Have windows not usually associated with READ, such as Browse and Modify Memo windows, participate in the READ along with active GETs;
- Create an event-driven interface, like that of FoxPro 2, in which applications are launched from the System menu.

In addition to activating GETs, READ now can be used to insert a *wait state* into your program, in much the same way as the Command window is FoxPro's "wait state." From the Command window, FoxPro recognizes and acts upon your keystrokes and menu selections. Your applications now can respond to events, such as selections made by the user from the System menu. Because you can incorporate modules of your application into the System menu, you can create a truly seamless environment in which the user can access the features of FoxPro 2 and your application, while retaining control over what is available and when it is available.

Most of the required interaction among your menus, screens, and other programs is coordinated for you by the Project Manager, covered in Chapter 14.

This section discusses the tasks required to establish the framework of your application and to provide a smooth transition to and from the user's environment. The next section, "Developing Programming Techniques," covers some of the FoxPro commands that you can use in the programs activated by making selections from your menus.

Saving, Setting, and Restoring the Environment

When you rent a summer cottage, it's considered polite to leave things the way you found them. (Perhaps the owner has a good reason for keeping the dishes in the washing machine!)

If, upon exiting your application, the user may return to the interactive FoxPro 2 environment or to another FoxPro application that uses yours as a module in a larger application, you must restore the environment settings to the values they held when your application was first run.

Consider the SAFETY setting, which controls whether or not FoxPro asks your permission before overwriting or erasing an existing file. From within an application, you usually are in control of which files can be erased with impunity, such as when you erase temporary files. Therefore, you usually should SET SAFETY OFF at the top of your program.

However, you cannot make any assumptions about the proper setting for SAFETY outside of your application. The best practice is to leave the SAFETY setting the way you found it.

FoxPro 2 has several built-in functions that return the current value of some setting. The most versatile of these functions is SET(), which enables you to save the current SETting of most, but not all, of the many SET commands.

The syntax for the SET() function is as follows:

```
SET(<expC> [,1])
```

The only reason to save a setting is that you are going to set it to some value that may be different from the current value. Because SET() always returns the current setting, you have to save what it returns to a variable before you change it. You then use this variable to restore the previous setting.

In APPSHELL.PRG, TALK is SET OFF to suppress the screen display of the value of the assignment statements (e.g., more = .T.) that follow. You can amend this program to save and restore the current TALK setting as follows:

```
PARAMETERS fname
curr_talk = SET('TALK')
SET TALK OFF
. (the rest of the program goes here)
.
.
IF curr_talk = 'ON'
   SET TALK ON
ENDIF
```

SET() has an optional argument (the number 1) that can be used with *a few* of the settings to return additional information. Generally, the additional information is what the setting has been SET TO. For example, you can save the name of the current Help file, as set by SET HELP TO <*file name*>, with:

```
curr_help = SET('HELP',1)
```

So far, this section has covered saving the environment settings at the top of the application and restoring them before exiting. The types of settings that you usually would save in this manner include TALK, SAFETY, and BELL.

You will want to save, change, and restore other settings often throughout your application. One such setting is presented in Chapter 12, which covers the Screen Builder. In the data entry validation code snippets, you save the index order of the particular lookup table, set the order to what you required to do your lookup, and then restored the table to its previous value before returning. To do this, you use FoxPro's ORDER( ) function, which returns the master index file name or master tag name for the table in the currently selected work area:

```
morder = ORDER()
SET ORDER TO prodcode
* save the current table order
* so you can set it up the way you want to
* but restore it afterwards

IF SEEK(mcode)
.
.
.
ENDIF

* now put things back the way you found them
SET ORDER TO (morder)
```

FoxPro has several other functions that enable you to put things back the way they were. Some of the most often used are as follows:

- ALIAS( ) Returns the alias of a work area
- RECNO( ) Returns the number of the current record
- SELECT( ) Returns the number of the selected work area

Some of the ways in which you use these functions are explored in Part V, "Getting To Know FoxPro 2 Commands and Functions."

Selecting Work Areas and Opening Tables

Before you can work with a table, you have to open the table in a work area. You can do this in one of two ways:

- Restore the environment, including open tables and index files, that you saved with the CREATE VIEW command by using SET VIEW TO <*view file*>.
- Use the USE command.

Chapter 3, "Exploring Databases and Tables" discusses CREATE VIEW and SET VIEW TO. From within a program, it is more typical to open the specific tables and indexes that the application requires. This section discusses the USE command and its options.

If you are coming to FoxPro 2 from dBASE III, FoxBASE+, or FoxPro 1, be advised that the simple USE command found in those products has acquired a few new features, among them the capability to open a table in more than one work area. Although this chapter covers most of the typical uses of the command, you should refer to the FoxPro 2 *Commands & Functions* reference guide or the Help file for complete information on this enhanced command.

Unless you specify a particular work area, USE opens the table in the current work area, which defaults to 1 if you haven't yet selected any others. You may use the IN clause to specify a particular work area. Work areas are referred to by number (1-25). Work areas 1 through 10 also may be referenced by a letter (A-J).

FoxPro 2 can open the same table in more than one work area. This capability is useful when you want to view the table in more than one Browse window simultaneously.

Each work area is assigned an *alias*, by which the table open in that work area may be referred. The default alias is the name of the table. If you open a table in more than one work area using the AGAIN clause, the work area letter (or a combination of "W" and the work area number for areas above 10) is assigned as the alias.

For example, open some of the tables used in the Omnipresent Widget application, each in its own work area:

USE BUDGET	IN 1	Assigned alias is BUDGET.
USE BUDCAT	IN 2	Assigned alias is BUDCAT.
USE CUSTOMER	IN C	Assigned alias is CUSTOMER.
USE CUSTOMER	IN D AGAIN	CUSTOMER is now open in two work areas; its alias in area D is "D".
USE DEPT	IN 5	Assigned alias is DEPT.
USE SALES	IN 11	Assigned alias is SALES.
USE SALES	IN 12 AGAIN	SALES is now open in two work areas; its alias in area 12 is "W12".

Usually, no good reason exists to use both numbers and letters (1 and C) when referring to work areas. Nor does it usually make sense to assign tables to work areas in anything other than a sequential fashion.

Type *DISPLAY STATUS* in the Command window to view the current status of the open work areas. Note the alias assigned to each work area.

You may assign an alternative alias to a table with the ALIAS clause, as long as that alias has not already been assigned to a currently open table in a different work area. Assigning an alternative alias can be especially useful when opening a table in two work areas, such as the SALES table. For example, when the SALES table was opened in work area 12, you could have assigned it an alias such as SALES_A:

```
USE SALES IN 12 AGAIN ALIAS SALES_A
```

Notice that if the SALES table were opened in a second work area, using the View window, FoxPro assigns SALES_A as the table's alias in that work area.

The whole point of alias names is that you don't have to know, or care, which area a particular table is in. You now can refer to the second instance of the SALES table as SALES_A, rather than having to remember that you opened the table in area 12. Using alternative aliases becomes particularly important when using SQL SELECT statements in your program, or through the RQBE facility, because SQL SELECT opens tables in work areas indiscriminately.

You should be aware of a little-known fact concerning aliases. Some legal DOS file names cannot be translated into a legal alias. Table names that begin with a digit, for example, are assigned the work area letter as their default alias, rather than the table name.

For example, create a table such as *1991DATA*. Now activate the View Window. Notice that the new table's alias is the work area letter, not "1991DATA," as you may have expected. If you try to select the table with *SELECT 1991DATA*, FoxPro displays an error message, because no such alias exists.

When you display the current work area status after entering the USE commands in the Command window, notice that each of the tables has an open index file, even though you didn't specify any INDEX clause in your USE commands. These indexes are *structural indexes*, created when you first created each of the tables in the Omnipresent Widget sample application. Structural indexes are opened when the related table is opened. For that reason, structural indexes are preferable to stand-alone index files.

Keep in mind, however, that when a table with a structural index is opened, none of the index tags are set as the controlling, or *master* index. To set a specific one as the master index, use the ORDER clause to specify the desired index tag. For example, the following command sets the DEPTCODE tag as the controlling index tag:

```
USE DEPT IN 1 ORDER DEPTCODE
```

FoxPro 2 is the first version of FoxPro to use structural indexes. Earlier versions were limited to using stand-alone index files, which must specifically be opened along with the related table, using the INDEX <*.idx file list*> clause of the USE command or the SET INDEX TO <*.idx file list*> command. For example, the following command opens the index files MYDATA1 and MYDATA2 along with the table MYDATA:

```
USE MYDATA INDEX MYDATA1, MYDATA2
```

The first index in the index file list, MYDATA1 in this case, automatically becomes the master index. Structural index files, however, require that the desired index order be specified using the ORDER clause or the SET ORDER TO command.

Refer to Chapter 4, "Database Management Fundamentals," for more information on the different types of indexes you can create with FoxPro 2.

Using Menus To Present Choices

The environment has been set—like a backdrop—and the tables, like actors, have been called to take their places. Now you can establish your menu, which provides the series of acts for the "play" about to be performed.

You learn how to create a menu system in Chapter 14, "Organizing and Packaging Your Applications." If you create your menus through the Menu Builder system, as most people using FoxPro 2 do, enabling your menu is a simple matter of adding the following command at this point in your program:

```
DO your_menu.mpr
```

FoxPro 2 also can create many other forms of menus—from simple popups to complete menu systems. Whichever menu form you choose, your program executes its main menu now.

A FoxPro 2 application is like certain forms of improvisational or experimental drama; the actors and the audience (the users) can determine a different order for the acts every time the program is performed. Your menu system should be flexible enough to enable your users to do their work in a way that seems natural to them, rather than the way that seems natural to you.

Developing Programming Techniques

Earlier in this chapter, you moved some commands from the Command window into a program file and ran the program. Placing the commands into a program enabled you to achieve your objective, without having to retype the commands each time you wanted to use them.

You could just as easily have stored these commands in a *macro* file and played the macro. You wouldn't have had to retype the commands, and you could have inserted a pause in the macro to enable you to type the desired customer code.

What makes a program more powerful than a macro is the ability it gives users to take different actions based upon the truth or falsehood of a *condition*. The condition may be set by an action that the user takes during the program execution, or the condition may depend upon the current values of the data in your tables.

This section explores FoxPro 2's *structured programming* commands and functions that are used to control program execution and branching within a FoxPro program. The following commands and functions are included:

- IF ... ENDIF
- IIF()
- DO WHILE ... ENDDO
- SCAN ... ENDSCAN
- DO CASE ... ENDCASE
- FOR ... ENDFOR

The discussion provides one or more examples of how to use each of these commands. As you gain in knowledge of, and experience with, the FoxPro programming language, you will begin to recognize the situations in which one command may be preferable to another.

Trying to control program execution without understanding what a memory variable is, is like trying to drive a car without a steering wheel. This section, therefore, defines memory variables (in a linguistic and a programmatic sense) and shows you how to use memory variables in your programs.

This section also covers commands that use a *scope*, a FOR, or a WHILE clause to perform an action on a group of records in a table. Among these commands are COUNT, SUM, and REPLACE.

Last, but not least, you are introduced to *procedures*, and your knowledge of user-defined functions (UDF's), some of which you already have used as code snippets in the Screen Builder and Menu Builder chapters, is expanded. Procedures and UDF's are indispensable allies in the battle to produce readable, verifiable, and maintainable code.

Understanding and Using Memory Variables

If you followed along with the examples in Chapter 10, "Using the Report Writer and Label Designer," you already have seen and used memory variables.

Think of a memory variable as a bucket, to which you affix a gummed label with the name "My_Bucket" printed on it. Into this bucket, you put three marbles. When your mother asks you, "Have you lost your marbles?" You reply, "No, they're in My_Bucket!"

When you want to refer to those three marbles, you can use the name My_Bucket in place of the contents of the actual bucket. When you type *IF My_Bucket = 3*, FoxPro looks in the variable My_Bucket, sees the value 3 stored there, and *evaluates* the expression as follows:

```
IF 3 = 3
```

This statement is true. Because the expression evaluates to true, the commands that follow IF and precede ELSE (if you specified an ELSE) or ENDIF (if you did not specify an ELSE) are executed.

As the word implies, a variable may be changed at any time. You can increment a variable, decrement a variable, store a completely different value to a variable, or copy a variable's value to another variable:

mvar = 0	create the variable mvar and set it to 0
mvar = mvar + 1	add 1 to mvar and save the result back to mvar
mvar = mvar - 1	subtract 1 from mvar and save the result to mvar
My_Bucket = mvar	create the variable My_Bucket and copy the value of mvar to it

After entering these commands in the Command window (the comments are not necessary), My_Bucket equals 0 (maybe your mother was right!).

NOTE FoxPro has two ways of assigning values to memory variables and array elements, = and the STORE command. The STORE command has the following syntax:

STORE <*expression*> to <*memory variable list*> | <*array*>

Both = and STORE do the same thing. Which one to use is mostly a matter of personal preference. Some programmers consider STORE to be preferable, as this command is more descriptive of its function: to store values. Those who have programmed in other languages usually are more comfortable with =.

The one clear advantage of STORE over = is its capability to store a value to more than one variable. Because STORE accepts a list of variables or array elements, multiple assignments of *the same value* to more than one variable or array element can be accomplished with a single line of code, as in the following:

```
STORE .F. to mvar1, mvar2, mvar3
```

FoxPro, as well as most of the other X-Base dialects, differs from many other languages in that you need not define a variable and specify its data type before you actually create the variable. In the preceding example, the first time you assign a value to *mvar*, FoxPro creates the variable if it does not already exist.

You also can change the data type of a variable after it has been created, something which is prohibited in most languages. You can do this by assigning to the variable a value of the new data type. To demonstrate this procedure, activate the Command window and type the following lines:

```
mvar = 0
? TYPE('mvar')
```

FoxPro displays `N` on-screen (or in the active window), indicating that the variable *mvar* is of numeric type. Type the following:

```
mvar = "Hello, world!"
? TYPE('mvar')
```

As you can see, *mvar* is now of character (C) type.

In computer science terms, the X-Base language has "weak type checking," which means that the compiler cannot catch your mistake when you unintentionally assign a value of the wrong data type to a memory variable. The compiler cannot flag the assignment as an error, because you may have *intended* to change the variable's data type. The ability to change a variable's data type can be used to great advantage, but this ability also can get you into trouble.

This weak type checking applies also to arrays but does not extend to fields in tables. You cannot change the data type of a field by REPLACEing the value with a value of a different data type. If you try to store a value of the wrong data type to a field, you will trigger an error.

You need to understand the following rules when creating and using memory variables:

- Memory variables must begin with a letter or the underscore (_) character. Avoid beginning memory variable names with the underscore character, however, because your variable names may conflict with FoxPro's system memory variables and menu bar names.
- You can use a name longer than 10 characters, but only the first 10 are significant. To avoid error and confusion, limit your variable names to 10 characters.
- You may create a memory variable with the same name as a field in the currently selected table. Indeed, FoxPro 2 does this when

you use the SCATTER MEMVAR command. However, when you use a command that can take its arguments from the field or the memory variable, precede the memory variable name with the *M.* or *M->* prefix to tell FoxPro to use the value of the memory variable. Otherwise, FoxPro gives precedence to the field and uses the field value.

- You may store the contents of a memo field as a character string in a memory variable, but keep in mind that a character string has a length limitation. The exact limit depends upon which version (Standard or Extended) of FoxPro 2 you are using. In the Standard version, character strings can be a maximum of 64K (65,536) characters. In the Extended version, character strings have a theoretical maximum of *2 gigabytes* (2 billion bytes). The practical limit is the amount of available RAM (random-access memory) in your computer.

Now that you understand what memory variables are, you can use them to construct conditional expressions that can be evaluated by FoxPro's structured programming commands.

Using Commands That Evaluate Conditions

You already have seen some simple examples of using IF ... ENDIF and DO WHILE ... ENDDO to test for certain conditions and to perform actions suitable to each set of circumstances. Knowing when you need to evaluate a condition is the easy part. The hard part is understanding how to properly *express* the condition, or combination of conditions, to be tested.

The condition always takes the form of a *logical expression*, one that can be evaluated as true or false. You can construct a logical expression by using one of the following:

- A table field of logical type
- A memory variable or array element that holds a logical value
- A function (built-in or user-defined) that returns a logical value
- Other expression types (character, numeric, or date) separated by a *relational operator* (such as <, >, =, <=, !=, and so on)

You also can use *.T.* or *.F.* to construct a logical expression.

To illustrate some of these, refer to the APPSHELL.PRG example one more time:

```
* APPSHELL is part of the FoxApp system.
* This is a routine to display a list of APP files and
* prompt the user for the one to run.
* It does not display the list
* of files if a file name is passed as a parameter.

PARAMETERS fname
SET TALK OFF
IF PARAMETERS() = 1
   DO (fname)
ENDIF

more = .T.
DO WHILE more
   fname = GETFILE('APP','Application to run')
   IF !EMPTY(fname)
    DO (fname)
    CLEAR PROGRAM
    more = .T.
   ELSE
    more = .F.
   ENDIF
ENDDO
```

This program uses two of the five means of constructing a logical expression. APPSHELL.PRG uses a function that returns a logical value (EMPTY(), an expression that evaluates to a logical value (PARAMETERS() = 1), and a memory variable that contains a logical value.

The version of APPSHELL that grew out of the pseudocode example uses a pair of non-logical expressions compared to each other using a relational operator (in this case !=_) and a logical value, .T.:

```
do while .t.
   fname = getfile('APP','Application to run')
   if "" != fname
    * run the program, and then clear it from memory
    do (fname)
    clear program
   else
    EXIT
   endif
enddo
```

Examine the IF construct first. If the user presses Esc while in the Getfile dialog, the GETFILE() function returns *the null string* (""), which is stored into variable *fname*. You then can compare *fname* to the null string to determine whether or not to run another program.

What does `do while .t.` mean? This instruction specifies a logical value, rather than an expression that must be evaluated to a logical value. You can just as easily say `do while 3 = 3`. You are telling FoxPro, "This is not the right time to decide whether or not to continue. I'll let you know somewhere else when I want to leave this loop."

This type of construct is called an *infinite loop*. Without some other means of exiting, a program with an infinite loop goes on forever. As its name implies, the EXIT command enables you to break out of the infinite loop. When the user presses **Esc** in GETFILE(), the expression `"" != fname` becomes false (fname now contains the null string); the ELSE is activated; and EXIT is executed.

Using IF ... ENDIF To Choose Your Path

By now, you have seen many examples of how to use the IF ... ENDIF construct to make a decision. IF ... ENDIF has two formats:

Format 1: IF ... ENDIF

```
* Evaluate a condition, and perform one or more steps
* only if it is true

IF <condition>  <optional comment>

  commands to be executed if <condition> is true

ENDIF                   <optional comment>
```

Format 2: IF ... ELSE ... ENDIF

```
* Evaluate a condition
* Perform one series of steps if it is true,
* and a different series of steps if it is false

IF <condition>  <optional comment>

  commands to be executed if <condition> is true

ELSE                    <optional comment>

  commands to be executed if <condition> is false

ENDIF                   <optional comment>
```

Comments may be placed at the *end* of any line. Comments that appear on the same line as a command or expression *must* be preceded by a double ampersand (&&), which tells FoxPro not to evaluate the remainder of the line. A comment that appears on a line by itself must be preceded by a double ampersand, the word NOTE, or, more traditionally, by one or more asterisks (*).

IF statements also may be *nested*; that is, one or more of the commands to be executed may itself be an IF statement, which also can have one or more IF statements nested within it:

```
* GLADHAND.PRG
* An example of a nested IF
*
input "How old are you (in years) ? " to your_age
if your_age < 40
  if your_age < 30
        if your_age < 20
        ? "Gee, I wish I was a kid like you again!"
        else
        ? "Your twenties are the best years of your life!"
        endif
  else
        ? "Your thirties are the best years of your life!"
  endif
else
  if your_age > 49
        if your_age > 59
        ? "Gee, you don't look a day over 30!"
        else
        ? "Your fifties are the best years of your life!"
        endif
  else
        ? "Your forties are the best years of your life!"
  endif
endif
return
```

When each condition in an IF ... ELSE ... ENDIF performs the same operation with a different expression, you can use the IIF() (usually read as “Immediate If”) function to evaluate the condition and return the desired expression. IIF() requires three arguments and is structured as follows:

IIF(<*condition*>, <*expression1*>, <*expression2*>)

The condition is evaluated. If it is true, *<expression1>* is returned, and if it is false, *<expression2>* is returned. Because the returned expression is not very useful by itself, you assign the expression to a variable or pass it along as the argument of another command or function. You can rewrite the GLADHAND procedure using IIF( ) as follows:

```
* GLADHAND.PRG
* An example of a nested IF using IIF()
*
input "How old are you (in years) ? " to your_age
? iif(your_age < 40, ;
  iif(your_age < 30, ;
        iif(your_age < 20, ;
              "Gee, I wish I was a kid like you again!", ;
              "Your twenties are the best years of your life!"), ;
        "Your thirties are the best years of your life!"),;
  iif(your_age > 49, ;
        iif(your_age > 59, ;
              "Gee, you don't look a day over 30!",;
              "Your fifties are the best years of your life!"),;
        "Your forties are the best years of your life!"))
return
```

This program *looks* much more complicated, but the logic is the same. The real difference is that it is harder to read, because the ELSE is *implied* in the construction of the IIF() function's arguments, rather than printed in the appropriate place in the program. Actually, if you adopt a formatting convention like the one shown and use that convention every time you use IIF(), the program becomes just as easy to read as an IF ... ELSE ... ENDIF:

```
IIF(condition, ;
  expression to return if condition is true, ;
  expression to return if condition is false)
```

The logic of the GLADHAND program is clear and fairly easy to follow. In a more complicated case, the use of multiple nested IF's can make the program hard to understand.

FoxPro has a command, DO CASE, that makes it much easier to follow the logic of a program that must choose among more than two possible cases.

Making Multiple Choice Decisions with DO CASE

FoxPro's DO CASE command is similar to the CASE command in Pascal and the SWITCH() function in C. DO CASE evaluates a series of conditions and performs the ones that follow the first condition, if any, that is true:

```
DO CASE
   CASE <condition 1>
         <statements>
   [CASE <condition 2>
         <statements>
   ...
   CASE <condition n>
         <statements>]
   [OTHERWISE
         <statements>]
ENDCASE
```

The brackets ([and]) indicate that these parts of the construct are optional. A DO CASE can contain one CASE to be evaluated, in which case it would be functionally identical to an IF ... ENDIF. However, DO CASE is rarely used in this fashion.

The following restructure of the GLADHAND program is a more typical usage of DO CASE:

```
* GLADHAND.PRG
* An example of using DO CASE
*
input "How old are you (in years) ? " to your_age
do case
   case your_age < 20
         ? "Gee, I wish I was a kid like you again!"
   case between(your_age, 20, 29)
         ? "Your twenties are the best years of your life!"
   case between(your_age, 30, 30)
         ? "Your thirties are the best years of your life!"
   case between(your_age, 40, 49)
         ? "Your forties are the best years of your life!"
   case between(your_age, 50, 59)
         ? "Your fifties are the best years of your life!"
   otherwise
         ? "Gee, you don't look a day over 30!"
endcase
return
```

When a condition that evaluates to True is found, the conditions that follow it are not evaluated; unlike C, in which the program *falls through* to all of the other statements in the SWITCH() function call.

The optional OTHERWISE clause enables you to specify a default series of steps to be taken. The commands that follow OTHERWISE are executed only if none of the stated conditions evaluates to True.

Using Commands That Operate on a Range of Records

When using commands that operate on records in a table, such as REPLACE, COPY and COUNT, you usually can limit the records the command processes to a certain range. The records to be included in the range are specified by attaching a *scope*, FOR, and/or WHILE clause to the command. If the range to be affected by the command can be specified in this manner, you should do it this way, rather than using one of the looping constructs to skip through the table, because FoxPro only needs to evaluate the condition once.

Table 16.1 shows the commands that take a scope, FOR, and WHILE clause. Table 16.2 shows the scope clauses you can use with these commands.

Table 16.1 Commands That Use a Scope, FOR and WHILE Clause

Command	Command	Command	Command
AVERAGE	COPY TO ARRAY	LABEL	REPORT
CALCULATE	COUNT	LIST	SCAN
CHANGE	DELETE	LOCATE	SORT
CONTINUE	DISPLAY	RECALL	SUM
COPY TO	EXPORT	REPLACE	TOTAL

Table 16.2 The Scope Clauses

Clause	Range of Records Affected	Record Pointer Lands At
ALL	All records in the table	End of File
NEXT <n>	The next <n> records, beginning with the current record	Last record processed
RECORD <n>	Only the record whose record number is <n>	Record <n>
REST	From the current record to the last one in the table	End of File

Keep in mind that the order in which the records are processed is affected by the master index, if any. If you use the command *REPLACE NEXT 3 ...*, the replacements are made in the current record and in the two records that follow it *in the current index order*.

Be especially careful when using the REPLACE command to change the value of any field contained in the current master index expression. Because REPLACE updates all active indexes, a scope, FOR, or WHILE clause should never be used with REPLACE when updating any field that is part of the master index expression.

Repeating Your Actions with DO WHILE, SCAN, and FOR

FoxPro 2 has three commands that enable you to repeat certain actions as long as some condition remains True. While similar in function, each is more appropriate than the others in certain circumstances.

The venerable DO WHILE command is the most versatile of the looping commands and has the distinction of being able to replace the other two under all conditions.

The format of DO WHILE ... ENDDO is the same as that of IF ... ENDIF. The following evaluates a condition and executes one or more commands if it is True:

```
DO WHILE <condition>
  commands to execute if condition is true
ENDDO
```

The difference is that, after the commands have been executed, FoxPro reevaluates the condition and keeps executing the commands until the condition evaluates to False. When that happens, program execution control passes to the line that follows ENDDO.

SCAN works much like DO WHILE but is designed specifically for moving through a table. SCAN automatically advances the record pointer on each successive loop. SCAN also reselects the table it is SCANning if you change the active work area within the loop. The default scope for SCAN is ALL, meaning that you don't have to explicitly position the record pointer at the top of the file. You also can specify any of the other scope clauses (REST, NEXT <n>, or RECORD <n>) to restrict the records to be SCANned to a range. Because it works only on tables, SCAN is more limited in what you can do with it than DO WHILE.

The first of the following code fragments uses DO WHILE and is functionally identical to the second fragment, which uses SCAN:

```
SELECT A
GO TOP
DO WHILE !EOF()
  SELECT B
  < some commands >
  SELECT A
  SKIP
ENDDO

SELECT A
SCAN
  SELECT B
  < some commands >
ENDSCAN
```

Although not required, you can explicitly reselect work area A before repeating the loop in the second code fragment. You must remember, however, not to use SKIP with SCAN, unless you are sure that you actually want to skip over a record.

FOR ... ENDFOR executes one or more commands in a loop a specified number of times. To use the FOR command, you have to set a memory variable, which acts as a counter, to some initial value and specify a limit value that, when exceeded by the counter, causes the FOR to be exited. By default, the counter is incremented by one after each pass through the loop. If the counter variable does not exist, FoxPro creates the counter variable for you.

You can increment the counter by a value other than one by specifying a STEP value. You can STEP *downward* from an initial value by specifying a negative increment.

FOR, shown in the following examples, is easier to illustrate than to explain:

```
* turn off the function keys F1 through F10
FOR j = 1 TO 10         && STEP 1 is implied
  SET FUNCTION j TO *
ENDFOR


* display the letters from "A" to "Z"
FOR j = ASC("A") TO ASC("Z") && STEP 1 is implied
  ? CHR(j)
ENDFOR

* display every other letter from ";A" to "Z"
FOR j = ASC("A") TO ASC("Z") STEP 2
  ? CHR(j)
ENDFOR

* display only the consonants, in reverse order
* from "Z" to "A"
vowels = "AEIOU"
FOR j = ASC("Z") TO ASC("A") STEP -1
  IF ! (CHR(j) $ vowels)
        ? CHR(j)
  ENDIF
ENDFOR
```

In each case, the counter *j* is initialized to some value and incremented by the STEP value *after* each pass through the loop. The commands in the loop are executed as long as the counter is less than or equal to the limit value. If you have specified a negative STEP value, the counter must be **greater** than or equal to the limit.

As was the case with SCAN, you also can use DO WHILE to accomplish all of these things:

```
* turn off the function keys F1 through F10
j = 1
DO WHILE j <= 10
  SET FUNCTION j TO *
  j = j + 1
ENDDO
```

The FOR command is preferable in this instance. Not only is the program using FOR two lines shorter, its form more clearly states the objective of the loop.

As a general rule, choose SCAN or FOR over DO WHILE whenever they can do the job, because SCAN and FOR's more limited functionality makes what is going on much clearer.

Changing the Program Flow with LOOP, EXIT, and RETURN

Each of the looping commands has two clauses, LOOP and EXIT, that enable you to alter the normal sequence of events within the loop.

LOOP tells FoxPro to disregard the remaining statements in the loop and to return to the DO WHILE, SCAN, or FOR line to reevaluate the condition. LOOP often is used within an IF statement that tests for a condition that, if true, obviates the intended function of the remaining statements in the loop.

```
* process the SALES table, disregarding "house" accounts
* House accounts begin with a "Z"
SELECT SALES
SCAN
  IF UPPER(LEFT(CUSTCODE,1)) = "Z"
        LOOP
  ENDIF
* it's not a house account, so process it
< statements >
ENDSCAN
```

EXIT, which is used in the sample version of the APPSHELL program, transfers program control to the line that follows the ENDDO, ENDSCAN, or ENDFOR. EXIT often is used to break out of an infinite loop created by DO WHILE .T.

RETURN transfers control to the program that called the current one or to the Command window if the current program is the first (or only) module in your application. When RETURN appears at the end of a procedure or UDF, the command is not altering the natural flow of the program. When one program ends, it is natural for the program that called this one to resume execution.

When RETURN appears within the *body* of a program, however, FoxPro disregards all of the following statements in the program. You can think of RETURN used in this manner as a LOOP that works with programs and subprocedures, rather than with the various looping commands. As with LOOP, RETURN is most often used when some condition exists that makes it unnecessary to continue with the program. An example of this is when a PACK routine is called, and the table to be PACKed is empty.

You should understand that you are *never* required to use *any* of these program control altering devices. You always can write a program so that they are not needed. However, writing a program without these devices sometimes requires you to use IF's, which can become nested to an uncomfortable level.

When, or whether, to use LOOP, EXIT, and RETURN is a matter of personal preference. Their judicious use can enhance the readability of your programs. If well-defined conditions under which you don't want to proceed appear, just say so, and get out of there! Try writing some routines that use LOOP, EXIT, and RETURN, as well as some routines that avoid using them, to see which ones seem more natural to you.

Using Structured Programming Commands: an Extended Example

You may wonder why the discussion of commands that act on a range of records, such as REPLACE, is positioned between the discussion of the different types of structured programming commands. The reason is that DO WHILE also can operate on a range of records but provides you with much more flexibility in determining which records are processed and which processes are applied to them.

When you use a command such as the following, the condition (custcode = "A001") is evaluated *once*.

```
REPLACE salesman WITH "B023" FOR custcode = "A001"
```

The CUSTCODE field of each record in the SALES table is compared to "B023". If they are the same, the replacement is made. The condition specified in a DO WHILE command, on the other hand, is evaluated the first time it is encountered in the program and on *each successive pass* through the loop.

The elements that make up the condition can be changed by any of the commands contained between the DO WHILE and ENDDO, giving you a much greater degree of control over which records are processed.

For example, if you want to calculate the commission due to the sales manager on house accounts for the previous fiscal quarter, you can write a program to perform the calculation. The rules for calculating the sales manager's commissions are as follows:

- The manager's commission percentage is a flat 8% of gross sales to house accounts.
- All house accounts start with Z in the CUSTCODE field.

- The total commission for the quarter cannot exceed $10,000.
- The commission earned on any one account cannot exceed $1,000.

The following example illustrates one way to write this in pseudocode:

```
* CALCCOMM.PRG

Purpose: To calculate the commission due to the sales
manager for a specified fiscal period. The rules to be
used in the calculation are:

(restate the above rules)

Steps:

accept the fiscal period from the calling program

open the SALES table

create a temporary index so that the sales are limited
to those made in the specified fiscal period to house
accounts

initialize memory variables to hold the commission
rate, the maximum commission amounts, and the commis-
sion balance

while there are more sales records to be processed, and
the total commission for the quarter has not exceeded
the maximum

  keep track of the current account

  while you're on the same account

        if the commissions for this account have not
        exceeded the maximum for each account

        add the commission rate * the amount of the
        sale to the running total for this account

ifthe commission for this account
  +  the commission for all accounts
  <= the maximum total commission

  add the commission for this account to the running
        total for all accounts
otherwise
  set the total commission equal to the maximum
  commission

erase the temporary file and return
```

Refined, the preceding example now appears as follows:

```
accept the fiscal period from the calling program

if the SALES table is already open
  select it
else
  open it in the next available work area
endif

get a temporary file name for your temporary index

index SALES on upper(CUSTCODE) for sales made in the
  specified fiscal period to customers which are house
  accounts to
  (temporary file)

initialize memory variables to hold the commission rate,
the maximum commission amounts, and the commission balance

do while there are more house accounts to be processed,
  and the total commission for the quarter has not
  exceeded the maximum

  keep track of the current account

  scan the records for this account

        if the commissions for this account have not
        exceeded the maximum for each account

              add the commission rate * the amount of the
              sale to the running total for this account

        endif

  endscan

  if    the commission for this account
        +  the commission for all accounts
        <= the maximum total commission

        add the commission for this account to the running
        total for all accounts

  else
        set the total commission equal to the maximum
        commission
  endif

enddo

erase the temporary file
return the commission amount due
```

Now you are ready to write the program:

```
* CALCCOMM.PRG
*
* Calculate and return the commission due to the sales
* manager for the fiscal period specified, as an
* integer, in parameter mperiod.
*
parameters mperiod

if used('SALES')
  select SALES
else
  * open the sales table in an available work area
  use SALES in select(1)
endif

* get a unique file name for our temporary index
temp = sys(3) + ".$$$"

* limit the records to sales made in the previous fiscal
* period to customers which are house accounts
index on upper(CUSTCODE) ;
  for    upper(left(CUSTCODE,1)) = "Z" ;
      and pd(DATESOLD) = mperiod ;
  to (temp)

* initialize memory variables to hold the commission rate, the
* maximum commission amounts, and the total commission balance
comm_rate = 0.08
max_comm  = 10000
max_each  =  1000
tot_comm  =     0

do while     !eof() ;
         and tot_comm < max_comm

  curr_cust = CUSTCODE
  this_comm = 0

  scan while CUSTCODE == curr_cust

         if this_comm <= max_each
                * add the commission rate * the amount of the
                * sale to the running total for this account
                this_comm = this_comm + comm_rate * QUANTITY * PRICE
```

```
            endif
      endscan

      if this_comm > max_each
         this_comm = max_each
      endif

      if this_comm + tot_comm < max_comm
            tot_comm = tot_comm + this_comm
      else
            tot_comm = max_comm
      endif

   enddo

   set index to           && close the temporary index
   erase (temp)           && erase the temporary index file

   return tot_comm
```

NOTE The UDF PD(), used to determine which fiscal period a particular date is part of, comes from examples in Chapter 13 in which the UDF is part of a VALID clause code snippet.

Notice that a good deal of the work was performed before you entered the DO WHILE loop, by the construction of an index that limited the table's visible records to those that may be needed to calculate the commission. This step reduces the task to a matter of skipping through the records by customer group, performing calculations and testing simple conditions along the way.

Using Subroutines To Manage the Tasks

Procedures and UDF's are programs, just like any other program. A program is called a *procedure* when used by another program to perform a particular task and a UDF when used to calculate and return a value to a calling program.

Procedures and UDF's have more in common than they have differences, so this discussion refers to both as procedures.

A procedure can be part of a program file, part of a separate procedure file, or a stand-alone program. Unless it is a stand-alone program, a procedure must start with a label that enables FoxPro to find it. You assign a label to a procedure by preceding the label with `PROCEDURE` or `FUNCTION` (e.g. `PROCEDURE My_Proc`).

Which one you use is not important. Procedure My_Proc may be labelled as `FUNCTION My_Proc` or `PROCEDURE My_Proc`. Likewise, both PROCEDUREs and FUNCTIONs may return a value or not. For style and readability, use `PROCEDURE` for routines that do not return a value and `FUNCTION` for those that do.

At the beginning of this chapter, you created a program called SHOWORDS by moving some commands from the Command window into a separate program file. SHOWORDS is limited to displaying the records for a single customer, because you had *hard coded* the customer number into the program. To use this program to display sales records for other customers, you need to include a PARAMETERS statement.

The PARAMETERS statement serves as a communication link between a procedure and the programs that call the procedure. If present, PARAMETERS must be the first line in the procedure and must be followed by a list of one or more variable names. PARAMETERS creates *local memory variables* or arrays using these names and assigns to each the value passed to the procedure by the calling program.

The data type of each variable or array created is the same as that of the value in the same position within the list of values sent to the procedure. The list that follows a PARAMETERS statement can be longer than the list of parameters actually passed to the procedure. Any parameter names that cannot be filled with data from the calling program are created as logical variables and are set equal to `.F.`. If your parameter list has three names, for example, but you call the procedure with a list of only two values, the third parameter is set equal to a logical False.

You can modify SHOWORDS to use parameters and then call SHOWORDS with a parameter list:

```
* SHOWORDS.PRG
*
* Accept the order of the index to be used
* to perform a BROWSE KEY, and the "key" value to be
* displayed, from the calling program.
*
* The table to be used is currently selected.
*
PARAMETERS morder, mkey

* if the second parameter was not passed
if type(;mkey') = 'L'
   * set mkey to the null string, which will cause
```

```
        * BROWSE KEY to display all records in the table
        mkey = ""
    endif

    * set the proper index as the master index
    set order to morder

    *display the desired records
    browse key mkey

    return
```

To use the new version of the program from the Command window, type the following:

```
USE SALES IN 1
DO SHOWORDS WITH "CUSTCODE", "A001"
```

Then try:

```
DO SHOWORDS WITH "CUSTCODE"
```

You now have transformed the rigid command sequence into a useful program that displays any or all index key values, as long as you tell the program which structural index tag to set as the master index.

The PARAMETERS statement in the procedure created the variables *morder* and *mkey* and then stored into each the value of the related item in the parameter list of the calling program (or Command window, in this case). However, you also can create the variables in the Command window and not use the PARAMETERS statement. In the Command window, you can type the following and delete the PARAMETERS statement from SHOWORDS:

```
morder = "CUSTCODE"
mkey = "A001"
USE SALES IN 1
DO SHOWORDS
```

So why should you use parameters? Using parameters enables you to do the following:

- Use procedures and UDF's without having to remember the names used to refer to the values that you want the procedure to manipulate (*morder* and *mkey* in the example)
- Hide the variables that you are using in the program from the procedure and prevent their values from being changed by the commands contained in the procedure

Two Ways To Call a Subroutine

When you want a subroutine to perform a task without returning a value, you use the following:

DO <procedure name> [WITH <argument list>]

When you want the subroutine to return a value, you can use the following form:

<UDF name> ([argument list])

The value returned by the UDF usually is assigned to a memory variable or used as an argument to a built-in FoxPro command or function. Not all of FoxPro's commands, nor all clauses of those that do, accept a UDF. Refer to the "User-Defined Functions (UDFs)" entry in the FoxPro *Commands & Functions* manual for a complete list of the commands and clauses that support UDF's.

The return value of built-in functions and UDFs also may be discarded by using the = command, which evaluates an expression consisting of one or more function calls. You may choose to use this command if you are only interested in a *side effect* of the function, such as moving the record pointer to a specific record in a table.

Passing Parameters by Value and by Reference

One possible side effect of a procedure or UDF is that it may change the value of any of its parameters within the body of the subroutine. If the modified parameter received its original value from the calling program in the form of a memory variable or an array (as in "DO SHOWORDS WITH morder"), as opposed to a constant (such as "DO SHOWORDS WITH 'PRODCODE'"), the memory variable or array may or may not retain the changes when the subroutine ends.

If parameters are *passed by value*, the subroutine makes a *copy* of the original variables for use within the subroutine. When the subroutine ends, these temporary variables are released from memory. The original variables are not affected.

If parameters are *passed by reference*, the subroutine does *not* create a copy of the original variables but refers to them by the names used in the parameter list. Any changes made to the parameters within the subroutine actually are made to the original variables.

Which type of parameter passing is used for a particular subroutine call depends upon one or both of the following factors:

- The form used to call the subroutine (DO <procedure name> WITH <parameter list> or <function name> (<parameter list>))
- The current SETting of UDFPARMS

Variables passed to a subroutine using DO <procedure> ... are always passed by reference, unless you specify that pass by value should be used for a particular variable by enclosing its name in parentheses. Variables passed to a subroutine using <function> (<parameter list>) are passed by value, unless UDFPARMS is SET to REFERENCE or the variable name is preceded by the AT symbol (@). The default setting of UDFPARMS is VALUE.

Arrays also are affected by the calling format and by UDFPARMS. Although the rules are not difficult to understand, the manipulation of arrays passed as parameters is an advanced subject covered in Chapter 20, "Using Arrays and the Low-Level File Functions." For now, just be aware that a single element of an array (as opposed to the array itself) is always passed by value.

Chapter Summary

This chapter covers many of the basics of programming in FoxPro 2. You learned about the structure of a program, how to use pseudocode to outline the steps the program will take, and how to use FoxPro's structured programming commands to test conditions and repeat actions.

You also learned more about memory variables: what they are, when they are created, and how you can use them in programs. Finally, you learned the basics of using procedures and user-defined functions to break the tasks of the program into smaller pieces that make the application easier to read and to debug.

In the next chapter, the discussion expands upon the knowledge and skills gained in this chapter and introduces you to some more advanced programming techniques.

17

CHAPTER

Using Advanced FoxProgramming Techniques

Chapter 16 introduced some programming structure and design concepts. Pseudocode was used to clarify the steps that a program needed to take, and a few programs that used FoxPro's structured programming techniques were examined.

This chapter reinforces all the concepts and techniques used to this point and introduces you to a few more advanced techniques. This chapter also introduces you to FoxPro 2's text merge features, which you can use to create program templates.

This chapter begins by discussing the two types of memory variables that you can create and the circumstances under which you would use each of them.

Using Public and Private Variables

Chapter 16 defined memory variables and gave you some rules for using them. To manage memory variables in an application, you need to know more about how FoxPro resolves potential conflicts between variable names used more than once in different routines of your application.

Consider the following code fragment:

```
PROCEDURE mainproc
   x = 1
   y = factorial(5)
   ? x    <== the current value of x is now 120!
return

FUNCTION factorial
   *
   * return the factorial of mnum
   *
   parameters mnum

   x = 1
   for j=mnum to 1 step -1
       x = x * j
   endfor

return x
```

(Note that FACTORIAL handles the special case of 0 but does not handle negative numbers properly.)

Procedure MAINPROC stores the constant value 1 to a variable called *x*. When FoxPro encounters this statement, FoxPro looks for *x* in its internal list of variable names. If FoxPro doesn't find the variable, it creates the variable and stores the desired value to it. The variable *x*, therefore, is created in procedure MAINPROC.

When FoxPro encounters the statement `x=1` in function FACTORIAL, FoxPro again looks in its list. This time, the name *x* already is there, so FoxPro doesn't have to create the variable. FoxPro simply changes the value of *x* from whatever it was to the new value—in this case, the constant value 0. FACTORIAL increments *x* by *x* times *j* until *j* becomes equal to 1. When FACTORIAL returns control to MAINPROC, *x* is equal to 120.

When you called FACTORIAL, you didn't know that it referenced a variable named x. What can you do to prevent these unintentional changes in variables? Well, you could keep your own list of variable names currently in use and make sure that you never use the same one twice, or you can tell FoxPro that *x* is really two different variables that have the same name.

FoxPro is an example of a *block structured language*. A procedure is a block of program statements. Variables created in a particular procedure are visible only in the current procedure. Because the procedure may contain calls to other procedures, however, the procedure's variables also are visible to all of its subroutines unless you specifically hide the variable names from the subroutines. You hide variable names by using the PRIVATE command, as follows:

```
PRIVATE <memory variable list>
```

PRIVATE instructs FoxPro to create a separate instance of any variable contained in the `<memory variable list>` the first time a value is stored to the variable name in the current procedure. The PRIVATE command does not create the variable. The command simply hides the name of previously defined variables having the same name as a variable in the list so that the variables are not changed by the current procedure or by any subroutines called by the current procedure.

The example code fragment can be rewritten so that the value of *x* in MAINPROC is not affected by any changes made to a variable of the same name in MAINPROC's subroutines:

```
PROCEDURE mainproc
   x = 1
   y = factorial(5)
   ? x    <== now the value of x is still 1!
return

FUNCTION factorial
   *
   * return the factorial of mnum
   *
   parameters mnum
   PRIVATE x, j  && don't change any other x's or j's

   x = 1
   for j=mnum to 1 step -1
        x = x * j
   endfor

return x
```

When FoxPro encounters the statement x=1 in FACTORIAL, it creates a new variable named *x* and uses this variable to store the values assigned to *x* in the body of FACTORIAL. When FACTORIAL terminates, its private copies of both *x* and *j* automatically are released from memory, and references to *x* in MAINPROC once again refer to the copy of *x* created in MAINPROC.

This approach works fine, but it also creates a few problems of its own. Sometimes you want each procedure in an application to refer to the same copy of a variable name. You may, for example, have the user enter his or her name and then display that name at the top of each of your screens. You want to be able to access the variable in which the user's name is stored. How do you make sure that this variable is available throughout the application?

There are two ways you can do this. By applying the rules of block structure, you can ensure that the variable name is visible to all routines in the application by creating the variable in the top-most procedure, the one first called by FoxPro when the application is run. This approach has some advantages—variables used throughout the application are declared up front—but this approach also has some disadvantages. If, for example, the application has many such variables, the main program can become cluttered with variable declarations.

The other way to ensure that variables are available throughout the application is to use the PUBLIC command, as follows:

```
PUBLIC [ARRAY] <memory variable list/ array list>
```

As opposed to PRIVATE, PUBLIC actually creates the memory variables and arrays. Public (or global) variables and arrays are intialized to False (.F.). A variable that has been declared public is visible to all procedures in the application, regardless of the nesting level of the procedure in which it was created.

Declaring a variable as public doesn't prevent you from declaring a private variable by the same name. The public variable will be hidden from view in the procedure that creates the private variable. When the procedure terminates, the private variable is released, and the public variable once again is visible.

The reverse, however, is not true. If you try to declare a public variable or array with the same name as an existing private variable or array, an error occurs.

Public variables and arrays are not released by the RELEASE ALL command, and they are not released when you return to the Command window. Public variables can be removed from memory only by including their names in the memory variable list used with RELEASE <memory variable list> or by using the CLEAR ALL or CLEAR MEMORY commands.

Using Regional Variables

A *regional variable* is a special type of private variable. Regional variables conform to the same scope rules that private variables do, but, in conjunction with the #REGION compiler directive, regional variables can coexist with other regional variables that have the same name in the same program.

Regional variables are useful mainly when creating screen sets through the Screen Builder. Each of the screens in the set can use variables that have the same name as variables in one or more of the other screens.

When the screen program generator, GENSCRN, creates the single screen (SPR) program from the screen information tables (SCX), GENSCRN automatically resolves any conflicts between regional variables declared in other parts of the screen program. GENSCRN does this by padding the name of the second variable with underscores followed by the number of the region in which the variable was declared. So, for example, if variable *myvar* was declared as a regional variable in both region 0 and region 1, the instance of *myvar* in region 1 would be created as the private variable *myvar____1*.

Regional variables are not very useful in areas of the program over which you have direct control and need not be discussed further in the context of writing programs.

Using Subroutines To Describe the Steps of Your Program

In the section of Chapter 16 that covered pseudocode, it was suggested that you use pseudocode statements that cannot be translated into a single statement as a comment for the series of statements required to perform a task. When the task requires few statements, and its function is specific to a particular program, this type of program structuring usually works fine.

At other times, a task may require many steps, or the task may be required in other parts of your application. In both these instances, you should consider moving the statements into a subroutine. By doing so, you accomplish two things:

- You keep your main program small.
- You localize the functions of your program so that if the code requires changes, you have to change it in only one place.

If you have reviewed the sample programs included on your FoxPro 2 disks, you may have noticed that some of them begin with many lines of setup statements, such as saving the existing environment and opening data files. Although these statements are necessary for the proper functioning of the program, they don't have any direct bearing on the purpose of the program.

Rather than include the details of the program setup at the top of the program, you can move those statements to one or more subroutines. You can use descriptive names for the subroutines to indicate their function and then quickly get into the meat of the program.

The following code is an example of a typical program with the setup details included:

```
* save user's environment
if set("TALK") = "ON"
   set talk off
   talk_stat = "ON"
else
   talk_stat = "OFF"
endif
safe_stat = set("SAFETY")
set safety off
<other environment-saving statements>

* set global variables
PUBLIC m.g_var1, m.g_var2, m.g_var3
m.g_var1 = 1
m.g_var2 = 2
m.g_var3 = 3

* open tables
use BUDGET in 1
use BUDCAT in 2
<other table-opening statements>
```

```
*
* body of program goes here
*

* restore user's environment
if talk_stat = "ON"
  set talk on
endif
<other environment-restoring statements>
```

Instead, you can use the following code:

```
do save_env       && save user's environment
do set_global     && set global variables
do open_data      && open tables
*
* body of program goes here
*
do restor_env     && restore user's environment
```

Note that, with this approach, procedure SAVE_ENV must declare its variables as PUBLIC so that they will not be released when SAVE_ENV terminates and so that they are available for use by RESTOR_ENV.

One way to look at this method is that you are using subroutines in the same way that you use built-in FoxPro commands. For example, you don't care how the PACK command works; you care only that PACK removes deleted records from a table. After you have written your own procedures that save and restore the user's working environment (SAVE_ENV and RESTOR_ENV, in this case), you can treat them as built-in commands.

The previous example uses statements that usually are executed only once in your application. However, many of the programs and subroutines that make up your application will perform tests for certain conditions which, if true, make the remaining statements in the program unnecessary.

You may, for example, have a program that uses FoxPro's low-level file functions to open an input file, verify that it contains some information to be processed, and then create an output file to save the results of the operations. You can write the code as follows:

```
private in_name, out_name, in_handle, out_handle

in_name  = "INPUT.TXT"
out_name = "OUTPUT.TXT"

* open the input file, and store its file handle
* in in_handle
```

```
in_handle = fopen(in_name)
if in_handle < 0
   wait window "Unable to open file " + in_name + "!" ;
      timeout 5
   RETURN
endif

* make sure that the input file is not empty
if feof(in_handle)
   wait window "File " + in_name + " is empty!" ;
      timeout 5
   = fclose(in_handle)
   RETURN
endif

* create the output file, and store its file handle
* in out_handle
out_handle = fcreate(out_name)
if out_handle < 0
   wait window "Output file " + out_name + ;
      " could not be created!"
   = fclose(in_handle)
   RETURN
endif
```

You also can write the code in this way:

```
private in_name, out_name, in_handle, out_handle

in_name  = "INPUT.TXT"
out_name = "OUTPUT.TXT"
store 0 to in_handle, out_handle

if           ! open_file(in_name, @in_handle) ;
          or   file_empty(in_name, in_handle) ;
          or ! make_file(out_name, @out_handle)
   = fclose(in_handle)
   RETURN
endif

FUNCTION open_file
   *
   * open the f_name file, and store its file handle
   * in f_handle; return the success or failure of
   * the operation
   *
   parameters f_name, f_handle
```

```
      f_handle = fopen(f_name)
      if f_handle < 0
          wait window "Unable to open file " + f_name + "!" ;
          timeout 5
      endif
   return f_handle > 0

   FUNCTION file_empty
      *
      * is the f_name file empty?
      *
      parameters f_name, f_handle

      if feof(f_handle)
          wait window "File " + f_name + " is empty!" ;
          timeout 5
      endif
   return feof(f_handle)

   FUNCTION make_file
      *
      * create the f_name file, and store its file handle
      * in f_handle;
      * return the success or failure of the operation
      *
      parameters f_name, f_handle

      f_handle = fcreate(f_name)
      if f_handle < 0
          wait window "Output file " + f_name + ;
          " could not be created!" timeout 5
      endif
   return f_handle > 0
```

Writing your code this way accomplishes the objective stated previously: the code tells you that there are three conditions under which you do not want to proceed, describes those conditions by using descriptive procedure names and then tells you at a glance what the program will do if any of these conditions is true. The code also provides you with some generic file-handling routines that you can use in any application you write.

This approach to program structure is an example of the concept of *abstraction*. The following section explores this important concept further and shows you how to use abstraction to your advantage in writing applications that are easily understood and maintained.

Using Abstraction To Create Readable Programs

It is important that your programs be both readable and maintainable. To make a program readable, you use variable names and procedure names that help describe the purpose of the variable or subroutine, and you use comments when your purpose cannot be so succinctly expressed.

For a program to be maintainable, it must be able to adapt to changes in its working environment. As used here, the term *working environment* includes input devices (such as the keyboard), output devices (such as the display screen), and the data the application manipulates.

The following section discusses using variables to hold constant values and introduces you to some built-in FoxPro functions that give you control over the ever-changing FoxPro environment.

Avoiding Hard Coded Values in Your Programs

Do you know what number is returned by the LASTKEY() function when you press the Backspace key? Probably not. Why would you want to? You can create your own table, mapping to a variable name each of the keystrokes commonly used in your applications. The following procedure creates these global variables:

```
PROCEDURE set_keys
  *
  * map inkey()/lastkey() values to descriptive variable names
  *
  PUBLIC ik_enter,  ik_esc, ik_up, ik_down, ik_left, ;
         ik_bksp, ik_pgup, ik_pgdn, ik_home, ik_end, ;
         ik_del, ik_clear, ik_ctlend, ik_tab

  ik_enter  =  13
  ik_esc    =  27
  ik_up     =   5
  ik_down   =  24
  ik_left   =  19
  ik_bksp   = 127
```

```
    ik_pgup   =  18
    ik_pgdn   =   3
    ik_home   =   1
    ik_end    =   6
    ik_del    =   7
    ik_clear  =  25
    ik_ctlend =  23
    ik_tab    =   9
return
```

Storing constant values to variables serves three purposes:

- It reduces the constant to an abstraction (you want to know whether the user pressed Backspace; you don't care what number FoxPro's INKEY() function returns).
- It makes your application more portable to other environments, such as UNIX, which may or may not use the same values.
- It makes your program more readable (the reader doesn't need to know that LASTKEY()=27 means the user pressed Esc).

This last point will undoubtedly draw some fire from the programmers in the audience. You can, of course, put a comment in the code, as follows:

```
if lastkey()=27          && the user pressed the Esc key
```

But why clutter up the program with unnecessary comments?

Referencing Screen Positions in a Relative Way

Back in the "old days" of dBASE III Plus and FoxBASE+, things were simpler. When you wanted to display a message at the bottom of the screen, you could use the following command:

```
@ 24,0 say "Press Esc to return to the Main menu"
```

If you wanted to center the message on the line, you could change this command to:

```
msg = "Press Esc to return to the Main menu"
@ 24,40-len(msg)/2 say msg
```

With FoxPro, however, the concept of a screen has been changed from that of a single output device of known proportions to a series of one or more windows that can be moved and sized under interactive and program control and that may have as many as 50 rows and 132 columns.

Luckily, FoxPro has many built-in functions that tell you the current dimensions of the screen and any other defined windows and enable you to address these windows in a relative way. Although it is always a good idea to avoid *hard-coding* values in your programs, it is absolutely imperative that you avoid making assumptions about window positions and dimensions.

Using SET DISPLAY, SROWS(), and SCOLS()

Many common video cards and monitors can display more than 25 rows and 80 columns, and many applications enable users to avail themselves of these larger screen displays. You can ensure that your applications always run in standard (25 rows by 80 columns) mode, but because you have the tools required to handle different screen sizes, why not let the user choose his or her own screen dimensions? Besides, the capability of handling different screen sizes always makes a good impression and adds another measure of professionalism to your applications.

To switch from one display mode to another, use the SET DISPLAY command, as follows:

```
SET DISPLAY TO CGA ¦ COLOR ¦ EGA25 ¦ EGA 43 ¦ MONO ¦ VGA 25 ¦ VGA 50
```

If the selected mode is not supported by your hardware, FoxPro displays the error message `Display mode not available`. If you are setting the display mode from within your application, you can avoid this embarrassment by using the SYS(2006) function to determine the type of video card and monitor installed in the machine. SYS(2006) returns the card/monitor combination as a character string, such as `EGA/Color`. The following code fragment uses SYS (2006) to determine which command to use to set the display to the maximum number of rows possible:

```
*
* set the display to use the maximum number of rows possible
* on the user's computer
*
do case
   case "VGA" $ upper(sys(2006))
          set display to VGA50
   case "EGA" $ upper(sys(2006))
          set display to EGA43
endcase
```

Note that, if the user's video card supports neither VGA nor EGA mode, the screen display remains in normal 25-row mode.

Now that you have set the display mode, you need a way to position windows and objects so that they fill the screen the way you want. FoxPro's SROWS() and SCOLS() functions provide you with this information.

SROWS() returns the number of available screen rows, and SCOLS() returns the number of available screen columns. You can use these functions to define a window that will appear in the center of the screen, as follows:

```
PROCEDURE center_win
  *
  * define and activate a window of wheight rows and
  * wlength columns, using SROWS() and SCOLS() to
  * provide the number of available screen rows and columns
  *
  parameters wheight, wlength
  private trow, brow, lcol, rcol

  trow = (srows() - wheight) / 2
  brow = trow + wheight - 1
  lcol = (scols()-wlength) / 2
  rcol = lcol + wlength - 1

  define window center_win ;
     from trow,lcol to brow,rcol ;
     none shadow color scheme 4

  activate window center_win
return
```

You now have a routine to create and activate a window of specifiable proportions in the center of the screen, regardless of its current dimensions. You could use this routine to display a message to the user, as follows:

```
if !seek(this_rec)
  win_msg = "That record is not in the table!"
  do center_win with 1, len(win_msg) + 4
  wait win_msg timeout 5
  release window center_win
endif
```

Notice that if you change the message, the width of the center_win window also changes.

Using WROWS() and WCOLS()

In the CENTER_WIN procedure, you created the message window on each call to the procedure, enabling you to create a window a little wider than the particular message to be displayed.

Creating and releasing windows takes some extra time, though. The delay may not be much, but the window may not “snap” onto the screen the way you would like it to. Perhaps you don’t really need to size the window differently for each message. You could create a window that is wide enough to hold most of your messages at the top of the application and just activate the window as needed.

In this case, you need to know how wide the window is to be able to center your message in it. You could store the width to a global variable, or you could use FoxPro’s WCOLS() function.

WCOLS('my_win') returns the number of available columns in the window whose name is my_win, not the number of screen columns the window occupies. The difference between the two is the number of columns occupied by the window’s border, which is either two or zero. So, if you define a window as follows,

```
define window my_win ;
   from 10,10 to 20,70&& by default windows have a border
```

WCOLS('my_win') returns 59 (11 through 69, inclusive). If, however, you define the window without a border,

```
define window my_win ;
   from 10,10 to 20,70 ;
   none        && create this window without a border
```

the number of available columns is 61 (10 through 70, inclusive).

This difference also applies to the WROWS() function, which returns the number of available rows in a window. Both these functions can be used with or without a window name. If the window name is not specified, the currently active window is assumed. If the currently active window is the screen, then WROWS() and WCOLS() return the same values as SROWS() and SCOLS(), respectively.

If you need to know whether or not a window has a border, use the WBORDER() function. WBORDER() returns true if a window has a border and false if it does not.

Using LEN() and FSIZE() To Determine the Length of a Field

Sometimes you need to know the length of a particular field in a table. You may want to pop up a window, get a value into a memory variable, and eventually replace the field with the value of the variable. You want the GET to be properly sized to hold the required data.

FoxPro has two functions that return the length of a field, LEN() and FSIZE(). FSIZE() can be used with only database fields; LEN() can take either a database field or a memory variable as an argument. LEN(), however, can be used with only character expressions; FSIZE() also returns the size of a numeric field. (You don't need to determine the size of date, logical, and memo fields—they are always 8, 1, and 10 in length, respectively.)

Although these functions can be used interchangeably with character type fields, the proper usage of LEN() differs from that of FSIZE(). The following example demonstrates the difference by GETting a value to a memory variable, using each of these two functions. The example uses LEN() to determine the size of the character field (PRODCODE) and uses FSIZE() to determine the size of a numeric field (QUANTITY):

```
*
* GET the product code and quantity manufactured
* for a new entry into the MANUFACT table
*
m.prodcode = space(LEN(manufact.prodcode))
m.quantity = 0

do while empty(m.prodcode)
   activate window get_win    && previously defined
   @ 0,1 say "Product code:   " get m.prodcode picture "@!"
   @ 1,1 say "Production qty: " get m.quantity ;
       picture replicate("9",FSIZE("quantity","manufact"))
       * the picture clause serves to determine the
       * proper display size of the GET for m.quantity
   read
   if mod(readkey(),256) = rk_esc
       EXIT
   endif
enddo
```

If you had chosen to SELECT the MANUFACT table before issuing the GETs so that the reference to the table's alias name was not required, the only difference between the two functions would have been that FSIZE() requires that the field name be enclosed in quotation marks. When referencing alias names, however, FSIZE takes the alias name as its second argument (also in quotation marks), and LEN() takes the alias as part of a full field name (the_table.the_field, or the_table->the_field).

Selecting the Next Available Work Area with SELECT() and SELECT 0

As you know, a table must be opened in a work area before it can be used by the commands in your program. In previous examples, you opened all of your application's tables at once near the beginning of the program and assigned them to work areas sequentially, starting with work area 1.

At some point in your program, you probably will need to open one or more additional tables in an unused work area. You might, for example, want to create a temporary copy of selected records from a table and then manipulate the records in this temporary table. When you open the table, you must be sure that you are not using a work area that already has a table open in it, so you can avoid unintentionally closing that table.

In dBASE III Plus, FoxBASE+, and FoxPro 1, the SELECT command was used with an argument of 0 to tell the DBMS that you wanted to select the lowest available work area. You also can use this feature in FoxPro 2 to accomplish this task. For example:

```
temp_dbf = sys(3) + ".$$$"        && get a unique file name
select BUDGET
copy to (temp_dbf) next 3         && create the temporary table
SELECT 0                          && select the lowest unused
                                  && work area
use (temp_dbf) alias TEMP_DBF     && open the temp table without
                                  && closing any other table
```

In FoxPro 2, you can use the SELECT() function with an argument of 1 to return the number of the highest available work area. You can use the SELECT() function as part of the USE command, enabling you to open a table in an unused work area with a single command. This approach, however, does not activate the new work area automatically. You must still select the work area, using its alias name, as follows:

```
temp_dbf = sys(3) + ".$$$"
select BUDGET
copy to (temp_dbf) next 3
use (temp_dbf) alias TEMP_DBF in SELECT(1)
select TEMP_DBF
```

You also can use SELECT() without an argument, or with an argument of 0 (SELECT(0)), to return the number of the currently selected work area.

Combined with the use of work area alias names, SELECT(0) and SELECT(1) enable you to place the responsibility for the management of work areas where it belongs, on the shoulders of the DBMS. Which work area a table is open in should not concern you.

Using Macro Substitution, Indirect Referencing, and EVALUATE()

Many of FoxPro's commands require that you supply them with a name or other character string literal. Sometimes, however, the programmer doesn't know what the literal value is, such as when you use the SYS(3) function to get a unique file name. You need a way to tell FoxPro to use the contents of a memory variable or array element as the string literal. Macro substitution, indirect referencing, and the EVALUATE() function provide the means to do this.

Of the three methods, macro substitution is both the most flexible and the slowest to execute. The ampersand character (&) represents the macro substitution function. When a character type memory variable or array element is preceded by &, FoxPro treats the contents of the variable or array element as a character string literal and substitutes that value in place of the variable.

dBASE III Plus does not support arrays. Advanced programmers used macro substitution to simulate one-dimensional arrays. The following code fragment, for example, enabled a programmer to GET input from the user in a row-and-column format, storing the data in memory variables whose names were constructed "on the fly":

```
x = 1                       && your "pseudo array" element counter
firstrow =  5               && start GETting values on row 5
lastrow   = 20              && don't go below row 20
mrow = firstrow             && start at the top
```

```
do while mrow <= lastrow
   * create the memory variable names
   * (e.g. arr_one1, arr_one2)
   curr_get1 = "arr_one" + ltrim(str(x))
   curr_get2 = "arr_two" + ltrim(str(x))

   * now create and initialize the actual variables
   &curr_get1 = space(5)      && e.g. ARR_ONE1 = space(5)
   &curr_get2 = 0             && e.g. ARR_TWO1 = 0

   * issue the GETs
   @ mrow,10 say str(x,2)
   @ mrow,15 get &curr_get1 picture "!!!!!"
   @ mrow,25 get &curr_get2 picture "99999"

   * increment the "element number"
   x = x + 1

   * move to the next screen row
   mrow = mrow + 1
enddo
READ
```

As incredible as it may seem, this method actually works. Using this technique, you could not only simulate arrays, you also could simulate a Browse of a small table. The “table” was limited by the amount of memory that you could allocate to create all of these variables.

Unlike dBASE III Plus, FoxBASE+ supports both one- and two-dimensional arrays. As long as you had a good idea of the maximum size of the array and had enough memory available to create an array of that size, pseudo-arrays such as those used in dBASE III Plus were no longer necessary.

In spite of this capability, macro substitution is still of great value in FoxBASE+. Macro substitution most often is used to refer to files whose actual names could vary, depending on the circumstances. If, for example, you need to create a temporary table, you could use macro substitution to supply both the COPY command and the USE command with the actual name of the file, as follows:

```
temp_table = sys(3) + ".$$$"  && get a unique file name
copy to &temp_table
select 0
use &temp_table alias temp_table
```

Although you can still use macro substitution to supply file names to commands in FoxPro, FoxPro 1 introduced a more elegant and efficient method. You can use indirect referencing in any command or function that takes a name, such as a file name or a window name, as an argument. To use indirect referencing, simply enclose in parentheses the name of the variable that holds the string literal. Using this approach, you could open your temporary table, as follows:

```
temp_table = sys(3) + ".$$$"      && get a unique file name
copy to (temp_table)
select 0
use (temp_table) alias temp_table
```

Indirect referencing is more limited than macro substitution. You cannot use indirect referencing to evaluate an expression and substitute the value of the expression in a program statement. Because FoxPro knows it doesn't have to call its expression evaluator, however, indirect referencing executes faster and should be used in place of macro substitution wherever possible.

The EVALUATE() function evaluates a character expression and returns its result. EVALUATE(), like indirect referencing, is much more efficient than macro substitution and should be used in its place whenever possible.

EVALUATE() cannot replace the & function in all cases, however. You cannot, for example, restore the previous setting of TALK with either the following code:

```
SET TALK ON
talk_stat = SET('TALK')
SET TALK EVALUATE(talk_stat)
```

or with this code:

```
SET TALK ON
talk_stat = SET('TALK')
SET TALK EVALUATE('talk_stat')
```

In the first case, FoxPro tries to evaluate the name (ON), which is stored in talk_stat. Because no such variable exists, an error occurs. In the second case, FoxPro evaluates talk_stat itself, the value of which is ON. But you cannot say:

```
SET TALK "ON"
```

This results in a syntax error. You still have to use macro substitution to accomplish this in a single command, as follows:

```
SET TALK &talk_stat
```

Both EVALUATE() and macro substitution can be tricky to use properly. If your statements are not producing the anticipated results, execute them in the Command window (after setting TALK to ON), and observe the results of each level of assignment.

Some Advanced Techniques To Consider

FoxPro 2's *Commands & Functions* reference manual, although very complete in terms of specifying the syntax of the commands, doesn't give you very many real-world examples of how you can use these commands to create useful programs. In this section, you learn a few routines that show some of the ways you can use the power of the FoxPro programming language. All the routines come from working programs.

Most of the examples use several FoxPro commands and functions that may be unfamiliar to you. The comments in the code should be sufficient for you to understand the purpose of these commands, even if you do not yet understand how they work. If you haven't already, you should begin familiarizing yourself with the *Commands & Functions* manual—you will need it when you reach Part V, "Getting To Know FoxPro 2's Commands and Functions."

The authors do not intend for you to slap these routines into your programs. They are food for thought. Critique their approach to the problems they are designed to solve. Is the approach solid? Can you think of a better, clearer way to accomplish the task? Does the programming style enhance or detract from your understanding of the code?

Using INKEY() and ON KEY LABEL To Trap Keystrokes

INKEY() is one of several FoxPro functions that pauses for user input. Unlike most of the other functions, INKEY() waits for a single key press and then returns a number indicating which key was pressed. You learned some of INKEY()'s return values earlier in the chapter, when you mapped them to memory variables.

ON KEY LABEL is different from INKEY(). Actually, the only thing they have in common is that they react to a key press. ON KEY LABEL is one of FoxPro's event-handling commands. It intercepts certain keystrokes and executes a specified command. The command can be a call to a UDF, or it may be something as simple as a STORE command.

In this section, two routines are presented, one that uses INKEY() to accept a user's password and one that uses ON KEY LABEL to remap the Enter key and mark records in a table from a Browse.

Using INKEY() To Simulate a GET with GETPASS()

Access to an application that deals with sensitive information, such as a payroll program, is often restricted. Access to the data can be restricted by putting the computer containing the data files in a room accessible to only certain people.

Sometimes this is not a feasible approach. A single computer may have to serve the needs of everyone in a small business. Even within the application, some people may have the authority to view the information, but not to change it.

Passwords have long been used to restrict access to those who have the proper authority. Valid passwords can be stored in a table, along with a related user identification code, and compared to a user's password entry each time the application is run. FoxPro is certainly capable of accepting this information through a simple GET and READ, so why would anyone want to use INKEY() instead?

Because it often is impossible to restrict the view of the screen to the person who is using the computer, the actual characters that make up the password are never displayed. In applications written in the X-Base language, the display color is often set to the same color for both the foreground and background (such as blue on blue), preventing anyone from seeing the user's password entry. The only problem with this is that the user cannot see the password and cannot know whether or not each character of the password has been recognized and accepted by the computer.

The solution to this problem is to display a visual indicator, such as an asterisk, as a place holder for each keystroke that has been accepted by the password routine. GETPASS() uses this approach and uses a hashing algorithm that encrypts the user's entry before storing it, as follows:

```
Structure for database : USERS.DBF
     Field    Field Name       Type            Width
         1    ID               Character           3
         2    PASSWORD         Character           5
         3    FULLNAME         Character          30
** Total **                                       39

FUNCTION getpass
```

```
*
* get and verify the password for the user on whose
* record in USERS.DBF you are currently positioned;
* if the user enters a valid password, return True
* otherwise, return False
*
private hours_stat, chour, mornafteve, wheight, ;
        wlength, trow, brow, lcol, rcol, mpass

* save the current SETting of HOURS
hours_stat = set("hours")

* what part of the day is it?
set hours to 24
chour = val(substr(time(),1,2))
mornafteve = iif(chour < 12, ;
                 " morning, ", ;
                 iif(chour < 18, ;
                      " afternoon, ", ;
                      " evening, "))
set hours to (hours_stat)

wheight = 4
wlength = 40
trow = (srows() - wheight) / 2
brow = trow + wheight -1
lcol = (scols()-) / 2
rcol = lcol + wlength - 1

define window pass_win ;
   from trow,lcol to brow,rcol ;
   none shadow color scheme 10

do while .t.
    activate window pass_win noshow
    clear
    @ 1,1 say "Good" + mornafteve + fullname
    @ 2,1 say "Please enter your password: "
    show window pass_win

    * get the user's password and store it in mpass
    * if the user presses Esc, getkeys() will return
    * the null string
    mpass = getkeys(len(PASSWORD))

    if empty(mpass)
      * the user pressed Escape
      EXIT
```

```
      endif

      * user entered a password
      * hash the entered password
      mpass = hashit(mpass, len(PASSWORD))

      * now compare the hashed password to the entry
      * stored in the PASSWORD field of the current record
      if mpass == PASSWORD
         * you've got a valid password
         EXIT
      else
          ?? chr(7)                     && ring the bell
          wait window "Incorrect password entered, " + ;
               "please start over." nowait
      endif
  enddo

  release window pass_win
return ("" = mpass)


FUNCTION getkeys
  *
  * get user's password, using the inkey() function
  *
  parameters max_len
  private j, mpass

  j = 0
  mpass = ""

  do while len(mpass) <= max_len
     j = inkey(0)                        && get a keystroke
     do case
        case        (isalpha(chr(j)) or isdigit(chr(j)));
               and len(mpass) < max_len
            * user typed a valid password character ;
            * acknowledge acceptance by displaying an asterisk
            mpass = mpass + lower(chr(j))
            @ $,$ say "*"

        case j = ik_esc or j = ik_enter
            * either you're done or the user wants to cancel
            * the password entry
            EXIT
```

```
          case j = ik_bksp
              * user wants to edit the entry ;
              * simulate the backspace key
                  do case
                      case len(mpass) = 1
                          mpass = ""
                          @ $,$-1 say " "
                          @ $,$-1 say ""

                      case len(mpass) > 1
                          mpass = substr(mpass,1,len(mpass)-1)
                          @ $,$-1 say " "
                          @ $,$-1 say ""
                  endcase
          otherwise
             ?? chr(7)          && ring the bell
             wait window "A valid password may contain " + ;
                 "only letters and digits." nowait

              endcase
   enddo

   if j = ik_esc
      * zap the password entry
      mpass = ""
   endif

return mpass


FUNCTION hashit
   *
   * calculate hash code for password entered by user
   *
   parameters hashstr, str_len
   private j, hashcode

   hashcode = 0

   for j = 1 to len(hashstr)
             hashcode = hashcode + asc(substr(hashstr,j,1)) * j
   endfor

   hashstr = str(hashcode * 11, str_len, 0)
return hashstr
```

If you took the time to look up the $ command in the *Command & Functions* manual, you may be a little confused by how it is used in this example. The $ command has a dual nature. $ can be used to mean "is a substring of" (as in `if 'A' $ vowels`), or, as in the preceding routine, as a shorthand notation for the ROW() or COL() functions. FoxPro determines the proper usage for the command, based on the context in which you use it.

Notice that the HASHIT() function creates a string that could be the result of more than one possible password entry. Therefore, there is no way to reconstruct the user's actual password from the hashed password. If an unauthorized person uses either FoxPro or a DOS text viewer to view the contents of the USERS table, the password that appears in the table bears no relationship to the actual password, rendering it virtually indecipherable.

The other side of this coin, however, is that, if the user should forget the password, a new password must be assigned by someone who has supervisor or administrator status. Note that a complete user-authorization system must contain procedures that are not contained in the example program.

Using ON KEY LABEL To Remap the Keyboard

One of the most important enhancements to the X-Base language that FoxPro 1 provided was its BROWSE command. Browse, which rarely was used in a program, became an important tool in every FoxPro programmer's toolkit, attaining near-equal status with the READ command.

The ON KEY LABEL command immediately became an indispensable supporting player to both BROWSE and READ. ON KEY LABEL enabled the user to perform ancillary tasks without exiting the Browse. Of equal importance, the Browse window reflected any changes made to the table when program control returned to it.

With the release of FoxPro 2, ON KEY LABEL has lost a bit of its former luster. The programmer can now customize the FoxPro system menu to include options that call the same subroutines an ON KEY LABEL can call, also without exiting the Browse. You can even assign the same control key shortcut to the menu option.

ON KEY LABEL still serves some very useful purposes, however. For example, it gives you control over the function of the Enter key. When you want the user of your application to select one or more items from a list, using the Enter key as a marking device seems very natural.

Suppose that your application revolves around a personnel table, containing such items as each person's first name, last name, and Social Security number. The user selects the wanted record and then enters all the available information about that person before going on to the next record. Obviously, the first thing the user needs to do is to select a person from the personnel table.

Using BROWSE to display the personnel table seems like a natural choice. You can instruct the user to move the highlight bar to the desired person's name and then press Enter to confirm the selection.

To use the ON KEY LABEL method of selection, you first need to remap the Enter key to do the same thing as the Esc key, as follows:

```
select people
set order to tag lastname

wait window "Highlight the desired name, " + ;
  "then press Enter" nowait

on key label enter keyboard chr(ik_esc)
browse ;
  fields firstname :h="First Name", ;
         lastname  :h="Last Name", ;
         ssno      :h="Soc. Sec. #" ;
  nomodify noappend nodelete
on key label enter
```

When the user presses Enter, the command `KEYBOARD CHR(IK_ESC)` is executed. (Remember that ik_esc is a memory variable you created earlier in this chapter to hold the number returned by pressing the Esc key.)

The KEYBOARD command stuffs the specified character into the keyboard buffer, just as though the user had entered the character from the keyboard. When the user presses Enter, the Browse window responds to the presence of the Esc key character in the keyboard buffer, and the Browse is exited, leaving the record pointer on the user's selection.

The following example also uses ON KEY LABEL to remap the Enter key. This time, however, pressing Enter does not exit the Browse. The F7 function key is used for that purpose.

When the user presses Enter, a UDF named MARKREC is executed. MARKREC replaces the value of a logical field (SELECTED) in the current record, with the opposite of its current state—True or False. The Enter key, therefore, becomes a toggle.

The table used is a REPORTS table, which has the following structure:

```
Structure for database : REPORTS.DBF
     Field     Field Name        Type           Width
         1     CODE              Character      6
         2     DESCRIP           Character      50
         3     REPT_FORM         Memo           10
         4     REPT_MEMO         Memo           10
         5     SELECTED          Logical        1
**Total**                                       78
```

All the reports used in this application are stored in this table. Each record represents a different report. The report form table (FRX) is stored in the REPT_FORM memo field, and the report form's memo file (FRT) is stored in another memo field, REPT_MEMO.

Rather than printing reports one at a time, you let the user select as many reports as needed. Then, one by one, you copy the report's table and memo file to the disk and print the report! You can tell which reports have been selected by evaluating the current contents of the SELECTED field, as follows:

```
PROCEDURE print_rpts
  *
  * let the user select which reports to print;
  * for each selected report, copy the report table
  * and memo file to disk from the record's memo fields
  *
  private temp_form, temp_memo, conditions

  * get some temporary file names
  temp_form = sys(3) + ".$$$"
  temp_memo = sys(3) + ".$$$"

  * list the reports alphabetically by description
  select reports
  set order to tag DESCRIP

  * tell the user what to do
  wait window "Use the Enter key to select reports, " + ;
       "press F7 when done" nowait

  * remap the Enter and F7 keys
  on key label enter do markrec
  on key label F7 keyboard chr(ik_ctlend)
```

```
* display the available reports
* window rpt_list has already been defined
browse window rpt_list ;
    fields check=iif(selected, "√", " "), ;
           descrip :h= "Report Description" ;
    freeze descrip ;
    nomodify noappend nodelete

* restore default key actions
on key label enter
on key label F7 *

* print the selected reports
select reports
scan for selected
    * copy the report files to disk
    copy memo rept_form to (temp_form)
    copy memo rept_memo to (temp_memo)

    * build a string containing the user's report choices
    * e.g. "for STATE = 'CA'"
    * NOTE: function get_conds() is not presented as
    *       part of this example
    conditions = get_conds(code)

    * print the report, using macro substitution
    * to expand the conditions variable into the
    * string of desired report options
    report form (temp_form) &conditions

endscan

* erase any temporary files
if file(temp_form)
    erase (temp_form)
    erase (temp_memo)
endif
return

PROCEDURE markrec
*
* mark or unmark a record by replacing the "selected"
* logical field with the opposite of its current value
*

* disable the Enter key until we're done here
on key label enter *
```

```
   * "flip" the flag
   replace selected with !selected

   * move to the next record, or to the first
   * if we are on the last
   skip
   if eof()
      go top
   endif

   * reset the Enter key to call markrec
   on key label enter do markrec

return
```

Notice that you reset the F7 key with the line `ON KEY LABEL F7 *`. The asterisk prevents the specified key from performing any action. The F7 key, by default, is mapped to a macro that stuffs the DISPLAY MEMORY command into the keyboard buffer, followed by the Enter key to execute it. One of the first things you usually do in an application is to turn off all the function keys except the F1 (Help) key. If you just used `ON KEY LABEL F7`, the default macro would be reinstated.

Using a Data Compression Technique

Through its new Rushmore technology, FoxPro 2 can handle huge databases. This capability makes downsizing mainframe applications to PC's feasible. However, storing the tremendous amount of data that is typically generated by a mainframe application on a PC's hard disk can be a problem. One way to overcome this problem is to use a data compression technique.

A data compression algorithm encodes information in such a way that the information can be stored in fewer bytes than would otherwise be required. A related decompression algorithm then is used to translate and restore the data to its original form. This section explores one such data compression technique in depth.

Suppose that Omnipresent Widgets manufactures its own line of shoes. They make shoes in eight different sizes (5 through 12) and three different widths (narrow, medium, and wide). Whenever they receive an order from a customer, they need to know whether each style on the order is made in the sizes and widths that the customer has requested. How do you accomplish this?

To do this, you need to store the combinations of sizes and widths for each style and compare the ordered size and width combinations to the stored list.

If you were designing a paper form to hold this information for each style, you would probably set up a grid, with the sizes across the top and the widths down the left side. For each combination of a size and width, you would put a check mark in the box if the style was available and leave the box blank if it was not. That's fine for paper forms, but how would you store this information in a table?

The most readily apparent method would be to create a table to hold a separate record for each combination of style, size, and width. You could use a structure like the following:

```
Structure for database: STYLES.DBF
    Field     Field Name        Type            Width
        1     STYLE_CODE        Character       6
        2     WIDTH             Character       1
        3     SIZE              Character       2
**Total**                                       10
```

Because each record requires 10 bytes and there are a maximum of 24 possible combinations of 3 widths and 8 sizes, each style's available size and width information could require as many as 240 bytes to store.

What if you store the data in the same way that it appears on the form? The sizes could be logical fields ("available" or "not available") in the table, and the width would still be a character field. You would need one record for each of the three widths for each style. Now your table looks like the following:

```
Structure for database: STYLES.DBF
    Field     Field Name        Type            Width
        1     STYLE_CODE        Character       6
        2     WIDTH             Character       1
        3     S5                Logical         1
        4     S6                Logical         1
        5     S7                Logical         1
        6     S8                Logical         1
        7     S9                Logical         1
        8     S10               Logical         1
        9     S11               Logical         1
       10     S12               Logical         1
**Total**                                       16
```

Although each record now requires 16 bytes, each style has only 3 records (one for each width), reducing your storage requirements to 48 bytes per style. This is a big improvement, but you probably can do better.

Look at the paper form again. If you erase the vertical lines separating the different size columns, your table would seem to need only two fields, in addition to the style code. You could store the size information in an eight-character string, with each position in the string representing a different size. If the style of shoe is available in a particular size and width, you indicate this by storing an X in the proper position in a SIZES character field. Your table is as follows:

```
Structure for database: STYLES.DBF
    Field     Field Name       Type          Width
        1     STYLE_CODE       Character     6
        2     WIDTH            Character     1
        3     SIZES            Character     8
**Total**                      16
```

This seems like a good approach, but it still requires the same 16 bytes of storage space as your previous version of the table.

The only remaining way to significantly reduce the space requirement is to find a way to store more than one piece of information in a single byte. In this case, you want to store all the available widths for each size of shoe in a single character position of a SIZE_GRID field, thereby reducing the number of records for each style from three to one.

You can do this by replacing the X marker with a decimal number between 0 and 7. Each of these numbers represents the decimal number equivalent of a binary string, a string composed only of the binary digits 0 and 1 (for example, 101 equals the decimal number 5).

The key to the technique is realizing that the information to be stored is binary. That is, it can only have two possible values, True or False, On or Off, or, the way computers think, 0 or 1. Just as each position in the SIZE_GRID field represents a different size, so too each position in the binary string can represent a different width. The following chart illustrates this idea:

```
Sizes       5     6     7     8      9     10     11    12
Decimal#    0     0     3     0      5      0      7     0
            |           |            |             |
Binary     000         011          101           111
Widths     NMW         NMW          NMW           NMW
```

From this chart, you can see that this style of shoe is available in size 7 (medium and wide), size 9 (narrow and wide), and size 11 (all three widths).

The final version of your table looks like this:

```
Structure for database: STYLES.DBF
    Field     Field Name       Type           Width
        1     STYLE_CODE       Character      6
        2     SIZE_GRID        Character      8
**Total**                                     15
```

No matter how many size and width combinations are available for each style, you can now store the information in only 15 bytes, a 94 percent improvement over the original 240 bytes.

There is one problem with this scheme, however. This method works fine as long as there are only three possible widths. If Omnipresent Widgets develops an extra-wide shoe, this approach will not work, because the decimal equivalent of the binary string 1111 (one binary digit per width) is 15, which requires two bytes (or character positions) instead of one.

The following program solves this problem by storing the decimal number as its related ASCII character. If you activate FoxPro's ASCII Chart from the System menu, you see that the ASCII equivalent of 14 is a musical note (♪). If size 5 of a style is available in narrow, medium, and wide, but not extra wide, the binary string would be 1110; the decimal number would be 14; and the SIZE_GRID field for this style would contain "♪" in the first position.

The conversions from decimal numbers to binary digits and back is handled by the NUM2BIN and BIN2NUM procedures, respectively. The conversion between decimal numbers and their ASCII equivalents is performed using FoxPro's CHR() and ASC() functions.

In addition to the STYLES table, the program uses a WIDTHS table, which holds the available width codes. Its structure is as follows:

```
Structure for database: WIDTHS.DBF
    Field     Field Name       Type           Width
        1     WIDTH_CODE       Character      1
        2     DESCRIP          Character      10
** Total **                                   12
```

GETSIZES requires some sample data to run. Create the STYLES table and add a record to the table, filling in just the STYLE CODE field. GETSIZES stores the proper information in the SIZE_GRID field. Then create the WIDTHs table and add three records using "M", "N", and "W" as the WIDTH_CODE entries. Entries in the DESCRIP field are optional.

```
* GETSIZES.PRG
* This program allows the user to enter the size / width
* combinations for the current style in a grid-like
* fashion, with sizes shown across the top and widths
* down the left side.
*
private malias, depth, trow, brow, lcol, rcol, ;
        msgline, npairs, was_chgd, kp, ;
        ik_ctlend, ik_tab

* store keys to memory variables
  ik_ctlend = 23
  ik_tab    =  9

  * open the tables
  use styles in select(1)
use widths in select(1)
select styles

wait window "Creating size grid.  Just a moment..." nowait

* create a temporary table (a "cursor") to hold the size
* and width selections; use "malias" as the table's alias
malias = sys(2015)
do makegrid with malias
select (malias)

* create a window in which to display the grid
depth = min(reccount()+4, srows()-5)
trow  = (srows()-depth) / 2
brow  = trow + depth
lcol  = max(0,(scols()-len("Width")-(fcount()-1)*4-9) / 2)
rcol  = min(scols(),lcol + len("Width")+(fcount()-1)*4 + 9)

define window size_win ;
  from trow,lcol to brow,rcol ;
  title "Available Sizes for " + trim(styles.style_code) ;
  none shadow color scheme 10

* create a window in which to display the number of
* available size/width combinations for this style
define window pairs_win ;
  from trow-2,rcol-10 to trow-2,rcol ;
  none color scheme 7

* create a window in which to display a message
msgline = set("message")
define window msg_win ;
  from msgline,0 to msgline,scols()-1 ;
  none color w+/r
```

```
do while .t.
  * fill the grid for the current style
  wait window "Filling the grid..." nowait
  npairs = fillgrid(malias, styles.size_grid)
  select (malias)
  go top

  activate window msg_win
  @ 0,0 say padc("Enter:Toggle Mark
F7:Done",wcols())

  * display # of pairs in size run
  activate window pairs_win
  @ 0,1 say "Pairs: " + padl(ltrim(str(npairs)),3)

  * set a flag which will be set to True in markgrid
  * if the user made a change
  was_chgd = .f.
  on key label enter do markgrid with npairs
  on key label F7 keyboard chr(ik_ctlend)

  * get size run information
  select (malias)
  activate window size_win
  browse in window size_win ;
     nomodify noappend nodelete noclear

  on key label enter
  on key label F7 *

  * save the key used to exit the Browse
  kp = lastkey()

  * let user save settings
  if was_chgd
     wait window "Save these settings? (Y/N)" to choice
     if upper(choice) = "Y"
        do savegrid with malias
     endif
  endif

  * Did the user press F7 to exit the Browse?
  if kp = ik_ctlend
     wait window "Are we done? (Y/N)" to choice
     if upper(choice) = "Y"
        EXIT
     endif
  endif

enddo (while .t.)
```

```
* release the windows and erase the "cursor" table by
* closing it
release windows size_win, pairs_win, msg_win
select (malias)
use

* close the other tables
select styles
use
select widths
use

return


PROCEDURE makegrid
  *
  * create a temporary table to hold the user's size and
  * width selections for a particular style
  *
  parameters fname
  private j, smallest, largest, struc_arr

  * store the smallest and largest sizes in variables
  smallest =  5
  largest  = 12

  * create an array to hold the structure of the
  * temporary grid table, and fill the array with
  * the table structure information
  dimension struc_arr[largest - smallest + 2, 4]

  * we need a field to hold the width code
  struc_arr[1,1] = "WIDTH"
  struc_arr[1,2] = "C"
  struc_arr[1,3] =  2
  struc_arr[1,4] =  0

  * we need a field for each size
  k = 2
  for j = smallest to largest
      struc_arr[k,1] = "S" + ltrim(str(j))
      struc_arr[k,2] = "C"
      struc_arr[k,3] =  1
      struc_arr[k,4] =  0
      k = k + 1
  endfor
```

```
   * create the grid table in fname
   create cursor (fname) from array struc_arr

   * create a record in the grid table for
   * each available width
   select widths
   scan
      select (fname)
      append blank
      replace width with widths.width_code
   endscan

return


FUNCTION fillgrid
   *
   * fill the grid table with a check mark for each
   * currently selected size and width for the current style
   *
   * return the total number of available sizes and
   * widths for this style in fill_num
   *
   parameters gridfile, mgrid
   private n, j, k, nfields, nwidths, fill_num, ;
           b_str, grid_name, asize

   select (gridfile)
   nfields = fcount()
   nwidths = reccount("widths")
   fill_num = 0

   for j=1 to nwidths           && for each width
      go j
      scatter to asize
      for k=2 to nfields        && for each size
            n = asc(substr(mgrid,k-1,1))
            b_str = num2bin(n,nwidths)
            asize[k] = iif(substr(b_str,j,1)="1", ;
                           "√", ;
                           " ")
      fill_num = iif(asize[k] = "√", ;
                     fill_num+1, ;
                     fill_num)
      endfor
      gather from asize
   endfor

return fill_num
```

```
PROCEDURE savegrid
  *
  * save the current grid table by converting the
  * check marks and spaces back into ASCII characters,
  * then saving the resulting string in the size_grid
  * field for the current style
  *
  parameters gridfile, savefile
  private mgrid, nfields, nwidths, b_str, j, k

  select (gridfile)
  mgrid = ""
  nfields = fcount()
  nwidths = reccount("widths")

  * construct the new grid in mgrid
  for k=2 to nfields          && for each size
      b_str = ""

      * construct the binary string in b_str
      for j=1 to nwidths      && for each width
          go j
          scatter to asize
          b_str = b_str + iif(asize[k] = "√", ;
                              "1", ;
                              "0")
     endfor
     n = bin2num(b_str)
     mgrid = mgrid + chr(n)
  endfor

  select styles
  replace size_grid with mgrid

return


FUNCTION num2bin
  *
  * convert a decimal number between 0 and 255 (n) into
  * a string representation of its binary equivalent
  *
  * slen holds the number of "significant characters"
  * in the binary string
  *
  * e.g. 7 = "111"
  *
  parameters n, slen
  private s, x
```

```
   s = ""
   for x=7 to 0 step -1
      if n / 2^x >= 1
          s = s + "1"
          n = n - 2^x
      else
          s = s + "0"
      endif
   endfor
return right(s,slen)

FUNCTION bin2num
   *
   * convert the string representation of a decimal number
   * (b_str) between 0 and 255 back into its decimal equivalent
   *
   * e.g. "111" = 7
   *
   parameters b_str
   private n, x, j

   n = 0
   x = 1
   for j=len(b_str) to 1 step -1
      n = n + val(substr(b_str,j,1)) * x
      x = x * 2
   endfor
return n


FUNCTION markgrid
   *
   * toggle the state of the current field in
   * the temp grid table
   *
       parameters npairs
   private curfield

   * turn off the Enter key until we're done here
   on key label enter *

   if !(upper(field(1)) == upper(varread()))
      curfield = varread()
      replace &curfield with iif(&curfield="√", ;
                                  " ", ;
                                 "√")
```

```
        * display revised # of size/width combinations
        npairs = iif(&curfield="√", npairs+1, npairs-1)
        activate window pairs_win
        @ 0,1 say "Pairs: " + padl(ltrim(str(npairs)),3)
        activate window Available

        was_chgd = .t.
    endif

    * stuff the Tab character into the keyboard buffer
    * to move the cursor to the next field in the Browse;
    * the key won't be "read" by FoxPro until the Browse
    * is once again active
    keyboard chr(ik_tab)

    * remap the Enter key once again
    on key label enter do markgrid with npairs

return .t.
```

The GETSIZES program demonstrates that the FoxPro language provides you with a level of power and flexibility usually associated with "real" languages like C. When you consider the additional capabilities of FoxPro's low-level file functions, and the capability to link third-party utilities through the Application Programmer's Interface (API), there is very little you cannot do in FoxPro 2.

Creating Templates with FoxPro's Text-Merge Features

Template languages and program generators are nothing new. They have been around for a long time, and they're all limited in some fashion. You must do things their way, and there is always something you want to do that they don't provide for.

Fox Software has given the FoxPro programmer complete control over program code generation by using the one language that all FoxPro programmers know—the FoxPro language!

FoxPro is not only a programming language, but also its own template language. If you can write a program in FoxPro using a text editor, you also can create a program template.

The FoxPro language is powerful and easy to use. The few commands you need to learn to create a template as are follows:

- `SET TEXTMERGE ON TO <filename>`
- `SET TEXTMERGE DELIMITERS TO [<delimiter characters>]`
- `\ and \\`

That's it! You tell FoxPro the name of the file you want to hold the generated program, the characters you are using to delimit (enclose) any field names, the memory variables or expressions that FoxPro should evaluate, and which lines are to be written out to the program file.

FoxPro itself uses templates to create screen and menu programs from the tables in which it stores your choices. GENSCRN creates screen programs, and GENMENU creates menu programs. You can learn more about the kinds of logical decisions you must make in deciding how to best construct a template by reviewing these templates. The templates are located in the root FOXPRO 2 directory.

When you feel comfortable with the textmerge commands, you see how the GENMENU.PRG and GENSCRN.PRG templates are used to create "table-driven" programs, by writing lines of code from the information in each record of the MNX or SCX table. If either template does not fit your needs, just edit them until they do! (If you save your edited versions to new names, tell FoxPro to use your programs when it generates menus and screens by assigning the new filenames to the system variables _GENMENU and _GENSCRN.)

For example, suppose you want each menu object to have a message line on-screen, to give the user a fuller description of what each choice does. Menu-defining commands in FoxPro have an optional MESSAGE clause which provide such a line, but the Menu Builder does not provide a place for you to put this information.

However, you can add it to the "Comment" for each menu object, using its Options checkbox. Whatever you type in the Comment edit box is stored in a Comment memo field in the object's MNX record. In case you want to include other information in the Comment field at the same time, pick a special _delimiting character_ that will tell your version of GENMENU that the text it surrounds is a MESSAGE. (In the following code, the delimiter used is "%".)

Now look at GENMENU. For each line of code that DEFINEs a BAR or PAD, there are subprocedures called to add any optional clauses, as follows:

```
DO addkey
DO addskipfor
DO addmark
```

Wherever you see these commands, you add another one:

```
DO addmsg
```

Now add PROCEDURE addmsg to the end of the GENMENU program:

```
PROCEDURE addmsg

* does this object have a message clause?
IF AT("%",Comment) # 0

  PRIVATE msg_start, msg_len, the_msg

       * get position of the message
       msg_start = AT("%",Comment)+1
       msg_len = RAT("%", Comment) - msg_start

       * parse out the message from the memo field
       the_msg = SUBSTR(Comment, msg_start, msg_len)

       \\  ;
       * don't forget the space before the semi-colon

       \ MESSAGE "<<the_msg>>"

ENDIF

RETURN
```

Documenting Your Program as You Write

FoxPro includes a powerful program documentation utility, FoxDoc, which provides you with formatted source code listings, variable cross-reference reports, tree diagrams, and much more. FoxDoc is the subject of a section in Chapter 18.

One thing that FoxDoc will not document for you, however, is the logic of your program. That responsibility remains squarely on the shoulders of the developer.

This book has discussed the need to make your programs understandable and maintainable. You have learned some of the techniques for achieving this goal, such as using variable names and procedure names that describe what information they store or what function they are intended to perform.

Comments also can provide information that makes your program more understandable. There is, however, no generally accepted method for commenting program code. You must develop your own style. Following are some thoughts on commenting:

- Comment your programs as you write them. There will never be a time when you understand the logic of a procedure or block of statements better than you do as you are actually writing the code.
- Don't use comments to compensate for obtuse code. If 5 lines of code requires you to write 10 lines of comments to explain them, something probably is wrong with your code.
- Commenting your program is a good way to check your understanding of the problem-solving process. If you cannot write a short comment that describes the process, you probably don't understand the process well enough. Check your code for flaws in logic or design.

Chapter Summary

This chapter has discussed the different types of memory variables and arrays and provided some guidelines for using them. You have learned the merits of using abstraction to avoid hard-coding values into your programs.

The programming examples presented have introduced you to some new commands, functions, and techniques. These examples should give you some perspective on the broad range of database management problems that you can solve using the FoxPro language.

Finally, the chapter introduced FoxPro's text-merge feature used as a template generator. The simplicity of this tool belies its power. With the text-merge feature, you can create programs that conform to the requirements of almost any application.

The next chapter covers using the FoxPro Help system as an adjunct to your applications, using FoxPro's Debug and Trace features to help you debug your programs, and using FoxDoc, a powerful program documentation tool.

18

CHAPTER

Enhancing the Applications You Program

In the preceding chapters, you learned about the structure of a FoxPro program, the basics of program control and execution, and quite a few commands, functions and techniques for developing applications.

This chapter focuses on additional tools that smooth the process of designing and maintaining an application.

With FoxPro 2's integrated help system, you can provide user support and document the requirements and intended usage of different elements in applications that you create.

With Fox's error-handling system, you can sleuth your way to the cause of the inevitable bugs that occur as you write the programs—even when the programs are only short snippets! You also can help users deal with any "infelicities" that remain after the application is in use. ("Infelicities" is Fox Software's term for the unintended consequences of programming; some people refer to them an "anomalies" or "bugs." Because even the best-tested application is bound to have one or two infelicities, you should be prepared with procedures to handle them.)

Finally, with FoxDoc providing permanent records of systems, you have a superb device for maintaining—and for investigating someone else's—applications, should you need to make modifications.

Adding FoxPro 2-Style Help Systems

The *perfect* user interface would be self-explanatory. Every task the user must perform, every control and every object on-screen, would be effortlessly interpreted with no error by all who use the program. Because the perfect interface is an unreachable goal, most developers add *on-line help*, or explanatory text the user can call on, in the program.

An on-line help system can be simple and, at the same time, provide both an overview—or macro-level—and a context-sensitive micro-level of help. You can write a text file that explains the whole system. A menu option, complete with hotkey, opens this file in a scrolling window for the user to read. You can use the MESSAGE clause for GETs, available through the Screen Builder for each kind of GET- object. A one-line explanation of each item appears on-screen as the cursor moves through a data-entry screen. (If you used previous versions of FoxPro and FoxBase, you will appreciate FoxPro 2's capability of directing this message line to any desired window.)

FoxPro, however provides far more flexible and sophisticated options. You are already familiar with FoxPro 2's extensive on-line help system. This section teaches you how to produce similar help systems for applications that you create.

As the ways in which you can design custom help systems are discussed here, remember that these systems are not intended as a *substitute* for, but rather as a *supplement* to, thoughtful interface design. Never assume that everyone is going to sit down and read all the help entries (much less a printed manual!) before beginning to use a program. Try to make the help system as inviting and as accessible as possible so that users will access this feature often, thoroughly, and successfully.

Building and Organizing the HelpFile

In the View window's On/Off panel, or in the Command window, SET HELP OFF. Now open FoxPro 2's helpfile, FOXHELP.DBF, as a table, which you find in the main program directory. Type **USE ?** in the

Command window as a shorthand way of getting to the Open File dialog. BROWSE the file to look at the structure and arrangement.

TIP

With HELP ON, you can actually open FoxHelp by typing the command **USE FOXHELP AGAIN**. But no advantage to this technique exists when you want to *edit* the helpfile; the copy of the file that you open with the USE AGAIN command is *read-only*. Develop the habit of SETting HELP OFF or just SETting HELP TO a different file before you begin working on a new help system.

You can write a quick program to perform this process, which SAVEs the state of help and the name of the current help file, SETs HELP OFF, USEs the file for editing, and finally restores help to the original state by using the techniques you learned in Chapter 16. This option is a good tool to add to the personally tailored version of SYSMENU you use during program development.

As you see in figure 18.1, the FoxHelp table consists of three fields:

- *TOPIC*, a character field that describes the contents of each help entry and is used in the help index. A character field of this nature is *required* as the first field in any helpfile you create that uses Fox Pro's built-in help system. Although you can give the topic any name or length, this book refers to this name as *the TOPIC field* in the following discussion.
- *DETAILS*, a memo field that holds the actual text for each help entry. This kind of memo field also must be the second field in the helpfiles and is referred to as DETAILS, but you can give the field any name you prefer.
- *CLASS*, a character field that Fox Pro's help system uses to categorize and select appropriate help topics for any task you are performing. A CLASS field is not required, but you may create at least one, and possibly several, fields that perform the same function for help systems. You can have as many extra fields, of any nature, as you need in the helpfile. These fields must not precede the two required fields.

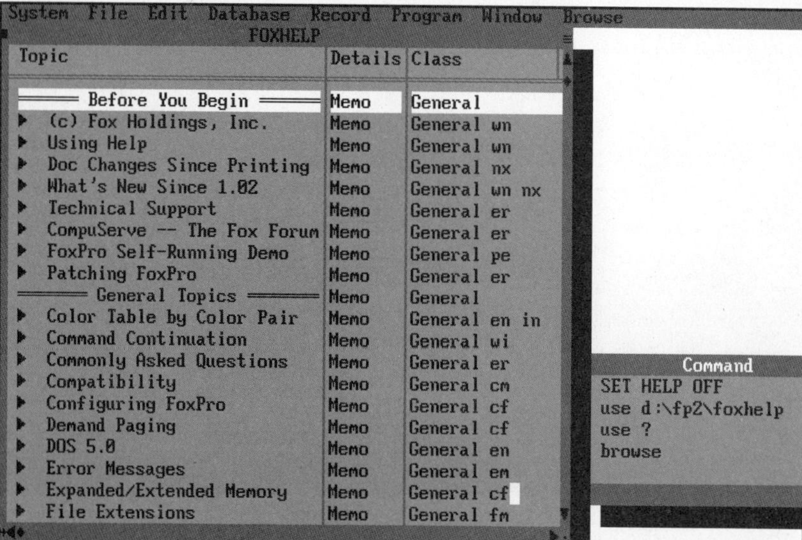

FIG. 18.1

The structure and contents of FOXHELP, FoxPro 2's internal helpfile.

A helpfile you build—with the two required fields and with all other fields you want—can be *assigned* to access Fox Pro's built-in help system simply by using the following commands:

SET HELP ON
SET HELP TO <*your filename*>

Thereafter, the *help* keypresses (Alt-F1, F1, and Alt-click), as well as the System pad Help option or any other menu option which was assigned the bar number **_MST_HELP**, will access **your** file, instead of FoxHelp, until you SET HELP TO FOXHELP once again.

The topics in FoxHelp are carefully arranged, and yours should be too, so that the Help index is useful. If you check the View window, you notice that FoxHelp doesn't have a structural index. The helpfile topics, or actually the records, are always shown in the natural order of the file, whether you are using the Help index or paging through Topics with `<Next>` and `<Previous>` buttons. FoxHelp uses the graphics characters ▶ (**ALT-16**) and ■ (**ALT-254**) to segregate some topics at the beginning and end of the listing, and the topics in between are alphabetically arranged, but the file was *sorted*, not indexed, on the Topics to maintain this order.

However, creating a helpfile with a structural index will not disturb the help system in any way. You can work on the helpfile like any other table, creating a CLASS or ORDER field that (perhaps along with the TOPIC field) determines the exact final arrangement. INDEX ON the appropriate expression as a TAG. COPY the file TO a new one while the ORDER you want is SET, and the new file will have the records in the order you want. The structural index on a helpfile can continue to be useful even after the file is complete, as you will see shortly.

What kinds of topic arrangements are useful? Put yourself in the users' position as much as possible here. When the user needs help, the user's concept may be entirely different from the way the problem looks from your perspective.

If you are writing an accounting system, suppose that you choose to put all information about printer setups under a general printing topic. This topic includes checking the character set the printer is set up to use, to make sure that the graphics characters in your attractive invoice forms print properly. A new user, however, may not realize that a problem that occurs while generating invoices is a system-wide printing question. The user wonders why the topic Invoices does not explain how to get the pretty boxes to print the way they appear in the documentation samples. As the user pages through the `<Next>` and `<Previous>` topics surrounding Invoices, and perhaps finds Billing Procedures, Invoice Numbers, and so on, the user may wander further and further away from finding the right information.

This difficulty, which even a sophisticated computer user may face when exploring a new system or beginning a new task, is the reason FoxPro 2 gives you the capability to provide alternative *paths* toward a topic using See Also references, which you previously used in FoxHelp. Just place the See Also references, as you have seen them in FoxHelp, after at least one carriage return (press Enter) at the end of the help text in the second required field (the memo field). Precede the list of references by the words **See Also:** (the colon is required), separated by commas. End the list with another carriage return. You can add spaces for readability and graphics characters to *set off* the list from the rest of the text, as FoxHelp does. FoxPro 2 places these entries in a popup control button in the Help window.

In the preceding example, you want any help topic that provides information on printed output, such as Invoices, to include a See Also reference to the Printing topic.

Develop the helpfile topics, the topic order, and suggestions for appropriate See Also references with the participation of as many different people as you can muster. Include information that is appropriate to all the kinds of users of the system and add as many cross references as you can. Because the help system is as easy to edit as other tables, correcting and even redesigning a help system should never seem an insurmountable task.

When the users pick a reference from the See Also popup control, FoxPro searches the list of topics for the *first* matching topic name. If the search finds a topic name that *begins* with the See Also reference, this topic is considered a match. You can see why identifying each record uniquely as a topic is important, which also is another reason—besides making the help index convenient for users—to be careful about the arrangement of the topics.

The list of topics can and should include records for all the fields and memory variables that are GETs in the system's data-entry boxes and dialogs. Filling out all these help entries doesn't have to be a last-minute undertaking when the system is completed. You can write help text in the Comments snippets for each GET as you design the screens. Then, you write a program to fill out the help text for all the *GET-level* entries by accessing the screen files (SCXs) as tables. Refer to the Appendixes of the *Developer's Guide* for the structures of the project and screen files, especially the TYPE field in a project and the OBJTYPE field in a screen as you read the following pseudocode for one method you can use:

```
SET HELP OFF
USE the help file
SELECT another workarea
USE the project file

SCAN FOR type = "S"
* look through all the
* screenfile records in the project

         SELECT another workarea
         USE the screen file (SCX)  ALIAS the_screen

         SCAN the records in the screen file
               IF objtype = 1
                     * it's the main (or header) record in
                     * the screen file; this record
                     * will provide screen-level help

                     STORE the window name & title to memvars,
                           make them all LOWER() case to make
                           comparisons easier later
                     SELECT the helpfile
                     APPEND BLANK
                     * add a record to the helpfile
                     REPLACE the DETAILS field WITH
                     the_screen->Comments
                     REPLACE extra fields WITH stored window
                           name and title if you plan to use them
                           to search for correct topics
                     REPLACE TOPIC field WITH
                     PROPER(screenfile name)

               ELSE
                     IF BETWEEN(objtype,11,16)
                           *these objtypes are the GET records
```

```
                        SELECT the help file
                        REPLACE DETAILS field from
                              the_screen->Message (if used)
                              + the_screen->Comments
                        REPLACE extra fields using stored
                              window name and title if you
                              use them

                        ************************************

                        REPLACE an extra field WITH
                              LOWER(the_screen->Name)
                              * this item will be
                              * what VARREAD() returns

                        ************************************


                        REPLACE Topic WITH
                        PROPER(the_screen->Name field )
                              * uniquely identify this GET in
                              * the topic list
                  ENDIF
                  * ignore other records like BOXes or SAYs

            ENDIF
            * SCAN automatically SELECTs the_screen
            * and SKIPs to the next record

      ENDSCAN

      USE
      * close the screenfile

   * SCAN reSELECTs project file
   * and SKIPs to next record
ENDSCAN

USE
* close the project file
```

In the preceding suggested pseudocode, you look at only the screens in the project; subsequently, you may want to do the same for other elements of the project (such as reports) to create more help entries. You may want to BROWSE through the helpfile, checking for empty DETAILS field entries (perhaps you neglected to include Comments for every GET), and you also may want to check and perhaps replace some TOPIC fields with *friendlier* topic titles where necessary. With the use of the PROPER( ) function to standardize capitalization, for example, the

BUDGET.SCX produces Topics similar to the following list:

Budcatcode
Query1
Saveit

You may want to make the Topics more readable by changing them to the following:

Budget Category Code
Budget Query #1
Save or Cancel Your Edit

These longer titles may be found in associated SAYs, or you may choose the MESSAGE clause to create and display these titles consistently on the screens. Another possibility is to make this line the first in the Help text entry, repeating the Topic as a heading for the Details, as FoxHelp does. Using the following replacement lines, you can easily adapt the preceding code to create more informative Topic entries, as shown in the following lines:

```
REPLACE Topic WITH the_screen->Message
```

or

```
REPLACE Topic ;
  WITH SUBSTR(the_screen->Comments,1,;
  AT(CHR(13),the_screen->Comments)-1)
* take the portion of the comments field up to
* the character just before the first carriage return
```

Look at the line in the pseudocoded procedure that is set off by lines of asterisks. You may remember that you used the function VARREAD( ) when you learned about the Screen Builder and data validation. VARREAD( ) returns the name of the current field, memory variable, or array element used in the current GET during a READ. Having an extra field in the helpfile that matches this value is the key to providing context-sensitive help on the GET- level. In the following section, you see just how you get the help system to respond with the correct entry at the right time.

Making the HelpFile Accessible

Fox's internal use of the helpfile uses some idiosyncratic methods to decide which topic to show you when you press F1. _MST_HELP, the system bar name associated with the help system. The program checks for highlighted text in the frontmost window first. If you have highlighted text, the topic list is searched for the text. If not, the topic search is carried out on the basis of an internal reference to the name or title of the frontmost window. You probably figured out that all the *interface* topics in FoxHelp are prefaced by the ■ (Alt-254) character. When FoxPro searches for the current activity among the topics by using a window reference, FoxPro prefaces the SEEK with this character followed by a space. When FoxPro subsequently checks See Also references from one interface topic, all the references are similarly prefaced with ■, with the result that the interface topics can only reference other interface topics.

If you try to extend this method, as suggested by the *Developer's Guide* section on "Customizing Help," you will find this method of limited utility. Window referencing, always a complicated subject where BROWSEs are concerned (as you may recall from working in the Screen Builder), becomes even more complicated with the help system. _MST_HELP checks a window title first and then a window name but also can pick the *image* window you DEFINEd for a BROWSE WINDOW rather than the actual BROWSE title. _MST_HELP also may be confounded by the addition of other graphics characters to the window title. Even if you forgo the use of window titles, if you are permitting GENSCRN to generate window *names*, you have another problem—which the #WNAME generator directive can't resolve. Further, adding the "■" to the beginning of the topic may not suit you, or you may not like the effect this addition has on the See Also list.

F1, in the internally defined role as _MST_HELP's shortcut key, also shows somewhat inconsistent performance during a READ. If you DO a filename.spr with no redefinition of the System menu at all, you will see that F1 no longer shows as the hotkey for the Help option on the System menu pad. Although you still can press Alt-S and then H to access help, pressing F1 terminates the READ instead!

Fortunately, FoxPro provides better methods of making the help system respond appropriately.

The simplest and most direct approach is to use the SET TOPIC command. You can SET TOPIC TO a character expression, in which case the TOPIC field (or whatever you named this field) is searched for a case-insensitive match to the expression.

To effectively use SET TOPIC, you must create a method of accessing Help. Instead of using the Bar _MST_HELP, just have the Help option on the SYSMENU issue the HELP command. If you use any other FoxPro menu systems, an ON KEY LABEL F1 HELP command can accomplish the same thing. Even if you use SYSMENU, an additional ON KEY LABEL F1 HELP command can ensure that the hotkey works consistently in a READ.

You also can SET TOPIC TO a logical expression, and the helpfile is searched for a record that causes the logical expression to RETURN .T. This expression is often complex and can reference the extra fields in the helpfile, as shown in the following examples.

Using the following command:

SET TOPIC TO <*a character expression*>

is very similar to using this command:

HELP <*the same character expression*>

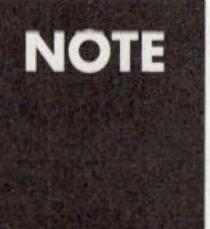

No matter which way you choose to SET TOPIC, remember that the rule you applied in the See Also Topic searches also applies here: the *first topic* that contains a match is the topic shown.

The SET TOPIC command, however, can be issued once (at the beginning of the program) and is *evaluated dynamically.* If the SET TOPIC expression (whether a logical or character type) contains functions or variables that you initialize in the program, the contents of the expression (and therefore the current Topic) changes, depending on the conditions prevailing when Help is accessed. If the Help table includes extra fields for the name of the current window and the current variable, as suggested in the preceding example, you can use a SET TOPIC expression in the following manner:

```
SET TOPIC TO wname = LOWER(WONTOP()) AND ;
  read_item = LOWER(VARREAD())
* wname and read_item are helpfile fields
```

NOTE

Notice that in both cases the *shorter* expression is placed on the *right* side of the comparison (the fields WNAME and READ_ITEM may be longer than WONTOP( ) and VARREAD( ), which contains no trailing spaces). If you refer to the SET EXACT entry in the *Commands and Functions* manual or Chapter 7 of this book, you find extensive discussion of *string comparisons*. As in other xBase dialects, if EXACT is SET OFF, which is the default, when you type the single Equals = sign to compare two character expressions, the expressions are compared only until *the one on the right side ends.*

In SET TOPIC expressions you find yet another use for the ubiquitous IIF( ) function. Suppose that you want to select a special set of help entries when users are just looking through menu options and not actually performing one of the tasks in the system. You can create these entries with Topics to match your menu pads and use the following expression:

```
SET TOPIC TO IIF(RDLEVEL() = 0,              ;
                   topic = PAD(),             ;
                   wname = LOWER(WONTOP()) AND ;
                     read_item = LOWER(VARREAD()))
```

This expression says "If you're not in a READ, find a topic that matches the current menu pad. Otherwise, use the active window and current GET to find a topic." (In Chapter 14 and in the FoxPro documentation, you learn about *Foundation READs*, which remain active while the user waits in a menu. If you use a foundation READ, however, you need to change the preceding expression to check *RDLEVEL()* > *1*.)

You also may want to create a special help topic that explains how to navigate in a BROWSE in the system. You can title all the BROWSEs consistently, perhaps by using a graphics character you use nowhere else, such as in the following expression:

```
BROWSE WINDOW <window name> ;
                  TITLE "↑↓"+PROPER(ALIAS())+ " Records
"
```

For the Budget.spr BROWSE, you see the following window title:

Budget Records

Now the SET TOPIC expression can be as follows:

```
SET TOPIC TO IIF("↑↓" $ WTITLE(),              ;
                   "Browsing Records",          ;
                   wname = LOWER(WONTOP()) AND  ;
                      read_item = LOWER(VARREAD()))
```

You can see, however, that the IIF( ) function limits you to only two kinds of TOPIC-SETting, and you may want a help system that considers more than two situations. As you may expect, you accomplish this with a CASE statement.

You can SET TOPIC directly TO a UDF( ) that RETURNs a logical or character expression based on the CASEs it evaluates. But it is far better to have the Help menu option (or ON KEY LABEL command) DO a special help procedure instead of simply calling HELP. This procedure can accept anything you need to establish your conditions as a list of passed parameters, for example, Do My_help WITH RDLEVEL( ), WONTOP( ),; WTITLE( ), VARREAD( ), PROGRAM( ). The help procedure includes the following instructions:

- Accept passed conditions in the form of a PARAMETERS statement

- Evaluate current conditions in a DO CASE structure and SET TOPIC accordingly
- If necessary, use PUSH KEY CLEAR to move any ON KEY LABEL assignments to the stack. Many people, for example, use the command ON KEY LABEL ENTER KEYBOARD CHR(23), which also can be expressed as KEYBOARD "{CTRL-W}", to select the currently highlighted record in a BROWSE for editing. This reassignment is awkward when the user tries to use the Enter key to select a Topic from the Help index!
- Issue the HELP command
- POP KEY to replace ON KEY LABEL assignments

PUSH and POP KEY are new FoxPro 2 commands. Using a specialized help procedure, you can add yet another new feature to the help system: you can use the new SET HELPFILTER TO command, which takes a logical expression. SET HELPFILTER is placed before the HELP command to restrict the topics that appear in the index. You previously saw a sophisticated use of this command in the HELPTREE.MPR program provided with FoxPro 2, and Chapter 14 briefly discussed the command's use when you explored the Menu Builder. Take time to investigate HELPTREE.MPR to get an idea of this command's potential for use with optional fields in helpfile's structure.

In the example helpfile structure, you may want to use the following command in at least one help CASEs:

```
SET HELPFILTER AUTOMATIC TO LOWER(WONTOP( )) $ wname
```

The AUTOMATIC keyword ensures that the filter is removed (that all topics are again accessible) after the Help window is closed. If you use AUTOMATIC, you avoid having to use a HELPFILTER in every CASE or SETting HELPFILTER TO <nothing> to turn off the filter after the HELP command.

Giving Users Control of the Help System

If the application uses passwords or restricts access to some features in any way, you can include a check for appropriate access in both the user-accessed printing procedure below and the SET HELPFILTER command. Many additional ways exist that you can use to help users feel in charge of the help system and (by extension) of the application as a whole.

Just as the helpfile is no substitute for proper interface design, don't rely entirely on on-line documentation. Many people prefer a manual that can be studied at leisure while away from the computer. You can easily include these user needs in your help system plans.

Using report forms, you can create a paper version of the helpfile. A UDF() in such a MANUAL.FRX, perhaps in the page header band, can transfer information about the output, including page numbers for the beginning of each topic (or groups of topics as defined by the report's control breaks) to another table while the report is created. You can choose to have this second table include one record for each page or one record for each topic or group. With such a table, imagine how easily you can create or revise a table of contents. The lists of See Also references, stored in one memo field of this support table also can form the basis of an index. A special TAG in the helpfile's structural index can reorder the topics for the manual, if necessary.

A special memo field in the helpfile can even store screen shots. If you used FoxPro's own Capture option to create them, the screen shots can be printed along with the help text in the usual way (remember to make the report expression wide enough to print them). If you use an external program to capture screens as graphics files, a memo field in the helpfile can still hold them so that they remain coordinated with the current topics. Better still, the extra helpfile memo field can store them as printing instructions, if you have the capability to print graphics files to disk.

Because manuals are always getting lost, you can remind users that they can use the File pad's Print... option to get a "hard copy" of any open window—and this of course includes the current help topic. If the application's version of SYSMENU doesn't make this option available, you can easily create a program to let them choose topics to print. In the following simple example, you can recognize a number of the techniques you have learned in this programming section:

```
old_prn = SET("PRINTER",1)
old_alias = ALIAS()
* save state of printer and work you have done

SELECT 0
USE widghelp AGAIN
* open the helpfile in an unused area
* USE... AGAIN is okay here, because you're not editing

SET ORDER TO doc_ord
* having the structural index helps us out here —
* the natural order of the table, which is used for
* proper use of the help index and SET TOPIC/See Also
* may not be the order you want for this job
```

```
* here you might want to add an option
* for printing ALL topics without seeing the
* popup and choosing them one at a time

  DEFINE POPUP widghelp FROM 5,5 TO 20,42 ;
   PROMPT FIELD topic
* set up a popup showing all topics

IF m.output # "P"
  * You have previously determined whether the user
  * wants to print to a file or to the printer

  * If to a file, the user has specified a filename
  * It is erased if it already exists and the user
  * doesn't want to append information to it;
  * the ADDITIVE keyword will allow the append
  * if the file is there

  SET PRINTER TO (m.helptext) ADDITIVE

ELSE
  SET PRINTER TO
  * restore to default (or set to a particular port
  * if you prefer)
ENDIF

ON SELECTION POPUP widghelp ;
  REPORT FORM widgdoc TO PRINT NEXT 1 OFF

m.pgcount = 0
* the report form will use a UDF, pageno(), below
* to print page numbers, because you will be printing
* topics as separate REPORT FORMs, one at a time
* You initialize the variable in the calling program
* Notes after the UDF offer an alternative approach

DO WHILE LASTKEY() # 27
  * continue until the user presses ESC
  ACTIVATE POPUP widghelp
ENDDO

  * put everything back the way you found it
RELEASE POPUP widghelp
SET PRINTER TO (old_prn)
USE
SELECT (old_alias)
RETURN
```

```
FUNCTION pageno
m.pgcount = m.pgcount + 1
RETURN ALLTRIM(STR(m.pgcount))
* this function is unnecessary if you design your report
* with persisting report variables, as described in
* Chapter 10. Initialize the report variable to
* m.pgcount+_PAGENO, and store
* m.pgcount+_PAGENO to it. This report variable
* becomes your page number in the report.
* Uncheck the option to Release After Report.
* In between report printings, change the value of
* m.pgcount to reflect the pages that have been printed,
* like this:
* ON SELECTION POPUP widghelp DO helpprint
* PROCEDURE helpprint
* REPORT FORM widgdoc TO PRINT NEXT 1 OFF
* m.pgcount = reportvar
* RETURN
```

You also can make sure that users feel in charge of the help system by providing ways in which a user can edit the file. Each user of the system, in fact, can have a personal copy of the help file, containing notes added by the user. Alternatively, you can add another memo field to the helpfile that (like Post-it notes) can contain the comments of all the users. The procedure you create to access help adds another menu option or hotkey to bring this additional field up in a MODIFY MEMO while the Help window is open. The helpfile's structural index can contain special filtered indexes (INDEX ON ... FOR...) to allow editing of help text by department or password level, as necessary.

Your application's APP file always contains the original (read only) copy of the helpfile, so no permanent damage can be done by users' editing. Remember that this edit requires that HELP be SET OFF first. If you are sharing a helpfile on a network, you must edit the file, using a procedure similar to the one suggested in Chapter 15 for editing a shared Resource file (see fig. 18.2).

A macro-level Overview topic that introduces the system users to the application can be a perfect place to provide an immediate sense that the user is in control of the system, with an *embedded menu* that takes advantage of FoxPro 2's Look Up feature. Just write some friendly paragraphs describing the system and the features. In the beginning of this introductory entry, you can explain how to use the help system and that users can find out more about many of the subjects you mention. Use the actual names of some of the other Topics directly in the text, perhaps set off with special marks as shown in figure 18.3. Along with the See Also listings, this technique provides a fairly simple system of the type sometimes called *hypertext*, which encourages your users to explore in many directions.

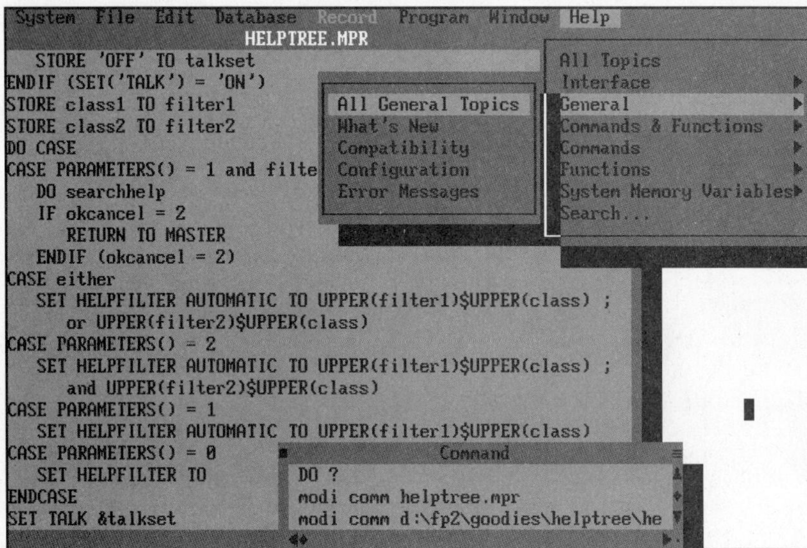

FIG. 18.2

HELPTREE.MPR demonstrates using the SET HELPFILTER command.

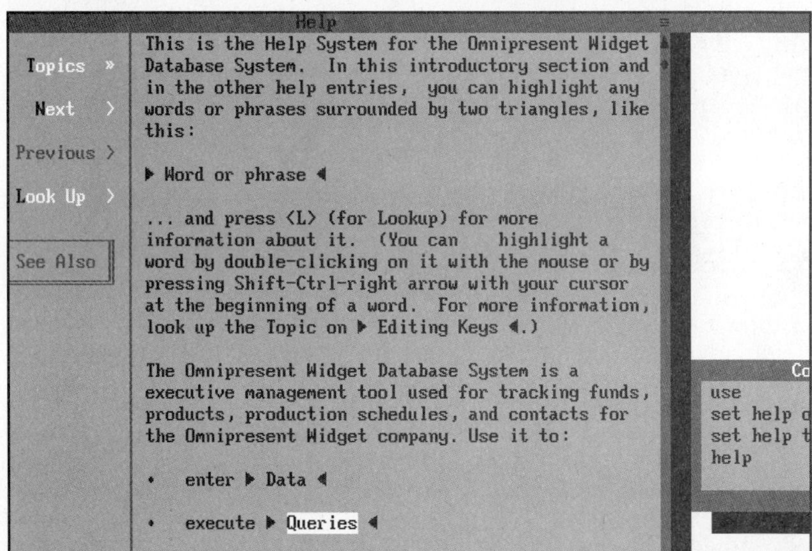

FIG. 18.3

An embedded menu-style introductory help topic.

Finding and Handling Program Errors

The perfect programmer never makes mistakes. She holds in her mind a complete conceptualization of all facets of the program to be written, is in complete control of all interrelationships within the program, and never types > when she means to type <.

Although a worthy goal, most programmers never attain this level of perfection. The programs usually contain errors in both execution logic and language usage. The process of finding and correcting these infelicities (or *bugs*) is known as *debugging*.

Debugging a program usually has at least three separate phases:

1. Correcting errors flagged by FoxPro as the program is compiled
2. Correcting obvious logic errors
3. Correcting hidden logic errors

When you compile a program, FoxPro tells how many errors were found in the program and saves the error messages in a text file that uses the same name as the program (or application) but with an ERR extension. You can view this error log by typing **MODIFY COMMAND *<program name>*.ERR** in the Command window or by opening the file, using the Open option on the File menu. Correcting these errors is usually a simple matter of locating the offending lines and retyping the incorrect parts of the statements.

After you successfully compile the program without errors, you can move on to the next step, finding and correcting obvious logic errors. As you test the application's features, you notice things that don't work as you intended, such as the positioning of windows and messages. You also may encounter run-time errors that can't be flagged at the compilation stage, such as trying to use a logical variable in a function that requires a numeric argument or referring to a field name that is not part of the current table.

The final stage of debugging usually requires some help from one or more people who weren't involved in the development of the application. Because you understand how the program is supposed to work, some errors may exist in the application that you can never catch. You may never have considered the possibility that a user may enter a negative order quantity in the New Sales Orders data-entry screen because you know that these adjustments are entered in the Credit Memos entry screen. If the program then uses that negative number in a function that accepts only positive numbers, the application may *bomb*. The inability of the developer(s) to anticipate every way in which the application will be used (or misused) is one reason for the lengthy beta test periods that all major commercial applications now undergo.

FoxPro has several tools that can help you debug programs. The most powerful tools are the Debug and Trace windows. The Debug window enables you to inspect the current value of variables and expressions contained in a program and to pause the execution of a program when one or more of these values changes. The Trace window displays program instructions and highlights each line as the line is executed. Both the Trace window and the Debug window may be used alone or in tandem with the other window.

TIP

Because FoxPro enables you to remap the keyboard with ON KEY and ON KEY LABEL, you may need a way to enter a command without using either Enter or the space bar if the program bombs after you have mapped one of these keys to do something other than the key's normal task. Many developers let the user select a record from a Browse by using either the space bar or the Enter key.

If you suddenly find yourself in this position, don't panic! You can get around the problem by typing **ON KEY** in the Command window, using Shift-space bar instead of the space bar, and Shift-Enter instead of Enter.

Using the Debug Window

You open the Debug window by selecting Debug from the Window menu. The Debug window resembles an empty split Browse window, in that this window also has a left and right partition and all the Browse window's control objects, such as a window splitter and scroll bars. Unlike a split Browse, however, only the left partition of a Debug window can be activated, as this is where you type the expressions that you want to inspect. The current value of the expression is displayed in the right partition.

Although you can activate the Debug window at any time the Window menu is selectable, the Debug window is usually activated either before running a program or from within a running program that is *suspended*, or paused in execution (see fig. 18.4). You can suspend a program by inserting the SUSPEND command into the program, by setting a *breakpoint* (discussed in the following paragraphs) in the Debug window, or by selecting `<Suspend>` from the FoxPro error-handling dialog that appears when a program error is encountered or when you press Esc—if ESCAPE is SET ON. FoxPro displays the message `Do suspended` in the system message window and returns you to the Command window.

To monitor the value of an expression, position the cursor in the left partition of the Debug window, type the expression, and press Enter. If the expression is longer than the displayed width of the partition, the text scrolls to the left as you type. Usually, the expression is a variable name but also can be a FoxPro function, such as PROGRAM(), which returns the name of the program currently executing.

If the expression is syntactically correct and if FoxPro can evaluate the expression, the value is displayed on the same row in the right partition. If the expression contains a syntax error, the computer beeps when you press Enter. If the expression is valid but currently has no value, FoxPro accepts the expression but doesn't display anything in the right partition. Please note that the Debug window cannot evaluate an expression that contains a macro substitution, such as *&field_name*.

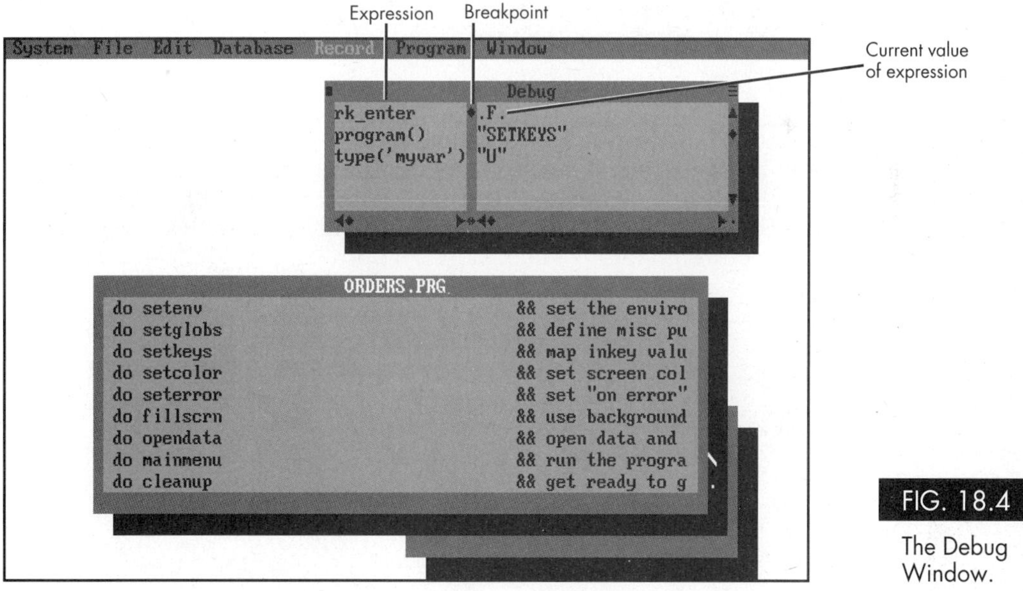

FIG. 18.4

The Debug Window.

You can resize the Debug window in the same manner as other windows. FoxPro assumes that you want to adjust the right partition and lengthens or shrinks the right side as you change the size of the window. You can adjust the relative size of the partitions by click-dragging on the window splitter control or by using the Tab key to move to the window splitter and then using the left- and right-arrow keys.

You also can use the Debug window to set program breakpoints based on the value of an expression. Setting a breakpoint instructs FoxPro to pause the program when the value of the expression on which the breakpoint is set changes.

To set a breakpoint with a mouse, click on the breakpoint column (the column that divides the left partition from the right) to the right of the desired expression. From the keyboard, press Tab or Shift-Tab until a highlighted block appears in the breakpoint column. Use the up- and down-arrow keys to position the block to the right of the desired expression and press the space bar. With either method, a diamond appears to indicate that a breakpoint is set. Because a breakpoint is a toggle (either on or off), you clear the breakpoint by repeating this process.

With a breakpoint set, program execution is suspended when the value of the expression changes. If you set a breakpoint on an expression that currently has no value (a field name in a table that has not yet been opened), the program is suspended when the expression acquires a value, and thereafter, when the expression changes to a different value.

When a program is suspended, the System menu becomes active, even if *turned off* from within the program. You can use the View window to see the currently open tables, the currently selected work area, the current master index, and so on. You also can work from the Command window by typing commands, such as **DISPLAY STATUS** to view items, such as the file search path, the default drive, open tables and indexes, and the current status of many FoxPro options. DISPLAY MEMORY lists the names and current values of all existing memory variables, including the system memory variables, such as _PDSETUP and _CUROBJ.

Using the Trace Window

The Trace window is a useful tool when you need to track down particularly elusive errors in program logic. Trace usually is used in conjunction with the Debug window. You enter the names of variables and expressions that the program manipulates in the Debug window and then use the Trace window to *step* through the program, watching the values that the variables hold at certain problem points.

If you used—and were disappointed with—the Trace feature in FoxPro 1, you are in for a pleasant surprise; in FoxPro 2, the Trace facility is greatly improved. You can now load a program into the Trace window, set the breakpoints, and then run the program directly from the Trace window. You also can see the complete program execution chain at the bottom of the Program menu popup.

The Trace window is opened by selecting Trace from the Window menu. The Trace window looks like a simple text editing window but has a menu bar that contains some special options, as shown in figure 18.5. Each menu pad has a hot key, but unlike the System menu, the hot key letter is not preceded by the Alt key. For example, to activate the Trace window's Program popup, just press the letter P. Alt-P still activates the Program pad that is part of the System menu.

The Program menu popup contains six options, as shown in figure 18.5. You can open a program file in the Trace window by selecting Open from the menu or by pressing Ctrl-E when the Trace window is active and then selecting the file from the Open File dialog. The name of the program is displayed in the bottom of the window's border. You can select Cancel to stop the execution of a suspended program.

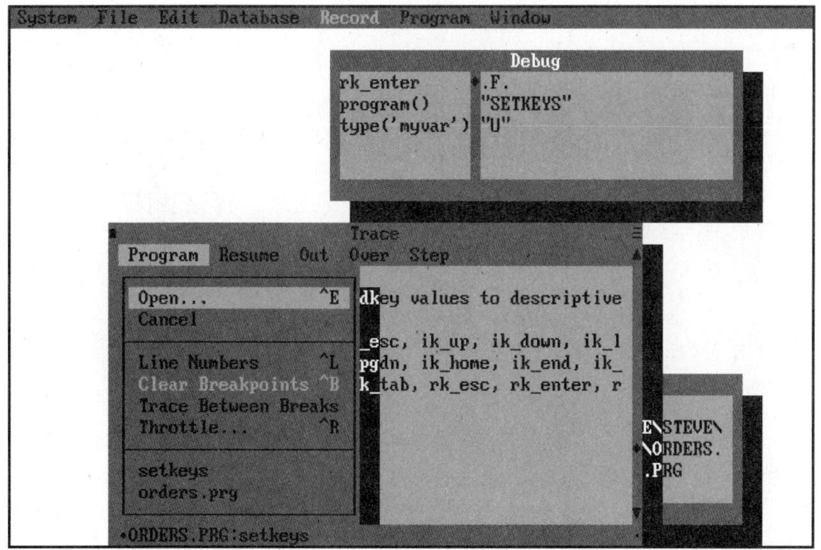

FIG. 18.5

The Program menu in the Trace window.

The Line Numbers option is a toggle that displays sequential line numbers before each line of the program in the Trace window. By default, line numbers are not displayed. You can clear, one at a time, any breakpoints you previously set, or you can select Clear Breakpoints to clear all the breakpoints at one time. Keep in mind, however, that selecting this option clears the breakpoints in all the program files. FoxPro *remembers* where you set breakpoints in a program—even breakpoints you replaced in the Trace window with another program.

One of Trace's nicest new features is the capability of executing the code between two breakpoints (or from the top of the program to the first breakpoint) without displaying each line in the Trace window. If you know that a problem lies in a particular segment of the program, you can quickly get to the segment by turning the Trace Between Breaks option *off* (the default state) and setting a breakpoint where you want to start the debugging session. Similar to the Line Numbers option, Trace Between Breaks also is a toggle and is *on* when a diamond (◆) appears immediately to the left of the menu prompt. When the option is on, each line of the program is displayed and highlighted as the program executes.

With the Throttle option, you can tell FoxPro to pause for a chosen number of seconds before moving from the current line to the next line. If you are debugging a large program, however, make sure that you set a breakpoint right after the code segment that you want to slowly step through. After you Do or Resume the program, all the menu options become disabled and, if you have SET ESCAPE OFF, you can't pause or even cancel the program.

Whenever a running program has been suspended, the Program menu popup expands to contain the chain of program execution, which is displayed beneath the Throttle option. The name of the current procedure is shown at the top of the list, followed by the names of the procedures or programs called to reach this point. This listing can be useful when debugging a module that is called by other routines in the program and that seems to exhibit problems only at certain times, depending on which routine called the module.

The Do option simply enables you to run a program. If you previously loaded a program in the Trace window, FoxPro starts executing the program. If you haven't loaded a program, you can select the program to Do from the Open File dialog that appears by default. When a running program has been suspended, Do is replaced by Resume. Selecting Resume causes the program to resume execution from the line following the line where the program was last paused.

When you *move off* the currently executing line (which is always highlighted when the cursor rests on the line), the position is marked with a right arrowhead (▶). To return to this point, possibly after reviewing other parts of the program and setting breakpoints, press the Home key. You cannot change the point at which a program resumes execution. To reach a certain point in the program, FoxPro must execute all the preceding statements.

One of the most frustrating aspects of using FoxPro 1's Trace facility is the amount of work and planning involved in avoiding stepping through routines that you know are not part of the problem. You either have to be sure that the breakpoints are all in place, or you have to constantly switch between SET STEP ON and SET STEP OFF. The new Out, Over, and Step options simplify the debugging process, and for the first time (in the author's opinion), make Fox's debugging utilities truly useful.

Over enables you to *step over* a current line that calls another program. FoxPro still executes the called program or procedure but doesn't display the program's lines in the Trace window. If you select Over on a line that doesn't call another program, Over moves to the next line, just as if you selected Skip.

The *Out* option *steps out* of the currently executing program and suspends program execution on the line that follows the line that called this program. This option is useful if you need to check the first few lines of a program to refresh your memory about what the program does and then, realizing that this program isn't the source of the problem, want to quickly return to the calling program. *Out* is only enabled when you are not in the top-level program of the application. You can't step out to the Command window (use Cancel for this purpose).

Step lets you *step through* the program to the next line. This option is the Trace feature that you will use most often in conjunction with the Debug window to nail down problems, after you isolate the part of the program where the problem occurs. Enter the variables that are set and evaluated by this portion of the program in the Debug window and note these values as each command is executed.

Error Trapping in an Application

By using the Trace and Debug windows and giving the program a thorough work-out, you can catch many program errors so that users never see them. But, just as you cannot design the perfect interface, you can never be sure (no matter how thoroughly you debug and no matter how sophisticated the tools you use) that the applications you create are 100 percent free from error.

A 0.00001 failure rate or a 15-year MTBF [mean time between failures] are totally meaningless when the product fails.

Insofar as the user is concerned, the failure rate instantly becomes 1.0000 and the MTBF becomes 0 microseconds when the gadget quits.

"The Alternate View: Quality," G. Harry Stine, *Analog Magazine*, May 1991

Inevitably, you encounter situations under which applications you create fail during normal use. You cannot test an application under every imaginable set of conditions and even if you could, you can't imagine all the possible sets of conditions! Beyond this limitation, some conditions, such as hardware failures, exist that you can imagine but still cannot control within the program.

Because software *does* fail, you want to write applications that fail as gracefully as possible.

Allowing users to encounter FoxPro's internally generated error messages is definitely not a good strategy. If you refer to the interface design discussion in Chapter 11 on the subject of effective language, you see that FoxPro error messages don't always meet the criteria of blamelessness, reversibility of action, and clear-cut choice. When an error occurs, just as during the acceptance testing period, you want to be especially sure that you communicate to the users that the program, *not the user*, failed.

In a FoxPro application, you can tell the program to intercept errors before FoxPro responds to them by using an *error-handling* program that you create to deal with all errors that occur.

An error-handling program is called with the special ON ERROR command, usually with several parameters that passes information about the state of the program at the moment the error occurs. This kind of command is shown in the following example:

```
ON ERROR DO widg_err WITH ;
  LINENO(1), PROGRAM(), ;
  MESSAGE(), MESSAGE(1), ERROR() ;
  WLAST(), WREAD(), WONTOP()
```

This list of parameters is by no means exhaustive. As you see shortly, an error-handling program can use many different FoxPro functions. A good general rule is to pass the function results that may be altered if the functions are called within the error procedure. If the error-handling procedure includes showing the user a message in an alert window (a recommended design), for example, you need to pass WLAST() and the other window functions so that these values aren't altered by the addition of the alert window. Some other functions passed in this ON ERROR example, such as MESSAGE(), rarely change their return values within the error-handling program—unless, of course, an error exists in the error-handling program itself!

NOTE Debugging an ON ERROR routine can be the trickiest part of creating an application. In FoxPro, after you're inside the program called by ON ERROR, you can neither rely on the program's own error-handling nor call a second ON ERROR routine to handle errors for you. Fortunately, the logic and arrangement of an ON ERROR routine is simple and clear-cut, and you will probably be able to use one ON ERROR procedure without significant change in every application you write.

The error-handling program usually contains a CASE structure, which enables the program to classify and handle errors according to type and severity. The CASE tests uses the ERROR() function to find out what has occurred. A number of similar errors may be handled by one CASE.

A good strategy for dealing with errors—how the CASEs handle each error—includes some evaluation of the error's *severity*, as well as the error type, as defined in the following list:

- *Trivial* errors, such as `Printer not ready`, that can be handled by the user adjusting the hardware in some way and continuing, which usually can be handled with a polite message and a RETRY command
- *Recoverable* errors, such as a missing or corrupted index, which often can be handled by a standby message as the program takes necessary corrective measures (such as re-creating the index file), followed by a RETURN command
- *Unrecoverable* errors, such as a corrupted database (perhaps due to a power failure) or a corrupted program file, should be handled with an explicit and clear explanatory message. Tell the users what has happened, what they can expect to happen next, and what to do about the error (especially where to look for help). Perform as graceful a cleanup as can be managed and then CANCEL or QUIT the program

These classifications are not as clear-cut as they may look. A lot of overlap exists between recoverable and unrecoverable errors; occasionally, a single procedure may not run properly, but you can give the users the option to continue with other program tasks. The RETURN TO MASTER command may be used in this case; make sure that you initialize the program just as if you were reloading the program.

If you use a Foundation READ, but your Foundation READ is in a backdrop-type screen called by your main program—or if it is not directly in the main program for any other reason—you should return to <*filename*>, explicitly specifying the program containing the Foundation READ rather than TO MASTER. With a Foundation READ, you also should be extremely careful to cancel any edits currently in progress. Your method of cancelling these edits will vary, as described in Chapter 12, depending on whether you choose direct or indirect READS for your application.

Some special CASEs among the recoverable errors also exist that do not actually mean a problem is encountered, although an error condition is created. If you issue the command SCATTER MEMVAR with the MEMO keyword, you may have insufficient memory to store a large memo field as a memory variable. The variable is created but is .F. (logical type). If you see an `Insufficient memory` message (Error # 43, passed using the ERROR() function), and the program line contains the word `SCATTER` (the line is passed using the MESSAGE(1) function), you can choose to create a temporary file with the COPY MEMO command. You can edit this file in the memory variable's stead, and then the memo field can be replaced with this file by using the APPEND MEMO command at a later time, if these changes are saved.

Unlike previous versions of FoxPro, Version 2.0's MESSAGE(1) command is useful even if you have distributed an application without source code. The command from the source code line will be returned. If a macro-substitution was used to create the line of code, the entire line (the result of the macro substitution) will be returned. The LINENO( ) function also was enhanced with an optional parameter so that you can receive a line number relative to the current procedure, rather than from the top of the entire program that you bound together with the BUILD APPLICATION command. In Appendix C, "Optimizing FoxPro 2's Performance," you can see one interesting use for the LINENO(1) function within the DEBUG window.

Another special kind of recoverable error that doesn't indicate a real problem with the program is the inability to lock a record or a file in a multi-user situation. You can use the error-handling routine to notify the user of the problem and RETRY the command until a lock is achieved or until the user decides not to proceed. You learn more about this problem, as well as the commands and functions provided in FoxPro to handle it, in Appendix B.

Every time the error-handling program is called and the cause is neither trivial nor one of these special cases, record the error for later examination. You can call a subprocedure in the appropriate CASEs to create this kind of log. The following code is for one method of error logging, which is part of an ON ERROR routine called WITH the preceding example parameter. Although seemingly unnecessarily thorough, and the log takes a few seconds to create, remember, however, that this subprocedure may not be used often—but when needed, every piece of information you can gather may be useful.

```
PARAMETERS errlineno, errprog, errmsg, errline, ;
         errno, lastwind, readwind, topwind
* a distinctive bell is sounded
* error cases are evaluated first.
* If the error is trivial or special-case,
* it has been handled and you RETURN at this point in the program.
* If not, you evaluate what kind of cleanup to do
* and perform the following logging procedure

SET PRINT OFF
SET CONSOLE ON
SET DEVICE TO SCREEN

* tell the user what's happening with
* a standard window procedure
DO wstandby WITH "A program exception has occurred.",;
  "Writing error log..."

SELECT errlog
* because it's very difficult to recover from errors in
* the error handling program, this file should be
* open (rather than trying to locate and USE it now)
* if at all possible

APPEND BLANK
SAVE WINDOWS ALL TO MEMO snapshot

REPLACE errdate WITH DATE()
REPLACE errtime WITH TIME()

* now build a string of information from the
* various elements of the current environment
* separated by CHR(13)'s (carriage returns)
* You can do multiple REPLACE Listing WITH...<expression> ADDITIVE commands
* rather than building this string
* if you prefer.

errdata = 'error number= '+ALLTRIM(STR(errno))
errdata = errdata+CHR(13)+'error message= '+errmsg
errdata = errdata+CHR(13)+'program= '+ errprog
errdata = errdata+CHR(13)+'lineno= '+;
   ALLTRIM(STR(errlineno))+":  "+errline
errdata = errdata+CHR(13)+'error parameter= '+ SYS(2018)
errdata = errdata+CHR(13)+'BOF()= '+IIF(BOF(),"YES","NO")
errdata = errdata+CHR(13)+'EOF()= '+IIF(EOF(),"YES","NO")
```

```
errdata = errdata+CHR(13)+'RECNO()= '+ALLTRIM(STR(RECNO()))
errdata = errdata+CHR(13)+'active window= '+topwind
errdata = errdata+CHR(13)+'windows in READ= '+readwind
errdata = errdata+CHR(13)+'last window= '+lastwind
errdata = errdata+CHR(13)+ ;
  'available diskspace='+ALLTRIM(STR(DISKSPACE(),25))
errdata = errdata+CHR(13)+ ;
  'total diskspace='+ALLTRIM(STR(SYS(2020)))

errdata = errdata+CHR(13)+ 'os='+OS()
errdata = errdata+CHR(13)+ 'ver='+VERSION(1)
errdata = errdata+CHR(13)+ ;
  ALLTRIM(STR(VAL(SYS(1016))/1024))+;
  "K memory in use by user objects"
errdata = errdata+CHR(13)+ ;
  ALLTRIM(STR(VAL(SYS(12))/1024))+;
  "K memory remaining"
errdata = errdata+CHR(13)+ ;
 ALLTRIM(STR(VAL(SYS(1001))/1024))+;
"K total memory available to Fox"
errdata = errdata+CHR(13)+ ;
  SYS(2019)+ "CONFIG.FP file"

errdata = errdata+CHR(13)+ 'processor='+ SYS(17)
errdata = errdata+CHR(13)+ 'video card/monitor='+SYS(2006)
errdata = errdata+CHR(13)+ 'FILES='+SYS(2010)
errdata = errdata+CHR(13)+CHR(13)+REPLICATE('=',50)
errdata = errdata+CHR(13)+'              Status listing'
errdata = errdata+CHR(13)+REPLICATE('=',50)

* put this string into a memo field
REPLACE listing WITH errdata

* add the contents of STATUS and MEMORY to the memo field

* first get a unique filename
errlog = SYS(3)+".err"
DO WHILE FILE(errlog)
errlog = SYS(3)+".err"
ENDDO

LIST STATUS NOCONSOLE TO (errlog)
APPEND MEMO listing FROM (errlog)
REPLACE listing WITH REPLICATE('=',50)+CHR(13)+;
   '  Memory listing'+CHR(13)+REPLICATE('=',50) ;  ADDITIVE
```

```
LIST MEMORY NOCONSOLE TO (errlog)
APPEND MEMO listing FROM (errlog)
* APPEND MEMO is ADDITIVE by default, unlike REPLACE
ERASE (errlog)

RELEASE WINDOW w_standby
* other cleanup and RETURN or RETURN TO MASTER go here
```

The error log table used by the preceding suggested procedure contains only a few fields, as shown in the following listing:

- ERRDATE and ERRTIME, date and character fields that tell you when the error occurred
- SNAPSHOT, a memo field that holds data on-screen so that you also can see the data (use the RESTORE WINDOW ALL FROM MEMO... command)
- LISTING, a memo field that holds a text description of the state of the program at the time of the error
- USERNOTES, another memo field, which can be used either within the ON ERROR routine or later to enable the user to *jot down* any facts the user thinks may help track down the problem. Instead of leaving this field empty when you create the error log record entry, you can fill the field with a helpful questionnaire for the user to complete. Because memo fields are unlimited in length, the user can add additional unstructured comments, including any information that might be helpful, at the bottom of the questionnaire.

You can make this file accessible to users with a menu option, just like any other table. Typically, useful choices include the following:

- A BROWSE of the file, with USERNOTES the only editable field. Here, you can add recollections or record a resolution of the problem, print the contents of LISTING, or give you pertinent information about the error over the phone.
- A REPORT on the contents of the file
- Error log maintenance. Users can delete old records of resolved problems or copy the file to a floppy disk to send to you (see fig. 18.6).

In case the problem is so severe that normal access through the application is impossible, you can create a special stand-alone procedure that, completely separate from the rest of the application, allows access to the error log and the associated tasks.

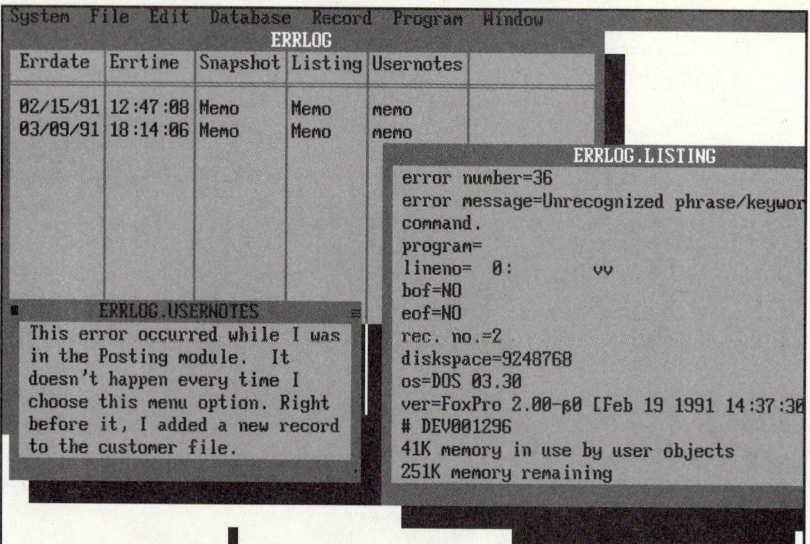

FIG. 18.6

An error log table currently undergoing editing by a user.

No error-handling procedures can guarantee you complete control of program behavior and a graceful exit under all conditions. If the error is `Insufficient memory` or `out of disk space`, you probably cannot create the Listing memo field in the error log. When the error type is `insufficient memory` or `out of disk space`, in fact, you can create an alternate log by sending information directly to the printer, after checking with the user to make sure a printer is available.

But no matter how many layers of insulation from errors you provide, the obvious conclusion is that some kinds of errors require *preventative* checking to avert them at points of the program in which they are likely to happen. With both preventative and remedial error-handling, users can endure the rare *total crash* with good humor and a cooperative attitude.

Quality is an overused, even abused, word. The Latin expression *sine qua non*—"without which nothing," an indispensable factor—may represent the most exact definition of quality. Most people do agree that products that aren't of a high quality shouldn't be built. The disagreement begins when you try to ascertain precisely what is indispensable to a high-quality product.

This section suggests that your definition of quality should include an awareness and an acceptance of problems. This definition is indispensable to a constructive response—on the part of the application and also the users—when problems inevitably occur.

Documenting Applications with FoxDoc

FoxDoc is a FoxPro-specific version of SNAP!, a shareware program written by Walter J. Kennamer. FoxDoc is a marvelous program documentation tool. All you do is supply FoxDoc with the name of the top-level program in the application (or the application's project name), set FoxDoc's options (or use the default settings), and run FoxDoc. FoxDoc then follows the program's execution from beginning to end and creates numerous useful reports, such as a variable cross-reference report, a database structure report, action diagrams, and a program tree structure diagram.

FoxDoc also can format the source code files, which makes this data more attractive and readable. FoxDoc can indent control structures (such as IF ... ENDIF blocks), capitalize and expand keywords, and add informative headings to each program and procedure in an application. Besides simple text (such as the program name, author and copyright notice), the headings also include the names of files that this program calls and files called from this program.

FoxDoc is a stand-alone executable file (FOXDOC.EXE) and, as such, can be run from DOS by typing **FOXDOC** at the DOS prompt. FoxPro includes a *hook* into FoxDoc, which makes FoxDoc accessible from FoxPro. You can run FoxDoc while in FoxPro by selecting FoxDoc from the Program menu or by entering the command FOXDOC in the Command window.

> **TIP**
>
> If the FoxDoc option on the Program menu is disabled, FoxPro can't find the FoxDoc files. Refer to the "Getting Started" section of the FoxDoc chapter in the FoxPro Developer's Guide for a list of the required files. With the exception of CONFIG.FXD, all these files must reside in the FoxPro home directory.

FoxDoc always looks for the configuration file CONFIG.FXD in the current directory. If this file is found, FoxDoc takes the default values from the file. If the file isn't found, FoxDoc uses the built-in defaults. You can (and should) create a configuration file for each of the applications and save the file in the application's main directory. When you subsequently run FoxDoc from the application's directory, this configuration file for the application is used.

To create a configuration file, run FoxDoc and fill in the fields on the system screen. Then press the F5 function key to save the entries. Accept the default configuration file name, and FoxDoc then creates the file. As you work through each of FoxDoc's option screens, always remember that you must save the settings if you want them used as the default values in the next FoxDoc session with this application.

The documentation for FoxDoc is located in Chapter 13 of the *FoxPro Developer's Guide*. The documentation is fairly straight-forward and complete. FoxDoc also has a very complete context-sensitive help system that you can always access by pressing F1. Rather than simply restating what you can learn about FoxDoc from reading the manuals and the help screens, the next section focuses on what may not be apparent and gives you a few pointers for getting the most from this impressive tool.

The FoxDoc System Screen

When you run FoxDoc, the first thing you see is a FoxPro logo screen. Press Enter, and the FoxDoc System screen appears. This screen is the only one in which you must enter information. FoxDoc requires the name of the *main*, or top-level program in the application, or the name of the application's project (PJX) file. Enter the name of this file in the field below the Copyright date.

If you haven't yet created a configuration file in the current directory, FoxDoc uses the current directory as the default value for all the paths, except for the "Path for FoxDoc files," which by default is the FoxPro home directory. If any directories are incorrect, you must change them so that FoxDoc can find the files. You can clear the current entry by pressing Ctrl-End and copy the contents of the previous field into the current field by pressing Ctrl-D.

After you fill in all the information, press F10 to activate FoxDoc's main menu. Now, FoxDoc verifies that all the directories you specified and the top-level program of the application can be found; otherwise, you receive an error message. Press Ctrl-C to exit FoxDoc or press any other key to return to the System screen.

Remember that FoxDoc can process only ASCII source code (PRG, MPR and SPR) files and project (PJX) files. FoxDoc can't read compiled source code (APP, EXE, or FXP) files. If you receive the error message `The main program must be a source code or project file`, you have either specified the wrong file extension, or the current directory contains only the compiled version of the program.

WARNING

Always specify an *output files* directory different from the *program source code* directory. If you don't, FoxDoc overwrites the original source code files with the formatted output files. Although FoxDoc will save the original files with a BAK extension, this protects you only once. When you next run FoxDoc on this application, the original source code files are overwritten and gone forever.

You can direct FoxDoc output files to a subdirectory named \DOC, beneath the directory that holds the program source code. If the program source code is in C:\MYPROGS, direct output files to C:\MYPROGS\DOC. If this directory does not exist, FoxDoc creates the \DOC directory.

NOTE

Some early release versions of FoxDoc 2.1 do not recover gracefully from this error. After an error occurs, nothing you can enter as the main program file is accepted as valid. Press any key to clear an error message from the screen and then press Ctrl-C. To exit FoxDoc at any time, press Ctrl-C.

The current FoxDoc version not only corrects this problem but also scans the current directory, looking for source code files with the file name you entered. If you entered ORDERS.APP as the main program file, FoxDoc looks for a related source code file, such as ORDERS.MPR, and processes the code instead of telling you that the APP file can't be read.

FoxDoc Configuration Options

FoxDoc has a few dozen configuration options that enable you to customize the reports, formatted source code listings, and output file names. Mostly, the default settings work fine and do not need to be changed. In this section, you focus on the few configuration options that really require you to decide what you want FoxDoc to do in certain situations.

Source Code Formatting Options

Run FoxDoc, enter the required information on the screen, and then press F10 to activate the main menu. Now select the Format option, and a screen entitled `FoxDoc Format and Action Diagram Options Screen` appears. You must be sure that four options on this screen are set properly before you run FoxDoc.

By default, FoxDoc follows the xBase formatting convention of using lowercase for tokens (i.e. variables, databases and other non-keywords) and uppercase for keywords (e.g. REPLACE). If the program formatting style doesn't follow this convention, then you need to change these settings. You can tell FoxDoc to use all uppercase, all lowercase, uppercase for the first letter only (leaving the other letters unchanged), or no capitalization (leave everything unchanged).

FoxDoc also assumes that you want to reindent control structures, such as DO WHILE ... ENDDO blocks. You can tell FoxDoc to insert either Tab characters or spaces in the output file to accomplish this, or you can tell FoxDoc not to change indentation.

If you are like the author, you capitalize and indent the programs the way you desire as you write the programs. Usually, you can indent test conditions that contain multiple expressions with the following:

```
DO WHILE          <condition 1> ;
              AND <condition 2>
```

If you don't want FoxDoc to change the program's appearance, be sure that you select N for all these options. Also be sure that you use the F5 function key to save the settings in CONFIG.FXD.

One situation in which you definitely want to use FoxDoc's formatting options is when you are taking over a project from someone else whose formatting conventions may differ from yours, or who didn't follow a consistent pattern of capitalization and indentation. Even if the listings aren't exactly the way you like, the consistent treatment of variable names and keywords makes the program much easier to follow.

The final formatting option to definitely consider is the *Graphics, ASCII or other characters?* option. By default, FoxDoc uses the IBM line drawing characters to create the action diagram lines, linking the beginning of a control structure to the ending. If the printer does not support these characters, type **A** in this field. FoxDoc now uses ASCII characters in drawing the lines.

Cross-Reference Options

One of FoxDoc's most useful reports is the cross-reference report. This report shows you the program module and line number where a particular variable or keyword appears in the application and how the variable or keyword was used at that point in the program. If you use a variable named MYVAR, FoxDoc tells you that in procedure SETUP, MYVAR was declared PRIVATE on line 1 and had a value STOREd to MYVAR on line 10. This information can be extremely useful when you changed a variable's name in one place (especially a PUBLIC variable's name) and want to make sure that you changed the name everywhere else. This report also is handy to ensure that any variable whose value is changed in a particular procedure is declared PRIVATE in this procedure so that you don't risk an inadvertent modification of a variable by the same name in a higher level procedure.

FoxDoc assumes that you want to cross-reference variables and other *tokens*, but not FoxPro keywords. To see where the keyword REPLACE is used in the application, change the `Cross reference FoxPro keywords` option from N to Y.

To create the global, system-wide cross-reference report, FoxDoc must maintain a table of all token names and locations in memory. In a large application, FoxDoc may lack enough memory to store all this information. You can work around this problem by setting the `Local cross-references only?` option to Y. This change tells FoxDoc to create a separate cross-reference report for each module in the application. You can see where the variable FOO (FoxDoc's author's favorite variable name) was referenced within a particular procedure, but you won't get a listing of every occurrence of FOO throughout the application.

Tree Diagram Options

Like the action diagrams, tree diagrams may use either graphic characters or ASCII characters to draw the lines in the diagram. If the printer does not support the IBM line drawing characters, set the `Characters for tree (G/A/N)?` option you see on-screen to either A (ASCII) or N (none).

If you select N, the diagram uses no lines to connect programs, but you still can tell which programs are called by other programs by the level of indentation at which they appear in the diagram.

Printing Options

For many developers, FoxDoc's formatted source code listings are the program's most valuable feature. Although many FoxDoc screens may be left unchanged, you almost certainly want to change at least one of the default printer setup options before printing the source code listings.

Reviewing an action diagram, for example, is helpful in tracking down a nesting error in a program that contains multiple nested IF's and DO WHILE's, but you don't always want to print these commands along with the source code. If so, you can set the `Create action diagrams?` option on the Format and Action Diagrams Options screen to Y so that action diagrams are created and then set the `Print action diagrams?` option here to N.

FoxDoc's line width, page length, and margin settings are all configured for a wide-carriage dot-matrix printer. If you use a laser printer, you may want to change most of the settings. Remember that the default page length for a Hewlett-Packard LaserJet is 60 lines per page, rather than 66, and that you can print 132 characters across the page only if you use compressed print.

To use compressed print without resetting the printer's default setup, you can enter the proper LaserJet escape code sequence in the `Printer setup string:` field. Information you enter here is sent to the printer before printing begins. If you enter a setup string, a good idea is to also enter a reset string in the field below the setup string. The contents of this field are sent to the printer after the print job is complete.

You can use the F2-List option to pick a printer from a small list of printers for which Fox Software has provided appropriate printer settings and printer control codes. The printers currently supported are Epson and Hewlett-Packard LaserJets and close compatibles that use the same setup strings as these printers. The printer setup codes are contained in the ASCII text file FXDPRT.FXD. If this file is not on the disk or if you want to add a printer to the file, you can create or modify this file. However, you must follow these formatting conventions for FoxDoc to *read* your setup. The following lines are at the top of the FXDPRT.FXD file:

```
* This is the FoxDoc printer default file. It is formatted like this:
*  Printer name
*  Line width
*  Page length
*  Top margin
*  Bottom margin
*  Left margin
*  Right margin
*  Tab expansion
*  Print line numbers?
*  Form feed before print?
*  Form feed after print?
*  Setup string
*  Reset string
```

```
************************************************************
Default printer
************************************************************
80
66
8
8
12
1
3
Y
Y
Y


************************************************************
Epson—pica
************************************************************
80
66
8
8
12
1
3
Y
Y
Y
\027@
\018
```

Note that the two blank lines that separate the last entry for `Default printer` and the row of asterisks above `Epson—pica` are part of the printer setup for "Default printer". The fact that these lines are blank indicates that this printer doesn't require either a setup or reset string.

Formatting Snippets with SNIPFMT.APP

Code snippets are new to FoxPro2. Snippets that you create in the Menu Builder and Screen Builder are stored in a table with the other information for the menu or screen. When you generate the source code, these snippets form part of the MPR or SPR source code file. FoxDoc treats code snippets just like any other procedure and formats them, according to the options you specified.

However, this doesn't change the original snippet, which is still located in the menu or screen table. FoxDoc's author, Walt Kennamer, has written a separate utility program to format code snippets, which you find in the FoxPro 2 home directory as SNIPFMT.APP. The SNIPFMT utility is more limited in capability than FoxDoc, but SNIPFMT indents and capitalizes the snippets by using the same settings that FoxDoc uses by default.

To change SNIPFMT's default behavior to a capitalization or identity format that you prefer, you must edit SNIPFMT itself. Like the template programs, GENSCRN and GENMENU, as well as the GENPD printer driver system, SNIPFMT is just an application written in FoxPro. To change it, you MODIFY the project that you find in the GOODIES\SNIPFMT directory. You edit the FMT procedure, located in SNIP.PRG (SNIPFMT's main file). You also can edit SNIPFMT to call one of several different FMT procedures to allow different styles, just as FoxDoc does.

You use SNIPFMT by running the SNIPFMT.APP file. SNIPFMT asks you to select the file that contains the snippets from the Open File dialog, load the keywords file, and start formatting each snippet in the file. SNIPFMT actually applies the formatting to a temporary copy of the original snippet but won't change the source code unless you select «Save» when the formatted text appears in a window. Review and then save the formatted snippet if you like what SNIPFMT did. That's all there is!

Chapter Summary

Help systems, Debug and Trace, ON ERROR, and FoxDoc—this chapter has covered some diverse features of FoxPro 2. All these features share one important characteristic—each is a high-quality tool designed for a distinctive role within the overall process of creating a superior application.

With these features, and with the wide-ranging options discussed in Part III, FoxPro 2 goes to great lengths to ensure that you always have *the right tool for the job* so that you can create systems in which the users have the right tools for the job.

Supporting all these tools, and intrinsic to each one of them, are the commands and functions that constitute the FoxPro programming language. You used some of them since you began Part I of this book, and you were gradually introduced to more commands and functions in the practice sessions in Parts II and III. In Part IV, you learned about the logic and structure that are essential to programming techniques.

In the following part, Part V, you cover some special categories of commands and functions in greater detail, with suggestions for their use and sample procedures to provide models, as you begin to develop programs to accomplish custom tasks.

Getting To Know FoxPro 2 Commands and Functions

19

CHAPTER

Using Commands and Functions To Manipulate Data

Many of FoxPro 2's commands and functions enable you to manipulate data elements of FoxPro's basic data types (character, numeric, date, and logical). You can convert lowercase letters to uppercase, extract a line from a memo field, convert one type of data element to another type, and determine whether a sequence of characters is contained in a character string. The list of data manipulation functions that FoxPro provides is long, and the possible combinations of these functions is almost endless.

FoxPro also provides commands that make it easy for you to locate records and create subsets of your data.

This chapter covers many of FoxPro's data manipulation commands and functions. Some of these you have already seen in previous chapters. Others you will see for the first time. The goal is not to provide a reference manual to FoxPro's commands and functions, but rather to organize them by their intended use, to provide you with concrete examples of their usage, and to show you some creative methods for employing them in your applications.

Manipulating Single Data Elements

This section covers the functions that manipulate single data elements, such as a memory variable or a single record in a table. For the most part, this section concentrates attention on those functions that transform the data in some way. Because many of FoxPro's commands and functions require their arguments to be of a particular data type, or in a certain format, data transformation is a very important subject.

Keep in mind that functions simply return values; the functions don't actually change the data. The UPPER() function, for example, doesn't change the case of its argument; the function simply makes the uppercase form of the data available for use by another command or function. To actually convert the data element to all uppercase, you must store the returned value of the UPPER() function back to the variable—for example:

```
m.Lastname = "smith"
seek upper(m.Lastname)            && m.Lastname is "smith"
m.Lastname = upper(m.Lastname)    && m.Lastname is "SMITH"
```

Manipulating Character Strings and Memo Fields

FoxPro excels at manipulating character strings. You can search a string for the presence of a substring, strip off file extensions, replace one substring with another, pad a string with spaces, and convert character strings to other data types. The list goes on and on. This section explains the commands and functions used with character-type data.

In the standard version of FoxPro2, character strings can be up to 64K in length; character strings can be much longer in the Extended version (up to whatever length your system's free memory can accept). By contrast, memo fields are limited only by your available disk space. For this reason, not all functions that you can use on character strings work properly on large memo fields; some of the functions only work on memo fields if the contents of the field remain within allowable string size. In tables 19.1 and 19.2, the functions that can be used on memo fields *regardless of their size* are marked with an asterisk.

Finding One String within Another

FoxPro has several functions that enable you to search a character string for the occurrence of a character or substring. These functions are listed in table 19.1.

Table 19.1 FoxPro's String Search Functions

Function	Description
*$	Returns .T. if a substring is contained in a string or memo field
*AT()	Returns an integer representing the position in a string where a specified occurrence of a substring was found, searching from left to right. AT() is case-sensitive.
*ATC()	This function works the same way as AT(), but it is case-insensitive
*ATLINE()	Returns the number of the line in a memo field where a substring was found. Although most often used with memo fields, this function also works with character strings. The current setting of MEMOWIDTH determines how many characters each line contains, subject to the effects of word wrapping.
*ATCLINE()	A case-insensitive form of ATLINE
RAT()	Works like AT() but searches the target string from right to left. This function is particularly useful when you need to strip a simple file name from a fully-qualified file name, using the \ character as the search substring. Because the rightmost \ character indicates the end of the path, you can strip the file name of its path by using RAT().
RATLINE()	The same as ATLINE(), but the search is performed starting with the last character and moving toward the first.

* Denotes functions that can be used on memo fields of any size.

The $ symbol, which Fox's documentation refers to as both a function and an operator, tells you whether one string is contained in another string. If it is, $ returns .T.; otherwise it returns .F. . AT() does the same job, but it also tells you where in the string the substring occurs. If the substring was not found, AT() returns 0. The following two lines are functionally equivalent:

```
if "Johnson" $ Lastname
if at("Johnson", Lastname) > 0
```

If all you need to do is test for the presence of a substring, which function you use is mostly a matter of personal preference. If you are performing substring searches on memo fields and the substrings can consist of more than one word, however, you want to be aware of some special capabilities of $, explained in the following ATLINE() example.

You use $ with two arguments in the following form:

```
<substring> $ <string>
```

This entire expression evaluates to either true or false. To test for the absence of a substring, you must apply a logical negative operator (! or NOT) to the entire expression, as follows:

```
if ! ("Johnson" $ Lastname)
```

The enclosing parentheses are not required, but they make the function easier to read.

The AT() function really comes into its own when you need to extract a series of characters from a string. You may, for example, have allowed the user of your application to create a comma-delimited list of fields on which you will create an index tag for the current table. To isolate each field in the list, you can use the AT() function as follows:

```
* fld_list is in the form "Last, First, Company"
do while at(",", fld_list) > 0
   * extract the field name from the beginning of the list
   index_fld = alltrim(left(fld_list, AT(",",fld_list)-1))

   * create the index on this field
   index on &index_fld tag (index_fld)

   * now remove this field, and the comma that follows it, * from
   the list
   fld_list = substr(fld_list, at(",", fld_list)+1)
enddo

* you now have a list that contains a single field name
* create the index on this field
index on &fld_list tag (fld_list)
```

Because you know that each field name is separated from the next by a comma, you use the AT() function to determine the number of characters that make up the field name, the LEFT() function to store the current field name to a variable (index_fld), and the SUBSTR() function to remove this field name from the list when you don't need it anymore. LEFT() uses AT() to determine how many characters to include in index_fld, and SUBSTR() uses AT() to determine the first character of the old fld_list that should be included in the new fld_list. LEFT() and SUBSTR() are described in the next section of this chapter.

The ATLINE() functions—and its relatives ATCLINE() and RATLINE()—often are used with the MLINE() function to display or store the contents of a particular line of a memo field, for example:

```
* find each record in the table that contains a certain
* string in the NOTES memo field, and display the first
* line in which the string was found
contact = "Jones"
locate for contact $ Notes
do while found()
  ? MLINE(Notes, ATLINE(contact,Notes))
  continue
enddo
```

The MLINE() function also is covered later in this section.

ATLINE() and its related functions are governed by the setting of MEMOWIDTH, as you can see in the following. What they return is subject to word wrap like all other memo field handling commands. This means that the technique shown in this example is limited to single words; if contact were "Bob Jones" instead of "Jones," the $ search would return .J. However, if the words "Bob" and "Jones" were at the end and beginning of two separate lines, the ATLINE() function returns to 0.

Changing the Length, Case, and Contents of Strings and Memo Fields

Besides simply searching for strings, you also can change their contents. You can change a string's length and case and substitute one set of characters for another. The FoxPro functions you can use for these purposes are listed in table 19.2.

Table 19.2 FoxPro's String Manipulation Functions

Function	Description
TRIM()	Strips trailing blanks
LTRIM()	Strips leading blanks
RTRIM()	Same as TRIM()
ALLTRIM()	The same as LTRIM(RTRIM(`<string>`))
PADC()	Pads the string to the left and right so that it is centered within a specified pad character or characters
PADL()	Pads the string to the left with a specified character or characters
PADR()	Pads the string to the right with a specified character or characters
REPLICATE()	Returns a string consisting of a specified number of copies of a given expression
SPACE()	Returns a character string containing a specified number of spaces
LOWER()	Converts a string to all lowercase characters
UPPER()	Converts a string to all uppercase characters
PROPER()	Changes the first character of each word to uppercase and the remaining characters to lowercase
*LEN()	Returns the length of string
LEFT()	Returns a specified number of characters, beginning with the first character in the string
RIGHT()	Returns a specified number of characters, counting from the last character in the string
*SUBSTR()	Returns a specified number of characters, beginning at a specified position within the string
*MEMLINES()	Returns the number of lines in a string or memo field as determined by the current setting of SET MEMOWIDTH
*MLINE()	Returns the contents of a specified line in a string or memo field. Which characters appear on the line is determined by the current setting of MEMOWIDTH
CHRTRAN()	Substitutes any occurrence of a character for a different one, using two character strings as a translation table

Function	Description
STRTRAN( )	Like CHRTRAN( ), but works with entire substrings, rather than individual characters. Any instance of the first substring is replaced by the second substring, or by the null string (" ") if a second string is not supplied.
STUFF( )	Like STRTRAN( ), but a specified number of characters are replaced, and the replacement begins at a specified character position.
TRANSFORM( )	Enables you to display formatted character or numeric expressions without using @ ... SAY/GET.

* Denotes function that can be used on memo fields of any size.

The “trimming” functions remove all blank spaces from one end or both ends of a string or memo field. Strings are usually trimmed before a comparison operation, to ensure that two strings which are the same are not regarded as different because of extraneous spaces. For example:

```
@ 10,10 say "Contact" get contact default space(20)
read
* user may have entered "   Bob Jones"
* use the LTRIM() function to strip any leading spaces
* before comparing the entry
if LTRIM(contact) = "Bob Jones"
  <statements>
endif
```

Note that the expression `if LTRIM(contact) = "Bob Jones"` may not return the same value as `if "Bob Jones" = LTRIM(contact)`. This is because of the way that all xBase dialects compare character strings. The expressions also are affected by the current setting of EXACT (ON or OFF). If EXACT is ON, the expressions are considered the same; if EXACT is OFF, they are not. Refer to Chapter 7, “Querying with SQL and Searching with Rushmore,” for a detailed analysis of the rules FoxPro follows to decide whether two strings are the same.

As opposed to removing spaces, you can use the “padding” functions to add spaces (or any other character or characters) to a string. The only difference among the functions is where the characters are added.

PADC() (pad center) is very useful for displaying a message centered within a window of unknown width, as follows:

```
activate window win1
@ 0,0 say padc("Reindexing tables...", wcols())
```

WCOLS() returns the number of columns in the active window (win1), and PADC() inserts the proper number of spaces before and after the message text so that the message will be centered within the window. To pad the message with something other than spaces, specify the pad character(s) as the third argument in the function call. For example:

```
@ 0,0 say padc(" Reindexing tables... ", wcols(), "*")
```

PADR() (pad right) can be used to ensure that a search expression has the same form as the current index expression. If, for example, you have the index key LASTNAME+FIRSTNAME and LASTNAME is 20 characters long, the index entries look like the following:

```
Jones                   Bob
Thompson                Michael
```

To find "Bob Jones" using this index, you must pad the last name with spaces, so that "Bob" appears in the same position in the search expression as it does in the index expression, as follows:

```
mlast  = "Jones"
mfirst = "Bob"
msearch = padr(mlast, fsize('LASTNAME')) + mfirst
seek msearch
```

The case-changing functions are used primarily to overcome the case-sensitive nature of FoxPro's comparison operators and searching functions. When updating a customer table, for example, you may want to avoid having two records for Bob Jones, one in proper case and one in upper- or lowercase. The following procedure provides an example of this type of validation.

```
* open the CUSTOMER table; the index key is
UPPER(CUSTOMER) use CUSTOMER

@ 10,10 say "Customer " get mcust default space(20)
read

* user may have entered "Bob Jones", "bob jones" or
* "BOB JONES"; use the UPPER() function to convert the
* search expression to the same case as the index en-
tries
if seek(upper(mcust))
  ?? chr(7)     && get the user's attention
  wait window "This customer is already on file!" nowait
endif
```

LEFT(), RIGHT(), and SUBSTR() all return a specified number of characters from a string or memo field. The difference is where in the string the substring to be returned will begin. LEFT() always starts at the first character; RIGHT() starts at the character whose position is equal to the length of the string minus the specified number of characters plus one; and SUBSTR() starts wherever you tell it to.

Suppose that you have a memory variable that holds a fully qualified file name (C:\FOXPRO2\CONFIG.FP, for example). You can extract the various parts of the file name using each of these substring functions, as follows:

```
* isolate the FoxPro configuration file's drive and
* subdirectory, base file name and file extension

* store the name of the config file
fullname = sys(2019)

* locate the last backslash character
bs_pos   = rat("\",fullname)

* locate the period in the file name
pd_pos   = rat(".",fullname)

dirname  = left(fullname,bs_pos)
basename = substr(fullname,bs_pos+1,pd_pos-bs_pos-1)
extname  = right(fullname,len(fullname)-pd_pos)
*
* if fullname = C:\FOXPRO2\CONFIG.FP, then
* dirname  = C:\FOXPRO2\
* basename = CONFIG
* extname  = FP
*
```

MLINE() returns the contents of a single line of a memo field or character string. MLINE() is like SUBSTR(), but it is specifically designed to respect word wrapping. How many characters are on each line is determined by the current setting of MEMOWIDTH. The following example illustrates how MLINE() works and how it differs from SUBSTR():

```
s = replicate("Nothing runs like the fox! ", 150)
set memowidth to 50
? len(s)               && 4050
? len(s) / 50          &&   81
? memlines(s)          &&   84
? substr(s,51,50)
  * ox! Nothing runs like the fox! Nothing runs like t
? mline(s,2)
  * fox! Nothing runs like the fox! Nothing runs like
```

If the MEMLINES() function did not respect the MEMOWIDTH setting and the resulting word wrapping of the text, MEMLINES() would return the same value as LEN(s) / 50. Instead, it returns the number of lines that would be displayed on-screen if you entered question marks (?) in the Command window.

SUBSTR() sees the memory variable *s* as a simple string of characters, as follows:

```
     0         1         2         3         4         5
     12345678901234567890123456789012345678901234567890
   0 Nothing runs like the fox! Nothing runs like the f
  50 ox! Nothing runs like the fox! Nothing runs like t
 100 he fox! Nothing runs like the fox! Nothing runs li
```

MLINE() and MEMLINES(), on the other hand, see *s* as a memo field that has been opened in a memo editing window, like this:

```
     0         1         2         3         4         5
     12345678901234567890123456789012345678901234567890
   0 Nothing runs like the fox! Nothing runs like the
  50 fox! Nothing runs like the fox! Nothing runs like
 100 the fox! Nothing runs like the fox! Nothing runs
```

The MLINE() function has been enhanced by the addition of an optional third argument that specifies an offset from a particular memo line and by a new system variable (_MLINE) that automatically is adjusted to hold the number of the last line returned by MLINE(). When printing a series of lines from a memo field, using 1 as the second argument and _MLINE as the third argument greatly improves the rate at which MLINE() returns memo field lines. See the MLINE() entry in the help file or the *Commands and Functions* manual for further details.

The STRTRAN() function is great for removing blank spaces from within a string or for swapping file extensions.

The trimming functions easily can strip blanks from the beginning and end of a string, but they can't help you when you need to remove spaces from within the string. You can use STRTRAN() to accomplish this task by specifying the null string (" ") as the third argument, or by not specifying a third argument, which tells FoxPro to use the null string as the replacement string. This feature can be very useful when you want to search a field that may contain any number of embedded spaces, as follows:

```
* search for a name in the CONTACT field; the user
might
* enter "Bob Jones" as "Bob   Jones", so you need to
* strip out the embedded spaces; you actually search
* for "BOBJONES," with all uppercase and no spaces
```

```
@ 10,10 say "Contact " get fullname default space(20)
read

locate for    upper(strtran(contact," ")) ;
             == upper(strtran(fullname," "))
```

When you create a temporary copy of a table that has a memo field, a memo file (FPT) also is created. If your application doesn't know whether the table has a memo field, you should check for the existence of a memo file when erasing the temporary files. Because the memo file has the same base name as the database file, you can use STRTRAN() to change the extension of the file name stored in a memory variable, as follows:

```
* get a unique file name and create a temporary copy
* of the current table
tempfile = sys(3) + ".$$$"    && (e.g. 55048985.$$$)
copy structure to (tempfile)

*
* data processing commands go here
*

* now you're ready to "clean up"

* erase the temporary database file whose name is
* held in tempfile
erase (tempfile)

* must also erase any memo file created
tempfile = strtran(tempfile, ".$$$", ".FPT")
* tempfile is now something like "55048985.FPT"
if file(tempfile)      && if there is a related memo
file
  erase (tempfile)    && erase the memo file
endif
```

You also can use the new CREATE CURSOR command to create a temporary table that automatically is erased when you close it. CREATE CURSOR is covered in the "Using FoxPro 2's SQL Commands" section of this chapter.

Converting Character Data to and from Other Data Types

FoxPro has several functions that convert character data to and from other data types. These functions are listed in table 19.3.

Table 19.3 Character Data Conversion Functions

Function	Converts From	To
CTOD( )	Character (using current SET DATE format)	Date
DTOC( )	Date	Character (using current SET DATE format)
DTOS( )	Date	Character (using YYYYMMDD format, suitable for indexing)
STR( )	Numeric	Character
VAL( )	Character	Numeric

Examples of CTOD(), DTOC() and DTOS() are included in this chapter's section "Manipulating Dates," and STR() and VAL() are discussed in "Manipulating Numeric Data."

Manipulating Numeric Data

Many of FoxPro's numeric data-handling functions perform mathematical, trigonometric, and financial operations on numeric data. Among them are ABS(), which returns the absolute value of a number, and PAYMENT(), which calculates the amount of each payment on a fixed-interest loan.

Most database applications have little need for the trigonometric and financial functions, and those that do require a more in-depth analysis of their usage than can be provided here. This book looks at the numeric functions that are more generally useful in database applications.

Using MAX( ) and MIN( ) To Define Boundaries

Often times, you may need to select the largest or smallest in a series of values. You can compare each of the values, two at a time, in a series of IF ... ENDIF's, or you can use FoxPro's MAX() and MIN() functions. The MAX() function returns the largest of a list of expressions; the MIN() function returns the smallest of a list of expressions.

Both functions accept a list of expressions. Although they are categorized as numeric functions, their arguments can be of any data type, as long as they are all of the same data type (to verify this, try typing **? max(.t., .f.)** in the Command window). The return value is the same data type as the argument list.

In the following example, both MAX() and MIN() are used to determine the proper width for a data-entry window. The size of each field in the table is compared to a variable that holds the size of the largest field seen so far, and then the size of the largest field is compared to the number of available screen columns to ensure that the window is completely contained in the visible screen area:

```
* create an array containing structure info on current
* table afields() automatically creates the array if it
* doesn't exist
= afields(fld_array)

* determine the largest field
max_len = 0
for j=1 to alen("fld_array",1)
  * the field length is held in the third
  * "column" of the array
  max_len = max(max_len, fld_array[j,3])
endfor

* adjust max_len to account for the field descriptions,
* the window borders, and some extra spacing
max_len = max_len + 16

* store the lesser of max_len or the screen width in
* win_width
win_width = min(max_len, scols())
```

This example uses two of FoxPro 2's new array-handling functions, AFIELDS() and ALEN(), to provide the required information about the current table. The array-handling functions are covered in detail in the next chapter.

Using the Rounding and Modulus Functions

You can round numbers up and down with ROUND(), CEILING(), and FLOOR() and drop the decimals from a number with INT(). MOD() and % are equivalent functions that return the modulus of a number. These functions are described in table 19.4.

Table 19.4 FoxPro's Rounding Functions

Function	Description
%	Also called the "Modulus operator," it returns the remainder obtained by dividing one number by another.
CEILING()	Returns the nearest integer that is greater than or equal to the specified number
FLOOR()	Returns the nearest integer that is less than or equal to the specified number
INT()	Returns the integer portion of a number
MOD()	A function that performs the same task as the Modulus operator (%)
ROUND()	Rounds a number to a specified number of decimal places

The % operator, which is new to FoxPro 2, provides the same functionality as the MOD() function. Each function returns the remainder obtained by dividing two numbers. MOD(5,2), for example, returns 1, as does 5 % 2.

The traditional example of a use for the modulus functions is to determine whether a year is a leap year. A leap year is one which is exactly divisible by four, unless it is a centennial year, in which case it must be exactly divisible by four hundred. You can determine whether a year is a leap year as follows:

```
curr_year = year(date())
  is_leap = iif(curr_year % 100 = 0, ;
  curr_year % 400 = 0, ;
  curr_year % 4 = 0)
```

You also can use % or MOD() to create a sample of records in a table. Suppose that you have a table of names and addresses of people from all over the United States that represents a mailing list. Before you spend money on postage and materials, you want to send a sample mailing to a cross-section of people, and you want your sample to contain people from each of the different states in the same proportion as the entire table. To create a sample table, you can sort on the STATE field and then copy every *n*th record to the sample table, as follows:

```
PROCEDURE makesamp
  *
  * Create a sample table containing samp_size number
  * of records from MAILLIST
  *
```

```
   parameters samp_size
   private tot_recs, samp_intvl, tempfile
   use MAILLIST
   tempfile = sys(3) + ".$$$"
   sort on STATE to (tempfile)
   use (tempfile)
   tot_recs = reccount()
   samp_intvl = int(tot_recs / samp_size)
   copy to SAMPLE for mod(recno(), samp_intvl) = 0
   use
   erase (tempfile)
   use SAMPLE
return
```

This example used the INT() function to make sure that you are always working with integers. You could have used ROUND(tot_recs / samp_size, 0) to obtain the same result.

Converting Numeric Data to and from Character Data

FoxPro has two functions that are useful for working with numeric data that needs to be treated as a string of digits and for character data on which you need to perform a numeric operation.

STR() converts numeric data into a character string of digits. VAL() performs the opposite function, converting character data into its numeric representation.

STR() is useful when you need to include a number as part of a character expression. When, for example, an index expression must be of a single data type. You cannot index on an expression that contains character strings and numeric data. You can, however, index on a character string plus the character representation of a number, such as:

```
index on CUSTNO + STR(AMOUNT,10,0) to INVBYAMT
```

In this example, STR() accepts two optional arguments with which you can specify the length of the string and the number of decimal places.

VAL() is used when you need to perform a computation on a character data element that consists, at least partially, of digits. A table, for example, may have a character field that holds an invoice number. In an order entry routine, you may want to display the next sequentially ordered invoice number as the default for the next order. Because you cannot increment a character string, you must convert the character string into a number, add 1 to it, and then convert the result back into character form. You use both VAL() and STR() in the process, as follows:

```
* open the ORDERS table and order it by invoice number,
* which is a character-type field
use ORDERS order INVOICENUM

* increment the last invoice number and use it as the
* default for the next order
go bottom
minvno = str(val(INVOICENUM)+1, len(INVOICENUM))
```

You might wonder why the invoice number is stored as a character string in the first place when it consists entirely of digits and you want to be able to perform a computation on it. There are several reasons for this.

First, the invoice number also may include one or more letters.

It is not uncommon for an invoice number to be prefaced by an identifier, such as XX1234, where XX might be the code for a particular division of the company. If a company that had been using invoice numbers that consisted of digits decided to include an identifier as part of the invoice number, you would not easily be able to accommodate this change if you had been storing the invoice number in a numeric field.

If you used an invoice numbering system of this nature, you strip the prefacing alphabetical characters from the invoice code before incrementing the invoice number in the earlier procedure, such as the following:

```
* invoice numbering system is "XX1234"
minvno = LEFT (INVOICENUM,2)+;
         STR(VAL(RIGHT(INVOICENUM),4)+1,4)
```

Second, although you may want to perform some type of computation on the invoice number, such as incrementing it by 1, there is no need to include the number in any table-wide computational database commands, such as SUM or AVERAGE. You will never need to keep a running total of invoice numbers. Just as with a Social Security number, the digits don't really have any numeric significance, other than to differentiate one record from the others.

Manipulating Dates

FoxPro provides a full complement of functions that manipulate dates. Many of the date functions return character strings that can be used in reports to display the current date as text (September 30, 1991, for example), rather than as digits (09/30/91). Other functions simply convert dates into character strings (perhaps for inclusion in a character index expression) and character strings into dates (for use in a "date math" calculation, or for comparison to a date type field or variable).

FoxPro treats dates as a special type of numeric data. This explains why you can add or subtract one date from another. If, for example, you type the following in the Command window:

```
? cdow({01/01/1901})
? cdow({01/01/1901} - 1)
```

you will see that the first New Year's Day of the 20th Century fell on a Tuesday, and that the last New Year's Eve of the 19th Century fell on a Monday.

For an in-depth analysis of FoxPro 2's internal handling of dates, see *Developing FoxPro 2 Applications*, by P.L. Olympia and Kathy Cea.

Displaying the Current Date and Time

FoxPro has built-in functions that return the current system date and time by reading the computer's system clock.

DATE() often is used to display the current date at the top of the screen and to print the current date on reports. DATE() also is used as the argument to those date functions that convert a date from digits to text, such as "January 1, 1992."

TIME() is used in much the same way as DATE(). TIME() returns the current time, as stored in the computer's system clock. You also can display the current system time on-screen with the SET CLOCK ON command. You change the position with SET CLOCK TO `<row>, <col>`.

Another time function, SECONDS(), returns the number of seconds that have elapsed since midnight. Using this function, you can determine, for example, how long it took FoxPro to execute a series of commands by saving the value returned by SECONDS() immediately before the first line of the block of commands and then displaying the difference between the current value of SECONDS() and the variable that holds the beginning time.

Displaying Dates as Text and Extracting a Day, Month, or Year

Because dates are treated like numbers, you can calculate any of the information provided by the functions shown in table 19.6, as long as you know the relevant information for some other date. To do this, you can use many IF...ELSE...ENDIF or DO CASE constructs.

Luckily, you don't have to calculate this information. These date functions take much of the headache out of calculating and displaying dates. Of particular interest are the MDY() and DMY() functions, which you can use to display a date in full spelled form, such as "October 12, 1991," or the equivalent European format "12 October 1991," respectively.

Because the uses of these functions are self-evident once you know what they do, table 19.5 simply describes the functions, and table 19.6 provides some usage information and sample output.

Table 19.5 Date Manipulation Functions

Function	Description
CDOW()	Returns the day of the week for a specified date as a name, such as "Saturday"
CMONTH()	Returns the name of the month for a specified date, such as "April"
DAY()	Returns the day of the month for a particular date
DMY()	Returns a date in European day-month-year format. The month is displayed as a name, and the number of digits in the year depends on the current setting of CENTURY.
DOW()	Returns the number of the day of the week for a date; Sunday is day 1.
GOMONTH()	Returns the date that is a specified number of months before or after a date. GOMONTH() takes the differing number of days in the intervening months into account so that the date it returns always has the same day of the month as the date supplied.
MDY()	The same as DMY() but uses American month-day-year format. With CENTURY set ON, MDY() and DMY() are useful for printing the current date on a letter.
MONTH()	Returns the month of the year for a particular date
YEAR()	Returns the year of a given date. The year is always returned as a four-digit number, regardless of the setting of CENTURY.

Table 19.6 Using the Date Manipulation Functions

Function	Takes	Returns	Example	Displays
CDOW()	Date	Char	? CDOW(DATE())	Saturday
CMONTH()	Date	Char	? CMONTH(DATE())	October
DAY()	Date	Num	? DAY(DATE())	12
DMY()	Date (with CENTURY set ON)	Char	? DMY(DATE()) 12 October 1991	12 October 91
DOW()	Date	Num	? DOW(DATE())	7
GOMONTH()	Date,Num	Date	? GOMONTH(DATE(),3)	01/12/92
MDY()	Date (with CENTURY set ON)	Char	? MDY(DATE()) October 12, 1991	October 12, 91
MONTH()	Date	Num	? MONTH(DATE())	10
YEAR()	Date	Num	? YEAR(DATE())	1991

Converting Dates to and from Character Data

You can convert dates to character strings and back using the functions shown in table 19.7.

Table 19.7 The Date Conversion Functions

Function	Description
CTOD()	Read as "character to date." Converts a character string, such as "01/01/91," to date type.
DTOC()	Read as "date to character." Converts a date into its equivalent character string.
DTOS()	Read as "date to string." Converts a date into an eight-digit string in the format YYYYMMDD, which is most suitable for ordering a table on a date field.

CTOD() converts a character string to date type. One instance in which this feature is valuable is filling a date field with dates that are currently stored in an ASCII text file as character strings in MM/DD/YY format.

Suppose that you are converting an application from another database management system to FoxPro 2, that the other DBMS's file format is incompatible with FoxPro, and that the file format is not one of the file formats supported by the IMPORT command. You can export the data to an ASCII text file from the other DBMS and then append the text to a character field in your FoxPro table, using the APPEND FROM command. For this example, assume that you have created an ASCII text file called OLD_DATA.TXT that looks like the following (of course, the ruler at the top is only for your reference):

```
0        1         2         3         4
1234567890123456789012345678901234567890123456789
Jones               William        05/23/54
Smith               Roger          09/15/62
Walters             Kenneth        10/07/56
```

To match the format of the text file, you create a table that has this structure:

```
Structure for database: C:\FOXPRO2\MODEL\PEOPLE.DBF

Field         Field Name    Type         Width  Dec  Index

 1            LASTNAME      Character    20

 2            FIRSTNAME     Character    15

 3            TEMP_DATE     Character    8

** Total **                              44
```

Now you're ready to import the data. Type the following in the Command window:

```
append from OLD_DATA.TXT type SDF
```

A new record is appended to your table for each row in the text file, and the fields are filled with the appropriate data, because you sized them according to the number of spaces in each column of the text file.

Notice that the date field, TEMP_DATE, is actually a character field. Because you cannot import text into a date field unless it is in YYYYMMDD format (FoxPro's internal date format), you must perform the conversion in two steps. First, you import the text into a character field, as you have just done. Then, you add a date type field to the table. Call it BIRTHDATE. Now you can use the CTOD() function to fill the date field with the intended date values, as follows:

```
replace all Birthdate with ctod(temp_date)
```

To complete the conversion, just remove the TEMP_DATE field from the table.

DTOC() converts dates to character strings. This function often is used when you want to concatenate a date field with one or more character fields, as in:

```
@ 10,10 say "Today's date is " + dtoc(date())
```

DTOC() accepts an optional second argument, the digit 1, that tells FoxPro to return the character string in the form of YYYYMMDD. This form is more appropriate than the MMDDYYYY form for creating an index that orders the records by a date field.

DTOC(date(),1) is equivalent to DTOS(date()). Both return an eight-digit string in YYYYMMDD format, regardless of the current setting of CENTURY. CTOD(), and DTOC() without the ",1" argument, both respect the current CENTURY setting.

Using TYPE() and EMPTY() To Test a Variable

In an event-driven environment such as FoxPro, you often need to know whether a variable currently exists, and, in the case of a global variable, whether it has been assigned a value. TYPE() and EMPTY() provide this information.

TYPE() returns a single letter code for the data type of an expression: C for character, N for numeric, D for date, L for logical, and U for undefined.

Because FoxPro 2 enables you to modify the system menu, you can allow the user of your application to launch the application by selecting it from the system menu. Your application becomes an addition to FoxPro. When not in the application, the user has complete access to all of FoxPro's commands and functions through the Command window and the menu popups.

One example application works in just this way. It installs itself into the FoxPro system menu and peacefully coexists with the other FoxPro menu options. Each menu option runs a separate program contained in an application (APP) file. Each of these programs must save any elements of the user's environment it needs to set a certain way and must restore the environment before exiting. Although the code to save the environment is contained within each of the programs, you can use a generic procedure called RESTENV to restore the environment. Each program calls this procedure before exiting.

RESTENV knows that each program that called it used the same name to save a particular environment setting, but RESTENV doesn't know whether the calling program actually created such a variable. RESTENV uses the TYPE() function to test for the existence and proper data type of each variable that it uses. For example, the following lines reset the previous setting of SAFETY and EXACT, but only if TYPE() verifies that a character type variable that stores the required information exists:

```
if type('safestat') = "C"
   set safety &safestat
endif

if type('exacstat') = "C"
   set exact &exacstat
endif
```

EMPTY() accepts an expression of any data type and returns .T. only if the expression is blank. The meaning of *blank* in this context depends on the data type of the expression. Table 19.8 defines *blank* for each of the data types, treating memo fields as a special form of character data.

Table 19.8 Values That Cause EMPTY() To Return True

Data Type	What FoxPro Considers to be a Blank
Character	Nulls, spaces, tabs, carriage returns, and line feeds
Numeric	0
Date	Null (e.g. { / / })
Logical	False (.F.)
Memo	Empty (no memo contents, including no spaces, carriage returns, or characters of any kind)

FoxPro enables you to pass a variable number of arguments to a procedure or UDF. From within the procedure, you often need to know whether a parameter was passed by the calling program, and, if so, whether it contains a value. The procedure CHIMES, for example, accepts up to five parameters. The pause parameter is optional. Any parameters that were not passed by the calling program are initialized to .F., so you need to know whether pause contains a value passed by the calling program before you try to use it:

```
PROCEDURE chimes
   *
   * ring bell, using different frequencies and durations
```

```
        parameters startfreq, endfreq, freqstep, duration,
        pause
        private j, bellstat

        bellstat = set("bell")
        set bell on

        for j=startfreq to endfreq step freqstep
               set bell to j,duration
               ?? chr(7)
               if !empty(pause)
                      = inkey(pause)
               endif
   endfor

   * restore bell SETtings
   set bell to 512,2
   set bell &bellstat
return
```

If you are familiar with the PARAMETERS() function, you may wonder why it wasn't used instead of EMPTY(). PARAMETERS() returns the number of parameters that were passed to the most recently called procedure, which is not necessarily the current procedure. If, for example, you had called a procedure to display a message in a window before executing the body of CHIMES, PARAMETERS() would thereafter have returned the number of parameters passed to the message-displaying procedure, rather than the CHIMES procedure. If you choose to use PARAMETERS() in your programs, make sure that you save its value to a memory variable at the top of the procedure and use the variable rather than the current value of PARAMETERS().

Manipulating Records

In addition to manipulating single data elements, FoxPro contains commands and functions that move to or search for a particular record and that manipulate a group of records or an entire table. These commands and functions are discussed in this section of the chapter.

Moving to or Locating a Particular Record

Each record in a table has a record number. The number of the current record is returned by the RECNO() function. RECNO() always returns a number between 1 and the number of records in the table (as returned by RECCOUNT()) plus 1. To position the record pointer on a particular record, you use the GOTO command, which is usually abbreviated as GO.

GO often is used in conjunction with RECNO() to reposition the record pointer on a particular record after you have used some other data manipulation command, such as SEEK, that has moved the record pointer to another record, or perhaps to the end of file (EOF) position. Before using any of the record-moving commands, you can save the current record position by storing the current value of RECNO() to a memory variable, as follows:

```
currec = iif(eof(), 0, recno())
```

The EOF() function, which tests for the end of file condition, returns true or .T. if the record pointer is positioned on what is known as the *phantom record*. The phantom record is a blank record beyond the last physical record stored in the table.

When positioned on the phantom record, RECNO() returns the number of records in the table plus 1. If you try to GO to that record, you receive the error message `Record out of range`. Because no record in the table has a record number of 0, you store 0 to the variable *currec* as an indicator that you are currently at EOF. When you later want to reposition the record pointer, you can compare *currec* to 0 to determine whether you were previously at EOF before trying to move the record pointer to a particular record:

```
currec = iif(eof(), 0, recno())
*
* (other commands)
*

* reposition the record pointer on the previously
* current record
if currec > 0
   go currec
else
   * you were previously at end of file, so
   * go back there
   go bottom
```

```
  if !eof()
        skip
  endif
endif
```

If the file contains no records, GO BOTTOM positions the record pointer on the phantom record, from which you cannot SKIP forward. You therefore need to test for EOF after going to the bottom before you skip because you already may be at EOF.

SEEK has always been xBase's searching workhorse. SEEK uses the currently active index to quickly locate the first record that matches the search expression. The search expression *type and format* must match the *type and format* of the index expression. If, for example, the index key *expression* of the current index is UPPER(Lastname), you must use the uppercase form of a search expression to locate the record, as follows:

```
use CUSTOMER order CUSTOMER
* the index key of tag CUSTOMER is upper(Lastname)

@ 10,10 say "Last Name " get m.Lastname ;
  default space(len(Lastname))
read
if empty(m.Lastname)
  RETURN
endif
seek upper(m.Lastname)
if found()
  (commands)
endif
```

The SEEK() function is a powerful combination of the SEEK command and the FOUND() function. Not only does SEEK() return a logical true or false, depending on whether the search expression was found in the current index, it also accepts a work area alias as an optional second argument. SEEK(), therefore, can search an unselected table and position the record pointer in that table on the desired record. That record is then available to all of FoxPro's other table-accessing commands. You could rewrite the previous example as follows:

```
@ 10,10 say "Last Name " get m.Lastname ;
  default space(len(Lastname))
read
if empty(m.Lastname)
  RETURN
endif
if seek(upper(m.Lastname), "CUSTOMER")
  (commands)
endif
```

Where the record pointer is positioned after an unsuccessful search depends on the current setting of NEAR. If NEAR is set ON, the record pointer is positioned on the closest matching record to the search expression. If NEAR is set OFF, the record pointer is positioned at EOF. Regardless of the setting of NEAR, RECNO(0) always returns the record number of the closest matching record after an unsuccessful search. The "closest matching record," in this context, does not mean a near match using an intelligent search, phonetic or otherwise. It simply means the first record with a key that is greater than the expression for which the seek was done.

The LOCATE command hardly ever was used in previous versions of FoxPro or FoxBASE+ because it always required that each record in the table be compared to the search expression. FoxPro 2, however, can use indexes to find LOCATE FOR expressions almost as quickly as it can SEEK search expressions, through its Rushmore technology.

CONTINUE tells FoxPro to find the next record in the table that matches the LOCATE FOR expression. Following is an example that uses LOCATE, CONTINUE, and GO. This example uses LOCATE / CONTINUE to find all the records in the current table that match a search expression. The record number of each matching record is stored in an array; each matching record is copied to a temporary table; the user selects a record from a Browse; and then the record pointer is positioned in the source table on the selected record, using GO. The key to the technique is the fact that the rows of the array correspond to the record numbers in the temporary table:

```
* get the search expression
@ 10,10 say "Last Name " get m.Lastname
read

* if the user pressed Esc or didn't enter a name,
* don't proceed
if lastkey() = 27 or empty(m.Lastname)
  RETURN
endif

* create a temporary table with the same structure
* as the current table
tempdbf = sys(3) + ".$$$"
copy structure to (tempdbf)

* limit the number of matching records and create an
* array with this many elements to hold the record

* numbers
max_recs = 100
```

```
dimension recs_arr[max_recs]
j = 1

* perform the search
locate for Lastname = m.Lastname
if !found()
  RETURN
endif

* copy the matching records to the temporary table
* and store their record numbers in an array
do while found() and j <= max_recs
  recs_arr[j,1] = recno()
  scatter memvar memo
  insert into (tempdbf) from memvar
  j = j + 1
  continue
enddo

* use the space bar to let the user select a record
save_key = on('key', 'space bar')
on key label space bar keyboard chr(23)

* Browse the temporary table
select (tempdbf)
go top

browse ;
  title "Press space bar to select, Esc to cancel" ;
  partition scols()-30 redit lpartition ;
  nomodify noappend nodelete ;
  color scheme 10

* restore the previous state of the space bar
if "" != save_key
  on key label space bar
else
  on key label space bar &save_key
endif

* if the user selected a record, position the record
* pointer in the source table on the selected record
if lastkey() != 27
  mrec = recs_arr[recno()]
  select (searcharea)
  go mrec
endif
```

Creating a Subset of Records

FoxPro provides two methods for viewing a subset of the records in a table. The SET FILTER command compares each record in the current table to a filter expression that you supply, such as State = "CA", and includes a record in the subset only if the expression is true for that record.

The other method is to use INDEX ON...FOR, again supplying a filter expression. Only those records that match the expression will be included in the index, and only the indexed records will be visible as long as the index is controlling the order of the records.

In previous versions of FoxPro and FoxBASE+, the preferred method was to create an index. Although it took some extra time to do this, once the index was in place, subsequent access to the records in the subset was much faster than using a filter, because FoxPro had to constantly evaluate records against the filter condition.

Thanks to its Rushmore technology, however, FoxPro 2 can use existing indexes to evaluate a filter condition, making SET FILTER the preferred method for creating a subset of your data, provided, of course, that you already have created an index that matches your filter condition.

SET FILTER is discussed in Chapter 3, "Exploring Databases and Tables;" INDEX ON is covered in Chapter 4, "Database Management Fundamentals."

Using FoxPro 2's SQL Commands

FoxPro 2 supports four Structured Query Language (SQL) commands that you can use in your programs to replace multiple FoxPro commands. These four commands are shown in table 19.9.

The SELECT command is covered in Chapter 7.

Although SELECT statements can be constructed interactively through the RQBE, SELECT also can be used within a program or from the Command window. It is just another, albeit powerful, FoxPro command. You can use a SELECT command anywhere you can use any other FoxPro command.

Table 19.9 FoxPro's SQL Commands

Command	Description
CREATE CURSOR	Creates a temporary table
CREATE TABLE	Creates a table
INSERT INTO	Appends a record to a table. The table can be open in the current work area, open in another work area, or it can be closed.
SELECT	Retrieves data from one or more tables

CREATE CURSOR and CREATE TABLE can be used to create a table. CREATE CURSOR creates a temporary table that exists until you close it. Unlike a cursor created by a SELECT command, a cursor created by CREATE CURSOR is editable. The table created by CREATE TABLE is permanent.

In previous versions of FoxPro, as well as in FoxBASE+, you had two methods for creating a table. You could use the COPY STRUCTURE TO command to create an empty table with the same structure as the current table, or you could use the COPY TO ... STRUCTURE EXTENDED form of the COPY TO command, followed by CREATE FROM. Both of these methods can still be used in FoxPro 2, but CREATE CURSOR and CREATE TABLE have the advantage of not requiring an existing table from which to create the new table. Furthermore, because the table created by CREATE CURSOR automatically is deleted when it is closed, it relieves you of the housekeeping chores associated with erasing temporary tables created otherwise.

Both commands use the same syntax, as shown in the FoxPro 2 help file:

```
CREATE CURSOR <dbf_name>

  (<fname1 <type> [(<precision>
  [, <scale>])
  [, <fname2> ... ]])
  ¦ FROM ARRAY <array>

CREATE TABLE ¦ DBF <dbf_name>
  (<fname1> <type> [(<precision>
  [, <scale>])
  [, <fname2> ... ]])
  ¦ FROM ARRAY <array>
```

Although the syntax of other commands and functions have not been presented, the syntax for these commands are shown because the terminology used to describe them differs from that of non-SQL commands.

Each field in the table is defined with a name, type, precision, and scale. These terms are equivalent to the field name, field type, field length, and number of decimals columns that you see when you use the CREATE command to create a table interactively. The terms used are different, but the idea is the same, and the resulting table is identical to one that you might have created interactively.

Appendix I contains the listing for a procedure that uses CREATE TABLE to create each of the tables in the Omnipresent Widget database. Please refer to Appendix I for examples of how to use CREATE TABLE. These examples work equally well with CREATE CURSOR.

INSERT INTO performs the same function as APPEND BLANK followed by a REPLACE command, but it doesn't require that the table be open in the current work area, or be open in any work area, for that matter. If the table is not currently open, INSERT INTO will open it in the next available work area. INSERT INTO never changes the current work area. Its syntax has two forms:

```
INSERT INTO <dbf_name>
  [(<fname1> [, <fname2>
        [, ...]])]
  VALUES (<expr1> [, <expr2>
        [, ...]])

INSERT INTO <dbf_name>
  FROM ARRAY <array> ¦ FROM MEMVAR
```

Because INSERT INTO performs an implicit REPLACE, you have to supply at least one value if you use the first form of the command. The replacements are made in the order that the fields appear in the table unless you specify the optional list of related field names, one per value in the VALUES list.

Note that, like CREATE TABLE and CREATE CURSOR, the field names and values lists must be enclosed within parentheses, even if the list contains only a single item.

The second form of INSERT INTO works like APPEND BLANK followed by either GATHER FROM `<array name>` or GATHER MEMVAR.

SQL commands are not always appropriate for the task at hand, but when they are, they perform their functions elegantly and with a minimum amount of programming.

Chapter Summary

FoxPro 2 contains a dizzying number of commands and functions. This chapter introduced you to some that help you manipulate your data into different forms. You learned how to search strings and memo fields, add and delete spaces in strings, convert one data type to another, and display dates as text in reports.

You also learned about FoxPro's record-positioning commands. The chapter briefly discussed the SQL commands that you can use to create a table or append a record to a table.

In the next chapter, you learn about the commands and functions that help you manage all kinds of files and how to use FoxPro 2's powerful new array-handling functions.

20

CHAPTER

Using Arrays and the Low-Level File Functions

FoxPro's primary data structure is the table. Storing data in a table has many benefits, among them the ability to create an index, which provides almost immediate access to any record in the table, and the capability to relate one table to any number of other tables.

An array is a type of data structure different from a table, although an array can be manipulated in some of the same ways, and, like a table, can be conceptualized as a collection of rows and columns. You already have seen some of the ways in which arrays can be used in FoxPro 2. In this chapter, you examine arrays in more depth and learn the array-handling commands and functions that FoxPro 2 provides.

This chapter also covers FoxPro's low-level file functions, which give you direct access to files and which are comparable to the file manipulation functions of general-purpose programming languages, such as C.

Using Arrays

An array usually is used to store and manipulate data that you don't need to save from one database management session to the next. A temporary table would serve the same purpose, but arrays have several advantages over tables. Some of these are as follows:

- Arrays can hold any type of data, so they're more flexible than a table, which has a fixed structure.
- Arrays are stored entirely in the computer's random access memory, access to which is much faster than to a hard disk.
- Arrays can be sorted "in place" and do not require extra disk space to perform the sort.

In this section of the chapter, you learn how to create an array, refer to the array's elements, and use FoxPro's array-handling functions to manipulate arrays. You also learn a few ways you can get into trouble when using arrays, so pay attention!

Creating Arrays

Like memory variables, arrays can be either public or private. A public array is created using the PUBLIC command; a private array is created using the DIMENSION/DECLARE or SCATTER TO command.

Following are a few examples:

```
DIMENSION array1(20), array2[10,2]
DECLARE array1[20], array2(10,2)
PUBLIC array1[20], array2[10,2]
SCATTER TO array1
```

Although DIMENSION and DECLARE are separate commands, they work exactly the same way. This chapter discusses only DIMENSION, but everything applies equally to DECLARE.

SCATTER TO can create only a single array at a time. The other commands can accept a list of arrays. You can have a maximum of 3,600 arrays in memory, unless you are using the Extended version of FoxPro 2, which can hold up to 65,000 arrays. (Of course, most computers do not have enough memory to store 3,600 arrays, even if you could find a reason to create that many.) Each array can have up to the same number (3,600 or 65,000) of elements.

SCATTER also can create memory variables instead of an array. The syntax for each form of the command can be somewhat confusing. In short, if you use SCATTER TO, you create an array. If you use SCATTER MEMVAR, you create memory variables. If you use SCATTER TO MEMVAR, you create an array called "memvar" when you obviously intend to create memory variables.

The array subscripts (20 and 10,2 in the example) must be enclosed in either parentheses or square brackets. Either is acceptable, as long as you don't mix them (array2(10,2], for example, is illegal).

You also can create an array using three of FoxPro's array-handling functions. These functions are shown in table 20.1, along with the commands that create arrays.

Table 20.1 Commands and Functions That Create Arrays

Command/Function	Description
ACOPY()	Copies one or more elements from one array to another, creating the target array if it doesn't exist
ADIR()	Places directory information into an array, creating it if it doesn't exist
AFIELDS()	Places table structure information into an array, creating it if it doesn't exist
DECLARE	Same as DIMENSION
DIMENSION	Creates a one- or two-dimensional array of specified dimensions
PUBLIC [ARRAY]	Creates a public array of specified dimensions
SCATTER TO	Creates an array containing the values of the fields in the current table

ACOPY() copies the contents of one array to another. If the target array does not exist, it is created with the same dimensions as the source array and is an exact duplicate of it. ACOPY() will not redimension an existing array, however. If you try to copy more elements from the source array than an existing target array can hold, those elements that fit are copied, and then you'll receive a `Subscript out of bounds` error message.

Suppose that you have an array that holds some customer names. You want to present the customer names in a list that's sorted alphabetically, but you don't want to change the original order of the names. You can create a copy of the array with ACOPY(), sort the copy array, and use the copy as the source for the @ ... GET FROM <array> command, as follows:

```
= acopy(names_arr, temp_arr)
= asort(temp_arr)
@ 10,10 get mchoice ;
from temp_arr ;
size 20,40 ;
default 1
read
```

The ASORT() function is discussed later in this chapter.

ACOPY() has three optional arguments, all numeric, which enable you specify the first element to be copied, the number of elements to be copied, and the number of the element in the target array where the copying will begin. ACOPY() returns the number of elements that were copied.

ADIR() stores information about a DOS directory in an array. Like ACOPY(), ADIR() creates the array if it doesn't exist, but, unlike ACOPY(), ADIR() redimensions an existing array to the exact size required to hold the information. The information stored is that which DOS displays when you enter DIR at the DOS prompt (file name, file size, the date and time of the last update, and the file's attributes). You can supply a file skeleton to restrict the list to certain files or access a directory other than the current one, and you can expand the list to include hidden files, system files and subdirectories, or store only the volume label for a drive.

The following procedure, SUBDIRS, creates an array containing the names of all subdirectories below the current default directory. This procedure uses ADIR() with the "D" code as the third argument, which expands the file list to include subdirectories:

```
* SUBDIRS.PRG
* procedure to find all subdirs of any drive/dir

* call:
* dime my_array(1,1)
* DO subdirs WITH my_array
* to find out about current default
* or DO subdirs WITH my_array, somepath

PARAMETERS subdir, mpath

IF PARAMETERS() = 1
    oldpath = ""
    drivepath = ""
    * you're finding out about current default directory
```

```
ELSE
   IF  TYPE("mpath") # "C"
      WAIT WINDOW "Invalid path specified!"
      * or RELEASE the array or do whatever you want--
      * Without releasing, you could check for
      * TYPE("my_array(1,1)") = "N" to indicate
      * various error conditions; stuff it with 0 for
      * no subdirs, -1 for invalid path, whatever
      RETURN
   ENDIF
   IF RIGHT(mpath,1) = "\" OR RIGHT(mpath,1) = ":"
      checkpath = mpath + "nul"
   ELSE
      checkpath = mpath + "\nul"
   ENDIF
   IF ! FILE(checkpath)
      WAIT WINDOW "Invalid path specified!"
      * see above note about RETURN
      RETURN
   ENDIF
   oldpath = SET("DEFAULT",1)+SYS(2003)
   IF RIGHT(mpath,1) = ":" OR AT(":",mpath) = 0
      SET DEFAULT TO (mpath)
      drivepath = ""
   ELSE
      SET DEFAULT TO (LEFT(mpath,1))
      drivepath = SYS(2003)
      SET DEFAULT TO (mpath)
   ENDIF
ENDIF

ndirs = ADIR(subdir,"","D")

* sort them in ascending order by the 1st column
* (file names) so . & .. come *first* if they exist
= ASORT(subdir,1,ndirs,0)
ndels = 0

IF ndirs # 0
   FOR xx = 1 TO 2
      * there can only be two of these
      IF subdir(1,1) = "."
         * EXACT should be OFF for this to work
         * this is a DOS entry for upper directories
         ndels = ndels + 1
         = ADEL(subdir,1)
         * this row should now be moved to the end of the
         array
      ENDIF
```

```
        ENDFOR
        ndirs = ndirs - ndels
        IF ndirs # 0
           DIME subdir(ndirs,5)
           * get rid of "." entries
        ENDIF
    ENDIF

    IF ndirs = 0
        WAIT WINDOW "No subdirectories!"
        * see above note about RETURN
    ENDIF

    IF ! EMPTY(drivepath)
        SET DEFAULT TO (drivepath)
        * set default directory back for this drive
    ENDIF

    IF ! EMPTY(oldpath)
        SET DEFAULT TO (oldpath)
    ENDIF

    RETURN
```

AFIELDS() stores information about the structure of the current table. The information stored is that required to create a table (field names, field types, field lengths, and the number of decimals for numeric fields). You can use AFIELDS() together with the CREATE TABLE FROM ARRAY command to replace the combination of COPY TO `<file>` STRUCTURE EXTENDED and CREATE FROM commands that you had to use in previous versions of FoxPro to programmatically create a table:

```
temp_table = sys(3) + ".$$$"
do copytabl with temp_table
* when copytable returns, the new table is open in a
* previously unopen work area, and that work area is
* now selected
PROCEDURE copytabl
*
* create a copy of the current table in table_name*
parameters table_name
private struc_info
* create the array that holds the file
* structure information
= afields(struc_info)
* create the table
create table (table_name) ;
from array struc_info
return
```

Many of FoxPro's array-handling commands and functions, such as ACOPY(), create an array if it does not already exist. The *Commands and Functions* manuals that were shipped with early releases of FoxPro are often inaccurate when they say that the array must already exist. The *Late Breaking News* booklet contains information about enhancements of this kind that were made to the product after the manuals were printed.

The SET COMPATIBLE command is very important in determining how certain array commands and functions will work. Although FoxPro always initializes array elements to the logical value .F., for example, if COMPATIBLE is set to OFF or FOXPLUS (the default setting, OFF and FOXPLUS being equivalent), you can initialize an entire array to a particular value simply by assigning the value to the array name, as follows:

```
dimension the_array[3,2]
the_array = "Hello world!"
display memory like the_array
* the following is displayed on the screen
THE_ARRAY       Pub    A
(   1,    1)     C  "Hello world!"
(   1,    2)     C  "Hello world!"
(   2,    1)     C  "Hello world!"
(   2,    2)     C  "Hello world!"
(   3,    1)     C  "Hello world!"
(   3,    2)     C  "Hello world!"
```

If you execute these same commands with COMPATIBLE set to ON or DB4, DISPLAY MEMORY shows the following:

```
THE_ARRAY   Pub    C  "Hello world!"
```

As you can see, the assignment statement replaced the_array with a variable by the same name. Therefore, you can initialize an array with a single assignment statement only if COMPATIBLE is set to OFF or FOXPLUS.

The setting of COMPATIBLE also is important when redimensioning an array or using an array function that might redimension an array. When COMPATIBLE is off, you can redimension an array without losing the data that the array contains. When COMPATIBLE is on, the array can still be redimensioned, but the array elements will be reinitialized to .F., thereby destroying any data stored in the array.

CAUTION: The ability to redimension an existing array is new in FoxPro 2. If you have written procedures that depend on arrays maintaining their original size in FoxPro 1.02, you have to revise your programs to account for this behavior.

Referring to Array Elements

To use arrays effectively, you must be able to conceptualize their appearance. The manner in which FoxPro actually stores an array in memory is of little importance. What is important is the way in which you must refer to a particular array element.

Think of an array as a temporary table that is stored in memory instead of on a disk. Just like tables, arrays have one or more rows and columns. As with an @ ... SAY/GET command, the row is referenced before the column. So, if you use the DIMENSION command to create a two-dimensional array as follows:

```
dimension the_array[5,2]
```

FoxPro creates an array consisting of five rows and two columns that looks like this:

	Col 1	Col 2
Row 1	1,1	1,2
Row 2	2,1	2,2
Row 3	3,1	3,2
Row 4	4,1	4,2
Row 5	5,1	5,2

If you type **DISPLAY MEMORY LIKE the_array** in the Command window, you see that FoxPro considers the_array to be a list of 10 data elements, all of which belong to the_array, as follows:

```
THE_ARRAY      Pub   A
( 1,  1)       L     .F.
( 1,  2)       L     .F.
( 2,  1)       L     .F.
( 2,  2)       L     .F.
( 3,  1)       L     .F.
( 3,  2)       L     .F.
( 4,  1)       L     .F.
```

```
( 4, 2)      L      .F.
( 5, 1)      L      .F.
( 5, 2)      L      .F.
```

Because you defined the array as two-dimensional, by supplying a second argument in DIMENSION, FoxPro gives you the alternative of referring to an array element by its row and column coordinates. However, you also can refer to an element by its element number, which is the same as its order in the list previously displayed. So, for example, you could refer to the sixth element in the list as either the_array[3,2] or as the_array[6].

You may assume that a one-dimensional array consists of the specified number of rows and a single column. In fact, it is just the opposite. The array will have one row that has the specified number of columns. This difference becomes important when using an array with the COPY TO ARRAY or APPEND FROM ARRAY commands. If, for example, you type **DIMENSION the_array[RECCOUNT( )]** in the Command window, the_array looks like this:

1	2	3	...	n

where *n* stands for the number of records in the table, and ... represents all the array elements between 3 and *n*.

If you use this array in a COPY TO ARRAY command, only one record will be copied, because the array has only one row.

Think of DIMENSION(*x*) as the same as DIMENSION(1,*x*), which creates an array of one row and *x* columns. To create an array of *x* rows and one column, use DIMENSION(*x*,1). In the previous example, you would have used **DIMENSION(RECCOUNT( ),1)**.

Table 20.2 shows several functions that enable you to refer to an array element indirectly, that is, without knowing the element number.

All of the array-handling functions take an array name as their first argument. You can refer to the array as either a variable name (AELEMENT(the_array,5,2)) or as a string literal (AELEMENT("the_array",5,2)).

AELEMENT() takes two additional numeric arguments, representing the row and column subscripts of the desired element number, and returns the number of the element that corresponds to the row and column subscripts. (Actually, the second numeric argument is optional, but because AELEMENT(<array>,*x*) always returns *x*, it's hard to imagine what you would use this for.)

Table 20.2 Functions that Let You Indirectly Reference an Array Element

Function	Description
AELEMENT()	Returns the number of an element in an array. Used to convert from two-dimensional subscripts to an element number for use in functions that take an element number as an optional argument, such as ACOPY(), ASCAN(), and ASORT.
ALEN()	Returns the number of elements, rows, or columns in an array. By default, returns the number of elements. Use a code, 1 or 2, as the optional second argument to return the number of rows or the number of columns, respectively.
ASCAN()	Returns the number of the element where a specified expression was found, or 0 if it was not found.
ASUBSCRIPT()	Given an element number and a code (1 or 2), returns either the row or the column subscript of the element.

The following example function returns an element at or near the midpoint of an array:

```
PARAMETERS a_rows, a_cols
DIMENSION the_array[a_rows,a_cols]
the_center = AELEMENT(the_array,a_rows/2,a_cols/2)
RETURN the_center
```

ALEN() returns the number of elements, rows, or columns in an array. Its most obvious use is as a RECCOUNT() function for arrays. If, for example, you use the SQL SELECT command and output the selected records to an array, you can use ALEN() to determine how many records were selected, as follows:

```
select * from customer into array cust_arr ;
where state = "CA"
CA_custs = alen(cust_arr,1)
```

ASCAN() locates an expression in an array. ASCAN() returns the number of the first element in the array that contains the expression. If the expression was not found, ASCAN() returns 0.

ASUBSCRIPT() converts an element number into its two-dimensional subscript form and then returns either the row or column component of the subscript. To get the row number, use “1" as the third argument and to get the column number, use “2.”

Chapter 13 presents an example that uses ASCAN() and ASUBSCRIPT() to initialize a variable, *m.dept*, with the row number of an array, deptarray, in which a particular department code, m.deptcode, was located. The following is that code fragment:

```
* get m.dept from the row number of the array
* deptarray in which m.deptcode can be found:

m.dept  =  iif(empty(m.deptcode),                ;
                 0,                              ;
                 asubscript(deptarray,           ;
                            ascan(deptarray,     ;
                                  m.deptcode),   ;
                            1))
```

If m.deptcode contains a value (is not EMPTY()), you use ASUBSCRIPT() to provide the row in the array where the value of m.deptcode was found. The row number is returned because "1" was used as the third argument to the function. ASCAN() returns the number of the element in deptarray where m.deptcode was found and provides the remaining piece of information that ASUBSCRIPT() requires.

Manipulating Arrays

Although arrays were very useful in FoxPro 1 and FoxBASE+, manipulating them often required you to write a series of array-handling UDF's. Many applications, for example, included a UDF that applied a sorting algorithm, such as Quicksort, to an array to keep its elements in alphabetical or numeric order. Because you couldn't pass an entire array to a UDF, you had to either "hard-code" the array name into the UDF, in which case it couldn't be used as a generic sorting routine, or pass the array's name to the UDF, and use macro substitution to access the array elements. Sorting a large array could really slow down your program.

FoxPro 2 includes several new functions that enable you to sort arrays and insert and delete array elements, rows, and columns. These functions are listed in table 20.3.

AINS() inserts an element into a one-dimensional array and inserts a row or column into a two-dimensional array. AINS() is like an INSERT BEFORE command for arrays. The insertion takes place at the specified position. The current contents of the array at that position are pushed down or, in the case of a column insertion, pushed to the right.

The inserted element(s) are always initialized to .F.. If you want to add information to the array at the point of insertion, you must do that as a separate step. Because it seems likely that most people will want to do this, this chapter presents a procedure, ADD2ARR, to do it for you.

Table 20.3 Functions That Sort Arrays and Insert and Delete Elements, Rows, and Columns

Function	Description
ASORT()	Sorts an array in either ascending (the default) or descending order. Two-dimensional arrays are sorted by row, using a specified element to indicate the column that controls the sort order.
AINS()	Inserts an element into a one-dimensional array, and a row or a column into a two-dimensional array. The trailing elements move toward the bottom of the array, and the last element, row, or column is dropped from the array.
ADEL()	Deletes an element from a one-dimensional array and deletes a row or column from a two-dimensional array. The following elements move toward the top of the array, and the last element, row, or column is reinitialized to .F..

Procedure ADD2ARR takes three arguments: the array in which the insertion is to be made, a one-dimensional array that holds the data to be inserted, and the row number at which the insertion is to be made. Of course, you must create the one-dimensional array before calling ADD2ARR. If the information to be added to the array is the contents of the current record in a table, you could do this easily with SCATTER TO <array>. Because you need access to the contents of more than a single array element, the arrays must be passed by reference (see "Passing Arrays to Procedures and UDF's" for a discussion of passing arrays). Procedure ADD2ARR is as follows:

```
PROCEDURE add2arr
*
* add an element or row (if targ_arr is two-dimensional)
* to array targ_arr, insert a blank element or row at
* row_num, then store the contents of src_arr to the
* new element or row
*
parameters targ_arr, src_arr, row_num
private a_rows, a_cols, j

* Determine the number of rows and columns in the
* targ_arr array.
*
* If targ_arr is one-dimensional, a_rows will be the
* number of elements, and a_cols will be 0.
* If targ_arr is two-dimensional, a_rows will be the
* number of rows, and a_cols will be the number of
* columns.
```

```
a_rows = alen(targ_arr,1)
a_cols = alen(targ_arr,2)

if a_cols > 0        && if array is two-dimensional
        * add a row to the array
        dimension targ_arr[a_rows+1,a_cols]
        * insert the new row
        =ains[targ_arr, row_num]

        * store the contents of src_arr to the new row
        for j=1 to a_cols
            targ_arr[row_num,j] = src_arr[j]
        endfor

else
        * add an element to the array
        dimension targ_arr[a_rows+1]
        * insert the new element
        =ains[targ_arr, row_num]

        * store the contents of src_arr to the new element
        targ_arr[row_num] = src_arr[1]
endif
return
```

Note that the call to AINS() is the same, whether targ_arr is one- or two-dimensional. AINS() automatically treats the second argument as a row number if the array is two-dimensional.

ASORT() sorts an array in either ascending or descending order. You can specify a position (an element or a row) at which to start the sort and the number of elements or rows to be sorted. The way in which FoxPro interprets the numbers you use for the second and third arguments depends on whether the array is one- or two-dimensional. The rules can be confusing. Tables 20.4 and 20.5 illustrate the differences with some examples. Array arr1 is one-dimensional, and arr2 is two-dimensional.

Table 20.4 Using ASORT() with One-Dimensional Arrays

Example	Description
ASORT(arr1)	Sorts the entire array, beginning with the first element
ASORT(arr1,5)	Sorts the remainder of the array, beginning with the fifth element

continues

Table 20.4 Continued

Example	Description
ASORT(arr1,5,3)	Sorts three elements, beginning with the fifth element
ASORT(arr1,1,–1,1)	Sorts the entire array in descending order. The –1 is a code indicating that you don't want to limit the sort to a particular number of elements.
ASORT(arr1,5,0,1)	Sorts the remainder of the array, beginning with the fifth element, in descending order. Although not documented, 0 seems to be equivalent to –1.

Table 20.5 Using ASORT() with Two-Dimensional Arrays

Example	Description
ASORT(arr2)	Sorts the entire array using the contents of the first column as the sort criterion. The values of the other columns are not taken into account in the sorting process.
ASORT(arr2,5)	Sorts the remainder of the array, beginning with the row that contains the fifth element, using the contents of the column that contains the fifth element as the sort criterion
ASORT(arr2,5,3)	Same as ASORT(arr2,5), but only three rows are sorted
ASORT(arr2,1,-1,1)	Sorts the entire array in descending order using the contents of the first column as the sort criterion. The –1 is a code indicating that you don't want to limit the sort to a particular number of rows.
ASORT(arr2,5,0,1)	Sorts the remainder of the array, beginning with the row that contains the fifth element, in descending order

Copying Arrays to Tables and Tables to Arrays

FoxPro 2 has commands that enable you to move records from a table into an array and from an array into a table. The command COPY TO ARRAY copies records in a table to rows and columns in an array.

APPEND FROM ARRAY adds rows and columns in an array as new records in a table.

COPY TO ARRAY copies records from the current table to an array. If the array does not exist, it is created. An existing array is not redimensioned. If the preexisting array has fewer elements than the records that meet the optional `<scope>`, FOR, or WHILE clause (ALL is the default), the records that don't fit are not copied. You can limit the fields to be copied by including the optional FIELDS list.

APPEND FROM ARRAY appends new records to the current table, filling the fields with the related column values in the order in which they exist in the array. You can use the FIELDS clause to provide a list of fields. The first field in the list receives the values from the first array column, the second field from the second column, and so forth. One record is appended for each array element (or row, in the case of a two-dimensional array).

Remember, if you specify a single field (such as COMPANY in the following example) in the COPY TO ARRAY command, FoxPro will create a one-dimensional array unless the array already exists. When you later use APPEND FROM ARRAY to add multiple records to the table, you will be surprised to find that only one record has been added!

Unless you are sure that FoxPro will create a two-dimensional array, you should create the array yourself with a command such as **DIMENSION the_array[RECCOUNT( ),1]**.

Following is an example that uses both COPY TO ARRAY and APPEND FROM ARRAY. In a data entry routine, suppose that you want to let the user add as many records as wanted, without having to confirm the addition after each one. When all of the new records have been added to the array, you want to prompt the user to confirm that all should be added. You could use a temporary table for this purpose, or you could use an array, as follows:

```
* open the CUSTOMER table in COMPANY order
* use CUSTOMER order COMPANY

* create the array; since you are only copying one
* field, you can't let FoxPro create the array "on
* the fly", because it will create a one-dimensional
* array, which will only append *one* record when you
* later use APPEND FROM ARRAY
dimension comp_list[reccount(),1]

* copy each company name to an array
copy to array comp_list fields COMPANY
```

```
* save the current number of companies, you'll
* need this later; in this case, you can use either
* alen() or reccount()
curr_tot = alen(comp_list)

* suppress the "Invalid input" message that would
* otherwise be displayed when updlist() returns .f.
set notify off

* get the company names that the user wants to add;
* precede the array name with the "@" symbol to
* ensure that the entire array is passed to updlist()
@ 10,10 say "New customer " get m.company ;
   default " " ;
   valid updlist(@comp_list, m.company)
read

set notify on

if alen(comp_list) > curr_tot   && at least 1 record added
   mchoice = "X"
   do while ! upper(mchoice) $ "YN"
      wait window "Add these new customers to the "+ ;
                  "Customers table? (Y/N)" to mchoice
   enddo
   if upper(mchoice) = "Y"
      * create an array that contains only the
      * new records
      = acopy(comp_list, updates, curr_tot+1)

      * append the new records to the table
      append from array updates
   endif
endif

FUNCTION updlist
   *
   * Search arr_list for mname. If not found,
   * add it to arr_list and re-sort the array.
   *
   parameters arr_list, mname

   if ascan(arr_list, mname) = 0
      * mname not in list, add it
      wait window "Adding new item to list..." nowait
      dimension arr_list[alen(arr_list)+1]
      arr_list[alen(arr_list)] = mname
      wait clear
```

```
    else
       ?? chr(7)    && ring bell to get the user's attention
       wait window "That item is already on the list." ;
                   timeout 2
    endif
return .f.
```

Passing Arrays to Procedures and UDF's

Previous versions of FoxPro and FoxBASE+ allowed you to pass an array element to a procedure or UDF, but you couldn't pass the entire array. If you needed to use more than a single element of an array in a UDF, you had to pass the name of the array and then use macro substitution to reference the individual array elements.

In FoxPro 2, an entire array may now be passed to a procedure or UDF. To do this, you pass the array by reference, as opposed to by value. If you use the calling format:

```
do <procedure> with <array name>
```

the array is passed by reference unless you enclose the array name in parentheses. If you use the calling format:

```
= <user defined function>(<parameter list>)
```

then, whether the array is passed by value or by reference depends on the current setting of UDFPARMS.

If UDFPARMS is set to REFERENCE, the entire array is passed. If UDFPARMS is set to VALUE, only the first element of the array is passed, and it is passed by value. You can override the UDFPARMS setting by prefacing the array name with the "@" symbol to pass the array by reference or by enclosing the array name in parentheses to pass it by value.

Individual elements of an array are always passed by value. See Chapter 16 for more information on parameter passing rules.

When you pass arrays between programs in a FoxPro 2 project, you also must tell the Project Manager where the arrays are declared to avoid `unresolved reference` warnings when you build your application. Although you safely can tell the Project Manager to ignore these errors when you are certain that you have defined your arrays correctly, see Chapter 14 for a discussion of how to use the EXTERNAL ARRAY statement to avoid the annoyance.

Understanding Some Limitations of Arrays

Arrays are very powerful tools in your database management arsenal, but they do have some limitations that you should keep in mind. The most important of them is that arrays consume precious amounts of RAM (random access memory). The more memory you use to hold arrays, the less you have available for storing other memory variables and for creating windows.

Even if you are currently using very little RAM for other purposes, you may not have enough available memory to store an entire table in an array. Because tables grow in size as users add records to them, the COPY TO `<array>` command that worked just find while you were testing the application may one day "blow up" your program because of insufficient memory to hold the current number of records in the table.

In general, if the size of an array may exceed the amount of RAM available to store it, you are probably better off using a temporary table instead of an array.

Using the Low-Level File Functions

FoxPro 2 provides 12 low-level file functions (LLFF's) that enable you to read from and write to any type of file or communications port (such as COM1). The LLFF's provide much of the same file access functionality as is provided in general-purpose programming languages, such as C and Pascal. These functions are listed in table 20.6.

Table 20.6 FoxPro 2's Low-Level File Functions

Function	Description
FCHSIZE()	Changes the size of a file that was opened with FOPEN() or created with FCREATE(). Returns the new size of the file in bytes, unless FCHSIZE() was unable to change the file's size, in which case it returns –1.
FCLOSE()	Closes a file or communications port after first *flushing* the file to disk. Returns .T. if the file was closed, .F. if it could not be closed.

Function	Description
	FoxPro uses a technique known as *buffering* to speed access to portions of a file in use. When a file is closed, flushing it saves any modifications that have been made to the actual version of the file residing on disk. In situations where it is crucial to write any change to disk immediately, you can open the file unbuffered. When you open a communications port rather than a file, the part should always be opened unbuffered.
FCREATE()	Creates and opens a file. Returns the file handle number that all other functions must use to access the file.
FEOF()	Determines whether the file pointer is currently at the end of a file. If so, it returns .T.; otherwise it returns .F..
FERROR()	Returns an error status code indicating the error condition of the previous low-level file function. If the last function did not cause an error, 0 is returned.
FFLUSH()	Flushes to disk the contents of a file opened with a low-level file function and releases the memory used by the file's I/O buffer. See FCLOSE().
FGETS()	Returns a specified number of bytes from a file or communications port, unless a carriage return character is encountered within the specified number of bytes, in which case it returns the characters between the starting file pointer position and the carriage return.
FOPEN()	Opens a file and returns a file handle that the other low-level file functions must use to access the file. FOPEN() accepts a code that specifies the file's read/write privileges and file I/O buffering type (buffered or unbuffered). See FCLOSE() for notes on buffering a file.
FPUTS()	Writes a character string to a file or communications port and adds carriage return and line feed characters to the end of the string.
FREAD()	Similar to FGETS() but does not stop reading the file when a carriage return is encountered
FSEEK()	Moves the file pointer a specified number of bytes from either the current file pointer position, the beginning of the file, or the end of the file. Returns the new file pointer position with respect to the beginning of the file.
FWRITE()	Similar to FPUTS() but does not write a carriage return and line feed at the end of the string. Returns the number of bytes written.

Files are either created with FCREATE() or opened with FOPEN(). Both of these functions return a numeric file handle, which you store to a memory variable for use with the other LLFF's. (LLFF's require that you specify the file handle as their first argument.) The file handle tells the function which file you want to access.

If the file cannot be created or opened, both FCREATE() and FOPEN() return the numeric value –1. Your applications should always verify that the returned value is greater than zero before proceeding.

Files are opened and created with certain specified file attributes. For example, a file can be opened as read only or read/write. If a file is opened as read only, which is the default, you cannot write to the file. On the other hand, files that you create with FCREATE() are read/write by default.

The best way to explain the LLFF's is by example. The remainder of this chapter contains several examples of some useful ways in which you can use these functions to read and write files.

The following is an installation program for an application that you supply on a disk. INSTALL.PRG creates a batch file that runs the application, copies each of the files that are listed in FILES.LST file on the disk, checks the FILES= setting in the user's CONFIG.SYS file, and changes CONFIG.SYS if it is too low (and if the user permits the change).

```
* INSTALL.PRG
* uses low-level file functions to write batch files
* and edit CONFIG.SYS —
* Note that this method does not take into account
* MEMORY MANAGERS such as Quarterdeck's QEMM
* that put FILES or BUFFERS management information
* into your AUTOEXEC.BAT. But the user is given
* an opportunity to refuse the CONFIG.SYS edit,
* so s/he can make the changes in an appropriate
* manner on his or her system.

CLEAR
SET ESCAPE OFF
SET TALK OFF
SET SAFETY OFF
SET SCOREBOARD OFF
SET STATUS OFF
SET CONFIRM ON
SET ECHO OFF
SET SYSMENU OFF
SET CONFIRM OFF
bdrive = "c:"
idrive = "a:"
```

```
* drives verified with the user in the full program
DEFINE WINDOW install FROM 5,10 TO 19,70 ;
   COLOR SCHEME 1 SHADOW ;
   TITLE " Welcome to the ABC Installation Program "
WAIT WINDOW NOWAIT ;
   "Creating batch file to start ABC program... "
IF FILE("ABC.BAT")
   ERASE ABC.BAT
   * in full program, ask for a new batch file name
ENDIF
fhandle = FCREATE("ABC.BAT")
= FPUTS(fhandle,"ECHO OFF")
= FPUTS(fhandle,"CLS")
= FPUTS(fhandle,SET("DEFAULT"))
= FPUTS(fhandle,"CD"+SYS(2003))
= FPUTS(fhandle,"foxr -t abcmain")
= FCLOSE(fhandle)
* create similar files if necessary to
* run the setup and initialization programs from DOS
* the last line above works for APP files;
* alter appropriately for executables
ACTIVATE WINDOW install
@ 1,2 SAY "A file called ABC.BAT has been created in your"
@ 2,2 SAY "program directory."
@ 4,2 SAY "You can rename this file to anything with a "
@ 5,2 SAY "BAT extension, and copy it to any directory"
@ 6,2 SAY "on your path. "
@ 8,2 SAY "Then type the file's NAME (currently ABC), and"
@ 9,2 SAY "press the ENTER key to start the ABC Program."
WAIT WINDOW

* in full program, check to see if data files already exist
* and if so check if okay to overwrite or get new datapath
okay =  .T.
datapath = ""
IF okay
   WAIT WINDOW NOWAIT "Installing new data files... "

   fhandle = FOPEN(idrive+"files.lst")
   * files.lst should be supplied on installation disk
   * with all files that need to be copied to the target disk
   * — files.lst can be created using the FLS.EXE utility
   * found in \goodies\misc on your application's
   * directory, or you can USE the application's PJX file and
   * use the low-level file functions to create files.lst
   * from the records in the project. In the second method,
   * don't forget to add their relevant memo files!
```

```
    DO WHILE !FEOF(fhandle)
       thisfile = FGETS(fhandle)
       COPY FILE (idrive+thisfile) TO (datapath+thisfile)
    ENDDO
    = FCLOSE(fhandle)
    WAIT CLEAR

ENDIF

* now check CONFIG.SYS file
cfgfile = bdrive+"\CONFIG.SYS"
chg_cfg = .F.
needfiles = 70
IF FILE(cfgfile)
    IF  val(sys(2010)) < needfiles
       CLEAR
       @ 1,2 SAY "This file:  "+cfgfile+;
                 ", which already exists, must"
       @ 2,2 SAY "contain certain settings "+ ;
                 "to run this program:  "
       @ 3,2 SAY "          FILES = "+ALLTRIM(STR(needfiles))
       @ 4,2 SAY "          BUFFERS = 20"
       @ 5,2 SAY "Your current CONFIG.SYS file contains "+ ;
                 "a FILES"
       @ 6,2 SAY "statement with too low a setting. "
       @ 8,2 SAY "Press <Y> to have this file altered for you;"
       @ 9,2 SAY "otherwise you can edit it yourself:  " ;
                GET chg_cfg PICTURE "Y"
       READ
       IF chg_cfg
          WAIT WINDOW NOWAIT ;
            "Renaming your "+cfgfile+;
            "to "+bdrive+"\EXCONFIG.SYS and rewriting... "
          COPY FILE (cfgfile) TO (bdrive+"\EXCONFIG.SYS")
          ERASE (cfgfile)
          fhandle = FOPEN(bdrive+"\EXCONFIG.SYS")
          csize = FSEEK(fhandle,0,2)
          = FSEEK(fhandle,0)
          cnewfile = FCREATE(cfgfile)
          ctext = FREAD(fhandle,csize)
          filespos = ATCLINE("files",ctext)
          IF filespos = 0
            ctext = "FILES = "+ALLTRIM(STR(needfiles))+;
                 CHR(13)+CHR(10)+ctext
          ELSE
            cline = MLINE(ctext,filespos)
            ctext = STRTRAN(ctext,cline, ;
                        "FILES = "+ALLTRIM(STR(needfiles)))
```

```
        ENDIF
        buffpos = ATCLINE("buffers",ctext)
        IF buffpos = 0
          ctext = "BUFFERS = 20"+CHR(13)+CHR(10)+ctext
        ELSE
          cline = MLINE(ctext,buffpos)
          ctext = STRTRAN(ctext,cline,"BUFFERS = 20")
        ENDIF
        = FWRITE(cnewfile,ctext)
        = FCLOSE(fhandle)
        = FCLOSE(cnewfile)
        CLEAR
        @ 5,2 SAY "Please REBOOT or RE-SET your system "
        @ 6,2 SAY "before starting to run the "
        @ 7,2 SAY "ABC program, since your CONFIG.SYS "
        @ 8,2 SAY "has been changed."
      ELSE
        @ 8,2 CLEAR
        @ 9,2 SAY  "Make sure you set your FILES "+ ;
                   "and BUFFERS at least"
        @ 10,2 SAY "this high before running "+ ;
                   "the ABC Program."
      ENDIF
      WAIT WINDOW
    ENDIF
ELSE
    WAIT WINDOW NOWAIT "Creating CONFIG.SYS file... "
    fhandle = FCREATE(cfgfile)
    = FPUTS(fhandle,"FILES = "+ALLTRIM(STR(needfiles)))
    = FPUTS(fhandle,"BUFFERS = 20")
    = FCLOSE(fhandle)
    CLEAR
    @ 1,2 SAY "A file called "+cfgfile+" has been added to"
    @ 2,2 SAY "the root directory of your boot drive."
    @ 3,2 SAY "It contains the following lines:"
    @ 4,2 SAY "        FILES = "+ALLTRIM(STR(needfiles))
    @ 5,2 SAY "        BUFFERS = 20"
    @ 7,2 SAY "If you need to change your CONFIG.SYS file for"
    @ 8,2 SAY "the needs of other programs, please do not "
    @ 9,2 SAY "erase these lines or lower the numbers."
    @ 10,2 SAY "PLEASE REBOOT or RESET YOUR COMPUTER before"
   @ 11,2 SAY "starting the ABC Program."
   WAIT WINDOW
ENDIF
QUIT
```

Notice that INSTALL.PRG assigns the returned value of the file creation function, FCREATE(), to a variable called fhandle, which is then used as the first argument in FPUTS() and FCLOSE(). Remember that you must store the file handle to be able to access the file.

The following program, MAXLINE, is a utility that compares the length of each line of text in a file against a specified maximum length and creates a report showing each of the lines that exceed the allowable length. Writers can use it to check their ASCII text submissions for their publisher's maximum allowable length. FoxPro programmers can use it to check for lines in their source code files that exceed the line length specified in FoxDoc.

```
* MAXLINE.PRG
* DO MAXLINE WITH "your prg name", # of lines

PARAMETERS the_file, the_length
SET ESCAPE OFF
IF PARAMETERS() # 2 .OR.;
      TYPE("the_file") # "C" .OR.;
      TYPE("the_length") # "N" .OR.;
      (TYPE("the_length") = "N" .AND.;
      INT(the_length) # the_length)
   WAIT WINDOW "You need two params: a filename "+;
   "(string) & a max line length (integer)."
   RETURN
ENDIF
the_file = UPPER(IIF(AT(".",the_file) # 0,;
   the_file,the_file+".PRG"))
fileh = FOPEN(the_file)
IF fileh = -1
   WAIT WINDOW "Could not find file "+the_file+". "
   RETURN
ENDIF
the_report = SUBSTR(the_file,1,;
   AT(".",the_file)-1)
IF FILE(the_report+".TXT")
   mext = "TXT"
   DEFINE WINDOW getit FROM 10,29 TO 15,51;
      PANEL TITLE " Report Name "
   DO WHILE FILE(the_report+"."+mext)
      WAIT WINDOW "File "+the_report+"."+mext;
         +" already exists.  Overwrite?  (y/n)" TO manswer
      IF UPPER(manswer) = "Y"
         ERASE (the_report+"."+mext)
      ELSE
         ACTIVATE WINDOW getit
         @ 1,4 SAY the_report+"." GET mext PICTURE "@!N"
```

```
          READ
          IF LASTKEY() = 27
             EXIT
          ENDIF
       ENDIF
    ENDDO
    RELEASE WINDOW getit
    IF FILE(the_report+"."+mext)
       * got an escape press
       = FCLOSE(fileh)
       RETURN
    ELSE
       the_report = the_report+"."+mext
    ENDIF
ELSE
    the_report = the_report+".TXT"
ENDIF
reporth = FCREATE(the_report)
= FPUTS(reporth,"This is a report of lines in "+;
    the_file)
= FPUTS(reporth,"that exceed the given maximum of "+;
    ALLTRIM(STR(the_length))+" characters.")
= FPUTS(reporth," ")
= FPUTS(reporth," ")
the_line = 0
overmax = 0
DO WHILE !FEOF(fileh)
    the_line = the_line + 1
    this_line = FGETS(fileh)
    IF LEN(this_line) > the_length
       = FPUTS(reporth,PADR("Line # ";
          +ALLTRIM(STR(the_line)),15)+this_line)
       overmax = overmax + 1
    ENDIF
ENDDO
= FCLOSE(reporth)
= FCLOSE(fileh)
?? CHR(7)
IF overmax = 0
    ERASE(the_report)
    WAIT WINDOW "No lines over the maximum of "+;
       ALLTRIM(STR(the_length))+;
       " chars were found.  Congrats!  :-)"
ELSE
    WAIT WINDOW "Report "+the_report+" shows "+;
```

```
      ALLTRIM(STR(overmax))+;
      IIF(overmax = 1," line"," lines");
      +" over the maximum of "+;
      ALLTRIM(STR(the_length))+" chars."
ENDIF
RETURN
```

MAXLINES checks for the existence of a report file and requests your permission to overwrite it before continuing. You should always check for the existence of any file that you are about to create because, regardless of the setting of SAFETY, FoxPro does not warn you that you are about to overwrite a file when you use the low-level file functions.

The following procedure, CONVERT, reads in an ASCII orders file that was created on a mainframe system and creates another ASCII file in the proper format to be appended to a FoxPro table.

```
PROCEDURE convert
   *
   * convert an ASCII orders file into another ASCII file
   * that holds just the record headers and detail line
   * items.
   *

   private in_name, out_name, in_file, out_file, ;
         blocksize, recsperblk, recsize, cblock, ;
         write_ok

   * get name of ASCII orders file
   in_name = getfile("","Select ASCII orders file to " +;
      "be processed")
   if "" = in_name    && no file selected
      RETURN
   endif

   * create variables to hold output file name, and input
   * and output file handles
   out_name = uniqfile() + ".$$$"
   in_file  = 0
   out_file = 0

   * check for error conditions
   wait window "Checking input file..." nowait

   if     !openfile(in_name, in_file) ;
      .or. filempty(in_name, in_file) ;
      .or. !okchars(in_name, in_file) ;
      .or. !makefile(out_name, out_file)
         = fclose(in_file)
```

```
      wait clear
      RETURN
endif
* end of error checking

* set block and record parameters
blocksize  = 840
recsperblk =   9
recsize    =  86
nblocks    =   0
nrecs      =   0
cblock     = ""

* read a block into cblock, then write the nine data
* records in the block to an output file; records are 90
* chars, but I'm stripping off the record number, which
* is the first 4 chars of the record.
wait window "Processing input file " + in_name + "..." ;
   nowait

write_ok = .t.
do while gotblock(cblock, in_file, blocksize, nblocks) ;
      .and. write_ok
   recpos = 17
   for j=1 to recsperblk
      currec = "  " + substr(cblock,recpos,recsize)
      if !empty(currec)
        bytesout = fputs(out_file, currec)
        if bytesout != recsize + 3  && "  "+CR+LF
             ?? chr(7)
             wait window "Error in writing records to "+;
               "output file "+out_name+" !" timeout 5
             write_ok = .f.
             EXIT
        endif
        nrecs = nrecs+1
      endif
      recpos = recpos + recsize + 4
   endfor
enddo

* close the input and output files
= fclose(in_file)
= fclose(out_file)

if write_ok    && if output file successfully created
   * display record and block counters, then pause for a
   * keystroke
```

```
        wait window "Created " + ltrim(str(nrecs)) + ;
            " records from " + ltrim(str(nblocks)) + ;
            " blocks." timeout 5

        if !addords(out_name)
            wait window "Order file not updated." timeout 5
        endif
    endif

    erase (out_name)
    wait clear

return

FUNCTION openfile
    *
    * can we open the file?
    *
    parameters f_name, f_handle

    f_handle = fopen(f_name)
    if f_handle < 0
      ?? chr(7)
    wait window "Unable to open file " + upper(f_name) +;
      "!" timeout 5
    endif
return f_handle > 0

FUNCTION filempty
    *
    * is the file empty?
    *
    parameters f_name, f_handle

    if feof(f_handle)
         ?? chr(7)
      wait window "File " + upper(f_name) + " is empty!" ;
         timeout 5
    endif
return feof(f_handle)

FUNCTION okchars
    *
    * verify that the input file contains only letters,
    * digits and spaces
    *
    parameters f_name, f_handle
    private b_str, all_ok, c

    all_ok = .t.
    do while !feof(f_handle) .and. all_ok
```

```
        b_str = fgets(f_handle, 1000)
        for j=1 to len(b_str)
            c = substr(b_str,j,1)
            if !isalpha(c) .and. !isdigit(c) .and. c != " "
                    ?? chr(7)
              wait window upper(f_name) + " contains " + ;
                    "an invalid character ("+c+")!" timeout 5
              all_ok = .f.
              EXIT
            endif
        endfor
    enddo

    * reset file pointer to top of file
    = fseek(f_handle, 0)
return all_ok

FUNCTION makefile
    *
    * can we create the file?
    *
    parameters f_name, f_handle

    f_handle = fcreate(f_name)

    if f_handle < 0
        ?? chr(7)
    wait window "Output file " + f_name + ;
        " could not be created!" timeout 5
    endif
return f_handle > 0

FUNCTION gotblock
    *
    * read a block of nbytes from a file; use fgets() to
    * stop at the carriage return character
    parameters b_str, f_handle, nbytes, nblocks

    b_str = fgets(f_handle, nbytes+10)
    nblocks = iif(len(b_str) = 0, nblocks, nblocks+1)

    if between(len(b_str), 1, nbytes-1)
        * we got 1 or more bytes, but we didn't get
        * as many as we should have!
            ?? chr(7)
        wait window "Block no. " + ltrim(str(nblocks)) + ;
            " has " + ltrim(str(len(b_str))) + " bytes.  " + ;
            ltrim(str(nbytes)) + " bytes are required!" ;
            timeout 5
    endif
return len(b_str) = nbytes
```

```
FUNCTION addords
    *
    * process ASCII file created from orders ASCII file by
    * convert.prg
    *
    parameters new_ascii
    private temp

    wait window "Updating orders table..." nowait

    * create temp dbf to hold line items in temp ASCII file
    temp = sys(3) + ".$$$"
    create cursor (temp) ;
       (status C(1), code C(2), text C(90))

    * append from temp orders ASCII file created by
    * convert.prg
    append from (new_ascii) type sdf
    go top

    *
    * code to analyze the orders data and update the
    * actual fields of the orders table would go here
    *
return
```

Of the three examples presented here, CONVERT is the most specialized. It assumes that the input file will have a specific file layout, that the records will always be of the same length, and that codes are used consistently to indicate the type of records being processed. CONVERT is a good example of the power that the low-level file functions provide for handling data manipulation jobs that were previously the exclusive domain of languages such as C.

Chapter Summary

This chapter covered FoxPro 2's array handling commands and functions, which enable you to create arrays, store information in them, sort them, retrieve data from them, and pass them to procedures and UDF's. The chapter discussed some of the strengths and weaknesses of arrays and showed you several ways to use arrays in an application.

You also learned about FoxPro's low-level file functions. The LLFF's enable you to manipulate files in ways that were not possible in FoxBASE+ and dBASE III Plus. LLFF's are a valuable tool in any application that requires access to files not stored in FoxPro's DBF file format.

The next chapter discusses the commands and functions FoxPro 2 provides to enable you to trap for the occurrence of an event and to control the environment in which your programs are executed.

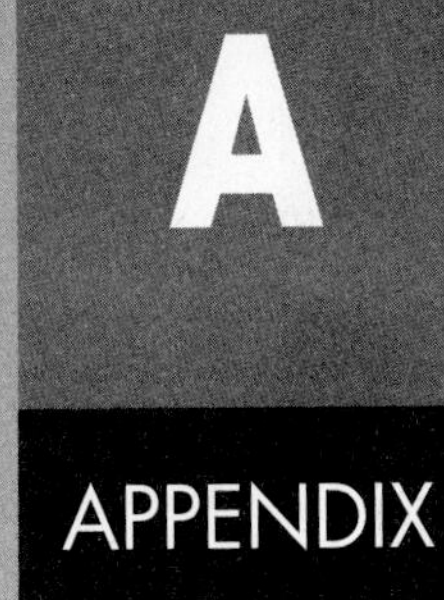

Installing FoxPro 2

In this appendix, you learn how to install FoxPro 2. Then you can move directly to Chapter 1, where you find complete instructions on loading the program and getting to work.

Establish the Base Product

FoxPro 2 comes on four installation disks if you have the 5 1/4-inch 1.2M set or 7 disks if you have the 3 1/2-inch 744k set. (Low-density 360k 5 1/4-inch disks also can be requested from Fox Software.)

A short pamphlet called the *Installation Guide* is included with your documentation. If you are installing FoxPro 2 on a network, you also should check the *Developer's Guide* for the chapter on "Multi-User FoxPro," which discusses additional system requirements, provides configuration compatibility tips, and explains the *AddUser* procedure for network use. The process described in this appendix, however, is the same for the single- and the multi-user product and for 5 1/4-inch and 3 1/2-inch disks.

Before you start, you should be aware that FoxPro 2 requires at least 480k free RAM and 6M of free space on your hard disk. The program runs much more smoothly if you give it more memory. With only 480K,

FoxPro 2 runs; however, your use of the FoxPro power tools and windowing capabilities is severely limited. You also need quite a bit more hard disk to install all the sample files and the Distribution Kit; a total of almost 19M is needed. FoxPro also needs some elbow room for its temporary work files.

Check the root directory of your boot drive (usually C:) for a file called CONFIG.SYS. This file is used by DOS to establish its own environment. If you do not have a CONFIG.SYS file, you should create a file with that name in your boot drive's root directory, containing the following lines:

```
FILES=40
BUFFERS=20
```

Use a text editor or a word processor that can create an *ASCII text file*—or you can use the DOS command *COPY CON*. See your DOS manual if you need more information on how to do this.

If you already have a CONFIG.SYS file, make sure that the file contains entries for FILES and BUFFERS. For FoxPro 2, Fox Software recommends setting BUFFERS between 20 and 40. A setting of 40 is the *minimum* recommended for FILES, and many people use much higher FILES settings. Add or edit your CONFIG.SYS file accordingly; copy your old file to a backup name first, in case you have a problem and need to start again.

NOTE

As you create more complex applications, you need to open more files at the same time. The FILES setting in CONFIG.SYS determines how many files DOS enables you to open at the same time. If you receive an error message from FoxPro, such as `Too many files open`, boost the setting of FILES in CONFIG.SYS.

If you use any applications that modify your CONFIG.SYS file, make sure that you check the file afterwards and that the settings of FILES and BUFFERS are still appropriate for FoxPro.

Note an important exception to this rule: *memory management software* alters your CONFIG.SYS and AUTOEXEC.BAT file to create non-standard FILES and BUFFERS settings. They often load FILES and BUFFERS in high memory, leaving only a minimal number in CONFIG.SYS and leaving more conventional memory free for applications such as FoxPro. If you are using memory management software, do not adjust your FILES and BUFFERS settings without consulting the manuals for these products.

If you need to make any adjustments to your CONFIG.SYS file, or if you do not have a CONFIG.SYS file, you need to accomplish one more task before you can proceed with installation: reboot your computer (by pressing Ctrl-Alt-Del or a re-set switch if you have one) so that your new CONFIG.SYS settings are in effect.

Next, make your *target* drive (the one in which you want FoxPro to be installed) your current *default* drive, by typing its letter and a colon at the DOS prompt. If your target drive is C (normal if you have only one hard disk) you type the following:

C:

(It does not matter whether you use lower- or uppercase.) Now insert the installation disk labelled `FoxPro` (or `FoxPro/LAN`) `Disk 1` into a floppy drive (your *source* drive). Type the letter of your source drive, followed by a colon and the word *install*:

A:INSTALL

After you read the message on the first installation screen you see, press any key on your keyboard to continue with installation.

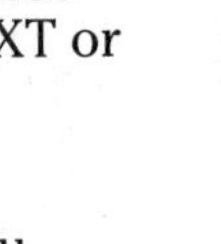

The next screen gives you a choice of products to install. If you have a 20386 or 20486 processor and 4M of memory or more, you benefit greatly from FoxPro 2's *Extended* version's capability to use extended memory, and you should install *FoxPro (X)*. If you have as little as 2M of memory and a 20386 or 20486 processor, you may want to install the Extended and the *Standard* version to see which gives you better performance. (You also may want to install both programs if you are a developer and need to check the programs you write for performance in both versions.) Finally, if you have an 8088 or 80286 processor (XT or AT class), or a 80386 or 80486 processor with less than 1.5M of memory, you should be using the Standard version only.

In all cases, you should install the FoxPro *Help File*. Not only do you need to have FoxPro's context-sensitive and comprehensive help available on-line, but the *Help File* also contains information on enhancements and changes that occurred after the manuals were printed.

After you have answered *Y* or *N*, indicating which of the three products you want to install, the program asks you into which directory you want FoxPro 2 installed. A default directory of `FOXPRO2` is shown, along with the name of the drive from which you started the installation process. If you press Enter to confirm, this directory becomes the FoxPro *main program* directory; many subdirectories are created under it to hold some of FoxPro's subsidiary programs and sample applications.

If you indicate a different directory in this screen (or even a different drive and directory), you are asked to confirm your choice. In either case, the directory is created if it does not already exist, as part of the installation process.

A message screen appears to let you know about the process of *branding* your copy of FoxPro 2 with your serial number.

If you have just purchased FoxPro 2, your package included a sealed *activation key envelope*; if you are upgrading, you are using your old activation key and serial number in the following instructions.

The outside of your activation envelope shows your serial number and a *demonstration activation key*. If you install with the demo key, you will have a fully functioning version of FoxPro 2 that is limited to 120 records in any one file. You can use your demo for up to 30 days and receive technical support from Fox Software, before you decide to finalize your purchase. To finalize, *open* the envelope, indicating agreement with Fox licensing terms as described in the *Installation Guide*. Use the *live* activation key and re-install.

FoxPro files are not copy protected in any other way. You may safely use disk optimizing programs that move your files to other physical locations on your hard disk or restore FoxPro files from a backup, and so on.

Don't lose your activation key envelope! You will need your serial number and activation key if you upgrade your copy of FoxPro 2, if you need to re-install, and if you install the Distribution Kit, either now or later.

Fox Software keeps track of registered serial numbers to help them inform their customers of product developments. After you have finalized your purchase of FoxPro by opening your activation key envelope and installing with the live key, return your *registration form* to make sure that you are notified of updates and other Fox news.

Press a key when you have read and understand the message about your serial number and activation key and type your serial number and either activation key in the next screen, as requested. (Don't worry if you make a mistake—you will see an error message like the Distribution Kit installation section, but you can re-type either number.)

When your serial number and activation key have been properly entered, all the required files are copied to your hard disk. You see a *thermometer* indicating progress as each product is installed, like the one in figure A.2. You also are asked to insert different disks as the copying progresses.

When the base products have been copied, you receive a confirming message. At this point, you can end the installation by pressing Esc or go on to install the supplemental products included with FoxPro 2. If you choose to stop now, the supplemental product installation can be run at any time from within FoxPro.

Whether you are stopping the installation process here or are continuing with the supplemental products, those of you who are upgrading from FoxPro 1 have an extra step to take after you have completed the installation. You need to run the FIXUSER program in the \GOODIES\MISC directory under your FoxPro 2 main program directory. SET RESOURCE TO your normal Resource file and DO FIXUSER to create 2.0 copies of all your 1.0 COLOR SET resources. Do this several times if you have several different Resource files you want to continue using.

Unfortunately, FoxPro 1-type BROWSE PREFERENCE resources are not converted by FIXUSER (you have to recreate them), but all other entries in your existing Resource files are readable in 2.0.

Add the Supplemental Files

The Supplemental Product Installation is actually a FoxPro application. If you have chosen to continue with it, FoxPro loads itself at this point. The screens you see next are all typical of the screens that FoxPro 2 presents later on and of the screens you can create.

You first are asked to choose a monitor type. Use the cursor (arrow) keys to move the *highlight* to your choice and press Enter. In most cases, your choice is `Generic Color` or `Generic Monochrome`, but several other options are provided for laptop users with special needs.

Next, you are asked to choose the supplemental, or optional, files you want to install. As you select different products from the list on the left (again, highlight your choice and press Enter), a check appears next to all the choices you have made. Watch the `Disk Statistics` shown at the bottom of the screen, and the `Descriptions` for each of the supplemental products as you make your choices. In figure A.1, all the options have been chosen.

Install as many of the supplemental products as you have space for on your hard disk. Some of these products are valuable tools, and all of them are invaluable examples. The discussions throughout the book refer to many of them and use many of the sample data files. Remember, however, that you can come back to the installation process and add some of these files later if you need them.

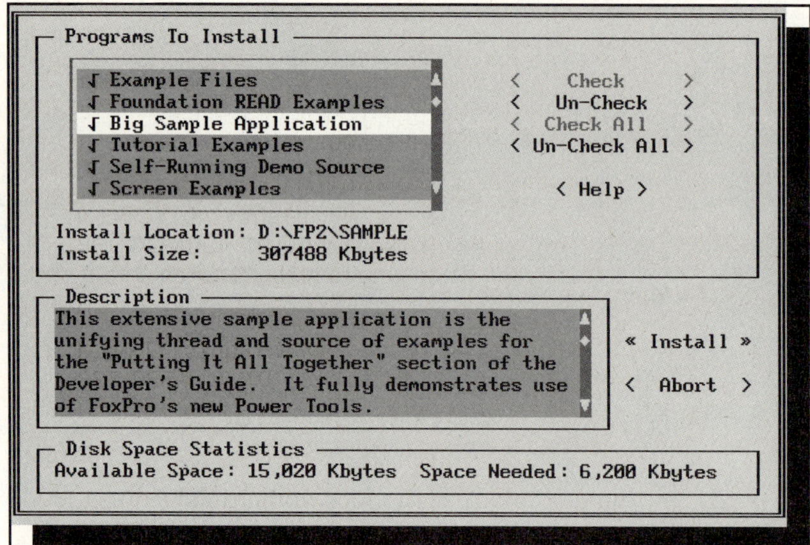

FIG. A.1

Choosing supplemental products.

When you have chosen your supplemental products, press the Tab key until the « `Install` » option is highlighted. Press Enter to begin the copying process.

If you have chosen more supplemental files than you have disk space for, FoxPro 2 warns you before the program continues. If you are re-installing FoxPro 2 over older versions of the same files, you may ignore the warning. Otherwise, choose to `Cancel` and de-select some of your choices.

The supplemental files are copied using the same procedures as the base products (as shown in fig. A.2). A final message tells you that installation has been completed. You can continue with the instructions in Chapter 1 on loading FoxPro 2.

Attach the Distribution Kit

To create and *distribute* applications to other users who do not own a development copy of FoxPro 2, you may have purchased the separate

FoxPro 2 Distribution Kit. After you have installed the base products, you can install the Distribution Kit. The process is much like the installation of the development version of FoxPro 2.

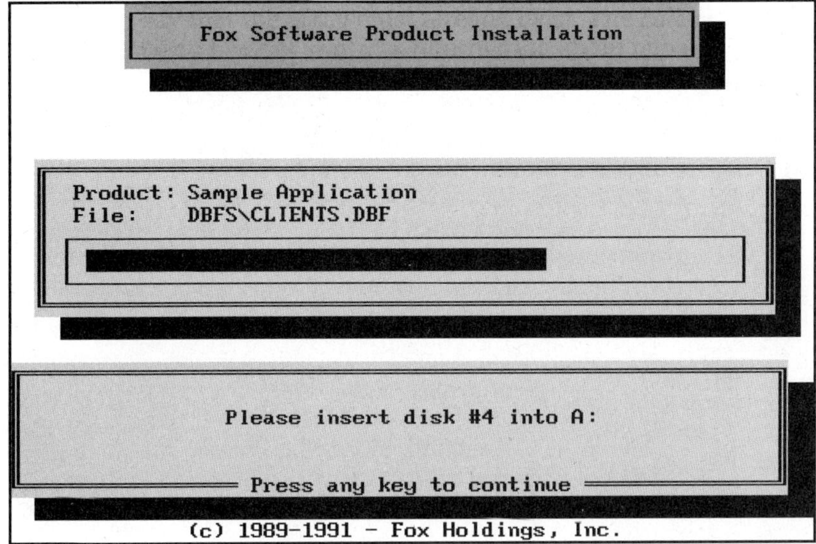

FIG. A.2

The thermometer shows you the progress as the files are copied.

You are asked to select the Distribution Kit products you want to install. Again, you have the choice of products that fit the Standard and Extended versions of FoxPro 2. You may choose either or both, depending on the environments for which you are developing applications.

For the Standard and Extended versions, FoxPro 2 can create *standalone* executable files, which can be large, as well as *compact* executable files and *runtime* compiled applications, which are much smaller but must be distributed with accompanying *support libraries.* Depending upon what kind of applications you are going to develop, choose the appropriate products. If you have the diskspace, install the standalone products and the support libraries so that you can try them.

After you have selected the products, you are asked to confirm the proper directory for installation. *This directory must be the same one into which you installed the development version of FoxPro 2.* The Distribution Kit installation alters your development version program files so that they can access the Distribution Kit features.

Next, you see another screen asking for your Distribution Kit serial number and activation key. (As before, if you are upgrading from FoxPro 1, use your old serial number and activation key.) After they are entered, you are asked for your development version's serial number and activation key.

Your development version's serial number installs the Distribution Kit in the proper form for multi- or single-user products. No *demo* key is provided for the Distribution Kit. However, when you give your development version activation key, you can use its demo version to create distributable demos that, like FoxPro 2, are limited to 120 records per file.

When both sets of serial numbers and activation keys are entered, the file copying process operates as before.

B

APPENDIX

Using FoxPro 2 in a Network Environment

FoxPro 2 is available in single-user and multi-user versions. The multi-user version, FoxPro/LAN, enables more than one person to access a table at the same time. When two or more people are running the same copy of FoxPro, several new configuration and control issues arise.

Managing File and Record Contention

In a network environment, users contend for network resources, such as a shared printer. This contention is managed by the network software. For example, most networks redirect output intended for the printer to a file on the network server. A separate program maintains a list of files in the queue and sends each to the printer in the order in which the files are created. This system prevents one person's output from becoming printed in the middle of someone else's.

In a multi-user database environment, users contend for database resources, primarily tables and records. Database contention is managed by the database manager, in this case FoxPro. Although FoxPro can automatically (implicitly) manage simultaneous access to tables and records, the program also provides several commands and functions that enable you to explicitly lock and unlock tables and records and to tailor the way in which FoxPro 2 responds when you try to access a resource currently in use by another. These multi-user commands and functions are listed in table B.1.

Table B.1 FoxPro 2's Multi-User Commands and Functions

Command/Function	Description
FLOCK()	Attempts to lock a table; returns `.T.` if successful; returns `.F.` if someone else currently has the table, or a record in the table, locked.
LOCK()	Attempts to lock one or more records in a table; returns `.T.` if successful; returns `.F.` if someone else currently has the record(s) or file locked. Whether or not you may lock more than one record simultaneously depends upon the current SETting of MULTILOCKS.
NETWORK()	Returns `.T.` if you are running FoxPro/LAN, the network version of FoxPro. This function *does not* tell you whether or not you are on a network.
ON ERROR	Determines the error-handling routine, if any, that is executed when FoxPro is unable to *implicitly* lock a table or record, such as when you try to edit a record in a Browse. The error routine is not activated when you use one of the explicit locking functions, because the inability of the function to gain the lock is not considered to be an error.
RLOCK()	The same as LOCK().
SET EXCLUSIVE	Determines whether or not tables are opened for exclusive use. Regardless of the SETting of EXCLUSIVE, you can explicitly open a table for exclusive use by including the EXCLUSIVE option with the USE command. By default, EXCLUSIVE is set ON. If you USE a file with EXCLUSIVE ON and then SET EXCLUSIVE OFF, the file continues to be USEd exclusively until it is closed.
SET LOCK	Determines whether or not certain database commands that don't change any of the table's information try to lock the table before proceeding. The default setting of LOCK is OFF.

Command/Function	Description
SET MULTILOCKS	Determines whether or not the current workstation can lock more than one record in a table at a time. By default, only one record at a time may be locked.
SET NOTIFY	If NOTIFY is set OFF, FoxPro does not display the message `Attempting to lock ...` while attempting to place a lock.
SET REFRESH <ExpN1>,<ExpN2>	First parameter determines when changes made by other users are reflected in a Browse/Edit window or in a MODIFY MEMO window. Second parameter determines when data buffers are automatically FLUSHed. The default values are 0, 5, in seconds. SET REFRESH has no effect upon active GETs or upon data displayed in any other manner.
SET REPROCESS	Determines how long FoxPro continues trying to lock a table or record after an unsuccessful first attempt.
SYS(0)	On FoxPro/LAN, returns the network machine `#/name` for the current workstation. The machine `#/name` must have been set by the network software, and the network shell must be loaded.
SYS(2011)	Returns a character string containing the current file or record lock status. The text returned is the same as that displayed in the system status bar (e.g. `File Locked`). Because SYS(2011) *does not* try to place a lock, unlock RLOCK() and FLOCK(). SYS(2011) also does not report whether another user placed a lock previously. It just lets you know whether you have locked this record or file previously.
UNLOCK	Releases file or record lock(s).
USE ... EXCLUSIVE	Opens a table for exclusive use.

At its simplest level, whether or not two people can access a table simultaneously depends upon the SETting of EXCLUSIVE. If EXCLUSIVE is set ON on either workstation, a table can be used only by the first person to open the table. This limitation also is in effect if the table is opened for exclusive use, regardless of the SETting of EXCLUSIVE, with the EXCLUSIVE option of the USE command (e.g., USE BUDGET EXCLUSIVE).

When a table has been opened for shared use, each user's access to records in the table is controlled by implicit and explicit locks.

Implicit locks are those that FoxPro places on records and tables. An implicit lock is placed under two types of conditions:

- When you begin to edit a record in a Browse/Edit or Modify Memo window
- When you issue certain database commands, such as READ or REPLACE

A table that has been opened for shared use can always be viewed in a Browse window, even if the file has been locked by someone else. FoxPro does not try to lock a record until you begin editing it. At that point, FoxPro tries to lock the record to prevent anyone else's changes from overwriting yours (or vice versa). The record is unlocked automatically when you move the record pointer off the current record.

Whether a file lock or a record lock is placed as a result of issuing a database command generally depends upon the number of records that may be affected. FoxPro is *smart* enough to know that REPLACE or REPLACE NEXT 1 affects only the current record, although REPLACE ALL or REPLACE NEXT 10 affects more than one record. REPLACE locks only the current record, but REPLACE <*scope*> locks the entire table. Implicit locks are released after the command has been executed.

Explicit locks are those placed by using the FLOCK( ), LOCK(), and RLOCK() functions. FLOCK() locks the entire table, but LOCK() and RLOCK(), which are functionally identical, lock one or more records. Records locked with LOCK() or RLOCK() are not released when you move the record pointer. Explicit record and file locks are only released by the following:

- Issuing an UNLOCK command releases file and record locks in the current table.
- UNLOCK ALL releases all file and record locks in all open tables.
- Locking a record releases the previous record lock, unless MULTILOCKS is ON.
- Changing the SETting of MULTILOCKS releases all locks in all open tables.
- Locking a table with FLOCK() releases any record locks in that table.
- Closing a table releases all locks in that table.

What FoxPro does when it is unable to place a lock depends upon the current SETting of REPROCESS, whether or not an ON ERROR routine is in effect, and whether the lock is being placed implicitly or explicitly. Table B.2 shows the different settings of REPROCESS and how long FoxPro continues to try to place the lock.

Table B.2 The Effects of Different REPROCESS SETtings

SET REPROCESS TO ...	#/Duration of Retries	ESC to Cancel?
0		
with ON ERROR	0	N/A
without ON ERROR	indefinitely	Yes
0 SECONDS	0	N/A
–1	indefinitely	No
<n>	<n> times	No
<n> SECONDS	<n> seconds	No
AUTOMATIC or -2	indefinitely	Yes

If REPROCESS is set to 0 (the default), and an ON ERROR routine is active, FoxPro does not retry the lock. Whether or not the ON ERROR routine is called depends upon whether the attempted lock was implicit or explicit. If you try to edit a locked record in a Browse (an implicit lock), the error routine is called. If you try to lock a record with the LOCK() function (an explicit lock), the error routine is not called, and the function returns the logical value `.F.`

Aside from its relationship to REPROCESS, an unsuccessful implicit lock triggers an error, and an unsuccessful explicit lock returns `.F.` The errors that may occur when you execute a READ (or DO a screen (SPR) program that always issues a READ) must be handled by an error-handling routine.

REFRESH controls how frequently changes being made to a table by others on the network are reflected in a Browse/Edit or memo editing window and how often data buffers are FLUSHed automatically (saving changes to disk). REFRESH has no effect on GETs activated with READ.

By default, the first parameter of REFRESH is set to 0, which means that others' changes are not reflected in your Browse unless you position the cursor on a changed record that has been unlocked by the other user. At that point, the changes made for *that* record become visible to you. Changes made to other records are still not reflected.

You can specify that a Browse/Edit or memo editing window be refreshed at some interval by SETting REFRESH TO a value between 1 and 3,600, representing the number of seconds in the interval. Follow this procedure especially if the users of your application spend a great deal of time in a Browse window. However, keep the following things in mind:

- Regardless of the SETting of REFRESH, changes made by others are not reflected in another user's Browse/Edit or memo editing window until the user who made the change unlocks the record.
- You can override the current REFRESH setting to disable the Browse window refreshing by including the NOREFRESH option in the BROWSE command.
- Setting REFRESH to a low value, such as 1, forces FoxPro to spend a great deal of time *polling* the network and may slow down an intensive data-entry application.

Unless each user needs to be aware of changes as they are made, a REFRESH setting between 60 and 300 (1 to 5 minutes) should be a good compromise between data timeliness and program efficiency.

The second parameter of SET REFRESH is set to 5 by default. This setting determines how long FoxPro goes between FLUSHing (or saving changes that may have been stored in memory for faster access to the disk version of your tables). The same considerations as described previously should be applied to your use of this value. Experiment with both settings in your own environment to determine their optimal values for your programs.

The NETWORK() function *does not* tell you whether or not the application is running on a network. This function tells you whether or not the network version of FoxPro (FoxPro/LAN) is running. Many developers use this function in the *setup* part of an application to determine the proper SETting of EXCLUSIVE:

```
if network()
   set exclusive off
endif
```

Printing to Network Queues

Support for network queues is a significant change in multi-user FoxPro 2. This support is provided through two forms of the SET PRINTER command:

```
SET PRINTER TO
   [\\<machine name>
   \<printer name> = <dest>]
SET PRINTER TO
   [\\SPOOLER [\NB]
      [\F = <expN>] [\B = <banner>]
      [\C = <expN>] [\P = <expN>]]
      [\S = <server>] [\Q = <queue>]
```

Although the printer driver system does not directly support any kind of network printing assignments, you can tailor printer driver setups to the different printers available on a network.

Standard FoxPro dialog windows can provide you with the ability to choose among the available printers and then issue the appropriate SET PRINTER TO command. After output has been directed to a printer, you can SET PDSETUP TO a printer driver setup appropriate for the printer you selected.

Figure B.1 shows you dialogs that are part of a network printer utility shared by its author, John Flynn Matthew of Patrick Media Group, Inc., on CompuServe's FoxForum. The latest source code for this program and many others is in the Forum libraries and message areas; read Appendix H for instructions on participating.

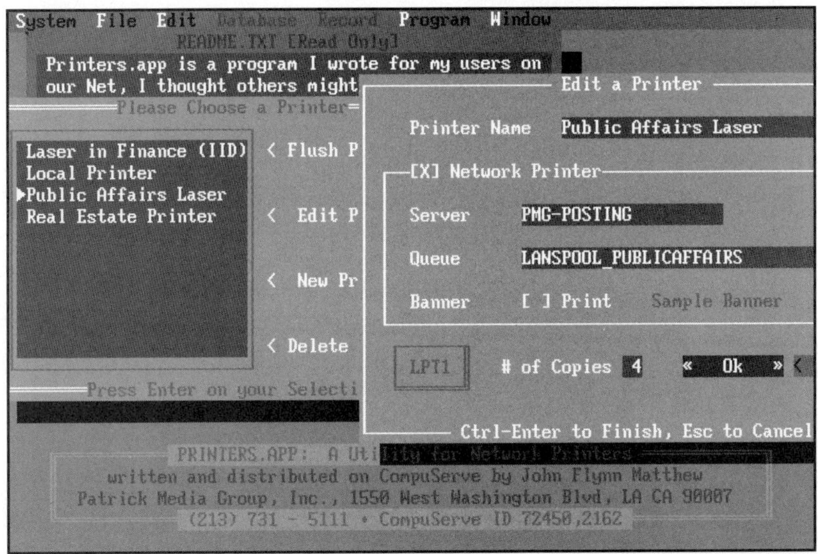

FIG. B.1

A Network printer utility available from the FoxForum Libraries on CompuServe.

The Network message section is one of the liveliest Forum areas, and the Forum members and staffers have a wide and invaluable range of experience. Often, you may have difficulty telling whether or not FoxPro has anything to do with a network problem. Someone on the Forum probably has encountered a similar hardware and software setup and will be glad to share what he has learned.

Using ADDUSER To Give Each User a Separate Configuration and Resource File

In a network environment, a single configuration (CONFIG.FP) file and Resource (FOXUSER.DBF) file may no longer be sufficient. FoxPro includes a program, called ADDUSER.APP, that facilitates the creation of a separate CONFIG.FP and FOXUSER.DBF for each user on the network. This utility application is located in the FoxPro 2 home directory.

To ease the process of setting up custom configuration files for each user, ADDUSER looks for two default files if the program cannot locate CONFIG.FP and/or FOXUSER.DBF in the directory that you specify in the ADDUSER configuration screen. You create these files yourself. CONFIG.DEF is a default configuration file that you can create with the FoxPro editor or any other text editor. DEFUSER.DBF is a default Resource file.

Although creating CONFIG.DEF is a simple matter, creating the default Resource file for a group of people takes a little more thought and work. One way you may approach this process is to create an empty DEFUSER.DBF table by copying the structure of an existing FOXUSER.DBF to DEFUSER.DBF. If you then made DEFUSER.DBF your Resource file (and made sure that RESOURCE is SET ON), you could open and Browse tables, create Browse preferences, and set up DEFUSER.DBF the way you want. Reset your Resource file, and you now have a DEFUSER.DBF that ADDUSER can copy to a separate directory for each user on the network.

Of course, if a single Resource file will suffice for everyone, you can allow each user to access that file by setting its file attributes to read-only—through FoxPro's Filer utility or with the DOS ATTRIB command. Information then can be read from the Resource file, but changes cannot be saved to it. You can read more about read-only Resource files in Chapter 15. Along with a CONFIG.FP file, a Resource file may be shared by including it in an APP or EXE.

Note that CONFIG.DEF and DEFUSER.DBF must reside in the directory from which ADDUSER was run for the program to find and use the files. Also note that the source code for ADDUSER (ADDUSER.PRG) is located in the \GOODIES\ADDUSER subdirectory under your FoxPro 2 home directory. As with the program-generating programs, such as GENSCRN and GENMENU, you can modify ADDUSER.PRG to work exactly the way you want the program to work and then rebuild the application (APP) file.

Converting an Application from Single-User to Multi-User

Although local area networks are increasingly used at all levels of business, most applications currently in use on personal computers began life as single-user programs. At some point, almost all developers must face the task of converting an application from single-user to multi-user. Luckily for those who develop applications with FoxPro, much of the conversion can be handled transparently by FoxPro's built-in record and file locking logic.

However, you have to take a few things into consideration when converting an application to run in a multi-user environment.

Providing for Record and File Locking

In an application running under the single-user version of FoxPro, all files are opened for exclusive use. In a shared data environment, you must provide for the required locking of tables and records to prevent users from overwriting each others' changes.

If your application uses *direct reads* (i.e., field values are edited directly, just as in a Browse), you can handle the conversion from single-user to multi-user fairly easily. Although the following procedure doesn't work in all situations, it should be sufficient in most:

1. Make sure that you have an ON ERROR routine that traps for network-related errors in effect at all times.
2. SET REPROCESS TO AUTOMATIC so that the users can decide for themselves how long they are willing to wait to edit the record.
3. Make sure that all READs contain a `TIMEOUT <n>` clause so that record locks are released if a user walks away from his workstation without moving off of a record that he has edited.

If you used the Screen Builder to create the screens, you can insert a `#READCLAUSES TIMEOUT <n>` generator directive into #SECTION 1 of your Setup procedure for each screen set (e.g., `#READCLAUSES TIMEOUT 60`) and then regenerate each of the SPR files. Note that this generator directive must begin in column one of the line.

At a minimum, your error-handling routine must trap for error # 108 (file is in use by another), error # 109 (record is in use by another), and error # 110 (exclusive open of file is required). The routine should inform the user of the problem and ask whether she wants to RETRY the lock. If the user decides that she doesn't want to wait any longer, you can execute a *cleanup* routine and RETURN TO MASTER or RETURN to <program name>, naming PRG or SPR that issued your foundation READ.

If your application uses *dirty,* or indirect, *reads* (i.e., a READ that GETs to memory variables or array elements), the waters become muddier. FoxPro does not try to lock the record into which the variables' values eventually are REPLACEd or GATHERed, and the user may be entering data that she cannot save when the edit is complete. In this situation, you must rewrite your program to use direct reads or insert a call to LOCK() before each of the READs in your application, testing the returned value of the function before executing the READ.

An alternative strategy for both direct and indirect READs is to issue the READ with a NOLOCK keyword. (NOLOCK is an option in your screen Generate Options dialog.) Use a menu option and/or a control button GET to enable the user to signal his readiness to edit a record. Issue an explicit RLOCK() and SHOW GETS LOCK at that time, informing the user if the record currently cannot be edited and offering choices such as the error-handling routine described above. Explicitly UNLOCK the record after the user is finished editing or when the READ ends because of a TIMEOUT or other reason.

FoxPro 2 supports *transaction processing* on networks running Novell Netware. Just as an indirect READ protects a record's contents by not changing the field values until the edit is confirmed as complete, in a transaction processing system, a whole series of instructions or procedures is made reversible by not *committing* them until the accumulated results have been confirmed as complete. (If the changes are not committed, the cancellation process is called a *rollback.*)

FoxPro can use Netware's Transactional Tracking system (TTS) only when the TTS has been loaded according to Novell's instructions for your system. FoxPro accesses the TTS, using an API library included with your installation files, beginning with the November 15, 1991 build of the product. This file is named NETWARE.PLB and includes the library functions TTSAVAIL(), TTSATTRIB(), BEGINTRAN(), COMMIT(), and RLLBACK(). To assess whether its use is feasible on your system, check SYS(12) to see how much memory is required to load this library. Read the section of the API in Chapter 15 for more information on using a library; use the on-line help for information on each NETWARE.PLB function.

Using SYS(3) To Obtain Unique Temporary File Names

In a single-user application, code fragments such as the following are not uncommon throughout the program:

```
* create a temporary index
index on <field name> to TEMP
```

When only one person is running the application and the data files are segregated from those of other applications, this strategy for creating a temporary file works fine. In a multi-user environment, temporary files with hard-coded names can get you into trouble.

To avoid this potential problem, always use the SYS(3) function to obtain a unique file name. SYS(3) uses the system date and time to return an eight-character name that you can use when creating temporary indexes and tables. SYS(3) does not, however, check the default drive for the existence of a file by that name. Therefore, use the FILE() function in conjunction with SYS(3) to be absolutely sure that the file is unique. The following example uses a user-defined function called UNIQFILE() to return unique file names:

```
* create a temporary index
tempidx = uniqfile()
index on <field name> to (tempidx)
*
* other code goes here
*
* erase the temporary index file
if file(tempidx)
  erase (tempidx)
endif
FUNCTION uniqfile
  *
  * return a unique file name
  *

  private mfile
  mfile = sys(3) + ".$$$"
  do while     file(mfile)
        mfile = sys(3) + ".$$$"
  enddo
return mfile
```

Note that you must store the name returned by UNIQFILE() (or SYS(3) if you don't use a user-defined function) to a variable, so that you will be able to refer to it when you want to delete the file.

Maintenance Routines in a Multi-User Environment

In a single-user application, deleted records often are removed from the tables by using the PACK command at the end of each data-entry session or by selecting an option on a Utilities menu. Although this operation takes a little time if the tables are large, it inconveniences only one individual and often can be started before that person leaves the office.

Because PACK (as well as REINDEX and ZAP) requires exclusive use of a table (a file lock is *not* sufficient), PACKING a table that is open throughout an application requires that only one person be running the program when the PACK is performed. If your application routinely PACKs tables, this operation can cause substantial inconvenience for your users.

You can handle this problem in several ways. One way to avoid using PACK is by *recycling* deleted records by blanking their contents and then deleting them. Before your application APPENDs a BLANK record, it first checks for the existence of a deleted record whose key field is blank and only APPEND BLANKs if one is not found (because the key field is blank, they all are at the *top* of the table). However, recycling deleted records may represent a major change in the way your application works—a change that you may not want to make in an existing application.

Another approach, one that applies to all maintenance routines, is to insert a routine at the top of your maintenance procedures that monitors the number of users who are currently running your application. If the application already uses a system wide table, you can add a numeric field such as USERS, which is incremented by one every time a new user runs the program and decremented by one before a user exits the program. If the value of this field is not one, you can display a message saying that no others are currently in the program, and RETURN.

You can approach this problem in a number of other ways, but, as with most other multi-user considerations, the important point is to realize that you need to address a problem.

Network Performance and Other Issues

Many factors, such as the amount of available memory and the speed of your hard disk, affect FoxPro's performance. In a network environment, additional factors come into play, such as the throughput of your network cards and the network topology. Although there are no hard and fast rules to follow when trying to optimize FoxPro's performance on a network, you should be aware of some general guidelines.

Novell's default FILES setting is 40. If you are receiving the error message `Too many files open`, and you have set `FILES=` in your CONFIG.SYS file to a high number, you should create a SHELL.CFG file on the boot disk of each workstation. Include the line `FILE HANDLES=104` in SHELL.CFG. FoxPro can open a maximum of 99 files, and DOS uses another five.

By default, FoxPro places its temporary files in the current working directory, which usually is on a network drive. In most cases, you want to direct FoxPro to place its temporary files on the workstation's local hard drive, which usually can be accessed more quickly than the network server. To do this, include one or more of the EDITWORK, SORTWORK, PROGWORK, and TMPFILES statements in each workstation's CONFIG.FP file (e.g., `EDITWORK = C:\TEMP`). Make sure that the specified directory has plenty of free disk space, as some of these temporary files (especially those created by the SORT command) can become quite large.

If the network includes diskless workstations with only 640K of memory, FoxPro 2 may run slowly, even on 386 machines. The best way to increase performance on such machines is to add as much additional RAM as you can afford, configured as Expanded Memory (unless you always use the Extended version of FoxPro 2). You may want to allocate some or all of this memory as a RAM disk and instruct FoxPro to place its overlay file and/or some of its temporary files on the RAM disk, or you may achieve better results by letting FoxPro use all of the memory.

Refer to Appendix C, "Optimizing FoxPro 2's Performance," for more information on general approaches to maximizing FoxPro's performance—in single-user and multi-user environments.

C

APPENDIX

Optimizing FoxPro 2's Performance

When first written, FoxBASE sped past dBASE II. Nearly a decade later, Fox Software remains the speed champion among companies producing PC-based database management systems. Today's high-end PCs are 20 to 100 times faster than their counterparts of nine years ago. Depending on what operation is taking place, FoxPro 2 is anywhere from 10 to 10,000 times faster than the original FoxBASE running on the same PC. For many people, FoxPro 2 runs fast enough for their needs—no matter how inexperienced the user or inefficient the code.

No matter how small your files or how modest your database needs, you can save some time (and even some wear and tear on your hard disk) if you try to apply the following simple rules:

- If you have to create temporary files—perhaps a subset of a table or an index required for a single report—try to do it through a SQL SELECT command, creating the table as a CURSOR. If you have a RAM disk, you also can create the temporary files there for increased speed.

- In the *Commands and Functions* volume of the FoxPro documentation, read the "Remarks" subheading for the entry of each programming instruction you investigate. If the entry says "Included for backward compatibility," use the recommended alternative. A short section entitled "General Performance Hints" in the *Developer's Guide* gives you additional guidance on specific commands to avoid any substitutions for them.
- Read Appendix B to learn about special considerations if you are running FoxPro 2 on a network.
- Read Appendix D on using your FoxPro 2 configuration file (the CONFIG.FP) to your best advantage.

For some users, however, FoxPro 2 using an 80486 processor with 24M of RAM is not fast enough right from the start. This appendix is intended to help appease the growing appetite for larger databases, more network users, and more sophisticated applications, with some hints on fine-tuning FoxPro 2 for the best possible performance.

The Challenge of Optimizing

Before rushing into benchmarking, changing all of your code because someone told you command X is 20 percent faster than command Y, or upgrading your hardware, you should know what you are up against.

Fox Software has created some of the most sophisticated algorithms in the database industry. These routines can dynamically adjust their performance characteristics during program execution.

When running network applications, remember that other programs also are running on this network. They may affect overall network performance, and you probably will have no control over when they run.

Specific advice from other users and programmers is not always useful to you because they are using different hardware or running different programs. The wide variety of hardware components and the multitude of FoxPro 2 commands and functions one can use, not to mention programming styles, can significantly impact performance issues.

You can use some general techniques to organize all this complexity in your quest for enhanced FoxPro 2 performance. These two rules are the essence of optimization:

- To make something faster, take out the slow parts.
- Try to understand everything you can about the relevant and potentially relevant aspects of your environment—including hardware, software, and people.

The Human Equation

A few questions at the beginning can result in large productivity gains. First ask these questions and then decide whether or not the time required for optimizing your application is cost-effective for you:

- Do I really need this procedure to work this way? Will performance increase dramatically if I take the procedure out?
- Does the intended user perceive a performance difference? (The user doesn't usually have a stopwatch lying around waiting to benchmark a routine.)
- How does management view the time and money spent to increase performance? (If you are a sole proprietor, what effect will this have on your bottom line? Are you in the business of enhancing performance, or is your business really centered on something else?)
- If the routines I am automating with FoxPro 2 previously took days, weeks, or weren't even done, will anybody care that it now takes 30 minutes to do them without optimizing?

If the answers to all the questions above are "No," do not optimize for the sake of optimizing—you are wasting, not saving time. However, optimization can bring you additional benefits besides the immediate increase in performance. Add these questions to factor in other possible positive outcomes:

- Will optimizing my routines lead to new breakthroughs in my systems, opening up possibilities previously thought impossible?
- How will this affect your image as an innovator? Is the competition lagging, or do I need every possible performance aid?

If the preceding questions show you benefits that are not easily quantified, you must weigh these benefits against the money and time that will be spent, along with any measurable performance gains that may be realized. Only then can you decide whether optimization is a worthwhile investment for you.

The Hard Questions about Hardware

Despite the common perception that disk speed is the most important bottleneck to database applications, FoxPro's architecture makes disk speed less relevant. Because hard drives are much slower than memory, FoxPro does everything possible to reduce disk accesses. As a simple test, listen and watch your hard drive light while running various FoxPro routines. If you want a more detailed benchmark, run *Personal Measure* available from The Spirit of Performance. This utility watches all CPU, disk, keyboard, and printer usage to give you details and graphics of these categories (see fig. C.1).

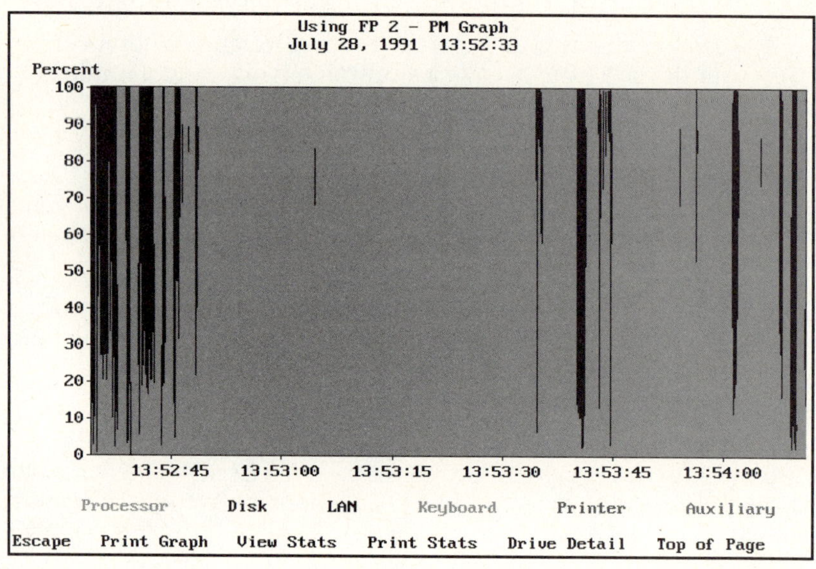

FIG. C.1

Typical usage of hardware registered by Personal Measure.

FoxPro makes extensive use of memory to minimize hard disk accesses. Using its own internal algorithms, FoxPro decides which files and parts of files are used most often and stores this data in memory. FoxPro can store many megabytes of data in this manner. This technique generally is known as *caching*.

The speed of the memory in your computer can be important. Fox Software has a program called MEM2.EXE that measures this speed. Some surprising results can be obtained from PCs that aren't up to snuff. You can obtain this program on Fox's CompuServe forum (see Appendix H).

CPU speed is important but sometimes overrated with respect to FoxPro 2. Having enough memory to bring data into memory is often a more important factor in data retrieval. When memory is used efficiently, CPU speed again becomes a factor in these operations. Nondata operations, such as drawing the screen and executing a program line, are always affected by CPU speed.

FoxPro 2 Extended version runs in 386 *protected* mode, which enables data to be moved 32 bits at a time, as opposed to the Standard version that moves data 16 bits at a time. This difference may contribute to speed differences on a 16 Mhz 286 versus a 16 Mhz 386 with all other factors being equal.

On a network, wire traffic is usually the final bottleneck after all other issues have been addressed. FoxPro LAN passes a fairly large amount of data to local work stations for processing. One method to reduce this traffic is to put temporary files on a local hard drive via the `TMPFILES=<drive>` setting in the FoxPro 2 configuration file, CONFIG.FP. The use of 16-bit network adapter cards also can alleviate traffic problems.

Math coprocessors, once touted as calculation cure-alls, are no longer viewed as important factors in performance tuning. They still may be useful where vast amounts of advanced calculations are used (SIN, LOG, COS, EXPONENTIAL, and so on). Additions and subtractions are unaffected by them, and most data operations' total times overwhelm the small amount of time required to handle the actual calculations.

RAM Disks, Disk Caches, and DOS

RAM disks are used widely and effectively with less advanced applications. But RAM disks tend to be counterproductive in FoxPro because these disks require memory that FoxPro would otherwise manage, using its own aggressive and sophisticated scheme. A RAM disk creates a disk that resides entirely in memory. You may encounter several problems with RAM disks:

- They must be created at boot time. When no longer needed for an application, their memory cannot be reclaimed until you reconfigure the computer and reboot. Super PC-Kwik's RAM disk is a major exception. This program shares memory with its other tools for disk caching, print spooling, and so on.
- Because RAM disks behave like physical DOS disks in most other respects, only complete files can be copied to them. If your file is larger than the RAM disk, the entire file must remain on a slower hard disk.
- If all of the file isn't accessed frequently, it becomes wasteful to have that much memory storing data that isn't being used. Caching algorithms were created to solve this problem. They can move to memory only the parts of files that are used frequently, and many more tables can exist in memory if none of it has been allocated to a RAM disk.

- FoxPro still caches files on a RAM disk if it is present. This double dipping of memory is wasteful although it's probably harmless if you have memory to burn. With sufficient memory, you may even have enough extra memory to put FoxPro's EXE file on the RAM disk; most PCs, however, do not have this luxury.

Despite these warnings, you may want to create a RAM disk in certain instances. For FoxPro's Standard version, you may want to put the overlay file (FoxPro.OVL) on a RAM disk. If you perceive *significant* speed differences, consider keeping the RAM disk. If you cannot tell the difference, give all expanded memory to the FoxPro Standard version. Expanded memory is more flexible and likely to improve overall system performance over the RAM disk option. This is especially true for those doing interactive work.

General purpose external disk caches aren't useful for FoxPro and take memory away from the program. If you can unload the cache before starting FoxPro, do so. Caching controller boards have the same problem. If purchased primarily to make FoxPro faster, the money is better spent elsewhere (for example, on system memory).

One specific type of general cache often useful to FoxPro is DOS 5's FASTOPEN command. This command caches directory entries. If you have many files in a subdirectory, any program that opens and closes files takes time just to find the file. FASTOPEN stores the most frequently used file names in memory to facilitate searching, taking little memory itself.

Better yet, reduce the number of files in a subdirectory. After 150 files, performance starts to degrade. If you get into the hundreds, it can take a very long time. This rule doesn't apply to files residing on a Novell disk drive.

Tips on FoxPro 2 Performance

The following observations are guidelines, not firm rules. Fox Software continues to optimize FoxPro, so these guidelines are subject to change.

- Sequential data access is faster than indexed access. When Rushmore operates on very large tables, this is particularly true. The discussion of Rushmore and SQL in Chapter 7 elaborates on these issues and should help you optimize your database search and query techniques.

- Opening and closing tables frequently is a performance drain. FoxPro caches data from those tables upon opening them to speed up subsequent operations. If you close them immediately, that data may have to be written back to disk. The same rule goes for using FLUSH and SET AUTOSAVE ON. This procedure increases writing memory back to disk. FoxPro is generally intelligent enough to determine when it's best to do this automatically. Overriding this on machines with a great deal of memory for caching can severely impact performance.

- More commands in a program usually means slower execution. If you can consolidate commands that perform in a loop into fewer commands, performance increases. This is especially true for sets of table commands that can be replaced with a single SQL SELECT.

- If you are using macros extensively, look at indirect referencing and the EVALUATE() function as a possible replacement. This doesn't always help, as the overhead of actually executing the command outweighs the speed up in part of the command by getting rid of macros.

FoxPro's use of memory has limits. At some point, increasing memory has no effect on performance. A curve comparing the memory to the execution time looks like figure C.2.

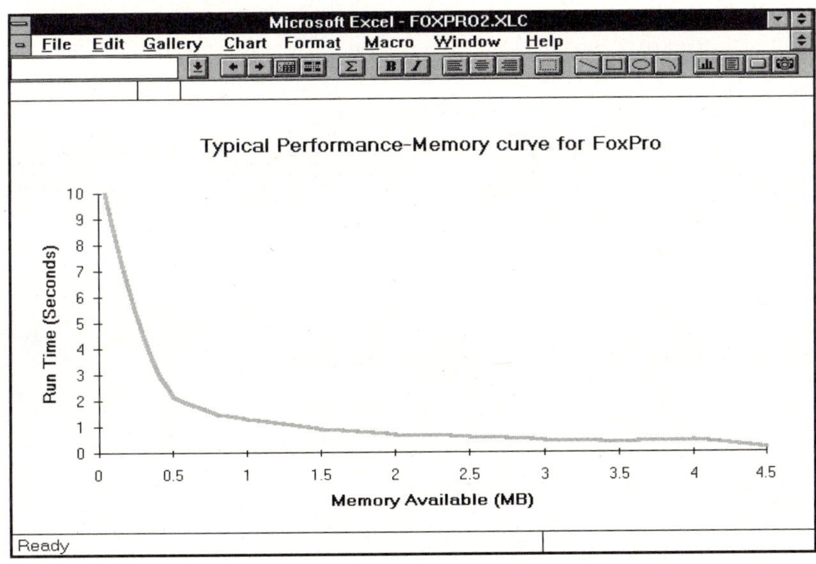

FIG. C.2

Memory versus execution time.

If you decrease your available memory by 25 percent and notice significant performance loss, you may benefit from having more memory.

Tools for Optimizing FoxPro

A single function may do more for your optimization efforts than any other. Before running a program, type the following in the Command window:

```
logfile = FCREATE('RUNTIME.LOG')
```

The variable *logfile* now contains a number, the *file handle* that FoxPro's FCREATE() function has just assigned to the file it has opened. Now open the Debug window and place the following expression in the left partition (all on one line—the partition scrolls as you type):

```
FPUTS(logfile,PADR(PROGRAM(),12)+STR(LINENO(1),6,0) +
    "  "+STR(SECONDS(),9,3))
```

Then execute your program. This expression creates a log file tracking every statement executed and at what time.

When you are finished, issue the following command in the Command window:

```
= FCLOSE(logfile)
```

`MODIFY FILE runtime.log` shows you the results, as shown in figure C.3.

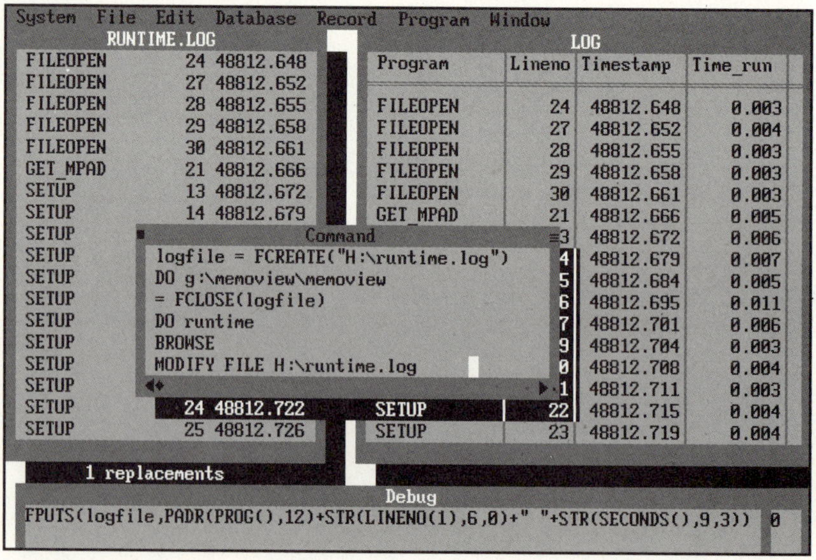

FIG. C.3

Use the Debug window to create a log of your program's commands.

RUNTIME.LOG is an ASCII text file, containing a list of commands run (denoted by their program and the line number of the command within the program) and a *timestamp* when the command was executed. You can bring this data into a table using a short program. Include an extra field to show the time it took to run each program instruction:

```
CREATE TABLE Log ;
  (program C(12),    ;
  lineno C(6),       ;
  timestamp N(10,3),;
  time_run N(9,3))
APPEND FROM runtime.log TYPE SDF
* bring the information in from the text file
old_time = 0
SCAN
  REPLACE time_run WITH timestamp - old_time
  * subtract successive timestamps
  old_time = timestamp
ENDSCAN
```

Now you can get a good idea of how long each command takes to run, as well as which commands are being executed most often.

This technique is known as an *execution profiler*. You should be aware of two limitations to this technique:

- There can be measurement inaccuracies due to the time it takes to write a line in the file RUNTIME.LOG. Minimize these inaccuracies, if you can, by creating the RUNTIME.LOG file on a RAM disk.

- If your program encounters a CLOSE ALL command, it closes the RUNTIME.LOG file, effectively ending your profiling. Consider replacing the CLOSE ALL command with something like CLOSE DATABASES or CLEAR ALL. Sometimes CLOSE ALL does more than you need it too.

For single SQL statements, SET TALK ON gives the run-time of that command. You also can insert ? SECONDS() commands in your programs, but you have to remove them later.

You would do better to rely on tests like these, supplemented by your own general impression drawn from your personal database use patterns using your own configuration, rather than published benchmarks of any kind. Take published benchmarks and comparison tests with a grain of salt. Carefully read the sections that discuss the exact environment in use during the tests before you draw any conclusions.

A benchmark to determine the speed of a single command or small routine can be useful *ONLY* if you are reasonably sure you have eliminated all contributing factors when you interpret the results.

FoxPro's dynamic caching algorithms further confound the common benchmarking technique of running the test repeatedly. The theory is that random effects will distort the measurement of a single iteration of a command. To combat this, the command may be run in a loop 1000 times, and the average time is taken. This usage may not be representative of normal situations. FoxPro's SECONDS() command is accurate to three decimal places. Consider running the command once unless the run-time is close to 0.005 seconds. If the command doesn't take much time, in fact, why measure it at all?

FoxPro naturally attracts users and programmers intrigued by speed. Trying to enhance performance is normal and enjoyable, and tinkering with all the contributing factors can be a rewarding process. Just remember that although any one factor mentioned in this appendix could be a pivotal in any specific circumstance, you can never find an ideally optimized configuration—so don't continue optimizing if you're not having any fun.

D

APPENDIX

Customizing the CONFIG.FP File

In Appendix A, you read about the CONFIG.SYS file used by DOS to set its environment. FoxPro uses a similar file to set certain factors of its own environment, usually called its CONFIG.FP file.

Among the FoxPro environment options you can control from the CONFIG.FP are all the options for which there are SET commands. In the CONFIG.FP file, however, their syntax is slightly different. Instead of the following lines in the CONFIG.FP file

```
SET RESOURCE TO d:\fox\model\q_user
SET RESOURCE ON
```

you include the following:

```
RESOURCE = d:\fox\model\q_user
RESOURCE = ON
```

Any such statements in the CONFIG.FP take precedence over FoxPro's internal SET defaults.

Special CONFIG.FP Configuration Statements

In addition to the SET values, the CONFIG.FP has a number of special statements that control elements of the environment not accessible to you from within FoxPro.

The `COMMAND` = statement enables you to execute a command as soon as FoxPro starts up. You can directly issue one FoxPro command, such as the following:

```
COMMAND = FILER
```

Or, you can indicate that a whole range of activities should be carried out:

COMMAND = DO *STARTUP*

STARTUP is any program name, usually a program or application that sets up your environment and/or begins immediate execution of other application tasks without any intervention by the user. In Chapter 15, you find an example of such a program being used to load default macros for each user.

A number of CONFIG.FP options enable you to specify the locations of files used by FoxPro. The following statement uses a copy of FoxPro's overlay file (OVL) in a location of your choosing:

```
OVERLAY = C:\directory
```

The Extended version of FoxPro does not use this switch because it doesn't have an overlay file, but for the Standard version, copying the OVL file to a RAM disk can result in faster performance. If the file is not present, or the one available has an earlier date than the one in your main FoxPro directory, the overlay is copied to your specified location. Use the keyword OVERWRITE to have the file copied without a request for permission.

Similar statements can be used to direct the temporary files used by FoxPro to a RAM disk or fast hard drive to improve performance. You can put them all in the same place with the `TMPFILES` = statement, or you can specify different locations with `PROGWORK` = (which locates the program cache), `EDITWORK` = (which locates the temporary files used by the text editor), and `SORTWORK` = (which locates various temporary files created with commands such as SORT during processing).

The TMPFILES redirection can specify only a drive (any path included in the statement is ignored). However, EDITWORK, SORTWORK, and PROGWORK can send files to a specific directory, as well as a drive.

Although the space required by PROGWORK is relatively small, the size of SORTWORK and EDITWORK files is determined by the size of the files with which you are working. It is usually better to put these files on your fastest hard disk (on a network, usually a local disk) rather than on a RAM disk.

NOTE If you use the RUN command, the temporary files created by FOXSWAP are not redirected by any of these assignments.

The following statements can be used to tell FoxPro where to find some of its component programs if you do not use their default names and locations:

```
_GENGRAPH = C:\directory\program_name
_GENMENU  = C:\directory\program_name
_GENPD    = C:\directory\program_name
_GENSCRN  = C:\directory\program_name
_GENXTAB  = C:\directory\program_name
_FOXDOC   = C:\directory\program_name
_FOXGRAPH = C:\directory\program_name
```

If you do not use FOXDOC or FOXGRAPH and don't have them installed on your disk, you can speed FoxPro's load time by specifying the null string (" ") for these two items. You also can tell FoxPro not to look for a default printer driver setup to load:

```
PDSETUP = "-"
```

(Of course you can use the `PDSETUP =` statement, like other SET commands, to load a specific setup at load time.)

Three statements enable you to specify nondefault extensions for three types of FoxPro files, without explicitly identifying them every time you use these files:

```
INDEX = <extension, where the default is IDX>
LABEL =  <extension, where the default is LBX>
REPORT = <extension, where the default is FRX>
```

The `TEDIT =` statement enables you to specify an outside editor to be called when you choose to MODIFY COMMAND or FILE. In the Standard version of FoxPro, you can add a /<*expN*> switch to specify how much memory is made available to your editor. The more memory you specify, the slower the swap between programs appears. You can get the maximum amount of memory by using the following line:

```
TEDIT = /0 <your editor>
```

DOSMEM = is used to regulate FoxPro's Extended version's use of DOS memory. By default DOSMEM = OFF, and most DOS memory is still available for programs to be run from within FoxPro. You can set DOSMEM = ON instead, to have DOS memory accessed and used by the Extended version along with your extended memory, or you can set DOSMEM = <expN> to reserve some memory for a run command and have some accessible to FoxPro.

By contrast, EMS = and EMS64 = are used only by the Standard version of FoxPro and regulate its use of expanded memory, where available. EMS = ON is the default, but you can reserve all or some of EMS for use by other programs with EMS = OFF or EMS = <expN>. Use EMS64 = OFF if your EMS emulator and FoxPro don't appear compatible. There are several entries in the Fox help file on this topic, and these entries are updated regularly as new information becomes available. If you have an unusual configuration, however, and are experiencing problems with memory management, you may want to contact Fox Software directly. See Appendix H for tips on getting in touch and getting the fastest possible response.

MVCOUNT = <expN> can be set to any value from 128 to 3,600 (for the Standard version) or 65,000 (for the Extended version) through the CONFIG.FP. This option sets the number of variables FoxPro can handle. MVCOUNT's default is 256, which often is too low for a complex application. Because the higher you set MVCOUNT, the more RAM is reserved for memory variables, you may have to experiment with the best setting for your use.

Two more options specify certain aspects of keyboard handling in FoxPro. Use F11F12 = OFF if you have an old-style keyboard and do not see a cursor when you load FoxPro. (See Appendix F for more information about how FoxPro tests keyboards.) Use OUTSHOW = OFF to disable the keypress Ctrl-Shift-Alt, which hides all windows in front of the current output (WOUTPUT()) window by default.

One special CONFIG.FP statement, TIME = <expN>, specifies the number of retries FoxPro makes if a print device is not ready when it sends a character, which can become an issue when you are printing over a network. The value can range from 1 to 1,000,000 and defaults to 6,000.

Users of other, earlier, Fox products will note that there are some items missing from this list. MVARSIZ, which was used in FoxPro 1, and the FILES and BUCKETS statements used in FoxBase's CONFIG.FX file are no longer needed.

If you add these statements to your FoxPro 2.0 CONFIG.FP file, they are ignored. Similarly, if you spell one of the allowable statements wrong, it is ignored. No error is ever generated, except from the `COMMAND =` statement, because that is the only statement actually interpreted by FoxPro. If you use a particular SET equivalent or any of the special CONFIG.FP statements more than once in your file, the last one is the one that takes effect.

When you edit your CONFIG.FP file, you should test to make sure that your new settings are in force and that all its statements are being used in the way you expect. Use the View window, the About... panels, and the SET() and SYS() functions to check ON/OFF status of various environmental features, memory, and file locations. Use the Filer to find Foxpro's temporary work files (they appear unselectable, with the extension TMP).

Specifying a CONFIG.FP File

Whether you run FoxPro on a stand-alone machine or a network, multiple CONFIG.FP files can enable different user preferences, hardware, and application requirements to be managed with ease. To use multiple CONFIG.FP files, you need to understand where and how FoxPro looks for the one to use.

When you load FoxPro from DOS, FoxPro looks for a file named CONFIG.FP in the current directory. If one is not found, the main FoxPro program directory, and then other directories along the DOS path, are checked. *If you load FoxPro with the name of an APP or EXE file to run, FoxPro looks for a file named CONFIG.FP that has been included in the APP or EXE file first.*

Although FoxPro searches in these locations for a file named CONFIG.FP by default, you can specify any name or location for your FoxPro configuration file. You can set a specific DOS environment variable, FOXPROCFG, equal to the name and full path of the file you want to use, in your AUTOEXEC.BAT file, in another batch file, or at the DOS command line. Use the following format:

```
SET FOXPROCFG=C:\DIR\FILENAME
```

Substitute the drive, directory, and file names you want to use for your CONFIG.FP. Notice that no spaces are around the equal sign. You can use the default filename (CONFIG.FP) but still specify the location with the following format:

```
SET FOXPROCFG=C:\DIR\
```

Notice the final backslash (otherwise FoxPro thinks you want to use a file named DIR in the root directory).

If you want to know if this environmental variable has been created on your system, you can issue the DOS SET command without parameters to see all such assignments. From within FoxPro, use *WAIT WINDOW GETENV("FOXPROCFG")* to see whether the variable exists.

Even if you have SET a FOXPROCFG, you can change the configuration file used by FoxPro at the time you load by using the *-C* switch. This switch has the highest priority of all CONFIG.FP assignments. No matter which of the FoxPro *loaders* you use, the syntax is as follows:

```
FOX -CC:\DIR\FILENAME
```

(The first C is the switch, and the second is the drive.) Refer to Appendix E to find out about other such switches and about using the loaders.

E

APPENDIX

Using Command Line Options and the FoxPro 2 Loaders

Because FoxPro is available in Extended and Standard editions in single- and multi-user versions and in Extended and Standard editions of the distributable (run-time) version which can be configured as single- or multi-user, you can load FoxPro in a lot of different ways.

Specifying the Version of FoxPro To Load

FoxPro is supplied with four small files called *loaders*. Without any instructions from you, each loader checks the FoxPro versions available on your disk and your available memory to decide which version should be run.

Within the type of versions each loader supports, the Extended version is loaded by preference over the Standard version if your system supports the Extended version. The multi-user version is loaded by preference over the single-user version if it is found. Note that the version with the highest priority, not the version found first along your DOS path, is loaded.

The loader files are as follows:

FOX.EXE, which checks all versions

FOXS.EXE, which loads only the single-user versions

FOXL.EXE, which loads only multi-user versions

FOXR.EXE, which loads only run-time versions

Within the types of files checked by each loader, however, you can make additional decisions by adding one or more *switches*, each separated by a space and preceded by a hyphen. These switches affect which version is loaded:

+L	Loads the LAN (multi-user) version, where permitted by the loader
-L	Doesn't load the LAN version, even if permitted and available
+R	Forces the load of the run-time version
-R	Doesn't load the run-time version
+X	Forces the load of the Extended version
-X	Doesn't load the Extended version, even if memory is available
-M<n>	Runs the Extended version only if <*n*> kilobytes of memory are available (the default check is for 2000 kilobytes)
-Y	Exits immediately after having set the DOS error level to 1 if the Extended version can be run (for use within batch files and is followed by an explicit load of a particular version)

You also can execute any of the loaders with a -? or /? switch to get a help message reminding you of the switches that can be used by that loader. Try this with your own copy of FoxPro; the -M and -Y switches were added after the initial introduction of FoxPro 2. Your copy may not allow them, or perhaps new ones have been added since this book was written.

If you use the FOX.EXE loader with a -V switch, you get a message that tells you what the loaders see when they check your system and files available. The last line of the message tells you which version is run if you don't force a different choice.

The loader files are convenient when you are running FoxPro on a network and need to tailor the use of the product to many different situations, without knowing in advance what they are. However, the loaders take as much as 20K of memory. If you know in advance which version of the product is best for your situation, load that version directly and dispense with the loaders. If you don't know which is best for you, you can still use FOX -V to find out which version is *recommended* by the loaders and then load that version directly.

The following are the executable files for each version of the FoxPro 2 product that can be run directly:

FOXPRO.EXE	Standard version of the single-user product
FOXPROX.EXE	Extended version of the single-user product
FOXPROL.EXE	Standard version of the multi-user product
FOXPROLX.EXE	Extended version of the multi-user product

FOXR.EXE is used for all versions of the run-time.

Using Additional Command Line Options

A few more switches affect loading in additional ways. These switches can be used with the loader files or the actual executable files for each version:

- The -C switch, discussed in Appendix D, enables you to specify the name and location of the CONFIG.FP file to be used.
- The -E switch prevents the use of expanded memory, like the EMS = OFF option in the CONFIG.FP.
- The -K switch, like F11F12 = OFF in the CONFIG.FP, prevents FoxPro from attempting to use Function Keys 11 and 12 on older keyboards with BIOS that erroneously report their existence.

- The -T switch suppresses the appearance of Fox's normal sign-on logo screen and the normal shutdown message when you QUIT. (The same effect can be created for executable distributed applications by unchecking the Logo box on the Project Options screen.)

You can create a DOS environmental variable, FOXPROSWX, that specifies the default use of these switches for you. Just as the FOXPROCFG variable is overridden by an explicit -C switch when you load FoxPro, all the switches listed in the FOXPROSWX variable can be countermanded by new instructions at load time. As with FOXPROCFG, you should not put a space between the name of the variable you are creating, but spaces should be added before each switch. For example, the following instructions in FOXPROSWX to use one CONFIG.FP file are overridden at load time by another:

```
SET FOXPROSWX= -T +S -CG:\MODEL\WIDGET.FP

FOX -CG:\NEWCFG.FP -M3000
```

The single-user version is loaded, and no sign-on logo is shown, because of the additional switches in FOXPROSWX. The Extended version is loaded only if 3000 kilobytes of memory are available, because of the additional command line option specified with the loader.

Specifying a Program or Application at Start-Up Time

One additional option is available, along with any of the switches, and with the loaders or the normal executable FoxPro files: a name of a program to be started as soon as the program is loaded. Any other information added when you load FoxPro from the DOS prompt, aside from the allowable switches, is assumed to be such a program and its parameters. Parameters are added after the name of the program, separated by spaces.

For example, the ASK.SPR program used in the Widget application (in Chapter 14) has three parameters. This program can be called from the command line as follows:

```
FOX ask.spr Value: 100 99999
```

Notice that no delimiters are used, and data types are not specified in any way. (The *Distribution Kit* pamphlet indicates that multiword string-type parameters can be enclosed in single quotation marks, but this does not appear to work in the present version.) Because parameters are separated by spaces, it seems to be impossible to pass a single parameter such as `Enter the value to use:`. If ASK.SPR had really been designed to be run from the DOS command line, you would redesign its first parameter to use a string of words concatenated with some rarely used character, as follows:

```
FOX ask.spr Enter~the~value~to~be~used: 100 9999
```

Within the ASK.SPR, you can use the STRTRAN() function to replace all instances of this character with spaces. Similar tricks can be used to specify the data type for the second parameter from the command line and to determine it within ASK.SPR.

If you have specified a program to be run from the `COMMAND =` statement of the CONFIG.FP file, the program named on the DOS command line is executed after the `CONFIG.FP COMMAND =` statement.

F

APPENDIX

Key Codes, Key Labels, and Special Key Usage in FoxPro 2

This appendix contains a chart to show you the different ways individual keypresses are referred to and used in FoxPro 2.

The *ASCII values* are shown in the first column, in decimal form. This form is returned by FoxPro's ASC( ) function when you use it to determine the ASCII value of a character or by the CHR( ) function when you use ASCII values to tell FoxPro about a character. This column corresponds to the first column in the ASCII chart desk accessory of the System menu popup. Items with no ASCII values shown cannot be added to an ASCII text file.

The INKEY/LASTKEY column corresponds to the values returned by FoxPro's INKEY( ) and LASTKEY( ) functions when you use them to tell you what key was pressed. INKEY( ) also tells you about a mouse click if you use its M parameter. The E parameter also can be used to have INKEY( ) return the first keystroke in a macro, instead of the macro itself, if the keypress received called a macro. You use it to *wait* for a keypress and then to test what you have; whereas LASTKEY( ) is used to find out about a keypress received *before* you called the LASTKEY( ) function.

The INKEY/LASTKEY( ) values are the same as the ASCII values in many cases, but you can use INKEY( ) and LASTKEY( ) to get information about many keypresses for which you cannot use or get an ASCII value directly.

The READKEY/NO UPDATE column corresponds to the value that the READKEY( ) function returns when you use it to tell you what key was used to exit a READ. The values in this column are returned for the corresponding keypresses when no changes to the data are made in the course of the READ. The next column, READKEY/UPDATE, shows you the values returned for each keypress if changes to the data are made.

READKEY( ) now can take an optional parameter, for which you can use any number (even 0). If you use this parameter, the READKEY( ) function can be used to test the reason why the READ was concluded, which can have a number of possible causes besides the normal exit keystrokes in FoxPro 2.

If READKEY (<expN>) returns:	**You know that the READ was exited because:**
2	The program issued a CLEAR READ command.
3	The user selected a terminating control (or the program selected it for him/her).
4	The READ window was closed by a command or by the user.
5	The READ's DEACTIVATE clause returned TRUE.
6	The READ's TIMEOUT was reached.
1	None of the above (a normal conclusion of the READ, using exit keystrokes, was reached).

The *KEY LABEL* column shows you the way you would refer to this keypress in an ON KEY LABEL command. Additionally, in FoxPro 2, key labels can be used in the KEYBOARD command, surrounded by curly braces and quotation marks, as follows:

```
ON KEY LABEL F10 KEYBOARD "{F9}"
```

Formerly, the KEYBOARD command could only be used with ASCII values using the CHR( ) function, as follows:

```
ON KEY LABEL F10 KEYBOARD CHR(65)+CHR(90)
```

Strings of characters also can be KEYBOARDed in quotation marks, so the last command could have been written as follows:

```
ON KEY LABEL F10 KEYBOARD "AZ"
```

The ability to KEYBOARD actual key labels, using the braces inside the quotation marks, enables you to KEYBOARD function keys and other shifted keystrokes that don't have ASCII values you can use. Because the braces are FoxPro's special key label delimiters, the braces themselves have special key labels, as shown in the chart.

Key labels for keypresses that are shifted (for which you have to press more than one key at a time) seem to work equally well in all cases whether the keys to be pressed are joined together with the + or – character. Although they must be enclosed by the curly braces for KEYBOARDing, or inside a macro you are editing, to indicate that they are labels rather than actual keystrokes, they then can be delimited (like any other character strings) with single quotation marks, double quotation marks, or brackets ([]). Key labels also are case-insensitive. You can use [{Ctrl-F1}] if you prefer it to {CTRL+F1}; it won't make any difference to the way FoxPro understands the label.

The fact that labels are case-insensitive has one undesirable side-effect: you cannot create ON KEY LABEL statements for a letter of the alphabet and have them react differently for the lower- and uppercase versions of the letter. Because you can KEYBOARD them as character strings, or by using their ASCII values, the KEYBOARD command respects upper- and lowercase. The two preceding commands have a different effect than the following two:

```
ON KEY LABEL F10 KEYBOARD CHR(97)+CHR(122)

ON KEY LABEL F10 KEYBOARD "az"
```

You can KEYBOARD far more key labels than are shown in this chart, because key labels can contain multiple shift keys, as follows:

```
ON KEY LABEL F10 KEYBOARD "{SHIFT+CTRL+F9}"
```

(This command enables you to use the F10 key to dock your active window.) Multiple shift combinations can be used in macros, both as the keystrokes to which the macro is assigned and as keystrokes that the macro plays back. The list of shifted combinations allowed is not completely consistent, and you may have to experiment a bit to make sure that the ones you want are available. For example, you can use a shifted tab as part of a macro or assign an ON KEY LABEL command to it, using its label {BACKTAB}, but you cannot assign a macro directly to this keypress.

If a Key Label column is empty for an item, it cannot be used in an ON KEY LABEL command.

Be careful not to create multiple assignments for one key combination. However, if you do inadvertently designate one keypress to accomplish different tasks in your program, you should be aware that any ON KEY LABEL command for a keypress takes precedence over other assignments. In the absence of an ON KEY LABEL, a macro assigned to a keypress takes precedence over the KEY clause on a DEFINE POPUP or a menu shortcut defined through SYSMENU and the Menu Builder.

Some keypresses such as Ctrl-Tab cannot be assigned ON KEY LABEL statements or macros on all systems, because some systems' keyboard BIOS do not return a key code to FoxPro for them. You can check your system's keyboard BIOS by noting the return value of FKMAX( ). This function returns 12 if you have your system BIOS support an Extended keyboard, which returns more key codes than the original IBM PC keyboard. The 12 indicates twelve function keys, but your motherboard may support an Extended keyboard and the associated key codes even if you have an old-style keyboard with 10 function keys. In such cases, you still can refer to the full range of keypresses.

FoxPro may not function properly with an old keyboard if the motherboard supports Extended keyboards. For example, a program may check FKMAX( ) and make a key assignment for F12 based on the results, but the user cannot find an F12 key. In such cases, you can use the -K switch on the DOS command line to tell FoxPro that your keyboard is old-style. (Refer to Appendix E on the use of DOS command line switches.)

Upon loading, FoxPro also checks your system for its keyboard configuration, which is different for people using DOS computers with different languages. European keyboard configurations are not supported by the US/Canadian version of the product. Fox offers language-specific versions of FoxPro 2, which do not run if the keyboard is found to be configured for the wrong language. The company's stated reason for this policy is to discourage gray market competition with legitimate foreign distributors of each language-specific version of their product. However, if a registered user can demonstrate a reasonable need for a version of FoxPro supporting all keyboards, Fox has a policy to accommodate this problem and supplies such a version.

When you edit macros you have created that access the FoxPro system dialogs, you may see key labels that you cannot identify. In some of the system dialogs, FoxPro *stuffs* the keyboard with keystrokes in between the keys you press to perform special jobs. Try recording a macro while you tab through the entries in the View window's Misc panel and then edit the macro. You see a sequence that includes the following keystrokes: `{x00FD}{TAB}{TAB}{x00FD}{TAB}`. The unfamiliar key labels are a hexadecimal representation of the keystrokes that FoxPro added. You should not use these keystrokes yourself—and you should not remove them from your macros when you see them.

The INTERFACE NOTES column contains special uses for various keypresses in the FoxPro 2 interface. Some of these uses are not available all the time, and some keypresses have multiple uses depending on the task you are performing. Remember that all the menu shortcuts refer to SYSMENU in its default configuration only! If SYSMENU is OFF or if you have changed it, the shortcuts shown here may not work for you.

FoxPro contains a default macro set that includes assignments for the first 10 unshifted function keys (they are commonly used FoxPro commands, such as LIST). These are included in the INTERFACE NOTES column as well, although if you have CLEARed MACROs or have created a different macro set and specified it as your DEFAULT, these macros do not work for you.

Your \GOODIES\MISC directory contains a second macro file, called FOXPLUS.FKY. This file changes some of the editing and interface keystrokes to match those of FoxBase+. If you use applications originally written in FoxBase+, these programs may test LASTKEY( ) or READKEY( ) and expect the results received in FoxBase+. In this situation, you have to RESTORE MACROS FROM FOXPLUS.FKY to enable these programs to continue to function. The effects of FOXPLUS.FKY on various keystrokes also are noted in the INTERFACE NOTES column.

Table F.1 Key Codes, Key Labels, and Special Key Usage

KEY NAME	ASCII VALUE	INKEY & LASTKEY	READKEY NOUP/UPD	KEY LABEL	INTERFACE NOTES
No Key Press		0	20/276		READKEY() values refer to a READ ended because of a TIMEOUT clause which specified the number of secodns the READ could continue with no editing keystrokes. The INKEY() value of 0, similarly, is returned if INKEY() "time," having reached the number of seconds specified in its numeric parameter.
Ctr-Alt-Shft					Hides all windows except output window or screen.
Mouse				MOUSE	ON KEY LABEL MOUSE traps every mouseclick, regardless of which button is used.
Left Click		151		LEFTMOUSE	Only INKEY() returns 151 for the left mouse click; LASTKEY() returns 13 as if it were an ENTER press. The "M" argument checks INKEY() for a left mouse click. See GOODIES\MISC\DBLCLICK.PRG to see how to use it to check for a double click. The system variable _DBLCLICK affects how quickly clicks have to follow each other to be "considered together" as a double click. A left click activates a menu choice, window, record in a Browse, or object in a READ on which you have clicked. A double left click is often used for object selection. See the chapters on the FoxPro interface, the Screen Builder, and the Report Writer for other special uses, especially for selection techniques in the editor and selection/sizing techniques that use the "click-drag."
Shift Left Click					Shift-click is used to make multiple selections.
Alt Left Click					Alt-LeftClick activates the help system.
Ctrl Left Click					Size an object in the Screen Builder and Report Writer.
Right Click				RIGHTMOUSE	Right-doubleclick will activate SYSMENU.
F1		28	36/292	F1	Default key for the help system. If the system bar name _MST_HELP is used, this key also will exit a READ. To prevent this behavior, include an ON KEY LABEL F1 statement that directs the F1 key to run your own help program, as described in Chapter 18.
Shift F1		84		ShIFT+F1	
Alt F1		104		ALT+F1	
Ctrl F1		94		CTRL+F1	Menu shortcut to cycle through available windows.
F2		-1		F2	Types "SET" if the default macros are not cleared.
Shift F2		85		SHIFT+F2	
Alt F2		105		ALT+F2	
Ctrl F2		95		CTRL+F2	Menu shortcut to activate Command window.
F3		-2		F3	Types "LIST" if the default macros are not cleared.
Shift F3		86		SHIFT+F3	
Alt F3		106		ALT+F3	
Ctrl F3		96		CTRL+F3	
F4		-3		F4	Types "DIR" if the default macros are not cleared.
Shift F4		87		SHIFT+F4	
Alt F4		107		ALT+F4	
Ctrl F4		97		CTRL+F4	
F5		-4		F5	Types "DISPLAY STRUCTURE" if the default macros are not cleared.
Shift F5		88		SHIFT+F5	
Alt F5		108		ALT+F5	
Ctrl F5		98		CTRL+F5	
F6		-5		F6	Types "DIPSLAY STATUS" if the default macros are not cleared.
Shift F6		89		SHIFT+F6	
Alt F6		109		ALT+F6	
Ctrl F6		99		CTRL+F6	
F7		-6		F7	Types "DISPLAY MEMORY" if the default macros are not cleared.
Shift F7		90		SHIFT+F7	
Alt F7		110		ALT+F7	
Ctrl F7		100		CTRL+F7	Menu shortcut to move the active window.
F8		-7		F8	Types "DISPLAY" if the default macros are not cleared.
Shift F8		91		SHIFT+F8	
Alt F8		111		ALT+F8	
Ctrl F8		101		CTRL+F8	Menu shortcut to size the active window.
F9		-8		F9	Types "APPEND" if the default macros are not cleared.

KEY NAME	ASCII VALUE	INKEY & LASTKEY	READKEY NOUP/UPD	KEY LABEL	INTERFACE NOTES
Shift F9		92		SHIFT+F9	
Alt F9		112		ALT+F9	
Ctrl F9		102		CTRL+F9	Menu shortcut to minimize the active window or recall from minimized state. Shift-Ctrl-F9 docks a window or recalls it from docked state.
F10		-9		F10	Used to access SYSMENU.
Shift F10		93		SHIFT+F10	Default key to call up macro definition dialog; may be changed with SET MACKEY TO.
Alt F10		113		ALT+F10	Calls up the "Play Macro" dialog.
Ctrl F10		103		CTRL+F10	Menu shortcut to zoom the active window.
F11		133		F11	
Shift F11		135		SHIFT+F11	
Alt F11		139		ALT+F11	
Ctrl F11		137		CTRL+F11	
F12		134		F12	
Shift F12		136		SHIFT+F12	
Alt F12		140		ALT+F12	
Ctrl F12		138		CTRL+F12	
Right Arrow		4	1/257	RIGHTARROW	Editing key: move one character right.
Shift Right Arrow		54		SHIFT+RIGHTARROW	Editing key: select one character, moving right. Use with Ctrl key to select to end of word.
Alt Right Arrow		157		ALT+RIGHTARROW	
Ctrl Right Arrow		2	15/271	CTRL+RIGHTARROW	Same READKEY() values returned if field is filled and CONFIRM is OFF. Editing key: move one word right.
Left Arrow		19	0/256	LEFTARROW	Editing key: move one character left.
Shift Left Arrow		52		SHIFT+LEFTARROW	Editing key: select one character, moving left. Use with Ctrl key to select to beginning of word.
Alt Left Arrow		155		ALT+LEFTARROW	
Ctrl Left Arrow		26		CTRL+LEFTARROW	Editing key: move one word left.
Up Arrow		5	4/260	UPARROW	Editing key: move one line up.
Shift Up Arrow		56		SHIFT+UPARROW	
Alt Up Arrow		152		ALT+UPARROW	
Ctrl Up Arrow		141		CTRL+UPARROW	
Down Arrow		24	5/261	DNARROW	Editing key: move one line down.
Shift Down Arrow		50		SHIFT+DNARROW	
Alt Down Arrow		160		ALT+DNARROW	
Ctrl Down Arrow		145		CTRL+DNARROW	
End		6	3/259	END	Editing key: move to end of line.
Shift End		49			Editing key: select to end of line. Use with Ctrl key to select to the end of file from current cursor position.
Ctrl End		23	/270	CTRL+END	Editing key: move to the end of file. Exit and save in a BROWSE.
Home		1	2/258	HOME	Editing key: move to beginning of line.
Shift Home		55			Editing key: select to beginning of line. Use with Ctrl key to select from beginning of file to current cursor position.
Ctrl Home		29	33/289	CTRL+HOME	Access a memo field in BROWSE or READ. Editing key: move to beginning of file.
Page Down		3	7/263	PGDN	Editing key: move one window of text down. Calendar: move ahead one month.
Shift Page Down		51			Editing key: select to end of current window of text. Calendar: move back one year.
Ctrl Page Down		30	35/291	CTRL+PGDN	Access a memo field in a BROWSE or READ.
Page Up		18	6/262	PGUP	Editing key: move one window of text up. Calendar: move back one month.
Shift Page Up		57			Editing key: select to bottom of current window. Calendar: move ahead one year.
Ctrl Page Up		31	34/290	CTRL+PGUP	Access a memo field in a BROWSE or READ.
Delete		7		DEL	
Shift Delete		46			
Ctrl Delete		147		CTRL+DEL	
Insert		22		INS	
Shift Insert		48			
Ctrl Insert		146		CTRL+INS	
Escape		27	12/268	ESC or ESCAPE	Used throughout the interface to exit without saving changes.

continues

Table F.1 Continued

KEY NAME	ASCII VALUE	INKEY & LASTKEY	READKEY NOUP/UPD	KEY LABEL	INTERFACE NOTES
Shift Escape		27			
Ctrl Escape		27			
Backspace	127	127	0/256	BACKSPACE	
Shift Backspace		127			
Ctrl Backspace		127			
Tab	9	9	5/261	TAB	Move from Calendar to Diary.
Shift Tab		15	4/260	BACKTAB	Move from Diary to Calendar.
Alt Tab		165			
Ctrl Tab		148		CTRL+TAB	
Enter	13	13	15/271	ENTFR	Same READKEY() values returned if field is filled and CONFIRM is OFF.
Shift Enter		13			Can be used to execute a command, like regular Enter keypress; useful if Enter has been re-defined with an ON KEY LABEL or macro. (Shift-Enter cannot be re-defined.)
Ctrl Enter		10	5/261	CTRL+ENTER	Accept default choice in a dialog.
Spacebar	32	32		SPACEBAR	The spacebar is the keyboard analog of a left mouse click in FoxPro 2. It can be used to activate a menu choice, window, record in a Browse, or object in a READ. A "double-spacebar" is often used for object selection. See the chapters on the FoxPro interface, the Screen Builder, and the Report Writer for other special uses of the spacebar.
Shift Spacebar		32			Can be used to type commands in the Command window, like regular Spacebar keypress; useful if Spacebar has been re-defined with an ON KEY LABEL or macro. (Shift-Spacebar cannot be re-defined.) Like Shift-Leftclick, used to make multiple selections.
Ctrl Spacebar		32		CTRL+SPACEBAR	Size an object in the Screen Builder and Report Writer.
0	48	48		0	
Alt 0		19		ALT+0	
1	49	49		1	
Alt 1		120		ALT+1	
2	50	50		2	
Alt 2		121		ALT+2	
3	51	51		3	
Alt 3		122		ALT+3	
4	52	52		4	
Alt 4		123		ALT+4	
5	53	53		5	
Alt 5		124		ALT+5	
6	54	54		6	
Alt 6		125		ALT+6	
Ctrl 6		30			
7	55	55		7	
Alt 7		126		ALT+7	
8	56	56		8	
Alt 8		127		ALT+8	
9	57	57		9	
Alt 9		128		ALT+9	
a	97	97		A	
A	65	65		A	
Alt A		30		ALT+A	
Ctrl A		1	2/258	CTRL+A	READKEY() values returned if SYSMENU is OFF or FOXPLUS.FKY is loaded. If SYSMENU is ON, it selects all text. Macros menu shortcut: clear all macros. Filer menu shortcut: tag all files. Project Manager menu shortcut: add a file.
b	98	98		B	
B	66	66		B	
Alt B		48		ALT+B	Access Browse pad on SYSMENU when available.
Ctrl B		2		CTRL+B	Report/Screen menu shortcut: Box/Line drawing. Expression Builder menu shortcut: Database popup. Project Manager menu shortcut: Build dialog.
c	99	99		C	
C	67	67		C	
Alt C		46		ALT+C	Access Screen pad on SYSMENU when available.
Ctrl C		3	7/263	CTRL+C	Copies selected text to the clipboard (system variable _CLIPTEXT). Macros menu shortcut: clear a macro. Filer menu shortcut: copy files. Project Manager menu shortcut: toggle included/excluded status.

KEY NAME	ASCII VALUE	INKEY & LASTKEY	READKEY NOUP/UPD	KEY LABEL	INTERFACE NOTES
d	100	100		D	
D	68	68		D	
Alt D		32		ALT+D	Access the Database pad on SYSMENU.
Ctrl D		4	1/257	CTRL+D	READKEY() values returned if SYSMENU is OFF or FOXPLUS.FKY is loaded. If SYSMENU is ON, Ctrl-D is the menu shortcut to DO a program. Expression Builder menu shortcut: Date function popup. Macros menu shortcut: set a default macro set. File menu shortcut: delete files. Modify Structur menu shortcut: delete fields.
e	101	101		E	
E	69	69		E	
Alt E		18		ALT+E	Access the Edit pad on SYSMENU.
Ctrl E		5	4/260	CTRL+E	READKEY () values returned if SYSMENU is OFF or FOXPLUS.FKY is loaded. If SYSMENU is ON, replaces text with value specified in the Find... dialog and fins next occurrence. Expression Builder menu shortcut: Verify option. Label Designer menu shortcut: Field expressions. Macros menu shortcut: edit a macro. Filer menu shortcut: edit tagged files. Menu Builder menu shortcut: delete item. Project Manager menu shortcut: edit the highlighted file.
f	102	102		F	
F	70	70		F	
Alt F		33		ALT+F	Access the File pad on SYSMENU.
Ctrl F		6	3/259	CTRL+F	Menu shortcut for Find... dialog when SYSMENU is on or when Filer is in use. Report/Screen menu shortcut: Field expression. Expression Builder menu shortcut: Fields list.
g	103	103		G	
G	71	71		G	
Alt G		34		ALT+G	
Ctrl G		7		CTRL+G	Menu shortcut for "find next occurrence" of text specified in the Find... dialog. Report/Screen menu shortcut: bring selected object(s) to front.
h	104	104		H	
H	72	72		H	
Alt H		35		ALT+H	
Ctrl H		8	0/256	CTRL+h	Filer menu shortcut: change directories. Browse menu shortcut: switch partitions. Screen menu shortcut: create a push button.
i	105	105		I	
I	73	73		I	
Alt I		9		ALT+I	Access Filer pad on SYSMENU when available.
Ctrl I		23	5/261	CTRL+I	Report/Label menu shortcut: Preview. Screen menu shortcut: create an invisible button. Menu Builder menu shortcut: insert item. Project Manager menu shortcut: information screen for highlighted file. Modify Structure menu shortcut: insert fields.
j	106	106		J	
J	74	74		J	
Alt J		36		ALT+J	
Ctrl J		10	5/261	CTRL+J	Report/Screen menu shortcut: send selected object(s) to back. Project Manager menu shortcut: project information screen.
k	107	107		K	
K	75	75		K	
Alt K		37		ALT+k	
Ctrl K		11	4/260	CTRL+K	READKEY() values returned if SYSMENU is OFF or FOXPLUS.FKY is loaded. If SYSMENU is ON, Ctrl-K is the menu shortcut for CONTINUE if a LOCATE has been executed. Filer menu shortcut: make a directory. Screen Builder menu shortcut: create a check box.
l	108	108		L	
L	76	76		L	
Alt L		38		ALT+L	Access Label pad on SYSMENU when availalbe.
Ctrl L		12	1/257	CTRL+L	Expression Builder menu shortcut: Logical function popup. Label Designer menu shortcut: Layouts. Filer menu shortcut: switch between "tree" and "files" views. Screen Builder menu shortcut: create a list.
m	109	109		M	
M	77	77		M	
Alt M		50		ALT+M	Access Macros pad on SYSMENU when available. Access menu pad on SYSMENU when available.

continues

Table F.1 Continued

KEY NAME	ASCII VALUE	INKEY & LASTKEY	READKEY NOUP/UPD	KEY LABEL	INTERFACE NOTES
Ctrl M		13	15/271	CTRL+M	Same READKEY() values returned if field is filled and CONFIRM is OFF. If a program has been suspended, Ctrl-M is the menu shortcut to RESUME executing the program. Expression Builder menu shortcut: Math function popup. Macros menu shortcut: record a macro.
n	110	110		N	
N	78	78		N	
Alt N		49		ALT+N	
Ctrl N		14		CTRL+N	Report Writer menu shortcut: add a line. Label Designer menu shortcut: Environment options. Macros menu shortcut: new macro. Filer menu shortcut: un-tag all files. If Browse menu pad is in use and NOAPPEND has not been used on the BROWSE, menu shortcut to append a record. Screen Builder menu shortcut: create a radio button.
o	111	111		O	
O	79	79		O	
Alt O		24		ALT+O	Access Report pad on SYSMENU when available. Access Project pad on SYSMENU when available.
Ctrl O		15		CTRL+O	If a program file is being edited in the active window, Ctrl-O is the menu shortcut to DO the program. Report Writer menu shortcut: remove a line. Filer menu shortcut: move files. Screen Builder menu shortcut: create a popup. Project Manager menu shortcut: Options dialog.
p	112	112		P	
P	80	80		P	
Alt P		25		ALT+P	Access the Program pad on SYSMENU.
Ctrl P		16		CTRL+P	Not allowed as a menu shortcut because it's reserved by DOS for printer control. You can use it in an ON KEY LABEL command or assign a macro to it, but this is not recommended.
q	113	113		Q	
Q	81	81		Q	
Alt Q		16		ALT+Q	Access RQBE pad on SYSMENU when available.
Ctrl Q		17	12/268	CTRL+Q	Exit without saving changes.
r	114	114		R	
R	82	82		R	
Alt R		19		ALT+R	Access the Record pad on SYSMENU.
Ctrl R		18	6/262	CTRL+R	READKEY() values returned if SYSMENU is OFF or FOXPLUS.FKY is loaded. If SYSMENU is ON, menu shortcut to re-do last text editing un-done by Ctrl-U. Expression Builder menu shortcut: Variables list. Macros menu shortcut: restore a macro. Filer menu shortcut: rename files.
s	115	115		S	
S	83	83		S	
Alt S		31		ALT+S	Access the System pad on SYSMENU.
Ctrl S		19	0/256	CTRL+S	Expression Builder menu shortcut: String function popup. Macros menu shortcut: save a macro. Filer menu shortcut: sort files. Screen Builder menu shortcut: open all snippets (with Shift, close all snippets). Project Manager menu shortcut: show errors.
t	116	116		T	Move to today's date in the Calendar.
T	84	84		T	
Alt T		20		ALT+T	Access the Modify Structure pad on SYSMENU when available.
Ctrl T		20		CTRL+T	Report/Screen menu shortcut: begin Text typing. Filer menu shortcut: change file attributes. If Browse menu pad is in use and NODELETE option has not been used on the BROWSE, menu shortcut to delete a record.
u	117	117		U	
U	85	85		U	
Alt U		22		ALT+U	
Ctrl U		21		CTRL+U	Un-do a text editing action.
v	118	118		V	
V	86	86		V	
Alt V		47		ALT+V	
Ctrl V		22		CTRL+V	Paste an item from the clipboard (_CLIPTEXT system variable). Filer menu shortcut: invert all tag states. Project Manager menu shortcut: remove a file.

KEY NAME	ASCII VALUE	INKEY & LASTKEY	READKEY NOUP/UPD	KEY LABEL	INTERFACE NOTES
w	119	119		W	
W	87	87		W	
Alt W		17		ALT+W	Access the Window pad on SYSMENU.
Ctrl W		23	/270	CTRL+W	Exit and save.
x	120	120		X	
X	88	88		X	
Alt X		45		ALT+X	Access Expression pad on SYSMENU when available.
Ctrl X		23	5/261	CTRL+X	READKEY () values returned if SYSMENU is OFF or FOXPLUS.FKY is loaded. When SYSMENU is ON, menu shortcut for "cut" (delete selected text from current location and save on clipboard in _CLIPTEXT system variable).
y	121	121		Y	
Y	89	89		Y	
Alt Y		21		ALT+Y	Access the Diary pad on SYSMENU when Calendar/Diary window is active.
Ctrl Y		25		CTRL+Y	Label Designer menu shortcut: Styles.
z	122	122		Z	
Z	90	90		Z	
Alt Z		44		ALT+Z	
Ctrl Z		26		CTRL+Z	Filer menu shortcut: see file sizes for all tagged files.
'	96	96		'	Type the left-quote character followed by a character to type the ctrl-character equivalent where these cannot be typed directly; i.e., the Ctrl-G character, can be typed 'G. (This technique doesn't work in a BROWSE or READ, just in an editing window holding a FILE, MEMO, or COMMAND. You also can type these characters by holding down the ALT key and typing their ASCII values on the numeric keypad; the latter technique will work on both situations.)
~	126	126		~	
!	33	33		!	
@	64	64		@	
#	35	35		#	
$	36	36		$	
%	37	37		%	
^	94	94		^	Ctrl+^ returns 35 for READKEY () if not updated and 291 for READKEY () if updated, like Ctrl+PgUp.
&	38	38		&	
*	42	42		*	
(	40	40		(	
)	41	41		)	
-	45	45		-	Ctrl+- returns 34 for READKEY() if not updated and 290 for READKEY() if updated, like Ctrl_PgUp.
_	95	95		_	
=	61	61		=	
+	43	43		+	
\	92	92		\	Used by the Find/Replace dialog to search for special characters in text: \r to find a carriage return; \t to find a tab; \n to find a line feed. Use \\ to find the '\' character itself.
|	124	124		|	
[	91	91		[	
{	123	123		LBRACE	Along with having a spcial key label because the curly braces are FoxPro's label delimiter, this character can be surrounded by a pair of braces to be used in instructions sent to the printer with the ??? command, like this: ???"{{}"
]	93	93		]	Ctrl-] returns 33 for READKEY() if not updated and 289 for READKEY() if updated, like Ctrl-Home.
}	125	125		RBRACE	Along with having a special key label because the curly braces are FoxPro's label delimiter, this character can be surrounded by a pair of braces to be used in instructions sent to the printer with the ??? command, like this: ??? "{}}"
;	59	59		;	
:	58	58		:	
'	39	39		'	
"	34	34		"	
,	44	44		,	
<	60	60		<	
.	46	46		.	
>	62	62		>	
/	47	47		/	
?	63	63		?	

G

APPENDIX

Installation Disk Files and File Extensions

If you have been using the Filer or another disk utility program to explore the directories FoxPro's installation process creates, you know that FoxPro 2 comes supplied with an astonishing variety of sample programs and other "goodies."

Table G.1 will help you become familiar with the default file extensions for each type of file created by FoxPro so that you know what to do with the treasures you find. If you do not specify other extensions, the defaults will become standard for your own FoxPro files.

Take some time to investigate the directories. If they are not all available on your disk, you may not have installed all the sample directories when you installed FoxPro. As explained in Chapter 1, you can DO INSTALL.APP from the main FoxPro directory to add these directories, singly or all together. If you have limited disk space, the notes in this appendix should help you decide which directories will prove most valuable to you.

Main (Home) FoxPro Program Directory

This directory contains all the files required to run FoxPro. In addition to the executable versions of the program and its overlays and loaders (described in Appendix E), FoxPro expects to find a number of other files at startup. Some of these files can be moved by indicating new locations for them in your CONFIG.FP file, as explained in Appendix D.

Included here are all the files required by FOXDOC, a program documenting utility covered in Chapter 18, the GENMENU and GENSCRN template programs, the default printer driver (GENPD.APP), the self-running demo (DEMO.APP), the application generator (FOXAPP.APP) and the crosstab-generating program (GENXTAB) and snippet-formatting program (SNIPFMT.APP). If you have the multi-user version of FoxPro, an application to configure it for individual users (ADDUSER.APP) is included.

In addition, your original Resource file and the FoxPro help file are in this directory. Your default macro set (DEFAULT.FKY) also is saved in this directory by default.

If you own the Distribution Kit, quite a number of support files are required to compile and link stand-alone applications. Most of these files have the extensions LIB, but two executable files (WLINK8.EXE and FOXLDR.EXE) are used by the Distribution Kit as well. The Distribution Kit installation process also places the run-time support files, which have the extensions ESO and ESL, in your main FoxPro directory. These files must be used to distribute APP files and compact EXEs.

The small PROAPI16.EXE file provides support for the API library used by GENPD. If you distribute a stand-alone application that uses the default printer driver system, remember to distribute GENPD.APP along with the application. If it is an Extended version stand-alone, you also need to distribute PROAPI16.EXE.

If you distribute applications that use the RUN command, make sure that you add FOXSWAP.COM to the files on your distribution disk. This file also is found in FoxPro's main directory. This file is used to make extra memory available to the programs being executed with the RUN command by SWAPping portions of FoxPro to disk. Read the entry for the RUN command in your *Commands and Functions* manual for more information.

In addition, some applications may require certain files to be located in your main FoxPro directory; add the files to this directory as part of their installation process. These applications generally are designed to become part of your interactive menu, like developers' tools. Locating files in the main FoxPro directory is the surest way to make sure that they are always available, no matter what changes the user makes to the current path or defaults.

Sample File Directories

Three directories located under your FoxPro main directory hold distinct groups of sample files.

\SAMPLE and its subsidiary directories holds the ORGANIZE files. You use these extensive sample applications in Chapter 1 and borrow a data file from \GOODIES\SAMPLE\DBFS in Chapter 9.

\TUTORIAL files give you all the sample data and other work files required to go through the tutorial in the *Getting Started* volume of the documentation. You use some data from this directory in Chapter 6.

\COMMFUNC contains the sample files used to create the procedures and code snippets you see in the *Commands and Functions* manual and the on-line help file.

The \GOODIES Directories

Directly under your main FoxPro program directory, one additional directory called \GOODIES holds a number of sub-directories, containing a wide assortment of useful files.

The \GOODIES\DEMO directory holds the project file for the self-running demo program. Under this directory, several additional subdirectories hold the project's associates menus, screens, and so on.

The \GOODIES directory contains a number of other subdirectories holding sample projects, most of which, in turn, have subdirectories holding their required files by type.

The \GOODIES\FOXAPP directory holds the project file for the applications generator. In Chapter 13, you use a table-ordering utility screen called GETORDER from the \GOODIES\FOXAPP\ files. The \GOODIES\LASER directory holds three applications and projects (LASER1, LASER2, and LASER3) showing three variations on one simple application theme. In Chapter 12, you use a *control panel* screen you find in \GOODIES\LASER\SCREENS. The \GOODIES\FNDATION directory holds three applications and projects (EX1, EX2, and INV) that demonstrate the use of a Foundation READ. In addition, its text files, GETLESS.TXT and GETANS.TXT, are a tutorial on the use of Foundation READs.

The \GOODIES\HELPTREE directory contains the menu files for the HELPTREE utility described briefly in Chapter 14. The \GOODIES\SNIPFMT directory contains the simple application that you can use to format your code snippets consistently. The GOODIES\PDRIVERS directory contains the GENPD project and all subsidiary files for the default drivers. These three directories have no subsidiary directories.

The final subdirectory, \GOODIES\MISC, contains a number of utilities that are unclassifiable.

LMOUSE.SYS/COM and MMOUSE.COM are mouse drivers. If you have a mouse that is using an older driver which does not work well with FoxPro, try one of these.

FOX210.PRG/MEM is an interface emulator for those who really prefer the old-style dot prompt to the Command window.

CONFIG.FOX and FOXPLUS.FKY are provided for use with programs originally written for FoxBASE+. They provide greater keyboard and environment compatibility with FoxBASE+ than the standard FoxPro 2 defaults.

SETSAVE.PRG and SETSET.PRG provide models for you to use in saving and restoring the program environment.

DBLCLICK.PRG is an example of double-mouse-click detection within a program.

FIXUSER.PRG should be run to convert any FoxPro 1 color sets you want to use under FoxPro 2.

FLS.EXE provides a simple file list of any directory, which can be redirected to a text file. This file can be useful in the creation of automatic compilation and installation routines, as shown in PROCOMP.BAT/PRG.

Table G.1 Default File Extensions in FoxPro 2

Extension (2 extensions signify a related memo file)	Generated source program	Generated compiled program	Backup	Description
CDX	—	—	—	Compound index file; has same filename as associated table if a structural index
DBF/FPT	—	—	BAK*/TBK	Standard table; backup created if you MODIFY STRUCTURE

Extension (2 extensions signify a related memo file)	Generated source program	Generated compiled program	Backup	Description
DBF/DBT	——	——	BAK*/TBK	Standard table with vanilla memo fields that can be read by non-FoxPro xBase dialects

NOTE This type of table can be read and written by FoxPro without change and created within FoxPro by a COPY TO... TYPE FOXPLUS command. It also can be read and written by other xBase dialects. If you MODIFY the STRUCTURE of this type of table, the modified file has a FoxPro-style FPT memo file, but the backup (TBK) retains its old format, in spite of the fact that the file is given the same extension as the backup of a FoxPro-style memo file.

Extension	Generated source program	Generated compiled program	Backup	Description
ERR*	——	——	——	Error files created for programs during compilation (file name is same as associated program)

NOTE All errors for files being compiled at the same time can be directed to one filename you specify.

Extension	Generated source program	Generated compiled program	Backup	Description
FKY	——	——	——	Macro sets SAVEd TO a file
FMT	——	PRX*	——	Data-entry format file

NOTE These files are supported in FoxPro 2 for backward compatibility and are not discussed in this book.

Extension	Generated source program	Generated compiled program	Backup	Description
FRX/FRT	——	——	——	Report file created through Report Writer or CREATE REPORT... FROM "quick report" command

continues

Table G.1 Continued

Extension (2 extensions signify a related memo file)	Generated source program	Generated compiled program	Backup	Description

NOTE A file with an FRX extension but no associated FRT may be a FoxPro 1.0x report form, which has a different (non-table) format. FoxPro 1.0x reports also may have an associated FRV file, a special VUE file with the report's environment. This default extension may be changed in your CONFIG.FP (see Appendix D).

Extension (2 extensions signify a related memo file)	Generated source program	Generated compiled program	Backup	Description
IDX	—	—	—	Single index file; may be read by FoxPro 1.0x if not created COMPACT. Extension may be changed in CONFIG.FP.
LBX/LBT	—	—	—	Label file created through Label Designer. Extension may be changed in CONFIG.FP.

NOTE A file with an LBX extension but no associated LBT may be a FoxPro 1.0x label form, which has a different (non-table) format. FoxPro 1.0x labels also may have an associated LBV file, a special VUE file with the label's environment.

Extension (2 extensions signify a related memo file)	Generated source program	Generated compiled program	Backup	Description
MEM	—	—	—	Memory variables SAVEd TO a file
MNX/MNT	MPR	MPX*	—	Menu file created with Menu Builder
PJX/PJT	—	APP*	—	Project file created through the Project Manager or the BUILD PROJECT... FROM command

NOTE This type of output is compiled file only; no bound program file of source code is created.

Extension (2 extensions signify a related memo file)	Generated source program	Generated compiled program	Backup	Description
PLB	—	—	—	API library file, which you can SET LIBRARY TO, the product of OBJ and LIB files compiled using the Library Construction Kit. Ordinarily files of this type are given an EXE extension when compiled.
PRG	—	FXP*	BAK*	Program usually created with MODIFY COMMAND
PRT	—	—	—	File created by designating a file as SET PRINT target device from the File menu's Printer Setup dialog
QPR	—	QPX*	—	Query file usually created with the RQBE but can be created or edited like any other program or ASCII file (creates a BAK backup file, if edited directly)
SCX/SCT	SPR	SPX*	—	Screen file created with Screen Builder or by CREATE SCREEN ... FROM "quick screen" command

continues

Table G.1 Continued

Extension (2 extensions signify a related memo file)	Generated source program	Generated compiled program	Backup	Description
TMP	—	—	—	Temporary workfiles created during processing. If the program is QUIT normally, these files are erased after each session.
TXT	—	—	BAK*	ASCII file usually created with MODIFY FILE
TXT	—	—	—	ASCII output file created by REPORT/ LABEL FORM/ DISPLAY MEMORY and other commands sent TO a FILE command or SET ALTERNATE is used

NOTE No default extension is used when you use SET PRINT TO <*filename*> in the command window instead; however, see PRT in the this table.

Extension	Generated source program	Generated compiled program	Backup	Description
VUE	—	—	—	View file, saving FoxPro environment settings and open files
WIN	—	—	—	Window definitions SAVEd TO a file

* This extension is required. All listed memo file extensions are required by the main files associated with them. All other file extensions listed are defaults that can be overridden by specifying a different extension when you create or edit the file.

H

APPENDIX

Finding Available Help

As you work in FoxPro, you will have many reasons for wanting to communicate your experiences to other people. Sometimes a command or a tool does not work exactly as you expect it to, and you need advice. At other times, you are happy about your progress, and you want to share a technique you have developed or learned.

Sitting down to a computer alone is the only way that you are going to create applications and write programs. Reading this book and working through its examples will help you, and there are many other valuable books and database-oriented publications. (A *Third Party Book List* is available from Fox Software.)

The process of learning about applications and programs usually takes the support and encouragement of other people. The more perspectives on the same problem you have, the sooner, and the more effectively, you will solve the problem.

If you live in an area with many other FoxPro users, there may be a FoxPro-oriented *user's group* near you. In a user's group, people with a mutual interest get together on a regular basis to share ideas. The Event Coordination Department at Fox Software can tell you if there is a Fox user's group in your area or help you start one if there isn't.

Fox also publishes a *Developers Directory*, which contains a list of consultants who can help you and with whom you may have a common interest. This directory includes a geographical listing. A special insert lists Fox professionals who specialize in training FoxPro users.

You also can attend the *Fox Software Developer's Conference*, to meet people from all over the world. You can share your tips in the computer labs, see new versions of Fox products, and learn from experts on all aspects of developing in FoxPro.

Even without meeting people in person, you can be part of a diverse and talented group of folks who "meet" electronically on *CompuServe's FOXFORUM*. Because the forum is sponsored by Fox Software, its *sysops* (managing staff) are Fox Technical Support and Sales and Service personnel. They provide you with a direct line to the company. This method is by far the fastest way to get an answer when you need one (you can even order an upgrade on-line)—and it has the added advantage of many on-line volunteers who add their expertise to the sysops'.

The forum *libraries* are stocked with programs and tips shared by forum members over time, and its *message area* covers the latest information on every aspect of Fox products, with between 300 and 1,000 messages posted every day.

With FoxPro 2, Fox Software has instituted a new practice of posting new *patch files* on FOXFORUM every time changes are made to the release version of the product. You can download three small files (PATCH.DBF, PATCH.EXE, and READ.ME) from the Updates Library (Library 5), to find out what you need to do to patch the build of FoxPro you are currently using. Then go back on-line to download the files you need to patch your FoxPro files.

If you already are a CompuServe member, GO FOXFORUM to access this forum. If you are not, you can get a free introductory CompuServe membership because you use a Fox product. CompuServe representatives can help you get started if you have never communicated electronically before (and you can GO PRACTICE to work on your forum skills in an area free of connect time charges). After you have accessed FOXFORUM, be sure to read the file FFINFO.TXT in Library 1 (or download FFINFO.ZIP), by Nancy Jacobsen, for complete information on getting the most out of the Forum and CompuServe in general. Your Foxhelp file includes most of FFINFO.TXT in a special topic about the Forum, labeled ■ *CompuServe—The Fox Forum*. Also included in this topic is information on receiving the free introductory CompuServe membership.

If you prefer to contact Fox Software privately by telephone or mail, Appendix A of the *Developer's Guide* gives you a list of the different customer support departments and what kinds of help each department offers.

Whether you have a problem or a new idea, and whether you share this problem with your user's group, a consultant or trainer, with the Fox community at large on FoxForum, or directly with Fox Software by phone or mail, you are most likely to get the help you need if you do some groundwork first.

Be sure that you have the details of your hardware and software within reach. The answer to your question could depend on the particular video board you use or your memory manager. Make sure to have the contents of your CONFIG.FP, CONFIG.SYS, and AUTOEXEC.BAT files available; network users often have other configuration files that must be checked.

Use the FoxPro About... screens for details of your use of FoxPro. Write down the figures you see on all five of its screens, or (on many systems) press Shift-PrtSc to print them.

Make sure to mention which version (FoxPro single- or multi-user, Standard or Extended) you are using, as well as any other programs, especially *RAM-resident* or popup programs, that may be in use at the same time. Use the VERSION(1) function to find out exactly what build of the product you are using.

If you have to supply sample files, try to cut the problem down to a simple example; many times, just following this procedure helps you figure out the answer. If sample data is needed, provide the minimum quantity of data required to demonstrate the problem. If a complex procedure or many sub-procedures must be used, try re-creating the problem yourself from the files you are uploading or sending by mail, in a temporary directory, to make sure you have included everything necessary.

Be specific about what your problem or question is. Asking "How do I create a screen?" isn't likely to generate as helpful a response as "I want to display a calculated total on my screen; how do I make it refresh when a new figure is entered?" Remember that you can always ask a second question, and a third, when you understand the answer to the first one.

Be optimistic, too. Don't say "FoxPro doesn't work!" Instead say, "This command doesn't work the way I think it should. Here's what I did—what's going on?" Chances are you will find a quick and constructive answer.

People who work for Fox Software and people who work with FoxPro are genuinely glad to talk about what they do with the product and what they can do to help you. Soon your own comments will enrich the collective experience as you share what you learn.

I

APPENDIX

Example Database Structures and Procedures

The Omnipresent Widget Limited application used in this book is provided as a model of an extensive system of related files. Most of the tables are not needed for the examples in the text. The procedure that follows, however, shows you the structures for all the tables in the system. Create and fill as many of these structures as you like:

```
PROCEDURE CREATET

*
*                    Executive Information System for
*
*                      The Omnipresent Widget, Ltd.

* codes in the system are created from initial letters
* plus tie-breaking digits for sub-groups
```

```
CREATE TABLE Budget        ;
    (Deptcode    C(4),    ;
     Prodcode    C(5),    ;
     Budcatcode  C(4),    ;
     Period      D,       ;
     Budgetamt   N(7,0),  ;
     Final       L,       ;
     Notes       M)
INDEX ON Prodcode   TAG Prodcode
INDEX ON Deptcode   TAG Deptcode
INDEX ON Budcatcode TAG Budcatcode
INDEX ON Period     TAG Period
INDEX ON Budgetamt  TAG Budgetamt
INDEX ON Final      TAG Final

CREATE TABLE Dept          ;
     (Deptcode   C(4),    ;
      Deptname   C(30))
INDEX ON Deptcode TAG Deptcode
INDEX ON Deptname Tag Deptname

CREATE TABLE Product       ;
     (Prodcode   C(5),    ;
      Prodname   C(20),   ;
      Photo            M)

INDEX ON Prodname TAG Prodname
INDEX ON Prodcode TAG Prodcode

CREATE TABLE Budcat        ;
     (Budcatcode C(4),    ;
      Budcat     C(20))   ;
INDEX ON Budcatcode TAG Budcatcode
INDEX ON Budcat     TAG Budcat

CREATE TABLE Manufact      ;
     (Prodcode   C(5),    ;
      Proddate   D,       ;
      Shift      C(1),    ;
      Quantity   N(4,0),  ;
      Rejects    N(4,0))

CREATE TABLE Prodmix       ;
     (Prodcode   C(5),    ;
      Rawmatter  C(20),   ;
      Weight     N(7,0))

CREATE TABLE Rawdeliv      ;
      (Invoice    C(5),   ;
       Vendorcode C(4),   ;
```

```
      Rawmatter  C(20),   ;
      Cost       N(10,2),;
      Delivdate  D,       ;
      Paiddate   D)

CREATE TABLE Material     ;
     (Rawmatter C(20))

CREATE TABLE Vendor       ;
     (Vendorcode C(4),    ;
      Company    C(30),   ;
      President  C(30),   ;
      Phone      C(10))

CREATE TABLE Capexp       ;
     (Capcode    C(4),    ;
      Deptcode   C(4),    ;
      Prodcode   C(5),    ;
      Period     C(5),    ;
      Depnperiod N(2,0),  ;
      Amount     N(10,2),;
      Notes      M)

CREATE TABLE Wages        ;
     (Deptcode   C(4),    ;
      Prodcode   C(5),    ;
      Wagetype   C(1),    ;
      Shift      C(1),    ;
      Periodwk   C(5),    ;
      Amount     N(11,2))

CREATE TABLE Sales        ;
     (Invoice    C(5),    ;
      Prodcode   C(5),    ;
      Datesold   D,       ;
      Quantity   N(5,0),  ;
      Price      N(7,2),  ;
      Salesman   C(4),    ;
      Custcode   C(4))

CREATE TABLE Salesman     ;
     (Salesman   C(4),    ;
      Name       C(30))

CREATE TABLE Customer     ;
     (Custcode   C(4),    ;
      Company    C(35),   ;
      Address1   C(30),   ;
      Address2   C(30),   ;
      City       C(20),   ;
```

```
        State       C(2),    ;
        Zip         C(5),    ;
        Lastname    C(20),   ;
        Firstname   C(15),   ;
        Prefix      C(3),    ;
        Phone       C(10))
   RETURN
```

The first four tables created in this procedure are the ones you need for the examples in the text. The data used in creating the examples follows:

Record#	DEPTCODE	PRODCODE	BUDCATCODE	PERIOD	BUDGETAMT	FINAL	NOTES
1	SLS1	BBM0	ADV0	01/01/91	2000	.T.	Call NJ at the Jacobsen agency. We want to mount an entirely new campaign for the Bobometers, with a much more positive, upbeat tone than the previous ads.
2	FIN0	DSQ0	INS0	04/01/91	1000	.F.	The cost of Dream Sequencer insurance is expected to rise dramatically this year, for obvious reasons.
3	MFT0	DSQ0	PLT0	01/01/91	1500	.F.	
4	PER0	JLD0	LHR0	01/01/91	10000	.F.	
5	SLS1	LLD0	ADV0	01/01/91	1500	.T.	
6	PER0	LLD0	LHO0	04/01/91	2000	.F.	There's always a production rush on Log Ladles as orders come in right before taxes are due—not sure why they are so popular at this season every year.
7	FIN0	WGT1	TRV0	01/01/91	3000	.F.	An extended trip to Calistoga will be necessary to check out the cost-cutting procedures in use at Amalgamated Gadgets. They are stealing a lion's share of the LapTop Widget Market that is rightfully ours! This is our flagship product!
8	PER0	WGT1	LSL0	04/01/91	11000	.F.	
9	MFT0	WGT1	PLT0	04/01/91	23000	.F.	Manufacturing anticipates a need to update equipment for the LapTop Widget Production Line in the second quarter, but final estimates are not in yet.
10	SLS2	WGT2	LCM0	01/01/91	3000	.T.	The Mainframe Widget specialist sales force will no doubt be selling maintenance contracts as reliably as ever in the first quarter. Since we are no longer producing the Mainframe line, one wonders how long this gravy train will hold out.
11	MFT0	WZL1	PLT0	04/01/91	5000	.F.	

```
     12   SLS2        WZL2        ADV0          01/01/91 1000        .T.      Marketing strategy for the
                                                                               Weazlette line should feature
                                                                               the upcoming Industrial
                                                                               Strength version of the product
                                                                               along with our current House-
                                                                               hold brand.

     13   SLS3        WZL3        LCM0          04/01/91 2500        .F.

Record#   DEPTCODE    DEPTNAME

      1   SLS1        Sales SouthEast Division
      2   SLS2        Sales NorthEast Division
      3   SLS3        Sales Western Division
      4   FIN0        Finance
      5   MFT0        Manufacturing
      6   PER0        Personnel

Record#   PRODCODE    PRODNAME    PHOTO

      1   WGT2        Mainframe Widgets          memo
      2   WGT1        Laptop Widgets             memo
      3   DSQ0        Dream Sequencers           memo
      4   BBM0        Bobometers                 memo
      5   LLD0        Log Ladles (pine)          memo
      6   JLD0        Jeli-Do Nuts & Bolts       memo
      7   WZL1        Pine Weazlettes            memo
      8   WZL2        Lemon Weazlettes           memo
      9   WZL3        Floral Weazlettes          memo
     10   WZL4        Unscented Weazlettes       memo

Record#   BUDCATCODE  BUDCAT

      1   INS0                    Insurance
      2   LHR0                    Labor, Hourly Reg
      3   LHO0                    Labor, Hourly Over
      4   LSL0                    Labor, Salary
      5   LCM0                    Labor, Commission
      6   TRV0                    Travel
      7   ADV0                    Advertising
      8   PLT0                    Plant
```

Most FoxPro code required by the examples in this book are listed in the text. The snippets for the generic ASK procedure used in Chapter 14, however, are listed here. The comments explain how to create an SCX that generates the appropriate SPR file.

ASK can be used as a function or a procedure. However, when you generate the code, you have to specify the (non-default) extension of PRG for ASK to be used as a function.

Following the code for ASK is a short procedure named UNALIAS.PRG. This program shows you how you can strip alias information from a table Fox uses to build a screen or report form, as suggested in Chapters 10 and 13.

The last code listing is STARTOFF.PRG, referred to in Chapter 13. Along with showing you an alternative approach to integrating a BROWSE in a READ CYCLE that puts the user in the BROWSE first, this listing demonstrates a solution for one key limitation in FoxPro 2: it is not possible to DEFINE child windows for use within a READ CYCLE. The active GET must always be in the window that is literally on top, not just WONTOP(). The command ACTIVATE WINDOW BOTTOM or SAME does not enable a window with the current GET to be behind a smaller child window in the READ. The result is that the child window seems to disappear when a GET in the parent window is edited.

If you run STARTOFF.PRG, you see a BROWSE window that appears to be a child of a larger READ window. The larger window is really painted on-screen, and the GETs that appear to be in that window are in a much smaller window with no border and the same background color. This trick enables you to add many windows that appear to be children (containing GETs as well as a BROWSE) to a READ. Any GETs that should appear to be in the parent should be DEFINed with no border, as in the example, while DEFINition of apparent child windows should include borders and distinctive COLOR SCHEMEs. The READ's DEACTIVATE and ACTIVATE clauses can include checks for WBORDER(WLAST()), WBORDER(MWINDOW()), and WBORDER(WONTOP()) if the movement between child and parent windows has any special significance in your program.

```
*****************************************************

* code for ASK.SPR/PRG

* The ASK screen contains one GET, a dummy variable.
* The GET's WHEN calls the *real* READ, with a
* GET that is properly formatted and placed
* using the information passed to the .SPR

* Since the WHEN RETURNs .F., the dummy variable is
* never entered.

* The dummy is one character long, and centered on
* line 3. The "real" READ, in the WHEN, is at least 1
* character long, and also centered on line 3,
* so the dummy is never seen.

* ASK also contains one SAY, the passed question.
* It is centered on line 1 by using
* PADC(the_passed_question,the_length_of_the_SAY)
* as the SAY expression.

* ASK requires three code snippets, as follows.

*****************************************************

* SETUP snippet for ASK.SPR/PRG
#section1
PARAMETERS m.question, m.value,m.valid
novalid = (PARAMETERS() = 2)

#section2
m.dummy =" "
```

```
**************************************************

* WHEN snippet for ASK.SPR/PRG

PRIVATE temp, msize, getcol
DO CASE
CASE TYPE("m.value") = "C" AND (! novalid) AND ;
   "@" $ m.valid AND " " $ m.valid
   temp = LEN(m.valid)-AT(" ",m.valid)
CASE TYPE("m.value") = "C" AND (novalid OR "@" $
m.valid)
   temp = LEN(ALLTRIM(m.value))
CASE TYPE("m.value") = "C"
   temp = LEN(ALLTRIM(m.valid))
CASE TYPE("m.value") = "N"
   temp = IIF(novalid,LEN(ALLTRIM(STR(m.value))),;
             LEN(m.valid)-AT(" ",m.valid))
CASE TYPE("m.value") = "D"
   temp = IIF(SET("CENTURY") = "ON",10,8)
CASE TYPE("m.value") = "L"
   temp = 1
ENDCASE
getcol = 23-INT(temp/2)
msize = "1,"+ALLTRIM(STR(temp))
IF novalid
  @3,getcol GET m.value SIZE &msize
ELSE
   temp = ALLTRIM(m.valid)
   @3,getcol GET m.value PICTURE (temp) SIZE &msize
ENDIF
READ
CLEAR READ
RETURN .F.

**************************************************

* CLEANUP snippet for ASK.SPR/PRG
* used only when the program is called as a function
* but it doesn't do any harm when ASK is called as
* a procedure

RETURN m.value

**************************************************

PROCEDURE Unalias
* unchecking the alias in a screen or report form
* isn't going to change the fact that your objects
* *were* created with aliases. It will just affect
```

```
* any new objects you design.
* Instead of manually editing each object, you can
* USE the SCX or FRX and get rid of all aliases at
* once.

USE GETFILE("scx",;
  "Pick a Screen File for Alias Removal or Esc")
DO WHILE LASTKEY() # 27
  REPLACE ALL Name WITH ;
           SUBSTR(Name,AT(".",Name)+1) ;
           FOR "." $ Name AND Objtype > 10
  * if you were inconsistent, include old-style
  * alias referencing (using "->"):
  REPLACE ALL Name WITH ;
           SUBSTR(Name,AT(">",Name)+1) ;
           FOR "->" $ Name AND Objtype > 10
  * include checks here for Expr field
  * containing aliases as well:
  BROWSE FIELDS Expr FOR "." $ Expr OR ;
           "->" $ Expr
  USE GETFILE("scx",;
           "Pick a Screen File for Alias Removal or Esc")
ENDDO

**************************************************
**************************************************
* STARTOFF.PRG
* Demonstrates use of apparent child/parent
* windows in a READ CYCLE,
* and starting a READ off from an included BROWSE
SET DELETED OFF
SET TALK OFF
USE
USE ?
IF EMPTY(ALIAS())
  RETURN
ENDIF

ACTIVATE SCREEN
@ 0,0 FILL TO SROWS()-1,SCOLS()-1 COLOR SCHEME 3
@ 03,9 TO 22,71 DOUBLE
mtitle = " Parent Window "
@ 03, (80-LEN(mtitle))/2 SAY mtitle
@ 03,9 FILL TO 22,71 COLOR SCHEME 1

DEFINE WINDOW hbrow FROM 05,10 TO 16,70 ;
  COLOR SCHEME 10
DEFINE WINDOW hedit FROM 20,10 TO 20,70 ;
```

```
  COLOR SCHEME 1 NONE
ACTIVATE WINDOW hedit
startoff = .T.
editmode = .F.
action = 1

@ 0,3 GET action ;
  PICTURE "@*HN Add;Edit/Browse;Delete;Finished" ;
  SIZE 1,13,1 ;
  VALID v_action() WHEN actbrow()

READ CYCLE ACTI checkbrow()
RELEASE WINDOWS hbrow, hedit, (ALIAS())
CLEAR
RETURN

FUNCTION v_action
DO CASE
CASE M.action = 1
  APPEND BLANK
  * this keyboard "{ctrl-f1}" and
  * all the other ones are unnecessary
  * if you want to stay in the control
  * panel once you're there; the assumption
  * in this program is that you want to *stay*
  * in the browse while using buttons.
  KEYBOARD "{CTRL-F1}"
CASE M.action = 2
  * this one is unnecessary if you allow
  * access to the browse menu, of course
  IF editmode
          editmode = .F.
          BROWSE WINDOW hbrow NOWAIT NOMENU
          * use two different PREFERENCES
          * for the BROWSE and EDIT
          * if you want to save user
          * alterations to each
  ELSE
          editmode = .T.
          EDIT WINDOW hbrow NOWAIT
  ENDIF
  KEYBOARD "{CTRL-F1}"
CASE M.action = 3
  IF DELETED()
          RECALL
  ELSE
          DELETE
```

```
   ENDIF
   KEYBOARD "{CTRL-F1}"
CASE M.ACTION == 4
   RELEASE WINDOWS hbrow, hedit, (ALIAS())
ENDCASE
RETURN .T.

FUNCTION actbrow
IF startoff
   startoff = .F.
   BROWSE WINDOW hbrow SAVE NOMENU
   KEYBOARD "{CTRL-F1}{CTRL-F1}"
   * this part is necessary to make it
   * work the first time through
ENDIF
RETURN .T.

FUNCTION checkbrow
IF ! WVISIBLE(ALIAS()) AND ! startoff
   CLEAR READ
ENDIF
RETURN .T.
```

INDEX

Symbols

A

B

C

D

E

G

H

I

M

N

O

P

Q

R

S

T

U

V

W

X–Z

Free Catalog!

Mail us this registration form today, and we'll send you a free catalog featuring Que's complete line of best-selling books.

Name of Book ____________________

Name ____________________

Title ____________________

Phone ( ) ____________________

Company ____________________

Address ____________________

City ____________________

State __________ ZIP __________

Please check the appropriate answers:

1. Where did you buy your Que book?
   - ☐ Bookstore (name: __________)
   - ☐ Computer store (name: __________)
   - ☐ Catalog (name: __________)
   - ☐ Direct from Que
   - ☐ Other: __________

2. How many computer books do you buy a year?
   - ☐ 1 or less
   - ☐ 2-5
   - ☐ 6-10
   - ☐ More than 10

3. How many Que books do you own?
   - ☐ 1
   - ☐ 2-5
   - ☐ 6-10
   - ☐ More than 10

4. How long have you been using this software?
   - ☐ Less than 6 months
   - ☐ 6 months to 1 year
   - ☐ 1-3 years
   - ☐ More than 3 years

5. What influenced your purchase of this Que book?
   - ☐ Personal recommendation
   - ☐ Advertisement
   - ☐ In-store display
   - ☐ Price
   - ☐ Que catalog
   - ☐ Que mailing
   - ☐ Que's reputation
   - ☐ Other: __________

6. How would you rate the overall content of the book?
   - ☐ Very good
   - ☐ Good
   - ☐ Satisfactory
   - ☐ Poor

7. What do you like *best* about this Que book?

   ____

   ____

8. What do you like *least* about this Que book?

   ____

   ____

9. Did you buy this book with your personal funds?
   - ☐ Yes ☐ No

10. Please feel free to list any other comments you may have about this Que book.

    ____

    ____

    ____

QUE

Order Your Que Books Today!

Name ____________________

Title ____________________

Company ____________________

City ____________________

State __________ ZIP __________

Phone No. ( ) ____________________

Method of Payment:

Check ☐ (Please enclose in envelope.)

Charge My: VISA ☐ MasterCard ☐

American Express ☐

Charge # ____________________

Expiration Date ____________________

Order No.	Title	Qty.	Price	Total

You can **FAX** your order to **1-317-573-2583.** Or call **1-800-428-5331, ext. ORDR** to order direct.
Please add $2.50 per title for shipping and handling.

Subtotal	
Shipping & Handling	
Total	

QUE

NO POSTAGE
NECESSARY
IF MAILED
IN THE
UNITED STATES

BUSINESS REPLY MAIL
First Class Permit No. 9918 Indianapolis, IN

Postage will be paid by addressee

11711 N. College
Carmel, IN 46032

NO POSTAGE
NECESSARY
IF MAILED
IN THE
UNITED STATES

BUSINESS REPLY MAIL
First Class Permit No. 9918 Indianapolis, IN

Postage will be paid by addressee

11711 N. College
Carmel, IN 46032